The Complete Mediterranean Diet
Cookbook for Beginners 2022

1000+ Quick and Easy Mediterranean Recipes to Build Healthy Habits and Change your Eating Lifestyle |16 Weeks Flexible Meal Plan Included!

Ellen Marino

© Copyright 2022 by Ellen Marino - All rights reserved.

This paper is geared towards providing exact and reliable information regarding the topic and issue at hand. The publication is sold with the idea that the publisher is not required to render accounting, officially permitted, or otherwise, qualified services. If advice, legal or professional, is needed, you should seek the advice of a person experienced in the profession.

From a statement of principles that has been accepted and approved equally by a committee of the American Bar Association and a committee of publishers and associations.

It is not legal in any way to reproduce, duplicate, or transmit any part of this document in either electronic or printed media. Recording of this publication is strictly prohibited, and any storage of this document is not permitted except with the written permission of the publisher. All rights reserved.

The information provided herein is stated to be true and consistent, in that any liability, in terms of inattention or otherwise, for any use or misuse of any policy, process, or direction contained within is the sole and total responsibility of the receiving reader. Under no circumstances will any legal liability or fault be held against the publisher for any repair, damage, or monetary loss due to the information contained herein, either directly or indirectly.

The respective authors own all copyrights not held by the publisher.

The information contained herein is offered for informational purposes only and is universal as such. The presentation of the information is without contract or any type of warranty assurance.

Trademarks used are without consent, and publication of the trademark is without permission or endorsement from the trademark owner. All trademarks and brands within this book are for clarification purposes only and are the property of the owners themselves, not affiliated with this document.

DISCLAIMER

The information contained in the Book is for informational purposes only, and in no way constitutes the making of a diagnosis or prescription for treatment.

The information contained in this book is not intended and should not in any way replace the direct relationship doctor-patient or specialist examination.

It is recommended that you always seek the advice of your physician and/or specialists for any reported indication.

CONTENTS

- 7 INTRODUCTION
- 8 BRIEF HISTORY OF MEDITERRANEAN DIET
- 8 MAIN BENEFITS OF THE MEDITERRANEAN DIET
- 11 WHAT IS MEDITERRANEAN DIET PYRAMID
- 12 FAQ
- 13 THE #1 SECRET TO WEIGHT LOSS

15 RECIPES

- 16 SAUCES, DIPS AND DRESSING
- 24 BREAKFAST
- 36 FISH & SEAFOOD
- 59 POULTRY
- 86 BEEF, PORK AND LAMB
- 106 VEGETABLES
- 124 SIDES
- 133 BEANS
- 137 GRAINS & RICE
- 155 SOUP & SALAD
- 176 DESSERT
- 187 APPETIZERS & SNACKS
- 196 HOLIDAY & PIZZA
- 206 16 WEEKS FLEXIBLE MEAL PLAN
- 215 THE PYRAMID METHOD

217 CONCLUSION

Cooking Measurement Chart

Weight

Imperial	Metric
1/2 oz	15 g
1 oz	29 g
2 oz	57 g
3 oz	85 g
4 oz	113 g
5 oz	141 g
6 oz	170 g
8 oz	227 g
10 oz	283 g
12 oz	340 g
13 oz	369 g
14 oz	397 g
15 oz	425 g
1 lb	453 g

Measurement

Cup	Onces	Milliliters	Tablespoons
8 cup	64 oz	1895 ml	128
6 cup	48 oz	1420 ml	96
5 cup	40 oz	1180 ml	80
4 cup	32 oz	960 ml	64
2 cup	16 oz	480 ml	32
1 cup	8 oz	240 ml	16
3/4 cup	6 oz	177 ml	12
2/3 cup	5 oz	158 ml	11
1/2 cup	4 oz	118 ml	8
3/8 cup	3 oz	90 ml	6
1/3 cup	2.5 oz	79 ml	5.5
1/4 cup	2 oz	59 ml	4
1/8 cup	1 oz	30 ml	3
1/16 cup	1/2 oz	15 ml	1

Temperature

Farenheit	Celsius
100 °F	37 °C
150 °F	65 °C
200 °F	93 °C
250 °F	121 °C
300 °F	150 °C
325 °F	160 °C
350 °F	180 °C
375 °F	190 °C
400 °F	200 °C
425 °F	220 °C
450 °F	230 °C
500 °F	260 °C
525 °F	274 °C
550 °F	288 °C

INTRODUCTION

These days, we spend a large part of our life at a frenzied pace. However, far too often, we don't have much time to dedicate to our health. As a result, diseases become a tormenting issue and, very often, one of the leading causes is a lack of nutrition in our diet.

Though we hardly notice, what we eat every day plays a vital role in living a healthy life, especially with the hectic lifestyle we have. But you don't need to worry.

The solution to all of these problems is the Mediterranean diet, and everything you need to know can be found in this book. In the following pages, I will show you, step by step, everything you need to best follow the No. 1 diet in the world. I will explain all its benefits and what sets it apart from other diets. I will also help you through a 16-week meal plan and 1000 delicious recipes to achieve the shape you want. I'll reveal the secrets no one tells you about weight loss and a valuable trick to enjoy any meal without feeling guilty! I have structured this book so that you can easily understand this information.

Here's a sneak peek of what you'll find inside:

A quick (but important) introduction to the Mediterranean diet, its history, and the Mediterranean lifestyle:
- Over 1000 easy and delicious recipes
- An easy to follow 16-week meal plan
- All the health benefits of the Mediterranean diet
- FAQ section on the Mediterranean diet
- Complete nutritional information for each recipe
- Conversion table for weight, measurement, and temperature.

The recipes contained in this book are all effortless to follow and prepare. Get ready to cook delicious meals for your entire family in under 30 minutes.
Is not it amazing? Start by diving in to the following chapters!

Brief History of Mediterranean diet

The Mediterranean diet consists of food patterns typical of the Mediterranean Basin, including southern Europe, northern Africa and Latin America. The origins of Mediterranean diet started with a study conducted by Ancel Keys in the 1970s, when he revealed that countries around the Mediterranean Sea had lower rates of cardiovascular disease compared to other parts of Europe. From then on, the Mediterranean diet was generally connected with the lower rates of cardiovascular disease and cancer. Mediterranean diet is rich in fruits and vegetables, whole grains, legumes, nuts, and beans, as well as high in seafood, olive oil, and moderate in alcohol.

What is Mediterranean Diet?

The Mediterranean diet is more than just a simple diet, it's a real lifestyle.
The diet is composed of meals that include lots of fresh fruits, vegetables, fish, olive oil, low-fat vegetable oils, moderate consumption of red wine with meals, and an active lifestyle. It is also rich in antioxidants and low in cholesterol. Among its many benefits, many studies have shown that the Mediterranean diet prevents cancer, cardiovascular disease and diabetes. The diet has been studied by scientists since the 1950s, and continues to be considered one of the healthiest diets to promote health.

The Mediterranean diet focuses mainly on choosing the correct foods, while the caloric aspect plays a secondary role. This diet also has a positive impact on our emotional, physical and mental health.

Main Benefits of the Mediterranean diet

The principles of this diet are the best defense against diseases such as atherosclerosis, hypertension, heart attack, and stroke. This diet will help you manage your hunger without getting rid of delicious foods. The Mediterranean diet includes a major reduction in unhealthy foods such as red meat, junk food (fast food), processed food and sugar. Instead, you'll eat a healthy portion of vegetables, fruits, seeds, fish, and legumes. Weight loss isn't the only benefit of this diet, you can maintain your healthy weight and see many health results that don't involve weight. The Mediterranean diet can help people who suffer from cardiovascular problems, skin problems, diabetes, or people who just want to stay healthy and lower the risk of deadly diseases like cancer. This diet is for anyone who wants to live a healthy lifestyle.

Let's take a look at the health benefits this diet offers.

Prevents Cardiovascular Diseases

Emphasizing meals in this diet that contain healthy amounts of fruits, vegetables, oils and fewer processed foods is the safest way to stay healthy. A 2013 study in the New England Journal of Medicine followed more than 7,000 people (men and women) in Spain who had type 2 diabetes. They were at high risk for cardiovascular disease; those who followed the Mediterranean diet (lots of vegetables, fruits, fish, and olive oil) had about a 30% lower risk of a heart attack . Researchers did not ask the participants to exercise, so the results are based on the effects of the Mediterranean diet alone. Replacing red meat with fish is the key to a healthy heart!

Prevents Alzheimer's disease

Following the Mediterranean diet not only helps prevent cardiovascular disease but also neurodegenerative diseases. Our brain activity begins to decrease dramatically as we age.

The human brain needs energy and, therefore, food to function properly, and when this food is not suitable, you are more likely to develop Alzheimer's disease. In 2016, the Journal Frontiers in Nutrition studied the effects of the Mediterranean diet on cognitive function. The results showed that this diet improves brain function by about 30%, while also slowing down developing neurodegenerative diseases.

Manage Type 2 Diabetes

People who have type 2 diabetes also have a lot to gain from the Mediterranean diet. People with type 2 diabetes are usually instructed to follow a low diet low in carbohydrates and sugar. This diet is all about whole grains and healthy carbohydrates, which do not raise blood sugar levels and do not stimulate the hormone called "insulin". Several studies have shown that people between the ages of 50 and 80 who did not have diabetes and followed the Mediterranean diet for three to four years did not develop the disease. These studies found that among people who used olive oil and nuts and generally ate fresh foods and fish instead of processed foods and meats, they had a 52% lower risk for type 2 diabetes.

Burn Fat

Following the Mediterranean diet means following a healthy, but most importantly, natural lifestyle. The menu of this diet consists of foods that are native to the area (Spain, France, Italy, Balkan countries), especially fruits, vegetables, seeds, fish, nuts and herbs. What makes this eating pattern perfect for weight loss is that it suggests eating fresh, whole foods without preservatives or additives. Preservatives and additives actually make you crave more unhealthy foods. These fresh foods help you cleanse your body of fat and cholesterol while also aiding in the weight loss process. Healthy fats provide the brain and body with enough energy, while the rest are not layered in fat throughout the body. Enjoying this diet for five years will keep your weight balanced and your brain in excellent condition. If your goal is to lose more weight, you can combine exercise and a little calorie restriction with this diet.

Let's start!

The best way to get great results is to pair the Mediterranean diet some regular exercise (I recommend at least 30 minutes of walking a day three times a week), lots of rest and fun.

The secret to enjoying good health in the long run is balancing these three aspects.

Consume seafood

Seafood is one of the key ingredients of the Mediterranean diet. One of the benefits of this diet is precisely encouraging the consumption of this type of food, which has a high protein value. If you are a vegetarian, consider taking fish oil supplements so your body gets healthy ome.

Consume meat (monthly)

In the past, red meat was a luxury for people in the Mediterranean. Although, it is best consumed in moderation. I recommend consuming it at most no more than three times a month. The reason is straightforward: you should avoid consuming too many "bad" fats from red meat (it contains saturated fats and omega-6 fatty acids). A healthier choice is to combine an excellent side dish to increase the sense of satiety and eat at most a couple of slices per month, without overdoing it.

Eating healthy fats

The Mediterranean diet is very similar to the Keto diet in some ways because it includes high consumption of fats, which are good for the heart. However, keep in mind that: not all fats are equal. Some fats are considered "good" and some fats are considered "bad". Monosaturated fats and polyunsaturated fatty acids (omega-3), for example, are considered "good" fats. On the other hand, omega-6 polyunsaturated fats and saturated fats are considered "bad" fats (most often found in unhealthy foods). For example, in the United States, it is estimated that about 10/15% of total calories consumed come from saturated fat. This is a very high number compared to the average of people who instead follow the Mediterranean diet, who consume about 8% of their calories through saturated fat. For a healthier lifestyle, start by eliminating foods like butter and replacing them with olive oil, an obviously healthier choice as it is rich in healthy fats.

Drink wine!

I have great news for wine lovers. In the Mediterranean diet, it is recommended to have at least one glass of wine with dinner. Red wine contains nutrients that are especially good for your heart, so consuming at least a couple of glasses a week is actually a healthy choice. Of course, just like for anything else, red wine should be consumed in moderation! If you already suffer from any pathology, it is good to consult your doctor to ask for advice.

Make your body work

As we already covered, exercise should be paired with diet. I advise you to walk for at least 30 minutes for a minimum of 3 times a week. Simple alternatives like walking instead of driving or taking the stairs instead of the elevator are easy ways to make your body work more, and you don't even need to go to the gym. Adding more movement to your day creates a daily caloric deficit (and consequently weight loss). So, be creative and work your body when you can. You'll see the benefits in no time!

Enjoy it with friends and family

Taking a few minutes a day to spend with loved ones doing something fun is a great way to lower stress levels. This part of the diet should not be underestimated. Today, we don't appreciate the importance of this, and people tend to feel lonely. When we are stressed, our body produces a hormone called "cortisol", also known as the "stress hormone."
In some cases, this hormone has negative consequences on our body by lowering and slowing down our basal metabolic rate. When this happens, we have a hard time losing weight. So, dedicating some time to yourself and cherishing happy moments with your loved ones can solve a considerable chunk of problems.

Meal planning

If you are new to the Mediterranean diet and have never attempted it before, in this case, you will need to identify what changes you need to make to your current diet. Eventually, the Mediterranean diet will come naturally to you, but before you start, you'll need to plan. Start by figuring out your weight, size, and which foods you like to eat. The changes may seem small, but they will benefit you in the long run. Meal planning involves carefully monitoring your meals, food preparation and what you will need to buy. It may seem difficult at first, but it will make it much easier when you start following the diet. Meal planning is essential because:

- It's a time saver
- Your food will stay fresh
- You don't have to think about what to cook every day
- You can reduce food waste

Meal planning techniques and shopping list

Meal planning is a process that can be perfected over time if you're not used to it. Below I will list some of the most common ways to plan your meals:

- If you like to be thorough with your planning, you can write down what you will eat for breakfast, lunch, and dinner for each day of the week. Also include snacks.

- On the other hand, if you like to plan the whole month once, this may take a little more work and time. Just make sure you don't plan too long and make a new plan to incorporate seasonal foods each season.

- Once you get used to the diet, you'll start having Mediterranean foods in your kitchen all the time, and you won't need to spend as much time meal planning.

You can also try to create a big shopping list and try to choose organic products if possible, but only if they are within your budget.
An example of a shopping list would be as follows:

- Walnuts, cashews, almonds
- Pumpkin and sunflower seeds
- Turmeric, cinnamon, salt, pepper
- Yogurt and Greek yogurt
- Potatoes and sweet potatoes
- chicken
- Eggs
- Olive oil
- Olive oil and avocado oil
- Shrimps and shellfish
- Cabbage, garlic, spinach, arugula, onions, carrots
- Fruits such as grapes, oranges, apples and bananas
- Blueberries, strawberries, raspberries
- Frozen vegetables
- Whole wheat pasta, whole wheat bread
- Beans, lentils, chickpeas
- Mackerel, trout, tuna, salmon and sardines
- Cheese

Remember that the best quality foods are fresh and in season.

What is Mediterranean Diet Pyramid

The Mediterranean Diet Pyramid is a nutritional guide that was developed by the World Health Organization in 1993. It was also worked on by the Harvard School of Public Health, and the Oldways Preservation Trust. It is a visual tool that summarizes the Mediterranean Diet's suggested eating pattern. The pyramid gives a guide to how often specific tools should be eaten. This allows you to break healthy eating habits without overdoing it on too many calories.

How is the pyramid laid out? Let's go over each tier.

OLIVE OIL, FRUITS, VEGETABLES, WHOLE GRAINS, LEGUMES, BEANS, NUTS & SEEDS, SPICES & HERBS: These are the types of food that form the base of the pyramid. These foods are mostly from plant sources. You should attempt to include a few variations of these items into each meal you eat. Olive oil should be your number one fat in your cooking and your dishes, so use that instead of butter. Generous portions of herbs and spices are also encouraged to season your food and add flavor as an alternative to salt. If you don't have access to fresh herbs, you can get dried herbs instead. Always be sure to read the nutrition labels to ensure no other ingredients are mixed with the herbs. Fresh ginger and garlic are also great flavor enhancers for your meals and you can easily store them in the freezer.

FISH & SEAFOOD: With the Mediterranean diet, fish and seafood is your main protein source. You want to try and include these in your diet at least two times a week. Try new types of fish, either frozen or fresh. Also eat seafood like mussels, crab, and shrimp into your diet. Canned tuna is also great to include on sandwiches or throw in a salad with fresh vegetables.

CHEESE, YOGURT, EGGS & POULTRY: You should eat a smaller amount of these foods when on the Mediterranean diet. Depending on the food, they should be used sparingly throughout the week. Keep in mind that if you are using eggs in baking or cooking, those will also be counted in your weekly limit. When eating cheeses, stick to more healthy cheese like Parmesan, ricotta, or feta that you can add as a topping or garnish on your dishes.

RED MEAT & SWEETS: These items will be consumed less frequently when on the Mediterranean diet. Eat small quantities of these foods and choose lean meats with less fat.

Most studies recommend a maximum of 12 to 16 ounces per month. You can still have red meat on occasion to add some variety to your diet, but you want to reduce how often you have it. There are health concerns that come with eating red meat and sugar The Mediterranean diet is working to improve cardiovascular health and reduce blood pressure, while red meat tends to be dangerous in cardiac health. Greece's

residents eat fish or seafood as their main source of protein and eat very little red meat.

WATER: The Mediterranean diet encourages you to stay hydrated, which means drinking more than your usual intake of water. The Institute of Medicine recommends a total of 9 cups each day for women, and 13 cups for men. That number should be increased for women who are pregnant or breastfeeding.

WINE: Moderate consumption of wine with meals is encouraged on the Mediterranean diet. Studies have shown that moderate consumption of alcohol can reduce the risk of heart disease. That can mean about 1 glass per day for women. Men tend to have higher body mass so they can consume 1 to 2 glasses. Talk to your doctor about recommended wine consumption based on your health and family history.

FAQ

Below are the most commonly asked questions (and their answers) about the Mediterranean diet. It is good to check them if you have any concerns or questions.

Why follow this diet?
Unlike every other diet, the Mediterranean diet has scientifically proven health benefits for our body that have been confirmed by health experts for years.

It has been shown that those who follow the Mediterranean diet live healthier and longer lives

How do you follow this diet?
The best way to follow this diet is to eat more foods with a high satiating power (being very high in fiber) and rich in nutrients, such as fruits and vegetables. Of course, you can also eat meat, dairy, beans, and grains.

But remember the importance of healthy quantities.

Will it help me lose weight?
The Mediterranean diet offers a large number of products that have high satiating power. The secret to following your diet is to focus on these foods (such as fruits, nuts, grains, vegetables, and seafood) to reset your metabolism and lose weight faster. The first results can usually be seen after 3-4 weeks.

Can I eat everything on this diet?
It is possible to eat everything included in this diet if you are careful about the portion sizes. To better understand this concept, check out the Mediterranean diet pyramid shown at the beginning of this chapter.

Why is this diet called "Mediterranean"?
The answer is straightforward: The diet is named after the regions surrounded by the Mediterranean Sea, such as Italy, Spain, Greece, France, and other countries.

How to Buy the Right Ingredients for Your Meals

After you understand how the Mediterranean diet works, you will realize that this diet promotes the consumption of fresh fruits and vegetables and emphasizes smaller amounts of meat, dairy, and sugar. Therefore, it is important to immediately research the ingredients to prepare the dish you have chosen.

Buy fresh seasonal fruits and vegetables and buy organic foods when possible.

Avoid preserved foods and limit meat or chicken products (maximum once or twice per month).
Instead, buy nuts and beans in decent quantities.
Lastly, don't forget to make a checklist when you go shopping.

Hunger or appetite?

When we are on a diet, are we "hungry," or do we have an "appetite"?
Unfortunately, both things. Let me explain more fully.

Hunger is the physiological need to feed, while appetite is the psychological need to satisfy.
When we create an energy (or caloric) deficit through the diet, our body is hungry because we are eating (in terms of quantity) less food than before. Then we fill up (literally) with low energy density foods, i.e., foods with a good volume to fill the stomach but few calories. These foods are fruits or vegetables, which are highly hydrated foods.

The issue is that the psychological need for food satisfaction remains. As a result, we
eventually give in to our cravings. Instead, we can divide what we eat into 80% healthy food (with low energy density) and 20% "free" food which allows us to satisfy both the physiological need for hunger and the psychological need for appetite.

Do not feel guilty when you eat a piece of cake or a biscuit because it is a natural psychological need to reward yourself with a "prize."
In the next chapter, I'll explain how you can eat the foods you want in moderate amounts so you don't feel guilty or ruin your results.

The #1 Secret to Weight Loss.

When we follow a diet plan to lose weight, we often mistakenly assume that we must go hungry.
Of course, this does not make us feel good. Following a diet literally means a lifestyle change, but that doesn't mean we have to be miserable or feel guilty if we eat something that is not part of our meal plan!

Remember what I told you earlier: 80% healthy foods and 20% "free" foods.
This means that if you sometimes want to have a treat here and there in order to satisfy your "psychological" need, go for it!

Do you want to eat a sweet treat? Eat it! You don't have to feel guilty.
Now I'll explain why.

Our body constantly works to maintain a consistent balance and perform all the functions it needs.

This balance is controlled by our basal metabolism, in other words, the energy consumption of our body at rest to perform all the functions it needs (functioning of the organs, regulation of body temperature, etc.). This is very important because it allows us to know our daily calorific needs. If our daily calorie requirement is 2000kcal and we have 2500kcal every day, we automatically gain weight. This is because our body does not know what to do with those extra 500kcal. And from that point, we begin to gain weight and put on those extra pounds that bother us.

Now, if I start taking 1300kcal per day instead of 2000kcal, we begin to "break" that balance to which our body was accustomed to, and as a result we will lose weight.
It's a matter of numbers. We simply have to balance what the "income" and the "expenses" are. Which translated means how many calories I'm taking in and how many I'm consuming.

Yes, ok, but how do I know how many calories I am consuming?
It's very straightforward, I'll explain it to you.

We assume that our basal metabolism consumes 65/70% of our daily calories. The remaining calories we consume when we start moving and doing other physical activity. And here is the "secret" that will prevent you from feeling guilty when you eat ice cream or pizza with friends. We have to move and break the balance. When we do so, our bodies will be forced to consume the excess calories that we have introduced. It will no longer be able to accumulate fat.
residents eat fish or seafood as their main source of protein and eat very little red meat.

WATER: The Mediterranean diet encourages you to stay hydrated, which means drinking more than your usual intake of water. The Institute of Medicine recommends a total of 9 cups each day for women, and 13 cups for men. That number should be increased for women who are pregnant or breastfeeding.

WINE: Moderate consumption of wine with meals is encouraged on the Mediterranean diet. Studies have shown that moderate consumption of alcohol can reduce the risk of heart disease. That can mean about 1 glass per day for women. Men tend to have higher body mass so they can consume 1 to 2 glasses. Talk to your doctor about recommended wine consumption based on your health and family history.

SAUCES, DIPS AND DRESSING

1

1. Walnut Pesto

Prep time: 5 minutes | Cook time: 0 minutes | Serves 6

INGREDIENTS:

- 1/3 cup shredded Parmesan cheese
- 1 1/2 garlic cloves, peeled
- 4 1/2 cups packed arugula
- 3/4 cup chopped walnuts
- 1/3 teaspoon salt
- 3/4 cup extra-virgin olive oil
- 3/4 cup fresh rocket

DIRECTIONS:

1. In a food processor, combine the rocket, walnuts, cheese and garlic and chop finely then season with salt. While the processor is running, pour in the olive oil until well blended.
2. If the mixture feels too thick, add lukewarm water, 1 tablespoon at a time, until the mixture is smooth and creamy. Store in a sealed container in the refrigerator until ready to serve.
3. Enjoy!

NUTRITION:

calories: 296 | fat: 31g | protein: 4g | carbohydrates: 2g | fiber: 1g | sodium: 206mg

2. Tzatziki Sauce

Prep time: 5 minutes | Cook time: 0 minutes | Serves 4

INGREDIENTS:

- 1 teaspoon salt, divided, plus more
- 1 lemon, juiced
- 2 medium cucumbers, peeled, seeded and diced
- 2 tablespoon chopped fresh parsley
- 1 teaspoon dried minced garlic
- 1 cup plain, unsweetened, full-fat Greek yogurt
- 1 teaspoon dried dill
- Freshly ground black pepper, to taste

DIRECTIONS:

1. Put the cucumbers in a colander. Season with ¼ teaspoon of salt and mix. Let the cucumbers sit at room temperature in the colander for 30 minutes.
2. Rinse the cucumbers in cold water and place it in a single layer on several layers of paper towels to remove excess liquid.
3. In a food processor, blend the cucumbers to finely chop it and drain the excess liquid.
4. Pour the cucumbers into a bowl, add the yogurt, lemon juice, parsley, garlic, dill and the remaining ¼ teaspoon of salt. Season with salt and pepper to taste and blend the ingredients. Refrigerate in an airtight container until ready to serve.

NUTRITION:

calories: 77 | fat: 3g | protein: 6g | carbohydrates: 6g | fiber: 1g | sodium: 607mg

3. Herb Butter

Prep time: 5 minutes | Cook time: 0 minutes | Makes 1 cup

INGREDIENTS:

- 1 cup almond butter, at room temperature
- 2 garlic cloves, finely minced
- 4 teaspoons finely chopped fresh rosemary
- 2 teaspoons finely chopped fresh oregano
- 1 teaspoon salt

DIRECTIONS:

1. In a food processor, combine all the ingredients and blend until well blended, smooth and creamy, scraping the sides if necessary. Alternatively, you can whip the ingredients together with an electric mixer.
2. Using a spatula, scrape the almond butter mixture into a small bowl or glass container and cover. Store in the refrigerator for up to 1 month or until ready to serve.

NUTRITION:

calories: 103 | fat: 12g | protein: 0g | carbohydrates: 0g | fiber: 0g | sodium: 227mg

4. Tahini Dressing

Prep time: 5 minutes | Cook time: 0 minutes | Serves 6

INGREDIENTS:

- 1/3 cup tahini
- 1/4 cup freshly squeezed lemon juice (about 2 to 3 lemons)
- 1/4 cup extra-virgin olive oil
- 3/4 garlic clove, finely minced or 1/2 teaspoon garlic powder
- 1 1/2 teaspoons salt

DIRECTIONS:

1. In a glass jar with a lid, combine the ingredients. Cover and shake well until the mixture is smooth and creamy. Store in the refrigerator for up to 2 weeks or until ready to serve.

NUTRITION:

calories: 121 | fat: 12g | protein: 2g | carbohydrates: 2g | fiber: 1g | sodium: 479mg

5. Spanakopita Sauce

Prep time: 15 minutes | Cook time: 14 minutes | Serves 4

INGREDIENTS:

- 4 tablespoons minced white onion
- 4 garlic cloves, minced
- Olive oil cooking spray
- 6 tablespoons olive oil, divided
- 8 ounces (113 g) feta cheese, divided
- Zest of 1 lemon
- 1/2 teaspoon ground nutmeg
- 8 cups fresh spinach
- 8 ounces (113 g) cream cheese, softened
- 2 teaspoon dried dill
- 1 teaspoon salt
- Pita chips, carrot sticks, or sliced bread for serving (optional)

DIRECTIONS:

1. Preheat the air fryer to 360°F (182°C). Coat the inside of a baking dish around 6-inch or baking sheet with cooking spray olive oil.
2. In a large skillet over medium heat, heat 1 tablespoon of olive oil. Add the onion, cook for around 1 minute.
3. Add the garlic and cook, stirring again for 1 minute.
4. Reduce the heat to low and add the spinach and water. Cook for 2 to 3 minutes or until the spinach has wilted. Remove the pan from the heat.
5. In a medium bowl, combine the cream cheese, 2 ounces of feta and the remaining 2 tablespoons of olive oil, along with the lemon zest, nutmeg, dill, and salt. Mix until just combined.
6. Add the vegetables to the cheese base and mix until combined.
7. Pour the sauce mixture into the prepared pan and garnish with the remaining 2 ounces of feta cheese.
8. Place the sauce in the basket of the air fryer and cook for 10 minutes, or until warm and boiling.
9. Serve with pita chips, carrot sticks or sliced bread.

NUTRITION:

calories: 550 | fat: 52g | protein: 14g | carbohydrates: 9g | fiber: 2g | sodium: 113mg

6. Piemontese Sauce

Prep time: 5 minutes | Cook time: 20 minutes | Serves 6

INGREDIENTS:

- 6 anchovy fillets, very finely chopped
- 3 large garlic cloves, finely minced
- 3 tablespoons (1/2 stick) butter (optional)
- 1/3 teaspoon salt
- 1/3 cup extra-virgin olive oil
- 1/3 teaspoon freshly ground black pepper

DIRECTIONS:

1. In a small saucepan, heat the olive oil and butter (if desired) over medium-low heat until the butter melts.
2. Add the anchovies and garlic and toss to combine. Season with salt and pepper and reduce the heat to low. Cook, stirring occasionally, until the anchovies are very soft and the mixture very fragrant, about 20 minutes.
3. Serve hot, topped with steamed vegetables, as a dip for raw vegetables or cooked artichokes, or use as a salad dressing. Store leftovers in an airtight container in the refrigerator for up to 2 weeks or until ready to serve.

NUTRITION:

calories: 181 | fat: 20g | protein: 1g | carbohydrates: 1g | fiber: 0g | sodium: 333mg

7. Rosemary Garlic

Prep time: 5 minutes | Cook time: 30 minutes | Makes 2 cup

INGREDIENTS:

- 8 large garlic cloves, smashed
- 2 cup extra-virgin olive oil
- 8 (4- to 5-inch) sprigs rosemary

DIRECTIONS:

1. In a medium skillet, heat the ingredients over low heat. Cook until the garlic is fragrant and tender, 30 to 45 minutes, stirring occasionally. Don't let the oil get too hot or the garlic will burn and become bitter.
2. Remove from heat and allow to cool slightly. Remove the garlic and rosemary with a slotted spoon and pour the oil into a glass container. Allow

to cool completely before covering. Store covered at room temperature for up to 3 months or until ready to serve.

NUTRITION:

calories: 241 | fat: 26g | protein: 0g | carbohydrates: 1g | fiber: 0g | sodium: 1mg

8. Grapefruit Dressing

Prep time: 5 minutes | Cook time: 0 minutes | Serves 6

INGREDIENTS:

- 1 1/2 teaspoon dried tarragon or 1 tablespoon chopped fresh tarragon
- 3/4 cup avocado oil mayonnaise
- 3 tablespoons Dijon mustard
- 1/3 teaspoon freshly ground black pepper
- Zest and juice of 1/2 grapefruit (2 tablespoons juice)
- 3/4 teaspoon salt
- 1 1/2 to 2 tablespoons water (optional)

DIRECTIONS:

1. In a large glass jar or glass measuring cup, combine the ingredients and beat well with a fork until smooth and creamy. If you prefer a thinner dressing, dilute with water, serve when ready.

NUTRITION:

calories: 86 | fat: 7g | protein: 1g | carbohydrates: 6g | fiber: 0g | sodium: 390mg

9. Polenta With Chives and Parmesan

Prep time: 5 minutes | Cook time: 15 minutes | Serves 6

INGREDIENTS:

- 1 1/2 teaspoon olive oil
- 1/3 cup minced shallot
- 3/4 cup white wine
- 5 cups water
- 1 1/8 cup cornmeal
- 4 1/2 tablespoons grated Parmesan cheese
- 3/4 teaspoon kosher salt
- 1/3 cup chopped chives

DIRECTIONS:

1. Heat the oil in a saucepan over medium heat. Once the oil is simmering, add the shallot and sauté for 2 minutes. Add the wine and water and bring to a boil.
2. Pour the cornmeal in a thin, even stream into the liquid, stirring continuously until the mixture starts to thicken.
3. Reduce the heat to low and continue to cook for 10 to 12 minutes, whisking every 1 to 2 minutes.
4. Turn the heat off and stir in the cheese, salt, and chives. Cool.
5. Place about ¾ cup of polenta in each of containers.
6. Store covered containers in the refrigerator for up to 5 days or until ready to serve.

NUTRITION:

calories: 110 | fat: 7g | protein: 3g | carbohydrates: 16g | fiber: 1g | sodium: 29g

10. Fruit Salad with Mint

Prep time: 5 minutes | Cook time: 10 minutes | Serves 6

INGREDIENTS:

- 3 cups cantaloupe, cut into 1-inch cubes
- 3 cups hulled and halved strawberries
- 3/4 teaspoon orange blossom water
- 3 tablespoons chopped fresh mint

DIRECTIONS:

1. In a large bowl, toss all the ingredients together.
2. Place 1 cup of fruit salad in each of 5 containers.
3. Store covered containers in the refrigerator for up to 5 days or until ready to serve.

NUTRITION:

calories: 52 | fat: 1g | protein: 1g | carbohydrates: 12g | fiber: 2g | sodium: 10mg

11. Artichoke-olive Compote

Prep time: 5 minutes | Cook time: 15 minutes | Serves 2 cups

INGREDIENTS:

- 2 (6-ounce) jar marinated artichoke hearts, chopped
- 2/3 cup chopped pitted green olives (8 to 9 olives)
- 6 tablespoons chopped fresh basil
- 1 teaspoon freshly squeezed lemon juice
- 4 teaspoons olive oil

DIRECTIONS:

1. Place all the ingredients in a medium mixing bowl and stir to combine.
2. Place the compote in a container and refrigerate.
3. Store covered containers in the refrigerator for up to 7 days or until ready to serve.

NUTRITION:

calories: 8 | fat: 7g | protein: 1g | carbohydrates: 5g | fiber: 1g | sodium: 350mg

12. Green Olive and Spinach Tapenade

Prep time: 5 minutes | Cook time: 20 minutes | Serves 2 cups

INGREDIENTS:

- 2 cup pimento-stuffed green olives, drained
- 6 packed cups baby spinach
- 4 teaspoon chopped garlic
- 1 teaspoon dried oregano
- 2/3 cup packed fresh basil
- 4 tablespoons olive oil
- 4 teaspoons red wine vinegar

DIRECTIONS:

1. Place all the ingredients in the bowl of a food processor and pulse until the mixture looks finely chopped but not puréed.
2. Scoop the tapenade into a container and refrigerate.
3. Store covered containers in the refrigerator for up to 5 days or until ready to serve.
4. Enjoy!

NUTRITION:

calories: 80 | fat: 8g | protein: 1g | carbohydrates: 1g | fiber: 1g | sodium: 6mg

13. Bulgur Pilaf with Almonds

Prep time: 10 minutes | Cook time: 20 minutes | Serves 6

INGREDIENTS:

- 1 cup uncooked bulgur
- 2 cups water
- 1/3 cup sliced almonds
- 1 1/2 cup small diced red bell pepper
- 1/2 cup chopped fresh cilantro
- 1 1/2 tablespoon olive oil
- 1/3 teaspoon salt

DIRECTIONS:

1. Place the bulgur and water in a saucepan and bring the water to a boil. Once the water is at a boil, cover the pot with a lid and turn off the heat. Let the covered pot stand for 20 minutes.
2. Transfer the cooked bulgur to a large mixing bowl and add the almonds, peppers, cilantro, oil, and salt. Stir to combine.
3. Place about 1 cup of bulgur in each of 4 containers.
4. Store covered containers in the refrigerator for up to 5 days or until ready to serve. Bulgur can be either reheated or eaten at room temperature.
5. Enjoy!

NUTRITION:

calories: 17 | fat: 7g | protein: 4g | carbohydrates: 25g | fiber: 6g | sodium: 152mg

14. Honey-Lemon Vinaigrette

Prep time: 10 minutes | Cook time: 5 minutes | Serves 1 cup

INGREDIENTS:

- 1/2 cup freshly squeezed lemon juice
- 2 teaspoon honey
- 4 teaspoons Dijon mustard
- 1/4 teaspoon kosher salt
- 1/2 cup olive oil

DIRECTIONS:

1. Place the lemon juice, honey, mustard, and salt in a small bowl and whisk to combine.
2. Whisk in the oil, pouring it into the bowl in a thin steam.
3. Pour the vinaigrette into a container and refrigerate.
4. Store the covered container in the refrigerator for up to 2 weeks or until ready to serve. Allow the vinaigrette to come to room temperature and shake before serving.
5. Enjoy!

NUTRITION:

calories: 131 | fat: 14g | protein: 1g | carbohydrates: 3g | fiber: 1g | sodium: 133mg

15. Garlic Yogurt Sauce

Prep time: 10 minutes | Cook time: 5 minutes | Serves 2 cup

INGREDIENTS:

2 cup low-fat (2%) plain Greek yogurt
1 teaspoon garlic powder
4 tablespoons freshly squeezed lemon juice
2 tablespoon olive oil
1/2 teaspoon kosher salt

DIRECTIONS:

1. Mix all the ingredients in a medium bowl until well combined.
2. Spoon the yogurt sauce into a container and refrigerate.
3. Store the covered container in the refrigerator for up to 7 days or until ready to serve.
4. Enjoy!

NUTRITION:

calories: 75 | fat: 5g | protein: 6g | carbohydrates: 3g | fiber: 0g | sodium: 173mg

16. Cinnamon Couscous

Prep time: 10 minutes | Cook time: 10 minutes | Serves 6

INGREDIENTS:

3 teaspoons olive oil
1/3 cup minced shallot
3/4 cup freshly squeezed orange juice (from 2 oranges)
3/4 cup water
1/4 teaspoon ground cinnamon
1/3 teaspoon kosher salt
3 cup whole-wheat couscous

DIRECTIONS:

1. Heat the oil in a saucepan over medium heat. Once the oil is simmering, add the shallot and cook for 2 minutes, stirring frequently. Add the orange juice, water, cinnamon, and salt, and bring to a boil.
2. Once the liquid is boiling, add the couscous, cover the pan, and turn off the heat. Leave the couscous covered for 5 minutes. When the couscous is done, fluff with a fork.
3. Place ¾ cup of couscous in each of 4 containers.
4. Store covered containers in the refrigerator for up to 5 days. Freeze for up to 2 months or until ready to serve.
5. Enjoy!

NUTRITION:

calories: 21 | fat: 4g | protein: 8g | carbohydrates: 41g | fiber: 5g | sodium: 147mg

17. Raspberry Red Wine Sauce

Prep time: 10 minutes | Cook time: 20 minutes | Serves 2 cups

INGREDIENTS:

4 teaspoons olive oil
4 tablespoons finely chopped shallot
3 cups frozen raspberries
2 cup dry, fruity red wine
2 teaspoon thyme leaves, roughly chopped
2 teaspoon honey
1/2 teaspoon kosher salt
1 teaspoon unsweetened cocoa powder

DIRECTIONS:

1. In a skillet, heat the oil over medium heat. Add the shallot and cook until soft, about 2 minutes.
2. Add the raspberries, wine, thyme, and honey and cook on medium heat until reduced, about 15 minutes.
3. Stir in the salt and cocoa powder.
4. Transfer the sauce to a blender and blend until smooth. Depending on how much you can scrape out of your blender, this recipe makes ¾ to 1 cup of sauce.
5. Scoop the sauce into a container and refrigerate.
6. Store the covered container in the refrigerator for up to 7 days or until ready to serve.
7. Enjoy!

NUTRITION:

calories: 107 | fat: 3g | protein: 1g | carbohydrates: 1g | fiber: 4g | sodium: 148mg

18. Roasted Cherry Tomato

Prep time: 10 minutes | Cook time: 40 minutes | Serves 2 cups

INGREDIENTS:

4 pints cherry tomatoes (20 ounces total)
4 teaspoons olive oil, plus 3 tablespoons
1/2 teaspoon kosher salt
1 teaspoon chopped garlic
1/2 cup fresh basil leaves

DIRECTIONS:

1. Preheat the oven to 350°F | 180°C | Fan 160°C. Line a sheet pan with a silicone baking mat or parchment paper.
2. Place the tomatoes on the lined sheet pan and toss with teaspoons of oil. Roast for 40 minutes, shaking the pan halfway through.
3. While the tomatoes are still warm, place them in a medium mixing bowl and add the salt, the garlic, and the remaining tablespoons of oil. Mash the tomatoes with the back of a fork. Stir in the fresh basil.
4. Scoop the sauce into a container and refrigerate.
5. Store the covered container in the refrigerator for up to 2 days or until ready to serve.
6. Enjoy!

NUTRITION:

calories: 141 | fat: 13g | protein: 1g | carbohydrates: 7g | fiber: 2g | sodium: 158mg

19. Basil, Almond, And Celery Heart Pesto

Prep time: 10 minutes | Cook time: 10 minutes | Serves 2 cups

INGREDIENTS:

1 cup raw, unsalted almonds
4 cups fresh basil leaves, (about 1 1/2 ounces)
1 cup chopped celery hearts with leaves
1/2 teaspoon kosher salt
2 tablespoons freshly squeezed lemon juice
1/2 cup olive oil
6 tablespoons water

DIRECTIONS:

1. Place the almonds in the bowl of a food processor and process until they look like coarse sand.
2. Add the basil, celery hearts, salt, lemon juice, oil and water and process until smooth. The sauce will be somewhat thick. If you would like a thinner sauce, add more water, oil, or lemon juice, depending on your taste preference.
3. Scoop the pesto into a container and refrigerate.
4. Store the covered container in the refrigerator for up to 2 weeks. Pesto may be frozen for up to 6 months or until ready to serve.
5. Enjoy!

NUTRITION:

calories: 231 | fat: 22g | protein: 4g | carbohydrates: 6g | fiber: 3g | sodium: 178mg

20. Sautéed Kale with Garlic and Lemon

Prep time: 10 minutes | Cook time: 7 minutes | Serves 6

INGREDIENTS:

1 1/2 tablespoon olive oil
4 1/2 bunches kale, stemmed and roughly chopped
3 teaspoons chopped garlic
1/3 teaspoon kosher salt
1 1/2 tablespoon freshly squeezed lemon juice

DIRECTIONS:

1. Heat the oil in a skillet over medium-high heat. Once the oil is simmering, add as much kale as will fit in the pan. You will probably only fit half the leaves into the pan at first. Mix the kale with tongs so that the leaves are coated with oil and start to wilt. As the kale wilts, keep adding more of the raw kale, continuing to use tongs to mix. Once all the kale is in the pan, add the garlic and salt and continue to cook until the kale is tender. Total cooking time from start to finish should be about 7 minutes.
2. Mix the lemon juice into the kale. Add additional salt and/or lemon juice if necessary.
3. Place 1 cup of kale in each of 4 containers and refrigerate.
4. Store covered containers in the refrigerator for up to 5 days or until ready to serve.
5. Enjoy!

NUTRITION:

calories: 8 | fat: 1g | protein: 6g | carbohydrates: 17g | fiber: 4g | sodium: 214mg

21. Red Wine Vinaigrette

Prep time: 10 minutes | Cook time: 5 minutes | Serves 2 cups

INGREDIENTS:

4 teaspoons Dijon mustard
4 tablespoons red wine vinegar
2 tablespoons of water
1/2 teaspoon dried oregano
1/2 teaspoon chopped garlic
1/4 teaspoon kosher salt
1/2 cup olive oil

DIRECTIONS:

1. Place the mustard, vinegar, water, oregano, garlic, and salt in a small bowl and whisk to combine.
2. Whisk in the oil, pouring it into the mustard-vinegar mixture in a thin steam.
3. Pour the vinaigrette into a container and refrigerate.
4. Store the covered container in the refrigerator for up to 2 weeks. Allow the vinaigrette to come to room temperature and shake before serving or until ready to serve.
5. Enjoy!

NUTRITION:

calories: 123| fat: 14g | protein: 0g | carbohydrates: 0g | fiber: 0g | sodium: 133mg

22. Romesco Sauce

Prep time: 10 minutes | Cook time: 10 minutes | Serves 2 cups

INGREDIENTS:

1 cup raw, unsalted almonds
8 medium garlic cloves (do not peel)
(12-ounce) jar of roasted red peppers, drained
1 cup canned diced fire-roasted tomatoes, drained
2 teaspoons smoked paprika
1 teaspoon kosher salt
Pinch cayenne pepper
4 teaspoons red wine vinegar
4 tablespoons olive oil

DIRECTIONS:

1. Preheat the oven to 350° F | 180°C | Fan 160°C.
2. Place the almonds and garlic cloves on a sheet pan and toast in the oven for 10 minutes. Remove from the oven and peel the garlic when cool enough to handle.
3. Place the almonds in the bowl of a food processor. Process the almonds until they resemble coarse sand, for 45 seconds. Add the garlic, peppers, tomatoes, paprika, salt, and cayenne. Blend until smooth.
4. Once the mixture is smooth, add the vinegar and oil and blend until well combined. Taste and add more vinegar or salt if needed.
5. Scoop the romesco sauce into a container and refrigerate.
6. Store the covered container in the refrigerator for up to 7 days or until ready to serve.
7. Enjoy!

NUTRITION:

calories: 158| fat: 13g | protein: 4g | carbohydrates: 10g | fiber: 3g | sodium: 292mg

23. Tzatziki Sauce

Prep time: 10 minutes | Cook time: 15 minutes | Serves 4 cups

INGREDIENTS:

4 English cucumber
4 cups low-fat (2%) plain Greek yogurt
2 tablespoon olive oil
4 teaspoons freshly squeezed lemon juice
1 teaspoon chopped garlic
1 teaspoon kosher salt
1/4 teaspoon freshly ground black pepper
4 tablespoons chopped fresh dill
4 tablespoons chopped fresh mint

DIRECTIONS:

1. Place a sieve over a medium bowl. Grate the cucumber, with the skin, over the sieve. Press the grated cucumber into the sieve with the flat surface of a spatula to press as much liquid out as possible.
2. In a separate medium bowl, place the yogurt, oil, lemon juice, garlic, salt, pepper, dill, and mint and stir to combine.
3. Press on the cucumber one last time, then add it to the yogurt mixture. Stir to combine. Taste and add more salt and lemon juice if necessary.
4. Scoop the sauce into a container and refrigerate.
5. Store the covered container in the refrigerator for up to days or until ready to serve.
6. Enjoy!

NUTRITION:

calories: 51 | fat: 2g | protein: 5g | carbohydrates: 3g | fiber: 1g | sodium: 137mg

24. Mocha-nut Stuffed Dates

Prep time: 10 minutes | Cook time: 10 minutes | Serves 6

INGREDIENTS:

3 tablespoons creamy, unsweetened, unsalted almond butter
1 1/2 teaspoon unsweetened cocoa powder
3 tablespoons walnut pieces
3 tablespoons water
1/3 teaspoon honey
1 1/8 teaspoon instant espresso powder
15 Medjool dates, pitted

DIRECTIONS:

1. In a small bowl, combine the almond butter, cocoa powder, and walnut pieces.
2. Place the water in a small microwaveable mug and heat on high for 30 seconds. Add the honey and espresso powder to the water and stir to dissolve.
3. Add the espresso water to the cocoa bowl and combine thoroughly until a creamy, thick paste forms.
4. Stuff each pitted date with 1 teaspoon of mocha filling.
5. Place 2 dates in each of 5 small containers.
6. Store covered containers in the refrigerator for up to 5 days or until ready to serve.
7. Enjoy!

NUTRITION:

calories: 205 | fat: 2g | protein: 3g | carbohydrates: 39g | fiber: 4g | sodium: 1mg

25. Roasted Eggplant Dip

Prep time: 10 minutes | Cook time: 45 minutes | Serves 4 cups

INGREDIENTS:

4 eggplants (close to 1 pound each)
2 teaspoon chopped garlic
4 tablespoons unsalted tahini
1/2 cup freshly squeezed lemon juice
2 tablespoon olive oil
1 teaspoon kosher salt

DIRECTIONS:

1. Preheat oven to 450°F. | 230°C | Fan 210°C. Line a sheet pan with a silicone baking mat or parchment paper.
2. Prick the eggplants in many places with a fork, place on the sheet pan, and roast in the oven until extremely soft, about 45 minutes. The eggplants should look like they are deflating.
3. When the eggplants are cool, cut them open and scoop the flesh into a large bowl. You may need to use your hands to pull the flesh away from the skin. Discard the skin. Mash the flesh very well with a fork.
4. Add the garlic, tahini, lemon juice, oil, and salt. Taste and adjust the seasoning with additional lemon juice, salt, or tahini if needed.
5. Scoop the dip into a container and refrigerate.
6. Store the covered container in the refrigerator for up to 5 days or until ready to serve.

NUTRITION:

calories: 8 | fat: 5g | protein: 2g | carbohydrates: 10g | fiber: 4g | sodium: 156mg

26. Antipasti Shrimp Skewers

Prep time: 10 minutes | Cook time: 10 minutes | Serves 6

INGREDIENTS:

24 pitted kalamata or green olives
24 fresh mozzarella balls (ciliegine)
24 cherry tomatoes
24 medium (41 to 50 per pound) precooked peeled, deveined shrimp
12 (8-inch) wooden or metal skewers

DIRECTIONS:

1. Alternate 2 olives, 2 mozzarella balls, 2 cherry tomatoes, and 2 shrimp on 8 skewers.
2. Place skewers in each of 4 containers.
3. Store covered containers in the refrigerator for up to 4 days or until ready to serve.

NUTRITION:

calories: 108 | fat: 6g | protein: 9g | carbohydrates: 2g | fiber: 1g | sodium: 328mg

27. Eggs With Sun-dried Tomatoes

Prep time: 10 minutes | Cook time: 15 minutes | Serves 6

INGREDIENTS:

7 1/2 large eggs
4 1/2 tablespoons prepared pesto

1/3 teaspoon white vinegar
3 tablespoons low-fat (2%) plain Greek yogurt
7 1/2 teaspoons sliced sun-dried tomatoes

DIRECTIONS:

1. Place the eggs in a saucepan and cover with water. Bring the water to a boil. As soon as the water starts to boil, place a lid on the pan and turn the heat off. Set a timer for 2 minutes.
2. When the timer goes off, drain the hot water and run cold water over the eggs to cool.
3. Peel the eggs, slice in half vertically, and scoop out the yolks. Place the yolks in a medium mixing bowl and add the pesto, vinegar, and yogurt. Mix well, until creamy.
4. Scoop about 1 tablespoon of the pesto-yolk mixture into each egg half. Top each with ½ teaspoon of sun-dried tomatoes.
5. Place 2 stuffed egg halves in each of 2 separate containers.
6. Store covered containers in the refrigerator for up to 5 days or until ready to serve.

NUTRITION:

calories: 124 | fat: 9g | protein: 8g | carbohydrates: 2g | fiber: 1g | sodium: 204mg

28. Spiced Sautéed Cabbage

Prep time: 10 minutes | Cook time: 10 minutes | Serves 6

INGREDIENTS:

3 teaspoons olive oil
1 1/2 small head green cabbage (about 1 1/2 to 2 pounds), cored and thinly sliced
1 1/2 teaspoon ground coriander
1 1/2 teaspoon garlic powder
3/4 teaspoon caraway seeds
3/4 teaspoon ground cumin
1/3 teaspoon kosher salt
Pinch red chili flakes
1 1/2 teaspoon freshly squeezed lemon juice

DIRECTIONS:

1. Heat the oil in a skillet over medium-high heat. Once the oil is hot, add the cabbage and cook down for 3 minutes. Add the coriander, garlic powder, caraway seeds, cumin, salt, and chili flakes (if using) and stir to combine. Continue cooking the cabbage for about 7 more minutes.
2. Stir in the lemon juice and cool.
3. Place 1 heaping cup of cabbage in each of 4 containers.
4. Store covered containers in the refrigerator for up to 5 days or until ready to serve.

NUTRITION:

calories: 69 | fat: 3g | protein: 8g | carbohydrates: 11g | fiber: 4g | sodium: 178mg

29. Blueberry, Flax, And Sunflower Butter Bites

Prep time: 10 minutes | Cook time: 10 minutes | Serves 4

INGREDIENTS:

1/8 cup ground flaxseed
1/3 cup unsweetened sunflower butter, preferably unsalted
1/4 cup dried blueberries
1 1/3 tablespoons all-fruit blueberry preserves
Zest of 1 lemon
1 1/3 tablespoons unsalted sunflower seeds
1/4 cup rolled oats

DIRECTIONS:

1. Mix all the ingredients in a medium mixing bowl until well combined.
2. Form balls, slightly smaller than a golf ball, from the mixture and place on a plate in the freezer for about 20 minutes to firm up.
3. Place 2 bites in each of 6 containers and refrigerate.
4. Store covered containers in the refrigerator for up to 5 days. Bites may also be stored in the freezer for up to 3 months or until ready to serve.

NUTRITION:

calories: 229 | fat: 14g | protein: 7g | carbohydrates: 26g | fiber: 3g | sodium: 1mg

30. Mascarpone With Strawberries

Prep time: 10 minutes | Cook time: 10 minutes | Serves 6

INGREDIENTS:

1 1/2 (8-ounce) container mascarpone cheese
3 teaspoons honey
1/3 teaspoon ground cardamom
3 tablespoons milk
1 1/2-pound strawberries (should be 24 strawberries in the pack)

DIRECTIONS:

1. Combine the mascarpone, honey, cardamom, and milk in a medium mixing bowl.
2. Mix with a spoon until super creamy, about 30 seconds.
3. Place 6 strawberries and 2 tablespoons of the mascarpone mixture in each of 4 containers.
4. Store covered containers in the refrigerator for up to 5 days or until ready to serve.

NUTRITION:

calories: 289 | fat: 2g | protein: 1g | carbohydrates: 11g | fiber: 3g | sodium: 26mg

31. White Bean and Mushroom Dip

Prep time: 10 minutes | Cook time: 8 minutes | Serves 6

INGREDIENTS:

4 teaspoons olive oil, plus 2 tablespoons
16 ounces button or cremini mushrooms, sliced
2 teaspoon chopped garlic
4 tablespoon fresh thyme leaves
4 (15.5-ounce) cans cannellini beans, drained and rinsed
4 tablespoons plus 1 teaspoon freshly squeezed lemon juice
1 teaspoon kosher salt

DIRECTIONS

1. Heat 2 teaspoons of oil in a skillet over medium-high heat. Once the oil is simmering, add the mushrooms and sauté for 6 minutes. Add the garlic and thyme and continue cooking for 2 minutes.
2. While the mushrooms are cooking, place the beans and lemon juice, the remaining tablespoons of oil, and the salt in the bowl of a food processor. Add the mushrooms as soon as they are done cooking and blend everything until smooth. Scrape down the sides of the bowl if necessary and continue to process until smooth.
3. Taste and adjust the seasoning with lemon juice or salt if needed.
4. Scoop the dip into a container and refrigerate.
5. Store the covered container in the refrigerator for up to 2 days. Dip can be frozen for up to 3 months or until ready to serve.

NUTRITION:

calories: 192 | fat: 2g | protein: 9g | carbohydrates: 25g | fiber: 7g | sodium: 197mg

32. Candied Maple-cinnamon Walnuts

Prep time: 10 minutes | Cook time: 15 minutes | Serves 6

INGREDIENTS:

3 cup walnut halves
3/4 teaspoon ground cinnamon
3 tablespoons pure maple syrup

DIRECTIONS:

1. Preheat oven to 325°F. | 170°C | Fan 150°C. Line a baking sheet with a silicone baking mat or parchment paper.
2. In a small bowl, mix the walnuts, cinnamon, and maple syrup until the walnuts are coated.
3. Pour the nuts onto the baking sheet, making sure to scrape out all the maple syrup. Bake for 15 minutes. Allow the nuts to cool completely.
4. Place ¼ cup of nuts in each of 4 containers or resealable sandwich bags.
5. Store covered containers at room temperature for up to 7 days or until ready to serve.

NUTRITION:

calories: 190 | fat: 17g | protein: 4g | carbohydrates: 10g | fiber: 2g | sodium: 2mg

33. Smoked Paprika and Olive Oil–Marinated Carrots

Prep time: 10 minutes | Cook time: 15 minutes | Serves 6

INGREDIENTS:

(1-pound) bag baby carrots (not the petite size)
3 tablespoons olive oil
3 tablespoons red wine vinegar
1/3 teaspoon garlic powder
1/3 teaspoon ground cumin
1/3 teaspoon smoked paprika
1/4 teaspoon red pepper flakes
1/3 cup chopped parsley
1/3 teaspoon kosher salt

DIRECTIONS:

1. Pour enough water into a saucepan to come ¼ inch up the sides. Turn the heat to high, bring the water to a boil, add the carrots, and cover with a lid. Steam the carrots for 5 minutes, until crisp and tender.
2. After the carrots have cooled, mix with the oil, vinegar, garlic powder, cumin, paprika, red pepper, parsley, and salt.
3. Place ¾ cup of carrots in each of 4 containers.
4. Store covered containers in the refrigerator for up to 5 days or until ready to serve.

NUTRITION:

calories: 109 | fat: 7g | protein: 2g | carbohydrates: 11g | fiber: 3g | sodium: 234mg

34. Chermoula Sauce

Prep time: 10 minutes | Cook time: 10 minutes | Serves 2 Cups

INGREDIENTS:

2 cup packed parsley leaves
2 cup cilantro leaves
1 cup mint leaves
2 teaspoon chopped garlic
1 teaspoon ground cumin
1 teaspoon ground coriander
1 teaspoon smoked paprika
1/4 teaspoon cayenne pepper
1/4 teaspoon kosher salt
6 tablespoons freshly squeezed lemon juice
6 tablespoons water
1 cup extra-virgin olive oil

DIRECTIONS:

1. Place all the ingredients in a blender or food processor and blend until smooth.
2. Pour the chermoula into a container and refrigerate.
3. Store the covered container in the refrigerator for up to 5 days or until ready to serve.

NUTRITION
calories: 257 | fat: 27g | protein: 1g | carbohydrates: 4g | fiber: 2g | sodium: 96mg

35. Apple Dressing

Prep time: 5 minutes | Cook time: 0 minutes | Serves 4

INGREDIENTS:

4 tablespoons apple cider vinegar
2/3 lemon, juiced
2/3 lemon, zested
Salt and freshly ground black pepper, to taste

DIRECTIONS:

1. In a jar, combine the vinegar, lemon juice, and zest. Season with salt and pepper, cover and shake well.
2. Serve when ready.

NUTRITION

calories: 4 | fat: 0g | protein: 0g | carbohydrates: 1g | fiber: 0g | sodium: 0mg

36. Vinaigrette

Prep time: 5 minutes | Cook time: 0 minutes | Serves 4

INGREDIENTS:

1/2 cup plus 2 tablespoons extra-virgin olive oil
4 tablespoons red wine vinegar
2 tablespoon apple cider vinegar
4 teaspoons honey
4 teaspoons Dijon mustard
1 teaspoon minced garlic
1/4 teaspoon kosher salt
1/4 teaspoon freshly ground black pepper

DIRECTIONS:

1. In a jar, combine the vinegar, lemon juice, and zest. Season with salt and pepper, cover and shake well.
2. Serve when ready.

NUTRITION

calories: 386 | fat: 41g | protein: 0g | carbohydrates: 6g | fiber: 0g | sodium: 198mg

37. Spicy Harissa Sauce

Prep time: 10 minutes | Cook time: 20 minutes | Serves 4

INGREDIENTS:

1 1/3 cup vegetable broth
1 1/3 tablespoon tamari
1 1/3 teaspoon ground cumin
2 2/3 tablespoons tomato paste
1 1/3 yellow onion, cut into thick rings
1 1/3 large red bell pepper, deseeded, cored, and cut into chunks
5 1/3 garlic cloves, peeled
1 1/3 tablespoon Hungarian paprika

DIRECTIONS:

1. Preheat oven to 450°F. | 230°C | Fan 210°C. Line a baking sheet with parchment paper.
2. Place the pepper on the prepared baking sheet, meat side up, and space the onion and garlic around the pepper.
3. Roast in the preheated oven for 20 minutes. Transfer to a blender.
4. Add the vegetable stock, tomato paste, tamari, cumin and paprika. Puree until smooth.
5. Sauce can be served warm or cold.

NUTRITION

calories: 15 | fat: 1g | protein: 1g | carbohydrates: 3g | fiber: 1g | sodium: 201mg

38. Oregano Cucumber Dressing

Prep time: 5 minutes | Cook time: 0 minutes | Serves 4

INGREDIENTS:

2 tablespoon dried, minced garlic
2 cucumbers, seeded and peeled
3 cups plain, unsweetened, full-fat Greek yogurt
1 lemon, juiced and zested
1 tablespoon dried dill
4 teaspoons dried oregano
Salt, to taste

DIRECTIONS:

1. In a food processor, combine the yogurt, cucumber, lemon juice, garlic, dill, oregano and a pinch of salt and mix until smooth. Adjust toppings as needed and transfer to serving bowl.

NUTRITION

calories: 209 | fat: 10g | protein: 18g | carbohydrates: 14g | fiber: 2g | sodium: 69mg

39. Sweet Pineapple Salsa

Prep time: 10 minutes | Cook time: 0 minutes | Serves 8

INGREDIENTS:

1 1/3 bunch cilantro or mint, leaves only, chopped
1 1/3 pound (454 g) fresh or thawed frozen pineapple, finely diced, juices reserved
1 1/3 white or red onion, finely diced
1 1/3 jalapeño, minced (optional)
Salt, to taste

DIRECTIONS:

1. Mix the pineapple with its juice, onion, cilantro and jalapeño (if desired) in a medium bowl. Season with salt to taste and serve.
2. The sauce can be stored in the refrigerator in an airtight container for up to 2 days.

NUTRITION

calories: 55 | fat: 0g | protein: 1g | carbohydrates: 12g | fiber: 2g | sodium: 20mg

40. Marinara Dip

Prep time: 15 minutes | Cook time: 40 minutes | Makes 10 cups

INGREDIENTS:

1 1/4 small onion, diced
1 1/4 small red bell pepper, stemmed, seeded and chopped
2 1/2 tablespoons plus 1/4 cup extra-virgin olive oil, divided
2 1/2 tablespoons butter (optional)
5 to 6 garlic cloves, minced
2 1/2 teaspoon salt, divided
2/3 teaspoon freshly ground black pepper
2 1/2 (32-ounce / 907-g) cans crushed tomatoes (with basil, if possible), with their juices
2/3 cup thinly sliced basil leaves, divided
2 1/2 tablespoons chopped fresh rosemary
1 1/4 to 2 teaspoons crushed red pepper flakes (optional)

DIRECTIONS:

1. In a food processor, combine the onion and pepper and whisk until very finely chopped.
2. In a large skillet, heat 2 tablespoons of olive oil and butter (if desired) over medium heat. Add the chopped onion and red pepper and sauté until it starts to turn tender, about 5 minutes.
3. Add the garlic, salt and pepper and sauté until fragrant, for another 1 to 2 minutes.
4. Reduce the heat to low and add the tomatoes and their juices, 1 cup remaining olive oil, ¼ cup basil, rosemary and red pepper flakes (if using). Stir to mix, then bring to a boil and cover. Cook over low heat for 30-60 minutes to allow the flavors to blend.

5. Add ¼ cup of chopped fresh basil remaining after removing from heat, stirring to combine or until ready to serve.

NUTRITION
calories: 256| fat: 20g | protein: 4g | carbohydrates: 19g | fiber: 5g | sodium: 803mg

41. Yogurt Dressing
Prep time: 5 minutes | Cook time: 0 minutes | Serves 6

INGREDIENTS:
1 teaspoon kosher salt
1/2 teaspoon garlic powder
2 tablespoon apple cider vinegar
1 lemon, juiced
2 tablespoon chopped fresh oregano
2 cup plain, unsweetened, full-fat Greek yogurt
1 cup extra-virgin olive oil
1 teaspoon dried parsley
1/2 teaspoon freshly ground black pepper

DIRECTIONS:
In a large bowl, combine the yogurt, olive oil, vinegar, lemon juice, oregano, parsley, salt, garlic powder and pepper and beat well.
Once all ingredients are combined you may serve your dressing.

NUTRITION
calories: 402| fat: 40g | protein: 8g | carbohydrates: 4g | fiber: 0g | sodium: 417mg

42. Orange Dressing
Prep time: 5 minutes | Cook time: 0 minutes | Serves 4

INGREDIENTS:
1 teaspoon salt
2 oranges, zested
1/2 cup extra-virgin olive oil
2 teaspoon garlic powder
4 tablespoons freshly squeezed orange juice
1 1/2 teaspoon za'atar seasoning
1/2 teaspoon Dijon mustard
Freshly ground black pepper, to taste

DIRECTIONS:
1. In a jar, combine the olive oil, orange juice and zest, garlic powder, za'atar, salt and mustard. Season with pepper and shake vigorously until completely absorbed or until ready to serve.

NUTRITION
calories: 283| fat: 27g | protein: 1g | carbohydrates: 11g | fiber: 2g | sodium: 597mg

43. Herbed Oil
Prep time: 5 minutes | Cook time: 0 minutes | Serves 4

INGREDIENTS:
1 cup extra-virgin olive oil
2 teaspoon dried basil
2 teaspoon dried parsley
2 teaspoon fresh rosemary leaves
4 teaspoons dried oregano
1/4 teaspoon salt

DIRECTIONS:
1. Pour the oil into a small bowl and add the basil, parsley, rosemary, oregano and salt while whisking the oil with a fork.
2. Once mixed, oil is ready to be served.

NUTRITION
calories: 486| fat: 54g | protein: 1g | carbohydrates: 2g | fiber: 1g | sodium: 78mg

44. Onion Dip
Prep time: 10 minutes | Cook time: 12 minutes | Serves 6

INGREDIENTS:
1/3 teaspoon black pepper
1/4 teaspoon red pepper flakes
3 cups peeled pearl onions
3/4 teaspoon salt
1 1/2 cup nonfat plain Greek yogurt
4 1/2 garlic cloves
4 1/2 tablespoons olive oil, divided
1 1/2 tablespoon lemon juice
Pita chips, vegetables, or toasted bread for serving (optional)

DIRECTIONS:
1. Preheat the air fryer to 360°F (182°C)
2. In a large bowl, combine the spring onions and garlic with 2 tablespoons of olive oil until the onions are well coated.
3. Pour the garlic and onion mixture into the basket of the air fryer and roast for 12 minutes.
4. Transfer the garlic and onions to a food processor. Blend the vegetables several times, until the onions are chopped, but still have some pieces.
5. In a large bowl, combine the garlic and onions and the remaining tablespoon of olive oil, along with the salt, yogurt, lemon juice, black pepper, and red pepper flakes.
6. Cover and chill for 1 hour before serving with pita chips, vegetables, toast or as you desire.

NUTRITION
calories: 150| fat: 10g | protein: 7g | carbohydrates: 7g | fiber: 1g | sodium: 3mg

45. Bitter-sweet Romesco Sauce
Prep time: 10 minutes | Cook time: 0 minutes | Serves 12

INGREDIENTS:
1 1/4 (12-ounce / 340-g) jar roasted red peppers, drained
1 1/4 (14 1/2-ounce / 411-g) can diced tomatoes, undrained
2/3 cup dry-roasted almonds
2 1/3 garlic cloves
2 1/3 teaspoons red wine vinegar
1 1/4 teaspoon smoked paprika or 1/2 teaspoon cayenne pepper
1/3 teaspoon kosher or sea salt
1/3 teaspoon freshly ground black pepper
1/3 cup extra-virgin olive oil
²/₃ cup torn, day-old bread or toast
Assortment of sliced raw vegetables such as carrots, celery, cucumber, green beans, and bell peppers, for serving

DIRECTIONS:
1. In a high-powered blender or food processor, combine the roasted peppers, tomatoes and their juices, almonds, garlic, vinegar, smoked paprika, salt and pepper.
2. Start blending the ingredients at medium speed and slowly pour in the oil while the blender is running. Continue to blend until the sauce is well blended.
3. Add the bread and puree.
4. Serve with raw vegetables to soak, alternatively store in a lidded jar for up to a week in the refrigerator.

NUTRITION
calories: 96| fat: 7g | protein: 3g | carbohydrates: 8g | fiber: 3g | sodium: 2mg

46. Cucumber Yogurt Dip
Prep time: 4 minutes | Cook time: 0 minutes | Serves 4

INGREDIENTS:
2 tablespoon chopped fresh mint
1 cup cucumber, peeled, seeded, and diced
2 cup plain, unsweetened, full-fat Greek yogurt
2 tablespoons freshly squeezed lemon juice
2 small garlic cloves, minced
Salt and freshly ground black pepper, to taste

DIRECTIONS:
1. In a food processor, combine the yogurt, cucumber, lemon juice, mint and garlic. Blend several times to combine, leaving noticeable pieces of cucumber.
2. Taste and season with salt and pepper.
3. Then serve when ready.

NUTRITION
calories: 128| fat: 6g | protein: 11g | carbohydrates: 7g | fiber: 0g | sodium: 47mg

BREAKFAST RECIPES

Breakfasts

47. Sweet Potato Toast

Prep time: 5 minutes | Cook time: 15 minutes | Serves 6

INGREDIENTS:

- Salt and freshly ground black pepper, to taste
- 3 large sweet potatoes, sliced lengthwise
- 3 plum tomatoes, halved
- 9 tablespoons extra-virgin olive oil, divided
- 1 1/2 cup fresh spinach
- 12 medium asparagus, trimmed
- 6 tablespoons pesto
- 6 large cooked eggs or egg substitute (poached, scrambled, or fried)
- 1 1/2 cup arugula
- 6 tablespoons shredded Asiago cheese

DIRECTIONS:

1. Preheat oven to 450°F.| 230°C | Fan 210°C
2. On a baking sheet, brush the halves of the cherry tomatoes with 2 tablespoons of olive oil and season with salt and pepper. Roast the tomatoes in the oven for about 15 minutes, then take them out of the oven and let them rest.
3. Place the sweet potato slices on a separate baking tray and brush about 2 tablespoons of oil on each side and season with salt and pepper. Cook the sweet potato slices for about 15 minutes, turning once after 5-7 minutes, until tender. Remove from the oven and set aside.
4. In a skillet, heat the remaining 2 tablespoons of olive oil over medium heat and sauté the fresh spinach until wilted. Remove from the pan and let it rest on a plate lined with paper towels. In the same pan add the asparagus and sauté them, turning them over. Transfer to a paper towel lined plate.
5. Arrange the grilled sweet potato slices on serving plates and divide the spinach and asparagus equally between the slices. Place a prepared egg on top of the spinach and asparagus. Top this with ¼ cup of arugula.
6. Finish with 1 tablespoon of pesto and sprinkle with 1 tablespoon of cheese.
7. Serve with 1 roasted datterino tomato.

NUTRITION

calories: 441| fat: 35g | protein: 13g | carbohydrates: 23g | fiber: 4g | sodium: 481mg

48. Mini Frittatas

Prep time: 10 minutes | Cook time: 25 minutes | Serves 8

INGREDIENTS:

- 1/3 cup chopped red bell pepper
- 1/3 cup asparagus, sliced lengthwise in half and chopped
- 1/3 cup chopped red potatoes (about 3 small)
- 1/3 cup minced onions
- Nonstick cooking spray
- 2 tablespoons extra-virgin olive oil
- 5 1/3 large eggs
- 5 1/3 large egg whites
- 2/3 cup unsweetened almond milk
- Salt and freshly ground black pepper, to taste
- 2/3 cup shredded low-moisture, part-skim Mozzarella cheese, divided

DIRECTIONS:

1. Preheat oven to 350°F | 180°C | Fan 160°C. Using non-stick cooking spray, prepare a 12-point muffin pan.
2. In a medium skillet, heat the oil over medium heat and sauté the potatoes and onions for about 4 minutes, until the potatoes are tender.
3. Add the pepper and asparagus and sauté for about 4 minutes, until tender. Transfer the contents of a pan to a paper towel lined plate to cool.
4. In a bowl, beat the eggs, egg whites and milk together. Season with salt and pepper.
5. Once the vegetables have cooled to room temperature, add the vegetables and ¼ cup of mozzarella.
6. Using a spoon or ladle, evenly distribute the contents of the bowl into the prepared muffin pan, about halfway filling the cups.
7. Sprinkle the remaining ¼ cup of cheese over the cups.
8. Cook for 20-25 minutes or until the eggs reach a core temperature of 145°F (63°C) or the center is firm.
9. Let the mini omelettes rest for 5-10 minutes before removing them from the muffin pan.
10. Serve when ready.

NUTRITION

calories: 133| fat: 9g | protein: 10g | carbohydrates: 4g | fiber: 1g | sodium: 151mg

49. Vanilla Raspberry Oats

Prep time: 10 minutes | Cook time: 0 minutes | Serves 4

INGREDIENTS:

- ²/₃ cup vanilla, unsweetened almond milk
- 1/3 cup rolled oats
- 1/2 cup raspberries
- 2 teaspoon honey
- 1/2 teaspoon turmeric
- 1/4 teaspoon ground cinnamon
- Pinch ground cloves

DIRECTIONS:

1. In a mason jar, combine the almond milk, oats, raspberries, honey, turmeric, cinnamon, and cloves and shake well.
2. Store in the refrigerator for 8 to 24 hours.
3. Serve cold or heated.

NUTRITION

calories: 82| fat: 2g | protein: 2g | carbohydrates: 14g | fiber: 3g | sodium: 98mg

50. Bulgur Bowls with Fruits

Prep time: 5 minutes | Cook time: 15 minutes | Serves 8

INGREDIENTS:

- 2 2/3 cups unsweetened almond milk
- 2 cups uncooked bulgur
- 1 1/3 cup water
- 2/3 teaspoon ground cinnamon
- 2 2/3 cups frozen (or fresh, pitted) dark sweet cherries
- 10 2/3 dried (or fresh) figs, chopped
- 2/3 cup chopped almonds
- 1/3 cup loosely packed fresh mint, chopped

DIRECTIONS:

1. Combine the milk, bulgur, water, and cinnamon in a medium saucepan, stirring, and bring just to a boil.
2. Cover, reduce the heat to medium-low, and allow to simmer for 10 minutes, or until the liquid is absorbed.
3. Turn off the heat, but keep the pan on the stove, and stir in the frozen cherries (no need to thaw), figs, and almonds. Cover and let the hot bulgur thaw the cherries and partially hydrate the figs, about 1 minute.
4. Fold in the mint and stir to combine.
5. Serve when ready.

NUTRITION

calories: 207| fat: 6g | protein: 8g | carbohydrates: 32g | fiber: 4g | sodium: 82mg

51. Pistachio Smoothie

Prep time: 10 minutes | Cook time: 0 minutes | Serves 2

INGREDIENTS:

- 1 cup plain whole-milk Greek yogurt
- 1 cup unsweetened almond milk, plus more as needed
- Zest and juice of 1 clementine or 1/2 orange
- 2 tablespoon extra-virgin olive oil or MCT oil
- 2 tablespoon shelled pistachios, coarsely chopped
- 2 to 2 teaspoons monk fruit extract or stevia (optional)
- 1/2 to 1/2 teaspoon ground allspice or unsweetened pumpkin pie spice
- 1/2 teaspoon ground cinnamon
- 1/2 teaspoon vanilla extract

DIRECTIONS:

1. In a blender or a large wide-mouth jar, if using an immersion blender, combine the yogurt, ½ cup almond milk, clementine zest and juice, olive oil, pistachios, monk fruit extract (if using), allspice, cinnamon, and vanilla and blend until smooth and creamy, adding more almond milk to achieve your desired consistency.
2. Serve when ready.

NUTRITION

calories: 264| fat: 22g | protein: 5g | carbohydrates: 12g | fiber: 1g | sodium: 127mg

52. Greek Yogurt with Nuts

Prep time: 10 minutes | Cook time: 0 minutes | Serves 4

INGREDIENTS:

- 2 cup plain whole-milk Greek yogurt
- 8 tablespoons heavy whipping cream
- 1 cup frozen berries, thawed with juices
- 2 teaspoon vanilla or almond extract (optional)
- 1 teaspoon ground cinnamon (optional)
- 4 tablespoon ground flaxseeds
- 8 tablespoons chopped nuts (walnuts or pecans)

DIRECTIONS:

1. In a small bowl or glass, combine the yogurt, heavy whipping cream, thawed berries in their juice, vanilla or almond extract (if using), cinnamon (if using), and flaxseed and stir well until smooth.
2. Top with chopped nuts and enjoy.
3. Then serve when ready.

NUTRITION

calories: 267 | fat: 19g | protein: 11g | carbs: 12g | fiber: 3g | sodium: 63mg

53. Chickpea and Hummus Patties

Prep time: 15 minutes | Cook time: 13 minutes | Serves 6

INGREDIENTS:

1 1/2 (15-ounce / 425-g) can chickpeas, drained and rinsed	1 1/2 tablespoon extra-virgin olive oil
3/4 cup lemony garlic hummus or 1/2 cup prepared hummus	1 1/2 cucumber, unpeeled (or peeled if desired), cut in half lengthwise
3/4 cup whole-wheat panko bread crumbs	1 1/2 (6-ounce / 170-g) container 2% plain Greek yogurt
1 1/2 large egg	1 1/2 garlic clove, minced
3 teaspoons dried oregano	3 whole-wheat pita breads, cut in half
1/3 teaspoon freshly ground black pepper	1 1/2 medium tomato, cut into 4 thick slices

DIRECTIONS:

1. In a large bowl, mash the chickpeas with a potato masher or fork until coarsely smashed. Add the hummus, bread crumbs, egg, oregano, and pepper. Stir well to combine. With your hands, form the mixture into 4 (½-cup-size) patties. Press each patty flat to about ¾ inch thick and put on a plate.
2. In a large skillet over medium-high heat, heat the oil until very hot, about 3 minutes. Cook the patties for 5 minutes, then flip with a spatula. Cook for an additional 5 minutes.
3. While the patties are cooking, shred half of the cucumber with a box grater or finely chop with a knife. In a small bowl, stir together the shredded cucumber, yogurt, and garlic to make the tzatziki sauce. Slice the remaining half of the cucumber into ¼-inch-thick slices and set aside.
4. Toast the pita breads. To assemble the sandwiches, lay the pita halves on a work surface. Into each pita, place a few slices of cucumber, a chickpea patty, and a tomato slice, then drizzle the sandwich with the tzatziki sauce.
5. Then serve when ready.

NUTRITION

calories: 288 | fat: 22g | protein: 4g | carbohydrates: 8g | fiber: 2g | sodium: 271mg

54. Cardamom-Cinnamon Oats

Prep time: 10 minutes | Cook time: 0 minutes | Serves 4

INGREDIENTS:

1 cup vanilla, unsweetened almond milk (not Silk brand)	sweetener
1 cup rolled oats	2 teaspoon chia seeds
4 tablespoons sliced almonds	1/2 teaspoon ground cardamom
4 tablespoons simple sugar liquid	1/2 teaspoon ground cinnamon

DIRECTIONS:

1. In a mason jar, combine the almond milk, oats, almonds, liquid sweetener, chia seeds, cardamom, and cinnamon and shake well. 2. Store in the refrigerator for 8 to 24 hours.
3. Then serve when ready heated or cold.

NUTRITION

calories: 131 | fat: 6g | protein: 5g | carbohydrates: 17g | fiber: 4g | sodium: 45mg

55. Spinach Pie

Prep time: 10 minutes | Cook time: 20 minutes | Serves 6

INGREDIENTS:

Non-stick cooking spray	1/4 teaspoon ground nutmeg
1 1/2 tablespoons extra-virgin olive oil	3 large eggs, divided
3/4 onion, chopped	3/4 cup grated Parmesan cheese, divided
3/4 pound (454 g) frozen spinach, thawed	1 1/2 puff pastry doughs, (organic, if available), at room temperature
1/4 teaspoon garlic salt	3 hard-boiled eggs, halved
1/4 teaspoon freshly ground black pepper	

DIRECTIONS:

1. Preheat oven to 350°F | 180°C | Fan 160°C. Spray a baking sheet with non-stick cooking spray and set aside.
2. Heat a large sauté pan or skillet over medium-high heat. Put in the oil and onion and cook for about 5 minutes, until translucent.
3. Squeeze the excess water from the spinach, then add to the pan and cook, uncovered, so that any excess water from the spinach can evaporate. Add the garlic salt, pepper, and nutmeg. Remove from heat and set aside to cool.
4. In a small bowl, crack 3 eggs and mix well. Add the eggs and ½ cup Parmesan cheese to the cooled spinach mix.
5. On the prepared baking sheet, roll out the pastry dough. Layer the spinach mix on top of dough, leaving 2 inches around each edge.
6. Once the spinach is spread onto the pastry dough, place hard-boiled egg halves evenly throughout the pie, then cover with the second pastry dough. Pinch the edges closed.
7. Crack the remaining egg in a small bowl and mix well. Brush the egg wash over the pastry dough.
8. Bake for 15 to 20 minutes, until golden brown and warmed through.
9. Then serve when ready.

NUTRITION

calories: 417 | fat: 28g | protein: 17g | carbohydrates: 25g | fiber: 3g | sodium: 490mg

56. Pancakes with Berry Sauce

Prep time: 5 minutes | Cook time: 10 minutes | Serves 6

INGREDIENTS:

1 1/2 cup almond flour	Zest and juice of 1 lemon
1 1/2 teaspoon baking powder	3/4 teaspoon vanilla extract
1/3 teaspoon salt	Berry Sauce:
9 tablespoon extra-virgin olive oil, divided	1 1/2 cup frozen mixed berries
3 large eggs, beaten	1 1/2 tablespoon water, plus more as needed

DIRECTIONS:

1. In a large bowl, combine the almond flour, baking powder, and salt and stir to break up any clumps.
2. Add 4 tablespoons olive oil, beaten eggs, lemon zest and juice, and vanilla extract and stir until well mixed.
3. Heat 1 tablespoon of olive oil in a large skillet. Spoon about 2 tablespoons of batter for each pancake. Cook until bubbles begin to form, 4 to 5 minutes. Flip and cook for another 2 to 3 minutes. Repeat with the remaining 1 tablespoon of olive oil and batter.
Berry Sauce
4. Combine the frozen berries, water, and vanilla extract in a small saucepan and heat over medium-high heat for 3 to 4 minutes until bubbly, adding more water as needed. Using the back of a spoon or fork, mash the berries and whisk until smooth.
5. Serve the pancakes with the berry sauce.
6. Enjoy!

NUTRITION

calories: 275 | fat: 26g | protein: 4g | carbohydrates: 8g | fiber: 2g | sodium: 271mg

57. Blueberry & Chia Seeds Smoothie

Prep time: 10 minutes | Cook time: 0 minutes | Serves 2

INGREDIENTS:

2 cup unsweetened almond milk, plus more as needed	2 tablespoon extra-virgin olive oil or avocado oil
1/2 cup frozen blueberries	2 to 2 teaspoons stevia or monk fruit extract (optional)
4 tablespoons unsweetened almond butter	1 teaspoon vanilla extract
2 tablespoon ground flaxseed or chia seeds	1/2 teaspoon ground cinnamon

DIRECTIONS:

1. In a blender or a large wide-mouth jar, if using an immersion blender, combine the almond milk, blueberries, almond butter, flaxseed, olive oil, stevia (if using), vanilla, and cinnamon and blend until smooth and creamy.
2. Adding more almond milk to achieve your desired consistency.
3. Then serve when ready.

NUTRITION

calories: 460 | fat: 40g | protein: 8g | carbs: 20g | fiber: 9g | sodium: 147mg

58. Green Smoothie

Prep time: 10 minutes | Cook time: 0 minutes | Serves 2

INGREDIENTS:

2 small very ripe avocado, peeled and pitted

2 cup almond milk or water, plus more as needed
2 cup tender baby spinach leaves, stems removed
1 medium cucumber, peeled and seeded
2 tablespoon extra-virgin olive oil or avocado oil
16 to 10 fresh mint leaves, stems removed
2 to 2 tablespoons juice of 1 lime

DIRECTIONS:

1. In a blender or a large wide-mouth jar, if using an immersion blender, combine the avocado, almond milk, spinach, cucumber, olive oil, mint, and lime juice and blend until smooth and creamy.
2. Adding more almond milk or water to achieve your desired consistency.
3. Then serve when ready.

NUTRITION

calories: 330 | fat: 30g | protein: 4g | carbohydrates: 19g | fiber: 8g | sodium: 36mg

59. Frittata

Prep time: 10 minutes | Cook time: 7 minutes | Serves 4

INGREDIENTS:

8 large eggs
4 tablespoons fresh chopped herbs, such as rosemary, thyme, oregano, basil or 1 teaspoon dried herbs
1/2 teaspoon salt
Freshly ground black pepper, to taste
8 tablespoons extra-virgin olive oil, divided
2 cup fresh spinach, arugula, kale, or other leafy greens
8 ounces (113 g) quartered artichoke hearts, rinsed, drained, and thoroughly dried
16 cherry tomatoes, halved
1 cup crumbled soft goat cheese

DIRECTIONS:

1. Preheat the oven to broil on low.
2. In a small bowl, combine the eggs, herbs, salt, and pepper and whisk well with a fork. Set aside.
3. In a 4- to 5-inch oven-safe skillet or omelette pan, heat 2 tablespoons olive oil over medium heat. Add the spinach, artichoke hearts, and cherry tomatoes and sauté until just wilted, 1 to 2 minutes.
Pour in the egg mixture and let it cook undisturbed over medium heat for 3 to 4 minutes, until the eggs begin to set on the bottom.
4. Sprinkle the goat cheese across the top of the egg mixture and transfer the skillet to the oven.
5. Broil for 4 to 5 minutes, or until the frittata is firm in the centre and golden brown on top.
6. Remove from the oven and run a rubber spatula around the edge to loosen the sides. Invert onto a large plate or cutting board and slice in half. Serve warm and drizzled with the remaining 2 tablespoons olive oil.
7. Then serve when ready.

NUTRITION

calories: 527 | fat: 47g | protein: 21g | carbs: 10g | fiber: 3g | sodium: 760mg

60. Cheese Frittata with Vegetables

Prep time: 15 minutes | Cook time: 25 minutes | Serves 4

INGREDIENTS:

2 tablespoon olive oil
1 pint cherry or grape tomatoes
4 garlic cloves, minced
10 large eggs, beaten
6 tablespoons unsweetened almond milk
1 teaspoon salt
Pinch freshly ground black pepper
4 tablespoons minced fresh oregano
4 tablespoons minced fresh basil
4 ounces (57 g) crumbled goat cheese (about 1/2 cup)

DIRECTIONS:

1. Heat the oil in a non-stick skillet over medium heat. Add the tomatoes. As they start to cook, pierce some of them so they give off some of their juice. Reduce the heat to medium-low, cover the pan, and let the tomatoes soften.
2. When the tomatoes are mostly softened and broken down, remove the lid, add the garlic and continue to sauté.
3. In a medium bowl, combine the eggs, milk, salt, pepper, and herbs and whisk well to combine.
4. Turn the heat up to medium-high. Add the egg mixture to the tomatoes and garlic, then sprinkle the goat cheese over the eggs.
5. Cover the pan and let cook for about 7 minutes.
6. Uncover the pan and continue cooking for another 7 to 10 minutes, or until the eggs are set. Run a spatula around the edge of the pan to make sure they won't stick.
7. Let the frittata cool for about 5 minutes before serving. Cut it into wedges and serve.
8. Enjoy!

NUTRITION

calories: 417 | fat: 31g | protein: 26g | carbs: 12g | fiber: 3g | sodium: 867mg

61. Poached Eggs

Prep time: 5 minutes | Cook time: 15 minutes | Serves 4

INGREDIENTS:

2/3 tablespoon extra-virgin olive oil
2/3 cup chopped onion
1 1/3 garlic cloves, minced
1 1/3 (14.5-ounce / 411-g) cans no-salt-added Italian diced tomatoes, undrained
4 large eggs
1/3 cup chopped fresh flat-leaf parsley

DIRECTIONS:

1. Heat the olive oil in a large skillet over medium-high heat.
2. Add the onion and sauté for 5 minutes, stirring occasionally. Add the garlic and cook for 1 minute more.
3. Pour the tomatoes with their juices over the onion mixture and cook for 2 to 3 minutes until bubbling.
4. Reduce the heat to medium and use a large spoon to make six indentations in the tomato mixture. 5. Crack the eggs, one at a time, into each indentation.
6. Cover and simmer for 6 to 7 minutes, or until the eggs are cooked to your preference.
7. Serve with the parsley sprinkled on top.
8. Enjoy!

NUTRITION

calories: 89 | fat: 6g | protein: 4g | carbs: 4g | fiber: 1g | sodium: 77mg

62. Sweet Potato Toast

Prep time: 5 minutes | Cook time: 15 minutes | Serves 6

INGREDIENTS:

3 plum tomatoes, halved
9 tablespoons extra-virgin olive oil, divided
Salt and freshly ground black pepper, to taste
3 large sweet potatoes, sliced lengthwise
1 1/2 cup fresh spinach
12 medium asparagus, trimmed
6 large cooked eggs or egg substitute (poached, scrambled, or fried)
1 1/2 cup arugula
6 tablespoons pesto
6 tablespoons shredded Asiago cheese

DIRECTIONS:

1. Preheat oven to 450°F.| 230°C | Fan 210°C.
2. On a baking sheet, brush the plum tomato halves with 2 tablespoons of olive oil and season with salt and pepper. Roast the tomatoes in the oven for approximately 15 minutes, then remove from the oven and allow to rest.
3. Put the sweet potato slices on a separate baking sheet and brush about 2 tablespoons of oil on each side and season with salt and pepper. Bake the sweet potato slices for about 15 minutes, flipping once after 5 to 7 minutes, until just tender. Remove from the oven and set aside.
4. In a sauté pan or skillet, heat the remaining 2 tablespoons of olive oil over medium heat and sauté the fresh spinach until just wilted. Remove from the pan and rest on a paper towel-lined dish. In the same pan, add the asparagus and sauté, turning throughout. Transfer to a paper towel-lined dish.
5. Place the slices of grilled sweet potato on serving plates and divide the spinach and asparagus evenly among the slices. Place a prepared egg on top of the spinach and asparagus. Top this with ¼ cup of arugula.
6. Finish by drizzling with 1 tablespoon of pesto and sprinkle with 1 tablespoon of cheese. Serve with 1 roasted plum tomato.
7. Enjoy!

NUTRITION

calories: 441 | fat: 35g | protein: 13g | carbs: 23g | fiber: 4g | sodium: 481mg

63. Ricotta with Honey

Prep time: 5 minutes | Cook time: 25 minutes | Serves 6

INGREDIENTS:

1 1/2 (1-pound / 454-g) container whole-milk ricotta cheese
3 large eggs
1/3 cup whole-wheat pastry flour
1 1/2 tablespoon sugar
1 1/2 teaspoon vanilla extract
1/3 teaspoon ground nutmeg
1 1/2 pear, cored and diced

3 tablespoons water
1 1/2 tablespoon honey
Non-stick cooking spray

DIRECTIONS:

1. Preheat oven to 400°F | 200°C | Fan 180°C Spray four ramekins with non-stick cooking spray.
2. Beat together the ricotta, eggs, flour, sugar, vanilla, and nutmeg in a large bowl until combined.
3. Spoon the mixture into the ramekins.
4. Bake in the preheated oven for 22 to 25 minutes, or until the ricotta is just set.
5. Meanwhile, in a small saucepan over medium heat, simmer the pear in the water for 10 minutes, or until slightly softened. Remove from the heat, and stir in the honey.
6. Remove the ramekins from the oven and cool slightly on a wire rack. Top the ricotta ramekins with the pear and serve.
7. Enjoy!

NUTRITION

calories: 329 | fat: 19g | protein: 17g | carbs: 23g | fiber: 3g | sodium: 109mg

64. Banana Corn Fritters

Prep time: 5 minutes | Cook time: 10 minutes | Serves 4

INGREDIENTS:

1 cup yellow cornmeal
1/2 cup flour
4 small ripe bananas, peeled and mashed
4 tablespoons unsweetened almond milk
2 large eggs, beaten
1 teaspoon baking powder
1/2 to 1/2 teaspoon ground chipotle chili
1/2 teaspoon ground cinnamon
1/2 teaspoon sea salt
2 tablespoon olive oil

DIRECTIONS:

1. Stir together all ingredients except for the olive oil in a large bowl until smooth.
2. Heat a non-stick skillet over medium-high heat. Add the olive oil and drop about 2 tablespoons of batter for each fritter. Cook for 2 to 3 minutes until the bottoms are golden brown, then flip.
3. Continue cooking for 1 to 2 minutes more, until cooked through. Repeat with the remaining batter.
4. Serve warm.
5. Enjoy!

NUTRITION

calories: 396 | fat: 10g | protein: 7g | carbs: 68g | fiber: 4g | sodium: 307mg

65. Cheesy Mini Frittatas

Prep time: 10 minutes | Cook time: 25 minutes | Serves 4

INGREDIENTS:

Non-stick cooking spray
1 tablespoon extra-virgin olive oil
1/8 cup chopped red potatoes (about 3 small)
1/8 cup minced onions
1/8 cup chopped red bell pepper
1/8 cup asparagus, sliced lengthwise in half and chopped
2 2/3 large eggs
2 2/3 large egg whites
1/3 cup unsweetened almond milk
Salt and freshly ground black pepper, to taste
1/3 cup shredded low-moisture, part-skim Mozzarella cheese, divided

DIRECTIONS:

1. Preheat oven to 350°F | 180°C | Fan 160°C. Using non-stick cooking spray, prepare a 12-count muffin pan.
2. In a medium sauté pan or skillet, heat the oil over medium heat and sauté the potatoes and onions for about 4 minutes, until the potatoes are fork-tender.
3. Add the bell pepper and asparagus and sauté for about 4 minutes, until just tender. Transfer the contents of a pan onto a paper-towel-lined plate to cool.
4. In a bowl, whisk together the eggs, egg whites, and milk. Season with salt and pepper.
5. Once the vegetables are cooled to room temperature, add the vegetables and ¼ cup of Mozzarella cheese.
6. Using a spoon or ladle, evenly distribute the contents of the bowl into the prepared muffin cups, filling the cups about halfway.
7. Sprinkle the remaining ¼ cup of cheese over the top of the cups.
8. Bake for 20 to 25 minutes, or until eggs reach an internal temperature of 145°F (63°C) or the centre is solid.
9. Allow the mini frittatas to rest for 5 to 10 minutes before removing from muffin pan and serving.
10. Enjoy!

NUTRITION

calories: 396 | fat: 10g | protein: 7g | carbs: 68g | fiber: 4g | sodium: 307mg

66. Feta and Pepper Frittata

Prep time: 10 minutes | Cook time: 20 minutes | Serves 6

INGREDIENTS:

Olive oil cooking spray
12 large eggs
1 1/2 medium red bell pepper, diced
3/4 teaspoon salt
3/4 teaspoon black pepper
1 1/2 garlic clove, minced
3/4 cup feta, divided

DIRECTIONS:

1. Preheat oven to 350°F | 180°C | Fan 160°C. Lightly coat the inside of a 6-inch round cake pan with olive oil cooking spray.
2. In a large bowl, beat the eggs for 1 to 2 minutes, or until well combined.
3. Add the bell pepper, salt, black pepper, and garlic to the eggs, and mix together until the bell pepper is distributed throughout.
4. Fold in ¼ cup of the feta cheese.
5. Pour the egg mixture into the prepared cake pan, and sprinkle the remaining ¼ cup of feta over the top.
6. Place into the air fryer and bake for 18 to 20 minutes, or until the eggs are set in the centre.
7. Remove from the air fryer and allow to cool for 5 minutes before serving.
8. Then serve when ready.

NUTRITION

calories: 204 | fat: 14g | protein: 16g | carbs: 4g | fiber: 1g | sodium: 606mg

67. Vegetarian Stuffed Hash Browns

Prep time: 10 minutes | Cook time: 20 minutes | Serves 6

INGREDIENTS:

Olive oil cooking spray
1 1/2 tablespoon plus 2 teaspoons olive oil, divided
6 ounces (113 g) baby bella mushrooms, diced
1 1/2 scallion, white parts and green parts, diced
1 1/2 garlic clove, minced
3 cups shredded potatoes
3/4 teaspoon salt
1/3 teaspoon black pepper
1 1/2 Roma tomato, diced
3/4 cup shredded Mozzarella

DIRECTIONS:

1. Preheat the air fryer to 380°F (193°C). Lightly coat the inside of a 6-inch cake pan with olive oil cooking spray.
2. In a small skillet, heat 2 teaspoons olive oil over medium heat. Add the mushrooms, scallion, and garlic, and cook for 4 to 5 minutes, or until they have softened and are beginning to show some color. Remove from heat.
3. Meanwhile, in a large bowl, combine the potatoes, salt, pepper, and the remaining tablespoon olive oil. Toss until all potatoes are well coated.
4. Pour half of the potatoes into the bottom of the cake pan. Top with the mushroom mixture, tomato, and Mozzarella. Spread the remaining potatoes over the top.
5. Bake in the air fryer for 12 to 15 minutes, or until the top is golden brown.
6. Remove from the air fryer and allow to cool for 5 minutes before slicing and serving.
7. Then serve when ready.

NUTRITION

calories: 164 | fat: 9g | protein: 6g | carbs: 16g | fiber: 3g | sodium: 403mg

68. Apple Toast

Prep time: 5 minutes | Cook time: 0 minutes | Serves 2

INGREDIENTS:

4 slices whole-wheat bread, toasted
4 tablespoons tahini
2 small apples of your choice, cored and thinly sliced
2 teaspoon honey

DIRECTIONS:

1. Spread the tahini on the toasted bread.
2. Place the apple slices on the bread and drizzle with the honey. Serve immediately.
3. Enjoy!

NUTRITION

calories: 458 | fat: 17g | protein: 11g | carbs: 63g | fiber: 10g | sodium: 285mg

69. Bruschetta with Prosciutto
Prep time: 10 minutes | Cook time: 20 minutes | Serves 6

INGREDIENTS:

- 1/3 teaspoon kosher or sea salt
- 9 cups broccoli rabe, stemmed and chopped (about 1 bunch)
- 1 1/2 tablespoon extra-virgin olive oil
- 3 garlic cloves, minced (about 1 teaspoon)
- 1 1/2-ounce (28 g) prosciutto, cut or torn into 1/2-inch pieces
- 1/3 teaspoon crushed red pepper
- Nonstick cooking spray
- 4 1/2 large eggs
- 1 1/2 tablespoon unsweetened almond milk
- 1/3 teaspoon freshly ground black pepper
- 6 teaspoons grated Parmesan or Pecorino Romano cheese
- 1 1/2 garlic clove, halved
- 12 (3/4-inch-thick) slices baguette-style whole-grain bread or 4 slices larger Italian-style whole-grain bread

DIRECTIONS:

1. Bring a large stockpot of water to a boil. Add the salt and broccoli rabe, and boil for 2 minutes. Drain in a colander.
2. In a large skillet over medium heat, heat the oil. Add the garlic, prosciutto, and crushed red pepper, and cook for 2 minutes, stirring often. Add the broccoli rabe and cook for an additional 3 minutes, stirring a few times. Transfer to a bowl and set aside.
3. Place the skillet back on the stove over low heat and coat with non-stick cooking spray.
4. In a small bowl, whisk together the eggs, milk, and pepper. Pour into the skillet. Stir and cook until the eggs are soft scrambled, 3 to 5 minutes. Add the broccoli rabe mixture back to the skillet along with the cheese. Stir and cook for about 1 minute, until heated through. Remove from the heat.
5. Toast the bread, then rub the cut sides of the garlic clove halves onto one side of each slice of the toast. (Save the garlic for another recipe.) Spoon the egg mixture onto each piece of toast and serve.
6. Enjoy!

NUTRITION

calories: 313 | fat: 10g | protein: 17g | carbs: 38g | fiber: 8g | sodium: 559mg

70. Veggie Sandwiches
Prep time: 10 minutes | Cook time: 0 minutes | Serves 6

INGREDIENTS:

- 12 slices whole-grain or whole-wheat bread
- 1 1/2 ripe avocado, halved and pitted
- 1/3 teaspoon freshly ground black pepper
- 1/3 teaspoon kosher or sea salt
- 6 romaine lettuce leaves, torn into 8 pieces total
- 1 1/2 large, ripe tomato, sliced into 8 rounds
- 3 ounces (57 g) prosciutto, cut into 8 thin slices

DIRECTIONS:

1. Toast the bread and place on a large platter.
2. Scoop the avocado flesh out of the skin into a small bowl. Add the pepper and salt. Using a fork or a whisk, gently mash the avocado until it resembles a creamy spread. Spread the avocado mash over all 8 pieces of toast.
3. To make one sandwich, take one slice of avocado toast, and top it with a lettuce leaf, tomato slice, and prosciutto slice. Top with another slice each of lettuce, tomato, and prosciutto, then cover with a second piece of avocado toast (avocado-side down on the prosciutto). Repeat with the remaining ingredients to make three more sandwiches and serve.
4. Enjoy!

NUTRITION:

calories: 262 | fat: 12g | protein: 8g | carbs: 35g | fiber: 10g | sodium: 162mg

71. Avocado Toast with Poached Eggs
Prep time: 5 minutes | Cook time: 7 minutes | Serves 6

INGREDIENTS:

- Olive oil cooking spray
- 6 large eggs
- Salt and black pepper, to taste
- 6 pieces whole grain bread
- 1 1/2 avocado
- Red pepper flakes (optional)

DIRECTIONS:

1. Preheat the air fryer to 320°F (160°C). Lightly coat the inside of four small oven-safe ramekins with olive oil cooking spray.
2. Crack one egg into each ramekin, and season with salt and black pepper.
3. Place the ramekins into the air fryer basket. Close and set the timer to 7 minutes.
4. While the eggs are cooking, toast the bread in a toaster.
5. Slice the avocado in half lengthwise, remove the pit, and scoop the flesh into a small bowl. Season with salt, black pepper, and red pepper flakes, if desired. Using a fork, smash the avocado lightly.
6. Spread a quarter of the smashed avocado evenly over each slice of toast.
7. Remove the eggs from the air fryer, and gently spoon one onto each slice of avocado toast before serving.
8. Enjoy!

NUTRITION:

calories: 232 | fat: 14g | protein: 11g | carbohydrates: 18g | fiber: 6g | sodium: 175mg

72. Sandwich
Prep time: 5 minutes | Cook time: 4 minutes | Serves 2

INGREDIENTS:

- 2 large eggs
- 1/2 teaspoon baking powder
- 1 teaspoon dried rosemary, oregano, basil, thyme, or garlic powder (optional)
- 6 tablespoons almond flour
- 2 tablespoon extra-virgin olive oil
- 1/4 teaspoon salt

DIRECTIONS:

1. In a microwave-safe dish, combine the almond flour, olive oil, egg, rosemary (if using), baking powder, and salt. Mix well with a fork.
2. Microwave for 90 seconds at maximum power.
3. Run a knife around the edges of the cup and turn it to remove the bread.
4. Cut in half with a serrated knife if you want to use it to make a sandwich.
5. Enjoy!

NUTRITION:

calories: 232 | fat: 22g | protein: 8g | carbohydrates: 1g | fiber: 0g | sodium: 450mg

73. Veggie Sandwiches with Prosciutto, Avocado
Prep time: 10 minutes | Cook time: 0 minutes | Serves 6

INGREDIENTS:

- 12 slices whole-grain or whole-wheat bread
- 1 1/2 ripe avocado, halved and pitted
- 6 romaine lettuce leaves, torn into 8 pieces total
- 1 1/2 large, ripe tomato, sliced into 8 rounds
- 1/3 teaspoon freshly ground black pepper
- 1/3 teaspoon kosher or sea salt
- 3 ounces (57 g) prosciutto, cut into 8 thin slices

DIRECTIONS:

1. Toast the bread and place it on a large plate.
2. Collect the avocado pulp from the skin in a small bowl. Add the pepper and salt. Using a fork or whisk, gently mash the avocado until you get a spread. Spread the avocado puree over all 8 pieces of toast.
3. To make a sandwich, take a slice of avocado toast and cover it with a lettuce leaf, a tomato slice and a slice of ham. Cover with another wedge of lettuce, tomato and ham, then cover with a second piece of avocado toast (avocado side down on the ham). Repeat with the other ingredients to make three more sandwiches and serve.
4. Enjoy!

NUTRITION:

calories: 262 | fat: 12g | protein: 8g | carbohydrates: 35g | fiber: 10g | sodium: 162mg

74. Scrambled Eggs with Feta and Olives
Prep time: 10 minutes | Cook time: 5 minutes | Serves 4

INGREDIENTS:

- 2 tablespoon unsweetened almond milk
- 8 large eggs
- 2 tablespoon olive oil
- 1/2 cup crumbled feta cheese
- Sea salt and freshly ground pepper, to taste
- 20 Kalamata olives, pitted and sliced
- Small bunch fresh mint, chopped, for garnish

DIRECTIONS:

1. Beat the eggs in a bowl until they are combined. Add the milk and a pinch

of sea salt and mix well.
2. Heat a medium non-stick skillet over medium-high heat and add the olive oil.
3. Pour in the egg mixture and stir constantly, or until they begin to curdle and harden, about 2 minutes. Add the feta cheese and the olive slices and mix until smooth. Season with salt and pepper.
4. Divide the mixture into 2 plates and serve garnished with chopped fresh mint.
5.Enjoy!

NUTRITION:
calories: 244 | fat: 21g | protein: 8g | carbohydrates: 3g | fiber: 0g | sodium: 339mg

75. Vegetarian Stuffed Hash Browns
Prep time: 10 minutes | Cook time: 20 minutes | Serves 6

INGREDIENTS:

6 ounces (113 g) baby Bella mushrooms, diced	Olive oil cooking spray
1 1/2 garlic clove, minced	1 1/2 tablespoon plus 2 teaspoons olive oil, divided
3 cups shredded potatoes	1/3 teaspoon black pepper
3/4 teaspoon salt	1 1/2 Roma tomato, diced
1 1/2 scallion, white parts and green parts, diced	3/4 cup shredded Mozzarella

DIRECTIONS:
1. Preheat the air fryer to 380ºF (193ºC). Lightly coat the inside of a 6-inch cake pan with olive oil cooking spray.
2. In a small skillet, heat 2 teaspoons of olive oil over medium heat. Add the mushrooms, shallots and garlic and cook for 4-5 minutes, or until soft and starting to show some color. Remove from the heat.
3. Meanwhile, in a large bowl, combine the potatoes, salt, pepper and the remaining spoonful of olive oil. Stir until all the potatoes are well coated.
4. Pour half of the potatoes into the bottom of the pan. Garnish with the mixture of mushrooms, tomato and mozzarella. Spread over the remaining potatoes.
5. Cook in the air fryer for 12-15 minutes or until the top is golden brown.
6. Remove from deep fryer and allow to cool for 5 minutes before slicing and serving.
7.Enjoy!

NUTRITION
calories: 164 | fat: 9g | protein: 6g | carbohydrates: 16g | fiber: 3g | sodium: 403mg

76. Arugula, Figs, Cheese and Polenta
Prep time: 10 minutes | Cook time: 40 minutes | Serves 6

INGREDIENTS:

1 1/2 teaspoon minced fresh thyme or 1/4 teaspoon dried	4 1/2 tablespoons extra-virgin olive oil, divided
3 ounces (57 g) baby arugula	3/4 teaspoon table salt
6 figs, cut into 1/2-inch-thick wedges	1 1/2 cup coarse-ground cornmeal
3/4 cup oil-packed sun-dried tomatoes, chopped	1 1/2 tablespoon balsamic vinegar
1/3 teaspoon pepper	3 ounces (57 g) blue cheese, crumbled
	3 tablespoons pine nuts, toasted

DIRECTIONS:
1. Place the trivet included with the Instant Pot in the base of the insert and add 1 cup of water. Fold the aluminium foil into a 16 x 6-inch sling, then place a 1½-quart round souffle plate in the centre of the sling. Whisk 4 cups of water, cornmeal, tomatoes, thyme, salt and pepper together in a bowl, then transfer the mixture to a souffle dish. Using the sling, lower the souffle into the pot and onto the trivet; let the narrow edges of the harness rest along the sides of the insert.
2. Lock the lid in place and close the pressure release valve. Select the high-pressure cooking function and cook for 40 minutes. Turn off Instant Pot and quick release pressure. Carefully remove the lid, allowing the steam to escape.
3. Using the sling, transfer the souffle plate to a wire rack. Beat 1 tablespoon of oil into the polenta, smoothing out any lumps. Let it sit until it thickens slightly, about 10 minutes. Season with salt and pepper to taste.
4. Mix the rocket and figs with the vinegar and the remaining 2 tablespoons of oil in a bowl and season with salt and pepper to taste. Divide the polenta into individual serving plates and sprinkle with the rocket, gorgonzola and pine nut mixture.
5.Enjoy!

NUTRITION
calories: 360 | fat: 21g | protein: 7g | carbohydrates: 38g | fiber: 8g | sodium: 510mg

77. Vegetables and Goat Cheese Frittata
Prep time: 15 minutes | Cook time: 25 minutes | Serves 4

INGREDIENTS:

1 teaspoon salt	10 large eggs, beaten
Pinch freshly ground black pepper	2 tablespoon olive oil
4 tablespoons minced fresh basil	1 pint cherry or grape tomatoes
4 ounces (57 g) crumbled goat cheese (about 1/2 cup)	6 tablespoons unsweetened almond milk
4 garlic cloves, minced	4 tablespoons minced fresh oregano

DIRECTIONS:
1. Heat the oil in a non-stick pan over medium heat. Add the tomatoes. When they start cooking, pierce a few so that they release some of their juice. Reduce the heat to medium-low, cover the pan and allow the tomatoes to soften.
2. When the tomatoes are mostly softened and chopped, remove the lid, add the garlic and continue to brown.
3. In a medium bowl, combine the eggs, milk, salt, pepper and herbs and beat well to combine.
4. Turn up the heat to medium-high. Add the egg mixture to the tomatoes and garlic, then sprinkle the goat cheese over the eggs.
5. Cover the pan and cook for about 7 minutes.
6. Uncover the pan and continue cooking for another 7-10 minutes or until the eggs have set. Run a spatula around the edge of the pan to make sure they don't stick.
7. Let the omelette cool for about 5 minutes before serving. Cut it into wedges and serve.
8.Enjoy!

NUTRITION
calories: 417 | fat: 31g | protein: 26g | carbohydrates: 12g | fiber: 3g | sodium: 867mg

78. Chickpea and Hummus Patties
Prep time: 15 minutes | Cook time: 13 minutes | Serves 6

INGREDIENTS:

3/4 cup lemony garlic hummus or 1/2 cup prepared hummus	3 teaspoons dried oregano
3 whole-wheat pita breads, cut in half	1/3 teaspoon freshly ground black pepper
1 1/2 tablespoon extra-virgin olive oil	1 1/2 large egg
1 1/2 cucumber, unpeeled (or peeled if desired), cut in half lengthwise	1 1/2 garlic clove, minced
3/4 cup whole-wheat panko bread crumbs	1 1/2 (6-ounce / 170-g) container 2% plain Greek yogurt
1 1/2 (15-ounce / 425-g) can chickpeas, drained and rinsed	1 1/2 medium tomato, cut into 4 thick slices

DIRECTIONS:
1. In a large bowl, mash the chickpeas with a potato masher or fork until coarsely mashed (they should still be a little thick). Add the hummus, breadcrumbs, egg, oregano and pepper. Mix well to combine. With your hands, form 4 meatballs (half a cup) with the mixture. Press each meatball about 1inch thick and place it on a plate.
2. In a large skillet over medium-high heat, heat the oil until very hot, about 3 minutes. Cook the meatballs for 5 minutes, then turn them with a spatula. Cook for another 5 minutes.
3. While the meatballs are cooking, chop half the cucumber with a grater or chop finely with a knife. In a small bowl, mix the chopped cucumber, yogurt, and garlic together to make the tzatziki sauce. Cut the remaining half of the cucumber into half a centimetre thick slice and set aside.
4.Toast the pita bread. To assemble the sandwiches, lay the pita halves on a work surface. In each pita, place a few slices of cucumber, a chickpea pie and a slice of tomato, then top the sandwich with the tzatziki sauce and serve.
5.Enjoy!

NUTRITION
calories: 308 | fat: 8g | protein: 15 g | carbohydrates: 45 g | fiber: 78g | sodium: 321 mg

79. Feta and Pepper Frittata
Prep time: 10 minutes | Cook time: 20 minutes | Serves 6
INGREDIENTS:
- 3/4 teaspoon black pepper
- 1 1/2 garlic clove, minced
- 1 1/2 medium red bell pepper, diced
- 3/4 teaspoon salt
- Olive oil cooking spray
- 12 large eggs
- 3/4 cup feta, divided

DIRECTIONS:
1. Preheat the air fryer to 360ºF (182ºC). Lightly coat the inside of a 6-inch round cake pan with cooking spray olive oil.
2. In a large bowl, beat the eggs for 1 to 2 minutes, or until well blended.
3. Add the pepper, salt, black pepper and garlic to the eggs and stir until the pepper is distributed throughout.
4. Incorporate cup of feta cheese.
5. Pour the egg mixture into the prepared pan and sprinkle the remaining ¼ cup of feta cheese on top.
6. Place in the air fryer and cook for 18-20 minutes or until the eggs are set in the center.
7. Remove from deep fryer and allow to cool for 5 minutes before serving.
8. Enjoy!

NUTRITION
calories: 204 | fat: 14g | protein: 16g | carbohydrates: 4g | fiber: 1g | sodium: 606mg

80. Orange French Toast
Prep time: 5 minutes | Cook time: 15 minutes | Serves 4
INGREDIENTS:
- 1/8 teaspoon ground cardamom
- 2 large eggs
- 1 1/3 teaspoons grated orange zest
- 1/8 teaspoon ground cinnamon
- 2/3 cup unsweetened almond milk
- 2/3 teaspoon vanilla extract
- 2/3 loaf of boule bread, sliced
- 2/3 inch thick (gluten-free preferred)
- 2/3 banana, sliced
- 1/8 cup Berry and Honey Compote

DIRECTIONS:
1. Heat a large non-stick skillet or skillet over medium-high heat.
2. In a large, shallow dish, combine the milk, eggs, orange zest, vanilla, cardamom, and cinnamon. Working in batches, pass the slices of bread in the egg mixture and place in the hot pan.
3. Cook for 5 minutes on each side, until golden brown. Serve, garnished with banana and topped with honey compote.
4. Enjoy!

NUTRITION
calories: 394 | fat: 6g | protein: 17g | carbohydrates: 68g | fiber: 3g | sodium: 716mg

81. Avocado with Eggs Toast
Prep time: 5 minutes | Cook time: 7 minutes | Serves 6
INGREDIENTS:
- Salt and black pepper, to taste
- 6 pieces whole grain bread
- Olive oil cooking spray
- 6 large eggs
- 1 1/2 avocado
- Red pepper flakes (optional)

DIRECTIONS:
1. Preheat the air fryer to 160ºC (320ºF). Lightly coat the inside of four small baking molds with olive oil cooking spray.
2. Break an egg into each mold and season with salt and black pepper.
3. Place the molds in the basket of the air fryer. Close and set the timer to 7 minutes.
4. While the eggs are cooking, toast the bread in a toaster.
5. Cut the avocado in half lengthwise, remove the stone and collect the pulp in a small bowl. Season with salt, black pepper and red pepper flakes if desired. Using a fork, lightly mash the avocado.
6. Spread one quarter of the mashed avocado evenly over each slice of toast.
7. Remove the eggs from the deep fryer and gently place one on each slice of avocado toast before serving.
8. Enjoy!

NUTRITION
calories: 232 | fat: 14g | protein: 11g | carbohydrates: 18g | fiber: 6g | sodium: 175mg

82. Honey Granola with Pumpkin Layers
Prep time: 5 minutes | Cook time: 0 minutes | Serves 6
INGREDIENTS:
- 1 1/2 cup honey granola
- 1 1/2 teaspoon pumpkin pie spice
- 1/3 teaspoon ground cinnamon
- 6 teaspoons honey, additional to taste
- 1 1/2 (15-ounce / 425-g) can pure pumpkin purée
- 3 cups plain, unsweetened, full-fat Greek yogurt

DIRECTIONS:
1. In a large bowl, mix the pumpkin puree, honey, pumpkin pie spices, and cinnamon. Cover and refrigerate for at least 2 hours.
2. To make parfaits, add ¼ cup of pumpkin mix, ¼ cup of yogurt and ¼ cup of granola into each cup. Repeat the layers of Greek yogurt and pumpkin and garnish with honey granola.
3. Enjoy!

NUTRITION
calories: 264 | fat: 9g | protein: 15g | carbohydrates: 35g | fiber: 6g | sodium: 90mg

83. Warm Bulgur Breakfast Bowls
Prep time: 5 minutes | Cook time: 15 minutes | Serves 4
INGREDIENTS:
- 1½ cups uncooked bulgur
- 2 cups frozen (or fresh, pitted) dark sweet cherries
- 8 dried (or fresh) figs, chopped
- 1 cup water
- 2 cups unsweetened almond milk
- ½ teaspoon ground cinnamon
- ½ cup chopped almonds
- ¼ cup loosely packed fresh mint, chopped

DIRECTIONS:
1. Combine the milk, bulgur, water and cinnamon in a medium saucepan, stirring and bring to a boil.
2. Cover, reduce heat to medium-low and simmer for 10 minutes or until liquid is absorbed.
3. Turn off the heat, but keep the pan over the heat and add the frozen cherries (no need to defrost them), figs and almonds. Cover and let the hot bulgur thaw the cherries and partially hydrate the figs, about 1 minute.
4. Incorporate the mint and stir to combine, then serve. Enjoy!

NUTRITION
calories: 207 | fat: 6g | protein: 8g | carbohydrates: 32g | fiber: 4g | sodium: 82mg

84. Marinara Poached Eggs
Prep time: 5 minutes | Cook time: 15 minutes | Serves 4
INGREDIENTS:
- 2/3 tablespoon extra-virgin olive oil
- 1 1/3 garlic cloves, minced
- 1 1/3 (14.5-ounce / 411-g) cans no-salt-added Italian diced tomatoes, undrained
- 2/3 cup chopped onion
- 4 large eggs
- 1/3 cup chopped fresh flat-leaf parsley

DIRECTIONS:
1. Heat the olive oil in a large skillet over medium-high heat.
2. Add the onion and sauté for 5 minutes, stirring occasionally. Add the garlic and cook for 1 minute longer.
3. Pour the tomatoes with their juices over the onion mixture and cook for 2 or 3 minutes until it boils.
4. Reduce the heat to medium and use a large spoon to make six indentations in the tomato mixture. Break the eggs, one at a time, into each indentation.
5. Cover and simmer for 6-7 minutes or until eggs are cooked to your preference.
6. Serve with the parsley sprinkled on top.
7. Enjoy!

NUTRITION
calories: 89 | fat: 6g | protein: 4g | carbohydrates: 4g | fiber: 1g | sodium: 77mg

85. Baked Ricotta with Honey Pears Honey
Prep time: 5 minutes | Cook time: 25 minutes | Serves 6
INGREDIENTS:
- 3 large eggs
- 1/3 cup whole-wheat pastry flour
- 1 1/2 teaspoon vanilla extract
- 1/3 teaspoon ground nutmeg
- 1 1/2 pear, cored and diced
- 3 tablespoons water
- 1 1/2 (1-pound / 454-g) container whole-milk ricotta cheese

1 1/2 tablespoon sugar
1 1/2 tablespoon honey
Non-stick cooking spray

DIRECTIONS:

1. Preheat oven to 400°F | 200°C | Fan 180°C Spray four molds with non-stick cooking spray.
2. Beat the ricotta, eggs, flour, sugar, vanilla and nutmeg in a large bowl until combined. Pour the mixture into the molds.
3. Bake in a preheated oven for 22-25 minutes, or until the ricotta is just set.
4. Meanwhile, in a small saucepan over medium heat, simmer the pear in the water for 10 minutes or until it softens slightly. Remove from the heat and stir in the honey.
5. Remove the molds from the oven and allow to cool slightly on a wire rack. Garnish the ricotta molds with the pear and serve.
6. Enjoy!

NUTRITION

calories: 329 | fat: 19g | protein: 17g | carbohydrates: 23g | fiber: 3g | sodium: 109mg

86. Cardamom-Cinnamon Overnight Oats

Prep time: 10 minutes | Cook time: 0 minutes | Serves 4

INGREDIENTS:

4 tablespoons sliced almonds
1 cup vanilla, unsweetened almond milk (not Silk brand)
1 cup rolled oats
2 teaspoon chia seeds
4 tablespoons simple sugar liquid sweetener
1/2 teaspoon ground cardamom
1/2 teaspoon ground cinnamon

DIRECTIONS:

1. In a glass jar, combine the almond milk, oats, almonds, liquid sweetener, chia seeds, cardamom, and cinnamon and shake well. Refrigerate for 8-24 hours, then serve cold or reheated.
2. Enjoy!

NUTRITION

calories: 131 | fat: 6g | protein: 5g | carbohydrates: 17g | fiber: 4g | sodium: 45mg

87. Breakfast Bruschetta

Prep time: 10 minutes | Cook time: 20 minutes | Serves 6

INGREDIENTS:

6 teaspoons grated Parmesan or Pecorino Romano cheese
1 1/2 garlic clove, halved
1 1/2 tablespoon extra-virgin olive oil
1/3 teaspoon crushed red pepper
1/3 teaspoon kosher or sea salt
9 cups broccoli rabe, stemmed and chopped (about 1 bunch)
Non-stick cooking spray
4 1/2 large eggs
3 garlic cloves, minced (about 1 teaspoon)
1 1/2-ounce (28 g) prosciutto, cut or torn into 1/2-inch pieces
1 1/2 tablespoon unsweetened almond milk
1/3 teaspoon freshly ground black pepper
12 (3/4-inch-thick) slices baguette-style whole-grain bread or 4 slices larger Italian-style whole-grain bread

DIRECTIONS:

1. Heat the oil in a non-stick pan over medium heat. Add the tomatoes. When they start cooking, pierce a few so that they release some of their juice. Reduce the heat to medium-low, cover the pan and allow the tomatoes to wilt.
2. When the tomatoes are mostly softened and chopped, remove the lid, add the garlic and continue to brown.
3. In a medium bowl, combine the eggs, milk, salt, pepper and herbs and beat well to combine.
4. Turn up the heat to medium-high. Add the egg mixture to the tomatoes and garlic, then sprinkle the goat cheese over the eggs.
5. Cover the pan and cook for about 7 minutes.
6. Uncover the pan and continue cooking for another 7-10 minutes or until the eggs have set. Run a spatula around the edge of the pan to make sure they don't stick.
7. Let the omelette cool for about 5 minutes before serving. Cut it into wedges and serve.
8. Enjoy!

NUTRITION

calories: 313 | fat: 10g | protein: 17g | carbohydrates: 38g | fiber: 8g | sodium: 559mg

88. Berry-Honey Compote with Fruity Pancakes

Prep time: 10 minutes | Cook time: 4 minutes | Serves 6

INGREDIENTS:

3 tablespoons extra-virgin olive oil
1 1/2 sliced banana or 1 cup sliced strawberries, divided
3 large eggs, beaten
1 1/2 cup almond flour
1 1/2 cup plus 2 tablespoons skim milk
1/3 cup honey
1 1/2 teaspoon baking soda
1/3 teaspoon salt
3 tablespoons berry and honey compote

DIRECTIONS:

1. In a bowl, mix the almond flour, milk, eggs, honey, baking soda, and salt.
2. In a large skillet or skillet, heat the olive oil over medium-high heat and pour ½ cup of pancake batter into the pan. Cook for 2 to 3 minutes. Just before the pancake is ready to flip, add half of the fresh fruit and flip to cook for 2 to 3 minutes on the other side, until cooked through.
3. Garnish with the remaining fruit, drizzle with the berry and honey compote and serve.
4. Enjoy!

NUTRITION

calories: 415 | fat: 24g | protein: 12g | carbohydrates: 46g | fiber: 4g | sodium: 526mg

89. Hearty Honey-Apricot Granola

Prep time: 15 minutes | Cook time: 30 minutes | Serves 4

INGREDIENTS:

1/8 to 1/3 cup raw honey, plus more for drizzling
1/8 cup walnuts, chopped
2/3 cup rolled oats
1/8 cup dried apricots, diced
1/8 cup almond slivers
2/3 tablespoon olive oil
1/8 cup pumpkin seeds
1/8 cup hemp hearts
2/3 teaspoon ground cinnamon
1/8 teaspoon ground nutmeg
1/8 teaspoon salt
1 1/3 tablespoons sugar-free dark chocolate chips (optional)
2 cups non-fat plain Greek yogurt

DIRECTIONS:

1. Preheat the air fryer to 260ºF (127ºC). Line the air fryer basket with parchment paper.
2. In a large bowl, combine the oats, apricots, almonds, walnuts, pumpkin seeds, hemp hearts, honey, olive oil, cinnamon, nutmeg and salt, mixing so that the honey, oil and spices are well distributed.
3. Pour the mixture onto the parchment paper and spread it out in an even layer.
4. Cook for 10 minutes, then shake or mix and distribute again in an even layer. Continue cooking for another 10 minutes, then repeat the process of stirring the mixture. Cook for another 10 minutes before removing from the air fryer.
5. Allow the granola to cool completely before adding the chocolate chips (if used) and pour into an airtight container for storage.
6. For each serving, add ½ cup of Greek yogurt with ⅓ cup of granola and a drizzle of honey if needed.
7. Enjoy!

NUTRITION

calories: 342 | fat: 16g | protein: 20g | carbohydrates: 31g | fiber: 4g | sodium: 162mg

90. Blueberry and Chia Seeds Smoothie

Prep time: 10 minutes | Cook time: 0 minutes | Serves 2

INGREDIENTS:

2 to 2 teaspoons stevia or monk fruit extract (optional)
1 teaspoon vanilla extract
2 tablespoon ground flaxseed or chia seeds
1/2 cup frozen blueberries
4 tablespoons unsweetened almond butter
2 tablespoon extra-virgin olive oil or avocado oil
2 cup unsweetened almond milk, plus more as needed
1/2 teaspoon ground cinnamon

DIRECTIONS:

1. In a blender or a large wide-mouth jar, if using an immersion blender, combine the almond milk, blueberries, almond butter, flaxseed, olive oil, stevia (if using), vanilla, and cinnamon and blend until smooth and creamy.

2. Adding more almond milk to achieve your desired consistency.
3. Enjoy!

NUTRITION

calories: 460 | fat: 40g | protein: 8g | carbohydrates: 20g | fiber: 9g | sodium: 147mg

91. Spicy Almond and Pistachio Smoothie

Prep time: 10 minutes | Cook time: 0 minutes | Serves 2

INGREDIENTS:

2 to 2 teaspoons monk fruit extract or stevia (optional)
1/2 to 1/2 teaspoon ground allspice or unsweetened pumpkin pie spice
1 cup unsweetened almond milk, plus more as needed
Zest and juice of 1 clementine or 1/2 orange
1 cup plain whole-milk Greek yogurt
2 tablespoon extra-virgin olive oil or MCT oil
2 tablespoon shelled pistachios, coarsely chopped
1/2 teaspoon ground cinnamon
1/2 teaspoon vanilla extract

DIRECTIONS:

1. In a blender or a large wide-mouth jar, if using an immersion blender, combine the yogurt, ½ cup almond milk, clementine zest and juice, olive oil, pistachios, monk fruit extract (if using), allspice, cinnamon, and vanilla and blend until smooth and creamy.
2. Adding more almond milk to achieve your desired consistency.
3. Enjoy!

NUTRITION

calories: 264 | fat: 22g | protein: 5g | carbohydrates: 12g | fiber: 1g | sodium: 127mg

92. Salad Sandwich with Tuna and Avocado

Prep time: 10 minutes | Cook time: 2 minutes | Serves 6

INGREDIENTS:

1 1/2 very ripe avocado, peeled, pitted, and mashed
3 (4-ounce/ 113-g) cans tuna, packed in olive oil
3 tablespoons roasted garlic aioli, or avocado oil mayonnaise with 1 to 2 teaspoons freshly or
1 1/2 tablespoon chopped fresh capers (optional)
6 versatile sandwich rounds
3 squeezed lemon juice and/or zest
1 1/2 teaspoon chopped fresh dill or 1/2 teaspoon dried dill

DIRECTIONS:

1. Prepare some rods according to the recipe. Cut each round in half and set aside.
2. In a medium bowl, place the tuna and oil from the cans. Add the aioli, avocado, capers (if used) and dill and blend well with a fork.
3. Toast sandwiches and fill them with a quarter of the tuna salad.
4. Then serve when ready.

NUTRITION

calories: 436 | fat: 36g | protein: 23g | carbohydrates: 5g | fiber: 3g | sodium: 790mg

93. Shakshuka

Prep time: 15 minutes | Cook time: 18 minutes | Serves 6

INGREDIENTS:

1 1/2 (14 1/2-ounce / 411-g) can diced tomatoes, drained
1/3 teaspoon turmeric
1 1/2 cup chopped red bell peppers
1 1/2 cup finely diced potato
3 tablespoons extra-virgin olive oil
1 1/2 cup chopped shallots
1 1/2 teaspoon garlic powder
1/3 teaspoon paprika
1/3 teaspoon ground cardamom
6 large eggs
1/3 cup chopped fresh cilantro

DIRECTIONS:

1. Preheat oven to 350°F | 180°C | Fan 160°C.
2. In a skillet or non-stick skillet, heat the olive oil over medium-high heat and sauté the shallots, stirring occasionally, for about 3 minutes, until fragrant. Add the peppers, potatoes and garlic powder. Cook, uncovered, for 10 minutes, stirring every 2 minutes.
3. Add the tomatoes, turmeric, paprika and cardamom to the pan and mix well. Once it boils, remove from heat and break the eggs into the pan so that the yolks are facing up.
4. Place the pan in the oven and cook for another 5-10 minutes, until the eggs are cooked to your preference. Garnish with cilantro and serve.
5. Then serve when ready.

NUTRITION

calories: 224 | fat: 12g | protein: 9g | carbohydrates: 20g | fiber: 3g | sodium: 278mg

94. Pancakes with Sauce

Prep time: 5 minutes | Cook time: 10 minutes | Serves 6

INGREDIENTS:

1/3 teaspoon salt
3 large eggs, beaten
Zest and juice of 1 lemon
9 tablespoon extra-virgin olive oil, divided
1 1/2 cup almond flour
1 1/2 teaspoon baking powder
3/4 teaspoon vanilla extract
Berry Sauce:
1 1/2 cup frozen mixed berries
1 1/2 tablespoon water, plus more as needed
3/4 teaspoon vanilla extract

DIRECTIONS:

1. In a large bowl, combine the almond flour, baking powder and salt and mix to break up any lumps.
2. Add 4 tablespoons of olive oil, beaten eggs, lemon zest and juice and vanilla extract and mix until well blended.
3. Heat 1 tablespoon of olive oil in a large skillet. Pour about 2 tablespoons of batter for each pancake. Cook until bubbles start to form, 4-5 minutes. Turn and cook for another 2 to 3 minutes. Repeat with the remaining 1 tablespoon of olive oil and the batter.
Berry Sauce
4. Combine the frozen berries, water and vanilla extract in a small saucepan and heat over medium-high heat for 3-4 minutes until boiling, adding more water as needed. Using the back of a spoon or fork, mash the berries and whisk until smooth.
5. Serve the pancakes with the berry sauce.
6. Enjoy!

NUTRITION

calories: 275 | fat: 26g | protein: 4g | carbohydrates: 8g | fiber: 2g | sodium: 271mg

95. Vanilla Raspberry Oats

Prep time: 10 minutes | Cook time: 0 minutes | Serves 4

INGREDIENTS:

2 teaspoon honey
1/2 cup raspberries
²/₃ cup vanilla, unsweetened almond milk
1/4 teaspoon ground cinnamon
¹/₃ cup rolled oats
1/2 teaspoon turmeric
Pinch ground cloves

DIRECTIONS:

1. In a glass jar, combine the almond milk, oats, raspberries, honey, turmeric, cinnamon and cloves and shake well.
2. Refrigerate for 8-24 hours, then serve cold or reheated.
3. Enjoy!

NUTRITION

calories: 82 | fat: 2g | protein: 2g | carbohydrates: 14g | fiber: 3g | sodium: 98mg

96. Spinach Pie with Parmesan

Prep time: 10 minutes | Cook time: 20 minutes | Serves 6

INGREDIENTS:

1 1/2 puff pastry doughs, (organic, if available), at room temperature
3 hard-boiled eggs, halved
3/4 onion, chopped
Nonstick cooking spray
1 1/2 tablespoons extra-virgin olive oil
1/4 teaspoon freshly ground black pepper
1/4 teaspoon ground nutmeg
3 large eggs, divided
3/4 pound (454 g) frozen spinach, thawed
1/4 teaspoon garlic salt
3/4 cup grated Parmesan cheese, divided

DIRECTIONS:

1. Preheat oven to 350°F | 180°C | Fan 160°C. Spray a baking sheet with non-stick cooking spray and set aside.
2. Heat a large skillet or skillet over medium-high heat. Add the oil and onion and cook for about 5 minutes, until they become translucent.
3. Squeeze the excess water from the spinach, then add to the pan and cook, uncovered, so that the excess water from the spinach can evaporate. Add the garlic, salt, pepper and nutmeg. Remove from heat and set aside to cool.
4. In a small bowl, break 3 eggs and mix well. Add the eggs and ½ cup of

Parmesan to the cooled spinach mix.
5. On the prepared baking tray, roll out the shortcrust pastry. Spread the spinach mixture over the dough, leaving 2 inches around each edge.
6. Once the spinach has spread over the shortcrust pastry, arrange the hard-boiled egg halves evenly over the entire cake, then cover with the second shortcrust pastry. Pinch the closed edges.
7. Break the remaining egg into a small bowl and mix well. Brush the beaten egg over the shortcrust pastry.
8. Cook for 15-20 minutes, until golden and hot.
3. Enjoy!

NUTRITION

calories: 417 | fat: 28g | protein: 17g | carbohydrates: 25g | fiber: 3g | sodium: 490mg

97. Green Smoothie
Prep time: 10 minutes | Cook time: 0 minutes | Serves 2

INGREDIENTS:

2 small very ripe avocado, peeled and pitted	2 tablespoon extra-virgin olive oil or avocado oil
2 cup almond milk or water, plus more as needed	16 to 10 fresh mint leaves, stems removed
2 cup tender baby spinach leaves, stems removed	4 to 2 tablespoons juice of 1 lime (is it 1?)
1 medium cucumber, peeled and seeded	

DIRECTIONS:

1. In a blender or large, wide-mouthed jar, if using a hand blender, combine the avocado, almond milk, spinach, cucumber, olive oil, mint and juice of lime and whisk until smooth and creamy.
2. Adding more almond milk or water to achieve the desired consistency.
3. Enjoy!

NUTRITION

calories: 330 | fat: 30g | protein: 4g | carbohydrates: 19g | fiber: 8g | sodium: 36mg

98. Greek Yogurt with Nuts
Prep time: 10 minutes | Cook time: 0 minutes | Serves 2

INGREDIENTS:

1 teaspoon vanilla or almond extract (optional)	1 cup plain whole-milk Greek yogurt
1/2 teaspoon ground cinnamon (optional)	4 tablespoons heavy whipping cream
	2 tablespoon ground flaxseeds
1/2 cup frozen berries, thawed with juices	4 tablespoons chopped nuts (walnuts or pecans)

DIRECTIONS:

1. In a small bowl or glass, combine the yogurt, heavy whipping cream, defrosted berries in their juice, vanilla or almond extract (if used), cinnamon (if used) and flax seeds and mix well until the mixture is smooth.
2. Complete with chopped walnuts.
3. Enjoy!

NUTRITION

calories: 267 | fat: 19g | protein: 11g | carbohydrates: 12g | fiber: 3g | sodium: 63mg

99. Herb Frittata
Prep time: 10 minutes | Cook time: 7 minutes | Serves 4

INGREDIENTS:

16 cherry tomatoes, halved	2 cup fresh spinach, arugula, kale, or other leafy greens
1 cup crumbled soft goat cheese	8 large eggs
8 tablespoons extra-virgin olive oil, divided	Freshly ground black pepper, to taste
4 tablespoons fresh chopped herbs, such as rosemary, thyme, oregano, basil or 1 teaspoon dried herbs	8 ounces (113 g) quartered artichoke hearts, rinsed, drained, and thoroughly dried
1/2 teaspoon salt	

DIRECTIONS:

1. Preheat the oven to cook over low heat.
2. In a small bowl, combine the eggs, herbs, salt and pepper and beat well with a fork. To put aside.
3. In a 4- to 5-inch skillet or omelette pan, heat 2 tablespoons of olive oil over medium heat. Add the spinach, artichoke hearts and cherry tomatoes and sauté until wilted, 1 to 2 minutes.
4. Pour in the egg mixture and cook undisturbed over medium heat for 3 to 4 minutes, until the eggs begin to settle on the bottom.
5. Sprinkle the goat cheese on top of the egg mixture and transfer the pan to the oven.
6. Cook for 4 to 5 minutes, or until the omelette is firm in the center and golden on the top.
7. Remove from the oven and run a rubber spatula around the edge to loosen the sides. Flip onto a large plate or cutting board and cut in half.
8. Serve hot and seasoned with the remaining 2 tablespoons of olive oil.

NUTRITION

calories: 527 | fat: 47g | protein: 21g | carbohydrates: 10g | fiber: 3g | sodium: 760mg

100. Apple-Tahini Toast
Prep time: 5 minutes | Cook time: 0 minutes | Serves 2

INGREDIENTS:

4 slices whole-wheat bread, toasted	4 tablespoons tahini
2 small apples of your choice, cored and thinly sliced	2 teaspoon honey

DIRECTIONS:

1. Spread the tahini on the toast.
2. Arrange the apple slices on the bread and drizzle with honey.
3. Serve immediately.

NUTRITION

calories: 458 | fat: 17g | protein: 11g | carbohydrates: 63g | fiber: 10g | sodium: 285mg

101. Pumpkin Muffins
Prep time: 15 minutes | Cook time: 15 minutes | Makes 18 Muffins

INGREDIENTS:

3/4 cup plain, unsweetened, full-fat yogurt	Pinch nutmeg
3/4 cup butter, melted (optional)	1 1/8 cup all-purpose flour
3/4 cup sugar	3 teaspoons pumpkin pie spice
Nonstick cooking spray	4 1/2 mashed bananas
2 1/4 cups granulated sugar	1 1/2 (15-ounce / 425-g) can pure pumpkin purée
1 1/2 teaspoon baking soda	
1/3 teaspoon salt	3 large egg whites

DIRECTIONS:

1. Preheat oven to 350°F | 180°C | Fan 160°C. Spray a muffin mold with cooking spray.
2. In a large bowl, combine the sugars, flour, pumpkin pie spices, baking soda, salt, and nutmeg. In a separate bowl, mix the bananas, pumpkin puree, yogurt, and butter (if desired). Slowly mix the wet ingredients into the dry ingredients.
3. In a large glass bowl, using a mixer on top, beat the egg whites until stiff and fold into the batter.
4. Pour the batter into a muffin pan, filling each cup halfway. Bake for 15 minutes, or until a fork inserted in the centre comes out clean.
5. Enjoy!

NUTRITION

calories: 259 | fat: 8g | protein: 3g | carbohydrates: 49g | fiber: 3g | sodium: 226mg

102. Banana Corn Fritters
Prep time: 5 minutes | Cook time: 10 minutes | Serves 4

INGREDIENTS:

1 teaspoon baking powder	4 small ripe bananas, peeled and mashed
4 tablespoons unsweetened almond milk	1 cup yellow cornmeal
1/2 teaspoon ground cinnamon	2 large eggs, beaten
1/2 to 1/2 teaspoon ground chipotle chili	1/2 teaspoon sea salt
1/2 cup flour	2 tablespoon olive oil

DIRECTIONS:

1. Mix all ingredients except the olive oil in a large bowl until smooth.
2. Heat a non-stick skillet over medium-high heat. Add the olive oil and pour about 2 tablespoons of batter for each pancake. Cook for 2 to 3 minutes until the bottom is golden, then flip. Continue cooking for 1 or 2 minutes more, until completely cooked. Repeat with the remaining batter.

3. Serve hot and enjoy!

NUTRITION

calories: 396 | fat: 10g | protein: 7g | carbohydrates: 68g | fiber: 4g | sodium: 307mg

103. Avocado Smoothie

Prep time: 2 minutes | Cook time: 0 minutes | Serves 4

INGREDIENTS:

2 large avocados
3 cups unsweetened coconut milk
4 tablespoons honey

DIRECTIONS:

1. Put all the ingredients in a blender and blend until smooth and creamy.
2. Serve immediately.

NUTRITION

calories: 686 | fat: 57g | protein: 6g | carbohydrates: 35g | fiber: 10g | sodium: 35mg

FISH & SEAFOOD RECIPES

Fish and Seafood

104. Fish Fillet on Lemons

Prep time: 5 minutes | Cook time: 6 minutes | Serves 6

INGREDIENTS:

1 1/2 tablespoon extra-virgin olive oil
Nonstick cooking spray
1/3 teaspoon freshly ground black pepper
6 (4-ounce/ 113-g) fish fillets, such as tilapia, salmon, catfish, cod, or your favorite fish
4 1/2 to 4 medium lemons
1/3 teaspoon kosher or sea salt

DIRECTIONS:

1. Using paper towels, dry the fillets and let them rest at room temperature for 10 minutes. Meanwhile, coat the cold grill cooking rack with non-stick cooking spray and preheat the grill to 205°C (400°F) or medium-high heat. Or preheat a grill over medium-high heat on the stove.
2. Cut a lemon in half and set half aside. Cut the remaining half of that lemon and the remaining lemons into ¼-inch thick slices. (You should have 12 to 16 lemon slices.) In a small bowl, squeeze 1 tablespoon of juice from the reserved lemon half.
3. Add the oil to the bowl with the lemon juice and mix well. Brush both sides of the fish with the oil mixture and sprinkle evenly with pepper and salt.
4. Carefully arrange the lemon slices on the grill (or grill pan), arranging 3 or 4 slices together in the shape of a fish fillet, and repeat with the remaining slices. Place the fish fillets directly on top of the lemon slices and grill with the lid closed. (If you're grilling on the stove, cover with a large lid or aluminum foil.) Turn the fish halfway through the cooking time only if the fillets are more than half an inch thick.
5. The fish is ready and ready to serve when it begins to separate into flakes (pieces) when gently pressed with a fork.

NUTRITION

calories: 208 | fat: 11g | protein: 21g | carbohydrates: 2g | fiber: 0g | sodium: 249mg

105. Tilapia Fillet with Onion and Avocado

Prep time: 5 minutes | Cook time: 3 minutes | Serves 6

INGREDIENTS:

1 1/2 tablespoon freshly squeezed orange juice
6 (4-ounce/113-g) tilapia fillets, more oblong than square, skin-on or skinned
1/3 cup chopped red onion
1 1/2 tablespoon extra-virgin olive oil
1/3 teaspoon kosher or sea salt
1 1/2 avocado, pitted, skinned, and sliced

DIRECTIONS:

1. In a 9-inch glass cake pan, use a fork to mix the oil, orange juice, and salt. Working one fillet at a time, place them in the pan and turn them to cover them from all sides. Arrange the fillets in a wagon wheel formation, so that one end of each fillet is in the centre of the plate and the other end is temporarily draped over the edge of the plate. Cover each fillet with 1 tablespoon of onion, then fold the end of the fillet that hangs from the edge above the onion in half. When finished, you should have 4 folded fillets with the crease against the outside edge of the plate and the ends all in the centre.
2. Cover the dish with cling film, leaving a small part open at the edge to let the steam escape. Microwave on high for about 3 minutes. The fish is ready when it starts to separate into flakes (pieces) when gently pressed with a fork.
3. Garnish the fillets with the avocado.
4. Serve when ready.

NUTRITION

calories: 210 | fat: 10g | protein: 25g | carbohydrates: 5g | fiber: 3g | sodium: 240mg

106. Garlic Shrimp Black Bean Pasta

Prep time: 10 minutes | Cook time: 15 minutes | Serves 6

INGREDIENTS:

6 tablespoons extra-virgin olive oil
1 1/2 onion, finely chopped
4 1/2 garlic cloves, minced
1 1/2 pound (454 g) black bean linguine or spaghetti
1 1/2 pound (454 g) fresh shrimp, peeled and deveined
1/3 cup basil, cut into strips

DIRECTIONS:

1. Bring a large pot of water to a boil and cook the pasta according to the instructions on the package.
2. In the last 5 minutes of cooking the pasta, add the prawns to the hot water and cook for 3-5 minutes. When they turn pink, remove them from hot water and, if you think they are too hot, run them under cold water. To put aside.
3. Save 1 cup of the pasta cooking water and drain the noodles. In the same pan, heat the oil over medium-high heat and cook the onion and garlic for 7-10 minutes. Once the onion is translucent, add the pasta again and mix well.
4. Serve the pasta, then garnish with the prawns and garnish with the basil.
5. Enjoy!

NUTRITION

calories: 668 | fat: 19g | protein: 57g | carbohydrates: 73g | fiber: 31g | sodium: 615mg

107. Almond-Crusted Swordfish

Prep time: 25 minutes | Cook time: 15 minutes | Serves 6

INGREDIENTS:

3/4 to 1 teaspoon salt, divided
3 pounds (907 g) Swordfish, preferably 1 inch thick
3/4 cup almond flour
1/3 cup crushed Marcona almonds
1 1/2 large egg, beaten (optional)
1/3 cup pure apple cider
7 1/2 medium baby portobello mushrooms, chopped (optional)
6 or 5 chopped scallions, both green and white parts
1/3 cup extra-virgin olive oil, plus more for frying
4 1/2 to 4 sprigs flat-leaf parsley, chopped
1 1/2 lemon, juiced
1 1/2 tablespoon Spanish paprika
4 1/2 to 4 garlic cloves, peeled
1/3 cup chopped pitted Kalamata olives

DIRECTIONS:

1. On a flat plate, spread the flour and the chopped Marcona almonds and add the salt. Alternatively, pour the flour, almonds and teaspoon of salt into a large plastic food bag. Add the fish and coat it with the flour mixture. If you want a thicker layer, repeat this step after dipping the fish in the egg (if used).
2. In a measuring cup, combine the apple cider, 1 cup of olive oil, parsley, lemon juice, paprika and 1 teaspoon of salt. Mix well and set aside.
3. In a large, heavy-bottomed skillet or skillet, pour the olive oil to a depth of ⅛ inch and heat over medium heat. Once the oil is hot, add the fish and sauté for 3-5 minutes, then flip the fish and add the mushrooms (if used), shallots, garlic and olives. Cook for another 3 minutes. When the other side of the fish is golden, remove the fish from the pan and set aside.
4. Pour the cider mixture into the pan and mix well with the vegetables. Place the fried fish in the pan on top of the mixture and cook with the sauce over medium-low heat for 10 minutes, until the fish flakes easily with a fork. Carefully remove the fish from the pan and plate. Pour the sauce over the fish.
5. Serve with white rice or home-fried potatoes.

NUTRITION

calories: 305 | fat: 13g | protein: 54g | carbohydrates: 12g | fiber: 3g | sodium: 170mg

108. Fideos with Seafood

Prep time: 15 minutes | Cook time: 20 minutes | Serves 8

INGREDIENTS:

2/3 cup shredded Parmesan cheese
1/3 cup chopped fresh flat-leaf Italian parsley, for garnish
8 cups zucchini noodles, roughly chopped (2 to 3 medium zucchini)
1 1/3-pound (454 g) shrimp, peeled, deveined and roughly chopped
8 to 8 ounces (170 to 227 g) canned chopped clams, drained
5 1/3 ounces (113 g) crab meat
2/3 cup crumbled goat cheese
2/3 cup crumbled feta cheese
1 1/3 (28-ounce / 794-g) can chopped tomatoes, with their juices
2 2/3 tablespoons extra-virgin olive oil, plus 1/2 cup, divided
1 1/3 teaspoon salt
1 1/3 teaspoon garlic powder
2/3 teaspoon smoked paprika

DIRECTIONS:

1. Preheat oven to 375° F | 190°C | Fan 170°C.
2. Pour 2 tablespoons of olive oil into the bottom of a 9x13 inch pan and shake to coat the bottom.
3. In a large bowl, combine the courgette noodles, prawns, clams and crab meat.
4. In another bowl, combine the goat cheese, feta and 1 cup of olive oil and

mix to combine well. Add the canned tomatoes and their juices, salt, garlic powder and paprika and mix well. Add the mixture to the courgette and seafood mixture and toss to combine.
5. Pour the mixture into the prepared pan, distributing it evenly. Spread the grated Parmesan over the top and drizzle with the remaining ¼ cup of olive oil. Cook until boiling, 20 to 25 minutes.
6. Serve hot, garnished with chopped parsley.

NUTRITION

calories: 434 | fat: 31g | protein: 29g | carbohydrates: 12g | fiber: 3g | sodium: 712mg

109. Thyme Whole Roasted Red Snapper

Prep time: 5 minutes | Cook time: 45 minutes | Serves 6

INGREDIENTS:

6 or 5 sprigs of thyme	scaled
4 1/2 cloves garlic, sliced	3 lemons, sliced (about 10 slices)
1 1/2 (2 to 2 1/2 pounds / 907 g to 1.1 kg) whole red snapper, cleaned and	4 1/2 tablespoons cold salted butter, cut into small cubes, divided (optional)

DIRECTIONS:

1. Preheat oven to 350°F | 180°C | Fan 160°C.2. Cut a piece of aluminum foil the size of your pan; put the foil on the baking sheet.
3. Make a horizontal slice across the belly of the fish to create a pocket.
4. Place 3 lemon slices on the aluminum foil and the fish on top of the lemons.
5. Stuff the fish with garlic, thyme, 3 lemon slices and butter. Reserve 3 pieces of butter.
6. Place the reserved 3 pieces of butter on top of the fish and 3 or 4 lemon slices on top of the butter. Gather the foil and seal it to make a pocket around the fish.
7. Place the fish in the oven and cook for 45 minutes.
8. Serve with the remaining fresh lemon slices.

NUTRITION

calories: 345 | fat: 13g | protein: 54g | carbohydrates: 12g | fiber: 3g | sodium: 170mg

110. Fast Seafood Paella

Prep time: 20 minutes | Cook time: 20 minutes | Serves 6

INGREDIENTS:

2 1/4 cups medium-grain Spanish paella rice or arborio rice	2 1/4 tablespoons garlic powder
3 carrots, finely diced	1 1/2 tablespoon sweet paprika
Salt, to taste	12 ounces (227 g) lobster meat or canned crab
1 1/2 large onion, finely chopped	3/4 cup frozen peas
1/3 cup plus 1 tablespoon extra-virgin olive oil	4 1/2 cups chicken stock, plus more if needed
1 1/2 cup dry white wine	1/3 pound (136 g) calamari rings
9 jumbo shrimp, unpeeled	1 1/2 lemon, halved
3 tomatoes, peeled and chopped	

DIRECTIONS:

1. In a large skillet (16-inch ideal), heat the oil over medium heat until small bubbles begin to come out of the oil. Add the onion and cook for about 3 minutes, until fragrant, then add the tomatoes and garlic powder. Cook for 5-10 minutes, until the tomatoes have reduced by half and the consistency is sticky.
2. Incorporate the rice, carrots, salt, paprika, lobster and peas and mix well. In a microwave-safe pot or bowl, heat the chicken broth almost to a boil, then add it to the rice mixture. Bring to a boil, then add the wine.
3. Smooth out the rice in the bottom of the pan. Cover and cook over low heat for 10 minutes, stirring occasionally, to prevent burning.
4. Cover the rice with the prawns, cover and cook for another 5 minutes. Add more broth to the pan if the rice looks dry.
5. Just before removing the pan from the heat, add the squid rings. Stir the ingredients frequently. In about 2 minutes, the rings will look dull. Remove the pan from the heat immediately (if you don't want the paella to overcook). Squeeze the fresh lemon juice onto the plate.
6. Serve when ready.

NUTRITION

calories: 632 | fat: 20g | protein: 34g | carbohydrates: 71g | fiber: 5g | sodium: 920mg

111. Shrimp with Garlic and Mushrooms

Prep time: 10 minutes | Cook time: 15 minutes | Serves 6

INGREDIENTS:

1/3 cup chopped fresh flat-leaf Italian parsley
1 1/2 pound (454 g) peeled and deveined fresh shrimp
12 large garlic cloves, thinly sliced
6 ounces (113 g) sliced mushrooms (shiitake, baby bella, or button)
3/4 teaspoon red pepper flakes
1 1/2 teaspoon salt
1 1/2 cup extra-virgin olive oil
Zucchini noodles or riced cauliflower, for serving

DIRECTIONS:

1. Rinse the shrimp and dry them. Place in a small bowl and sprinkle with salt.
2. In a large, thick-sided skillet, heat the olive oil over medium-low heat. Add the garlic and heat until very fragrant, 3-4 minutes, reducing the heat if the garlic starts to burn.
3. Add the mushrooms and sauté for 5 minutes, until soft. Add the shrimp and chili flakes and saute until the shrimp start to turn pink, another 3 to 4 minutes.
4. Remove from the heat and stir in the parsley.
5. Serve on courgette noodles or cauliflower rice.

NUTRITION

calories: 620 | fat: 56g | protein: 24g | carbohydrates: 4g | fiber: 0g | sodium: 736mg

112. Sea Bass Crusted with Moroccan Spices

Prep time: 15 minutes | Cook time: 40 minutes | Serves 6

INGREDIENTS:

1 1/2 (15-ounce / 425-g) can chickpeas, drained and rinsed	pepper
2 1/4 cups low-sodium vegetable broth	1 1/2 large carrot, sliced on an angle
2 1/4 teaspoons ground turmeric, divided	3 sun-dried tomatoes, thinly sliced (optional)
1 1/8 teaspoon saffron	3 tablespoons tomato paste
2 1/4 pounds (680 g) sea bass fillets, about 1/2 inch thick	1/3 cup white wine
12 tablespoons extra-virgin olive oil, divided	3/4 lemon, juiced
12 garlic cloves, divided (4 minced cloves and 4 sliced)	3/4 lemon, cut into thin rounds
9 medium baby portobello mushrooms, chopped	6 to 5 rosemary sprigs or 2 tablespoons dried rosemary
3/4 teaspoon ground cumin	1 1/2 tablespoon ground coriander (optional)
1/3 teaspoon kosher salt	1 1/2 cup sliced artichoke hearts marinated in olive oil
1/3 teaspoon freshly ground black	3/4 cup pitted Kalamata olives
	Fresh cilantro, for garnish

DIRECTIONS:

1. In a small bowl, combine 1 teaspoon of turmeric, saffron and cumin. Season with salt and pepper. Season both sides of the fish with the spice mixture. Add 3 tablespoons of olive oil and work the fish to make sure it is well coated with the spices and olive oil.
2. In a large skillet or skillet, heat 2 tablespoons of olive oil over medium heat until it glistens but smokes. Brown the top of the sea bass for about 1 minute or until golden brown. Remove and set aside.
3. In the same pan, add the minced garlic and cook very briefly, stirring regularly, until it becomes fragrant. Add the mushrooms, carrot, dried tomatoes (if used) and tomato paste. Cook for 3 to 4 minutes over medium heat, stirring often, until it becomes fragrant. Add the chickpeas, stock, wine, coriander (if used) and sliced garlic. Stir in the remaining ½ teaspoon of ground turmeric. Turn up the heat if necessary and bring to a boil, then lower the heat to simmer. Cover part of the path and let the sauce simmer for about 20 minutes, until it thickens.
4. Carefully add the seared fish to the pan. Pour some sauce over the fish. Add the artichokes, olives, lemon juice and slices and the sprigs of rosemary. Cook another 10 minutes or until the fish is completely cooked and crumbly.
5. Garnish with fresh cilantro and serve when ready.

NUTRITION

calories: 259 | fat: 8g | protein: 3g | carbohydrates: 49g | fiber: 3g | sodium: 226mg

113. Italian Fried Shrimp

Prep time: 10 minutes | Cook time: 5 minutes | Serves 6

INGREDIENTS:

1 1/2 teaspoon salt
1 1/2 cup flour
3 large eggs
3 cups seasoned Italian bread crumbs
1 1/2 pound (454 g) large shrimp (21 to 25), peeled and deveined
Extra-virgin olive oil

DIRECTIONS:

1. In a small bowl, beat the eggs with 1 tablespoon of water, then transfer to a deep plate.
2. Add the breadcrumbs and salt to a separate deep plate; mix well.
3. Put the flour in a third deep plate.
4. Dip the prawns in the flour, then in the egg and finally in the breadcrumbs. Place on a plate and repeat with all the prawns.
5. Preheat a skillet over high heat. Pour in enough olive oil to coat the bottom of the pan. Cook the shrimp in the hot pan for 2 to 3 minutes per side. Remove the prawns and drain them on absorbent paper.
6. Serve hot.

NUTRITION

calories: 714 | fat: 34g | protein: 37g | carbohydrates: 63g | fiber: 3g | sodium: 1727mg

114. Classic Escabeche

Prep time: 10 minutes | Cook time: 20 minutes | Serves 6

INGREDIENTS:

12 tablespoons extra-virgin olive oil, divided
1 1/2 bunch asparagus, trimmed and cut into 2-inch pieces
1 1/2 (13 3/4-ounce / 390-g) can artichoke hearts, drained and quartered
6 large garlic cloves, peeled and crushed
1 1/2 pound (454 g) wild-caught Spanish mackerel fillets, cut into four pieces
1 1/2 teaspoon salt
3/4 teaspoon freshly ground black pepper
3 bay leaves
1/3 cup red wine vinegar
3/4 teaspoon smoked paprika

DIRECTIONS:

1. Sprinkle the fillets with salt and pepper and leave to rest at room temperature for 5 minutes.
2. In a large skillet, heat 2 tablespoons of olive oil over medium-high heat. Add the fish, skin side up, and cook for 5 minutes. Flip and cook 5 minutes on the other side, until golden brown and cooked. Transfer to a serving dish, pour the cooking oil over the fish and cover to keep warm.
3. Heat the remaining 6 tablespoons of olive oil in the same pan over medium heat. Add the asparagus, artichokes, garlic and bay leaves and saute until the vegetables are tender, 6 to 8 minutes.
4. Using a skimmer, season the fish with the cooked vegetables, keeping the oil in the pan. Add the vinegar and paprika to the oil and blend to mix well. Pour the vinaigrette over the fish and vegetables and let it sit at room temperature for at least 15 minutes, or marinate in the refrigerator for up to 24 hours for a deeper flavor. Remove the bay leaf before serving.
5. Serve when ready.

NUTRITION

calories: 578 | fat: 50g | protein: 26g | carbohydrates: 13g | fiber: 5g | sodium: 946mg

115. Lemon Rosemary Branzino

Prep time: 15 minutes | Cook time: 30 minutes | Serves 4

INGREDIENTS:

4 tablespoons paprika
4 teaspoons kosher salt
2 garlic cloves, minced
2 bunch scallions, white part only, thinly sliced
1 cup sliced pitted Kalamata or other good-quality black olives
2 large carrots, cut into 1/4-inch rounds
8 tablespoons extra-virgin olive oil, divided
4 (8-ounce / 227-g) branzino fillets, preferably at least 1 inch thick
1 tablespoon ground chili pepper, preferably Turkish or Aleppo
4 rosemary sprigs or 1 tablespoon dried rosemary
20 to 12 small cherry tomatoes, halved
1 cup dry white wine
2 small lemons, very thinly sliced

DIRECTIONS:

1. Heat a large, oven-safe skillet or skillet over high heat until hot, about 2 minutes. Carefully add 1 tablespoon of olive oil and heat until glistening, 10 to 15 seconds. Brown the sea bass fillets for 2 minutes, skin side up. Carefully flip the fillets skin side down and cook for another 2 minutes, until golden brown. To put aside.
2. Shake 2 tablespoons of olive oil around the pan to coat it evenly. Add the garlic, shallots, kalamata olives, carrot and tomatoes and sauté the vegetables for 5 minutes, until soft. Add the wine, stirring until all the ingredients are well integrated. Carefully place the fish on the sauce.
3 Preheat oven to 450°F. | 230°C | Fan 210°C
4. While the oven is heating up, brush the fillets with 1 tablespoon of olive oil and season with paprika, salt and chilli. Garnish each fillet with a sprig of rosemary and several slices of lemon. Sprinkle the olives on the fish and around the pan.
5. Roast until lemon wedges are golden or charred, about 10 minutes.
6. Serve when ready.

NUTRITION

calories: 725 | fat: 43g | protein: 58g | carbohydrates: 25g | fiber: 10g | sodium: 2954mg

116. Crispy Fried Sardines

Prep time: 5 minutes | Cook time: 5 minutes | Serves 6

INGREDIENTS:

1 1/2 teaspoon freshly ground black pepper
3 cups flour
Avocado oil, as needed
2 1/4 pounds (680 g) whole fresh sardines, scales removed
1 1/2 teaspoon salt

DIRECTIONS:

1. Preheat a deep skillet over medium heat. Pour in enough oil so that there is about 1 inch in the pan.
2. Season the fish with salt and pepper.
3. Dip the fish in the flour so that it is completely covered.
4. Slowly dip 1 fish at a time, being careful not to overcrowd the pan.
5. Cook for about 3 minutes on each side or until the fish begins to brown on all sides.
6. Serve hot.

NUTRITION

calories: 794 | fat: 47g | protein: 48g | carbohydrates: 44g | fiber: 2g | sodium: 1441mg

117. Roasted Shrimp-Gnocchi Bake

Prep time: 10 minutes | Cook time: 20 minutes | Serves 6

INGREDIENTS:

1 1/2 pound (454 g) fresh raw shrimp (or frozen and thawed shrimp), shells and tails removed
3 tablespoons extra-virgin olive oil
3 garlic cloves, minced
3/4 teaspoon freshly ground black pepper
1/3 teaspoon crushed red pepper
1 1/2 (12-ounce / 340-g) jar roasted red peppers, drained and coarsely chopped
1 1/2 pound (454 g) frozen gnocchi (not thawed)
1 1/2 cup chopped fresh tomato
3/4 cup cubed feta cheese
1/3 cup fresh torn basil leaves

DIRECTIONS:

1. Preheat oven to 400°F | 200°C | Fan 180°C
2. In a baking dish, mix the tomatoes, oil, garlic, black pepper and chopped red pepper. Roast in the oven for 10 minutes.
3. Stir in the roasted peppers and shrimp. Roast for another 10 minutes, until the shrimp turn pink and white.
4. While the shrimp are cooking, cook the gnocchi on the stove according to package directions. Drain in a colander and keep warm.
5. Remove the pan from the oven. Add the cooked gnocchi, feta and basil and serve.

NUTRITION

calories: 146 | fat: 4g | protein: 23g | carbohydrates: 1g | fiber: 0g | sodium: 1144mg

118. Fish and Orzo

Prep time: 10 minutes | Cook time: 35 minutes | Serves 6

INGREDIENTS:

1 1/2 teaspoon garlic, minced
1 1/2 teaspoon red pepper, crushed
3 shallots, chopped
1 1/2 tablespoon olive oil
3 teaspoon anchovy paste
3 tablespoon oregano, chopped
3 tablespoons black olives, pitted and chopped
3 tablespoons capers, drained
22 1/2 ounces canned tomatoes, crushed
A pinch of salt and black pepper
6 cod fillets, boneless
1 1/2-ounce feta cheese, crumbled
1 1/2 tablespoons parsley, chopped
4 1/2 cups chicken stock
1 1/2 cup orzo pasta
Zest of 1 lemon, grated

DIRECTIONS:

1. Heat a pan with the oil over medium heat, add the garlic, chilli and shallot and sauté for 5 minutes.
2. Add the anchovy paste, oregano, black olives, capers, tomatoes, salt and pepper, mix and cook for another 5 minutes.
3. Add the cod fillets, sprinkle with cheese and parsley, place in the oven and cook 375° F for an extra 15 minutes.
4. Meanwhile, put the broth in a saucepan, bring to a boil over medium heat, add the barley and lemon zest, bring to the boil, cook for 10 minutes, shell with a fork and divide into plates.
5. Top each portion with the fish mix.
6. Serve when ready.

NUTRITION:

calories: 402 | fat: 21g | protein: 31g | carbohydrates: 21g | fiber: 8g

119. Baked Sea Bass

Prep time: 10 minutes | Cook time: 12 minutes | Serves 6

INGREDIENTS:

6 sea bass fillets, boneless
Salt and black pepper to the taste
3 cups potato chips, crushed
1 1/2 tablespoon mayonnaise

DIRECTIONS:

1. Season the fish fillets with salt and pepper, brush them with mayonnaise and pass them in the chips.
2. Arrange the fillets on a baking sheet lined with parchment paper and bake at
400°F | 200°C | Fan 180°C for 12 minutes.
3. Divide the fish on plates.
4. Serve with a side salad.

NUTRITION

calories: 228 | fat: 8.6g | protein: 25g | carbohydrates: 9.3g | fiber: 0.6g

120. Fish and Tomato Sauce

Prep time: 10 minutes | Cook time: 30 minutes | Serves 6

INGREDIENTS:

6 cod fillets, boneless
3 garlic cloves, minced
3 cups cherry tomatoes, halved
1 1/2 cup chicken stock
A pinch of salt and black pepper
1/3 cup basil, chopped

DIRECTIONS:

1. Place the tomatoes, garlic, salt and pepper in a pan, heat over medium heat and cook for 5 minutes.
2. Add the fish and the rest of the ingredients, bring to a boil, cover the pan and cook for 25 minutes.
3. Divide the mix on plates.
4. Serve when ready.

NUTRITION:

calories: 180 | fat: 1.9g | protein: 33.8g | carbohydrates: 5.3g | fiber: 1.4g

121. Seafood Paella

Prep time: 20 minutes | Cook time: 20 minutes | Serves 6

INGREDIENTS:

1/3 cup plus 1 tablespoon extra-virgin olive oil
1 1/2 large onion, finely chopped
3 tomatoes, peeled and chopped
2 1/4 tablespoons garlic powder
2 1/4 cups medium-grain Spanish paella rice or arborio rice
3 carrots, finely diced
Salt, to taste
1 1/2 tablespoon sweet paprika
12 ounces (227 g) lobster meat or canned crab
3/4 cup frozen peas
4 1/2 cups chicken stock, plus more if needed
1 1/2 cup dry white wine
9 jumbo shrimp, unpeeled
$^1/_3$ pound (136 g) calamari rings
1 1/2 lemon, halved

DIRECTIONS:

1. In a large sauté pan or skillet (16-inch is ideal), heat the oil over medium heat until small bubbles start to escape from oil. Add the onion and cook for about 3 minutes, until fragrant, then add tomatoes and garlic powder. Cook for 5 to 10 minutes, until the tomatoes are reduced by half and the consistency is sticky.
2. Stir in the rice, carrots, salt, paprika, lobster, and peas and mix well. In a pot or microwave-safe bowl, heat the chicken stock to almost boiling, then add it to the rice mixture. Bring to a simmer, then add the wine.
3. Smooth out the rice in the bottom of the pan. Cover and cook on low for 10 minutes, mixing occasionally, to prevent burning.
4. Top the rice with the shrimp, cover, and cook for 5 more minutes. Add additional broth to the pan if the rice looks dried out.
5. Right before removing the skillet from the heat, add the calamari rings. Toss the Shopping List frequently. In about 2 minutes, the rings will look opaque. Remove the pan from the heat immediately (if you don't want the paella to overcook). Squeeze fresh lemon juice over the dish.
6. Serve when ready.

NUTRITION:

calories: 632 | fat: 20g | protein: 34g | carbohydrates: 71g | fiber: 5g | sodium: 920mg

122. Escabeche

Prep time: 10 minutes | Cook time: 20 minutes | Serves 6

INGREDIENTS:

1 1/2 pound (454 g) wild-caught Spanish mackerel fillets, cut into four pieces
1 1/2 teaspoon salt
3/4 teaspoon freshly ground black pepper
12 tablespoons extra-virgin olive oil, divided
1 1/2 bunch asparagus, trimmed and cut into 2-inch pieces
1 1/2 (13 3/4-ounce / 390-g) can artichoke hearts, drained and quartered
6 large garlic cloves, peeled and crushed
3 bay leaves
1/3 cup red wine vinegar
3/4 teaspoon smoked paprika

DIRECTIONS:

1. Sprinkle the fillets with salt and pepper and let sit at room temperature for 5 minutes.
2. In a large skillet, heat 2 tablespoons olive oil over medium-high heat. Add the fish, skin-side up, and cook 5 minutes. Flip and cook 5 minutes on the other side, until browned and cooked through. Transfer to a serving dish, pour the cooking oil over the fish, and cover to keep warm.
3. Heat the remaining 6 tablespoons olive oil in the same skillet over medium heat. Add the asparagus, artichokes, garlic, and bay leaves and sauté until the vegetables are tender, 6 to 8 minutes.
4. Using a slotted spoon, top the fish with the cooked vegetables, reserving the oil in the skillet. Add the vinegar and paprika to the oil and whisk to combine well. Pour the vinaigrette over the fish and vegetables and let sit at room temperature for at least 15 minutes, or marinate in the refrigerator up to 24 hours for a deeper flavor.
5. Remove the bay leaf before serving.

NUTRITION:

calories: 578 | fat: 50g | protein: 26g | carbohydrates: 13g | fiber: 5g | sodium: 946mg

123. Crispy Sardines

Prep time: 5 minutes | Cook time: 5 minutes | Serves 6

INGREDIENTS:

Avocado oil, as needed
2 1/4 pounds (680 g) whole fresh sardines, scales removed
1 1/2 teaspoon salt
1 1/2 teaspoon freshly ground black pepper
3 cups flour

DIRECTIONS:

1. Preheat a deep skillet over medium heat. Pour in enough oil so there is about 1 inch of it in the pan.
2. Season the fish with the salt and pepper.
3. Dredge the fish in the flour so it is completely covered.
4. Slowly drop in 1 fish at a time, making sure not to overcrowd the pan.
5. Cook for about 3 minutes on each side or just until the fish begins to brown on all sides.
6. Serve warm.

NUTRITION:

calories: 794 | fat: 47g | protein: 48g | carbohydrates: 44g | fiber: 2g | sodium: 1441mg

124. Roasted Salmon

Prep time: 10 minutes | Cook time: 25 minutes | Serves 6

INGREDIENTS:

3/4 cup extra-virgin olive oil, divided
3 tablespoons balsamic vinegar
3 tablespoons garlic powder, divided
1 1/2 tablespoon cumin seeds
1 1/2 teaspoon sea salt, divided
1 1/2 teaspoon freshly ground black
pepper, divided
3 teaspoons smoked paprika
6 (8-ounce / 227-g) salmon fillets, skinless
3 small red onion, thinly sliced
3/4 cup halved Campari tomatoes

1 1/2 small fennel bulb, thinly sliced lengthwise	3/4 lime, zested
1 1/2 large carrot, thinly sliced	Handful cilantro leaves
12 medium portobello mushrooms	3/4 cup halved pitted Kalamata olives
12 medium radishes, sliced 1/8 inch thick	1 1/2 orange, thinly sliced
3/4 cup dry white wine	6 roasted sweet potatoes, cut in wedges lengthwise

DIRECTIONS:

1. Preheat oven to 375° F | 190°C | Fan 170°C.
2. In a medium bowl, mix 6 tablespoons of olive oil, the balsamic vinegar, 1 tablespoon of garlic powder, the cumin seeds, ¼ teaspoon of sea salt, ¼ teaspoon of pepper, and the paprika. Put the salmon in the bowl and marinate while preparing the vegetables, about 10 minutes.
3. Heat an oven-safe sauté pan or skillet on medium-high heat and sear the top of the salmon for about 2 minutes, or until lightly brown. Set aside.
4. Add the remaining 2 tablespoons of olive oil to the same skillet. Once it's hot, add the onion, tomatoes, fennel, carrot, mushrooms, radishes, the remaining 1 teaspoon of garlic powder, ¾ teaspoon of salt, and ¾ teaspoon of pepper. Mix well and cook for 5 to 7 minutes, until fragrant. Add wine and mix well.
5. Place the salmon on top of the vegetable mixture, browned-side up. Sprinkle the fish with lime zest and cilantro and place the olives around the fish. Put orange slices over the fish and cook for about 7 additional minutes. While this is baking, add the sliced sweet potato wedges on a baking sheet and bake this alongside the skillet.
6. Remove from the oven, cover the skillet tightly, and let rest for about 3 minutes.
7. Serve when ready.

NUTRITION:

calories: 841 | fat: 41g | protein: 59g | carbohydrates: 60g | fiber: 15g | sodium: 908mg

125. Almond-Crusted Swordfish

Prep time: 25 minutes | Cook time: 15 minutes | Serves 6

INGREDIENTS:

3/4 cup almond flour	chopped
1/3 cup crushed Marcona almonds	1 1/2 lemon, juiced
3/4 to 1 teaspoon salt, divided	1 1/2 tablespoon Spanish paprika
3 pounds (907 g) Swordfish, preferably 1 inch thick	7 1/2 medium baby portobello mushrooms, chopped (optional)
1 1/2 large egg, beaten (optional)	6 or 5 chopped scallions, both green and white parts
1/3 cup pure apple cider	
1/3 cup extra-virgin olive oil, plus more for frying	4 1/2 to 4 garlic cloves, peeled
4 1/2 to 4 sprigs flat-leaf parsley,	1/3 cup chopped pitted Kalamata olives

DIRECTIONS:

1. On a dinner plate, spread the flour and crushed Marcona almonds and mix in the salt. Alternately, pour the flour, almonds, and ¼ teaspoon of salt into a large plastic food storage bag. Add the fish and coat it with the flour mixture. If a thicker coat is desired, repeat this step after dipping the fish in the egg (if using).
2. In a measuring cup, combine the apple cider, ¼ cup of olive oil, parsley, lemon juice, paprika, and ¼ teaspoon of salt. Mix well and set aside.
3. In a large, heavy-bottom sauté pan or skillet, pour the olive oil to a depth of ⅛ inch and heat on medium heat. Once the oil is hot, add the fish and brown for 3 to 5 minutes, then turn the fish over and add the mushrooms (If using), scallions, garlic, and olives. Cook for an additional 3 minutes. Once the other side of the fish is brown, remove the fish from the pan and set aside.
4. Pour the cider mixture into the skillet and mix well with the vegetables. Put the fried fish into the skillet on top of the mixture and cook with sauce on medium-low heat for 10 minutes, until the fish flakes easily with a fork. Carefully remove the fish from the pan and plate. Spoon the sauce over the fish.
5. Serve with white rice or home-fried potatoes.

NUTRITION:

calories: 620 | fat: 37g | protein: 63g | carbohydrates: 10g | fiber: 5g | sodium: 644mg

126. Lemon Rosemary Branzino

Prep time: 15 minutes | Cook time: 30 minutes | Serves 4

INGREDIENTS:

8 tablespoons extra-virgin olive oil, divided	4 (8-ounce / 227-g) branzino fillets, preferably at least 1 inch thick
2 garlic cloves, minced	4 tablespoons paprika
2 bunch scallions, white part only, thinly sliced	4 teaspoons kosher salt
1 cup sliced pitted Kalamata or other good-quality black olives	1 tablespoon ground chili pepper, preferably Turkish or Aleppo
2 large carrots, cut into 1/4-inch rounds	4 rosemary sprigs or 1 tablespoon dried rosemary
20 to 12 small cherry tomatoes, halved	2 small lemons, very thinly sliced
1 cup dry white wine	

DIRECTIONS:

1. Warm a large, oven-safe sauté pan or skillet over high heat until hot, about 2 minutes. Carefully add 1 tablespoon of olive oil and heat until it shimmers, 10 to 15 seconds. Brown the branzino fillets for 2 minutes, skin-side up. Carefully flip the fillets skin-side down and cook for another 2 minutes, until browned. Set aside.
2. Swirl 2 tablespoons of olive oil around the skillet to coat evenly. Add the garlic, scallions, kalamata olives, carrot, and tomatoes, and let the vegetables sauté for 5 minutes, until softened. Add the wine, stirring until all Shopping List are well integrated. Carefully place the fish over the sauce.
3. Preheat oven to 450°F. | 230°C | Fan 210°C
4. While the oven is heating, brush the fillets with 1 tablespoon of olive oil and season with paprika, salt, and chili pepper. Top each fillet with a rosemary sprig and several slices of lemon. Scatter the olives over fish and around the pan.
5. Roast until lemon slices are browned or singed, about 10 minutes.

NUTRITION:

calories: 725 | fat: 43g | protein: 58g | carbohydrates: 25g | fiber: 10g | sodium: 2954mg

127. Shrimp with Garlic and Mushrooms

Prep time: 10 minutes | Cook time: 15 minutes | Serves 6

INGREDIENTS:

1 1/2 pound (454 g) peeled and deveined fresh shrimp	(shiitake, baby bella, or button)
	3/4 teaspoon red pepper flakes
1 1/2 teaspoon salt	1/3 cup chopped fresh flat-leaf Italian parsley
1 1/2 cup extra-virgin olive oil	
12 large garlic cloves, thinly sliced	Zucchini noodles or riced cauliflower, for serving
6 ounces (113 g) sliced mushrooms	

DIRECTIONS:

1. Rinse the shrimp and pat dry. Place in a small bowl and sprinkle with the salt.
2. In a large rimmed, thick skillet, heat the olive oil over medium-low heat. Add the garlic and heat until very fragrant, 3 to 4 minutes, reducing the heat if the garlic starts to burn.
3. Add the mushrooms and sauté for 5 minutes, until softened. Add the shrimp and red pepper flakes and sauté until the shrimp begins to turn pink, another 3 to 4 minutes.
4. Remove from the heat and stir in the parsley.
5. Serve over zucchini noodles or riced cauliflower.

NUTRITION:

calories: 620 | fat: 56g | protein: 24g | carbohydrates: 4g | fiber: 0g | sodium: 736mg

128. Black Bean Pasta

Prep time: 10 minutes | Cook time: 15 minutes | Serves 6

INGREDIENTS:

1 1/2 pound (454 g) black bean linguine or spaghetti	6 tablespoons extra-virgin olive oil
	1 1/2 onion, finely chopped
1 1/2 pound (454 g) fresh shrimp, peeled and deveined	4 1/2 garlic cloves, minced
	1/3 cup basil, cut into strips

DIRECTIONS:

1. Bring a large pot of water to a boil and cook the pasta according to the package instructions.
2. In the last 5 minutes of cooking the pasta, add the shrimp to the hot water and allow them to cook for 3 to 5 minutes. Once they turn pink, take them out of the hot water, and, if you think you may have overcooked them, run them under cool water. Set aside.
3. Reserve 1 cup of the pasta cooking water and drain the noodles. In the same pan, heat the oil over medium-high heat and cook the onion and garlic for 7 to 10 minutes. Once the onion is translucent, add the pasta back in and toss well.
4. Plate the pasta, then top with shrimp and garnish with basil.
5. Serve when ready.

NUTRITION:
calories: 668 | fat: 19g | protein: 57g | carbohydrates: 73g | fiber: 31g | sodium: 615mg

129. Olive Tuna

Prep time: 5 minutes | Cook time: 45 minutes | Serves 6

INGREDIENTS:

1 1/2 cup extra-virgin olive oil, plus more if needed
6 (3- to 4-inch) sprigs fresh rosemary
12 (3- to 4-inch) sprigs fresh thyme
3 large garlic cloves, thinly sliced
3 (2-inch) strips lemon zest
1 1/2 teaspoon salt
3/4 teaspoon freshly ground black pepper
1 1/2 pound (454 g) fresh tuna steaks (about 1 inch thick)

DIRECTIONS:

1. Select a thick pot just large enough to fit the tuna in a single layer on the bottom. The larger the pot, the more olive oil you will need to use. Combine the olive oil, rosemary, thyme, garlic, lemon zest, salt, and pepper over medium-low heat and cook until warm and fragrant, 20 to 25 minutes, lowering the heat if it begins to smoke.
2. Remove from the heat and allow to cool for 25 to 30 minutes, until warm but not hot.
3. Add the tuna to the bottom of the pan, adding additional oil if needed so that tuna is fully submerged, and return to medium-low heat. Cook for 5 to 10 minutes, or until the oil heats back up and is warm and fragrant but not smoking. Lower the heat if it gets too hot.
4. Remove the pot from the heat and let the tuna cook in warm oil 4 to 5 minutes, to your desired level of doneness. For a tuna that is rare in the center, cook for 2 to 3 minutes.
5. Remove from the oil and serve warm, drizzling 2 to 3 tablespoons seasoned oil over the tuna.
6. To store for later use, remove the tuna from the oil and place in a container with a lid. Allow tuna and oil to cool separately. When both have cooled, remove the herb stems with a slotted spoon and pour the cooking oil over the tuna. Cover and store in the refrigerator for up to 1 week.
7. Bring to room temperature to allow the oil to liquify before serving.

NUTRITION:
calories: 363 | fat: 28g | protein: 27g | carbohydrates: 1g | fiber: 0g | sodium: 624mg

130. Sea Scallops with White Purée

Prep time: 10 minutes | Cook time: 10 minutes | Serves 4

INGREDIENTS:

8 tablespoons olive oil, divided
4 garlic cloves
4 teaspoons minced fresh rosemary
2 (15-ounce / 425-g) can white cannellini beans, drained and rinsed
1 cup low-sodium chicken stock
Salt, to taste
Freshly ground black pepper, to taste
12 (10 ounce / 283-g) sea scallops

DIRECTIONS:

1. To make the bean purée, heat 2 tablespoons of olive oil in a saucepan over medium-high heat. Add the garlic and sauté for 30 seconds, or just until it's fragrant. Don't let it burn. Add the rosemary and remove the pan from the heat.
2. Add the white beans and chicken stock to the pan, return it to the heat, and stir. Bring the beans to a boil. Reduce the heat to low and simmer for 5 minutes.
3. Transfer the beans to a blender and purée them for 30 seconds, or until they're smooth. Taste and season with salt and pepper. Let them sit in the blender with the lid on to keep them warm while you prepare the scallops.
4. Pat the scallops dry with a paper towel and season them with salt and pepper.
5. Heat the remaining 2 tablespoons of olive oil in a large sauté pan. When the oil is shimmering, add the scallops, flat-side down.
6. Cook the scallops for 2 minutes, or until they're golden on the bottom. Flip them over and cook for another 1 to 2 minutes, or until opaque and slightly firm.
7. To serve, divide the bean purée between two plates and top with the scallops.
8. Enjoy!

NUTRITION:
calories: 465 | fat: 28g | protein: 30g | carbohydrates: 21g | fiber: 7g | sodium: 319mg

131. Salmon with Tomatoes

Prep time: 5 minutes | Cook time: 8 minutes | Serves 6

INGREDIENTS:

3 tablespoons olive oil
6 (1 1/2-inch-thick) salmon fillets
3/4 teaspoon salt
1/3 teaspoon cayenne
1 1/2 teaspoon chopped fresh dill
3 Roma tomatoes, diced
1/3 cup sliced Kalamata olives
6 lemon slices

DIRECTIONS:

1. Preheat the air fryer to 375° F.
2. Brush the olive oil on both sides of the salmon fillets, and then season them lightly with salt, cayenne, and dill.
3. Place the fillets in a single layer in the basket of the air fryer, then layer the tomatoes and olives over the top. Top each fillet with a lemon slice.
4. Bake for 8 minutes, or until the salmon has reached an internal temperature of 145°F (63°C).
5. Serve when ready.

NUTRITION:
calories: 241 | fat: 15g | protein: 23g | carbohydrates: 3g | fiber: 1g | sodium: 595mg

132. Sea Bass Crusted

Prep time: 15 minutes | Cook time: 40 minutes | Serves 6

INGREDIENTS:

2 1/4 teaspoons ground turmeric, divided
1 1/8 teaspoon saffron
3/4 teaspoon ground cumin
1/3 teaspoon kosher salt
1/3 teaspoon freshly ground black pepper
2 1/4 pounds (680 g) sea bass fillets, about 1/2 inch thick
12 tablespoons extra-virgin olive oil, divided
12 garlic cloves, divided (4 minced cloves and 4 sliced)
9 medium baby portobello mushrooms, chopped
1 1/2 large carrot, sliced on an angle
3 sun-dried tomatoes, thinly sliced
(optional)
3 tablespoons tomato paste
1 1/2 (15-ounce / 425-g) can chickpeas, drained and rinsed
2 1/4 cups low-sodium vegetable broth
1/3 cup white wine
1 1/2 tablespoon ground coriander (optional)
1 1/2 cup sliced artichoke hearts marinated in olive oil
3/4 cup pitted Kalamata olives
3/4 lemon, juiced plus 1/2 lemon, cut into thin rounds
6 to 5 rosemary sprigs or 2 tablespoons dried rosemary
Fresh cilantro, for garnish

DIRECTIONS:

1. In a small mixing bowl, combine 1 teaspoon turmeric and the saffron and cumin. Season with salt and pepper. Season both sides of the fish with the spice mixture. Add 3 tablespoons of olive oil and work the fish to make sure it's well coated with the spices and the olive oil.
2. In a large sauté pan or skillet, heat 2 tablespoons of olive oil over medium heat until shimmering but not smoking. Sear the top side of the sea bass for about 1 minute, or until golden. Remove and set aside.
3. In the same skillet, add the minced garlic and cook very briefly, tossing regularly, until fragrant. 4. Add the mushrooms, carrot, sun-dried tomatoes (if using), and tomato paste. Cook for 3 to 4 minutes over medium heat, tossing frequently, until fragrant. Add the chickpeas, broth, wine, coriander (if using), and the sliced garlic. Stir in the remaining ½ teaspoon ground turmeric. Raise the heat, if needed, and bring to a boil, then lower heat to simmer. Cover part of the way and let the sauce simmer for about 20 minutes, until thickened.
5. Carefully add the seared fish to the skillet. Ladle a bit of the sauce on top of the fish. Add the artichokes, olives, lemon juice and slices, and rosemary sprigs. Cook another 10 minutes or until the fish is fully cooked and flaky.
6. Garnish with fresh cilantro and serve when ready.

NUTRITION:
calories: 696 | fat: 41g | protein: 48g | carbohydrates: 37g | fiber: 9g | sodium: 810mg

133. Golden Salmon Cakes

Prep time: 15 minutes | Cook time: 11 minutes | Serves 4

INGREDIENTS:

Tzatziki Sauce:
1 cup plain Greek yogurt
2 teaspoon dried dill
1/2 cup minced cucumber
Salt, to taste
Freshly ground black pepper, to taste
Salmon Cakes:
12 ounces (170 g) cooked salmon
6 tablespoons olive oil, divided
1/2 cup minced celery
1/2 cup minced onion
1 teaspoon dried dill
2 tablespoon fresh minced parsley
Salt, to taste

Freshly ground black pepper, to taste
2 eggs, beaten
1 cup unseasoned bread crumbs

DIRECTIONS:

Sauce
Combine the yogurt, dill, and cucumber in a small bowl. Season with salt and pepper and set aside.
Salmon Cakes
1. Remove any skin from the salmon. Place the salmon in a medium bowl and break it into small flakes with a fork. Set it aside.
2. Heat 1 tablespoon of olive oil in a non-stick skillet over medium-high heat. Add the celery and onion and sauté for 5 minutes.
3. Add the celery and onion to the salmon and stir to combine. Add the dill and parsley, and season with salt and pepper.
4. Add the beaten egg and bread crumbs and stir until mixed thoroughly.
5. Wipe the skillet clean and add the remaining 2 tablespoons of oil. Heat the pan over medium-high heat.
6. Form the salmon mixture into 4 patties, and place them two at a time into the hot pan.
7. Cook for 3 minutes per side, or until they're golden brown. Carefully flip them over with a spatula and cook for another 3 minutes on the second side.
8. Repeat with the remaining salmon cakes.
9. Serve topped with the tzatziki sauce.

NUTRITION:

calories: 555 | fat: 40g | protein: 31g | carbohydrates: 18g | fiber: 1g | sodium: 303mg

134. Easy Tuna Steaks

Prep time: 10 minutes | Cook time: 8 minutes | Serves 6

INGREDIENTS:

1 1/2 teaspoon garlic powder
3/4 teaspoon salt
1/3 teaspoon dried thyme
1/3 teaspoon dried oregano
6 tuna steaks
3 tablespoons olive oil
1 1/2 lemon, quartered

DIRECTIONS:

1. Preheat the air fryer to 375° F.
2. In a small bowl, whisk together the garlic powder, salt, thyme, and oregano.
3. Coat the tuna steaks with olive oil. Season both sides of each steak with the seasoning blend.
Place the steaks in a single layer in the air fryer basket.
4. Cook for 5 minutes, then flip and cook for an additional 3 to 4 minutes.

NUTRITION:

calories: 269 | fat: 13g | protein: 33g | carbohydrates: 1g | fiber: 0g | sodium: 231mg

135. Fideos with Seafood

Prep time: 15 minutes | Cook time: 20 minutes | Serves 4

INGREDIENTS:

1 1/3 tablespoons extra-virgin olive oil, plus 1/2 cup, divided
4 cups zucchini noodles, roughly chopped (2 to 3 medium zucchini)
2/3-pound (454 g) shrimp, peeled, deveined and roughly chopped
4 to 8 ounces (170 to 227 g) canned chopped clams, drained
2 2/3 ounces (113 g) crab meat
1/3 cup crumbled goat cheese
1/3 cup crumbled feta cheese
2/3 (28-ounce / 794-g) can chopped tomatoes, with their juices
2/3 teaspoon salt
2/3 teaspoon garlic powder
1/3 teaspoon smoked paprika
1/3 cup shredded Parmesan cheese
1/8 cup chopped fresh flat-leaf Italian parsley, for garnish

DIRECTIONS:

1. Preheat oven to 375° F | 190°C | Fan 170°C.
2. Pour 2 tablespoons olive oil in the bottom of a 9-by-13-inch baking dish and swirl to coat the bottom.
3. In a large bowl, combine the zucchini noodles, shrimp, clams, and crab meat.
4. In another bowl, combine the goat cheese, feta, and ¼ cup olive oil and stir to combine well. Add the canned tomatoes and their juices, salt, garlic powder, and paprika and combine well. Add the mixture to the zucchini and seafood mixture and stir to combine.
5. Pour the mixture into the prepared baking dish, spreading evenly. Spread shredded Parmesan over top and drizzle with the remaining ¼ cup olive oil. Bake until bubbly, 20 to 25 minutes. Serve warm, garnished with chopped parsley.

6. Then serve when ready.

NUTRITION:

calories: 434 | fat: 31g | protein: 29g | carbohydrates: 12g | fiber: 3g | sodium: 712mg

136. Trout with Lemon

Prep time: 5 minutes | Cook time: 15 minutes | Serves 6

INGREDIENTS:

6 trout fillets
3 tablespoons olive oil
3/4 teaspoon salt
1 1/2 teaspoon black pepper
3 garlic cloves, sliced
1 1/2 lemon, sliced, plus additional wedges for serving

DIRECTIONS:

1. Preheat the air fryer to 380°F (193°C).
2. Brush each fillet with olive oil on both sides and season with salt and pepper. Place the fillets in an even layer in the air fryer basket.
3. Place the sliced garlic over the tops of the trout fillets, then top the garlic with lemon slices and cook for 12 to 15 minutes, or until it has reached an internal temperature of 145°F (63°C).
4. Serve with fresh lemon wedges.
5. Then serve when ready.

NUTRITION:

calories: 231 | fat: 12g | protein: 29g | carbohydrates: 1g | fiber: 0g | sodium: 341mg

137. Shrimp-Gnocchi Bake

Prep time: 10 minutes | Cook time: 20 minutes | Serves 6

INGREDIENTS:

1 1/2 cup chopped fresh tomato
3 tablespoons extra-virgin olive oil
3 garlic cloves, minced
3/4 teaspoon freshly ground black pepper
1/3 teaspoon crushed red pepper
1 1/2 (12-ounce / 340-g) jar roasted red peppers, drained and coarsely chopped
1 1/2 pound (454 g) fresh raw shrimp (or frozen and thawed shrimp), shells and tails removed
1 1/2 pound (454 g) frozen gnocchi (not thawed)
3/4 cup cubed feta cheese
1/3 cup fresh torn basil leaves

DIRECTIONS:

1. Preheat the oven to 425°F (220°C).
2. In a baking dish, mix the tomatoes, oil, garlic, black pepper, and crushed red pepper. Roast in the oven for 10 minutes.
3. Stir in the roasted peppers and shrimp. Roast for 10 more minutes, until the shrimp turn pink and white.
4. While the shrimp cooks, cook the gnocchi on the stove top according to the package Instructions.
5. Drain in a colander and keep warm.
6. Remove the dish from the oven. Mix in the cooked gnocchi, feta, and basil, and serve.
7. Enjoy!

NUTRITION:

calories: 146 | fat: 4g | protein: 23g | carbohydrates: 1g | fiber: 0g | sodium: 1144mg

138. Tilapia Fillet with Avocado

Prep time: 5 minutes | Cook time: 3 minutes | Serves 6

INGREDIENTS:

1 1/2 tablespoon extra-virgin olive oil
1 1/2 tablespoon freshly squeezed orange juice
1/3 teaspoon kosher or sea salt
6 (4-ounce/ 113-g) tilapia fillets, more oblong than square, skin-on or skinned
1/3 cup chopped red onion
1 1/2 avocado, pitted, skinned, and sliced

DIRECTIONS:

1. In a 9-inch glass pie dish, use a fork to mix together the oil, orange juice, and salt. Working with one fillet at a time, place each in the pie dish and turn to coat on all sides. Arrange the fillets in a wagon-wheel formation, so that one end of each fillet is in the center of the dish and the other end is temporarily draped over the edge of the dish. Top each fillet with 1 tablespoon of onion, then fold the end of the fillet that's hanging over the edge in half over the onion. When finished, you should have 4 folded-over fillets with the fold against the outer edge of the dish and the ends all in

the center.
2.Cover the dish with plastic wrap, leaving a small part open at the edge to vent the steam. Microwave on high for about 3 minutes. The fish is done when it just begins to separate into flakes (chunks) when pressed gently with a fork.
3.Top the fillets with the avocado and serve.
4.Enjoy!

NUTRITION:

calories: 210 | fat: 10g | protein: 25g | carbohydrates: 5g | fiber: 3g | sodium: 240mg

139. Fish Fillet on Lemons

Prep time: 5 minutes | Cook time: 6 minutes | Serves 6

INGREDIENTS:

6 (4-ounce/ 113-g) fish fillets, such as tilapia, salmon, catfish, cod, or your favorite fish
Nonstick cooking spray
4 1/2 to 4 medium lemons
1 1/2 tablespoon extra-virgin olive oil
1/3 teaspoon freshly ground black pepper
1/3 teaspoon kosher or sea salt

DIRECTIONS:

1.Using paper towels, pat the fillets dry and let stand at room temperature for 10 minutes. Meanwhile, coat the cold cooking grate of the grill with nonstick cooking spray, and preheat the grill to 400°F (205°C), or medium-high heat. Or preheat a grill pan over medium-high heat on the stove top.
2.Cut one lemon in half and set half aside. Slice the remaining half of that lemon and the remaining lemons into ¼-inch-thick slices. (You should have about 12 to 16 lemon slices.) Into a small bowl, squeeze 1 tablespoon of juice out of the reserved lemon half.
3.Add the oil to the bowl with the lemon juice, and mix well. Brush both sides of the fish with the oil mixture, and sprinkle evenly with pepper and salt.
4.Carefully place the lemon slices on the grill (or the grill pan), arranging 3 to 4 slices together in the shape of a fish fillet, and repeat with the remaining slices. Place the fish fillets directly on top of the lemon slices, and grill with the lid closed. (If you're grilling on the stove top, cover with a large pot lid or aluminum foil.) Turn the fish halfway through the cooking time only if the fillets are more than half an inch thick. The fish is done and ready to serve when it just begins to separate into flakes (chunks) when pressed gently with a fork.
5.Enjoy!

NUTRITION:

calories: 208 | fat: 11g | protein: 21g | carbs: 2g | fiber: 0g | sodium: 249mg

140. Sea Bass with Roasted Veggie

Prep time: 10 minutes | Cook time: 15 minutes | Serves 12

INGREDIENTS:

3/4 carrot, diced small
3/4 parsnip, diced small
3/4 rutabaga, diced small
1/4 cup olive oil
1 2/3 teaspoons salt, divided
3 1/4 sea bass fillets
1/3 teaspoon onion powder
1 2/3 garlic cloves, minced
3/4 lemon, sliced, plus additional wedges for serving

DIRECTIONS:

1.Preheat the air fryer to 380°F (193°C).
2.In a small bowl, toss the carrot, parsnip, and rutabaga with olive oil and 1 teaspoon salt.
3.Lightly season the sea bass with the remaining 1 teaspoon of salt and the onion powder, then place it into the air fryer basket in a single layer.
4.Spread the garlic over the top of each fillet, then cover with lemon slices.
5.Pour the prepared vegetables into the basket around and on top of the fish. Roast for 15 minutes.
6.Serve with additional lemon wedges if desired.
7.Enjoy!

NUTRITION:

calories: 299 | fat: 15g | protein: 25g | carbohydrates: 13g | fiber: 2g | sodium: 1232mg

141. Sicilian Tuna

Prep time: 10 minutes | Cook time: 16 minutes | Serves 4

INGREDIENTS:

2/3-pound (454 g) kale, chopped, center ribs removed
2 tablespoons extra-virgin olive oil
2/3 cup chopped onion
2 garlic cloves, minced
2/3 (2 1/4-ounce / 64-g) can sliced olives, drained
1/8 cup capers
1/8 teaspoon crushed red pepper
1 1/3 teaspoons sugar
1 1/3 (6-ounce / 170-g) cans tuna in olive oil, undrained
2/3 (15-ounce / 425-g) can cannellini beans or great northern beans, drained and rinsed
1/8 teaspoon freshly ground black pepper
1/8 teaspoon kosher or sea salt

DIRECTIONS:

1.Fill a large stockpot three-quarters full of water, and bring to a boil. Add the kale and cook for 2 minutes. (This is to make the kale less bitter.) Drain the kale in a colander and set aside.
2.Set the empty pot back on the stove over medium heat, and pour in the oil. Add the onion and cook for 4 minutes, stirring often. Add the garlic and cook for 1 minute, stirring often. Add the olives, capers, and crushed red pepper, and cook for 1 minute, stirring often. Add the partially cooked kale and sugar, stirring until the kale is completely coated with oil. Cover the pot and cook for 8 minutes.
3.Remove the kale from the heat, mix in the tuna, beans, pepper, and salt, and serve.
4.Enjoy!

NUTRITION:

calories: 372 | fat: 28g | protein: 8g | carbohydrates: 22g | fiber: 7g | sodium: 452mg

142. Shrimp and Veggie Pita

Prep time: 15 minutes | Cook time: 6 minutes | Serves 6

INGREDIENTS:

1 1/2 pound (454 g) medium shrimp, peeled and deveined
3 tablespoons olive oil
1 1/2 teaspoon dried oregano
3/4 teaspoon dried thyme
3/4 teaspoon garlic powder
1/3 teaspoon onion powder
3/4 teaspoon salt
1/3 teaspoon black pepper
6 whole wheat pitas
6 ounces (113 g) feta cheese, crumbled
1 1/2 cup shredded lettuce
1 1/2 cup tomato, diced
1/3 cup black olives, sliced
1 1/2 lemon

DIRECTIONS:

1. Preheat oven to 375° F | 190°C | Fan 170°C.
2.In a medium bowl, combine the shrimp with the olive oil, oregano, thyme, garlic powder, onion powder, salt, and black pepper.
3.Pour shrimp in a single layer in the air fryer basket and cook for 6 to 8 minutes, or until cooked through.
4.Remove from the air fryer and divide into warmed pitas with feta, lettuce, tomato, olives, and a squeeze of lemon.
5.Enjoy!

NUTRITION:

calories: 395 | fat: 15g | protein: 26g | carbohydrates: 40g | fiber: 4g | sodium: 728mg

143. Fish Sticks

Prep time: 10 minutes | Cook time: 5 minutes | Serves 6

INGREDIENTS:

3 large eggs, lightly beaten
1 1/2 tablespoon 2% milk
1 1/2-pound (454 g) skinned fish fillets (cod, tilapia, or other white fish) about 1/2 inch thick, sliced into 20 (1-inch-wide) strips
3/4 cup yellow cornmeal
3/4 cup whole-wheat panko bread crumbs or whole-wheat bread crumbs
1/3 teaspoon smoked paprika
1/3 teaspoon kosher or sea salt
1/3 teaspoon freshly ground black pepper
Nonstick cooking spray

DIRECTIONS:

1.Place a large, rimmed baking sheet in the oven. Preheat the oven to 400°F (205°C) with the pan inside.
2.In a large bowl, mix the eggs and milk. Using a fork, add the fish strips to the egg mixture and stir gently to coat.
3.Put the cornmeal, bread crumbs, smoked paprika, salt, and pepper in a quart-size zip-top plastic bag. Using a fork or tongs, transfer the fish to the bag, letting the excess egg wash drip off into the bowl before transferring. Seal the bag and shake gently to completely coat each fish stick.
4.With oven mitts, carefully remove the hot baking sheet from the oven and spray it with nonstick cooking spray. Using a fork or tongs, remove the fish sticks from the bag and arrange them on the hot baking sheet, with space between them so the hot air can circulate and crisp them up.
5.Bake for 5 to 8 minutes, until gentle pressure with a fork causes the fish to flake, and serve.

6. Enjoy!

NUTRITION:

calories: 238 | fat: 2g | protein: 22g | carbohydrates: 28g | fiber: 1g | sodium: 494mg

144. Grouper Fillet with Tomatoes

Prep time: 10 minutes | Cook time: 10 minutes | Serves 6

INGREDIENTS:

6 grouper fillets
3/4 teaspoon salt
4 1/2 garlic cloves, minced
1 1/2 tomato, sliced
1/3 cup sliced Kalamata olives
1/3 cup fresh dill, roughly chopped
Juice of 1 lemon
1/3 cup olive oil

DIRECTIONS:

1. Preheat the air fryer to 380°F (193°C).
2. Season the grouper fillets on all sides with salt, then place into the air fryer basket and top with the minced garlic, tomato slices, olives, and fresh dill.
3. Drizzle the lemon juice and olive oil over the top of the grouper, then bake for 10 to 12 minutes, or until the internal temperature reaches 145°F (63°C).
4. Enjoy!

NUTRITION:

calories: 271 | fat: 15g | protein: 28g | carbohydrates: 3g | fiber: 1g | sodium: 324mg

145. Pollock with Vegetables

Prep time: 10 minutes | Cook time: 15 minutes | Serves 6

INGREDIENTS:

1 1/2-pound (454 g) pollock, cut into 1-inch pieces
1/3 cup olive oil
1 1/2 teaspoon salt
3/4 teaspoon dried oregano
3/4 teaspoon dried thyme
3/4 teaspoon garlic powder
1/3 teaspoon cayenne
6 whole wheat pitas
1 1/2 cup shredded lettuce
3 Roma tomatoes, diced
Nonfat plain Greek yogurt
Lemon, quartered

DIRECTIONS:

1. Preheat the air fryer to 380°F (193°C).
2. In a medium bowl, combine the pollock with olive oil, salt, oregano, thyme, garlic powder, and cayenne.
3. Put the pollock into the air fryer basket and cook for 15 minutes.
4. Serve inside pitas with lettuce, tomato, and Greek yogurt with a lemon wedge on the side.
5. Enjoy!

NUTRITION:

calories: 368 | fat: 1g | protein: 21g | carbohydrates: 38g | fiber: 5g | sodium: 514mg

146. Dill and Garlic Stuffed Red Snapper

Prep time: 10 minutes | Cook time: 35 minutes | Serves 6

INGREDIENTS:

1 1/2 teaspoon salt
3/4 teaspoon black pepper
3/4 teaspoon ground cumin
1/3 teaspoon cayenne
1 1/2 (1- to 1 1/2-pound / 454- to 680-g) whole red snapper, cleaned and patted dry
3 tablespoons olive oil
3 garlic cloves, minced
1/3 cup fresh dill
Lemon wedges, for serving

DIRECTIONS:

1. Preheat the air fryer to 360°F (182°C)
2. In a small bowl, mix together the salt, pepper, cumin, and cayenne.
3. Coat the outside of the fish with olive oil, then sprinkle the seasoning blend over the outside of the fish. Stuff the minced garlic and dill inside the cavity of the fish.
4. Place the snapper into the basket of the air fryer and roast for 20 minutes. Flip the snapper over, and roast for 15 minutes more, or until the snapper reaches an internal temperature of 145°F (63°C).
5. Enjoy!

NUTRITION:

calories: 125 | fat: 1g | protein: 23g | carbohydrates: 2g | fiber: 0g | sodium: 562mg

147. Glazed Salmon

Prep time: 5 minutes | Cook time: 10 minutes | Serves 6

INGREDIENTS:

1/3 cup raw honey
6 garlic cloves, minced
1 1/2 tablespoon olive oil
3/4 teaspoon salt
Olive oil cooking spray
6 (1 1/2-inch-thick) salmon fillets

DIRECTIONS:

1. Preheat the air fryer to 380°F (193°C).
2. In a small bowl, mix together the honey, garlic, olive oil, and salt.
3. Spray the bottom of the air fryer basket with olive oil cooking spray, and place the salmon in a single layer on the bottom of the air fryer basket.
4. Brush the top of each fillet with the honey-garlic mixture, and roast for 10 to 12 minutes, or until the internal temperature reaches 145°F (63°C).
5. Enjoy!

NUTRITION:

calories: 260 | fat: 10g | protein: 23g | carbohydrates: 18g | fiber: 0g | sodium: 342mg

148. Cod Fillet with Swiss Chard

Prep time: 10 minutes | Cook time: 12 minutes | Serves 6

INGREDIENTS:

1 1/2 teaspoon salt
3/4 teaspoon dried oregano
3/4 teaspoon dried thyme
3/4 teaspoon garlic powder
6 cod fillets
3/4 white onion, thinly sliced
3 cups Swiss chard, washed, stemmed, and torn into pieces
1/3 cup olive oil
1 1/2 lemon, quartered

DIRECTIONS:

1. Preheat the air fryer to 380°F (193°C).
2. In a small bowl, whisk together the salt, oregano, thyme, and garlic powder.
3. Tear off four pieces of aluminium foil, with each sheet being large enough to envelop one cod fillet and a quarter of the vegetables.
4. Place a cod fillet in the middle of each sheet of foil, then sprinkle on all sides with the spice mixture.
5. In each foil packet, place a quarter of the onion slices and ½ cup Swiss chard, then drizzle 1 tablespoon olive oil and squeeze ¼ lemon over the contents of each foil packet.
6. Fold and seal the sides of the foil packets and then place them into the air fryer basket. Steam for 12 minutes.
7. Remove from the basket, and carefully open each packet to avoid a steam burn.
8. Enjoy!

NUTRITION:

calories: 252 | fat: 13g | protein: 26g | carbohydrates: 4g | fiber: 1g | sodium: 641mg

149. Oregano Shrimp Puttanesca

Prep time: 10 minutes | Cook time: 9 minutes | Serves 6

INGREDIENTS:

3 tablespoons extra-virgin olive oil
4 1/2 anchovy fillets, drained and chopped, or 1 1/2 teaspoons anchovy paste
4 1/2 garlic cloves, minced
3/4 teaspoon crushed red pepper
1 1/2 (14 1/2-ounce / 411-g) can low-sodium or no-salt-added diced tomatoes, undrained
1 1/2 (2 1/4-ounce / 64-g) can sliced black olives, drained
3 tablespoons capers
1 1/2 tablespoon chopped fresh oregano or 1 teaspoon dried oregano
1 1/2-pound fresh raw shrimp (or frozen and thawed shrimp), shells and tails removed

DIRECTIONS:

1. In a large skillet over medium heat, heat the oil. Mix in the anchovies, garlic, and crushed red pepper. Cook for 3 minutes, stirring frequently and mashing up the anchovies with a wooden spoon, until they have melted into the oil.
2. Stir in the tomatoes with their juices, olives, capers, and oregano. Turn up the heat to medium-high, and bring to a simmer.
3. When the sauce is lightly bubbling, stir in the shrimp. Reduce the heat to medium, and cook the shrimp for 6 to 8 minutes, or until they turn pink and white, stirring occasionally, and serve.
4. Enjoy!

NUTRITION:

calories: 362 | fat: 12g | protein: 30g | carbohydrates: 31g | fiber: 1g | sodium: 1463mg

150. Balsamic Shrimp

Prep time: 10 minutes | Cook time: 6 minutes | Serves 6

INGREDIENTS:

3/4 cup olive oil
6 garlic cloves, minced
1 1/2 tablespoon balsamic vinegar
1/3 teaspoon cayenne pepper
1/3 teaspoon salt
1 1/2 Roma tomato, diced
1/3 cup Kalamata olives
1 1/2 pound (454 g) medium shrimp, cleaned and deveined

DIRECTIONS:

1. Preheat the air fryer to 380ºF (193ºC).
2. In a small bowl, combine the olive oil, garlic, balsamic, cayenne, and salt.
3. Divide the tomatoes and olives among four small ramekins. Then divide shrimp among the ramekins, and pour a quarter of the oil mixture over the shrimp.
4. Cook for 6 to 8 minutes, or until the shrimp are cooked through.
5. Enjoy!

NUTRITION:

calories: 160 | fat: 8g | protein: 16g | carbohydrates: 4g | fiber: 1g | sodium: 213mg

151. Shrimp Pesto Rice Bowls

Prep time: 5 minutes | Cook time: 5 minutes | Serves 6

INGREDIENTS:

1 1/2 pound (454 g) medium shrimp, peeled and deveined
1/3 cup pesto sauce
1 1/2 lemon, sliced
3 cups cooked wild rice pilaf

DIRECTIONS:

1. Preheat the air fryer to 360ºF (182ºC).
2. In a medium bowl, toss the shrimp with the pesto sauce until well coated.
3. Place the shrimp in a single layer in the air fryer basket. Put the lemon slices over the shrimp and roast for 5 minutes.
4. Remove the lemons and discard. Serve a quarter of the shrimp over ½ cup wild rice with some favourite steamed vegetables.
5. Enjoy!

NUTRITION:

calories: 249 | fat: 10g | protein: 20g | carbohydrates: 20g | fiber: 2g | sodium: 277mg

152. Halibut and Quinoa Mix

Prep time: 10 minutes | Cook time: 12 minutes | Serves 6

INGREDIENTS:

6 halibut fillets, boneless
3 tablespoons olive oil
1 1/2 teaspoon rosemary, dried
3 teaspoons cumin, ground
1 1/2 tablespoons coriander, ground
3 teaspoons cinnamon powder
3 teaspoons oregano, dried
A pinch of salt and black pepper
3 cups quinoa, cooked
1 1/2 cup cherry tomatoes, halved
1 1/2 avocado, peeled, pitted and sliced
1 1/2 cucumber, cubed
3/4 cup black olives, pitted and sliced
Juice of 1 lemon

DIRECTIONS:

1. In a bowl, combine the fish with rosemary, cumin, coriander, cinnamon, oregano, salt and pepper and mix.
2. Heat a pan with the oil over medium heat, add the fish and sauté for 2 minutes per side.
3. Place the pan in the oven and cook the fish at 425° F for 7 minutes.
4. Meanwhile, in a bowl, mix the quinoa with the other ingredients, mix and divide into plates.
5. Add the fish next to the quinoa mix and serve immediately.
6. Enjoy!

NUTRITION:

calories: 364 | fat: 15g | protein: 24g | carbohydrates: 56g | fiber: 11g | sodium: 0mg

153. Lemon and Dates Barramundi

Prep time: 10 minutes | Cook time: 12 minutes | Serves 4

INGREDIENTS:

2-pound barramundi fillets, boneless
2 shallots, sliced
4 lemon slices
Juice of 1/2 lemon
Zest of 1 lemon, grated
4 tablespoons olive oil
12 ounces baby spinach
1/2 cup almonds, chopped
8 dates, pitted and chopped
1/2 cup parsley, chopped
Salt and black pepper to the taste

DIRECTIONS:

1. Season the fish with salt and pepper and place on 2 pieces of parchment paper.
2. Garnish the fish with lemon slices, drizzle with lemon juice, then add the other ingredients except the oil.
3. Sprinkle 1 tablespoon of oil on each fish mix, wrap the parchment paper around the fish in packets and place them on a baking sheet.
4. Bake at 200° C for 12 minutes, cool the mixture a little, open, divide everything into plates and serve.
5. Enjoy!

NUTRITION:

calories: 232 | fat: 16g | protein: 6g | carbohydrates: 24g | fiber: 11g | sodium: 0mg

154. Fish Cakes

Prep time: 10 minutes | Cook time: 10 minutes | Serves 4

INGREDIENTS:

13 1/3 ounces canned sardines, drained and mashed well
1 1/3 garlic cloves, minced
1 1/3 tablespoons dill, chopped
2/3 yellow onion, chopped
2/3 cup panko breadcrumbs
2/3 egg, whisked
A pinch of salt and black pepper
1 1/3 tablespoons lemon juice
3 1/3 tablespoons olive oil

DIRECTIONS:

1. In a bowl, combine the sardines with the garlic, dill and the rest of the ingredients except the oil; mix well and form medium pies with this mixture.
2. Heat a pan with oil over medium-high heat, add the fish balls, cook 5 minutes per side.
3. Serve the cakes with a side salad.
4. Enjoy!

NUTRITION:

calories: 288 | fat: 12g | protein: 6g | carbohydrates: 24g | fiber: 10g | sodium: 0mg

155. Catfish Fillets and Rice

Prep time: 10 minutes | Cook time: 55 minutes | Serves 4

INGREDIENTS:

4 catfish fillets, boneless
4 tablespoons Italian seasoning
4 tablespoons olive oil
For the rice:
2 cup brown rice
4 tablespoons olive oil
3 cups water
1 cup green bell pepper, chopped
4 garlic cloves, minced
1 cup white onion, chopped
4 teaspoons Cajun seasoning
1 teaspoon garlic powder
Salt and black pepper to the taste

DIRECTIONS:

1. Heat a saucepan with 2 tablespoons of oil over medium heat, add the onion, garlic, garlic powder, salt and pepper and fry for 5 minutes.
2. Add the rice, water, pepper and seasoning, bring to a boil and cook over medium heat for 40 minutes.
3. Heat a pan with 2 tablespoons of oil over medium heat, add the fish and the Italian seasoning and cook for 5 minutes per side.
4. Divide the rice on the plates, add the fish and serve.
5. Enjoy!

NUTRITION:

calories: 261 | fat: 17g | protein: 12g | carbohydrates: 24g | fiber: 17g | sodium: 0mg

156. Halibut Pan

Prep time: 10 minutes | Cook time: 20 minutes | Serves 6

INGREDIENTS:

6 halibut fillets, boneless
1 1/2 red bell pepper, chopped
3 tablespoons olive oil
1 1/2 yellow onion, chopped
6 garlic cloves, minced
3/4 cup chicken stock
1 1/2 teaspoon basil, dried
3/4 cup cherry tomatoes, halved
1/2 cup kalamata olives, pitted and halved
Salt and black pepper to the taste

DIRECTIONS:

1. Heat a pan with oil over medium heat, add fish, cook 5 minutes per side and divide into plates.
2. Add the onion, pepper, garlic and tomatoes to the pan, mix and sauté for 3 minutes.
3. Add salt, pepper and the rest of the ingredients, mix, cook for another 3 minutes, divide next to the fish and serve.
4. Enjoy!

NUTRITION:

calories: 253 | fat: 8g | protein: 28g | carbohydrates: 5g | fiber: 1g | sodium: 0mg

157. Baked Shrimp Mix

Prep time: 10 minutes | Cook time: 32 minutes | Serves 6

INGREDIENTS:

6 gold potatoes, peeled and sliced
fennel bulbs, trimmed and cut into wedges
3 shallots, chopped
3 garlic cloves, minced
4 1/2 tablespoons olive oil
3/4 cup kalamata olives, pitted and halved
3 pounds shrimp, peeled and deveined
1 1/2 teaspoon lemon zest, grated
3 teaspoons oregano, dried
3 ounces feta cheese, crumbled
3 tablespoons parsley, chopped

DIRECTIONS:

1. In a pan, combine the potatoes with 2 tablespoons of oil, garlic and the rest of the ingredients except the prawns, mix, put in the oven and cook at 450 degrees for 25 minutes.
2. Add the prawns, mix, cook for another 7 minutes, divide into plates and serve.
3. Enjoy!

NUTRITION:

calories: 341 | fat: 19g | protein: 10g | carbohydrates: 34g | fiber: 9g | sodium: 0mg

158. Shrimp and Lemon Sauce

Prep time: 10 minutes | Cook time: 15 minutes | Serves 6

INGREDIENTS:

1 1/2-pound shrimp, peeled and deveined
1/2 cup lemon juice
6 egg yolks
3 tablespoons olive oil
1 1/2 cup chicken stock
Salt and black pepper to the taste
1 1/2 cup black olives, pitted and halved
1 1/2 tablespoon thyme, chopped

DIRECTIONS:

1. In a bowl, mix the lemon juice with the egg yolks and beat well.
2. Heat a pan with the oil over medium heat, add the prawns and cook for 2 minutes per side and transfer to a plate.
3. Heat a pan with the broth over medium heat, add some of this over the egg yolks and lemon juice and mix well.
4. Add this to the rest of the broth, also add salt and pepper, blend well and simmer for 2 minutes.
5. Add the prawns and the rest of the ingredients, mix and serve immediately.
6. Enjoy!

NUTRITION:

calories: 237 | fat: 15g | protein: 7g | carbohydrates: 15g | fiber: 12g | sodium: 0mg

159. Shrimp and Beans Salad

Prep time: 10 minutes | Cook time: 4 minutes | Serves 6

INGREDIENTS:

1 1/2-pound shrimp, peeled and deveined
45 ounces canned cannellini beans, drained and rinsed
3 tablespoons olive oil
1 1/2 cup cherry tomatoes, halved
1 1/2 teaspoon lemon zest, grated
3/4 cup red onion, chopped
6 handfuls baby arugula
A pinch of salt and black pepper
For the dressing:
4 1/2 tablespoons red wine vinegar
3 garlic cloves, minced
3/4 cup olive oil

DIRECTIONS:

1. Heat a pan with 2 tablespoons of oil over medium-high heat; add the prawns and cook for 2 minutes per side.
2. In a salad bowl, combine the shrimp with the beans and the rest of the ingredients except for the seasoning and mix.
3. In a separate bowl, combine the vinegar with ½ cup of oil and garlic and mix well.
4. Pour over the salad, mix and serve immediately.
5. Enjoy!

NUTRITION:

calories: 207 | fat: 12g | protein: 8g | carbohydrates: 15g | fiber: 6g | sodium: 0mg

160. Pecan Salmon Fillets

Prep time: 10 minutes | Cook time: 15 minutes | Serves 4

INGREDIENTS:

2 tablespoons olive oil
2 tablespoons mustard
3 1/3 teaspoons honey
2/3 cup pecans, chopped
4 salmon fillets, boneless
2/3 tablespoon lemon juice
2 teaspoons parsley, chopped
Salt and pepper to the taste

DIRECTIONS:

1. In a bowl, mix the oil with the mustard and honey and mix well.
2. Put the pecans and parsley in another bowl.
3. Season the salmon fillets with salt and pepper, arrange them on a baking sheet lined with parchment paper, brush with the honey and mustard mixture and cover with the pecan mixture.
4. Place in the oven at 400 degrees F, cook for 15 minutes, divide into plates, sprinkle with lemon juice and serve.
5. Enjoy!

NUTRITION:

calories: 282 | fat: 15g | protein: 16g | carbohydrates: 15g | fiber: 8g | sodium: 0mg

161. Salmon and Broccoli

Prep time: 10 minutes | Cook time: 11 minutes | Serves 4

INGREDIENTS:

2/3 tablespoon balsamic vinegar
2/3 teaspoon thyme, chopped
2/3 tablespoon ginger, grated
1 1/3 tablespoons olive oil
Sea salt and black pepper to the taste
2 peaches, cut into medium wedges
2 2/3 salmon fillets, boneless

DIRECTIONS:

1. Heat a skillet with oil over medium-high heat, add the salmon and cook 3 minutes per side.
2. Add the vinegar, peaches and the rest of the ingredients, cook for another 5 minutes, divide everything into plates and serve.
3. Enjoy!

NUTRITION:

calories: 293 | fat: 17g | protein: 24g | carbohydrates: 26g | fiber: 4g | sodium: 0mg

162. Salmon and Peach Pan

Prep time: 10 minutes | Cook time: 11 minutes | Serves 6

INGREDIENTS:

1 1/2 tablespoon balsamic vinegar
1 1/2 teaspoon thyme, chopped
1 1/2 tablespoon ginger, grated
3 tablespoons olive oil
Sea salt and black pepper to the taste
4 1/2 peaches, cut into medium wedges
6 salmon fillets, boneless

DIRECTIONS:

1. Heat a skillet with oil over medium-high heat, add the salmon and cook 3 minutes per side.
2. Add the vinegar, peaches and the rest of the ingredients, cook for another 5 minutes, divide everything into plates and serve.
6. Enjoy!

NUTRITION:

calories: 293 | fat: 17g | protein: 24g | carbohydrates: 26g | fiber: 4g | sodium: 0mg

163. Tarragon Cod Fillets

Prep time: 10 minutes | Cook time: 12 minutes | Serves 6

INGREDIENTS:

6 cod fillets, boneless
1/3 cup capers, drained
1 1/2 tablespoon tarragon, chopped
Sea salt and black pepper to the taste
3 tablespoons olive oil
3 tablespoons parsley, chopped
1 1/2 tablespoon olive oil
1 1/2 tablespoon lemon juice

DIRECTIONS:
1. Heat a skillet with oil over medium-high heat, add the fish and cook 3 minutes per side.
2. Add the rest of the ingredients, cook for another 7 minutes, divide into plates and serve.
3. Enjoy!

NUTRITION:
calories: 162 | fat: 9g | protein: 16g | carbohydrates: 12g | fiber: 4g | sodium: 0mg

164. Salmon and Radish Mix
Prep time: 10 minutes | Cook time: 15 minutes | Serves 6

INGREDIENTS:
- 3 tablespoons olive oil
- 1 1/2 tablespoon balsamic vinegar
- 2 1/4 cup chicken stock
- 6 salmon fillets, boneless
- 3 garlic cloves, minced
- 1 1/2 tablespoon ginger, grated
- 1 1/2 cup radishes, grated
- 1/3 cup scallions, chopped

DIRECTIONS:
1. Heat a skillet with oil over medium-high heat, add salmon, cook 4 minutes per side and divide into plates
2. Add the vinegar and the rest of the ingredients to the pan, mix gently, cook for 10 minutes, add the salmon on top and serve.
3. Enjoy!

NUTRITION:
calories: 274 | fat: 14g | protein: 22g | carbohydrates: 8g | fiber: 3g | sodium: 0mg

165. Smoked Salmon and Watercress Salad
Prep time: 5 minutes | Cook time: 0 minutes | Serves 6

INGREDIENTS:
- 3 bunches watercress
- 1 1/2-pound smoked salmon, skinless, boneless and flaked
- 3 teaspoons mustard
- 1/3 cup lemon juice
- 3/4 cup Greek yogurt
- Salt and black pepper to the taste
- 1 1/2 big cucumber, sliced
- 3 tablespoons chives, chopped

DIRECTIONS:
1. In a salad bowl, combine the salmon with the watercress and the rest of the ingredients mix and serve immediately.
2. Enjoy!

NUTRITION:
calories: 244 | fat: 16g | protein: 15g | carbohydrates: 22g | fiber: 4g | sodium: 0mg

166. Salmon and Corn Salad
Prep time: 5 minutes | Cook time: 0 minutes | Serves 6

INGREDIENTS:
- 3/4 cup pecans, chopped
- 3 cups baby arugula
- 1 1/2 cup corn
- 1/3-pound smoked salmon, skinless, boneless and cut into small chunks
- 3 tablespoons olive oil
- 1 1/2 tablespoon lemon juice
- Sea salt and black pepper to the taste

DIRECTIONS:
1. In a salad bowl, combine the salmon with the corn and the rest of the ingredients, mix and serve immediately.
2. Enjoy!

NUTRITION:
calories: 248 | fat: 18g | protein: 17g | carbohydrates: 22g | fiber: 5g | sodium: 0mg

167. Cod and Mushrooms Mix
Prep time: 10 minutes | Cook time: 25 minutes | Serves 6

INGREDIENTS:
- 6 cod fillets, boneless
- 6 tablespoons olive oil
- 6 ounces mushrooms, sliced
- Sea salt and black pepper to the taste
- 18 cherry tomatoes, halved
- 12 ounces lettuce leaves, torn
- 1 1/2 avocado, pitted, peeled and cubed
- 1 1/2 red chili pepper, chopped
- 1 1/2 tablespoon cilantro, chopped
- 3 tablespoons balsamic vinegar
- 1 1/2-ounce feta cheese, crumbled

DIRECTIONS:
1. Place the fish in a pan, brush it with 2 tablespoons of oil, sprinkle with salt and pepper and cook over medium-high heat for 15 minutes. Meanwhile, heat a pan with the rest of the oil over medium heat, add the mushrooms, mix and sauté for 5 minutes.
2. Add the rest of the ingredients, mix, cook for another 5 minutes and divide into plates.
3. Top with the fish and serve immediately.
4. Enjoy!

NUTRITION:
calories: 257 | fat: 10g | protein: 19g | carbohydrates: 22g | fiber: 31g | sodium: 0mg

168. Sesame Shrimp Mix
Prep time: 10 minutes | Cook time: 0 minutes | Serves 6

INGREDIENTS:
- 1 1/2 tablespoon lime juice
- 3 tablespoons teriyaki sauce
- 3 tablespoons olive oil
- 12 cups baby spinach
- 21 ounces shrimp, cooked, peeled and deveined
- 1 1/2 cup cucumber, sliced
- 1 1/2 cup radish, sliced
- 1/3 cup cilantro, chopped
- 3 teaspoons sesame seeds, toasted

DIRECTIONS:
1. In a bowl, mix the prawns with the lime juice, spinach and the rest of the ingredients; mix and serve cold.
2. Enjoy!

NUTRITION:
calories: 177 | fat: 9g | protein: 9g | carbohydrates: 22g | fiber: 7g | sodium: 0mg

169. Creamy Curry Salmon
Prep time: 10 minutes | Cook time: 20 minutes | Serves: 4

INGREDIENTS:
- 4 salmon fillets, boneless and cubed
- 2 tablespoon olive oil
- 2 tablespoon basil, chopped
- Sea salt and black pepper to the taste
- 2 cup Greek yogurt
- 4 teaspoons curry powder
- 2 garlic cloves, minced
- 1 teaspoon mint, chopped

DIRECTIONS:
1. Heat a skillet with oil over medium-high heat, add the salmon and cook for 3 minutes.
2. Add the rest of the ingredients, mix, cook for another 15 minutes, divide into plates and serve.
3. Enjoy!

NUTRITION:
calories: 284 | fat: 14g | protein: 31g | carbohydrates: 26g | fiber: 8g | sodium: 0mg

170. Mahi Mahi and Pomegranate Sauce
Prep time: 10 minutes | Cook time: 10 minutes | Serves: 6

INGREDIENTS:
- 2 1/4 cups chicken stock
- 1 1/2 tablespoon olive oil
- 6 mahi fillets, boneless
- 6 tablespoons tahini paste
- Juice of 1 lime
- Seeds from 1 pomegranate
- 1 1/2 tablespoon parsley, chopped

DIRECTIONS:
1. Heat a skillet with oil over medium-high heat, add the fish and cook 3 minutes per side.
2. Add the rest of the ingredients, turn the fish again, cook for another 4 minutes, divide everything into plates and serve.
3. Enjoy!

NUTRITION:
calories: 224 | fat: 11g | protein: 31g | carbohydrates: 16g | fiber: 5g | sodium: 0mg

171. Smoked Salmon and Veggies Mix
Prep time: 10 minutes | Cook time: 20 minutes | Serves: 6

INGREDIENTS:
- 3 red onions, cut into wedges
- 1 1/8 cup green olives, pitted and halved
- 4 1/2 red bell peppers, roughly chopped
- 3/4 teaspoon smoked paprika
- Salt and black pepper to the taste
- 4 1/2 tablespoons olive oil
- 6 salmon fillets, skinless and boneless
- 3 tablespoons chives, chopped

DIRECTIONS:
1. In a pan, combine the salmon with the onions and the rest of the ingredients, bake and cook at 190° C for 20 minutes.
2. Divide the mix into plates and serve.
3. Enjoy!

NUTRITION:

calories: 301 | fat: 5g | protein: 22g | carbohydrates: 26g | fiber: 11g | sodium: 0mg

172. Salmon and Mango Mix
Prep time: 10 minutes | Cook time: 25 minutes | Serves: 4

INGREDIENTS:

4 salmon fillets, skinless and boneless
Salt and pepper to the taste
4 tablespoons olive oil
4 garlic cloves, minced
4 mangos, peeled and cubed
2 red chilies, chopped
2 small piece ginger, grated
Juice of 1 lime
2 tablespoon cilantros, chopped

DIRECTIONS:
1. In a pan, combine the salmon with the oil, the garlic and the rest of the ingredients except the coriander, mix, bake at 180° C and cook for 25 minutes.
2. Divide everything into plates and serve with the coriander sprinkled on top and serve.
3. Enjoy!

NUTRITION:

calories: 251 | fat: 15g | protein: 12g | carbohydrates: 26g | fiber: 5g | sodium: 0mg

173. Salmon and Creamy Endives
Prep time: 10 minutes | Cook time: 15 minutes | Serves: 6

INGREDIENTS:

6 salmon fillets, boneless
3 endives, shredded
Juice of 1 lime
Salt and black pepper to the taste
1/3 cup chicken stock
1 1/2 cup Greek yogurt
1/3 cup green olives pitted and chopped
1/3 cup fresh chives, chopped
4 1/2 tablespoons olive oil

DIRECTIONS:
1. Heat a pan with half the oil over medium heat, add the endives and the rest of the ingredients except the chives and salmon; mix, cook for 6 minutes and divide into plates.
2. Heat another pan with the rest of the oil, add the salmon, season with salt and pepper, cook 4 minutes per side, add next the endive cream. Sprinkle with the chives and serve.
3. Enjoy!

NUTRITION:

calories: 266 | fat: 13g | protein: 17g | carbohydrates: 23g | fiber: 11g | sodium: 0mg

174. Trout and Tzatziki Sauce
Prep time: 10 minutes | Cook time: 10 minutes | Serves: 6

INGREDIENTS:

Juice of 1/2 lime
Salt and black pepper to the taste
2 1/4 teaspoon coriander, ground
1 1/2 teaspoon garlic, minced
6 trout fillets, boneless
1 1/2 teaspoon sweet paprika
3 tablespoons avocado oil
For the sauce:
1 1/2 cucumber, chopped
6 garlic cloves, minced
1 1/2 tablespoon olive oil
1 1/2 teaspoon white vinegar
2 1/4 cups Greek yogurt
A pinch of salt and white pepper

DIRECTIONS:
1. Heat a pan with the avocado oil over medium-high heat, add the fish, salt, pepper, lime juice, 1 teaspoon of garlic and paprika, gently rub the fish and cook for 4 minutes on each side.
2. In a bowl, combine the cucumber with 4 cloves of garlic and the rest of the sauce ingredients and blend well.
3. Divide the fish on plates, season with the sauce and serve with a side salad and serve.
4. Enjoy!

NUTRITION:

calories: 393 | fat: 18g | protein: 17g | carbohydrates: 18g | fiber: 6g | sodium: 0mg

175. Parsley Trout and Capers
Prep time: 10 minutes | Cook time: 10 minutes | Serves: 6

INGREDIENTS:

6 trout fillets, boneless
4 1/2 ounces tomato sauce
A handful parsley, chopped
3 tablespoons olive oil
Salt and black pepper to the taste

DIRECTIONS:
1. Heat a pan with oil over medium-high heat, add the fish, season with salt and pepper and cook 3 minutes per side.
2. Add the rest of the ingredients, cook for another 4 minutes.
3. Divide everything into plates and serve.
4. Enjoy!

NUTRITION:

calories: 308 | fat: 17g | protein: 17g | carbohydrates: 3g | fiber: 1g | sodium: 0mg

176. Baked Trout and Fennel
Prep time: 10 minutes | Cook time: 22 minutes | Serves: 6

INGREDIENTS:

1 1/2 fennel bulb, sliced
3 tablespoons olive oil
1 1/2 yellow onion, sliced
3 teaspoons Italian seasoning
rainbow trout fillets, boneless
1/3 cup panko breadcrumbs
3/4 cup kalamata olives, pitted and halved
Juice of 1 lemon

DIRECTIONS:
1. Spread the fennel, onion and the rest of the ingredients except the trout and breadcrumbs on a baking sheet lined with parchment paper, turn them over and cook at 200° C for 10 minutes.
2. Add the breaded fish seasoned with salt and pepper and cook at 180° C for 6 minutes per side.
3. Divide the mix on plates and serve.
4. Enjoy!

NUTRITION:

calories: 306 | fat: 8g | protein: 14g | carbohydrates: 23g | fiber: 11g | sodium: 0mg

177. Lemon Rainbow Trout
Prep time: 10 minutes | Cook time: 15 minutes | Serves: 4

INGREDIENTS:

2 rainbow trout
Juice of 1 lemon
4 tablespoons olive oil
4 garlic cloves, minced
A pinch of salt and black pepper

DIRECTIONS:
1. Line a baking sheet with parchment paper, add the fish and the rest of the ingredients and rub.
2. Bake at 400° F for 15 minutes, divide into plates and serve with a side salad.
3. Enjoy!

NUTRITION:

calories: 521 | fat: 29g | protein: 52g | carbohydrates: 14g | fiber: 5g | sodium: 0mg

178. Trout and Peppers Mix
Prep time: 10 minutes | Cook time: 20 minutes | Serves: 6

INGREDIENTS:

6 trout fillets, boneless
3 tablespoons kalamata olives, pitted and chopped
1 1/2 tablespoon capers, drained
3 tablespoons olive oil
A pinch of salt and black pepper
2 1/4 teaspoons chili powder
1 1/2 yellow bell pepper, chopped
1 1/2 red bell pepper, chopped
1 1/2 green bell pepper, chopped

DIRECTIONS:
1. Heat a skillet with oil over medium-high heat, add the trout, salt and pepper and cook for 10 minutes.
2. Turn the fish, add the peppers and the rest of the ingredients, cook for another 10 minutes, divide everything into plates and serve.

3. Enjoy!

NUTRITION:

calories: 572 | fat: 17g | protein: 33g | carbohydrates: 71g | fiber: 6g | sodium: 0mg

179. Cod and Cabbage

Prep time: 10 minutes | Cook time: 15 minutes | Serves: 6

INGREDIENTS:

- 3 cups green cabbage, shredded
- 1 1/2 sweet onion, sliced
- A pinch of salt and black pepper
- 3/4 cup feta cheese, crumbled
- 6 teaspoons olive oil
- 6 cod fillets, boneless
- 1/3 cup green olives, pitted and chopped

DIRECTIONS:

1. Grease a pan with oil, add the fish, the cabbage and the rest of the ingredients, add to the pan and cook at 450° F for 15 minutes.
2. Divide the mix into plates and serve.
3. Enjoy!

NUTRITION:

calories: 270 | fat: 10g | protein: 31g | carbohydrates: 12g | fiber: 3g | sodium: 0mg

180. Mediterranean Mussels

Prep time: 10 minutes | Cook time: 10 minutes | Serves: 6

INGREDIENTS:

- 1 1/2 white onion, sliced
- 4 1/2 tablespoons olive oil
- 3 teaspoons fennel seeds
- 6 garlic cloves, minced
- 1 1/2 teaspoon red pepper, crushed
- A pinch of salt and black pepper
- 1 1/2 cup chicken stock
- 1 1/2 tablespoon lemon juice
- 3 3/4 pounds mussels, scrubbed
- 3/4 cup parsley, chopped
- 3/4 cup tomatoes, cubed

DIRECTIONS:

1. Heat a pan with the oil over medium-high heat, add the onion and garlic and sauté for 2 minutes.
2. Add the rest of the ingredients except the mussels, mix and cook for another 3 minutes.
3. Add the mussels, cook for another 6 minutes, divide everything into bowls and serve.
4. Enjoy!

NUTRITION:

calories: 276 | fat: 9g | protein: 20g | carbohydrates: 6g | fiber: 4g | sodium: 0mg

181. Mussels Bowls

Prep time: 10 minutes | Cook time: 10 minutes | Serves: 6

INGREDIENTS:

- 3 pounds mussels, scrubbed
- 1 1/2 tablespoon garlic, minced
- 1 1/2 tablespoon basil, chopped
- 1 1/2 yellow onion, chopped
- 9 tomatoes, cubed
- 1 1/2 cup heavy cream
- 3 tablespoons olive oil
- 1 1/2 tablespoon parsley, chopped

DIRECTIONS:

1. Heat a pan with the oil over medium-high heat, add the garlic and onion and sauté for 2 minutes.
2. Add the mussels and the rest of the ingredients; mix, cook for another 7 minutes, divide into bowls and serve.
3. Enjoy!

NUTRITION:

calories: 266 | fat: 11g | protein: 10g | carbohydrates: 16g | fiber: 5g | sodium: 0mg

182. Calamari and Dill Sauce

Prep time: 10 minutes | Cook time: 15 minutes | Serves: 6

INGREDIENTS:

- 2 1/4-pound calamari, sliced into rings
- 15 garlic cloves, minced
- 3 tablespoons olive oil
- Juice of 1 1/2 lime
- 3 tablespoons balsamic vinegar
- 4 1/2 tablespoons dill, chopped
- A pinch of salt and black pepper

DIRECTIONS:

1. Heat a skillet with oil over medium-high heat. Add the garlic, lime juice and other ingredients except squid and cook for 5 minutes.
2. Add the squid rings, cook for another 10 minutes, divide into plates and serve.
3. Enjoy!

NUTRITION:

calories: 282 | fat: 18g | protein: 18g | carbohydrates: 9g | fiber: 4g | sodium: 0mg

183. Chili Calamari and Veggie Mix

Prep time: 10 minutes | Cook time: 40 minutes | Serves: 6

INGREDIENTS:

- 1 1/2-pound calamari rings
- 3 red chili peppers, chopped
- 3 tablespoons olive oil
- 4 1/2 garlic cloves, minced
- 21 ounces canned
- 3 tomatoes, chopped
- 3 tablespoons tomato paste
- 1 1/2 tablespoon thyme, chopped
- Salt and black pepper to the taste
- 3 tablespoons capers, drained
- 18 black olives, pitted and halved

DIRECTIONS:

1. Heat a pan with the oil over medium-high heat, add the garlic and chilli and sauté for 2 minutes.
2. Add the rest of the ingredients except the olives and capers, mix, bring to the boil and cook for 22 minutes.
3. Add the olives and capers, cook for another 15 minutes. Divide everything into bowls and serve.
4. Enjoy!

NUTRITION:

calories: 272 | fat: 11g | protein: 15g | carbohydrates: 9g | fiber: 2g | sodium: 0mg

184. Cheesy Crab and Lime Spread

Prep time: 10 minutes | Cook time: 25 minutes | Serves: 6

INGREDIENTS:

- 3-pound crab meat, flaked
- 3 ounces cream cheese, soft
- 3/4 tablespoon chives, chopped
- 3/4 teaspoon lime juice
- 3/4 teaspoon lime zest, grated

DIRECTIONS:

1. In a pan greased with cooking spray, combine the crab with the rest of the ingredients and mix.
2. Place in the oven at 350° F, bake for 25 minutes, divide into bowls and serve.
3. Enjoy!

NUTRITION:

calories: 284 | fat: 14g | protein: 15g | carbohydrates: 16g | fiber: 5g | sodium: 0mg

185. Horseradish Cheesy Salmon Mix

Prep time: 10 minutes | Cook time: 0 minutes | Serves: 6

INGREDIENTS:

- 3/4 ounces feta cheese, crumbled
- 3 ounces cream cheese, soft
- 1 1/2 tablespoons already prepared horseradish
- 3/4-pound smoked salmon, skinless, boneless and flaked
- 1 1/2 teaspoons lime zest, grated
- 3/4 red onion, chopped
- 2 1/4 tablespoons chives, chopped

DIRECTIONS:

1. In the food processor, mix the cream cheese with the horseradish, goat cheese and lime zest and blend very well.
2. In a bowl, combine the salmon with the rest of the ingredients, mix and serve cold.
3. Enjoy!

NUTRITION:

calories: 281 | fat: 17g | protein: 25g | carbohydrates: 4g | fiber: 1g | sodium: 0mg

186. Greek Trout Spread

Prep time: 10 minutes | Cook time: 0 minutes | Serves: 6

INGREDIENTS:

- 2 1/4 ounces smoked trout, skinless, boneless and flaked
- 3/4 tablespoon lemon juice
- 3/4 cup Greek yogurt
- 3/4 tablespoon dill, chopped
- Salt and black pepper to the taste

A drizzle of olive oil

DIRECTIONS:

1. In a bowl, combine the trout with the lemon juice and the rest of the ingredients and whisk really well.
2. Divide the spread into bowls and serve.
3. Enjoy!

NUTRITION:

calories: 258 | fat: 4g | protein: 7g | carbohydrates: 5g | fiber: 2g | sodium: 0mg

187. Salmon and Green Beans

Prep time: 10 minutes | Cook time: 15 minutes | Serves: 6

INGREDIENTS:

4 1/2 tablespoons balsamic vinegar
3 tablespoons olive oil
1 1/2 garlic clove, minced
3/4 teaspoon red pepper flakes, crushed
3/4 teaspoon lime zest, grated
2 1/4 pounds green beans, chopped
Salt and black pepper to the taste
1 1/2 red onion, sliced
6 salmon fillets, boneless

DIRECTIONS:

1. Heat a pan with half the oil. Add the vinegar, onion, garlic and other ingredients except salmon, mix, cook for 6 minutes and divide into plates.
2. Heat the same pan with the rest of the oil over medium-high heat, add the salmon, salt and pepper, cook 4 minutes per side, add the green beans and serve.
3. Enjoy!

NUTRITION:

calories: 224 | fat: 15g | protein: 16g | carbohydrates: 22g | fiber: 8g | sodium: 0mg

188. Cayenne Cod and Tomatoes

Prep time: 10 minutes | Cook time: 25 minutes | Serves: 6

INGREDIENTS:

1 1/2 teaspoon lime juice
Salt and black pepper to the taste
1 1/2 teaspoon sweet paprika
1 1/2 teaspoon cayenne pepper
3 tablespoons olive oil
1 1/2 yellow onion, chopped
3 garlic cloves, minced
6 cod fillets, boneless
A pinch of cloves, ground
3/4 cup chicken stock
3/4-pound cherry tomatoes, cubed

DIRECTIONS:

1. Heat a skillet with oil over medium-high heat. Add cod, salt, pepper and cayenne pepper, cook 4 minutes per side and divide into plates.
2. Heat the same pan over medium-high heat, add the onion and garlic and sauté for 5 minutes.
3. Add the rest of the ingredients, mix, bring to a boil and cook for another 10 minutes.
4. Divide the mix next to the fish and serve.
5. Enjoy!

NUTRITION:

calories: 232 | fat: 16g | protein: 16g | carbohydrates: 24g | fiber: 11g | sodium: 0mg

189. Salmon and Watermelon Gazpacho

Prep time: 10 minutes | Cook time: 0 minutes | Serves: 6

INGREDIENTS:

1/3 cup basil, chopped
1 1/2-pound tomatoes, cubed
1 1/2-pound watermelon, cubed
1/3 cup red wine vinegar
1/2 cup avocado oil
3 garlic cloves, minced
1 1/2 cup smoked salmon, skinless, boneless and cubed
A pinch of salt and black pepper

DIRECTIONS:

1. In your blender, combine the basil with the watermelon and the rest of the ingredients except the salmon, blend well and divide into bowls.
2. Garnish each portion with salmon and serve cold.
3. Enjoy!

NUTRITION:

calories: 252 | fat: 16g | protein: 15g | carbohydrates: 24g | fiber: 9g | sodium: 0mg

190. Shrimp and Calamari Mix

Prep time: 10 minutes | Cook time: 12 minutes | Serves: 6

INGREDIENTS:

1 1/2-pound shrimp, peeled and deveined
Salt and black pepper to the taste
4 1/2 garlic cloves, minced
1 1/2 tablespoon avocado oil
3/4-pound calamari rings
3/4 teaspoon basil, dried
1 1/2 teaspoon rosemary, dried
1 1/2 red onion, chopped
1 1/2 cup chicken stock
Juice of 1 lemon
1 1/2 tablespoon parsley, chopped

DIRECTIONS:

1. Heat a pan with the oil over medium-high heat, add the onion and garlic and sauté for 4 minutes.
2. Add the prawns, squid and the rest of the ingredients except parsley, mix, simmer and cook for 8 minutes.
3. Add the parsley, divide everything into bowls and serve.
4. Enjoy!

NUTRITION:

calories: 288 | fat: 12g | protein: 6g | carbohydrates: 22g | fiber: 10g | sodium: 0mg

191. Shrimp and Dill Mix

Prep time: 10 minutes | Cook time: 10 minutes | Serves: 6

INGREDIENTS:

1 1/2-pound shrimp, cooked, peeled and deveined
3/4 cup raisins
1 1/2 cup spring onion, chopped
3 tablespoons olive oil
3 tablespoons capers, chopped
3 tablespoons dill, chopped
Salt and black pepper to the taste

DIRECTIONS:

1. Heat a pan with the oil over medium-high heat, add the onions and raisins and sauté for 2-3 minutes.
2. Add the prawns and the rest of the ingredients, mix, cook for another 6 minutes, divide into plates and serve with a side of salad.
3. Enjoy!

NUTRITION:

calories: 218 | fat: 12g | protein: 4g | carbohydrates: 22g | fiber: 6g | sodium: 0mg

192. Minty Sardines Salad

Prep time: 10 minutes | Cook time: 0 minutes | Serves: 6

INGREDIENTS:

4 ounces canned sardines in olive oil, skinless, boneless and flaked
2 teaspoons avocado oil
2 tablespoons mint, chopped
A pinch of salt and black pepper
1 avocado, peeled, pitted and cubed
1 cucumber, cubed
2 tomatoes, cubed
2 spring onions, chopped

DIRECTIONS:

1. In a bowl, combine the sardines with the oil and the rest of the ingredients, mix, divide into small bowls and refrigerate for 10 minutes before serving.
2. Enjoy!

NUTRITION:

calories: 261 | fat: 7g | protein: 12g | carbohydrates: 22g | fiber: 2g | sodium: 0mg

193. Salmon and Zucchini Rolls

Prep time: 10 minutes | Cook time: 0 minutes | Serves: 6

INGREDIENTS:

6 slices smoked salmon, boneless
1 1/2 zucchinis, sliced lengthwise in 8 pieces
3/4 cup ricotta cheese, soft
1 1/2 teaspoons lemon zest, grated
3/4 tablespoon dill, chopped
3/4 small red onion, sliced
Salt and pepper to the taste

DIRECTIONS:

1. In a bowl, mix the ricotta with the rest of the ingredients except the salmon and zucchinis and mix well.
2. Arrange the zucchini slices on a work surface and divide the salmon on top.
3. Spread the cheese mixture all over, roll up and secure with toothpicks

and serve immediately.
4. Enjoy!

NUTRITION:

calories: 297 | fat: 24g | protein: 11g | carbohydrates: 15g | fiber: 11g | sodium: 0mg

194. Chorizo Shrimp and Salmon Mix

Prep time: 10 minutes | Cook time: 20 minutes | Serves: 6

INGREDIENTS:

- 123 tablespoons olive oil
- 1 1/2-pound shrimp, peeled and deveined
- 1 1/2-pound salmon, skinless, boneless and cubed
- 6 ounces chorizo, chopped
- Salt and black pepper to the taste
- 4 1/2 cups canned tomatoes, crushed
- 1 1/2 red onion, chopped
- 3 garlic cloves, minced
- 1/3 teaspoon red pepper flakes, crushed
- 1 1/2 cup chicken stock
- 1 1/2 tablespoon cilantro, chopped

DIRECTIONS:

1. Heat a pan with olive oil over medium-high heat, add the chorizo and cook for 2 minutes.
2. Add salt, pepper, tomatoes and the rest of the ingredients except the shrimp, salmon and coriander, mix, bring to a boil and cook for 10 minutes.
3. Add the other ingredients, cook for another 8 minutes, divide into bowls and serve.
4. Enjoy!

NUTRITION:

calories: 232 | fat: 15g | protein: 16g | carbohydrates: 20g | fiber: 10g | sodium: 0mg

195. Garlic Scallops and Peas Mix

Prep time: 10 minutes | Cook time: 20 minutes | Serves: 4

INGREDIENTS:

- 8 ounces scallops
- 1 1/3 tablespoons olive oil
- 2 2/3 garlic cloves, minced
- A pinch of salt and black pepper
- 1/3 cup chicken stock
- 2/3 cup snow peas, sliced
- 1/3 tablespoon balsamic vinegar
- 2/3 cup scallions, sliced
- 2/3 tablespoon basil, chopped

DIRECTIONS:

1. Heat a skillet with half the oil over medium-high heat, add the scallops, cook for 5 minutes on each side and transfer to a bowl.
2. Heat the pan with the rest of the oil over medium heat, add the shallot and garlic and sauté for 2 minutes.
3. Add the rest of the ingredients, mix, bring to a boil and cook for another 5 minutes.
4. Add the scallops to the pan, cook for 3 minutes, divide into bowls and serve.
5. Enjoy!

NUTRITION:

calories: 296 | fat: 11g | protein: 20g | carbohydrates: 26g | fiber: 9g | sodium: 0mg

196. Kale, Beets and Cod Mix

Prep time: 10 minutes | Cook time: 20 minutes | Serves: 6

INGREDIENTS:

- 3 tablespoons apple cider vinegar
- 3/4 cup chicken stock
- 1 1/2 red onion, sliced
- 6 golden beets, trimmed, peeled and cubed
- 3 tablespoons olive oil
- Salt and black pepper to the taste
- 6 cups kale, torn
- 3 tablespoons walnuts, chopped
- 1 1/2-pound cod fillets, boneless, skinless and cubed

DIRECTIONS:

1. Heat a skillet with oil over medium-high heat, add the onion and beets and cook for 3-4 minutes.
2. Add the rest of the ingredients except the fish and nuts, mix, bring to a boil and cook for another 5 minutes.
3. Add the fish, cook for 10 minutes, divide into plates and serve.
4. Enjoy!

NUTRITION:

calories: 285 | fat: 7g | protein: 12g | carbohydrates: 16g | fiber: 6g | sodium: 0mg

197. Salmon, Calamari and Mango Mix

Prep time: 10 minutes | Cook time: 10 minutes | Serves: 6

INGREDIENTS:

- 3/4-pound smoked salmon, skinless, boneless and cubed
- 3/4-pound calamari rings
- 1 1/2 tablespoon garlic chili sauce
- 3 tablespoons olive oil
- 1/3 cup lime juice
- 3/4 teaspoon smoked paprika
- 3/4 teaspoon cumin, ground
- 3 garlic cloves, minced
- A pinch of salt and black pepper
- 1 1/2 cup mango, peeled and cubed

DIRECTIONS:

1. Heat a skillet with the oil over medium-high heat, add the garlic sauce, lime juice and the rest of the ingredients except the salmon and squid, mix and simmer for 3 minutes.
2. Add the other ingredients, cook for 7 minutes, divide into bowls and serve.
3. Enjoy!

NUTRITION:

calories: 274 | fat: 11g | protein: 15g | carbohydrates: 11g | fiber: 2g | sodium: 0mg

198. Squid and Cucumber Mix

Prep time: 10 minutes | Cook time: 15 minutes | Serves: 6

INGREDIENTS:

- 15 ounces squid, cut in medium pieces
- 3 cucumbers, chopped
- 4 1/2 tablespoons cilantro, chopped
- 1 1/2 hot jalapeno pepper, chopped
- 4 1/2 tablespoons balsamic vinegar
- 3 tablespoons olive oil
- A pinch of salt and black pepper
- 1 1/2 tablespoon dill, chopped

DIRECTIONS:

1. Heat a pan with the oil over medium-high heat, add the squid and cook for 5 minutes.
2. Add the cucumbers and the rest of the ingredients, mix, cook for another 10 minutes, divide into plates and serve.
3. Enjoy!

NUTRITION:

calories: 224 | fat: 14g | protein: 11g | carbohydrates: 22g | fiber: 11g | sodium: 0mg

199. Octopus and Radish Salad

Prep time: 10 minutes | Cook time: 1 hour & 30 minutes | Serves: 6

INGREDIENTS:

- 1 1/2 big octopus, cleaned and tentacles separated
- 3 ounces calamari rings
- 4 1/2 garlic cloves, minced
- 1 1/2 white onion, chopped
- 1 1/8 cup chicken stock
- 3 cups radicchio, sliced
- 3 cups radish, sliced
- 1 1/2 cup parsley, chopped
- 1 1/2 tablespoon olive oil
- Salt and black pepper to the taste

DIRECTIONS:

1. Put the octopus tentacles in a pot, add the broth, add the squid rings, season with salt and pepper. Bring to a boil and cook over medium heat for 1 hour and 30 minutes.
2. Drain everything, cut the tentacles into pieces and transfer them with the squid rings to a bowl.
3. Add the rest of the ingredients, mix and refrigerate the salad for 2 hours before serving.
4. Enjoy!

NUTRITION:

calories: 287 | fat: 9g | protein: 8g | carbohydrates: 22g | fiber: 5g | sodium: 0mg

200. Shrimp and Mushrooms Mix

Prep time: 10 minutes | Cook time: 12 minutes | Serves: 6

INGREDIENTS:

- 1 1/2-pound shrimp, peeled and deveined
- 3 green onions, sliced
- 3/4-pound white mushrooms, sliced
- 3 tablespoons balsamic vinegar
- 3 tablespoons sesame seeds, toasted
- 3 teaspoons ginger, minced
- 3 teaspoons garlic, minced
- 4 1/2 tablespoons olive oil
- 3 tablespoons dill, chopped

DIRECTIONS:

1. Heat a pan with oil over medium-high heat, add the spring onions and garlic and sauté for 2 minutes.
2. Add the rest of the ingredients except the prawns and cook for another 6 minutes.
3. Add the prawns, cook for 4 minutes, divide everything into plates and serve.
4. Enjoy!

NUTRITION:

calories: 245 | fat: 8g | protein: 17g | carbohydrates: 1g | fiber: 45g | sodium: 0mg

201. Scallops and Carrots Mix

Prep time: 10 minutes | Cook time: 15 minutes | Serves: 6

INGREDIENTS:

1 1/2-pound sea scallops, halved
3 celery stalks, sliced
3 tablespoons olive oil
4 1/2 garlic cloves, minced
Salt and black pepper to the taste
Juice of 1 lime
6 ounces baby carrots, trimmed
1 1/2 tablespoon capers, chopped
1 1/2 tablespoon mayonnaise
1 1/2 tablespoon rosemary, chopped
1 1/2 cup chicken stock

DIRECTIONS:

1. Heat a pan with oil over medium-high heat, add celery and garlic and sauté for 2 minutes.
2. Add the carrots and the rest of the ingredients except the scallops and mayonnaise, mix, bring to a boil and cook over medium heat for 8 minutes.
3. Add the scallops and mayonnaise, mix, cook for 5 minutes, divide into bowls and serve.
4. Enjoy!

NUTRITION:

calories: 305 | fat: 14g | protein: 7g | carbohydrates: 31g | fiber: 5g | sodium: 0mg

202. Lime Squid and Capers Mix

Prep time: 10 minutes | Cook time: 20 minutes | Serves: 6

INGREDIENTS:

1 1/2-pound baby squid, cleaned, body and tentacles chopped
3/4 teaspoon lime zest, grated
1 1/2 tablespoon lime juice
3/4 teaspoon orange zest, grated
4 1/2 tablespoons olive oil
1 1/2 teaspoon red pepper flakes, crushed
1 1/2 tablespoon parsley, chopped
6 garlic cloves, minced
1 1/2 shallot, chopped
3 tablespoons capers, drained
1 1/2 cup chicken stock
3 tablespoons red wine vinegar
Salt and black pepper to the taste

DIRECTIONS:

1. Heat a skillet with the oil over medium-high heat, add the lime zest, lime juice, orange zest and the rest of the ingredients except the squid and parsley.
2. Stir, bring to a boil and cook over medium heat for 10 minutes.
3. Add the remaining ingredients, stir, cook everything for 10 minutes more, divide into bowls and serve.
4. Enjoy!

NUTRITION:

calories: 302 | fat: 8g | protein: 11g | carbohydrates: 21g | fiber: 9g | sodium: 0mg

203. Cod and Brussels Sprouts

Prep time: 10 minutes | Cook time: 20 minutes | Serves: 6

INGREDIENTS:

1 1/2 teaspoon garlic powder
1 1/2 teaspoon smoked paprika
3 tablespoons olive oil
3 pounds Brussels sprouts, trimmed and halved
6 cod fillets, boneless
3/4 cup tomato sauce
1 1/2 teaspoon Italian seasoning
1 1/2 tablespoon chives, chopped

DIRECTIONS:

1. In a baking dish, combine the sprouts with the garlic powder and other ingredients except the cod and mix.
2. Place the cod on top, cover the pan with aluminum foil and bake at 450° F for 20 minutes.
3. Divide the mix on plates and serve.
4. Enjoy!

NUTRITION:

calories: 188 | fat: 12g | protein: 16g | carbohydrates: 22g | fiber: 9g | sodium: 0mg

204. Tarragon Trout and Beets

Prep time: 10 minutes | Cook time: 35 minutes | Serves: 6

INGREDIENTS:

1 1/2-pound medium beets, peeled and cubed
4 1/2 tablespoons olive oil
6 trout fillets, boneless
Salt and black pepper to the taste
1 1/2 tablespoon chives, chopped
1 1/2 tablespoon tarragon, chopped
4 1/2 tablespoon spring
3 onions, chopped
3 tablespoons lemon juice
3/4 cup chicken stock

DIRECTIONS:

1. Spread the beets on a baking sheet lined with parchment paper, add salt, pepper and 1 tablespoon of oil, stir and bake at 450° F for 20 minutes.
2. Heat a skillet with the rest of the oil over medium-high heat, add the trout and other ingredients and cook for 4 minutes on each side.
3. Add the beets to the oven, cook the mixture for another 5 minutes, divide everything into plates and serve.
4. Enjoy!

NUTRITION:

calories: 232 | fat: 5g | protein: 16g | carbohydrates: 20g | fiber: 7g | sodium: 0mg

205. Ginger Trout and Eggplant

Prep time: 10 minutes | Cook time: 22 minutes | Serves: 6

INGREDIENTS:

4 1/2 trout fillets, boneless
1 1/2 eggplant, sliced
1/3 cup tomato sauce
3 tablespoons olive oil
Salt and black pepper to the taste
3 teaspoons ginger, grated
3 tablespoons balsamic vinegar
3 tablespoons chives, chopped

DIRECTIONS:

1. Heat up a pan with the oil over medium heat, add the eggplant and the rest of the ingredients except the trout and cook for 10 minutes.
2. Add the fish on top, introduce the pan in the oven and bake at 450° F for 12 minutes.
3. Divide everything between plates and serve.
4. Enjoy!

NUTRITION:

calories: 282 | fat: 11g | protein: 14g | carbohydrates: 17g | fiber: 5g | sodium: 0mg

206. Sicilian Tuna and Veggie Bowl

Prep time: 10 minutes | Cook time: 16 minutes | Serves: 4

INGREDIENTS:

2 garlic cloves, minced
2/3 (2 1/4-ounce / 64-g) can sliced olives, drained
1 1/3 (6-ounce / 170-g) cans tuna in olive oil, undrained
2/3-pound (454 g) kale, chopped, centre ribs removed
2 tablespoons extra-virgin olive oil
2/3 cup chopped onion
2/3 (15-ounce / 425-g) can cannellini beans or great northern beans, drained and rinsed
1/8 teaspoon freshly ground black pepper
1/8 cup capers
1/8 teaspoon crushed red pepper
1 1/3 teaspoons sugar
1/8 teaspoon kosher or sea salt

DIRECTIONS:

1. Fill a large saucepan three quarters full with water and bring to a boil. Add the cabbage and cook for 2 minutes. (This is to make the cabbage less bitter.) Drain the cabbage in a colander and set aside.
2. Return the empty saucepan to medium heat and pour in the oil. Add the onion and cook for 4 minutes, stirring often. Add the garlic and cook for 1 minute, stirring often. Add the olives, capers and chopped chilli and cook for 1 minute, stirring often. Add the partially cooked cabbage and sugar, stirring until the cabbage is completely covered in oil. Cover the pot and cook for 8 minutes.
3. Remove the cabbage from the heat, add the tuna, beans, pepper and salt and serve.
4. Enjoy!

NUTRITION:

calories: 372 | fat: 28g | protein: 8g | carbohydrates: 22g | fiber: 7g |

sodium: 0mg

207. Grilled Lemon Shrimp

Prep time: 20 minutes | Cook time: 5 minutes | Serves: 6

INGREDIENTS:

3 pounds (907 g) jumbo shrimp (21 to 25), peeled and deveined
1/3 cup extra-virgin olive oil
4 1/2 tablespoons fresh Italian parsley, finely chopped
1 1/2 teaspoon salt
3 tablespoons garlic, minced
3/4 cup lemon juice

DIRECTIONS:

1. In a large bowl, mix the garlic, lemon juice, parsley, olive oil, and salt.
2. Add the shrimp to the bowl and mix to make sure all the pieces are covered with the marinade. Let the shrimp rest for 15 minutes.
3. Preheat a grill or lightly oiled skillet over high heat. While heating, thread about 5-6 pieces of shrimp onto each skewer.
4. Place the skewers on the wire rack, grill or pan and cook for 2 to 3 minutes on each side until cooked through. Serve hot.
5. Enjoy!

NUTRITION:

calories: 402 | fat: 18g | protein: 57g | carbohydrates: 4g | fiber: 0g | sodium: 0mg

208. Orange Roasted Salmon

Prep time: 10 minutes | Cook time: 25 minutes | Serves: 6

INGREDIENTS:

1 1/2 orange, thinly sliced
6 roasted sweet potatoes, cut in wedges lengthwise
1 1/2 teaspoon sea salt, divided
1 1/2 teaspoon freshly ground black pepper, divided
1 1/2 small fennel bulb, thinly sliced lengthwise
3/4 cup extra-virgin olive oil, divided
3 tablespoons balsamic vinegar
3 tablespoons garlic powder, divided
1 1/2 tablespoon cumin seeds
1 1/2 large carrot, thinly sliced
12 medium portobello mushrooms
12 medium radishes, sliced 1/8 inch thick
3/4 cup dry white wine
3 teaspoons smoked paprika
6 (8-ounce / 227-g) salmon fillets, skinless
3 small red onion, thinly sliced
3/4 cup halved Campari tomatoes
3/4 lime, zested
Handful cilantro leaves
3/4 cup halved pitted Kalamata olives

DIRECTIONS:

1. Preheat the oven to 190ºC (375ºF).
2. In a medium bowl, mix 6 tablespoons of olive oil, balsamic vinegar, 1 tablespoon of garlic powder, cumin seeds, teaspoon of sea salt, ¼ teaspoon of pepper and paprika. Place the salmon in the bowl and marinate while preparing the vegetables, about 10 minutes.
3. Heat a skillet over medium-high heat and sauté the top of the salmon for about 2 minutes, or until lightly browned. Put aside.
4. Add the remaining 2 tablespoons of olive oil to the same pan. Once it is hot, add the onion, tomatoes, fennel, carrot, mushrooms, radishes, the remaining 1 teaspoon of garlic powder, ¾ teaspoon of salt and ¾ teaspoon of pepper. Mix well and cook for 5-7 minutes, until it becomes fragrant. Add the wine and mix well.
5. Place the salmon on top of the vegetable mixture, golden side up. Sprinkle the fish with the lime zest and cilantro and arrange the olives around the fish. Put the orange slices on the fish and cook for about another 7 minutes. As it cooks, add the sliced sweet potato wedges to a baking sheet and cook them along with the pan.
6. Remove from the oven, cover the pan tightly and let it rest for about 3 minutes.
7. Enjoy!

NUTRITION:

calories: 841 | fat: 41g | protein: 59g | carbs: 60g | fiber: 15g | sodium: 908mg

209. Cilantro Lemon Shrimp

Prep time: 20 minutes | Cook time: 10 minutes | Serves: 6

INGREDIENTS:

4 1/2 tablespoons extra-virgin olive oil
1 1/2 teaspoon salt
1 1/2 cup fresh cilantro leaves
3/4 teaspoon ground coriander
⅓ cup lemon juice
6 garlic cloves
2 1/4 pounds (680 g) large shrimp (21 to 25), deveined and shells removed

DIRECTIONS:

1. In a food processor, blend the lemon juice, garlic, cilantro, coriander, olive oil and salt.
2. Place the shrimp in a bowl or zip-lock plastic bag, pour in the cilantro marinade and let it sit for 15 minutes.
3. Preheat a skillet over high heat.
4. Place the shrimp and marinade in the pan. Cook the prawns for 3 minutes per side. Serve hot.
5. Enjoy!

NUTRITION:

calories: 225 | fat: 12g | protein: 28g | carbs: 5g | fiber: 1g | sodium: 763mg

210. Baked Trout with Lemon

Prep time: 5 minutes | Cook time: 15 minutes | Serves: 6

INGREDIENTS:

3 tablespoons olive oil
3/4 teaspoon salt
6 trout fillets
1 1/2 teaspoon black pepper
3 garlic cloves, sliced
1 1/2 lemon, sliced, plus additional wedges for serving

DIRECTIONS:

1. Preheat the air fryer to 380ºF (193ºC).
2. Brush each fillet with olive oil on both sides and season with salt and pepper. Arrange the fillets in an even layer in the basket of the air fryer.
3. Place the sliced garlic on top of the trout fillets, then add the lemon sliced garlic and cook for 12-15 minutes, or until it reaches a core temperature of 145ºF (63ºC).
4. Serve with fresh lemon wedges.
5. Enjoy!

NUTRITION:

calories: 231 | fat: 12g | protein: 29g | carbs: 1g | fiber: 0g | sodium: 341mg

211. Olive Oil-Poached Tuna

Prep time: 5 minutes | Cook time: 45 minutes | Serves: 6

INGREDIENTS:

1 1/2 cup extra-virgin olive oil, plus more if needed
6 (3- to 4-inch) sprigs fresh rosemary
12 (3- to 4-inch) sprigs fresh thyme
3 large garlic cloves, thinly sliced
3 (2-inch) strips lemon zest
1 1/2 teaspoon salt
3/4 teaspoon freshly ground black pepper
1 1/2 pound (454 g) fresh tuna steaks (about 1 inch thick)

DIRECTIONS:

1. Choose a thick pot large enough to hold the tuna in a single layer at the bottom. The larger the pot, the more olive oil you will need to use. Combine the olive oil, rosemary, thyme, garlic, lemon zest, salt and pepper over medium-low heat and cook until hot and fragrant, 20 to 25 minutes, lowering the heat if it starts smoking.
2. Remove from heat and let cool for 25-30 minutes, until warm but not hot.
3. Add the tuna to the bottom of the pan, adding more oil as needed so that the tuna is completely submerged and return to medium-low heat. Cook for 5-10 minutes, or until the oil heats up again and is hot and fragrant but doesn't smoke. Lower the heat if it's too hot.
4. Remove the pan from the heat and cook the tuna in hot oil for 4-5 minutes, until the desired doneness. For a centered tuna, cook for 2 to 3 minutes.
5. Remove from the oil and serve hot, sprinkling 2-3 tablespoons of seasoned oil over the tuna.
6. To store for later use, remove the tuna from the oil and place it in a container with a lid. Leave the tuna and oil to cool separately. When both have cooled, remove the stems of the herbs with a slotted spoon and pour the cooking oil over the tuna. Cover and refrigerate for up to 1 week. Bring to room temperature to melt the oil before serving.
7. Enjoy!

NUTRITION:

calories: 363 | fat: 28g | protein: 27g | carbs: 1g | fiber: 0g | sodium: 624mg

212. Golden Salmon Cakes with Tzatziki Sauce

Prep time: 15 minutes | Cook time: 11 minutes | Serves: 4

INGREDIENTS:

For the Tzatziki Sauce:
2 teaspoon dried dill
1/2 cup minced cucumber
1 cup plain Greek yogurt
Salt, to taste
Freshly ground black pepper, to taste
For the Salmon Cakes:
1 teaspoon dried dill
6 tablespoons olive oil, divided
1/2 cup minced celery
2 tablespoon fresh minced parsley
Salt, to taste
Freshly ground black pepper, to taste
12 ounces (170 g) cooked salmon
1/2 cup minced onion
2 eggs, beaten
1 cup unseasoned bread crumbs

DIRECTIONS:
1. Make the Tzatziki Sauce
2. Combine the yogurt, dill, and cucumber in a small bowl. Season with salt and pepper and set aside.
3. Make the Salmon Cakes
4. Remove the skin from the salmon. Place the salmon in a medium bowl and break it into small flakes with a fork. Set it aside.
5. Heat 1 tablespoon of olive oil in a non-stick skillet over medium-high heat. Add the celery and onion and sauté for 5 minutes.
6. Add celery and onion to salmon and toss to combine. Add the dill and parsley and season with salt and pepper.
7. Add the beaten egg and breadcrumbs and mix until well blended.
8. Clean the pan and add the remaining 2 tablespoons of oil. Heat the skillet over medium-high heat.
9. Form 4 meatballs with the salmon mixture and place them two at a time in the hot pan.
10. Cook for 3 minutes on each side, or until golden brown. Turn them carefully with a spatula and cook for another 3 minutes on the second side.
11. Repeat with the remaining salmon cakes and serve topped with the tzatziki sauce.
12. Enjoy!

NUTRITION:
calories: 555 | fat: 40g | protein: 31g | carbs: 18g | fiber: 1g | sodium: 303mg

213. Salmon with Tomatoes and Olives
Prep time: 5 minutes | Cook time: 8 minutes | Serves: 6
INGREDIENTS:
3 Roma tomatoes, diced
1/3 cup sliced Kalamata olives
3 tablespoons olive oil
6 (1 1/2-inch-thick) salmon fillets
3/4 teaspoon salt
3/4 teaspoon cayenne
1 1/2 teaspoon chopped fresh dill
6 lemon slices

DIRECTIONS:
1. Preheat the air fryer to 380ºF (193ºC).
2. Brush the olive oil on both sides of the salmon fillets, then season them lightly with salt, cayenne pepper, and dill.
3. Arrange the fillets in a single layer in the basket of the air fryer, then stack the tomatoes and olives. Garnish each fillet with a lemon wedge.
4. Cook for 8 minutes, or until the salmon has reached an internal temperature of 145ºF (63ºC).
5. Enjoy!

NUTRITION:
calories: 241 | fat: 15g | protein: 23g | carbs: 3g | fiber: 1g | sodium: 595mg

214. Cod Saffron Rice
Prep time: 10 minutes | Cook time: 35 minutes | Serves: 6
INGREDIENTS:
1 1/2 teaspoon saffron threads
2 1/4 teaspoons salt
6 3/4 cups water
6 tablespoons extra-virgin olive oil, divided
1 1/2 large onion, chopped
4 1/2 cod fillets, rinsed and patted dry
1 1/2 teaspoon turmeric
3 cups long-grain rice, rinsed

DIRECTIONS:
1. In a large saucepan over medium heat, cook 2 tablespoons of olive oil and the onions for 5 minutes.
2. While the onions are cooking, preheat another large skillet over high heat. Add the remaining 2 tablespoons of olive oil and the cod fillets. Cook the cod for 2 minutes on each side, then remove from the pan and set aside.
3. Once the onions are cooked, add the water, saffron, salt, turmeric and rice, stirring to combine. Cover and cook for 12 minutes.
4. Cut the cod into 1-inch pieces. Place the cod pieces in the rice, mix lightly, cover and cook for another 10 minutes.
5. When cooked, shell the rice with a fork, cover and leave to rest for 5 minutes. Serve hot.
6. Enjoy!

NUTRITION:
calories: 564 | fat: 15g | protein: 26g | carbs: 78g | fiber: 2g | sodium: 945mg

215. Sea Bass with Roasted Root Veggie
Prep time: 10 minutes | Cook time: 15 minutes | Serves: 6
INGREDIENTS:
1 2/3 sea bass fillets
1/4 teaspoon onion powder
1/3 carrot, diced small
3/4 teaspoons salt, divided
3/4 garlic cloves, minced
1/3 parsnip, diced small
1/3 rutabaga, diced small
1/8 cup olive oil
1/3 lemon, sliced, plus additional wedges for serving

DIRECTIONS:
1. Preheat the air fryer to 380ºF (193ºC).
2. In a small bowl, season the carrot, parsnip and turnip with olive oil and 1 teaspoon of salt.
3. Lightly season the sea bass with the remaining 1 teaspoon of salt and the onion powder, then place it in the fryer basket in a single layer.
4. Spread the garlic over each fillet, then cover with lemon slices.
5. Pour the prepared vegetables into the basket around and on top of the fish. Roast for 15 minutes.
6. Serve with more lemon wedges if desired.
7. Enjoy!

NUTRITION:
calories: 299 | fat: 15g | protein: 25g | carbs: 13g | fiber: 2g | sodium: 1232mg

216. Shrimp Pesto Rice Bowls
Prep time: 5 minutes | Cook time: 5 minutes | Serves: 6
INGREDIENTS:
1/3 cup pesto sauce
1 1/2 lemon, sliced
1 1/2 pound (454 g) medium shrimp, peeled and deveined
3 cups cooked wild rice pilaf

DIRECTIONS:
1. Preheat the air fryer to 360ºF (182ºC).
2. In a medium bowl, mix the prawns with the pesto until well coated.
3. Arrange the shrimp in a single layer in the basket of the air fryer. Place the lemon slices on the shrimp and roast for 5 minutes.
4. Remove the lemons and discard them. Serve a quarter of the shrimp over ½ cup of wild rice with some favourite steamed vegetables.
5. Enjoy!

NUTRITION:
calories: 249 | fat: 10g | protein: 20g | carbs: 20g | fiber: 2g | sodium: 277mg

217. Pollock and Vegetable Pitas
Prep time: 10 minutes | Cook time: 15 minutes | Serves: 6
INGREDIENTS:
3/4 teaspoon garlic powder
3/4 teaspoon dried thyme
6 whole wheat pitas
1 1/2 cup shredded lettuce
3 Roma tomatoes, diced
1/3 teaspoon cayenne
1 1/2-pound (454 g) pollock, cut into 1-inch pieces
1/3 cup olive oil
1 1/2 teaspoon salt
3/4 teaspoon dried oregano
Non-fat plain Greek yogurt
Lemon, quartered

DIRECTIONS:
1. Preheat the air fryer to 380ºF (193ºC).
2. In a medium bowl, combine the pollock with the olive oil, salt, oregano, thyme, garlic powder, and cayenne pepper.
3. Place the pollock in the basket of the air fryer and cook for 15 minutes.
4. Serve inside the pitas with lettuce, tomato and Greek yogurt with a lemon wedge on the side.
5. Enjoy!

NUTRITION:
calories: 368 | fat: 1g | protein: 21g | carbs: 38g | fiber: 5g | sodium: 514mg

218. Hake Fillet in Saffron Broth

Prep time: 15 minutes | Cook time: 9 minutes | Serves: 6

INGREDIENTS:

- 1 1/8 cup water
- 3/4 cup dry white wine
- 6 ounces (113 g) Spanish-style chorizo sausage, sliced 1/4 inch thick
- 6 garlic cloves, minced
- 1 1/2 (8-ounce / 227-g) bottle clam juice
- 1 1/2 bay leaf
- 6 (6-ounce / 170-g) skinless hake fillets, 1 1/2 inches thick
- 3/4 teaspoon table salt
- 12 ounces (227 g) small red potatoes, unpeeled, quartered
- 1/3 teaspoon saffron threads, crumbled
- 3 tablespoons extra-virgin olive oil, divided, plus extra for drizzling
- 1 1/2 onion, chopped
- 1/3 teaspoon pepper
- 3 tablespoons minced fresh parsley

DIRECTIONS:

1. Using the highest sauté function, heat 1 tablespoon of oil in the Instant Pot until it glistens. Add the onion and chorizo and cook until the onion is soft and lightly browned, 5 to 7 minutes. Stir in the garlic and cook until fragrant, about 30 seconds. Combine the clam juice, water and wine, scraping off the golden pieces. Turn off the Instant Pot, then add the potatoes, saffron, and bay leaf.
2. Fold the aluminium foil into a 16 x 6-inch sling. Brush the hake with 1 tablespoon of the remaining oil and sprinkle with salt and pepper. Place the nose pad skin-down in the centre of the harness. Using the sling, lower the hake into the Instant Pot over the potato mixture; let the narrow edges of the harness rest along the sides of the insert. Lock the lid in place and close the pressure release valve. Select the high-pressure cooking function and cook for 3 minutes.
3. Turn off Instant Pot and Quick Release Press. Carefully remove the lid, allowing the steam to escape from you. Using the sling, transfer the hake to a large plate. Curtain with aluminium foil and let it rest while we finish the potato mixture.
4. Discard the bay leaf. Stir the parsley into the potato mixture and season with salt to taste. Serve the cod with the potato and broth mixture, sprinkling the individual portions with extra oil.
5. Enjoy!

NUTRITION:

calories: 410 | fat: 18g | protein: 39g | carbs: 14g | fiber: 1g | sodium: 287mg

219. Shrimp and Veggie Pita

Prep time: 15 minutes | Cook time: 6 minutes | Serves: 6

INGREDIENTS:

- 3/4 teaspoon dried thyme
- 3/4 teaspoon garlic powder
- 3/4 teaspoon salt
- 1/3 teaspoon black pepper
- 6 whole wheat pitas
- 6 ounces (113 g) feta cheese, crumbled
- 1 1/2 cup shredded lettuce
- 1 1/2 tomato, diced
- 1/3 teaspoon onion powder
- 1 1/2 pound (454 g) medium shrimp, peeled and deveined
- 3 tablespoons olive oil
- 1 1/2 teaspoon dried oregano
- 1/3 cup black olives, sliced
- 1 1/2 lemon

DIRECTIONS:

1. Preheat the oven to 380°F (193°C).
2. In a medium bowl, combine the shrimp with the olive oil, oregano, thyme, garlic powder, onion powder, salt, and black pepper.
3. Pour the shrimp in a single layer into the basket of the air fryer and cook for 6-8 minutes or until cooked through.
4. Remove from deep fryer and divide into heated pies with feta, lettuce, tomato, olives and a squeeze of lemon.
5. Enjoy!

NUTRITION:

calories: 395 | fat: 15g | protein: 26g | carbs: 40g | fiber: 4g | sodium: 728mg

220. Shrimp, Mushrooms, Basil Cheese Pasta

Prep time: 10 minutes | Cook time: 10 minutes | Serves: 4

INGREDIENTS:

- 2/3 pound (454 g) whole grain pasta
- 3 1/3 garlic cloves, minced
- 5 1/3 ounces (227 g) baby bella mushrooms, sliced
- 1/3 cup Parmesan, plus more for serving (optional)
- 2/3 teaspoon salt
- 1/3 teaspoon black pepper
- 2/3 pound (454 g) small shrimp, peeled and deveined
- 1/8 cup plus 1 tablespoon olive oil, divided
- 1/8 teaspoon garlic powder
- 1/8 teaspoon cayenne
- 1/3 cup fresh basil

DIRECTIONS:

1. Preheat the air fryer to 380°F (193°C).
2. In a small bowl, combine the shrimp, 1 tablespoon of olive oil, the garlic powder, and the cayenne pepper. Stir to coat the shrimp.
3. Place shrimp in air fryer basket and roast for 5 minutes. Remove the shrimp and set aside.
4. Cook the pasta according to package directions. When cooked, set aside half a glass of water from the pasta, then drain it.
5. Meanwhile, in a large skillet, heat ¼ cup of olive oil over medium heat. Add the garlic and mushrooms and cook for 5 minutes.
6. Pour the pasta, the pasta water set aside, the Parmesan, the salt, the pepper and the basil in the pan with the mixture of vegetables and oil and stir to season the pasta.
7. Add the shrimp and remove from the heat, then let the mixture rest for 5 minutes before serving with more Parmesan if desired.
8. Enjoy!

NUTRITION:

calories: 457 | fat: 14g | protein: 25g | carbs: 60g | fiber: 6g | sodium: 411mg

221. Cod with Green Salad and Dukkha

Prep time: 10 minutes | Cook time: 8 minutes | Serves: 6

INGREDIENTS:

- 2 1/4 pounds (680 g) small beets, scrubbed, trimmed, and cut into 1/2-inch wedges
- 3/4 cup chicken or vegetable broth
- 1/3 teaspoon table salt
- 6 (6-ounce / 170-g) skinless cod fillets, 1 1/2 inches thick
- 1 1/2 tablespoon dukkha, plus extra for sprinkling
- 1/3 cup extra-virgin olive oil, divided, plus extra for drizzling
- 1 1/2 shallot, sliced thin
- 3 garlic cloves, minced
- 1 1/2 tablespoon lemon juice
- 3 ounces (57 g) baby arugula

DIRECTIONS:

1. Using the highest sauté function, heat 1 tablespoon of oil in the Instant Pot until it glistens. Add the shallot and cook until softened, about 2 minutes. Stir in the garlic and cook until fragrant, about 30 seconds. Stir in the beets and broth. Lock the lid in place and close the pressure release valve. Select the high-pressure cooking function and cook for 3 minutes. Turn off Instant Pot and quick release pressure. Carefully remove the lid, allowing the steam to escape from you.
2. Fold the aluminium foil into a 16 x 6-inch sling. Combine 2 tablespoons of oil, dukkha and salt in a bowl, then brush the cod with the oil mixture. Arrange the cod skin side down in the centre of the harness. Using the sling, lower the cod into the Instant Pot; let the narrow edges of the harness rest along the sides of the insert. Lock the lid in place and close the pressure release valve. Select the high-pressure cooking function and cook for 2 minutes.
3. Turn off Instant Pot and Quick Release Press. Carefully remove the lid, allowing the steam to escape from you. Using the sling, transfer the cod to a large plate. Curtain with foil and let it rest while you finish the beet salad.
4. Combine the lemon juice and the remaining tablespoon of oil in a large bowl. Using a slotted spoon, transfer the beets to a bowl with the oil mixture. Add the rocket and mix gently to combine. Season with salt and pepper to taste. Serve the cod with salad, sprinkling individual portions with extra dukkha and drizzled with extra oil.
5. Enjoy!

NUTRITION:

calories: 340 | fat: 15g | protein: 33g | carbs: 14g | fiber: 3g | sodium: 231mg

222. Sea Scallops with White Bean Purée

Prep time: 10 minutes | Cook time: 10 minutes | Serves: 4

INGREDIENTS:

- 4 teaspoons minced fresh rosemary
- 2 (15-ounce / 425-g) can white cannellini beans, drained and rinsed
- 1 cup low-sodium chicken stock
- 8 tablespoons olive oil, divided
- 4 garlic cloves
- Salt, to taste
- Freshly ground black pepper, to taste
- 12 (10 ounce / 283-g) sea scallops

DIRECTIONS:

1. To make the bean puree, heat 2 tablespoons of olive oil in a saucepan over medium-high heat. Add the garlic and sauté for 30 seconds, or just until it becomes fragrant. Don't let it burn. Add the rosemary and remove the pan from the heat.

2. Add the white beans and chicken stock to the pan, return to the heat and stir. Bring the beans to a boil. Reduce the heat to low and simmer for 5 minutes.
3. Transfer the beans to a blender and blend them for 30 seconds, or until smooth. Taste and season with salt and pepper. Let them rest in the blender with the lid on to keep them warm while you prepare the scallops.
4. Dry the scallops with absorbent paper and season with salt and pepper.
5. Heat the remaining 2 tablespoons of olive oil in a large skillet. When the oil is shimmering, add the scallops, flat side down.
6. Cook the scallops for 2 minutes, or until golden on the bottom. Flip them over and cook for another 1 to 2 minutes, or until opaque and slightly firm.
7. To serve, divide the bean puree into two plates and garnish with the scallops.
8. Enjoy!

NUTRITION:
calories: 465 | fat: 28g | protein: 30g | carbs: 21g | fiber: 7g | sodium: 319mg

223. Dill and Garlic Stuffed Red Snapper
Prep time: 10 minutes | Cook time: 35 minutes | Serves: 6

INGREDIENTS:
1/3 teaspoon cayenne
1 1/2 (1- to 1 1/2-pound / 454- to 680-g) whole red snapper, cleaned and patted dry
3 tablespoons olive oil
1 1/2 teaspoon salt
3/4 teaspoon black pepper
3/4 teaspoon ground cumin
3 garlic cloves, minced
1/3 cup fresh dill
Lemon wedges, for serving

DIRECTIONS:
1. Preheat the air fryer to 360°F (182°C)
2. In a small bowl, mix the salt, pepper, cumin, and cayenne pepper.
3. Coat the outside of the fish with olive oil, then sprinkle the seasoning mixture on the outside of the fish. Stuff the minced garlic and dill inside the fish cavity.
4. Place snapper in air fryer basket and roast for 20 minutes. Turn the red snapper upside down and roast for another 15 minutes, or until the red snapper reaches a core temperature of 145°F (63°C).
5. Enjoy!

NUTRITION:
calories: 125 | fat: 1g | protein: 23g | carbs: 2g | fiber: 0g | sodium: 562mg

224. Cod Fillet with Swiss Chard
Prep time: 10 minutes | Cook time: 12 minutes | Serves: 6

INGREDIENTS:
3 cups Swiss chard, washed, stemmed, and torn into pieces
1 1/2 teaspoon salt
3/4 teaspoon dried oregano
3/4 teaspoon dried thyme
3/4 teaspoon garlic powder
1/3 cup olive oil
1 1/2 lemon, quartered
6 cod fillets
3/4 white onion, thinly sliced

DIRECTIONS:
1. Preheat the air fryer to 380°F (193°C).
2. In a small bowl, whisk together the salt, oregano, thyme, and garlic powder.
3. Tear off four pieces of aluminium foil, each of which is large enough to wrap a fillet of cod and a quarter of the vegetables.
4. Place a cod fillet in the centre of each foil sheet, then sprinkle all sides with the spice mixture.
5. In each foil packet, place a quarter of the onion slices and ½ cup of chard, then drizzle 1 tablespoon of olive oil and squeeze ¼ of a lemon over the contents of each foil packet.
6. Fold and seal the sides of the foil packets, then place them in the basket of the air fryer. Steam for 12 minutes.
7. Remove from basket and carefully open each package to avoid steam burns.
8. Enjoy!

NUTRITION:
calories: 252 | fat: 13g | protein: 26g | carbs: 4g | fiber: 1g | sodium: 641mg

225. Honey-Garlic Glazed Salmon
Prep time: 5 minutes | Cook time: 10 minutes | Serves: 6

INGREDIENTS:
1 1/2 tablespoon olive oil
3/4 teaspoon salt
Olive oil cooking spray
1/3 cup raw honey
6 garlic cloves, minced
6 (1 1/2-inch-thick) salmon fillets

DIRECTIONS:
1. Preheat the air fryer to 380°F (193°C).
2. In a small bowl, mix the honey, garlic, olive oil, and salt.
3. Spray the bottom of the air fryer basket with olive oil cooking spray and place the salmon in a single layer on the bottom of the air fryer basket.
4. Brush the top of each fillet with the honey and garlic mixture and roast for 10-12 minutes or until the core temperature reaches 145°F (63°C).
5. Enjoy!

NUTRITION:
calories: 260 | fat: 10g | protein: 23g | carbs: 18g | fiber: 0g | sodium: 342mg

226. Grouper Fillet with Tomato and Olive
Prep time: 10 minutes | Cook time: 10 minutes | Serves: 6

INGREDIENTS:
1 1/2 tomato, sliced
1/3 cup sliced Kalamata olives
1/3 cup fresh dill, roughly chopped
6 grouper fillets
3/4 teaspoon salt
4 1/2 garlic cloves, minced
Juice of 1 lemon
1/3 cup olive oil

DIRECTIONS:
1. Preheat the air fryer to 380°F (193°C).
2. Season the grouper fillets on all sides with salt, then place them in the basket of the air fryer and garnish with the chopped garlic, tomato slices, olives and fresh dill.
3. Pour the lemon juice and olive oil over the top of the grouper, then cook for 10-12 minutes or until the internal temperature reaches 145°F (63°C).
4. Enjoy!

NUTRITION:
calories: 271 | fat: 15g | protein: 28g | carbs: 3g | fiber: 1g | sodium: 324mg

227. Easy Tuna Steaks
Prep time: 10 minutes | Cook time: 10 minutes | Serves: 6

INGREDIENTS:
1/3 teaspoon dried oregano
6 tuna steaks
3 tablespoons olive oil
1 1/2 teaspoon garlic powder
3/4 teaspoon salt
1/3 teaspoon dried thyme
1 1/2 lemon, quartered

DIRECTIONS:
1. Preheat the air fryer to 380°F (193°C).
2. In a small bowl, whisk together the garlic powder, salt, thyme and oregano.
3. Cover the tuna steaks with olive oil. Season both sides of each steak with the seasoning mixture. Arrange the steaks in a single layer in the basket of the air fryer.
4. Cook for 5 minutes, then turn and cook for another 3-4 minutes.
5. Enjoy!

NUTRITION:
calories: 269 | fat: 13g | protein: 33g | carbs: 1g | fiber: 0g | sodium: 231mg

228. Salmon with Broccoli Rabe and Cannellini Beans
Prep time: 10 minutes | Cook time: 11 minutes | Serves: 6

INGREDIENTS:
3/4 cup chicken or vegetable broth
1/3 teaspoon red pepper flakes
1 1/2 lemon, sliced 1/4 inch thick, plus lemon wedges for serving
3/4 teaspoon table salt
1/3 teaspoon pepper
3 tablespoons extra-virgin olive oil, plus extra for drizzling
6 garlic cloves, sliced thin
6 (6-ounce / 170-g) skinless salmon fillets, 1 1/2 inches thick
1 1/2-pound (454 g) broccoli rabe, trimmed and cut into 1-inch pieces
1 1/2 (15-ounce / 425-g) can cannellini beans, rinsed

DIRECTIONS:
1. Using the highest sauté function, cook the oil and garlic in the Instant Pot until the garlic is fragrant and lightly browned, about 3 minutes. Using a skimmer, transfer the garlic to a plate lined with paper towels and season with salt to taste; set aside to serve. Turn off the Instant Pot, then add the

broth and pepper flakes.

2. Fold the aluminium foil into a 16 x 6-inch sling. Arrange the lemon slices width wise in 2 rows in the centre of the harness. Sprinkle the meat side of the salmon with salt and pepper, then arrange the skin side down on top of the lemon slices. Using the sling, lower the salmon into the Instant Pot; let the narrow edges of the harness rest along the sides of the insert. Lock the lid in place and close the pressure release valve. Select the high-pressure cooking function and cook for 3 minutes.

3. Turn off Instant Pot and Quick Release Press. Carefully remove the lid, allowing the steam to escape from you. Using the sling, transfer the salmon to a large plate. Curtain with plastic wrap and let it rest while we prepare the turnip greens mixture.

4. Stir the turnip greens and beans into the cooking liquid, partially cover and cook, using the highest sauté function, until the turnip greens are tender, about 5 minutes. Season with salt and pepper to taste. Gently lift and tilt the salmon fillets with the spatula to remove the lemon slices. Serve the salmon with the mixture of turnip greens and lemon wedges, sprinkling the individual portions with garlic flakes and drizzling with extra oil.

5. Enjoy!

NUTRITION:

calories: 510 | fat: 5g | protein: 43g | carbs: 15g | fiber: 5g | sodium: 232mg

229. Pressure-Cooked Mussels

Prep time: 10 minutes | Cook time: 6 minutes | Serves: 6

INGREDIENTS:

1 1/2 leek, ends trimmed, leek halved lengthwise, sliced 1 inch thick, and washed thoroughly	1 1/2 tablespoon extra-virgin olive oil, plus extra for drizzling
1/3 teaspoon red pepper flakes	1 1/2 fennel bulb, 1 tablespoon fronds minced, stalks discarded, bulb halved, cored, and sliced thin
3/4 cup dry white wine	
6 garlic cloves, minced	4 1/2 pounds (1.4 kg) mussels, scrubbed and debearded
4 1/2 sprigs fresh thyme	

DIRECTIONS:

1. Using the highest sauté function, heat the oil in the Instant Pot until it glistens. Add the fennel and leek and cook until soft, about 5 minutes. Stir in the garlic, thyme sprigs, and pepper flakes and cook until fragrant, about 30 seconds. Deglaze with the wine, then add the mussels.

2. Lock the lid in place and close the pressure release valve. Select the high-pressure cooking function and set the cooking time to 0 minutes. Once the Instant Pot has reached pressure, immediately turn off the pot and the quick release pressure. Carefully remove the lid, allowing the steam to escape from you.

3. Remove sprigs of thyme and any mussels that have not opened. Transfer the mussels to individual serving bowls, sprinkle with fennel fronds and drizzle with extra oil. To serve.

4. Enjoy!

NUTRITION:

calories: 380 | fat: 10g | protein: 42g | carbs: 22g | fiber: 1g | sodium: 342mg

230. Panko-Crusted Fish Sticks

Prep time: 10 minutes | Cook time: 5 minutes | Serves: 6

INGREDIENTS:

1/3 teaspoon kosher or sea salt	1/3 teaspoon smoked paprika
1/3 teaspoon freshly ground black pepper	1 1/2-pound (454 g) skinned fish fillets (cod, tilapia, or other white fish) about 1/2 inch thick, sliced into 20 (1-inch-wide) strips
3 large eggs, lightly beaten 1 tablespoon 2% milk	
3/4 cup whole-wheat panko bread crumbs or whole-wheat bread crumbs	3/4 cup yellow cornmeal
	Non-stick cooking spray

DIRECTIONS:

1. Place a large, rimmed baking sheet in the oven. Preheat the oven to 200º C with the pan inside.

2. In a large bowl, mix the eggs and milk. Using a fork, add the fish strips to the egg mixture and mix gently to coat.

3. Place the cornmeal, breadcrumbs, smoked paprika, salt and pepper in a one-quart plastic ziplock bag. Using a fork or tongs, transfer the fish to the bag, letting the excess egg drip into the bowl before transferring. Seal the bag and shake gently to completely coat each fish stick.

4. With oven gloves, carefully remove the hot pan from the oven and spray it with non-stick cooking spray. Using a fork or tongs, remove the fish sticks from the bag and place them on the hot pan, spacing them so that the hot air can circulate and make them crisp.

5. Cook for 5-8 minutes, until light pressure with a fork causes the fish to flake and serve.

6. Enjoy!

NUTRITION:

calories: 238 | fat: 2g | protein: 22g | carbs: 28g | fiber: 1g | sodium: 494mg

231. Oregano Shrimp Puttanesca

Prep time: 10 minutes | Cook time: 9 minutes | Serves: 6

INGREDIENTS:

3/4 teaspoon crushed red pepper	paste
1 1/2 (14 1/2-ounce / 411-g) can low-sodium or no-salt-added diced tomatoes, undrained	4 1/2 garlic cloves, minced
	3 tablespoons capers
1 1/2 (2 1/4-ounce / 64-g) can sliced black olives, drained	1 1/2 tablespoon chopped fresh oregano or 1 teaspoon dried oregano
3 tablespoons extra-virgin olive oil	1 1/2-pound fresh raw shrimp (or frozen and thawed shrimp), shells and tails removed
4 1/2 anchovy fillets, drained and chopped, or 1 1/2 teaspoons anchovy	

DIRECTIONS:

1. In a large skillet over medium heat, heat the oil. Combine the anchovies, garlic and chopped chilli. Cook for 3 minutes, stirring often and mashing the anchovies with a wooden spoon, until they have dissolved in the oil.

2. Mix the tomatoes with their juices, olives, capers and oregano. Turn the heat up to medium-high and bring to a boil.

3. When the sauce boils slightly, add the prawns. Reduce the heat to medium and cook the shrimp for 6-8 minutes, or until pink and white, stirring occasionally, and serve.

4. Enjoy!

NUTRITION:

calories: 362 | fat: 12g | protein: 30g | carbs: 31g | fiber: 1g | sodium: 1463mg

232. Balsamic Shrimp on Tomato and Olive

Prep time: 10 minutes | Cook time: 6 minutes | Serves 4

Shopping List

¼ teaspoon cayenne pepper	1 tablespoon balsamic vinegar
¼ teaspoon salt	¼ cup Kalamata olives
1 Roma tomato, diced	1 pound (454 g) mediumshrimp, cleaned and deveined
½ cup olive oil	
4 garlic cloves, minced	

Instructions

1. Preheat the air fryer to 380ºF (193ºC).

2. In a small bowl, combine the olive oil, garlic, balsamic vinegar, cayenne pepper, and salt.

3. Divide the tomatoes and olives into four small molds. Then divide the shrimp into molds and pour a quarter of the oil mixture over the shrimp.

4. Cook for 6-8 minutes, or until the shrimp are cooked through.

Nutrition:

calories: 160 | fat: 8g | protein: 16g | carbs: 4g | fiber: 1g | sodium: 213mg

4

POULTRY RECIPES

POULTRY

233. Lemon Chicken Thighs with Vegetables
Prep time: 15 minutes | Cook time: 45 minutes | Serves: 6

INGREDIENTS:
1 1/2 large carrot, thinly sliced
1/4 cup pitted Kalamata olives
12 pieces sun-dried tomatoes (optional)
1 1/2 tablespoon salt
3/4 tablespoon thyme
6 skin-on, bone-in chicken thighs
9 medium portobello mushrooms, quartered
9 tablespoons extra-virgin olive oil, divided
6 large garlic cloves, crushed
1 1/2 tablespoon dried basil
1 1/2 tablespoon dried parsley
1 1/2 large zucchini, sliced
3/4 cup dry white wine
1 1/2 lemon, sliced

DIRECTIONS:
1. In a small bowl, combine 4 tablespoons of olive oil, garlic cloves, basil, parsley, salt and thyme. Keep half of the marinade in a jar and, in a bowl, combine the remaining half to marinate the chicken legs for about 30 minutes.
2. Preheat the oven to 220° C (425° F).
3. In a large skillet or non-stick skillet, heat the remaining 2 tablespoons of olive oil over medium-high heat. Brown the chicken for 3-5 minutes on each side until golden brown and set aside.
4. In the same pan, sauté the portobello mushrooms, courgettes and carrots for about 5 minutes, or until lightly browned.
5. Add the chicken legs, olives and sun-dried tomatoes (if using). Pour the wine over the chicken legs.
6. Cover the pan and cook for about 10 minutes over medium-low heat.
7. Uncover the pan and transfer it to the oven. Cook for another 15 minutes, or until the skin of the chicken is crisp and the juices are clear. Garnish with lemon slices.
8. Enjoy!

NUTRITION:
calories: 544 | fat: 41g | protein: 28g | carbs: 20g | fiber: 11g | sodium: 1848mg

234. Chicken Skewers with Veggies
Prep time: 30 minutes | Cook time: 25 minutes | Serves: 6

INGREDIENTS:
1 1/2 teaspoon onion powder
1 1/2 teaspoon ground cumin
3/4 teaspoon dried oregano
1/3 cup olive oil
1 1/2 teaspoon garlic powder
3/4 teaspoon dried basil
1 1/2 red onion, cut into 1-inch pieces
1 1/2 zucchini, cut into 1-inch pieces
1/3 cup lemon juice
1 1/2 tablespoon apple cider vinegar
Olive oil cooking spray
1 1/2 pound (454 g) boneless skinless chicken thighs, cut into 1-inch pieces
1 1/2 red bell pepper, cut into 1-inch pieces
18 cherry tomatoes

DIRECTIONS:
1. In a large bowl, mix together the olive oil, garlic powder, onion powder, cumin, oregano, basil, lemon juice, and apple cider vinegar.
2. Spray six skewers with olive oil cooking spray.
3. On each skewer, thread a piece of chicken, then a piece of pepper, onion, courgette and finally a tomato and then repeat. Each skewer should have at least two pieces of each item.
4. Once all the skewers are prepared, place them in a 9x13 inch pan and pour the olive oil marinade over the skewers. Turn each skewer so that all sides of the chicken and vegetables are coated.
5. Cover the plate with cling film and put it in the refrigerator for 30 minutes.
6. After 30 minutes, preheat the air fryer to 380°F (193°C). (If you are using a grill accessory, make sure it is inside the air fryer during preheating.)
7. Remove the skewers from the marinade and lay them in a single layer in the basket of the air fryer. If your air fryer has a grill attachment, you can also place them on it.
8. Cook for 10 minutes. Turn the skewers, then cook them for another 15 minutes.
9. Remove the skewers from the air fryer and let them rest for 5 minutes before serving.
10. Enjoy!

NUTRITION:
calories: 304 | fat: 17g | protein: 27g | carbs: 10g | fiber: 3g | sodium: 62mg

235. Chicken Shish Tawook
Prep time: 15 minutes | Cook time: 15 minutes | Serves: 6

INGREDIENTS:
3/4 teaspoon freshly ground black pepper
3 pounds (907 g) boneless and skinless chicken (breasts or thighs)
3 tablespoons tomato paste
3 tablespoons garlic, minced
3/4 cup extra-virgin olive oil
2 1/4 teaspoons salt
1 1/2 teaspoon smoked paprika
3/4 cup lemon juice
Rice, tzatziki, or hummus, for serving (optional)

DIRECTIONS:
1. In a large bowl, add the garlic, tomato paste, paprika, lemon juice, olive oil, salt and pepper and whisk to combine.
2. Cut the chicken into 1/2-inch cubes and place them in the bowl; mix to coat with marinade. Set aside for at least 10 minutes.
3. To grill, preheat the grill on high. Place the chicken on the skewers and cook 3 minutes per side, for a total of 9 minutes.
4. To pan-fry, preheat the pan over high heat, add the chicken and cook for 9 minutes, turning the chicken with the tongs.
5. Serve the chicken with rice, tzatziki or hummus if desired.
6. Enjoy!

NUTRITION:
calories: 482 | fat: 32g | protein: 47g | carbs: 6g | fiber: 1g | sodium: 1298mg

236. Peach-Glazed Chicken Drumsticks
Prep time: 10 minutes | Cook time: 20 minutes | Serves: 6

INGREDIENTS:
1/3 cup honey
1/3 cup cider vinegar
4 1/2 garlic cloves
3/4 teaspoon smoked paprika
1/3 teaspoon kosher or sea salt
12 chicken drumsticks (2-pound / 907-g), skin removed
Nonstick cooking spray
1 1/2 (15-ounce / 425-g) can sliced peaches in 100% juice, drained
1/3 teaspoon freshly ground black pepper

DIRECTIONS:
1. Remove the chicken from the refrigerator.
2. Set an oven rack about 4 inches below the grill element. Preheat the oven to 500°F (260°C). Line a large, rimmed baking sheet with aluminum foil. Place a wire cooling grid on the aluminum foil and spray the grid with non-stick cooking spray. Put it aside.
3. In a blender, combine the peaches, honey, vinegar, garlic, smoked paprika, salt and pepper. Blend the ingredients until smooth.
4. Add the puree to a medium saucepan and bring to a boil over medium-high heat. Cook for 2 minutes, stirring constantly. Divide the sauce into two bowls. The first bowl will be brushed on the chicken; set aside the second bowl to serve on the table.
5. Brush all sides of the chicken with about half of the sauce (keeping half of the sauce for a second coating) and place the thighs on the prepared grill. Roast for 10 minutes.
6. Remove the chicken from the oven and set the rack on high. Brush the chicken with the remaining sauce from the first bowl. Return the chicken to the oven and cook for 5 minutes. Turn the chicken; cook for another 3-5 minutes, until the core temperature reaches 74°C (165°F) on a meat thermometer, or until the juices are clear. Serve with the reserved sauce.
7. Enjoy!

NUTRITION:
calories: 526 | fat: 22g | protein: 44g | carbs: 38g | fiber: 1g | sodium: 412mg

237. Greek Lemon Chicken Kebabs
Prep time: 15 minutes | Cook time: 20 minutes | Serves: 4

INGREDIENTS:
2 pound (454 g) boneless skinless chicken breasts, cut into 1 1/4-inch cubes
2 large red bell pepper, cut into 1 1/4-inch pieces
4 small zucchini (nearly 1 pound / 454 g), cut into rounds slightly under 1/2 inch thick
1 cup extra-virgin olive oil, divided
1 teaspoon za'atar seasoning
Salt and freshly ground black pepper, to taste
1 large lemon, juiced
4 garlic cloves, minced
4 large shallots, diced into quarters
Tzatziki sauce, for serving

DIRECTIONS:
1. In a bowl, whisk together ½ cup of olive oil, lemon juice, garlic, za'atar, salt and pepper.
2. Place the chicken in a medium bowl and pour the olive oil mixture over it. Press the chicken into the marinade. Cover and refrigerate for 45 minutes.

While the chicken is marinating, soak the wooden skewers in water for 30 minutes.
3. Season and season the pepper, courgettes and shallots with the remaining 2 and a half tablespoons of olive oil and season lightly with salt.
4. Preheat the oven to 500°F (260°C) and place a pan in the oven to heat.
5. On each skewer, slip a red pepper, courgette, scallion and 2 pieces of chicken and repeat twice. Place the skewers on the hot pan and cook for 7-9 minutes, or until the chicken is completely cooked. Turn once halfway through cooking. Serve the skewers hot with the tzatziki sauce.
6. Enjoy!

NUTRITION:

calories: 825 | fat: 59g | protein: 51g | carbs: 31g | fiber: 5g | sodium: 379mg

238. Poached Chicken Breast with Romesco Sauce

Prep time: 10 minutes | Cook time: 12 minutes | Serves: 4

INGREDIENTS:

2 sprigs fresh thyme or rosemary
2/3 cup romesco sauce
1/3 onion, halved
1 1/3 garlic cloves, smashed
1 pounds (680 g) boneless, skinless chicken breasts, cut into 6 pieces
2/3 carrot, halved
2/3 celery stalk, halved
1 1/3 tablespoons chopped fresh flat-leaf (Italian) parsley
1/8 teaspoon freshly ground black pepper

DIRECTIONS:

1. Place the chicken in a medium saucepan. Fill with water until there is about an inch of liquid on top of the chicken. Add the carrot, celery, onion, garlic and thyme. Cover and bring to a boil. Reduce the heat to low (covered) and cook for 12-15 minutes, or until the core temperature of the chicken reaches 74°C (165°F) on a meat thermometer and all juices come out.
2. Remove the chicken from the water and let it rest for 5 minutes.
3. When ready to serve, spread ¾ cup of romesco sauce on the bottom of a serving dish. Arrange the chicken breasts on top and drizzle with the remaining romesco sauce. Sprinkle the surface with parsley and pepper.
4. Enjoy!

NUTRITION:

calories: 270 | fat: 10g | protein: 13g | carbs: 31g | fiber: 2g | sodium: 647mg

239. Lemon-Garlic Whole Chicken and Potatoes

Prep time: 10 minutes | Cook time: 45 minutes | Serves: 6

INGREDIENTS:

1 1/2 teaspoon freshly ground black pepper
1 1/2-pound (454 g) fingerling or red potatoes
1 1/2 cup garlic, minced
2 1/4 cups lemon juice
1 1/2 whole chicken, cut into 8 pieces
1 1/2 cup plus 2 tablespoons extra-virgin olive oil, divided
2 1/4 teaspoons salt, divided

DIRECTIONS:

1. Preheat oven to 400°F | 200°C | Fan 180°C.
2. In a large bowl, whisk together the garlic, lemon juice, 1 cup of olive oil, 1 teaspoon of salt and pepper.
3. Place the chicken in a large roasting pan and pour half the lemon sauce over the chicken. Cover the pan with foil and bake for 20 minutes.
4. Cut the potatoes in half and season with 2 tablespoons of olive oil and 1 teaspoon of salt. Place them on a baking sheet and bake for 20 minutes in the same oven as the chicken.
5. Remove both the chicken and the potatoes from the oven. Using a spatula, transfer the potatoes to the pan with the chicken. Pour the remaining sauce over the potatoes and chicken. Bake for another 25 minutes.
6. Transfer the chicken and potatoes to a serving dish and pour the garlic and lemon sauce from the pan over them.
7. Enjoy!

NUTRITION:

calories: 959 | fat: 78g | protein: 33g | carbs: 37g | fiber: 4g | sodium: 1005mg

240. Parsley-Dijon Chicken and Potatoes

Prep time: 10 minutes | Cook time: 22 minutes | Serves: 4

INGREDIENTS:

1/8 teaspoon freshly ground black pepper
1/8 teaspoon kosher or sea salt
2/3 cup chopped fresh flat-leaf (Italian) parsley, including stems
2/3 tablespoon extra-virgin olive oil
1 1/3 garlic cloves, minced
1/8 cup dry white wine
1 pounds (680 g) boneless, skinless chicken thighs, cut into 1-inch cubes, patted dry
1 pounds (680 g) Yukon Gold potatoes, unpeeled, cut into 1/2-inch cubes
2/3 cup low-sodium or no-salt-added chicken broth
2/3 tablespoon Dijon mustard
2/3 tablespoon freshly squeezed lemon juice

DIRECTIONS:

1. In a large skillet over medium-high heat, heat the oil. Add the chicken and cook for 5 minutes, stirring only after the chicken has browned on one side. Remove the chicken and set aside on a plate.
2. Add the potatoes to the pan and cook for 5 minutes, stirring only after the potatoes are golden and crisp on one side. Push the potatoes to the side of the pan, add the garlic and cook, stirring constantly, for 1 minute. Add the wine and cook for 1 minute, until almost evaporated. Add the chicken stock, mustard, salt, pepper and the reserved chicken. Turn up the heat to high and bring to a boil.
3. When it boils, cover, reduce the heat to medium-low and cook for 10-12 minutes, until the potatoes are tender and the core temperature of the chicken is 74°C (165°F) on a meat thermometer and all juices are not coming out.
4. During the last minute of cooking, stir in the parsley. Remove from the heat, add the lemon juice and serve.
5. Enjoy!

NUTRITION:

calories: 324 | fat: 9g | protein: 16g | carbs: 45g | fiber: 5g | sodium: 560mg

241. Traditional Chicken Shawarma

Prep time: 15 minutes | Cook time: 15 minutes | Serves: 6

INGREDIENTS:

4 1/2 tablespoons minced garlic
3/4 cup extra-virgin olive oil
3/4 teaspoon freshly ground black pepper
3/4 teaspoon ground cardamom
2 1/4 teaspoons salt
3 pounds (907 g) boneless and skinless chicken
3/4 cup lemon juice
3/4 teaspoon cinnamon
Hummus and pita bread, for serving (optional)

DIRECTIONS:

1. Cut the chicken into 1-inch strips and place them in a large bowl.
2. In a separate bowl, whisk together the lemon juice, olive oil, garlic, salt, pepper, cardamom, and cinnamon.
3. Pour the dressing over the chicken and mix to coat all the chicken.
4. Let the chicken rest for about 10 minutes.
5. Heat a large skillet over medium-high heat and cook the chicken pieces for 12 minutes, turning the chicken with the tongs every few minutes.
6. Serve with hummus and pita bread if desired.
7. Enjoy!

NUTRITION:

calories: 477 | fat: 32g | protein: 47g | carbs: 5g | fiber: 1g | sodium: 1234mg

242. Moroccan Chicken Meatballs

Prep time: 10 minutes | Cook time: 10 minutes | Serves: 6

INGREDIENTS:

1 1/2 teaspoon ground cumin
3/4 teaspoon ground coriander
3/4 teaspoon salt
3/4 teaspoon freshly ground black pepper
1/4 teaspoon ground cardamom
1 1/2-pound (454 g) ground chicken
3 large shallots, diced
3 tablespoons finely chopped parsley
3 teaspoons paprika
3/4 teaspoon garlic powder
3/4 cup all-purpose flour, to coat
1/3 cup olive oil, divided

DIRECTIONS:

1. In a bowl, combine the shallot, parsley, paprika, cumin, coriander, garlic powder, salt, pepper, and cardamom. Mix well.
2. Add the chicken to the spice mixture and mix well. Roll into 1-inch balls flattened to about ½ inch thick.
3. Put the flour in a dredging bowl. Pass the balls in the flour until they are

61

covered.
4. Pour in enough oil to cover the bottom of a pan or skillet and heat over medium heat. Working in batches, cook the meatballs, turning them often, for 2 to 3 minutes per side, until cooked through. Add more oil between batches as needed. Serve in a pita, topped with lettuce topped with creamy yogurt sauce.
5. Enjoy!

NUTRITION:

calories: 405 | fat: 26g | protein: 24g | carbs: 20g | fiber: 1g | sodium: 387mg

243. Yogurt-Marinated Chicken

Prep time: 15 minutes | Cook time: 30 minutes | Serves: 4

INGREDIENTS:

6 garlic cloves, minced	Zest of 1 lemon
4 tablespoons minced fresh oregano (or 1 tablespoon dried oregano)	2 tablespoon olive oil
1 cup plain Greek yogurt	4 (4-ounce / 113-g) boneless, skinless chicken breasts
1 teaspoon salt	

DIRECTIONS:

1. In a medium bowl, add the yogurt, garlic, oregano, lemon zest, olive oil and salt and stir to combine. If the yogurt is very thick, you may need to add a few tablespoons of water or a splash of lemon juice to dilute it a little.
2. Add the chicken to the bowl and dip it in the marinade to coat it well. Cover and refrigerate the chicken for at least 30 minutes or overnight.
3. Preheat the oven to 350°F (180°C) and set the rack in the centre position.
4. Place the chicken in a roasting pan and roast for 30 minutes, or until the chicken reaches a core temperature of 165°F (74°C).
5. Enjoy!

NUTRITION:

calories: 255 | fat: 13g | protein: 29g | carbs: 8g | fiber: 2g | sodium: 694mg

244. Chicken Piccata with Mushrooms and Parsley

Prep time: 15 minutes | Cook time: 17 minutes | Serves: 6

INGREDIENTS:

1/3 cup roughly chopped capers	divided
3/4 teaspoon freshly ground black pepper	Zucchini noodles, for serving
6 tablespoons butter, divided (optional)	1/3 cup ground flaxseed
3 cups sliced mushrooms	1 1/2 pound (454 g) thinly sliced chicken breasts
3/4 cup dry white wine or chicken stock	2 1/4 teaspoons salt, divided
1/3 cup freshly squeezed lemon juice	1/3 cup chopped fresh flat-leaf Italian parsley, for garnish
3 tablespoons almond flour	
12 tablespoons extra-virgin olive oil,	

DIRECTIONS:

1. Season the chicken with 1 teaspoon of salt and pepper. On a plate, combine the ground flax seeds and almond flour and dip each chicken breast into the mixture. To put aside.
2. In a large skillet, heat 4 tablespoons of olive oil and 1 tablespoon of butter over medium-high heat. Working in batches, if necessary, brown the chicken, 3-4 minutes per side. Remove from the pan and keep warm.
3. Add the remaining 4 tablespoons of olive oil and 1 tablespoon of butter to the pan along with the mushrooms and sauté over medium heat until tender, 6 to 8 minutes.
4. Add the white wine, lemon juice, capers and the remaining ½ teaspoon of salt to the pan and bring to a boil, stirring to incorporate any golden bits that have stuck to the bottom of the pan. Reduce the heat to low and add the last 2 tablespoons of butter.
5. Return the browned chicken to a skillet, cover and simmer over low heat until the chicken is completely cooked and the sauce has thickened, 5 to 6 minutes more.
6. Serve the chicken and mushrooms hot on the courgette noodles, pour over the mushroom sauce and garnish with chopped parsley.
7. Enjoy!

NUTRITION:

calories: 538 | fat: 43g | protein: 30g | carbs: 8g | fiber: 3g | sodium: 1127mg

245. Moroccan Chicken Thighs and Vegetable Tagine

Prep time: 15 minutes | Cook time: 52 minutes | Serves: 4

INGREDIENTS:

2/3 red bell pepper, cut into 1-inch squares	or Spanish green work nicely)
1/3 cup extra-virgin olive oil, divided	1 1/3 medium tomatoes, chopped or 1 1/2 cups diced canned tomatoes
1 pounds (680 g) boneless skinless chicken thighs, cut into 1-inch chunks	2/3 cup water
1 teaspoons salt, divided	1 1/3 medium zucchini, sliced into 1/4-inch-thick half moons
1/3 teaspoon freshly ground black pepper	1/8 cup chopped fresh cilantro or flat-leaf Italian parsley
2/3 small red onion, chopped	Riced cauliflower or sautéed spinach, for serving
2/3 cup pitted halved olives (Kalamata	

DIRECTIONS:

1. In a Dutch oven or large-sided skillet, heat ¼ cup of olive oil over medium-high heat.
2. Season the chicken with 1 teaspoon of salt and pepper and sauté until golden brown on all sides for 6 to 8 minutes.
3. Add the onions and peppers and sauté until wilted, another 6-8 minutes.
4. Add the chopped tomatoes and water, bring to a boil and reduce the heat to low. Cover and simmer until the meat is cooked through and very tender, 30 to 45 minutes.
5. Add the remaining ¼ cup of olive oil, zucchini, olives and cilantro, stirring to combine. Continue to cook over low heat, uncovered, until the courgettes are tender, about 10 minutes.
6. Serve hot over cauliflower rice or a bed of sauteed spinach.
7. Enjoy!

NUTRITION:

calories: 358 | fat: 24g | protein: 25g | carbs: 8g | fiber: 3g | sodium: 977mg

246. Chicken Breast with Tomato and Basil

Prep time: 10 minutes | Cook time: 20 minutes | Serves: 6

INGREDIENTS:

1 1/2 cup shredded Mozzarella or 4 ounces fresh Mozzarella cheese, diced	1/3 teaspoon kosher or sea salt
1 1/2 (14 1/2-ounce / 411-g) can low-sodium or no-salt-added crushed tomatoes	1 1/2 large tomato, sliced thinly
	1 1/2 pound (454 g) boneless, skinless chicken breasts
Non-stick cooking spray	3 tablespoons extra-virgin olive oil
1/3 teaspoon freshly ground black pepper	3 tablespoons fresh torn basil leaves
	6 teaspoons balsamic vinegar

DIRECTIONS:

1. Set an oven rack about 4 inches below the grill element. Preheat the oven to 450°F (235°C). Line a large, rimmed baking sheet with aluminium foil. Place a wire cooling grid on the aluminium foil and spray the grid with non-stick cooking spray. Put aside.
2. Cut the chicken into 4 pieces (if they aren't already). Place the chicken breasts in a large zip-up plastic bag. With a rolling pin or meat mallet, pound the chicken so that it is evenly flattened, about ¼ inch thick. Add the oil, pepper and salt to the bag. Close the bag and rub the ingredients into the chicken. Take the chicken out of the bag and place it on the prepared grill.
3. Cook the chicken for 15-18 minutes, or until the core temperature of the chicken is 165°F (74°C) on a meat thermometer and the juices become clear. Turn on the high grill once. Arrange the tomato slices on each chicken breast and garnish with the mozzarella. Cook the chicken for another 2 to 3 minutes or until the cheese has melted (don't let the chicken burn on the edges). Remove the chicken from the oven.
4. While the chicken is cooking, pour the mashed tomatoes into a small microwave-safe bowl. Cover the bowl with a paper towel and microwave for about 1 minute on maximum power, until hot. When ready to serve, divide the tomatoes into four flat plates. Place each chicken breast on top of the tomatoes. Complete with basil and a drizzle of balsamic vinegar.
5. Enjoy!

NUTRITION:

calories: 258 | fat: 9g | protein: 14g | carbs: 28g | fiber: 3g | sodium: 573mg

247. Chicken and Olives

Prep time: 10 minutes | Cook time: 15 minutes | Serves: 6

INGREDIENTS:

6 chicken breasts, skinless and boneless
3 tablespoons garlic, minced
1 1/2 tablespoon oregano, dried
Salt and black pepper to the taste
3 tablespoons olive oil
3/4 cup chicken stock
Juice of 1 lemon
1 1/2 cup red onion, chopped
2 1/4 cups tomatoes, cubed
1/3 cup green olives, pitted and sliced
A handful parsley, chopped

DIRECTIONS:

1. Heat a pan with the oil over medium-high heat, add the chicken, garlic, salt and pepper and sauté for 2 minutes on each side.
2. Add the rest of the ingredients, mix, bring the mixture to a boil and cook over medium heat for 13 minutes.
3. Divide the mixture into plates and serve.
4. Enjoy!

NUTRITION:

calories: 135 | fat: 5g | protein: 9g | carbs: 12g | fiber: 3g | sodium: 573mg

248. Chicken Bake

Prep time: 10 minutes | Cook time: 30 minutes | Serves: 6

INGREDIENTS:

1½ pounds chicken thighs, skinless, boneless and cubed
2 garlic cloves, minced
1 tablespoon oregano, chopped
2 tablespoons olive oil
1 tablespoon red wine vinegar
½ cup canned artichokes, drained and chopped
1 red onion, sliced
1-pound whole wheat fusilli pasta, cooked
½ cup canned white beans, drained and rinsed
½ cup parsley, chopped
1 cup mozzarella, shredded
Salt and black pepper to the taste

DIRECTIONS:

1. Heat a pan with half the oil over medium-high heat, add the meat and sauté for 5 minutes.
2. Grease a pan with the rest of the oil, add the browned chicken and the rest of the ingredients except the pasta and mozzarella.
3. Spread the paste over the entire surface and mix gently.
4. Sprinkle the mozzarella and bake at 425° F for 25 minutes.
5. Divide the bake on plates and serve.
6. Enjoy!

NUTRITION:

calories: 195 | fat: 5g | protein: 11g | carbs: 12g | fiber: 3g | sodium: 573mg

249. Greek Chicken Rice

Prep time: 10 minutes | Cook time: 14 minutes | Serves: 6

INGREDIENTS:

4 1/2 chicken breasts, skinless, boned and cut into pieces
1/3 cup fresh parsley, chopped
1 1/2 zucchini, cut into slices
3 peppers, chopped
1 1/2 cup rice, rinsed and drained
2 1/4 cups chicken broth
1 1/2 tablespoon of oregano
4 1/2 tablespoons fresh lemon juice
1 1/2 tablespoon minced garlic
1 1/2 onion, diced
4 1/2 tablespoons olive oil

DIRECTIONS:

1. Add the oil to the inner pot of the Instant Pot and set the pot to sauté mode.
2. Add the onion and chicken and cook for 5 minutes.
3. Add the rice, oregano, lemon juice, garlic, broth, pepper and salt and mix well.
4. Seal the pot with the lid and cook over high heat for 4 minutes.
5. Once done, release the pressure using the quick release. Remove the lid.
6. Add the parsley, zucchini and peppers and mix well.
7. Seal the pot with the lid again and select manual and set the timer for 5 minutes.
8. Release the pressure using the quick release. Remove the cover.
9. Mix well and serve.
10. Enjoy!

NUTRITION:

calories: 500 | fat: 16g | protein: 38g | carbs: 48g | fiber: 3g | sodium: 573mg

250. Greek Lemon Chicken Kebabs

Prep time: 15 minutes | Cook time: 20 minutes | Serves: 4

INGREDIENTS:

1 cup extra-virgin olive oil, divided
1 large lemon, juiced
4 garlic cloves, minced
1 teaspoon za'atar seasoning
Salt and freshly ground black pepper, to taste
2 pound (454 g) boneless skinless chicken breasts, cut into 1 1/4-inch cubes
2 large red bell pepper, cut into 1 1/4-inch pieces
4 small zucchini (nearly 1 pound / 454 g), cut into rounds slightly under 1/2 inch thick
4 large shallots, diced into quarters
Tzatziki sauce, for serving

DIRECTIONS:

1. In a bowl, whisk together 1/2 cup of olive oil, lemon juice, garlic, za'atar, salt, and pepper.
2. Put the chicken in a medium bowl and pour the olive oil mixture over the chicken. Press the chicken into the marinade. Cover and refrigerate for 45 minutes. While the chicken marinates, soak the wooden skewers in water for 30 minutes.
3. Drizzle and toss the pepper, zucchini, and shallots with the remaining 2½ tablespoons of olive oil and season lightly with salt.
4. Preheat the oven to 500°F (260°C) and put a baking sheet in the oven to heat.
5. On each skewer, thread a red bell pepper, zucchini, shallot and 2 chicken pieces and repeat twice. Put the kebabs onto the hot baking sheet and cook for 7 to 9 minutes, or until the chicken is cooked through. Rotate once halfway through cooking. Serve the kebabs warm with the tzatziki sauce.
6. Enjoy!

NUTRITION:

calories: 825 | fat: 59g | protein: 51g | carbs: 31g | fiber: 5g | sodium: 379mg

251. Pesto Chicken Mix

Prep time: 10 minutes | Cook time: 40 minutes | Serves: 6

INGREDIENTS:

6 halves of chicken breast, skinless and boneless
4 1/2 tomatoes, diced
1 1/2 cup mozzarella, shredded
3/4 cup of basil pesto
A pinch of salt and black pepper
Cooking spray

DIRECTIONS:

1. Grease a baking sheet lined with baking paper with cooking spray.
2. In a bowl, mix chicken with salt, pepper and pesto and rub in well.
3. Place the chicken on the baking sheet, top with the tomatoes and shredded mozzarella and bake at 400° F for 40 minutes.
4. Divide the mix among plates and serve with a side salad.
5. Enjoy!

NUTRITION:

calories: 341 | fat: 20g | protein: 32g | carbs: 4g | fiber: 1g | sodium: 379mg

252. Bean Rice with Chicken Packed

Prep time: 10 minutes | Cook time: 15 minutes | Serves: 4

INGREDIENTS:

2/3-pound chicken breasts, skinless, boned and cut into pieces
9 1/3 ounces cannellini beans, rinsed and drained
2 2/3 cups chicken broth
1 1/3 cups brown rice
2/3 tablespoon Italian seasoning
2/3 small onion, chopped
2/3 tablespoon garlic, chopped
2/3 tablespoon olive oil
Pepper Salt

DIRECTIONS:

1. Add the oil to the inner pot of the Instant Pot and set the pot to sauté mode.
2. Add the garlic and onion and sauté for 3 minutes.
3. Add the remaining Ingredients and mix everything well.
4. Seal the pot with a lid and select manual and set the timer for 12 minutes.
5. Once done, release the pressure using the quick release. Remove the lid.
6. Mix well and serve.
7. Enjoy!

NUTRITION:

calories: 494 | fat: 11g | protein: 34g | carbs: 61g | fiber: 1g | sodium: 379mg

253. Spatchcock Chicken

Prep time: 20 minutes | Cook time: 45 minutes | Serves: 4

INGREDIENTS:

1/3 cup extra-virgin olive oil, divided
2/3 (3- to 4-pound / 1.4- to 1.8-kg)

roasting chicken
5 1/3 garlic cloves, roughly chopped
1 1/3 to 4 tablespoons chopped fresh rosemary
1 1/3 teaspoons salt, divided
2/3 teaspoon freshly ground black pepper, divided
1 1/3 lemons, thinly sliced

DIRECTIONS:

1. Preheat oven to 400°F | 200°C | Fan 180°C.
2. Pour 2 tablespoons olive oil in the bottom of a 9-by-13-inch baking dish or rimmed baking sheet and swirl to coat the bottom.
3. To spatchcock the bird, place the whole chicken breast-side down on a large work surface. Using a very sharp knife, cut along the backbone, starting at the tail end and working your way up to the neck. Pull apart the two sides, opening up the chicken. Flip it over, breast-side up, pressing down with your hands to flatten the bird. Transfer to the prepared baking dish.
4. Loosen the skin over the breasts and thighs by cutting a small incision and sticking one or two fingers inside to pull the skin away from the meat without removing it.
5. To prepare the filling, in a small bowl, combine ¼ cup olive oil, garlic, rosemary, 1 teaspoon salt, and ½ teaspoon pepper and whisk together.
6. Rub the garlic-herb oil evenly under the skin of each breast and each thigh. Add the lemon slices evenly to the same areas.
7. Whisk together the remaining 2 tablespoons olive oil, 1 teaspoon salt, and ½ teaspoon pepper and rub over the outside of the chicken.
8. Place in the oven, uncovered, and roast for 45 minutes, or until cooked through and golden brown. 9.Allow to rest 5 minutes before carving to serve.
9. Enjoy!

NUTRITION:

calories: 435 | fat: 34g | protein: 28g | carbs: 2g | fiber: 0g | sodium: 879mg

254. Paprika Chicken Mix

Prep time: 10 minutes | Cook time: 15 minutes | Serves: 6

INGREDIENTS:

3 cups of pineapple, peeled and diced
3 tablespoons of olive oil
1 1/2 tablespoon of smoked paprika
3 pounds of chicken breasts, skinless,
boned and diced
A pinch of salt and black pepper
1 1/2 tablespoon chives, chopped

DIRECTIONS:

1. Heat a skillet with oil over medium-high heat, add chicken, salt and pepper and brown for 4 minutes on each side.
2. Add the rest of the Shopping List, stir, cook for another 7 minutes, divide among plates and serve with a side salad.
3. Enjoy!

NUTRITION:

calories: 4264 | fat: 13g | protein: 15g | carbs: 25g | fiber: 8g | sodium: 879mg

255. Chicken with Tarragon Pasta

Prep time: 15 minutes | Cook time: 15 minutes | Serves: 4

INGREDIENTS:

4 tablespoons olive oil, divided
1 medium onion, minced
8 ounces (113 g) baby bella (cremini) mushrooms, sliced
4 small garlic cloves, minced
16 ounces (227 g) chicken cutlets
4 teaspoons tomato paste
4 teaspoons dried tarragon
4 cups low-sodium chicken stock
12 ounces (170 g) pappardelle pasta
1/2 cup plain full-fat Greek yogurt
Salt, to taste
Freshly ground black pepper, to taste

DIRECTIONS:

1. Heat 1 tablespoon of the olive oil in a sauté pan over medium-high heat. Add the onion and mushrooms and sauté for 5 minutes. Add the garlic and cook for 1 minute more.
2. Move the vegetables to the edges of the pan and add the remaining 1 tablespoon of olive oil to the center of the pan. Place the cutlets in the center and let them cook for about 3 minutes, or until they lift up easily and are golden brown on the bottom.
3. Flip the chicken and cook for another 3 minutes.
4. Mix in the tomato paste and tarragon. Add the chicken stock and stir well to combine everything. Bring the stock to a boil.
5. Add the pappardelle. Break up the pasta if needed to fit into the pan. Stir the noodles so they don't stick to the bottom of the pan.
6. Cover the sauté pan and reduce the heat to medium-low. Let the chicken and noodles simmer for 15 minutes, stirring occasionally, until the pasta is cooked and the liquid is mostly absorbed. If the liquid absorbs too quickly and the pasta isn't cooked, add more water or chicken stock, about ¼ cup at a time as needed.
7. Remove the pan from the heat.
8. Stir 2 tablespoons of the hot liquid from the pan into the yogurt. Pour the tempered yogurt into the pan and stir well to mix it into the sauce. Season with salt and pepper.
9. The sauce will tighten up as it cools, so if it seems too thick, add a few tablespoons of water.
10. Enjoy!

NUTRITION:

calories: 556 | fat: 17g | protein: 42g | carbs: 56g | fiber: 1g | sodium: 190mg

256. Moroccan Chicken Meatballs

Prep time: 10 minutes | Cook time: 10 minutes | Serves: 6

INGREDIENTS:

3 large shallots, diced
3 tablespoons finely chopped parsley
3 teaspoons paprika
1 1/2 teaspoon ground cumin
3/4 teaspoon ground coriander
3/4 teaspoon garlic powder
3/4 teaspoon salt
3/4 teaspoon freshly ground black pepper
1/4 teaspoon ground cardamom
1 1/2-pound (454 g) ground chicken
3/4 cup all-purpose flour, to coat
1/3 cup olive oil, divided

DIRECTIONS:

1. In a bowl, combine the shallots, parsley, paprika, cumin, coriander, garlic powder, salt, pepper, and cardamom. Mix well.
2. Add the chicken to the spice mixture and mix well. Form into 1-inch balls flattened to about ½-inch thickness.
3. Put the flour in a bowl for dredging. Dip the balls into the flour until coated.
4. Pour enough oil to cover the bottom of a sauté pan or skillet and heat over medium heat. Working in batches, cook the meatballs, turning frequently, for 2 to 3 minutes on each side, until they are cooked through. Add more oil between batches as needed. Serve in a pita, topped with lettuce dressed with Creamy Yogurt Dressing.
5. Enjoy!

NUTRITION:

calories: 405 | fat: 26g | protein: 24g | carbs: 20g | fiber: 1g | sodium: 387mg

257. Chicken Breasts

Prep time: 10 minutes | Cook time: 12 minutes | Serves: 6

INGREDIENTS:

4 1/2 chicken breasts, skinless and boneless
1 1/2 tablespoon basil pesto
1-1/2 tablespoon of cornstarch
1/3 cup roasted red peppers, chopped
1/2 cup heavy cream
1 1/2 teaspoon of Italian seasoning
1 1/2 teaspoon of minced garlic
1 1/2 cup of chicken broth
PepperHalls

DIRECTIONS:

1. Add the chicken to the Instant Pot. Season the chicken with Italian seasoning, pepper and salt. Sprinkle with the garlic.
2. Pour the broth over the chicken. Seal the pot with a lid and cook over high heat for 8 minutes.
3. Once done, let the pressure release naturally for 5 minutes then release the rest using the quick release. Remove the lid.
4. Transfer the chicken to a plate and clean the Instant Pot.
5. Set the Instant Pot to sauté mode. Add the heavy cream, pesto, cornstarch and red pepper to the pot and stir well and cook for 3-4 minutes.
6. Return the chicken to the pot and coat well with the sauce.
7. Enjoy!

NUTRITION:

calories: 341 | fat: 15g | protein: 43g | carbs: 4g | fiber: 1g | sodium: 387mg

258. Yogurt-Marinated Chicken

Prep time: 15 minutes | Cook time: 30 minutes | Serves: 4

INGREDIENTS:

1 cup plain Greek yogurt
6 garlic cloves, minced
4 tablespoons minced fresh oregano (or
1 tablespoon dried oregano)
Zest of 1 lemon
2 tablespoon olive oil

1 teaspoon salt
4 (4-ounce / 113-g) boneless, skinless chicken breasts

DIRECTIONS:

1. In a medium bowl, add the yogurt, garlic, oregano, lemon zest, olive oil, and salt and stir to combine. If the yogurt is very thick, you may need to add a few tablespoons of water or a squeeze of lemon juice to thin it a bit.
2. Add the chicken to the bowl and toss it in the marinade to coat it well. Cover and refrigerate the chicken for at least 30 minutes or up to overnight.
3. Preheat the oven to 350°F (180°C) and set the rack to the middle position.
4. Place the chicken in a baking dish and roast for 30 minutes, or until chicken reaches an internal temperature of 165°F (74°C).
5. Enjoy!

NUTRITION:

calories: 255 | fat: 13g | protein: 29g | carbs: 8g | fiber: 2g | sodium: 694mg

259. Stuffed Chicken Breasts

Prep time: 10 minutes | Cook time: 20 minutes | Serves: 6

INGREDIENTS:

1/3 cup cooked brown rice
1 1/2 teaspoon shawarma seasoning
6 (6-ounce / 170-g) boneless skinless chicken breasts
1 1/2 tablespoon harissa
4 1/2 tablespoons extra-virgin olive oil, divided
Salt and freshly ground black pepper, to taste
6 small dried apricots, halved
1/3 cup crumbled feta
1 1/2 tablespoon chopped fresh parsley

DIRECTIONS:

1. Preheat the oven to 375°F (190°C).
2. In a medium bowl, mix the rice and shawarma seasoning and set aside.
3. Butterfly the chicken breasts by slicing them almost in half, starting at the thickest part and folding them open like a book.
4. In a small bowl, mix the harissa with 1 tablespoon of olive oil. Brush the chicken with the harissa oil and season with salt and pepper. The harissa adds a nice heat, so feel free to add a thicker coating for more spice.
5. Onto one side of each chicken breast, spoon 1 to 2 tablespoons of rice, then layer 2 apricot halves in each breast. Divide the feta between the chicken breasts and fold the other side over the filling to close.
6. In an oven-safe sauté pan or skillet, heat the remaining 2 tablespoons of olive oil and sear the breast for 2 minutes on each side, then place the pan into the oven for 15 minutes, or until fully cooked and juices run clear. Serve, garnished with parsley.
7. Enjoy!

NUTRITION:

calories: 321 | fat: 17g | protein: 37g | carbs: 8g | fiber: 1g | sodium: 410mg

260. Chicken with Vegetable Pesto

Prep time: 10 minutes | Cook time: 25 minutes | Serves: 6

INGREDIENTS:

1-1/2 pounds chicken thighs, skinless, boned and cut into pieces
3/4 cup chicken broth
1/3 cup fresh parsley, chopped
3 cups cherry tomatoes, halved
1 1/2 cup basil pesto
1 1/8 lb asparagus, trimmed and cut in half
1 cup sun-dried tomatoes, drained and chopped
3 tablespoons olive oil

DIRECTIONS:

1. Add the oil to the inner pot of the Instant Pot and set the pot to sauté mode.
2. Add the chicken and sauté for 5 minutes.
3. Add remaining Shopping List except tomatoes and mix well.
4. Seal the pot with a lid and select manual and set the timer for 15 minutes.
5. Once done, release the pressure using the quick release. Remove the lid.
6. Add the tomatoes and mix well. Once again seal the pot and select manual and set the timer for 5 minutes.
7. Release the pressure using the quick release. Remove the cover.
8. Mix well and serve.
9. Enjoy!

NUTRITION:

calories: 459 | fat: 20g | protein: 9g | carbs: 14g | fiber: 1g | sodium: 410mg

261. Lemon Chicken Thighs

Prep time: 15 minutes | Cook time: 45 minutes | Serves: 6

INGREDIENTS:

9 tablespoons extra-virgin olive oil, divided
6 large garlic cloves, crushed
1 1/2 tablespoon dried basil
1 1/2 tablespoon dried parsley
1 1/2 tablespoon salt
3/4 tablespoon thyme
6 skin-on, bone-in chicken thighs
9 medium portobello mushrooms, quartered
1 1/2 large zucchini, sliced
1 1/2 large carrot, thinly sliced
1/4 cup pitted Kalamata olives
12 pieces sun-dried tomatoes (optional)
3/4 cup dry white wine
1 1/2 lemon, sliced

DIRECTIONS:

1. In a small bowl, combine 4 tablespoons of olive oil, the garlic cloves, basil, parsley, salt, and thyme. Store half of the marinade in a jar and, in a bowl, combine the remaining half to marinate the chicken thighs for about 30 minutes.
2. Preheat the oven to 425°F (220°C).
3. In a large skillet or oven-safe pan, heat the remaining 2 tablespoons of olive oil over medium-high heat. Sear the chicken for 3 to 5 minutes on each side until golden brown, and set aside.
4. In the same pan, sauté portobello mushrooms, zucchini, and carrot for about 5 minutes, or until lightly browned.
5. Add the chicken thighs, olives, and sun-dried tomatoes (if using). Pour the wine over the chicken thighs.
6. Cover the pan and cook for about 10 minutes over medium-low heat.
7. Uncover the pan and transfer it to the oven. Cook for 15 more minutes, or until the chicken skin is crispy and the juices run clear. Top with lemon slices.
8. Enjoy!

NUTRITION:

calories: 544 | fat: 41g | protein: 28g | carbs: 20g | fiber: 11g | sodium: 1848mg

262. Chicken Skewers with Vegetables

Prep time: 30 minutes | Cook time: 25 minutes | Serves: 6

INGREDIENTS:

1/3 cup olive oil
1 1/2 teaspoon garlic powder
1 1/2 teaspoon onion powder
1 1/2 teaspoon ground cumin
3/4 teaspoon dried oregano
3/4 teaspoon dried basil
1/3 cup lemon juice
1 1/2 tablespoon apple cider vinegar
Olive oil cooking spray
1 1/2 pound (454 g) boneless skinless chicken thighs, cut into 1-inch pieces
1 1/2 red bell pepper, cut into 1-inch pieces
1 1/2 red onion, cut into 1-inch pieces
1 1/2 zucchini, cut into 1-inch pieces
18 cherry tomatoes

DIRECTIONS:

1. In a large bowl, mix together the olive oil, garlic powder, onion powder, cumin, oregano, basil, lemon juice, and apple cider vinegar.
2. Spray six skewers with olive oil cooking spray.
3. On each skewer, slide on a piece of chicken, then a piece of bell pepper, onion, zucchini, and finally a tomato and then repeat. Each skewer should have at least two pieces of each item.
4. Once all of the skewers are prepared, place them in a 9-by-13-inch baking dish and pour the olive oil marinade over the top of the skewers. Turn each skewer so that all sides of the chicken and vegetables are coated.
5. Cover the dish with plastic wrap and place it in the refrigerator for 30 minutes.
6. After 30 minutes, preheat the air fryer to 380°F (193°C). (If using a grill attachment, make sure it is inside the air fryer during preheating.)
7. Remove the skewers from the marinade and lay them in a single layer in the air fryer basket. If the air fryer has a grill attachment, you can also lay them on this instead.
8. Cook for 10 minutes. Rotate the kebabs, then cook them for 15 minutes more.
9. Remove the skewers from the air fryer and let them rest for 5 minutes before serving.
8. Enjoy!

NUTRITION:

calories: 304 | fat: 17g | protein: 27g | carbs: 10g | fiber: 3g | sodium: 62mg

263. Duck and Tomato Sauce

Prep time: 10 minutes | Cook time: 120 minutes | Serves: 6

INGREDIENTS:

6 duck legs
3 yellow onions, sliced 4 cloves of garlic, minced
1/3 cup parsley, chopped
A pinch of salt and black pepper
1 1/2 teaspoon of Herbes de Provence
1 1/2 cup of tomato sauce
3 cups of black olives, pitted and sliced

DIRECTIONS:

1. In a baking dish, combine the duck legs with the onions, garlic and the rest of the Shopping List, place in the oven and bake at 370ºF for 2 hours.
2. Divide the mix among the plates and serve.
3. Enjoy!

NUTRITION:

calories: 300 | fat: 13g | protein: 15g | carbs: 16g | fiber: 3g | sodium: 62mg

264. Chicken Salad

Prep time: 10 minutes | Cook time: 0 minutes | Serves: 6

INGREDIENTS:

1 1/3 cup of rotisserie chicken, skinless, boneless and cubed
2/3 cup sun-dried tomatoes, chopped
2/3 cup marinated artichoke hearts, drained and chopped
1 1/3 cucumber, chopped
1/2 cup of kalamata olives, pitted and sliced
2 2/3 cups of arugula
1/3 cup parsley, chopped
1 1/3 avocado, peeled, pitted and cut into cubes
2/3 cup feta cheese, crumbled
5 1/3 tablespoons of red wine vinegar
2 2/3 tablespoons of Dijon mustard
1 1/3 tablespoon dried basil
1 1/3 clove garlic, minced
2 2/3 teaspoons honey
2/3 cup olive oil
Salt and black pepper to taste
4 tablespoons of lemon juice

DIRECTIONS:

1. In a salad bowl, mix the chicken with the tomatoes, artichokes, cucumber, olives, arugula, parsley and avocado and toss.
2. In another bowl, mix vinegar with mustard and remaining Shopping List except cheese, whisk well, add to salad and toss.
3. Sprinkle cheese on top and serve.
4. Enjoy!

NUTRITION:

calories: 326 | fat: 21g | protein: 8g | carbs: 24g | fiber: 1g | sodium: 62mg

265. Spicy Chicken

Prep time: 10 minutes | Cook time: 5 minutes | Serves: 6

INGREDIENTS:

1 1/2 lb tender, skinless chicken, boneless and cut into pieces
15 oz frozen vegetables
1/2 cup of flavorful Italian seasoning
3/4 teaspoon of Italian seasoning
1 1/2 cup of fried onions
1 cups of rice
1 1/2 cup of chicken broth

DIRECTIONS:

1. Add all Shopping List except the vegetables to the Instant Pot.
2. Meanwhile, cook frozen vegetables in the microwave according to package instructions.
3. Seal the pot with the lid and cook over high heat for 5 minutes.
4. Once done, let the pressure release naturally for 10 minutes then release the rest using the quick release. Remove the lid.
5. Add the cooked vegetables and mix well.
6. Enjoy!

NUTRITION:

calories: 482 | fat: 15g | protein: 38g | carbs: 40g | fiber: 1g | sodium: 62mg

266. Chicken and Olives

Prep time: 10 minutes | Cook time: 15 minutes | Serves: 6

INGREDIENTS:

6 chicken breasts, skinless and boneless
3 tablespoons minced garlic
1 1/2 tablespoon of dried oregano
Salt and black pepper to taste
3 tablespoons olive oil
3/4 cup chicken broth
Juice of 1 lemon
1 1/2 cup red onion, chopped
2 1/4 cups tomatoes, diced
1/3 cup green olives, pitted and sliced
A handful of parsley, chopped

DIRECTIONS:

1. Heat a skillet with the oil over medium-high heat, add the chicken, garlic, salt and pepper and brown for 2 minutes on each side.
2. Add the rest of the Shopping List, stir, bring the mixture to a simmer and cook over medium heat for 13 minutes.
3. Divide the mix among the plates and serve.
4. Enjoy!

NUTRITION:

calories: 135 | fat: 5g | protein: 38g | carbs: 12g | fiber: 3g | sodium: 62mg

267. Chili Chicken

Prep time: 10 minutes | Cook time: 18 minutes | Serves: 6

INGREDIENTS:

3 pounds chicken thighs, skinless and boneless
3 tablespoons olive oil
3 cups yellow onion, chopped
1 1/2 teaspoon onion powder
1 1/2 tablespoon of smoked paprika
1 1/2 teaspoon of chili pepper
3/4 teaspoon coriander seeds, ground
3 teaspoons oregano, dried
3 tablespoons of parsley flakes
45 ounces of canned tomatoes, chopped
3/4 cup black olives, pitted and halved

DIRECTIONS:

1. Set the Instant Pot to Sauté mode, add the oil, heat it, add the onion, onion powder and the rest of the Shopping List except the tomatoes, olives and chicken, stir and sauté for 10 minutes.
2. Add the chicken, tomatoes and olives, put the lid on and cook on High for 8 minutes.
3. Release pressure naturally 10 minutes, divide mixture into bowls and serve.
4. Enjoy!

NUTRITION:

calories: 153 | fat: 8g | protein: 12g | carbs: 9g | fiber: 2g | sodium: 62mg

268. Brown Rice with Chicken and Shallots

Prep time: 10 minutes | Cook time: 30 minutes | Serves: 6

INGREDIENTS:

1-1/2 cups brown rice
4 1/2 cups chicken broth
3 tablespoons of balsamic vinegar
1 1/2-pound chicken breast, boneless, skinless and diced
9 shallots, chopped
Salt and black pepper to taste
1 1/2 tablespoon sweet paprika
3 tablespoons of avocado oil

DIRECTIONS:

1. Heat a skillet with the oil over medium-high heat, add the chicken and sauté for 5 minutes.
2. Add the shallots and sauté for another 5 minutes.
3. Add the rice and the rest of the Shopping List, bring to a boil and cook over medium heat for 20 minutes.
4. Stir the mix, divide everything between plates and serve.
5. Enjoy!

NUTRITION:

calories: 300 | fat: 9g | protein: 23g | carbs: 18g | fiber: 11g | sodium: 62mg

269. Turkey with Walnuts

Prep time: 10 minutes | Cook time: 60 minutes | Serves: 6

INGREDIENTS:

1 1/2 turkey breast, skinless, boned and cut into slices
1/3 cup of chicken broth
1 1/2 tablespoon walnuts, chopped
1 1/2 red onion, chopped
Salt and black pepper to taste
3 tablespoons olive oil
6 peaches, pitted and cut into quarters
1 1/2 tablespoon coriander, chopped

DIRECTIONS:

1. In a pan greased with oil, combine the turkey and onion and the rest of the Shopping List except the cilantro, place in the oven and bake at 390º F for 1 hour.
2. Divide mixture among plates, sprinkle cilantro on top and serve.
3. Enjoy!

NUTRITION:

calories: 500 | fat: 14g | protein: 10g | carbs: 15g | fiber: 3g | sodium: 62mg

270. Chicken with Mushrooms

Prep time: 10 minutes | Cook time: 22 minutes | Serves: 4

INGREDIENTS:

1 1/3 lbs chicken breasts, skinless and boneless
1/3 cup heavy cream
1/4 cup of water
1/2 lb mushrooms, sliced
2 tbsp olive oil
2/3 teaspoon of Italian seasoning

DIRECTIONS:
1. Add the oil to the inner pot of the Instant Pot and set the pot to sauté mode.
2. Season chicken with Italian seasoning, pepper and salt.
3. Add the chicken to the pot and sauté for 5 minutes. Remove the chicken from the pot and set aside.
4. Add mushrooms and sauté for 5 minutes or until mushrooms are lightly browned.
5. Return the chicken to the pot. Add the water and mix well.
6. Seal the pot with a lid and select manual and set the timer for 12 minutes.
7. Once done, release the pressure using the quick release. Remove the lid.
8. Remove the chicken from the pot and place on a plate.
9. Set the pot to sauté mode. Add the heavy cream, stir well and cook for 5 minutes.
10. Pour the mushroom sauce over the chicken and serve.
11. Enjoy!

NUTRITION:
calories: 396 | fat: 22g | protein: 45g | carbs: 2g | fiber: 3g | sodium: 62mg

271. Chicken with Artichokes
Prep time: 10 minutes | Cook time: 20 minutes | Serves: 6

INGREDIENTS:
3 pounds chicken breast, skinless, boneless and sliced
A pinch of salt and black pepper
6 tablespoons of olive oil
12 ounces canned roasted artichoke hearts, drained
9 ounces sun-dried tomatoes, chopped
4 1/2 tablespoons capers, drained
3 tablespoons lemon juice

DIRECTIONS:
1. Heat a skillet with half the oil over medium-high heat, add artichokes and remaining Shopping List except chicken, stir and sauté for 10 minutes.
2. Transfer the mixture to a bowl, reheat the skillet with the rest of the oil over medium-high heat, add the meat and cook for 4 minutes on each side.
3. Return the vegetable mix to the skillet, toss, cook everything for another 2-3 minutes, divide among plates and serve.
4. Enjoy!

NUTRITION:
calories: 552 | fat: 28g | protein: 43g | carbs: 33g | fiber: 6g | sodium: 62mg

272. Chicken with Feta
Prep time: 10 minutes | Cook time: 25 minutes | Serves: 6

INGREDIENTS:
1 1/2 chicken breast, skinless, boned and cut into strips
1 1/2 red cabbage, shredded
3 tablespoons of olive oil
Salt and black pepper to taste
3 tablespoons of balsamic vinegar
2 1/4 cups tomatoes, diced
1 1/2 tablespoon chives, chopped
1/3 cup feta cheese, crumbled

DIRECTIONS:
1. Heat a skillet with the oil over medium-high heat, add the chicken and sauté for 5 minutes.
2. Add the rest of the Shopping List except the cheese, and cook over medium heat for 20 minutes, stirring often.
3. Add cheese, stir, divide between plates and serve.
4. Enjoy!

NUTRITION:
calories: 277 | fat: 15g | protein: 14g | carbs: 14g | fiber: 8g | sodium: 62mg

273. Creamy Chicken and Grapes
Prep time: 10 minutes | Cook time: 20 minutes | Serves: 6

INGREDIENTS:
1,5 kg of chicken breasts, skinned, boned and diced
3/4 cup almonds, chopped
1 1/2 cup green grapes, seedless and halved
3 tablespoons olive oil
Salt and black pepper to taste
1 1/2 cup heavy cream
1 1/2 tablespoon chives, chopped

DIRECTIONS:
1. Heat a skillet with oil over medium-high heat, add the chicken and brown for 3 minutes on each side.
2. Add the grapes and the rest of the Shopping List, bring to a boil and cook over medium heat for another 15 minutes.
3. Divide everything into bowls and serve.
4. Enjoy!

NUTRITION:
calories: 254 | fat: 19g | protein: 14g | carbs: 14g | fiber: 8g | sodium: 62mg

274. Baked chicken
Prep time: 10 minutes | Cook time: 30 minutes | Serves: 6

INGREDIENTS:
1-1/2 pounds of skinless chicken thighs, boned and diced
3 cloves of garlic, minced
1 1/2 tablespoon oregano, chopped
3 tablespoons olive oil
1 1/2 tablespoon of red wine vinegar
3/4 cup canned artichokes, drained and chopped
1 1/2 red onion, sliced
1 1/2 pound of whole wheat fusilli pasta, cooked
3/4 cup canned white beans, drained and rinsed
3/4 cup parsley, chopped
1 1/2 cup mozzarella, shredded
Salt and black pepper to taste

DIRECTIONS:
1. Heat a skillet with half of the oil over medium-high heat, add the meat and brown it for 5 minutes.
2. Grease a baking dish with the rest of the oil, add the browned chicken and the rest of the Shopping List except the pasta and mozzarella.
3. Spread the dough over the entire surface and toss gently.
4. Sprinkle mozzarella cheese on top and bake at 425° F for 25 minutes.
5. Divide the cake among the plates and serve.
6. Enjoy!

NUTRITION:
calories: 195 | fat: 5g | protein: 11g | carbs: 12g | fiber: 3g | sodium: 62mg

275. Chicken Kebab
Prep time: 10 minutes | Cook time: 20 minutes | Serves: 6

INGREDIENTS:
3 chicken breasts, skinless, boned and cut into cubes
1 1/2 red bell pepper, cut into squares
1 1/2 red onion, coarsely chopped into squares
3 teaspoons of sweet paprika
1 1/2 teaspoon nutmeg, ground
1 1/2 teaspoon Italian seasoning
1/3 teaspoon of smoked paprika
A pinch of salt and black pepper
1/3 teaspoon cardamom, ground
Juice of 1 lemon
4 1/2 garlic cloves, minced
3/4 cup olive oil

DIRECTIONS:
1. In a bowl, combine the chicken with the onion, bell pepper and other Shopping List, mix well, cover the bowl and refrigerate for 30 minutes.
2. Assemble skewers with chicken, peppers and onions, place on preheated grill and cook over medium heat for 8 minutes on each side.
3. Divide skewers among plates and serve with a side salad.
4. Enjoy!

NUTRITION:
calories: 262 | fat: 14g | protein: 20g | carbs: 14g | fiber: 2g | sodium: 62mg

276. Chicken with Rice
Prep time: 10 minutes | Cook time: 25 minutes | Serves: 6

INGREDIENTS:
1 1/2-pound chicken breasts, skinless and boneless
1 1/2 tablespoon olive oil
1 1/2 cup onion, diced
1 1/2 teaspoon minced garlic
6 carrots, peeled and sliced
3 tablespoons of Mediterranean spice mix
3 cups of brown rice, rinsed
3 cups of chicken broth Pepper

DIRECTIONS:
1. Add the oil to the inner pot of the Instant Pot and set the pot to sauté mode.
2. Add the garlic and onion and sauté until the onion is softened.
3. Add the broth, carrot, rice and Mediterranean spice mix and mix well.
4. Place chicken on top of rice mixture and season with pepper and salt. Do not stir.
5. Seal the pot with a lid and select manual and set the timer for 20 minutes.

6. Once done, let the pressure release naturally for 10 minutes then release the rest using the quick release. Remove the lid.
7. Remove the chicken from the pot and shred it with a fork.
8. Return the shredded chicken to the pot and mix well.
9. Enjoy!

NUTRITION:

calories: 612 | fat: 12g | protein: 41g | carbs: 81g | fiber: 2g | sodium: 62mg

277. Turkey Chunks

Prep time: 10 minutes | Cook time: 60 minutes | Serves: 6

INGREDIENTS:

1 1/2 cup apricots, pitted and diced
1/3 cup of chicken broth
1 1/2 large turkey breast, skinless, boned and cut into cubes
1 1/2 tablespoon balsamic vinegar
1 1/2 sweet onion, chopped
1/3 teaspoon red pepper flakes
3 tablespoons olive oil
Salt and black pepper to taste
3 tablespoons chopped parsley

DIRECTIONS:

1. Heat a skillet with the oil over medium-high heat, add the turkey and brown for 3 minutes on each side.
2. Add the onion, pepper flakes and vinegar and cook for another 5 minutes.
3. Add the remaining Shopping List except the parsley, stir, place the pan in the oven and bake at 380° F for 50 minutes.
4. Divide mixture among plates and serve with parsley sprinkled on top.
5. Enjoy!

NUTRITION:

calories: 292 | fat: 16g | protein: 14g | carbs: 24g | fiber: 8g | sodium: 62mg

278. Creamy chicken and mushrooms

Prep time: 10 minutes | Cook time: 30 minutes | Serves: 6

INGREDIENTS:

1 1/2 red onion, chopped
1 1/2 tablespoon olive oil
3 garlic cloves, minced
3 carrots, minced
Salt and black pepper to taste
1 1/2 tablespoon thyme, chopped
1 1/2 and 1/2 cups chicken broth
3/4 pound of Bella mushrooms, sliced
1 1/2 cup heavy cream
3 chicken breasts, skinless, boned and diced
3 tablespoons chives, chopped
3 tablespoons chopped parsley

DIRECTIONS:

1. Heat a Dutch oven with the oil over medium-high heat, add the onion and garlic and sauté for 5 minutes.
2. Add the chicken and mushrooms and sauté for another 10 minutes.
3. Add the rest of the Shopping List except the chives and parsley, bring to a boil and cook over medium heat for 15 minutes.
4. Add the chives and parsley, divide the mixture among the plates and serve.
5. Enjoy!

NUTRITION:

calories: 275 | fat: 11g | protein: 23g | carbs: 26g | fiber: 10g | sodium: 62mg

279. Chicken curry, artichokes and olives

Prep time: 10 minutes | Cook time: 7 hours | Serves: 4

INGREDIENTS:

2/3-pound chicken breasts, boneless, skinless and diced
8 ounces canned artichoke hearts, drained
2/3 cup chicken broth
2/3 chopped red onion
2/3 tablespoon of white wine vinegar
2/3 cup kalamata olives, pitted and chopped
2/3 tablespoon curry powder
1 1/3 tablespoons of dried basil
Salt and black pepper to taste
1/8 cup rosemary, chopped

DIRECTIONS:

1. In your slow cooker, combine the chicken with the artichokes, olives and the rest of the Shopping List, put the lid on and cook on low for 7 hours.
2. Divide the mix among plates and serve hot.
3. Enjoy!

NUTRITION:

calories: 275 | fat: 11g | protein: 18g | carbs: 19g | fiber: 7g | sodium: 62mg

280. Chicken with chives

Prep time: 10 minutes | Cook time: 30 minutes | Serves: 6

INGREDIENTS:

1 1/2 chicken breast, skinless, boned and cut into cubes
Salt and black pepper to taste
3 tablespoons olive oil
1 1/2 cup chicken broth
3/4 cup of tomato sauce
3/4-pound red radishes, diced
3 tablespoons chives, chopped

DIRECTIONS:

1. Heat a Dutch oven with the oil over medium-high heat, add the chicken and brown for 4 minutes on each side.
2. Add the rest of the Shopping List except the chives, bring to a boil and cook over medium heat for 20 minutes.
3. Divide the mixture among plates, sprinkle with chives and serve.
4. Enjoy!

NUTRITION:

calories: 277 | fat: 11g | protein: 33g | carbs: 20g | fiber: 9g | sodium: 62mg

281. Turkey, leeks and carrots

Prep time: 10 minutes | Cook time: 60 minutes | Serves: 6

INGREDIENTS:

1 1/2 large turkey breast, skinless, boned and diced
3 tablespoons avocado oil
Salt and black pepper to taste
1 1/2 tablespoon sweet paprika
3/4 cup chicken broth
1 1/2 leek, sliced
1 1/2 carrot, sliced
1 1/2 yellow onion, chopped
1 1/2 tablespoon lemon juice
1 1/2 teaspoon cumin, ground
1 1/2 tablespoon basil, chopped

DIRECTIONS:

1. Heat a skillet with the oil over medium-high heat, add the turkey and brown for 4 minutes on each side.
2. Add the leeks, carrot and onion and sauté for another 5 minutes.
3. Add the rest of the Shopping List, bring to a boil and cook over medium heat for 40 minutes.
4. Divide the mix among the plates and serve.
5. Enjoy!

NUTRITION:

calories: 249 | fat: 10g | protein: 17g | carbs: 23g | fiber: 11g | sodium: 62mg

282. Chicken and caper mix

Prep time: 10 minutes | Cook time: 7 hours | Serves: 6

INGREDIENTS:

3 chicken breasts, skinless, boned and halved
3 cups canned tomatoes, crushed
3 cloves garlic, minced
1 1/2 yellow onion, minced
3 cups chicken broth
3 tablespoons capers, drained
1/3 cup rosemary, chopped
Salt and black pepper to taste

DIRECTIONS:

1. In your slow cooker, combine the chicken with the tomatoes, capers and the rest of the Shopping List, put the lid on and cook on Low for 7 hours.
2. Divide the mix among the plates and serve.
3. Enjoy!

NUTRITION:

calories: 292 | fat: 9g | protein: 36g | carbs: 25g | fiber: 11g | sodium: 62mg

283. Chicken with herbs

Prep time: 10 minutes | Cook time: 40 minutes | Serves: 6

INGREDIENTS:

1 1/2 chicken breast, skinless, boned and sliced
3 red onions, chopped
3 tablespoons of olive oil
3 cloves of garlic, minced
3/4 cup of chicken broth
1 1/2 teaspoon oregano, dried
1 1/2 teaspoon basil, dried
1 1/2 teaspoon of dried rosemary
3 cup canned tomatoes, chopped
Salt and black pepper to taste

DIRECTIONS:

1. Heat a saucepan with the oil over medium-high heat, add the chicken and brown for 4 minutes on each side.

2. Add the garlic and onions and sauté for another 5 minutes.
3. Add the rest of the Shopping List, bring to a boil and cook over medium heat for 25 minutes.
4. Divide everything among plates and serve.
5. Enjoy!

NUTRITION:

calories: 251 | fat: 11g | protein: 9g | carbs: 15g | fiber: 15g | sodium: 62mg

284. Chicken with lentils

Prep time: 10 minutes | Cook time: 1 Hour | Serves: 10

INGREDIENTS:

1 1/4 tablespoon of olive oil
2 1/2 celery stalks, chopped
1 1/4 red onion, chopped
2 1/2 tablespoons of tomato paste
2 1/2 cloves of garlic, minced
2/3 cup chicken broth
2 1/2 cups French lentils
1 1/4-pound chicken thighs, boneless and skinless
Salt and black pepper to taste
1 1/4 tablespoon coriander, chopped

DIRECTIONS:

1. Heat a Dutch oven with the oil over medium-high heat, add the onion and garlic and sauté for 2 minutes.
2. Add the chicken and brown for 3 minutes on each side.
3. Add the rest of the Shopping List except the cilantro, bring to a boil and cook over medium-low heat for 45 minutes.
4. Add the cilantro, stir, divide the mixture into bowls.
5. Serve when ready.

NUTRITION:

calories: 249 | fat: 9.7g | protein: 24.3g | carbs: 25.3g | fiber: 11.9g | sodium: 0mg

285. Cucumber mix with chicken

Prep time: 10 minutes | Cook time: 20 minutes | Serves: 6

INGREDIENTS:

6 chicken breasts, boneless, skinless and diced
3 cucumbers, diced
Salt and black pepper to taste
1 1/2 tablespoon of grated ginger
1 1/2 tablespoon chopped garlic
3 tablespoons of balsamic vinegar
4 1/2 tablespoons of olive oil
1/3 teaspoon of chili paste
3/4 cup of chicken broth
3/4 tablespoon of lime juice
1 1/2 tablespoon chives, chopped

DIRECTIONS:

1. Heat a skillet with oil over medium-high heat, add the chicken and brown for 3 minutes on each side.
2. Add the cucumbers, salt, pepper and the rest of the Shopping List except the chives, bring to a boil and cook over medium heat for 15 minutes.
3. Divide the mix among plates.
4. Serve with the chives scattered on top.

NUTRITION:

calories: 288 | fat: 9.5g | protein: 28.6g | carbs: 25.6g | fiber: 12.1g | sodium: 0mg

286. Creamy coriander chicken

Prep time: 10 minutes | Cook time: 55 minutes | Serves: 6

INGREDIENTS:

1 1/2 pounds chicken breasts, boneless, skinless and halved
3 tablespoons avocado oil
3/4 teaspoon hot paprika 1 cup chicken broth
1 1/2 tablespoon almonds, chopped
3 spring onions, chopped
3 garlic cloves, minced
1/3 cup heavy cream
A handful of cilantros, chopped
Salt and black pepper to taste

DIRECTIONS:

1. Grease a baking dish with oil, add the chicken, paprika and the rest of the Shopping List except the cilantro and heavy cream, toss, introduce into the oven and bake at 350°F | 180°C | Fan 160°C for 40 minutes.
2. Add the cream and cilantro, toss, cook for another 15 minutes.
3. Divide among plates and serve.

NUTRITION:

calories: 225 | fat: 8.9g | protein: 17.5g | carbs: 20.8g | fiber: 10.2g | sodium: 0mg

287. Chicken Breast

Prep time: 10 minutes | Cook time: 12 minutes | Serves: 8

INGREDIENTS:

2 pounds (680 g) boneless, skinless chicken breasts, cut into 8 pieces
1 1/3 carrot, halved
1 1/3 celery stalk, halved
2/3 onion, halved
2 2/3 garlic cloves, smashed
4 sprigs fresh thyme or rosemary
1 1/3 cup romesco sauce
2 2/3 tablespoons chopped fresh flat-leaf (Italian) parsley
1/3 teaspoon freshly ground black pepper

DIRECTIONS:

1. Put the chicken in a medium saucepan. Fill with water until there's about one inch of liquid above the chicken.
2. Add the carrot, celery, onion, garlic, and thyme.
3. Cover and bring it to a boil. Reduce the heat to low (keeping it covered), and cook for 12 to 15 minutes, or until the internal temperature of the chicken measures 165°F (74°C) on a meat thermometer and any juices run clear.
4. Remove the chicken from the water and let sit for 5 minutes.
5. When you're ready to serve, spread ¾ cup of romesco sauce on the bottom of a serving platter.
6. Arrange the chicken breasts on top, and drizzle with the remaining romesco sauce.
7. Sprinkle the tops with parsley and pepper and serve when ready.

NUTRITION:

calories: 270 | fat: 10g | protein: 13g | carbs: 31g | fiber: 2g | sodium: 647mg

288. Chicken parmigiana

Prep time: 10 minutes | Cook time: 25 minutes | Serves: 6

INGREDIENTS:

2 1/4 pounds chicken breasts, skinless, boneless and diced
1 1/2 tablespoon olive oil
1 1/2 tablespoon coriander, ground
1 1/2 teaspoon parsley flakes
3 garlic cloves, minced
1 1/2 cup heavy cream
Salt and black pepper to taste
1/3 cup Parmesan cheese, grated
1 1/2 tablespoon basil, chopped

DIRECTIONS:

1. Heat a skillet with oil over medium-high heat, add chicken, salt and pepper and cook for 3 minutes on each side.
2. Add the garlic and cook for 1 more minute.
3. Add the rest of the Shopping List except the parmesan cheese and basil, cook everything over medium heat for 20 minutes and divide among the plates.
4. Sprinkle the basil and Parmesan cheese over the top.
5. Enjoy!

NUTRITION:

calories: 249 | fat: 16.6g | protein: 25.3g | carbs: 24.5g | fiber: 7.5g | sodium: 647mg

289. Chicken Sausage with Farro

Prep time: 10 minutes | Cook time: 45 minutes | Serves: 4

INGREDIENTS:

2 tablespoon olive oil
1 medium onion, diced
1/2 cup julienned sun-dried tomatoes packed in olive oil and herbs
16 ounces (227 g) hot Italian chicken sausage, removed from the casing
1 1/2 cup farro
3 cups low-sodium chicken stock
4 cups loosely packed arugula
8 to 5 large fresh basil leaves, sliced thin
Salt, to taste

DIRECTIONS:

1. Heat the olive oil in a sauté pan over medium-high heat.
2. Add the onion and sauté for 5 minutes.
3. Add the sun-dried tomatoes and chicken sausage, stirring to break up the sausage. Cook for 7 minutes, or until the sausage is no longer pink.
4. Stir in the farro. Let it toast for 3 minutes, stirring occasionally.
5. Add the chicken stock and bring the mixture to a boil.
6. Cover the pan and reduce the heat to medium-low. Let it simmer for 30 minutes, or until the farro is tender.
7. Stir in the arugula and let it wilt slightly. Add the basil, and season with salt.
8. Serve when ready.

NUTRITION:

calories: 491 | fat: 18g | protein: 31g | carbs: 53g | fiber: 6g | sodium: 765mg

290. Chicken with Roasted Artichokes

Prep time: 5 minutes | Cook time: 20 minutes | Serves: 6

INGREDIENTS:

3 large lemons
4 1/2 tablespoons extra-virgin olive oil, divided
3/4 teaspoon kosher or sea salt
3 large artichokes
6 (6-ounce / 170-g) bone-in, skin-on chicken thighs

DIRECTIONS:

1. Put a large, rimmed baking sheet in the oven. Preheat oven to 450°F. | 230°C | Fan 210°C with the pan inside. Tear off four sheets of aluminum foil about 8-by-10 inches each; set aside.
2. Using a Microplane or citrus zester, zest 1 lemon into a large bowl. Halve both lemons and squeeze all the juice into the bowl with the zest. Whisk in 2 tablespoons of oil and the salt. Set aside.
3. Rinse the artichokes with cool water, and dry with a clean towel. Using a sharp knife, cut about 1½ inches off the tip of each artichoke. Cut about ¼ inch off each stem. Halve each artichoke lengthwise so each piece has equal amounts of stem. Immediately plunge the artichoke halves into the lemon juice and oil mixture (to prevent browning) and turn to coat on all sides. Lay one artichoke half flat-side down in the center of a sheet of aluminum foil, and close up loosely to make a foil packet. Repeat the process with the remaining three artichoke halves. Set the packets aside.
4. Put the chicken in the remaining lemon juice mixture and turn to coat.
5. Using oven mitts, carefully remove the hot baking sheet from the oven and pour on the remaining tablespoon of oil; tilt the pan to coat.
6. Carefully arrange the chicken, skin-side down, on the hot baking sheet. Place the artichoke packets, flat-side down, on the baking sheet as well. (Arrange the artichoke packets and chicken with space between them so air can circulate around them.)
7. Roast for 20 minutes, or until the internal temperature of the chicken measures 165°F (74°C) on a meat thermometer and any juices run clear.
8. Before serving, check the artichokes for doneness by pulling on a leaf. If it comes out easily, the artichoke is ready.
9. Serve when ready.

NUTRITION:

calories: 882 | fat: 79g | protein: 19g | carbs: 11g | fiber: 4g | sodium: 544mg

291. Chicken and sweet potatoes

Prep time: 10 minutes | Cook time: 40 minutes | Serves: 8

INGREDIENTS:

2 2/3 pounds chicken breasts, skinless, boneless and sliced
2 2/3 tablespoons harissa dressing
Juice of 1 lemon
Peel of 1 lemon, grated
1/3 cup olive oil
Salt and black pepper to taste
2 2/3 sweet potatoes, peeled and roughly diced
1 1/3 sweet onion, chopped
2/3 cup feta cheese, crumbled
2/3 cup green olives, pitted and mashed

DIRECTIONS:

1. In a baking dish, combine the chicken with the seasoning and the rest of the Shopping List except the cheese and olives, stir and bake at 425 degrees F for 40 minutes.
2. In a bowl, combine the cheese with the crushed olives and mix well.
3. Divide the chicken and sweet potatoes among the plates, top each portion with the cheese and olive mixture.
4. Serve immediately.

NUTRITION:

calories: 303 | fat: 9.5g | protein: 13.6g | carbs: 21.5g | fiber: 9.2g | sodium: 0mg

292. Tahini Chicken

Prep time: 15 minutes | Cook time: 15 minutes | Serves: 6

INGREDIENTS:

1 1/2 cup uncooked instant brown rice
1/3 cup tahini or peanut butter (tahini for nut-free)
1/3 cup 2% plain Greek yogurt
3 tablespoons chopped scallions, green and white parts
1 1/2 tablespoon freshly squeezed lemon juice
1 1/2 tablespoon water
1 1/2 teaspoon ground cumin
1 1/8 teaspoon ground cinnamon
1/3 teaspoon kosher or sea salt
3 cups chopped cooked chicken breast
3/4 cup chopped dried apricots
3 cups peeled and chopped seedless cucumber
6 teaspoons sesame seeds
Fresh mint leaves, for serving (optional)

DIRECTIONS:

1. Cook the brown rice according to the package instructions.
2. While the rice is cooking, in a medium bowl, mix together the tahini, yogurt, scallions, lemon juice, water, cumin, cinnamon, and salt. Transfer half the tahini mixture to another medium bowl. Mix the chicken into the first bowl.
3. When the rice is done, mix it into the second bowl of tahini (the one without the chicken).
4. To assemble, divide the chicken among four bowls. Spoon the rice mixture next to the chicken in each bowl.
5. Next to the chicken, place the dried apricots, and in the remaining empty section, add the cucumbers.
6. Sprinkle with sesame seeds, and top with mint, if desired.
7. Serve when ready.

NUTRITION:

calories: 335 | fat: 10g | protein: 31g | carbs: 30g | fiber: 3g | sodium: 345mg

293. Chicken Piccata

Prep time: 15 minutes | Cook time: 17 minutes | Serves: 6

INGREDIENTS:

1 1/2 pound (454 g) thinly sliced chicken breasts
2 1/4 teaspoons salt, divided
3/4 teaspoon freshly ground black pepper
1/3 cup ground flaxseed
3 tablespoons almond flour
12 tablespoons extra-virgin olive oil, divided
6 tablespoons butter, divided (optional)
3 cups sliced mushrooms
3/4 cup dry white wine or chicken stock
1/3 cup freshly squeezed lemon juice
1/3 cup roughly chopped capers
Zucchini noodles, for serving
1/3 cup chopped fresh flat-leaf Italian parsley, for garnish

DIRECTIONS:

1. Season the chicken with 1 teaspoon salt and the pepper. On a plate, combine the ground flaxseed and almond flour and dredge each chicken breast in the mixture. Set aside.
2. In a large skillet, heat 4 tablespoons olive oil and 1 tablespoon butter over medium-high heat. Working in batches, if necessary, brown the chicken, 3 to 4 minutes per side. Remove from the skillet and keep warm.
3. Add the remaining 4 tablespoons olive oil and 1 tablespoon butter to the skillet along with mushrooms and sauté over medium heat until just tender, 6 to 8 minutes.
4. Add the white wine, lemon juice, capers, and remaining ½ teaspoon salt to the skillet and bring to a boil, whisking to incorporate any little browned bits that have stuck to the bottom of the skillet. Reduce the heat to low and whisk in the final 2 tablespoons butter.
5. Return the browned chicken to skillet, cover, and simmer over low heat until the chicken is cooked through and the sauce has thickened, 5 to 6 more minutes.
6. Serve chicken and mushrooms warm over zucchini noodles, spooning the mushroom sauce over top and garnishing with chopped parsley.
7. Enjoy!

NUTRITION:

calories: 538 | fat: 43g | protein: 30g | carbs: 8g | fiber: 3g | sodium: 1127mg

294. Chicken and Quinoa Mix

Prep time: 10 minutes | Cook time: 50 minutes | Serves: 6

INGREDIENTS:

6 chicken thighs, skinless and boneless
1 1/2 tablespoon olive oil
Salt and black pepper to taste
3 stalks of celery, chopped
3 spring onions, chopped 2 cups chicken broth
3/4 cup cilantro, chopped
3/4 cup of quinoa
3 tablespoons lime zest, grated

DIRECTIONS:

1. Heat a saucepan with the oil over medium-high heat, add the chicken and brown for 4 minutes on each side.
2. Add the onion and celery, stir and sauté for another 5 minutes.
3. Add the rest of the Shopping List, stir, bring to a boil and cook over medium-low heat for 35 minutes.
4. Divide everything among plates.
5. Serve when ready.

NUTRITION:

calories: 241 | fat: 12.6g | protein: 34.1g | carbs: 15.6g | fiber: 9.5g | sodium: 0mg

295. Grilled Chicken

Prep time: 10 minutes | Cook time: 20 minutes | Serves: 6

INGREDIENTS:

1/3 cup extra-virgin olive oil
3 tablespoons balsamic vinegar
1 1/2 teaspoon dried oregano, crushed between your fingers
1 1/2 pound (454 g) boneless, skinless chicken breasts, cut into 1 1/2-inch pieces
3 medium zucchinis, cut into 1-inch pieces
3/4 cup Kalamata olives, pitted and halved
3 tablespoons olive brine
1/3 cup torn fresh basil leaves
Non-stick cooking spray
Special Equipment:
21 to 15 (12-inch) wooden skewers, soaked for at least 30 minutes

DIRECTIONS:

1. Spray the grill grates with non-stick cooking spray. Preheat the grill to medium-high heat.
2. In a small bowl, whisk together the olive oil, vinegar, and oregano. Divide the marinade between two large plastic zip-top bags.
3. Add the chicken to one bag and the zucchini to another. Seal and massage the marinade into both the chicken and zucchini.
4. Thread the chicken onto 6 wooden skewers. Thread the zucchini onto 8 or 9 wooden skewers.
5. Cook the kebabs in batches on the grill for 5 minutes, flip, and grill for 5 minutes more, or until any chicken juices run clear.
6. Remove the chicken and zucchini from the skewers to a large serving bowl.
7. Toss with the olives, olive brine, and basil and serve when ready.

NUTRITION:

calories: 283 | fat: 15g | protein: 11g | carbs: 26g | fiber: 3g | sodium: 575mg

296. Chicken Drumsticks

Prep time: 10 minutes | Cook time: 20 minutes | Serves: 6

INGREDIENTS:

12 chicken drumsticks (2-pound / 907-g), skin removed
Nonstick cooking spray
1 1/2 (15-ounce / 425-g) can sliced peaches in 100% juice, drained
1/3 cup honey
1/3 cup cider vinegar
4 1/2 garlic cloves
3/4 teaspoon smoked paprika
1/3 teaspoon kosher or sea salt
1/3 teaspoon freshly ground black pepper

DIRECTIONS:

1. Remove the chicken from the refrigerator.
2. Set one oven rack about 4 inches below the broiler element. Preheat oven to 450°F. | 230°C | Fan 210°C
3. Line a large, rimmed baking sheet with aluminum foil. Place a wire cooling rack on the aluminum foil, and spray the rack with nonstick cooking spray. Set aside.
4. In a blender, combine the peaches, honey, vinegar, garlic, smoked paprika, salt, and pepper. Purée the Shopping List until smooth.
5. Add the purée to a medium saucepan and bring to a boil over medium-high heat. Cook for 2 minutes, stirring constantly. Divide the sauce among two small bowls. The first bowl will be brushed on the chicken; set aside the second bowl for serving at the table.
6. Brush all sides of the chicken with about half the sauce (keeping half the sauce for a second coating), and place the drumsticks on the prepared rack. Roast for 10 minutes.
7. Remove the chicken from the oven and turn to the high broiler setting. Brush the chicken with the remaining sauce from the first bowl. Return the chicken to the oven and broil for 5 minutes. Turn the chicken; broil for 3 to 5 more minutes, until the internal temperature measures 165°F (74°C) on a meat thermometer, or until the juices run clear.
8. Serve with the reserved sauce and enjoy!

NUTRITION:

calories: 526 | fat: 22g | protein: 44g | carbs: 38g | fiber: 1g | sodium: 412mg

297. Turkey Chorizo with Bok Choy

Prep time: 0 minutes | Cook time: 50 minutes | Serves: 6

INGREDIENTS:

6 mild turkey Chorizo, sliced
1/2 cup full-fat milk
9 ounces Gruyère cheese, preferably freshly grated
1 1/2 yellow onion, chopped
Coarse salt and ground black pepper, to taste
1 1/2-pound Bok choy, tough stem ends trimmed
1 1/2 cup cream of mushroom soup
1 1/2 tablespoon lard, room temperature

DIRECTIONS:

1. Melt the lard in a nonstick skillet over a moderate flame; cook the Chorizo sausage for about 5 minutes, stirring occasionally to ensure even cooking; reserve.
2. Add in the onion, salt, pepper, Bok choy, and cream of mushroom soup. Continue to cook for 4 minutes longer or until the vegetables have softened.
3. Spoon the mixture into a lightly oiled casserole dish. Top with the reserved Chorizo.
4. In a mixing bowl, thoroughly combine the milk and cheese. Pour the cheese mixture over the sausage.
5. Cover with foil and bake at 360 degrees F for about 35 minutes.
Storing
6. Cut your casserole into four portions. Place each portion in an airtight container; keep in your refrigerator for 3 to 4 days.
7. For freezing, wrap your portions tightly with heavy-duty aluminum foil or freezer wrap. Freeze up to 1 to 2 months. Defrost in the refrigerator.
8. Enjoy!

NUTRITION:

calories: 180 | fat: 12g | protein: 9.4g | carbs: 2.6g | fiber: 1g | sodium: 0mg

298. Duck Breasts in Boozy Sauce

Prep time: 0 minutes | Cook time: 20 minutes | Serves: 6

INGREDIENTS:

2 1/4 pounds duck breasts, butterflied
1 1/2 tablespoon tallow, room temperature
2 1/4 cups chicken consommé
3 tablespoons soy sauce
3 ounces vodka
3/4 cup sour cream
3 scallion stalks, chopped
Salt and pepper, to taste

DIRECTIONS:

1. Melt the tallow in a frying pan over medium-high flame. Sear the duck breasts for about 5 minutes, flipping them over occasionally to ensure even cooking.
2. Add in the scallions, salt, pepper, chicken consommé, and soy sauce. Partially cover and continue to cook for a further 8 minutes.
3. Add in the vodka and sour cream; remove from the heat and stir to combine well.
Storing
1. Place the duck breasts in airtight containers or Ziploc bags; keep in your refrigerator for up to 3 to 4 days.
2. For freezing, place duck breasts in airtight containers or heavy-duty freezer bags. Freeze up to 2 to 3 months. Once thawed in the refrigerator, reheat in a saucepan.
3. Enjoy!

NUTRITION:

calories: 351 | fat: 24g | protein: 22.1g | carbs: 6.6g | fiber: 0.6g | sodium: 0mg

299. Turkey Meatballs with Tangy Basil Chutney

Prep time: 0 minutes | Cook time: 30 minutes | Serves: 8

INGREDIENTS:

For the Meatballs
2 2/3 tablespoons sesame oil
2/3 cup Romano cheese, grated
1 1/3 teaspoon garlic, minced
2/3 teaspoon shallot powder
1/3 teaspoon dried thyme
2/3 teaspoon mustard seeds
2 2/3 small-sized eggs, lightly beaten
2 pounds ground turkey
2/3 teaspoon sea salt
1/3 teaspoon ground black pepper, or more to taste
4 tablespoons almond meal
For the Basil Chutney:
2 2/3 tablespoons fresh lime juice
1/3 cup fresh basil leaves
1/3 cup fresh parsley
2/3 cup cilantro leaves
2 2/3 teaspoon fresh ginger root, grated
2 2/3 tablespoons olive oil
2 2/3 tablespoons water
1 1/3 tablespoon habanero chili pepper, deveined and minced

DIRECTIONS:

1. In a mixing bowl, combine all Shopping List for the meatballs. Roll the mixture into meatballs and reserve.
2. Heat the sesame oil in a frying pan over a moderate flame. Sear the

meatballs for about 8 minutes until browned on all sides.
3. Make the chutney by mixing all the Shopping List in your blender or food processor.
Storing
1. Place the meatballs in airtight containers or Ziploc bags; keep in your refrigerator for up to 3 to 4 days.
2. Freeze the meatballs in airtight containers or heavy-duty freezer bags. Freeze up to 3 to 4 months. To defrost, slowly reheat in a frying pan.
3. Store the basil chutney in the refrigerator for up to a week.
4. Enjoy!!

NUTRITION:
calories: 390 | fat: 27.2g | protein: 37.4g | carbs: 1g | fiber: 0.3g | sodium: 0mg

300. Authentic Turkey Kebabs
Prep time: 0 minutes | Cook time: 30 minutes | Serves: 8

INGREDIENTS:
2/3 pounds turkey breast, cubed
4 Spanish peppers, sliced
2 2/3 zucchinis, cut into thick slices
1 1/3 onion, cut into wedges
2 2/3 tablespoons olive oil, room temperature
1 1/3 tablespoon dry ranch seasoning

DIRECTIONS:
1. Thread the turkey pieces and vegetables onto bamboo skewers. Sprinkle the skewers with dry ranch seasoning and olive oil.
2. Grill your kebabs for about 10 minutes, turning them periodically to ensure even cooking.
Storing
1. Wrap your kebabs in foil before packing them into airtight containers; keep in your refrigerator for up to 3 to days.
2. For freezing, place your kebabs in airtight containers or heavy-duty freezer bags. Freeze up to 2- 3 months. Defrost in the refrigerator.
3. Enjoy!

NUTRITION:
calories: 200 | fat: 13.8g | protein: 25.8g | carbs: 6.7g | fiber: 1.2g | sodium: 0mg

301. Parmesan Chicken Salad
Prep time: 0 minutes | Cook time: 20 minutes | Serves: 8

INGREDIENTS:
2 2/3 romaine hearts, leaves separated
Flaky sea salt and ground black pepper, to taste
1/3 teaspoon chili pepper flakes
2 2/3 teaspoon dried basil
1/3 cup Parmesan, finely grated
2 2/3 chicken breasts
Lebanese cucumbers, sliced
For the dressing:
2 2/3 large egg yolks
1 1/3 teaspoon Dijon mustard
2 2/3 tablespoon fresh lemon juice
1/3 cup olive oil
2 2/3 garlic cloves, minced

DIRECTIONS:
1. In a grilling pan, cook the chicken breast until no longer pink. Slice the chicken into strips.
Storing
1. Place the chicken breasts in airtight containers or Ziploc bags; keep in your refrigerator for to 4 days.
2. For freezing, place the chicken breasts in airtight containers or heavy-duty freezer bags. It will maintain the best quality for about 2 months.
3. Defrost in the refrigerator.
Preparing the Chicken Salad
1. Toss the chicken with the other Shopping List. Prepare the dressing by whisking all the Shopping List.
2. Dress the salad and enjoy!
3. Keep the salad in your refrigerator for 3 to 5 days.

NUTRITION:
calories: 183 | fat: 12.5g | protein: 16.3g | carbs: 0g | fiber: 0.9g | sodium: 0mg

302. Stuffed Chicken Breast
Prep time: 10 minutes | Cook time: 30 minutes | Serves: 6

INGREDIENTS:
12 tablespoons extra-virgin olive oil, divided
3 (6-ounce / 170 g) boneless, skinless chicken breasts
6 ounces (113 g) frozen spinach, thawed and drained well
1 1/2 cup shredded fresh Mozzarella cheese
1/3 cup chopped fresh basil
3 tablespoons chopped sun-dried tomatoes (preferably marinated in oil)
1 1/2 teaspoon salt, divided
1 1/2 teaspoon freshly ground black pepper, divided
3/4 teaspoon garlic powder
1 1/2 tablespoon balsamic vinegar

DIRECTIONS:
1. Preheat oven to 375° F | 190°C | Fan 170°C
2. Drizzle 1 tablespoon olive oil in a small deep baking dish and swirl to coat the bottom.
3. Make a deep incision about 3- to 4-inches long along the length of each chicken breast to create a pocket. Using your knife or fingers, carefully increase the size of the pocket without cutting through the chicken breast. (Each breast will look like a change purse with an opening at the top.)
4. In a medium bowl, combine the spinach, Mozzarella, basil, sun-dried tomatoes, 2 tablespoons olive oil, ½ teaspoon salt, ½ teaspoon pepper, and the garlic powder and combine well with a fork.
5. Stuff half of the filling mixture into the pocket of each chicken breast, stuffing down to fully fill the pocket. Press the opening together with your fingers. You can use a couple toothpicks to pin it closed if you wish.
6. In a medium skillet, heat 2 tablespoons olive oil over medium-high heat. Carefully sear the chicken breasts until browned, 3 to 4 minutes per side, being careful to not let too much filling escape. Transfer to the prepared baking dish, incision-side up. Scrape up any filling that fell out in the skillet and add it to baking dish. Cover the pan with foil and bake until the chicken is cooked through, 30 to 40 minutes, depending on the thickness of the breasts.
7. Remove from the oven and rest, covered, for 10 minutes. Meanwhile, in a small bowl, whisk together the remaining 3 tablespoons olive oil, balsamic vinegar, ½ teaspoon salt, and ½ teaspoon pepper.
8. To serve, cut each chicken breast in half, widthwise, and serve a half chicken breast drizzled with oil and vinegar.
9. Enjoy!

NUTRITION:
calories: 434 | fat: 34g | protein: 27g | carbs: 2g | fiber: 1g | sodium: 742mg

303. Chicken Tenders with Honey
Prep time: 10 minutes | Cook time: 20 minutes | Serves: 6

INGREDIENTS:
1 1/2 tablespoon honey
1 1/2 tablespoon whole-grain or Dijon mustard
1/3 teaspoon freshly ground black pepper
1/3 teaspoon kosher or sea salt
1 1/2 pound (454 g) boneless, skinless chicken breast tenders or tenderloins
1 1/2 cup almonds, roughly chopped
Nonstick cooking spray

DIRECTIONS:
1. Preheat oven to 450°F. | 230°C | Fan 210°C
2. Line a large, rimmed baking sheet with parchment paper. Place a wire cooling rack on the parchment-lined baking sheet, and spray the rack well with nonstick cooking spray.
3. In a large bowl, combine the honey, mustard, pepper, and salt. Add the chicken and toss gently to coat. Set aside.
4. Dump the almonds onto a large sheet of parchment paper and spread them out. Press the coated chicken tenders into the nuts until evenly coated on all sides. Place the chicken on the prepared wire rack.
5. Bake in the preheated oven for 15 to 20 minutes, or until the internal temperature of the chicken measures 165°F (74°C) on a meat thermometer and any juices run clear.
6. Cool for 5 minutes before serving.
7. Enjoy!

NUTRITION:
calories: 222 | fat: 7g | protein: 11g | carbs: 29g | fiber: 2g | sodium: 448mg

304. Chicken Soup
Prep time: 0 minutes | Cook time: 45 minutes | Serves: 6

INGREDIENTS:
1 1/2-pound whole chicken, boneless and chopped into small chunks 1/2 cup onions, chopped
3/4 cup rutabaga, cubed 2 carrots, peeled
3 celery stalks
Salt and black pepper, to taste 1 cup
chicken bone broth
3/4 teaspoon ginger-garlic paste
3/4 cup taro leaves, roughly chopped 1 tablespoon fresh coriander, chopped 3 cups water
1 1/2 teaspoon paprika

DIRECTIONS:
1. Place all Shopping List in a heavy-bottomed pot. Bring to a boil over the

highest heat.
2. Turn the heat to simmer. Continue to cook, partially covered, an additional 40 minutes.
Storing
1. Spoon the soup into four airtight containers or Ziploc bags; keep in your refrigerator for up to 3 to days.
2. For freezing, place the soup in airtight containers. It will maintain the best quality for about to 6 months. Defrost in the refrigerator.
3. Enjoy!

NUTRITION:
calories: 250 | fat: 12.9g | protein: 35.1g | carbs: 3.2g | fiber: 2.2g | sodium: 0mg

305. Chicken Breast with Tomato
Prep time: 10 minutes | Cook time: 20 minutes | Serves: 6

INGREDIENTS:

Nonstick cooking spray
1 1/2 pound (454 g) boneless, skinless chicken breasts
3 tablespoons extra-virgin olive oil
1/3 teaspoon freshly ground black pepper
1/3 teaspoon kosher or sea salt
1 1/2 large tomato, sliced thinly
1 1/2 cup shredded Mozzarella or 4 ounces fresh Mozzarella cheese, diced
1 1/2 (14 1/2-ounce / 411-g) can low-sodium or no-salt-added crushed tomatoes
3 tablespoons fresh torn basil leaves
6 teaspoons balsamic vinegar

DIRECTIONS:

1. Set one oven rack about 4 inches below the broiler element. Preheat oven to 450°F. | 230°C | Fan 210°C
2. Line a large, rimmed baking sheet with aluminum foil. Place a wire cooling rack on the aluminum foil, and spray the rack with non-stick cooking spray. Set aside.
3. Cut the chicken into 4 pieces (if they aren't already). Put the chicken breasts in a large zip-top plastic bag. With a rolling pin or meat mallet, pound the chicken so it is evenly flattened, about ¼-inch thick. Add the oil, pepper, and salt to the bag. Reseal the bag, and massage the Shopping List into the chicken. Take the chicken out of the bag and place it on the prepared wire rack.
4. Cook the chicken for 15 to 18 minutes, or until the internal temperature of the chicken is 165°F (74°C) on a meat thermometer and the juices run clear. Turn the oven to the high broiler setting. Layer the tomato slices on each chicken breast, and top with the Mozzarella. Broil the chicken for another 2 to 3 minutes, or until the cheese is melted (don't let the chicken burn on the edges). 5. Remove the chicken from the oven.
6. While the chicken is cooking, pour the crushed tomatoes into a small, microwave-safe bowl. Cover the bowl with a paper towel, and microwave for about 1 minute on high, until hot. When you're ready to serve, divide the tomatoes among four dinner plates. 7. Place each chicken breast on top of the tomatoes. Top with the basil and a drizzle of balsamic vinegar.
8. Serve when ready.

NUTRITION:
calories: 414 | fat: 22g | protein: 25g | carbs: 5g | fiber: 1g | sodium: 742mg

306. Chicken Liver Pâté
Prep time: 0 minutes | Cook time: 2 Hours 15 minutes | Serves: 6

INGREDIENTS:

1 1/2 yellow onion, finely chopped
15 ounces chicken livers
3/4 teaspoon Mediterranean seasoning blend
6 tablespoons olive oil
1 1/2 garlic clove, minced
For Flatbread:
1 1/2 cup lukewarm water
3/4 stick butter
3/4 cup flax meal
2 1/4 tablespoons psyllium husks
2 cups almond flour

DIRECTIONS:

1. Pulse the chicken livers along with the seasoning blend, olive oil, onion and garlic in your food processor; reserve.
2. Mix the dry Shopping List for the flatbread. Mix in all the wet Shopping List. Whisk to combine well.
3. Let it stand at room temperature for 2 hours. Divide the dough into 8 balls and roll them out on a flat surface.
4. In a lightly greased pan, cook your flatbread for 1 minute on each side or until golden.
Storing
1. Wrap the chicken liver pate in foil before packing it into airtight containers; keep in your refrigerator for up to 7 days.
2. For freezing, place the chicken liver pate in airtight containers or heavy-duty freezer bags. Freeze up to 2 months. Defrost overnight in the refrigerator.
3. As for the keto flatbread, wrap them in foil before packing them into airtight containers; keep in your refrigerator for up to 4 days.
4. Enjoy!

NUTRITION:
calories: 395 | fat: 30.2g | protein: 17.9g | carbs: 3.6g | fiber: 0.5g | sodium: 0mg

307. Turkey and avocado
Prep time: 10 minutes | Cook time: 1 Hour 10 minutes | Serves: 4

INGREDIENTS:

4 tablespoons of olive oil
2 turkey breast, boneless, skinless and cut in half
4 ounces cherry tomatoes, cut in half
A handful of cilantros, chopped Juice of 1 lime
Peel of 1 lime, grated
Salt and black pepper to taste
4 spring onions, chopped
4 avocados, pitted, peeled and cut into cubes

DIRECTIONS:

1. In a baking dish, combine the turkey with the oil and the rest of the Shopping List, place in the oven and bake at 375° F | 190°C | Fan 170°C for 1 hour and 10 minutes.
2. Divide among plates.
3. Serve when ready.

NUTRITION:
calories: 301 | fat: 8.9g | protein: 13.5g | carbs: 19.8g | fiber: 10.2g | sodium: 0mg

308. Greek Chicken Souvlaki
Prep time: 10 minutes | Cook time: 8 minutes | Serves: 6

INGREDIENTS:

3/4 cup extra-virgin olive oil, plus extra for serving
1/3 cup dry white wine (optional; add extra lemon juice instead, if desired)
9 garlic cloves, finely minced
Zest and juice of 1 lemon
1 1/2 tablespoon dried oregano
1 1/2 teaspoon dried rosemary
3/4 teaspoons salt
3/4 teaspoon freshly ground black pepper
1 1/2 pound (454 g) boneless, skinless chicken thighs, cut into 1 1/2-inch chunks
1 1/2 cup tzatziki, for serving

DIRECTIONS:

1. In a large glass bowl or resealable plastic bag, combine the olive oil, white wine (if using), garlic, lemon zest and juice, oregano, rosemary, salt, and pepper and whisk or shake to combine well. Add the chicken to the marinade and toss to coat. Cover or seal and marinate in the refrigerator for at least 1 hour, or up to 24 hours.
2. In a bowl, submerge wooden skewers in water and soak for at least 30 minutes before using.
3. To cook, heat the grill to medium-high heat. Thread the marinated chicken on the soaked skewers, reserving the marinade.
4. Grill until cooked through, flipping occasionally so that the chicken cooks evenly, 5 to 8 minutes. Remove and keep warm.
5. Bring the reserved marinade to a boil in a small saucepan. Reduce the heat to low and simmer 3 to 5 minutes.
6. Serve chicken skewers drizzled with hot marinade, adding more olive oil if desired, and tzatziki.
7. Enjoy!

NUTRITION:
calories: 493 | fat: 45g | protein: 19g | carbs: 3g | fiber: 0g | sodium: 385mg

309. Chicken Thighs with Vegetable
Prep time: 15 minutes | Cook time: 52 minutes | Serves: 8

INGREDIENTS:

2/3 cup extra-virgin olive oil, divided
2 pounds (680 g) boneless skinless chicken thighs, cut into 1-inch chunks
2 teaspoons salt, divided
2/3 teaspoon freshly ground black pepper
1 1/3 small red onion, chopped
1 1/3 red bell pepper, cut into 1-inch squares
2 2/3 medium tomatoes, chopped or 1 1/2 cups diced canned tomatoes
1 1/3 cup water
2 medium zucchini, sliced into 1/4-inch-thick half moons
1 1/3 cup pitted halved olives (Kalamata or Spanish green work nicely)

1/3 cup chopped fresh cilantro or flat-leaf Italian parsley
Riced cauliflower or sautéed spinach, for serving

DIRECTIONS:

1. In a Dutch oven or large rimmed skillet, heat ¼ cup olive oil over medium-high heat.
2. Season the chicken with 1 teaspoon salt and pepper and sauté until just browned on all sides, 6 to 8 minutes.
3. Add the onions and peppers and sauté until wilted, another 6 to 8 minutes.
4. Add the chopped tomatoes and water, bring to a boil, and reduce the heat to low. Cover and simmer over low heat until the meat is cooked through and very tender, 30 to 45 minutes.
5. Add the remaining ¼ cup olive oil, zucchini, olives, and cilantro, stirring to combine. Continue to cook over low heat, uncovered, until the zucchini is tender, about 10 minutes.
6. Serve warm over riced cauliflower or atop a bed of sautéed spinach.
7. Enjoy!

NUTRITION:

calories: 358 | fat: 24g | protein: 25g | carbs: 8g | fiber: 3g | sodium: 977mg

310. Chicken Meatballs with Parmesan

Prep time: 0 minutes | Cook time: 20 minutes | Serves: 8

INGREDIENTS:

For the Meatballs:	2 2/3 eggs, lightly beaten
1 2/3 pounds chicken, ground	Salt and ground black pepper
1 1/3 tablespoons sage leaves, chopped	2/3 teaspoon cayenne pepper
1 1/3 teaspoon shallot powder	For the sauce:
2 2/3 teaspoon porcini powder	2 2/3 tomatoes, pureed
2 2/3 garlic cloves, finely minced	1 1/3 cup chicken consommé
1/2 teaspoon dried basil	2/3 tablespoons lard, room temperature
1 cup Parmesan cheese, grated	1 1/3 onion, peeled and finely chopped

DIRECTIONS:

1. In a mixing bowl, combine all Shopping List for the meatballs. Roll the mixture into bite-sized balls.
2. Melt 1 tablespoon of lard in a skillet over a moderately high heat. Sear the meatballs for about 3 minutes or until they are thoroughly cooked; reserve.
3. Melt the remaining lard and cook the onions until tender and translucent. Add in pureed tomatoes and chicken consommé and continue to cook for 4 minutes longer.
4. Add in the reserved meatballs, turn the heat to simmer and continue to cook for 6 to 7 minutes.
Storing
1. Place the meatballs in airtight containers or Ziploc bags; keep in your refrigerator for up to 3 to 4 days.
2. Freeze the meatballs in airtight containers or heavy-duty freezer bags. Freeze up to 3 to 4 months. To defrost, slowly reheat in a saucepan.
3. Enjoy!

NUTRITION:

calories: 252 | fat: 9.7g | protein: 34.2g | carbs: 5.3g | fiber: 1.4g | sodium: 0mg

311. Pesto Chicken Mix

Prep time: 10 minutes | Cook time: 40 minutes | Serves: 6

INGREDIENTS:

6 chicken breast halves, skinless and boneless	3/4 cup basil pesto
4 1/2 tomatoes, cubed	A pinch of salt and black pepper
1 1/2 cup mozzarella, shredded	Cooking spray

DIRECTIONS:

1. Grease a baking sheet lined with parchment paper with cooking spray.
2. In a bowl, mix the chicken with salt, pepper and pesto and scrub well.
3. Place the chicken on the baking sheet, cover with tomatoes and shredded mozzarella and bake at 400 degrees F for 40 minutes.
4. Divide the mix on plates.
5. Serve with a side salad.

NUTRITION:

calories: 341 | fat: 20g | protein: 32g | carbs: 4g | fiber: 1g | sodium: 0mg

312. Chicken Wrap

Prep time: 10 minutes | Cook time: 0 minutes | Serves: 4

INGREDIENTS:

4 whole wheat tortilla flatbreads	4 provolone cheese slices 4 tomato slices
12 chicken breast slices, skinless, boneless, cooked and shredded A handful baby spinach	20 kalamata olives, pitted and sliced
	2 red onions, sliced
	4 tablespoons roasted peppers, chopped

DIRECTIONS:

1. Arrange the tortillas on a work surface and divide the chicken and other ingredients on each.
2. Roll up the tortillas.
3. Serve immediately.

NUTRITION:

calories: 190 | fat: 6.8g | protein: 6.6g | carbs: 15.1g | fiber: 3.5g | sodium: 0mg

313. Chicken and Artichokes

Prep time: 10 minutes | Cook time: 20 minutes | Serves: 6

INGREDIENTS:

3 pounds chicken breast, skinless, boneless and sliced	hearts, drained
	9 ounces sun-dried tomatoes, chopped
A pinch of salt and black pepper	4 1/2 tablespoons capers, drained
6 tablespoons olive oil	2 tablespoons lemon juice
12 ounces canned roasted artichoke	

DIRECTIONS:

1. Heat a skillet with half the oil over medium-high heat, add the artichokes and other ingredients except the chicken, stir and sauté for 10 minutes.
2. Transfer the mixture to a bowl, reheat the pan with the rest of the oil over medium-high heat, add the meat and cook 4 minutes per side.
3. Return the vegetable mix to the pan, stir, cook for another 2-3 minutes, divide into plates.
4. Serve when ready.

NUTRITION:

calories: 552 | fat: 28g | protein: 43g | carbs: 33g | fiber: 6g | sodium: 0mg

314. Chicken Kebabs

Prep time: 30 minutes | Cook time: 20 minutes | Serves: 6

INGREDIENTS:

3 chicken breasts, skinless, boneless and cubed	1/3 teaspoon smoked paprika
	A pinch of salt and black pepper
1 1/2 red bell pepper, cut into squares	1/3 teaspoon cardamom, ground Juice of 1 lemon
1 1/2 red onion, roughly cut into squares	
3 teaspoons sweet paprika	4 1/2 garlic cloves, minced
1 1/2 teaspoon nutmeg, ground	3/4 cup olive oil
1 1/2 teaspoon Italian seasoning	

DIRECTIONS:

1. In a bowl, combine the chicken with the onion, pepper and other ingredients, mix well, cover the bowl and refrigerate for 30 minutes.
2. Assemble the skewers with the chicken, peppers and onions, place them on the preheated grill and cook over medium heat for 8 minutes per side.
3. Divide the skewers on plates.
4. Serve with a side salad.

NUTRITION:

calories: 262 | fat: 14g | protein: 20g | carbs: 14g | fiber: 2g | sodium: 0mg

315. Chicken Salad and Mustard Dressing

Prep time: 10 minutes | Cook time: 0 minutes | Serves: 10

INGREDIENTS:

1 1/4 cup rotisserie chicken, skinless, boneless and cubed	1 1/4 avocado, peeled, pitted and cubed
	2/3 cup feta cheese, crumbled
2/3 cup sun-dried tomatoes, chopped	5 tablespoons red wine vinegar 2 tablespoons Dijon mustard
2/3 cup marinated artichoke hearts, drained and chopped 1 cucumber, chopped	1 1/4 teaspoon basil, dried
	1 1/4 garlic clove, minced
1/3 cup kalamata olives, pitted and sliced	2 1/2 teaspoons honey
	2/3 cup olive oil
2 1/2 cups baby arugula	Salt and black pepper to the taste 3 tablespoons lemon juice
1/3 cup parsley, chopped	

DIRECTIONS:

1. In a salad bowl, mix the chicken with the tomatoes, artichokes, cucumber, olives, rocket, parsley and avocado and mix.
2. In another bowl, mix the vinegar with the mustard and other ingredients except the cheese, whisk well, add to the salad and mix.

3. Sprinkle with cheese.
4. Serve when ready.

NUTRITION:

calories: 326 | fat: 21.7g | protein: 8.8g | carbs: 24.9g | fiber: 1.7g | sodium: 0mg

316. Chili Chicken Mix

Prep time: 10 minutes | Cook time: 18 minutes | Serves: 6

INGREDIENTS:

3 pounds chicken thighs, skinless and boneless
3 tablespoons olive oil
3 cups yellow onion, chopped 1 teaspoon onion powder
1 1/2 teaspoon smoked paprika 1 teaspoon chili pepper
3/4 teaspoon coriander seeds, ground 2 teaspoons oregano, dried
1 1/2 teaspoon parsley flakes
45 ounces canned tomatoes, chopped
3/4 cup black olives, pitted and halved

DIRECTIONS:

1. Set the Instant Pot to Sauté mode, add the oil, heat it, add the onion, onion powder and the rest of the ingredients except the tomatoes, olives and chicken, stir and sauté for 10 minutes.
2. Add the chicken, tomatoes and olives, cover and cook over high heat for 8 minutes.
3. Release the pressure naturally 10 minutes, divide the mixture into bowls.
4. Serve when ready.

NUTRITION:

calories: 153 | fat: 8g | protein: 12g | carbs: 9g | fiber: 2g | sodium: 0mg

317. Chicken Pilaf

Prep time: 10 minutes | Cook time: 30 minutes | Serves: 6

INGREDIENTS:

6 tablespoons avocado oil
3 pounds chicken breasts, skinless, boneless and cubed
3/4 cup yellow onion, chopped 4 garlic cloves, minced
12 ounces brown rice
6 cups chicken stock
3/4 cup kalamata olives, pitted
3/4 cup tomatoes, cubed
9 ounces baby spinach
3/4 cup feta cheese, crumbled
A pinch of salt and black pepper
1 1/2 tablespoon marjoram, chopped
1 1/2 tablespoon basil, chopped Juice of 1/2 lemon
1/3 cup pine nuts, toasted

DIRECTIONS:

1. Heat a pot with 1 tablespoon of avocado oil over medium-high heat, add the chicken, a little salt and pepper, brown for 5 minutes on each side and transfer to a bowl.
2. Reheat the pot with the rest of the avocado oil over medium heat, add the onion and garlic and sauté for 3 minutes.
3. Add the rice, the rest of the ingredients except the pine nuts, add the chicken again, stir, bring to a boil and cook over medium heat for 20 minutes.
4. Divide the mixture into plates, garnish each portion with pine nuts.
5. Serve when ready.

NUTRITION:

calories: 283 | fat: 12.5g | protein: 13.4g | carbs: 21.5g | fiber: 8.2g | sodium: 0mg

318. Chicken and Sweet Potatoes

Prep time: 10 minutes | Cook time: 40 minutes | Serves: 8

INGREDIENTS:

2 2/3 pounds chicken breasts, skinless, boneless and sliced
2 2/3 tablespoons harissa seasoning
Juice of 1 lemon
Zest of 1 lemon, grated
1/3 cup olive oil
Salt and black pepper to the taste
2 2/3 sweet potatoes, peeled and roughly cubed
1 1/3 sweet onion, chopped
2/3 cup feta cheese, crumbled
2/3 cup green olives, pitted and smashed

DIRECTIONS:

1. In a pan, combine the chicken with the seasoning and the rest of the ingredients except the cheese and olives, mix and bake at 425 degrees for 40 minutes.
2. In a bowl, combine the cheese with the crushed olives and mix well.
3. Divide the chicken and sweet potatoes on plates, garnish each portion with the cheese and olive mixture.
4. Serve immediately.

NUTRITION:

calories: 303 | fat: 9.5g | protein: 13.6g | carbs: 21.5g | fiber: 9.2g | sodium: 0mg

319. Paprika Chicken and Pineapple Mix

Prep time: 10 minutes | Cook time: 15 minutes | Serves: 6

INGREDIENTS:

3 cups pineapple, peeled and cubed
3 tablespoons olive oil
1 1/2 tablespoon smoked paprika
3 pounds chicken breasts, skinless, boneless and cubed
A pinch of salt and black pepper
1 1/2 tablespoon chives, chopped

DIRECTIONS:

1. Heat a skillet with oil over medium-high heat, add the chicken, salt and pepper and sauté for 4 minutes per side.
2. Add the rest of the ingredients, mix, cook for another 7 minutes, divide everything into plates.
3. Serve with a side of salad or as desired.

NUTRITION:

calories: 264 | fat: 13.2g | protein: 15.4g | carbs: 25.1g | fiber: 8.3g | sodium: 0mg

320. Chicken and Cashews Mix

Prep time: 10 minutes | Cook time: 30 minutes | Serves: 6

INGREDIENTS:

3- and 1/2-pounds chicken breasts, skinless, boneless and roughly cubed
6 spring onions, chopped
3 tablespoons olive oil
3 carrots, peeled and sliced
1/3 cup mayonnaise
3/4 cup Greek yogurt
1 1/2 cup cashews, toasted and chopped
A pinch of salt and black pepper

DIRECTIONS:

1. Heat a skillet with oil over medium-high heat, add the chicken and cook for 4 minutes on each side.
2. Add the onions, carrots and the rest of the ingredients except the cashews, mix, bring to a boil and cook over medium heat for 20 minutes.
3. Divide the mixture into bowls.
4. Serve with the cashews sprinkled on top.

NUTRITION:

calories: 304 | fat: 13.2g | protein: 15.4g | carbs: 19.1g | fiber: 6.5g | sodium: 0mg

321. Chicken, Corn and Peppers

Prep time: 5 minutes | Cook time: 1 Hour | Serves: 6

INGREDIENTS:

3 pounds chicken breast, skinless, boneless and cubed 2 tablespoons olive oil
3 garlic cloves, minced
1 1/2 red onion, chopped
3 red bell peppers, chopped
1/3 teaspoon cumin, ground
3 cups corn
3/4 cup chicken stock
1 1/2 teaspoon chili powder
1/3 cup cilantro, chopped

DIRECTIONS:

1. Heat a saucepan with the oil over medium-high heat, add the chicken and sauté for 4 minutes on each side.
2. Add the onion and garlic and sauté for another 5 minutes.
3. Add the rest of the ingredients, mix, bring to a boil over medium heat and cook for 45 minutes.
4. Divide into bowls.
5. Serve when ready.

NUTRITION:

calories: 332 | fat: 16.1g | protein: 17.4g | carbs: 25.4g | fiber: 8.4g | sodium: 0mg

322. Chicken and Apples Mix

Prep time: 10 minutes | Cook time: 40 minutes | Serves: 6

INGREDIENTS:

3/4 cup chicken stock
1 1/2 red onion, sliced
3/4 cup tomato sauce
3 green apples, cored and chopped
1 1/2-pound breast, skinless, boneless and cubed
1 1/2 teaspoon thyme, chopped
and 1/2 tablespoons olive oil

1 1/2 tablespoon chives, chopped

DIRECTIONS:

1. In a pan, combine the chicken with the tomato sauce, the apples and the rest of the ingredients except the chives, place the pan in the oven and bake at 425 degrees for 40 minutes.
2. Divide the mixture into plates, sprinkle with chives.
3. Serve when ready.

NUTRITION:

calories: 292| fat: 16.1g | protein: 16.4g | carbs: 15.g | fiber: 9.4g | sodium: 0mg

323. Walnut Turkey and Peaches

Prep time: 10 minutes | Cook time: 1 Hour | Serves: 6

INGREDIENTS:

- 1 1/2 turkey breasts, skinless, boneless and sliced
- 1/3 cup chicken stock
- 1 1/2 tablespoon walnuts, chopped 1 red onion, chopped
- Salt and black pepper to the taste
- 3 tablespoons olive oil
- 6 peaches, pitted and cut into quarters
- 1 1/2 tablespoon cilantro, chopped

DIRECTIONS:

1. In a pan greased with oil, combine the turkey and onion and the rest of the ingredients except the coriander, place in the oven and cook at 190° C for 1 hour.
2. Divide the mixture into plates, sprinkle with cilantro.
3. Serve when ready.

NUTRITION:

calories: 500| fat: 14g | protein: 10g | carbs: 15g | fiber: 3g | sodium: 0mg

324. Balsamic Turkey Bites and Apricots

Prep time: 5 minutes | Cook time: 1 Hour | Serves: 6

INGREDIENTS:

- 1 1/2 cup apricots, pitted and cubed
- 1/3 cup chicken stock
- 1 1/2 big turkey breast, skinless, boneless and cubed
- 1 1/2 tablespoon balsamic vinegar
- sweet onion, chopped
- 1/3 teaspoon red pepper flakes 2 tablespoons olive oil
- Salt and black pepper to the taste 2 tablespoons parsley, chopped

DIRECTIONS:

1. Heat a skillet with oil over medium-high heat, add the turkey and sauté for 3 minutes on each side.
2. Add the onion, pepper flakes and vinegar and cook for another 5 minutes.
3. Add the other ingredients except parsley, mix, place the pan in the oven and bake at 180 degrees C for 50 minutes.
4. Divide the mixture into plates.
5. Serve with the parsley sprinkled on top.

NUTRITION:

calories: 292| fat: 16.7g | protein: 14.4g | carbs: 24.8g | fiber: 8.6g | sodium: 0mg

325. Chipotle Turkey and Tomatoes

Prep time: 10 minutes | Cook time: 1 Hour | Serves: 6

INGREDIENTS:

- 3 pounds cherry tomatoes, halved
- 4 1/2 tablespoons olive oil
- 1 1/2 red onion, roughly chopped
- 1 1/2 big turkey breast, skinless, boneless and sliced
- 4 1/2 garlic cloves, chopped
- 4 1/2 red chili peppers, chopped
- 6 tablespoons chipotle paste
- Zest of 1/2 lemon, grated Juice of 1 lemon
- Salt and black pepper to the taste A handful coriander, chopped

DIRECTIONS:

1. Heat a skillet with oil over medium-high heat, add the turkey slices, cook 4 minutes per side and transfer to a pan.
2. Heat the skillet over medium-high heat, add the onion, garlic and chilli and sauté for 2 minutes.
3. Add the chipotle paste, sauté for another 3 minutes and pour over the turkey slices.
4. Mix the turkey slices with the chipotle mix, also add the rest of the ingredients except the coriander, place in the oven and cook at 400°F | 200°C | Fan 180°C for 45 minutes.
5. Divide everything into plates.
6. Sprinkle with coriander and serve.

NUTRITION:

calories: 264| fat: 13.2g | protein: 33.2g | carbs: 23.9g | fiber: 8.7g | sodium: 0mg

326. Parmesan Chicken and Cream

Prep time: 10 minutes | Cook time: 25 minutes | Serves: 6

INGREDIENTS:

- 1 1/2- and 1/2-pounds chicken breasts, skinless, boneless and cubed
- 1 1/2 tablespoon olive oil
- 1 1/2 teaspoon coriander, ground 1 teaspoon parsley flakes
- 3 garlic cloves, minced
- 1 1/2 cup heavy cream
- Salt and black pepper to the taste
- 1/3 cup parmesan cheese, grated 1 tablespoon basil, chopped

DIRECTIONS:

1. Heat a skillet with oil over medium-high heat, add the chicken, season with salt and pepper and cook for 3 minutes on each side.
2. Add the garlic and cook for 1 more minute.
3. Add the rest of the ingredients except the Parmesan and basil, cook over medium heat for 20 minutes and divide into plates.
4. Sprinkle the basil and Parmesan.
5. Serve when ready.

NUTRITION:

calories: 249| fat: 16.6g | protein: 25.3g | carbs: 24.5g | fiber: 7.5g | sodium: 0mg

327. Oregano Chicken and Zucchini Pan

Prep time: 10 minutes | Cook time: 30 minutes | Serves: 6

INGREDIENTS:

- 3 cups tomatoes, peeled and crushed
- 1 1/2- and 1/2-pounds chicken breast, boneless, skinless and cubed 2 tablespoons olive oil
- Salt and black pepper to the taste 1
- small yellow onion, sliced
- garlic cloves, minced
- 3 zucchinis, sliced
- 3 tablespoons oregano, chopped
- 1 1/2 cup chicken stock

DIRECTIONS:

1. Heat a skillet with oil over medium-high heat, add the chicken and sauté for 3 minutes on each side.
2. Add the onion and garlic and sauté for another 4 minutes.
3. Add the rest of the ingredients except the oregano, bring to a boil and cook over medium heat and cook for 20 minutes.
4. Divide the mixture into plates, sprinkle with oregano.
5. Serve when ready.

NUTRITION:

calories: 228| fat: 9.5g | protein: 18.6g | carbs: 15.6g | fiber: 9.1g | sodium: 0mg

328. Creamy Chicken and Grapes

Prep time: 10 minutes | Cook time: 20 minutes | Serves: 6

INGREDIENTS:

- 1 1/2- and 1/2-pounds chicken breasts, skinless, boneless and cubed
- 3/4 cup almonds, chopped
- 1 1/2 cup green grapes, seedless and halved
- 3 tablespoons olive oil
- Salt and black pepper to the taste
- 1 1/2 cup heavy cream
- 1 1/2 tablespoon chives, chopped

DIRECTIONS:

1. Heat a skillet with oil over medium-high heat, add the chicken and sauté for 3 minutes on each side.
2. Add the grapes and the rest of the ingredients, bring to a boil and cook over medium heat for another 15 minutes.
3. Divide everything into bowls.
4. Serve when ready.

NUTRITION:

calories: 292| fat: 16.7g | protein: 14.4g | carbs: 24.8g | fiber: 8.6g | sodium: 0mg

329. Chicken and Ginger Cucumbers Mix

Prep time: 10 minutes | Cook time: 20 minutes | Serves: 6

INGREDIENTS:

6 chicken breasts, boneless, skinless and cubed

3 cucumbers, cubed
Salt and black pepper to the taste
1 tablespoon ginger, grated
1 1/2 tablespoon garlic, minced
3 tablespoons balsamic vinegar
3 tablespoons olive oil
1/3 teaspoon chili paste
3/4 cup chicken stock
3/4 tablespoon lime juice
1 1/2 tablespoon chives, chopped

DIRECTIONS:

1. Heat a skillet with oil over medium-high heat, add the chicken and sauté for 3 minutes on each side.
2. Add the cucumbers, salt, pepper and the rest of the ingredients except the chives, bring to a boil and cook over medium heat for 15 minutes.
3. Divide the mixture into plates.
4. Serve with the chives sprinkled on top.

NUTRITION:

calories: 288| fat: 9.5g | protein: 28.6g | carbs: 25.6g | fiber: 12.1g | sodium: 0mg

330. Turmeric Chicken and Eggplant Mix

Prep time: 10 minutes | Cook time: 30 minutes | Serves: 6

INGREDIENTS:

3 cups eggplant, cubed
Salt and black pepper to the taste
3 tablespoons olive oil
1 1/2 cup yellow onion, chopped
2 tablespoons garlic, minced
2 tablespoons hot paprika
1 1/2 teaspoon turmeric powder
1 1/2 and 1/2 tablespoons oregano, chopped
1 1/2 cup chicken stock
1 1/2-pound chicken breast, skinless, boneless and cubed
1 cup half and half
1 1/2 tablespoon lemon juice

DIRECTIONS:

1. Heat a skillet with oil over medium-high heat, add the chicken and sauté for 4 minutes per side.
2. Add the eggplant, onion and garlic and sauté for another 5 minutes.
3. Add the rest of the ingredients, bring to a boil and cook over medium heat for 16 minutes.
4. Divide the mix on plates.
5. Serve when ready.

NUTRITION:

calories: 392| fat: 11.6g | protein: 24.2g | carbs: 21.1g | fiber: 8.3g | sodium: 0mg

331. Tomato Chicken and Lentils

Prep time: 10 minutes | Cook time: 1 Hour | Serves: 10

INGREDIENTS:

2 1/2 tablespoons olive oil
2 1/2 celery stalks, chopped
1 1/4 red onion, chopped
2 1/2 tablespoons tomato paste
2 garlic cloves, chopped
2/3 cup chicken stock
2 1/2 cups French lentils
1 1/4-pound chicken thighs, boneless and skinless
Salt and black pepper to the taste
1 1/4 tablespoon cilantro, chopped

DIRECTIONS:

1. Heat up a Dutch oven with the oil over medium-high heat, add the onion and the garlic and sauté for 2 minutes.
2. Add the chicken and brown for 3 minutes on each side.
3. Add the rest of the ingredients except the cilantro, bring to a simmer and cook over medium-low heat for 45 minutes.
4. Add the cilantro, stir, divide the mix into bowls and serve.
5. Enjoy!

NUTRITION:

calories: 249| fat: 9.7g | protein: 24.3g | carbs: 25.3g | fiber: 11.9g | sodium: 0mg

332. Turkey, Leeks and Carrots

Prep time: 10 minutes | Cook time: 1 hour | Serves: 6

INGREDIENTS:

1 1/2 big turkey breast, skinless, boneless and cubed
3 tablespoons avocado oil
Salt and black pepper to the taste
1 tablespoon sweet paprika
3/4 cup chicken stock
1 1/2 leek, sliced
1 1/2 carrot, sliced
1 1/2 yellow onion, chopped
1 1/2 tablespoon lemon juice
1 1/2 teaspoon cumin, ground
1 1/2 tablespoon basil, chopped

DIRECTIONS:

1. Heat a skillet with oil over medium-high heat, add turkey and sauté for 4 minutes on each side.
2. Add the leeks, carrot and onion and sauté for another 5 minutes.
3. Add the rest of the ingredients, bring to a boil and cook over medium heat for 40 minutes.
4. Divide the mix on plates and serve.
5. Enjoy!

NUTRITION:

calories: 249| fat: 10g | protein: 17g | carbs: 22g | fiber: 11g | sodium: 0mg

333. Chicken and Celery Quinoa Mix

Prep time: 10 minutes | Cook time: 50 minutes | Serves: 6

INGREDIENTS:

6 chicken thighs, skinless and boneless
1 1/2 tablespoon olive oil
Salt and black pepper to the taste
3 celery stalks, chopped
3 spring onions, chopped
2 cups chicken stock
3/4 cup cilantro, chopped
3/4 cup quinoa
1 1/2 teaspoon lime zest, grated

DIRECTIONS:

1. Heat a saucepan with the oil over medium-high heat, add the chicken and sauté for 4 minutes on each side.
2. Add the onion and celery, mix and brown for another 5 minutes.
3. Add the rest of the ingredients, mix, bring to a boil and cook over medium-low heat for 35 minutes.
4. Divide everything into plates and serve.
5. Enjoy!

NUTRITION:

calories: 241| fat: 12g | protein: 34g | carbs: 15g | fiber: 9g | sodium: 0mg

334. Herbed Chicken

Prep time: 10 minutes | Cook time: 40 minutes | Serves: 6

INGREDIENTS:

1 1/2-pound chicken breasts, skinless, boneless and sliced
2 red onions, chopped
3 tablespoons olive oil
3 garlic cloves, minced
3/4 cup chicken stock
1 1/2 teaspoon oregano, dried
1 teaspoon basil, dried
1 1/2 teaspoon rosemary, dried
1 1/2 cup canned tomatoes, chopped
Salt and black pepper to the taste

DIRECTIONS:

1. Heat a saucepan with the oil over medium-high heat, add the chicken and sauté for 4 minutes on each side.
2. Add the garlic and onions and sauté for another 5 minutes.
3. Add the rest of the ingredients, bring to a boil and cook over medium heat for 25 minutes.
4. Divide everything into plates and serve.
5. Enjoy!

NUTRITION:

calories: 251| fat: 11g | protein: 9g | carbs: 15g | fiber: 15g | sodium: 0mg

335. Chives Chicken and Radishes

Prep time: 10 minutes | Cook time: 30 minutes | Serves: 6

INGREDIENTS:

1 1/2-pound chicken breasts, skinless, boneless and cubed
Salt and black pepper to the taste
3 tablespoon olive oil
1 1/2 cup chicken stock
3/4 cup tomato sauce
3/4-pound red radishes, cubed
3 tablespoon chives, chopped

DIRECTIONS:

1. Heat a Dutch oven with oil over medium-high heat, add the chicken and brown for 4 minutes on each side.
2. Add the rest of the ingredients except the chives, bring to a boil and cook over medium heat for 20 minutes.
3. Divide the mixture into plates, sprinkle with chives and serve.
4. Enjoy!

NUTRITION:

calories: 277| fat: 15g | protein: 33g | carbs: 20g | fiber: 9g | sodium: 0mg

336. Feta Chicken and Cabbage
Prep time: 10 minutes | Cook time: 25 minutes | Serves: 6

INGREDIENTS:

1 1/2-pound chicken breasts, skinless, boneless and cut into strips
1 1/2 red cabbage, shredded
3 tablespoons olive oil
Salt and black pepper to the taste
2 tablespoons balsamic vinegar
1 1/2 and 1/2 cups tomatoes, cubed
1 tablespoon chives, chopped
1/3 cup feta cheese, crumbled

DIRECTIONS:

1. Heat a skillet with oil over medium-high heat, add the chicken and sauté for 5 minutes.
2. Add the rest of the ingredients except the cheese and cook over medium heat for 20 minutes, stirring often.
3. Add the cheese, mix, divide everything into plates and serve.
4. Enjoy!

NUTRITION:

calories: 277 | fat: 15g | protein: 14g | carbs: 14g | fiber: 8g | sodium: 0mg

337. Garlic Chicken and Endives
Prep time: 10 minutes | Cook time: 15 minutes | Serves: 6

INGREDIENTS:

1 1/2-pound chicken breasts, skinless, boneless and cubed
3 endives, sliced
3 tablespoons olive oil
6 garlic cloves, minced
3/4 cup chicken stock
3 tablespoons parmesan, grated
1 tablespoon parsley, chopped
Salt and black pepper to the taste

DIRECTIONS:

1. Heat a skillet with oil over medium-high heat, add the chicken and cook for 5 minutes.
2. Add the endives, garlic, broth, salt and pepper, mix, bring to a boil and cook over medium-high heat for 10 minutes.
3. Add the parmesan and parsley, mix gently, divide everything into plates and serve.
4. Enjoy!

NUTRITION:

calories: 280 | fat: 10g | protein: 14g | carbs: 21g | fiber: 10g | sodium: 0mg

338. Brown Rice, Chicken and Scallions
Prep time: 10 minutes | Cook time: 30 minutes | Serves: 6

INGREDIENTS:

1 1/2 and 1/2 cups brown rice
3 cups chicken stock
1 1/2 tablespoon balsamic vinegar
1 1/2-pound chicken breast, boneless, skinless and cubed
6 scallions, chopped
Salt and black pepper to the taste
1 tablespoon sweet paprika
3 tablespoons avocado oil

DIRECTIONS:

1. Heat a skillet with oil over medium-high heat, add the chicken and sauté for 5 minutes.
2. Add the shallots and sauté for another 5 minutes.
3. Add the rice and the rest of the ingredients, bring to a boil and cook over medium heat for 20 minutes.
4. Stir, divide everything into plates and serve.
5. Enjoy!

NUTRITION:

calories: 300 | fat: 9g | protein: 23g | carbs: 18g | fiber: 11g | sodium: 0mg

339. Creamy Chicken and Mushrooms
Prep time: 10 minutes | Cook time: 30 minutes | Serves: 6

INGREDIENTS:

1 1/2 red onion, chopped
1 1/2 tablespoon olive oil
3 garlic cloves, minced
3 carrots chopped
Salt and black pepper to the taste
1 tablespoon thyme, chopped
1 and 1/2 cups chicken stock
3/4-pound Bella mushrooms, sliced
1 1/2 cup heavy cream
1 1/2-pound chicken breasts, skinless, boneless and cubed
3 tablespoons chives, chopped
1 1/2 tablespoon parsley, chopped

DIRECTIONS:

1. Heat a Dutch oven with oil over medium-high heat, add the onion and garlic and sauté for 5 minutes.
2. Add the chicken and mushrooms and sauté for another 10 minutes.
3. Add the rest of the ingredients except the chives and parsley, bring to a boil and cook over medium heat for 15 minutes.
4. Add the chives and parsley, divide the mixture into plates and serve.
5. Enjoy!

NUTRITION:

calories: 275 | fat: 11g | protein: 23g | carbs: 26g | fiber: 10g | sodium: 0mg

340. Curry Chicken, Artichokes and Olives
Prep time: 10 minutes | Cook time: 7 hours | Serves: 4

INGREDIENTS:

2 pounds chicken breasts, boneless, skinless and cubed
12 ounces canned artichoke hearts, drained
1 cup chicken stock
1 red onion, chopped
1 tablespoon white wine vinegar
1 cup kalamata olives, pitted and chopped
1 tablespoon curry powder
2 teaspoons basil, dried
Salt and black pepper to the taste
1/4 cup rosemary, chopped

DIRECTIONS:

1. In your slow cooker, combine the chicken with the artichokes, olives and the rest of the ingredients, cover and cook over low heat for 7 hours.
2. Divide the mix on plates and serve hot.
3. Enjoy!

NUTRITION:

calories: 275 | fat: 11g | protein: 18g | carbs: 19g | fiber: 7g | sodium: 0mg

341. Slow Cooked Chicken and Capers Mix
Prep time: 10 minutes | Cook time: 7 hours | Serves: 6

INGREDIENTS:

3 chicken breasts, skinless, boneless and halved
3 cups canned tomatoes, crushed
3 garlic cloves, minced
1 1/2 yellow onion, chopped
2 cups chicken stock
3 tablespoons capers, drained
1/3 cup rosemary, chopped
Salt and black pepper to the taste

DIRECTIONS:

1. In your slow cooker, combine the chicken with the tomatoes, capers and the rest of the ingredients, cover and cook over low heat for 7 hours.
2. Divide the mix on plates and serve.
3. Enjoy!

NUTRITION:

calories: 292 | fat: 9g | protein: 36g | carbs: 25g | fiber: 11g | sodium: 0mg

342. Turkey and Chickpeas
Prep time: 10 minutes | Cook time: 5 hours | Serves: 6

INGREDIENTS:

3 tablespoons avocado oil
1 1/2 big turkey breast, skinless, boneless and roughly cubed
Salt and black pepper to the taste
1 1/2 red onion, chopped
22 1/2 ounces canned chickpeas, drained and rinsed
22 1/2 ounces canned tomatoes, chopped
1 1/2 cup kalamata olives, pitted and halved
3 tablespoons lime juice
1 1/2 teaspoon oregano, dried

DIRECTIONS:

1. Heat a skillet with oil over medium-high heat, add the meat and onion, sauté for 5 minutes and transfer to a slow cooker.
2. Add the rest of the ingredients, cover and cook on full power for 5 hours.
3. Divide on plates and serve immediately!
4. Enjoy!

NUTRITION:

calories: 352 | fat: 14g | protein: 26g | carbs: 25g | fiber: 11g | sodium: 0mg

343. Chicken Wings and Dates Mix
Prep time: 10 minutes | Cook time: 1 hours | Serves: 4

INGREDIENTS:

8 chicken wings, halved
1 1/3 garlic cloves, minced
Juice of 1 lime
Zest of 1 lime

1 1/3 tablespoons avocado oil
2/3 cup dates, pitted and halved 1 teaspoon cumin, ground
Salt and black pepper to the taste
1/3 cup chicken stock
2/3 tablespoon chives, chopped

DIRECTIONS:

1. In a pan, combine the chicken wings with the garlic, lime juice and the rest of the ingredients, mix, put in the oven and cook at 180F for 1 hour.
2. Divide everything into plates and serve with a side salad.
3. Enjoy!

NUTRITION:

calories: 294 | fat: 19g | protein: 17g | carbs: 21g | fiber: 11g | sodium: 0mg

344. Creamy Coriander Chicken

Prep time: 10 minutes | Cook time: 55 minutes | Serves: 6

INGREDIENTS:

1 1/2-pound chicken breasts, boneless, skinless and halved 2 tablespoons avocado oil
3/4 teaspoon hot paprika 1 cup chicken stock
1 1/2 tablespoon almonds, chopped 2 spring onions, chopped
3 garlic cloves, minced
1/3 cup heavy cream
A handful coriander, chopped
Salt and black pepper to the taste

DIRECTIONS:

1. Grease a pan with oil, add the chicken, paprika and the rest of the ingredients except coriander and cream, mix, put in the oven and cook at 180F for 40 minutes.
2. Add the cream and cilantro, mix, cook for another 15 minutes, divide into plates and serve.
3. Enjoy!

NUTRITION:

calories: 225 | fat: 8g | protein: 17g | carbs: 20g | fiber: 10g | sodium: 0mg

345. Lime Turkey and Avocado Mix

Prep time: 10 minutes | Cook time: 1 hour and 10 minutes | Serves: 4

INGREDIENTS:

4 tablespoons olive oil
4 turkey breast, boneless, skinless and halved
4 ounces cherry tomatoes, halved
A handful coriander, chopped
Juice of 1 lime
Zest of 1 lime, grated
Salt and black pepper to the taste
4 spring onions, chopped
2 avocadoes, pitted, peeled and cubed

DIRECTIONS:

1. In a pan, combine the turkey with the oil and the rest of the ingredients, bake and cook at 180 degrees F for 1 hour and 10 minutes.
2. Divide on plates and serve.
3. Enjoy!

NUTRITION:

calories: 301 | fat: 8g | protein: 13g | carbs: 19g | fiber: 10g | sodium: 0mg

346. Peanut and Chives Chicken Mix

Prep time: 10 minutes | Cook time: 25 minutes | Serves: 6

INGREDIENTS:

6 chicken breast halves, skinless and boneless
Salt and black pepper to the taste
3 tablespoons olive oil
3 tablespoons peanuts, chopped 1 tablespoon chives, chopped
3/4 cup tomato sauce
3/4 cup chicken stock

DIRECTIONS:

1. Heat up a pan with the oil over medium-high heat, add the chicken and brown for 4 minutes on each side.
2. Add the rest of the ingredients, bring to a simmer and cook over medium heat for 16 minutes.
3. Divide the mix between plates and serve.
4. Enjoy!

NUTRITION:

calories:294 | fat: 12g | protein: 12g | carbs: 25g | fiber: 9g | sodium: 0mg

347. Turkey and Salsa Verde

Prep time: 10 minutes | Cook time: 50 minutes | Serves: 6

INGREDIENTS:

1 1/2 big turkey breast, skinless, boneless and cubed
1 1/2 and 1/2 cups Salsa Verde
Salt and black pepper to the taste
1 1/2 tablespoon olive oil
1 1/2 and 1/2 cups feta cheese, crumbled
1/3 cup cilantro, chopped

DIRECTIONS:

1. In a pan greased with oil, combine the turkey with the sauce, salt and pepper and bake at 400° F for 50 minutes.
2. Add the cheese and coriander, mix gently, divide everything into plates and serve.
3. Enjoy!

NUTRITION:

calories: 332 | fat: 15g | protein: 34g | carbs: 22g | fiber: 10g | sodium: 0mg

348. Basil Turkey and Zucchinis

Prep time: 10 minutes | Cook time: 1 hour | Serves: 6

INGREDIENTS:

3 tablespoons avocado oil
1 1/2-pound turkey breast, skinless, boneless and sliced
Salt and black pepper to the taste
4 1/2 garlic cloves, minced 2 zucchinis, sliced
1 1/2 cup chicken stock
1/3 cup heavy cream
3 tablespoons basil, chopped

DIRECTIONS:

1. Heat a saucepan with the oil over medium-high heat, add the turkey and sauté for 5 minutes on each side.
2. Add the garlic and cook for 1 minute.
3. Add the rest of the ingredients except the basil, mix gently, bring to a boil and cook over medium-low heat for 50 minutes.
4. Add the basil, mix, divide the mixture into plates and serve.
5. Enjoy!

NUTRITION:

calories: 362 | fat: 9g | protein: 14g | carbs: 25g | fiber: 12g | sodium: 0mg

349. Duck and Tomato Sauce

Prep time: 10 minutes | Cook time: 2 hours | Serves: 6

INGREDIENTS:

6 duck legs
3 yellow onions, sliced
6 garlic cloves, minced
1/3 cup parsley, chopped
A pinch of salt and black pepper 1 teaspoon herbs de Provence
1 1/2 cup tomato sauce
3 cups black olives, pitted and sliced

DIRECTIONS:

1. In a pan, combine the duck legs with the onions, garlic and the rest of the ingredients, bake and cook at 180 degrees F for 2 hours.
2. Divide the mix on plates and serve.
3. Enjoy!

NUTRITION:

calories: 300 | fat: 13g | protein: 15g | carbs: 16g | fiber: 9g | sodium: 0mg

350. Cinnamon Duck Mix

Prep time: 10 minutes | Cook time: 20 minutes | Serves: 6

INGREDIENTS:

6 duck breasts, boneless and skin scored
Salt and black pepper to the taste
1 1/2 teaspoon cinnamon powder
3/4 cup chicken stock
4 1/2 tablespoons chives, chopped
2 tablespoons parsley, chopped 1 tablespoon olive oil
4 1/2 tablespoons balsamic vinegar 2 red onions, chopped

DIRECTIONS:

1. Heat a skillet with oil over medium-high heat, add the duck skin side down and cook for 5 minutes.
2. Add the cinnamon and the rest of the ingredients except the chives and cook for another 5 minutes.
3. Turn the duck breasts over again, bring everything to the boil and cook over medium heat for 10 minutes.
4. Add the chives, divide everything into plates and serve.
5. Enjoy!

NUTRITION:

calories: 310 | fat: 13g | protein: 15g | carbs: 16g | fiber: 9g | sodium: 0mg

351. Duck and Orange Warm Salad

Prep time: 10 minutes | Cook time: 25 minutes | Serves: 6

INGREDIENTS:

- 3 tablespoons balsamic vinegar
- 3 oranges, peeled and cut into segments
- 1 1/2 teaspoon orange zest, grated
- 3 tablespoons orange juice 3 shallot, minced
- 3 tablespoons olive oil
- Salt and black pepper to the taste
- 3 duck breasts, boneless and skin scored
- 3 cups baby arugula
- 3 tablespoons chives, chopped

DIRECTIONS:

1. Heat a skillet with oil over medium-high heat, add the duck breast skin side down and sauté for 5 minutes.
2. Turn the duck over, add the shallot and other ingredients except the rocket, orange and chives and cook for another 15 minutes.
3. Transfer the duck breasts to a cutting board, let them cool, cut them into strips and put them in a salad bowl.
4. Add the remaining ingredients, mix and serve hot.
5. Enjoy!

NUTRITION:

calories: 304 | fat: 15g | protein: 36g | carbs: 25g | fiber: 12g | sodium: 0mg

352. Orange Duck and Celery

Prep time: 10 minutes | Cook time: 40 minutes | Serves: 6

INGREDIENTS:

- 3 duck legs, boneless, skinless 1 tablespoon avocado oil
- 1 1/2 cup chicken stock
- Salt and black pepper to the taste 4 celery ribs, roughly chopped
- 3 garlic cloves, minced
- 1 1/2 red onion, chopped
- 3 teaspoons thyme, dried
- tablespoons tomato paste Zest of 1 orange, grated Juice of 2 oranges
- 3 oranges, peeled and cut into segments

DIRECTIONS:

1. Grease a pan with oil, add the duck legs, broth, salt, pepper and other ingredients, mix a little and mix at 450 degrees F for 40 minutes.
2. Divide everything into plates and serve hot.
3. Enjoy!

NUTRITION:

calories: 294 | fat: 12g | protein: 16g | carbs: 25g | fiber: 11g | sodium: 0mg

353. Duck and Blackberries

Prep time: 10 minutes | Cook time: 25 minutes | Serves: 6

INGREDIENTS:

- 6 duck breasts, boneless and skin scored
- 3 tablespoons balsamic vinegar
- Salt and black pepper to the taste
- 1 1/2 cup chicken stock
- 6 ounces blackberries
- 1/3 cup chicken stock
- 3 tablespoons avocado oil

DIRECTIONS:

1. Heat a skillet with the avocado oil over medium-high heat, add the duck breast, skin side down, and cook for 5 minutes.
2. Turn the duck over, add the rest of the ingredients, bring to a boil and cook over medium heat for 20 minutes.
3. Divide everything into plates and serve.
4. Enjoy!

NUTRITION:

calories: 239 | fat: 10g | protein: 33g | carbs: 21g | fiber: 10g | sodium: 0mg

354. Ginger Duck Mix

Prep time: 10 minutes | Cook time: 1 hour and 50 minutes | Serves: 6

INGREDIENTS:

- 6 duck legs, boneless
- 6 shallots, chopped
- 3 tablespoons olive oil
- 1 1/2 tablespoon ginger, grated
- 3 tablespoons rosemary, chopped
- 1 1/2 cup chicken stock
- 1 1/2 tablespoon chives, chopped

DIRECTIONS:

1. In a pan, combine the duck legs with the shallot and the rest of the ingredients except the chives, mix, bake at 250F and cook for 1 hour and 30 minutes.
2. Divide the mixture into plates, sprinkle with chives and serve.
3. Enjoy!

NUTRITION:

calories: 299 | fat: 10g | protein: 17g | carbs: 18g | fiber: 10g | sodium: 0mg

355. Duck, Cucumber and Mango Salad

Prep time: 10 minutes | Cook time: 50 minutes | Serves: 6

INGREDIENTS:

- Zest of 1 orange, grated
- 3 big duck breasts, boneless and skin scored
- 3 tablespoons olive oil
- Salt and black pepper to the taste
- 1 1/2 tablespoon fish sauce
- 1 1/2 tablespoon lime juice
- 1 1/2 garlic clove, minced
- 1 1/2 Serrano chili, chopped 1 small shallot, sliced
- 1 1/2 cucumber, sliced
- 3 mangos, peeled and sliced
- 1/3 cup oregano, chopped

DIRECTIONS:

1. Heat a skillet with oil over medium-high heat, add the duck breasts skin side down and cook for 5 minutes.
2. Add the orange zest, salt, pepper, fish sauce and the rest of the ingredients, bring to a boil and cook over medium-low heat for 45 minutes.
3. Divide everything into plates and serve.
4. Enjoy!

NUTRITION:

calories: 297 | fat: 9g | protein: 16g | carbs: 20g | fiber: 10g | sodium: 0mg

356. Turkey and Cranberry Sauce

Prep time: 10 minutes | Cook time: 50 minutes | Serves: 6

INGREDIENTS:

- 1 1/2 cup chicken stock
- 3 tablespoons avocado oil
- 3/4 cup cranberry sauce
- 1 1/2 big turkey breast, skinless, boneless and sliced
- 1 1/2 yellow onion, roughly chopped
- Salt and black pepper to the taste

DIRECTIONS:

1. Heat a pan with the avocado oil over medium-high heat, add the onion and sauté for 5 minutes.
2. Add the turkey and sauté for another 5 minutes.
3. Add the rest of the ingredients, mix, bake at 180°F and cook for 40 minutes
4. Enjoy!

NUTRITION:

calories: 382 | fat: 12g | protein: 17g | carbs: 26g | fiber: 9g | sodium: 0mg

357. Sage Turkey Mix

Prep time: 10 minutes | Cook time: 40 minutes | Serves: 6

INGREDIENTS:

- 3 big turkey breast, skinless, boneless and roughly cubed Juice of 1 lemon
- 3 tablespoons avocado oil 1 red onion, chopped
- 3 tablespoons sage, chopped 1 garlic clove, minced
- 1 1/2 cup chicken stock

DIRECTIONS:

1. Heat a pan with the avocado oil over medium-high heat, add the turkey and sauté for 3 minutes on each side.
2. Add the rest of the ingredients, bring to a boil and cook over medium heat for 35 minutes.
3. Divide the mixture into plates and serve with a side dish.
4. Enjoy!

NUTRITION:

calories: 382 | fat: 12g | protein: 33g | carbs: 16g | fiber: 9g | sodium: 0mg

358. Turkey and Asparagus Mix

Prep time: 10 minutes | Cook time: 30 minutes | Serves: 6

INGREDIENTS:

- 1 1/2 bunch asparagus, trimmed and halved
- 3 big turkey breast, skinless, boneless and cut into strips 1 teaspoon basil, dried
- 3 tablespoons olive oil
- A pinch of salt and black pepper
- 3/4 cup tomato sauce
- 1 1/2 tablespoon chives, chopped

DIRECTIONS:
1. Heat a skillet with oil over medium-high heat, add turkey and sauté for 4 minutes.
2. Add the asparagus and the rest of the ingredients except the chives, bring to a boil and cook over medium heat for 25 minutes.
3. Add the chives, divide the mixture into plates and serve.
4. Enjoy!

NUTRITION:
calories: 382 | fat: 12g | protein: 17g | carbs: 21g | fiber: 10g | sodium: 0mg

359. Herbed Almond Turkey
Prep time: 10 minutes | Cook time: 40 minutes | Serves: 6

INGREDIENTS:
- 1 1/2 big turkey breast, skinless, boneless and cubed
- 1 1/2 tablespoon olive oil
- 3/4 cup chicken stock
- 1 1/2 tablespoon basil, chopped
- 1 1/2 tablespoon rosemary, chopped
- 1 tablespoon oregano, chopped
- 1 tablespoon parsley, chopped
- 4 1/2 garlic cloves, minced
- 3/4 cup almonds, toasted and chopped
- 4 1/2 cups tomatoes, chopped

DIRECTIONS:
1. Heat a skillet with oil over medium-high heat, add the turkey and garlic and sauté for 5 minutes.
2. Add the broth and the rest of the ingredients, bring to a boil over medium heat and cook for 35 minutes.
3. Divide the mix on plates and serve.
4. Enjoy!

NUTRITION:
calories: 297 | fat: 11g | protein: 23g | carbs: 19g | fiber: 9g | sodium: 0mg

360. Thyme Chicken and Potatoes
Prep time: 10 minutes | Cook time: 50 minutes | Serves: 6

INGREDIENTS:
- 1 1/2 tablespoon olive oil
- 6 garlic cloves, minced
- A pinch of salt and black pepper
- 2 teaspoons thyme, dried
- 18 small red potatoes, halved
- 3 pounds chicken breast, skinless, boneless and cubed
- 1 cup red onion, sliced
- 1 1/8 cup chicken stock
- 3 tablespoons basil, chopped

DIRECTIONS:
1. In a pan greased with oil, add the potatoes, chicken and the rest of the ingredients, mix a little, put in the oven and cook at 200°F for 50 minutes.
2. Divide on plates and serve.
3. Enjoy!

NUTRITION:
calories: 281 | fat: 9.2g | protein: 13.6g | carbs: 21.6g | fiber: 10.9g | sodium: 0mg

361. Turkey, Artichokes and Asparagus
Prep time: 10 minutes | Cook time: 30 minutes | Serves: 6

INGREDIENTS:
- 3 turkey breasts, boneless, skinless and halved
- 4 1/2 tablespoons olive oil
- 1 1/2- and 1/2-pounds asparagus, trimmed and halved
- 1 1/2 cup chicken stock
- A pinch of salt and black pepper
- 1 1/2 cup canned artichoke hearts, drained
- 1/3 cup kalamata olives, pitted and sliced
- 1 1/2 shallot, chopped
- 4 1/2 garlic cloves, minced
- 4 1/2 tablespoons dill, chopped

DIRECTIONS:
1. Heat a skillet with oil over medium-high heat, add turkey and garlic and sauté for 4 minutes on each side.
2. Add the asparagus, stock and the rest of the ingredients except the dill, bring to a boil and cook over medium heat for 20 minutes.
3. Add the dill, divide the mixture into plates and serve.
4. Enjoy!

NUTRITION:
calories: 291 | fat: 16g | protein: 34.5g | carbs: 22.8g | fiber: 10.3g | sodium: 0mg

362. Lemony Turkey and Pine Nuts
Prep time: 10 minutes | Cook time: 30 minutes | Serves: 6

INGREDIENTS:
- 3 turkey breasts, boneless, skinless and halved
- A pinch of salt and black pepper
- 3 tablespoons avocado oil Juice of 2 lemons
- 1 1/2 tablespoon rosemary, chopped
- 4 1/2 garlic cloves, minced
- 1/3 cup pine nuts, chopped 1 cup chicken stock

DIRECTIONS:
1. Heat a skillet with oil over medium-high heat, add the garlic and turkey and sauté for 4 minutes on each side.
2. Add the rest of the ingredients, bring to a boil and cook over medium heat for 20 minutes.
3. Divide the mixture into plates and serve with a side salad.
4. Enjoy!

NUTRITION:
calories: 293 | fat: 12.4g | protein: 24.5g | carbs: 17.8g | fiber: 9.3g | sodium: 0mg

363. Yogurt Chicken and Red Onion Mix
Prep time: 10 minutes | Cook time: 30 minutes | Serves: 6

INGREDIENTS:
- 3 pounds chicken breast, skinless, boneless and sliced 3 tablespoons olive oil
- 1/3 cup Greek yogurt
- 3 garlic cloves, minced
- 3/4 teaspoon onion powder
- A pinch of salt and black pepper
- 6 red onions, sliced

DIRECTIONS:
1. In a pan combine the chicken with the oil, yogurt and other ingredients, bake at 180 degrees F and cook for 30 minutes.
2. Divide the chicken mix on plates and serve hot.
3. Enjoy!

NUTRITION:
calories: 278 | fat: 15g | protein: 23.3g | carbs: 15.1g | fiber: 9.2g | sodium: 0mg

364. Chicken and Mint Sauce
Prep time: 10 minutes | Cook time: 30 minutes | Serves: 6

INGREDIENTS:
- 3 and 1/2 tablespoons olive oil
- 3 pounds chicken breasts, skinless, boneless and halved
- 4 1/2 tablespoons garlic, minced
- 3 tablespoons lemon juice
- 1 1/2 tablespoon red wine vinegar 1/3 cup Greek yogurt
- 3 tablespoons mint, chopped
- A pinch of salt and black pepper

DIRECTIONS:
1. In a blender, combine the garlic with the lemon juice and other ingredients except the oil and the chicken and blend well.
2. Heat a skillet with oil over medium-high heat, add the chicken and sauté for 3 minutes on each side.
3. Add the mint sauce, bake and cook everything at 180 degrees F for 25 minutes.
4. Divide the mixture into plates.
5. Serve when ready.

NUTRITION:
calories: 278 | fat: 12g | protein: 13.3g | carbs: 18.1g | fiber: 11.2g | sodium: 0mg

365. Oregano Turkey and Peppers
Prep time: 10 minutes | Cook time: 1 Hour | Serves: 6

INGREDIENTS:
- 3 red bell peppers, cut into strips
- 3 green bell peppers, cut into strips
- 1 1/2 red onion, chopped
- 6 garlic cloves, minced
- 3/4 cup black olives, pitted and sliced
- 3 cups chicken stock
- 1 1/2 big turkey breast, skinless, boneless and cut into strips
- 1 1/2 tablespoon oregano, chopped
- 3/4 cup cilantro, chopped

DIRECTIONS:
1. In a baking dish, combine the peppers with the turkey and the rest of the ingredients, mix, bake at

200° C and roast for 1 hour.
2. Divide everything into plates and serve.
3. Enjoy!

NUTRITION:

calories: 229 | fat: 8.9g | protein: 33.6g | carbs: 17.8g | fiber: 8.2g | sodium: 0mg

366. Chicken and Mustard Sauce

Prep time: 10 minutes | Cook time: 26 minutes | Serves: 6

INGREDIENTS:

1/2 cup mustard	1 1/2 and 1/2 cups chicken stock
Salt and black pepper to the taste	6 chicken breasts, skinless, boneless and halved
1 1/2 red onion, chopped	
1 1/2 tablespoon olive oil	1/3 teaspoon oregano, dried

DIRECTIONS:

1. Heat a pan with the broth over medium heat, add the mustard, onion, salt, pepper and oregano, blend, bring to a boil and cook for 8 minutes.
2. Heat a skillet with oil over medium-high heat, add the chicken and sauté for 3 minutes on each side.
3. Add the chicken to the pan with the sauce, mix, simmer for another 12 minutes, divide into plates and serve.
4. Enjoy!

NUTRITION:

calories: 247 | fat: 15.1g | protein: 26.1g | carbs: 16.6g | fiber: 9.1g | sodium: 0mg

367. Chicken and Sausage Mix

Prep time: 10 minutes | Cook time: 50 minutes | Serves: 6

INGREDIENTS:

3 zucchinis, cubed	3 chicken breasts, boneless, skinless and halved
1 1/2-pound Italian sausage, cubed 2 tablespoons olive oil	Salt and black pepper to the taste
1 1/2 red bell pepper, chopped 1 red onion, sliced	3/4 cup chicken stock
3 tablespoons garlic, minced	1 1/2 tablespoon balsamic vinegar

DIRECTIONS:

1. Heat a skillet with half the oil over medium-high heat, add the sausages, brown for 3 minutes on each side and transfer to a bowl.
2. Heat the pan with the rest of the oil over medium-high heat, add the chicken and sauté for 4 minutes on each side.
3. Put the sausage back, add the rest of the ingredients, bring to the boil, put it in the oven and cook at 180 degrees for 30 minutes.
4. Divide everything into plates and serve.
5. Enjoy!

NUTRITION:

calories: 293 | fat: 13.1g | protein: 26.1g | carbs: 16.6g | fiber: 8.1g | sodium: 0mg

368. Coriander and Coconut Chicken

Prep time: 10 minutes | Cook time: 30 minutes | Serves: 6

INGREDIENTS:

pounds chicken thighs, skinless, boneless and cubed 2 tablespoons olive oil	tablespoon ginger, grated
	1/3 cup orange juice
Salt and black pepper to the taste	tablespoons coriander, chopped 1 cup chicken stock
tablespoons coconut flesh, shredded 1 and 1/2 teaspoons orange extract	1/3 teaspoon red pepper flakes

DIRECTIONS:

1. Heat a skillet with oil over medium-high heat, add the chicken and sauté for 4 minutes per side.
2. Add salt, pepper and the rest of the ingredients, bring to a boil and cook over medium heat for 20 minutes.
3. Divide the mix on plates and serve hot.
4. Enjoy!

NUTRITION:

calories: 297 | fat: 14.4g | protein: 25g | carbs: 22g | fiber: 9.6g | sodium: 0mg

369. Saffron Chicken Thighs and Green Beans

Prep time: 10 minutes | Cook time: 25 minutes | Serves: 6

INGREDIENTS:

3 pounds chicken thighs, boneless and skinless	3/4 cup Greek yogurt
	Salt and black pepper to the taste
3 teaspoons saffron powder	1 1/2 tablespoon lime juice
1 1/2-pound green beans, trimmed and halved	1 1/2 tablespoon dill, chopped

DIRECTIONS:

1. In a baking dish, combine the chicken with the saffron, the green beans and the rest of the ingredients, mix a little, put in the oven and cook at 200° F for 25 minutes.
2. Divide everything into plates and serve.
3. Enjoy!

NUTRITION:

calories: 274 | fat: 12.3g | protein: 14.3g | carbs: 20.4g | fiber: 5.3g | sodium: 0mg

370. Chicken and Olives Salsa

Prep time: 10 minutes | Cook time: 25 minutes | Serves: 6

INGREDIENTS:

1 1/2 tablespoon avocado oil	1 1/2 tablespoon balsamic vinegar
6 chicken breast halves, skinless and boneless	3 tablespoons parsley, chopped
	3 avocados, peeled, pitted and cubed
Salt and black pepper to the taste	3 tablespoons black olives, pitted and chopped
1 1/2 tablespoon sweet paprika 1 red onion, chopped	

DIRECTIONS:

1. Heat the grill over medium-high heat, add the chicken brushed with half the oil and seasoned with paprika, salt and pepper, cook 7 minutes per side and divide into plates.
2. Meanwhile, in a bowl, mix the onion with the rest of the ingredients and the remaining oil, mix, add the chicken on top and serve.
3. Enjoy!

NUTRITION:

calories: 289 | fat: 12.4g | protein: 14.3g | carbs: 23.8g | fiber: 9.1g | sodium: 0mg

371. Carrots and Tomatoes Chicken

Prep time: 10 minutes | Cook time: 1 hour 10 minutes | Serves: 6

INGREDIENTS:

3 pounds chicken breasts, skinless, boneless and halved	3 carrots, sliced
	4 1/2 tomatoes, chopped
Salt and black pepper to the taste	1/3 cup chicken stock
3 garlic cloves, minced	1 1/2 tablespoon Italian seasoning
3 tablespoons avocado oil 2 shallots, chopped	1 1/2 tablespoon parsley, chopped

DIRECTIONS:

1. Heat a skillet with oil over medium-high heat, add the chicken, garlic, salt and pepper and sauté for 3 minutes on each side.
2. Add the rest of the ingredients except the parsley, bring to a boil and cook over medium-low heat for 40 minutes.
3. Add the parsley, divide the mixture into plates and serve.
4. Enjoy!

NUTRITION:

calories: 309 | fat: 12.4g | protein: 15.3g | carbs: 23.8g | fiber: 11.1g | sodium: 0mg

372. Smoked and Hot Turkey Mix

Prep time: 10 minutes | Cook time: 40 minutes | Serves: 6

INGREDIENTS:

1 1/2 red onion, sliced	Salt and black pepper to the taste
3 big turkey breast, skinless, boneless and roughly cubed	3 tablespoons olive oil
	3/4 cup chicken stock
1 1/2 tablespoon smoked paprika	1 1/2 tablespoon parsley, chopped
3 chili peppers, chopped	1 1/2 tablespoon cilantro, chopped

DIRECTIONS:

1. Grease a pan with oil, add the turkey, onion, paprika and the rest of the

ingredients, mix, put in the oven and cook at 425 degrees F for 40 minutes.
2. Divide the mix on plates and serve immediately.
3. Enjoy!

NUTRITION:

calories: 310 | fat: 18.4g | protein: 33.4g | carbs: 22.3g | fiber: 10.4g | sodium: 0mg

373. Spicy Cumin Chicken

Prep time: 10 minutes | Cook time: 25 minutes | Serves: 6

INGREDIENTS:

3 teaspoons chili powder
3 and 1/2 tablespoons olive oil
Salt and black pepper to the taste 1 and 1/2 teaspoons garlic powder 1 tablespoon smoked paprika
3/4 cup chicken stock
1 1/2-pound chicken breasts, skinless, boneless and halved 2 teaspoons sherry vinegar
3 teaspoons hot sauce
3 teaspoons cumin, ground
3/4 cup black olives, pitted and sliced

DIRECTIONS:

1. Heat a skillet with oil over medium-high heat, add the chicken and sauté for 3 minutes on each side.
2. Add the chili powder, salt, pepper, garlic powder and paprika, mix and cook for another 4 minutes.
3. Add the rest of the ingredients, mix, bring to a boil and cook over medium heat for another 15 minutes.
4. Divide the mix on plates and serve.
5. Enjoy!

NUTRITION:

calories: 230 | fat: 18.4g | protein: 13.4g | carbs: 15.3g | fiber: 9.4g | sodium: 0mg

374. Chicken with Artichokes and Beans

Prep time: 10 minutes | Cook time: 40 minutes | Serves: 6

INGREDIENTS:

3 tablespoons olive oil
1 1/2-pound chicken breasts, skinless, boneless and halved Zest of 1 lemon, grated
3 garlic cloves, crushed Juice of 1 lemon
Salt and black pepper to the taste 1 tablespoon thyme, chopped
9 ounces canned artichokes hearts, drained
1 1/2 cup canned fava beans, drained and rinsed
1 1/2 cup chicken stock
A pinch of cayenne pepper
Salt and black pepper to the taste

DIRECTIONS:

1. Heat a skillet with oil over medium-high heat, add the chicken and sauté for 5 minutes.
2. Add the lemon juice, lemon zest, salt, pepper and the rest of the ingredients, bring to a boil and cook over medium heat for 35 minutes.
3. Divide the mix on plates and serve immediately.
4. Enjoy!

NUTRITION:

calories: 291 | fat: 14.9g | protein: 24.2g | carbs: 23.8g | fiber: 10.5g | sodium: 0mg

375. Chicken and Olives Tapenade

Prep time: 10 minutes | Cook time: 25 minutes | Serves: 6

INGREDIENTS:

3 chicken breasts, boneless, skinless and halved
1 1/2 cup black olives, pitted
3/4 cup olive oil
Salt and black pepper to the taste
3/4 cup mixed parsley, chopped
3/4 cup rosemary, chopped
Salt and black pepper to the taste
6 garlic cloves, minced
Juice of 1/2 lime

DIRECTIONS:

1. In a blender, combine the olives with half the oil and the rest of the ingredients except the chicken and blend well.
2. Heat a skillet with the rest of the oil over medium-high heat, add the chicken and brown for 4 minutes on each side.
3. Add the olive mix and cook for another 20 minutes, stirring often.
4. Enjoy!

NUTRITION:

calories: 291 | fat: 12.9g | protein: 34.2g | carbs: 15.8g | fiber: 8.5g | sodium: 0mg

376. Spiced Chicken Meatballs

Prep time: 10 minutes | Cook time: 20 minutes | Serves: 6

INGREDIENTS:

1 1/2 pound chicken meat, ground
1 1/2 tablespoon pine nuts, toasted and chopped
1 1/2 egg, whisked
3 teaspoons turmeric powder 2 garlic cloves, minced
Salt and black pepper to the taste 1 and 1/4 cups heavy cream
3 tablespoons olive oil
1/3 cup parsley, chopped
1 1/2 tablespoon chives, chopped

DIRECTIONS:

1. In a bowl, combine the chicken with the pine nuts and the rest of the ingredients except the oil and cream, mix well and form medium sized meatballs with this mixture.
2. Heat a skillet with oil over medium-high heat, add the meatballs and cook for 4 minutes per side.
3. Add the cream, mix gently, cook over medium heat for another 10 minutes, divide into plates and serve.
3. Enjoy!

NUTRITION:

calories: 283 | fat: 9.2g | protein: 34.5g | carbs: 24.4g | fiber: 12.8g | sodium: 0mg

377. Sesame Turkey Mix

Prep time: 10 minutes | Cook time: 25 minutes | Serves: 6

INGREDIENTS:

3 tablespoons avocado oil
1 1/2 and 1/4 cups chicken stock
1 1/2 tablespoon sesame seeds, toasted
Salt and black pepper to the taste
1 1/2 big turkey breast, skinless,
boneless and sliced
1/3 cup parsley, chopped
6 ounces feta cheese, crumbled
1/3 cup red onion, chopped 1 tablespoon lemon juice

DIRECTIONS:

1. Heat a skillet with oil over medium-high heat, add the meat and sauté for 4 minutes over high heat
each side.
2. Add the rest of the ingredients except the cheese and sesame seeds, bring to a boil and cook over medium heat for 15 minutes.
3. Add the cheese, mix, divide the mixture into plates, sprinkle with sesame seeds and serve.
4. Enjoy!

NUTRITION:

calories: 283 | fat: 13.2g | protein: 24.5g | carbs: 19.4g | fiber: 6.8g | sodium: 0mg

378. Cardamom Chicken and Apricot Sauce

Prep time: 10 minutes | Cook time: 7 hours | Serves: 6

INGREDIENTS:

Juice of 1/2 lemon
Zest of 1/2 lemon, grated
3 teaspoons cardamom, ground Salt and black pepper to the taste
3 chicken breasts, skinless, boneless and halved
3 tablespoons olive oil
3 spring onions, chopped
3 tablespoons tomato paste 2 garlic cloves, minced
1 1/2 cup apricot juice
3/4 cup chicken stock
1/3 cup cilantro, chopped

DIRECTIONS:

1. In your slow cooker, combine the chicken with the lemon juice, lemon zest and the other ingredients except the cilantro, toss, put the lid on and cook on Low for 7 hours.
2. Divide the mix between plates, sprinkle the cilantro on top.
3. Serve when ready.

NUTRITION:

calories: 323 | fat: 12g | protein: 16.4g | carbs: 23.8g | fiber: 11g | sodium: 0mg

379. Stuffed Chicken Breast with Caprese

Prep time: 10 minutes | Cook time: 30 minutes | Serves: 6

INGREDIENTS:

1 1/2 cup shredded fresh Mozzarella cheese
1/3 cup chopped fresh basil
12 tablespoons extra-virgin olive oil, divided
3 (6-ounce / 170 g) boneless, skinless chicken breasts
6 ounces (113 g) frozen spinach, thawed and drained well
3/4 teaspoon garlic powder

3 tablespoons chopped sun-dried tomatoes (preferably marinated in oil)
1 1/2 teaspoon salt, divided
1 1/2 teaspoon freshly ground black pepper, divided
1 1/2 tablespoon balsamic vinegar

DIRECTIONS:
1. Preheat oven to 375° F | 190°C | Fan 170°C
2. Pour 1 tablespoon of olive oil into a small deep pan and shake to coat the bottom.
3. Make a 3-4-inch-deep incision along the length of each chicken breast to create a pocket. Using your knife or your fingers, carefully increase the size of the pocket without cutting the chicken breast. (Each breast will look like a purse with an opening at the top.)
4. In a medium bowl, combine the spinach, mozzarella, basil, dried tomatoes, 2 tablespoons of olive oil, ½ teaspoon of salt, ½ teaspoon of pepper and the garlic powder and mix well with a fork. .
5. Fill half of the stuffing mixture into the pocket of each chicken breast, filling the pocket completely. Press the opening together with your fingers. If you wish, you can use a pair of toothpicks to pin it closed.
6. In a medium skillet, heat 2 tablespoons of olive oil over medium-high heat. Carefully brown the chicken breasts until golden brown, 3-4 minutes per side, being careful not to let too much stuffing out. Transfer to the prepared pan, with the incision facing up. Scrape the filling that fell into the pan and add it to the pan. Cover the pan with foil and cook until the chicken is cooked through, 30 to 40 minutes, depending on the thickness of the breasts.
7. Remove from the oven and leave to rest, covered, for 10 minutes. Meanwhile, in a small bowl, whisk together the remaining 3 tablespoons of olive oil, balsamic vinegar, ½ teaspoon of salt and ½ teaspoon of pepper.
8. To serve, cut each chicken breast in half, widthwise, and serve half a chicken breast drizzled with oil and vinegar.
9. Enjoy!

NUTRITION:
calories: 434 | fat: 34g | protein: 27g | carbs: 2g | fiber: 1g | sodium: 0mg

380. Feta Stuffed Chicken Breasts
Prep time: 10 minutes | Cook time: 20 minutes | Serves: 6

INGREDIENTS:
6 (6-ounce / 170-g) boneless skinless chicken breasts
1 1/2 tablespoon harissa
4 1/2 tablespoons extra-virgin olive oil, divided
⅓ cup cooked brown rice
1 1/2 teaspoon shawarma seasoning
Salt and freshly ground black pepper, to taste
6 small dried apricots, halved
⅓ cup crumbled feta
1 1/2 tablespoon chopped fresh parsley

DIRECTIONS:
1. Preheat oven to 375° F | 190°C | Fan 170°C
2. In a medium bowl, mix the rice and shawarma dressing and set aside.
3. Stuff the chicken breasts by cutting them almost in half, starting with the thickest part and folding them like a book.
4. In a small bowl, mix the harissa with 1 tablespoon of olive oil. Brush the chicken with harissa oil and season with salt and pepper. Harissa adds a nice warmth, so feel free to add a thicker coating for more spice.
5. On one side of each chicken breast, pour 1 or 2 tablespoons of rice, then layer 2 apricot halves on each breast. Divide the feta between the chicken breasts and fold the other side over the filling to close.
6. In a skillet or non-stick skillet, heat the remaining 2 tablespoons of olive oil and sauté the brisket for 2 minutes on each side, then place the pan in the oven for 15 minutes, or until cooked through and the juices flowed out.
7. Serve garnished with parsley.

NUTRITION:
calories: 321 | fat: 17g | protein: 37g | carbs: 8g | fiber: 1g | sodium: 0mg

381. Spatchcock Chicken with Lemon and Rosemary
Prep time: 20 minutes | Cook time: 45 minutes | Serves: 4

INGREDIENTS:
1 1/3 teaspoons salt, divided
2/3 teaspoon freshly ground black pepper, divided
1 1/3 lemons, thinly sliced
1/3 cup extra-virgin olive oil, divided
2/3 (3- to 4-pound / 1.4- to 1.8-kg) roasting chicken
5 1/3 garlic cloves, roughly chopped
1 1/3 to 4 tablespoons chopped fresh rosemary

DIRECTIONS:
1. Preheat oven to 450°F. | 230°C | Fan 210°C
2. Pour 2 tablespoons of olive oil into the bottom of a 9x13 inch pan or rimmed pan and shake to coat the bottom.
3. To spatchcock the bird, place the whole chicken breast side down on a large work surface. Using a very sharp knife, cut along the spine, starting at the tip of the tail and working up to the neck. Separate the two sides, opening the chicken. Flip it over, chest up, pressing with your hands to flatten the bird. Transfer to the prepared pan.
4. Loosen the skin on the breasts and thighs by making a small incision and inserting a finger or two inside to peel the skin off the flesh without removing it.
5. To prepare the filling, in a small bowl, combine 1 cup of olive oil, garlic, rosemary, 1 teaspoon of salt and ½ teaspoon of pepper and whisk together.
6. Rub the garlic and herb oil evenly under the skin of each breast and thigh. Add the lemon slices evenly in the same areas.
7. Whisk together the remaining 2 tablespoons of olive oil, 1 teaspoon of salt and ½ teaspoon of pepper and rub on the outside of the chicken.
8. Place in the oven, uncovered, and roast for 45 minutes, or until completely cooked and golden. Let it rest for 5 minutes before sculpting to serve.
9. Enjoy!

NUTRITION:
calories: 434 | fat: 34g | protein: 28g | carbs: 2g | fiber: 0g | sodium: 0mg

382. Greek Chicken Souvlaki with Tzatziki
Prep time: 10 minutes | Cook time: 8 minutes | Serves: 6

INGREDIENTS:
1 1/2 teaspoon dried rosemary
3/4 teaspoons salt
1/3 cup dry white wine (optional; add extra lemon juice instead, if desired)
3/4 cup extra-virgin olive oil, plus extra for serving
1 1/2 tablespoon dried oregano
9 garlic cloves, finely minced
1 1/2 pound (454 g) boneless, skinless chicken thighs, cut into 1 1/2-inch chunks
1 1/2 cup tzatziki, for serving
Zest and juice of 1 lemon
3/4 teaspoon freshly ground black pepper

DIRECTIONS:
1. In a large glass bowl or resealable plastic bag, combine the olive oil, white wine (if using), garlic, lemon zest and juice, oregano, rosemary, salt and pepper and whisk or shake to mix well. Add the chicken to the marinade and mix to coat. Cover or seal and marinate in the refrigerator for at least 1 hour or up to 24 hours.
2. In a bowl, dip the wooden skewers into the water and let them soak for at least 30 minutes before using them.
3. To cook, heat the grill over medium-high heat. Put the marinated chicken on the soaked skewers, keeping the marinade.
4. Grill until cooked, turning occasionally so the chicken cooks evenly, 5 to 8 minutes. Remove and keep warm.
5. Bring the reserved marinade to a boil in a small saucepan. Reduce the heat to low and simmer for 3 to 5 minutes.
6. Serve the chicken skewers topped with the hot marinade, adding more olive oil if desired and the tzatziki.
7. Enjoy!

NUTRITION:
calories: 493 | fat: 45g | protein: 19g | carbs: 3g | fiber: 0g | sodium: 0mg

383. Chicken Thigh with Roasted Artichokes
Prep time: 5 minutes | Cook time: 20 minutes | Serves: 6

INGREDIENTS:
3 large artichokes
3 large lemons
4 1/2 tablespoons extra-virgin olive oil, divided
3/4 teaspoon kosher or sea salt
6 (6-ounce / 170-g) bone-in, skin-on chicken thighs

DIRECTIONS:
1. Place a large, rimmed baking sheet in the oven. Preheat oven to 450°F. | 230°C | Fan 210°C
with the pan inside. Tear off four aluminum sheets of approximately 8 x 10 inches each; to put aside.
2. Using a Microplane or juicer, grate 1 lemon into a large bowl. Cut both lemons in half and squeeze all the juice into the bowl with the zest. Beat with 2 tablespoons of oil and salt. To put aside.
3. Rinse the artichokes with cold water and dry them with a clean cloth. Using a sharp knife, cut about 1½ inch from the tip of each artichoke. Cut about ¼ inch from each stem. Cut each artichoke in half lengthwise so that each piece has the same amount of stem. Immediately dip the artichoke halves into the lemon juice and oil mixture (to prevent them from blackening) and turn to coat on all sides.
Lay an artichoke halfway flat side down in the center of an aluminum foil

and close lightly to form an aluminum package. Repeat the process with the remaining three artichoke halves. Put the packages aside.
4. Place the chicken in the remaining lemon juice mixture and flip to coat.
5. Using oven gloves, carefully remove the hot pan from the oven and pour the remaining spoonful of oil over it; tilt the pan to coat. Carefully arrange the chicken, skin side down, on the hot pan. Also arrange the artichoke packets, with the flat side facing down, on the baking sheet. (Arrange the artichoke packets and chicken with a space between them so that air can circulate around them.)
6. Roast for 20 minutes, or until the core temperature of the chicken reaches 74°C (165°F) on a meat thermometer and all juices are clear. Before serving, check the cooking of the artichokes by pulling a leaf. If it comes out easily, the artichoke is ready.
7. Serve when ready.

NUTRITION:
calories: 832 | fat: 79g | protein: 19g | carbs: 11g | fiber: 4g | sodium: 544mg

384. Almond-Crusted Chicken Tenders with Honey
Prep time: 10 minutes | Cook time: 20 minutes | Serves: 6

INGREDIENTS:
1 1/2 cup almonds, roughly chopped
1/3 teaspoon freshly ground black pepper
1 1/2 tablespoon honey
1 1/2 tablespoon whole-grain or Dijon mustard
1 1/2 pound (454 g) boneless, skinless chicken breast tenders or tenderloins
1/3 teaspoon kosher or sea salt
Nonstick cooking spray

DIRECTIONS:
1. Preheat oven to 450°F. | 230°C | Fan 210°C. Line a large, rimmed baking sheet with parchment paper. Place a wire cooling rack on the parchment-lined baking sheet and spray the grill well with non-stick cooking spray.
2. In a large bowl, combine the honey, mustard, pepper and salt. Add the chicken and mix gently to coat. To put aside.
3. Pour the almonds onto a large sheet of baking paper and spread them out. Press the walnut-coated chicken tenders until they are evenly coated on all sides. Place the chicken on the prepared grill.
4. Bake in a preheated oven for 15-20 minutes, or until the core temperature of the chicken reaches 74°C (165°F) on a meat thermometer and all juices come out.
5. Cool for 5 minutes before serving Enjoy!

NUTRITION:
calories: 222 | fat: 7g | protein: 11g | carbs: 29g | fiber: 2g | sodium: 448mg

385. Grilled Chicken and Zucchini Kebabs
Prep time: 10 minutes | Cook time: 20 minutes | Serves: 6

INGREDIENTS:
1 1/2 teaspoon dried oregano, crushed between your fingers
1 1/2 pound (454 g) boneless, skinless chicken breasts, cut into 1 1/2-inch pieces
3/4 cup Kalamata olives, pitted and halved
3 tablespoons olive brine
1/3 cup torn fresh basil leaves
3 medium zucchinis, cut into 1-inch pieces
1/3 cup extra-virgin olive oil
3 tablespoons balsamic vinegar
Nonstick cooking spray

DIRECTIONS:
1. Spray the grill with non-stick cooking spray. Preheat the grill over medium-high heat.
2. In a small bowl, whisk together the olive oil, vinegar, and oregano. Divide the marinade between two large zip-up plastic bags.
3. Add the chicken in one bag and the courgettis in another. Seal and massage the marinade into both the chicken and the zucchini.
4. Place the chicken on 6 wooden skewers. Put the courgettis on 8 or 9 wooden skewers.
5. Cook the kebabs in batches on the grill for 5 minutes, flip and grill for another 5 minutes, or until the chicken juices have cleared.
6. Remove the chicken and courgettis from the skewers and place them in a large serving bowl. Season with olives, olive brine and basil and serve.
7. Enjoy!

NUTRITION:
calories: 283 | fat: 15g | protein: 11g | carbs: 26g | fiber: 3g | sodium: 575mg

386. Chicken Sausage and Tomato with Farro
Prep time: 10 minutes | Cook time: 45 minutes | Serves: 4

INGREDIENTS:
3 cups low-sodium chicken stock
2 tablespoon olive oil
1 medium onion, diced
16 ounces (227 g) hot Italian chicken sausage, removed from the casing
1 1/2 cup farro
1/2 cup julienned sun-dried tomatoes packed in olive oil and herbs
4 cups loosely packed arugula
8 to 5 large fresh basil leaves, sliced thin
Salt, to taste

DIRECTIONS:
1. Heat the olive oil in a skillet over medium-high heat. Add the onion and sauté for 5 minutes. Add the dried tomatoes and chicken sausage, stirring to break up the sausage. Cook for 7 minutes, or until the sausage is no longer pink.
2. Incorporate the spelled. Leave to cook for 3 minutes, stirring occasionally.
3. Add the chicken stock and bring to a boil. Cover the pan and reduce the heat to medium-low. Leave to simmer for 30 minutes, or until the farro is tender.
4. Incorporate the rocket and let it dry slightly. Add the basil and season with salt.
5. Serve when ready.

NUTRITION:
calories: 491 | fat: 18g | protein: 31g | carbs: 53g | fiber: 6g | sodium: 765mg

387. Chicken, Mushrooms, and Tarragon Pasta
Prep time: 15 minutes | Cook time: 15 minutes | Serves: 4

INGREDIENTS:
4 cups low-sodium chicken stock
1 medium onion, minced
8 ounces (113 g) baby bella (cremini) mushrooms, sliced
4 tablespoons olive oil, divided
16 ounces (227 g) chicken cutlets
4 teaspoons tomato paste
4 teaspoons dried tarragon
4 small garlic cloves, minced
12 ounces (170 g) pappardelle pasta
1/2 cup plain full-fat Greek yogurt
Salt, to taste
Freshly ground black pepper, to taste

DIRECTIONS:
1. Heat 1 tablespoon of olive oil in a skillet over medium-high heat. Add the onion and mushrooms and sauté for 5 minutes. Add the garlic and cook for 1 minute longer.
2. Move the vegetables to the edges of the pan and add the remaining tablespoon of olive oil to the center of the pan. Place the cutlets in the center and cook them for about 3 minutes, or until they lift easily and are golden on the bottom.
3. Flip the chicken and cook for another 3 minutes.
4. Add the tomato paste and tarragon. Add the chicken stock and mix well to mix everything. Bring the broth to a boil.
5. Add the pappardelle. If necessary, break up the pasta to get it into the pan. Stir the noodles so they don't stick to the bottom of the pan.
6. Cover the pan and reduce the heat to medium-low. Allow the chicken and noodles to simmer for 15 minutes, stirring occasionally, until the pasta is cooked and the liquid is mostly absorbed. If the liquid absorbs too quickly and the pasta is not cooked, add more water or chicken broth, about ¼ cup at a time, as needed.
7. Remove the pan from the heat.
8. Mix 2 tablespoons of the hot liquid from the pan into the yogurt. Pour the tempered yogurt into the pan and mix well to incorporate it into the sauce. Season with salt and pepper.
9. The sauce will shrink as it cools, so if it feels too thick, add a few tablespoons of water.
10. Serve when ready.

NUTRITION:
calories: 556 | fat: 17g | protein: 42g | carbs: 56g | fiber: 1g | sodium: 190mg

BEEF, PORK AND LAMB RECIPES

388. Beef, Pork, and Lamb

Prep time: 10 minutes | Cook time: 5 minutes | Serves: 6

INGREDIENTS:

1 1/2 pound (454 g) ground beef
1/3 teaspoon ground cumin
1 1/2 medium onion
1/3 cup fresh Italian parsley
1/3 teaspoon cinnamon
1 1/2 teaspoon salt
3/4 teaspoon freshly ground black pepper

DIRECTIONS:

1. Preheat a grill or grill pan to high temperature.
2. Chop the onion and parsley in a food processor until finely chopped.
3. In a large bowl, using your hands, combine the beef with the onion mix, ground cumin, cinnamon, salt and pepper.
4. Divide the meat into 6 portions. Shape each portion into a flat oval.
5. Place the meatballs on the grill or grill pan and cook for 3 minutes on each side.
6. Serve when ready.

NUTRITION:

calories: 203 | fat: 10g | protein: 24g | carbs: 3g | fiber: 1g | sodium: 655mg

389. Braised Veal Shanks

Prep time: 10 minutes | Cook time: 2 hours | Serves: 6

INGREDIENTS:

6 veal shanks, bone in
3/4 cup flour
6 tablespoons extra-virgin olive oil
1 1/2 large onion, chopped
7 1/2 cloves garlic, sliced
3 teaspoons salt
1 1/2 tablespoon fresh thyme
4 1/2 tablespoons tomato paste
9 cups water
Cooked noodles, for serving (optional)

DIRECTIONS:

1. Preheat oven to 350°F | 180°C | Fan 160°C
2. Dredge the veal shanks in the flour.
3. Pour the olive oil into a large oven-safe pot or pan over medium heat; add the veal shanks. Brown the veal on both sides, about 4 minutes each side. Remove the veal from pot and set aside.
4. Add the onion, garlic, salt, thyme, and tomato paste to the pan and cook for 3 to 4 minutes. Add the water, and stir to combine.
5. Add the veal back to the pan, and bring to a simmer. Cover the pan with a lid or foil and bake for 1 hour and 50 minutes. Remove from the oven and serve with cooked noodles, if desired.
6. Enjoy!

NUTRITION:

calories: 400 | fat: 19g | protein: 39g | carbs: 18g | fiber: 2g | sodium: 1368mg

390. Ground Pork Stuffed Peppers

Prep time: 0 minutes | Cook time: 40 minutes | Serves: 6

INGREDIENTS:

9 bell peppers, deveined
1 1/2 tablespoon vegetable oil 1 shallot, chopped
3/4 garlic clove, minced
3/4-pound ground pork
1/2-pound ground veal
1 1/2 ripe tomato, chopped
3/4 teaspoon mustard seeds
Sea salt and ground black pepper, to taste

DIRECTIONS:

1. Parboil the peppers for 5 minutes.
2. Heat the vegetable oil in a frying pan that is preheated over a moderate heat. Cook the shallot and garlic for 3 to 4 minutes until they've softened.
3. Stir in the ground meat and cook, breaking apart with a fork, for about 6 minutes. Add the chopped tomatoes, mustard seeds, salt, and pepper.
4. Continue to cook for 5 minutes or until heated through. Divide the filling between the peppers and transfer them to a baking pan.
5. Bake in the preheated oven at 375° F | 190°C | Fan 170°C for approximately 25 minutes.
Storing
1. Place the peppers in airtight containers or Ziploc bags; keep in your refrigerator for up to 3 to 4 days.
2. For freezing, place the peppers in airtight containers or heavy-duty freezer bags. Freeze up to 2 to 3 months. Defrost in the refrigerator.
3. Enjoy!

NUTRITION:

calories: 215 | fat: 20.5g | protein: 18.2g | carbs: 8.2g | fiber: 1.5g | sodium: 1368mg

391. Honey Pork Chops

Prep time: 10 minutes | Cook time: 16 minutes | Serves: 6

INGREDIENTS:

6 pork chops, boneless or bone-in
1/3 teaspoon salt
1/4 teaspoon freshly ground black pepper
4 1/2 tablespoons extra-virgin olive oil
7 1/2 tablespoons low-sodium chicken broth, divided
9 garlic cloves, minced
1/3 cup honey
3 tablespoons apple cider vinegar

DIRECTIONS:

1. Season the pork chops with salt and pepper and set aside.
2. In a large sauté pan or skillet, heat the oil over medium-high heat. Add the pork chops and sear for 5 minutes on each side, or until golden brown.
3. Once the searing is complete, move the pork to a dish and reduce the skillet heat from medium-high to medium. Add 3 tablespoons of chicken broth to the pan; this will loosen the bits and flavors from the bottom of the skillet.
4. Once the broth has evaporated, add the garlic to the skillet and cook for 15 to 20 seconds, until fragrant. Add the honey, vinegar, and the remaining 2 tablespoons of broth. Bring the heat back up to medium-high and continue to cook for 3 to 4 minutes.
5. Stir periodically; the sauce is ready once it's thickened slightly. Add the pork chops back into the pan, cover them with the sauce, and cook for 2 minutes.
6. Serve when ready.

NUTRITION:

calories: 302 | fat: 16g | protein: 22g | carbs: 19g | fiber: 0g | sodium: 753mg

392. Mediterranean Grilled Skirt Steak

Prep time: 10 minutes | Cook time: 10 minutes | Serves: 6

INGREDIENTS:

1 1/2-pound (454 g) skirt steak
1 1/2 teaspoon salt
3/4 teaspoon freshly ground black pepper
3 cups prepared hummus
1 1/2 tablespoon extra-virgin olive oil
3/4 cup pine nuts

DIRECTIONS:

1. Preheat a grill, grill pan, or lightly oiled skillet to medium heat.
2. Season both sides of the steak with salt and pepper.
3. Cook the meat on each side for 3 to 5 minutes; 3 minutes for medium, and 5 minutes on each side for well done. Let the meat rest for 5 minutes.
4. Slice the meat into thin strips.
5. Spread the hummus on a serving dish, and evenly distribute the beef on top of the hummus.
6. In a small saucepan, over low heat, add the olive oil and pine nuts. Toast them for 3 minutes, constantly stirring them with a spoon so that they don't burn.
7. Spoon the pine nuts over the beef and serve.
8. Enjoy!

NUTRITION:

calories: 602 | fat: 41g | protein: 42g | carbs: 20g | fiber: 8g | sodium: 1141m

393. Beef Kofta

Prep time: 10 minutes | Cook time: 5 minutes | Serves: 6

INGREDIENTS:

1 1/2 medium onion
1/3 cup fresh Italian parsley
1 1/2-pound (454 g) ground beef
1/3 teaspoon ground cumin
1/3 teaspoon cinnamon
1 1/2 teaspoon salt
3/4 teaspoon freshly ground black pepper

DIRECTIONS:

1. Preheat a grill or grill pan to high.
2. Mince the onion and parsley in a food processor until finely chopped.
3. In a large bowl, using your hands, combine the beef with the onion mix, ground cumin, cinnamon, salt, and pepper.
4. Divide the meat into 6 portions.
5. Form each portion into a flat oval.
6. Place the patties on the grill or grill pan and cook for 3 minutes on each side.
7. Serve when ready.

NUTRITION:

calories: 203 | fat: 10g | protein: 24g | carbs: 3g | fiber: 1g | sodium: 655mg

394. Beef and Potatoes with Tahini Sauce
Prep time: 10 minutes | Cook time: 30 minutes | Serves: 6

INGREDIENTS:

1 1/2-pound (454 g) ground beef
3 teaspoons salt, divided
3/4 teaspoon freshly ground black pepper
1 1/2 large onion, finely chopped
15 medium golden potatoes
3 tablespoons extra-virgin olive oil
4 1/2 cups Greek yogurt
1 1/2 cup tahini
4 1/2 cloves garlic, minced
3 cups water

DIRECTIONS:

1. Preheat oven to 450°F. | 230°C | Fan 210°C
2. In a large bowl, using your hands, combine the beef with 1 teaspoon salt, black pepper, and the onion.
3. Form meatballs of medium size (about 1-inch), using about 2 tablespoons of the beef mixture. Place them in a deep 8-by-8-inch casserole dish.
4. Cut the potatoes into ¼-inch-thick slices. Toss them with the olive oil.
5. Lay the potato slices flat on a lined baking sheet.
6. Put the baking sheet with the potatoes and the casserole dish with the meatballs in the oven and bake for 20 minutes.
7. In a large bowl, mix together the yogurt, tahini, garlic, remaining 1 teaspoon salt, and water; set aside.
8. Once you take the meatballs and potatoes out of the oven, use a spatula to transfer the potatoes from the baking sheet to the casserole dish with the meatballs, and leave the beef drippings in the casserole dish for added flavor.
9. Reduce the oven temperature to 375° F | 190°C | Fan 170°C and pour the yogurt tahini sauce over the beef and potatoes. Return it to the oven for 10 minutes. Once baking is complete, serve warm with a side of rice or pita bread.
10. Enjoy!

NUTRITION:

calories: 1078 | fat: 59g | protein: 58g | carbs: 89g | fiber: 11g | sodium: 1368mg

395. Mediterranean Lamb Bowls
Prep time: 15 minutes | Cook time: 15 minutes | Serves: 4

INGREDIENTS:

4 tablespoons extra-virgin olive oil
1/2 cup diced yellow onion
2-pound (454 g) ground lamb
2 teaspoon dried mint
2 teaspoon dried parsley
1 teaspoon red pepper flakes
1/2 teaspoon garlic powder
2 cup cooked rice
1 teaspoon za'atar seasoning
1 cup halved cherry tomatoes
2 cucumbers, peeled and diced
2 cup store-bought hummus
2 cup crumbled feta cheese
4 pita breads, warmed (optional)

DIRECTIONS:

1. In a large sauté pan or skillet, heat the olive oil over medium heat and cook the onion for about 2 minutes, until fragrant.
2. Add the lamb and mix well, breaking up the meat as you cook.
3. Once the lamb is halfway cooked, add mint, parsley, red pepper flakes, and garlic powder.
4. In a medium bowl, mix together the cooked rice and za'atar, then divide between individual serving bowls. Add the seasoned lamb, then top the bowls with the tomatoes, cucumber, hummus, feta, and pita (if using).
5. Serve when ready.

NUTRITION:

calories: 1312 | fat: 96g | protein: 62g | carbs: 62g | fiber: 12g | sodium: 1454mg

396. Smoked Pork Sausage
Prep time: 0 minutes | Cook time: 15 minutes | Serves: 4

INGREDIENTS:

1/2-pound smoked pork sausage, ground
2/3 teaspoon ginger-garlic paste
1 1/3 tablespoons scallions, minced
2/3 tablespoon butter, room temperature
2/3 tomato, pureed
2 2/3 ounces mozzarella cheese, crumbled
1 1/3 tablespoons flaxseed meal
5 1/3 ounces cream cheese, room temperature
Sea salt and ground black pepper, to taste

DIRECTIONS:

1. Melt the butter in a frying pan over medium-high heat. Cook the sausage for about 4 minutes, crumbling with a spatula.
2. Add in the ginger-garlic paste, scallions, and tomato; continue to cook over medium-low heat for a further 6 minutes.
3. Stir in the remaining Shopping List.
4. Place the mixture in your refrigerator for 1 to 2 hours until firm. Roll the mixture into bite-sized balls.
Storing
1. Transfer the balls to the airtight containers and place in your refrigerator for up to 3 days.
2. For freezing, place in a freezer safe container and freeze up to 1 month.
3. Enjoy!

NUTRITION:

calories: 386 | fat: 32g | protein: 16.7g | carbs: 5.1g | fiber: 1.7g | sodium: 0mg

397. Roasted Chicken with Cashew Pesto
Prep time: 0 minutes | Cook time: 35 minutes | Serves: 6

INGREDIENTS:

1 1/2 cup leeks, chopped
1 1/2-pound chicken legs, skinless
Salt and ground black pepper, to taste
3/4 teaspoon red pepper flakes
For the Cashew-Basil Pesto:
3/4 cup cashews
3 garlic cloves, minced
3/4 cup fresh basil leaves
3/4 cup Parmigiano-Reggiano cheese, preferably freshly grated
3/4 cup olive oil

DIRECTIONS:

1. Place the chicken legs in a parchment-lined baking pan. Season with salt and pepper, Then, scatter the leeks around the chicken legs.
2. Roast in the preheated oven at 390° F for 30 to 35 minutes, rotating the pan occasionally.
3. Pulse the cashews, basil, garlic, and cheese in your blender until pieces are small. Continue blending while adding olive oil to the mixture. Mix until the desired consistency is reached.
Storing
1. Place the chicken in airtight containers or Ziploc bags; keep in your refrigerator for up 3 to 4 days.
2. To freeze the chicken legs, place them in airtight containers or heavy-duty freezer bags. Freeze up to 3 months. Once thawed in the refrigerator, heat in the preheated oven at 375° F for 20 to 25 minutes.
3. Store your pesto in the refrigerator for up to a week.
4. Enjoy!

NUTRITION:

calories: 302 | fat: 44.8g | protein: 1g | carbs: 5g | fiber: 1g | sodium: 0mg

398. Creamed Greek-style Soup
Prep time: 0 minutes | Cook time: 30 minutes | Serves: 6

INGREDIENTS:

3/4 stick butter
3/4 cup zucchini, diced
3 garlic cloves, minced
6 3/4 cups roasted vegetable broth
Sea salt and ground black pepper, to season
2 1/4 cups leftover turkey, shredded
1/2 cup double cream
3/4 cup Greek-style yogurt

DIRECTIONS:

1. In a heavy-bottomed pot, melt the butter over medium-high heat. Once hot, cook the zucchini and garlic for 2 minutes until they are fragrant.
2. Add in the broth, salt, black pepper, and leftover turkey. Cover and cook for 15-20 minutes, stirring periodically.
3. Then, fold in the cream and yogurt. Continue to cook for 5 minutes more or until thoroughly warmed.
Storing
1. Spoon the soup into four airtight containers or Ziploc bags; keep in your refrigerator for up to 3 to 4 days.
2. For freezing, place the soup in airtight containers. It will maintain the best quality for about 4 months. Defrost in the refrigerator. 3. Enjoy!

NUTRITION:

calories: 256 | fat: 18.8g | protein: 15.8g | carbs: 5.4g | fiber: 0.2g | sodium: 0mg

399. Pork Wraps

Prep time: 0 minutes | Cook time: 15 minutes | Serves: 6

INGREDIENTS:

1 1/2-pound ground pork
3 garlic cloves, finely minced
1 1/2 chili pepper, deveined and finely minced
1 1/2 teaspoon mustard powder
2 1/4 tablespoon sunflower seeds
1 1/2 tablespoons champagne vinegar
1 1/2 tablespoon coconut aminos
Celery salt and ground black pepper, to taste
3 scallion stalks, sliced
1 1/2 head lettuce

DIRECTIONS:

1. Sear the ground pork in the preheated pan at 350° F for about 8 minutes. Stir in the garlic, chili pepper, mustard seeds, and sunflower seeds; continue to sauté for minute longer or until aromatic.
2. Add in the vinegar, coconut aminos, salt, black pepper, and scallions. Stir to combine well.
Storing
1. Place the ground pork mixture in airtight containers or Ziploc bags; keep in your refrigerator for up to 3 to days.
2. For freezing, place the ground pork mixture it in airtight containers or heavy-duty freezer bags. Freeze up to 2 to 3 months. 3. Defrost in the refrigerator and reheat in the skillet.
4. Add spoonful's of the pork mixture to the lettuce leaves, wrap them and serve.
5. Enjoy!

NUTRITION:

calories: 281 | fat: 19.4g | protein: 22.1g | carbs: 5.1g | fiber: 1.3g | sodium: 0mg

400. Ground Pork Skillet

Prep time: 0 minutes | Cook time: 25 minutes | Serves: 6

INGREDIENTS:

2 1/4 pounds ground pork
3 tablespoons olive oil
1 1/2 bunch kale, trimmed and roughly chopped
1 1/2 cup onions, sliced
1/3 teaspoon black pepper, or more to taste
1/3 cup tomato puree
1 1/2 bell pepper, chopped
1 1/2 teaspoon sea salt
1 1/2 cup chicken bone broth
1/3 cup port wine
3/4 cloves garlic, pressed
1 1/2 chili pepper, sliced

DIRECTIONS:

1. Heat tablespoon of the olive oil in a cast-iron skillet over a moderately high heat. Now, sauté the onion, garlic, and peppers until they are tender and fragrant; reserve.
2. Heat the remaining tablespoon of olive oil; once hot, cook the ground pork and approximately 5 minutes until no longer pink.
3. Add in the other Ingredients items and continue to cook for 15 to 17 minutes or until cooked through.
Storing
1. Place the ground pork mixture in airtight containers or Ziploc bags; keep in your refrigerator for up to 3 to 4 days.
2. For freezing, place the ground pork mixture in airtight containers or heavy-duty freezer bags. Freeze up to 2 to 3 months. Defrost in the refrigerator.
3. Enjoy!

NUTRITION:

calories: 349 | fat: 13g | protein: 45.3g | carbs: 4.4g | fiber: 1.2g | sodium: 0mg

401. Grilled Beef Kebabs

Prep time: 15 minutes | Cook time: 10 minutes | Serves: 4
INGREDIENTS:
1 1/3 pounds (907 g) beef fillet
1 teaspoons salt
2/3 teaspoon freshly ground black pepper
1/3 teaspoon ground allspice
1/3 teaspoon ground nutmeg
¹/₃ cup extra-virgin olive oil
2/3 large onion, cut into 8 quarters
2/3 large red bell pepper, cut into 1-inch cubes

DIRECTIONS:

1. Preheat a grill, grill pan, or lightly oiled skillet to high heat.
2. Cut the beef into 1-inch cubes and put them in a large bowl.
3. In a small bowl, mix together the salt, black pepper, allspice, and nutmeg.
4. Pour the olive oil over the beef and toss to coat the beef. Then evenly sprinkle the seasoning over the beef and toss to coat all pieces.
5. Skewer the beef, alternating every 1 or 2 pieces with a piece of onion or bell pepper.
6. To cook, place the skewers on the grill or skillet, and turn every 2 to 3 minutes until all sides have cooked to desired doneness, 6 minutes for medium-rare, 8 minutes for well done.
7. Serve warm.

NUTRITION:

calories: 485 | fat: 36g | protein: 35g | carbs: 4g | fiber: 1g | sodium: 1453mg

402. Turkey Wings With Gravy

Prep time: 0 minutes | Cook time: 6 hours | Serves: 4

INGREDIENTS:

1 1/3 pounds turkey wings
1/3 teaspoon cayenne pepper
2 2/3 garlic cloves, sliced
2/3 large onion, chopped Salt and pepper, to taste
2/3 teaspoon dried marjoram
2/3 tablespoon butter, room temperature
2/3 tablespoon Dijon mustard
For the Gravy:
2/3 cup double cream
Salt and black pepper, to taste
1/3 stick butter
1/2 teaspoon guar gum

DIRECTIONS:

1. Rub the turkey wings with the Dijon mustard and tablespoon of butter. Preheat a grill pan over medium-high heat.
2. Sear the turkey wings for 10 minutes on all sides.
3. Transfer the turkey to your Crock pot; add in the garlic, onion, salt, pepper, marjoram, and cayenne pepper. Cover and cook on low setting for 6 hours.
4. Melt 1/2 stick of the butter in a frying pan. Add in the cream and whisk until cooked through.
5. Next, stir in the guar gum, salt, and black pepper along with cooking juices. Let it cook until the sauce has reduced by half.
Storing
1. Wrap the turkey wings in foil before packing them into airtight containers; keep in your refrigerator for up to 3 to 4 days.
2. For freezing, place the turkey wings in airtight containers or heavy-duty freezer bags. Freeze up to 2 to 3 months. Defrost in the refrigerator.
3. Keep your gravy in refrigerator for up to 2 days.
4. Enjoy!

NUTRITION:

calories: 280 | fat: 22.2g | protein: 15.8g | carbs: 4.3g | fiber: 0.8g | sodium: 0mg

403. Saucy Boston Butt

Prep time: 0 minutes | Cook time: 1 hour 20 minutes | Serves: 6

INGREDIENTS:

3/4 tablespoon lard, room temperature
1 1/2 pounds Boston butt, cubed
Salt and freshly ground pepper
1/3 teaspoon mustard powder
A bunch of spring onions, chopped
1 1/2 garlic cloves, minced
1/3 tablespoon ground cardamom
1 1/2 tomatoes, pureed
3/4 bell pepper, deveined and chopped
1 1/2 jalapeno pepper, deveined and finely chopped
1/3 cup unsweetened coconut milk
1 1/2 cups chicken bone broth

DIRECTIONS:

1. In a wok, melt the lard over moderate heat. Season the pork belly with salt, pepper and mustard powder.
2. Sear the pork for 8 to 10 minutes, stirring periodically to ensure even cooking; set aside, keeping it warm.
3. In the same wok, sauté the spring onions, garlic, and cardamom. Spoon the sautéed vegetables along with the reserved pork into the slow cooker.
4. Add in the remaining Shopping List items, cover with the lid and cook for 1 hour 10 minutes over low heat.
Storing
1. Divide the pork and vegetables between airtight containers or Ziploc bags; keep in your refrigerator for up to 3 to 5 days.
2. For freezing, place the pork and vegetables in airtight containers or heavy-duty freezer bags. Freeze up to 4 months. Defrost in the refrigerator.
3. Enjoy!

NUTRITION:

calories: 369 | fat: 20.2g | protein: 41.3g | carbs: 2.9g | fiber: 0.7g | sodium: 0mg

404. Lamb Burgers

Prep time: 15 minutes | Cook time: 15 minutes | Serves: 6

INGREDIENTS:

- 1 1/2-pound (454 g) ground lamb
- 3/4 small red onion, grated
- 1 1/2 tablespoon dried parsley
- 1 1/2 teaspoon dried oregano
- 1 1/2 teaspoon ground cumin
- 1 1/2 teaspoon garlic powder
- 3/4 teaspoon dried mint
- 1/3 teaspoon paprika
- 1/3 teaspoon kosher salt
- 1/4 teaspoon freshly ground black pepper
- Extra-virgin olive oil
- 6 pita breads, for serving (optional)
- Tzatziki sauce, for serving (optional)
- Pickled onions, for serving (optional)

DIRECTIONS:

1. In a bowl, combine the lamb, onion, parsley, oregano, cumin, garlic powder, mint, paprika, salt, and pepper. Divide the meat into 4 small balls and work into smooth discs.
2. In a large sauté pan or skillet, heat a drizzle of olive oil over medium heat or brush a grill with oil and set it too medium. Cook the patties for 4 to 5 minutes on each side, until cooked through and juices run clear.
3. Serve the lamb burgers in pitas, topped with tzatziki sauce and pickled onions (if using).
4. Enjoy!

NUTRITION:

calories: 328 | fat: 27g| protein: 19g | carbs: 2g | fiber: 1g | sodium: 215mg

405. Sunday Chicken with Cauliflower Salad

Prep time: 0 minutes | Cook time: 20 minutes | Serves: 4

INGREDIENTS:

- 4 teaspoons hot paprika
- 4 tablespoons fresh basil, snipped
- 1 cup mayonnaise
- 4 teaspoon mustard
- 4 teaspoons butter
- 4 chicken wings
- 1 cup cheddar cheese, shredded
- Sea salt and ground black pepper, to taste
- 4 tablespoons dry sherry
- 2 shallots, finely minced
- 1 head of cauliflower

DIRECTIONS:

1. Boil the cauliflower in a pot of salted water until it has softened; cut into small florets and place in a salad bowl.
2. Melt the butter in a saucepan over medium-high heat. Cook the chicken for about 8 minutes or until the skin is crisp and browned. 3.Season with hot paprika salt, and black pepper.
4. Whisk the mayonnaise, mustard, dry sherry, and shallot and dress your salad. Top with cheddar cheese and fresh basil.
Storing
1. Place the chicken wings in airtight containers or Ziploc bags; keep in your refrigerator for up 3 to 4 days.
2. Keep the cauliflower salad in your refrigerator for up 3 days.
3. For freezing, place the chicken wings in airtight containers or heavy-duty freezer bags. Freeze up to 3 months. Once thawed in the refrigerator, reheat in a saucepan until thoroughly warmed.
4. Enjoy!

NUTRITION:

calories: 444 | fat: 36g| protein: 20.6g | carbs: 5.7g | fiber: 4.3g | sodium: 0mg

406. Turkey Bacon Bites

Prep time: 0 minutes | Cook time: 5 minutes | Serves: 6

INGREDIENTS:

- 6 ounces turkey bacon, chopped
- 6 ounces Neufchatel cheese
- 1 1/2 tablespoon butter, cold
- 1 1/2 jalapeno pepper, deveined and minced
- 1 1/2 teaspoon Mexican oregano
- 3 tablespoons scallions, finely chopped

DIRECTIONS:

1. Thoroughly combine all Shopping List items in a mixing bowl.
2. Roll the mixture into 8 balls.
Storing
1. Divide the turkey bacon bites between two airtight containers or Ziploc bags; keep in your refrigerator for up 3 to 5 days.
2. Enjoy!

NUTRITION:

calories: 190 | fat: 16.7g| protein: 8.8g | carbs: 2.2g | fiber: 0.3g | sodium: 0mg

407. Spare Ribs

Prep time: 0 minutes | Cook time: 3 hours 40 minutes | Serves: 4

INGREDIENTS:

- 2/3 pounds spare ribs
- 2/3 garlic clove, minced
- 1 1/3 teaspoon dried marjoram
- 2/3 lime, halved
- Salt and ground black pepper, to taste

DIRECTIONS:

1. Toss all Shopping List items in a ceramic dish.
2. Cover and let it refrigerate for 5 to 6 hours.
3. Roast the foil-wrapped ribs in the preheated oven at 275° F degrees for about 3 hours 30 minutes.
Storing
1. Divide the ribs into six portions. Place each portion of ribs in an airtight container; keep in your refrigerator for 3 days.
2. For freezing, place the ribs in airtight containers or heavy-duty freezer bags. Freeze up to 4 to months. Defrost in the refrigerator and reheat in the preheated oven.
3. Enjoy!

NUTRITION:

calories: 385 | fat: 29g| protein: 28.3g | carbs: 1.8g | fiber: 0.1g | sodium: 0mg

408. Cheesy Pork

Prep time: 0 minutes | Cook time: 20 minutes | Serves: 4

INGREDIENTS:

- 2/3 tablespoon sesame oil
- 1 pound's pork shoulder, cut into strips
- Himalayan salt and freshly ground black pepper, to taste
- 1/3 teaspoon cayenne pepper
- 1/3 cup shallots, roughly chopped
- 1 1/3 bell peppers, sliced
- 1/8 cup cream of onion soup
- 1/3 teaspoon Sriracha sauce
- 2/3 tablespoon tahini (sesame butter)
- 2/3 tablespoon soy sauce
- 2 2/3 ounces gouda cheese, cut into small pieces

DIRECTIONS:

1. Heat the sesame oil in a wok over a moderately high flame.
2. Stir-fry the pork strips for 3 to 4 minutes or until just browned on all sides. Add in the spices, shallots and bell peppers and continue to cook for a further 4 minutes.
3. Stir in the cream of onion soup, Sriracha, sesame butter, and soy sauce; continue to cook for to 4 minutes more.
4. Top with the cheese and continue to cook until the cheese has melted.
Storing
1. Place your stir-fry in six airtight containers or Ziploc bags; keep in your refrigerator for 3 to 4 days.
2. For freezing, wrap tightly with heavy-duty aluminum foil or freezer wrap. It will maintain the best quality for 2 to 3 months. 3.Defrost in the refrigerator and reheat in your wok.
4. Enjoy!

NUTRITION:

calories: 424 | fat: 29.4g |protein: 34.2g | carbs: 3g | fiber: 0.6g | sodium: 0mg

409. Pulled Pork

Prep time: 0 minutes | Cook time: 6 hours | Serves: 6

INGREDIENTS:

- 2 1/4 pounds pork shoulder
- 1 1/2 tablespoon liquid smoke sauce
- 1 1/2 teaspoon chipotle powder
- Au Jus gravy seasoning packet
- 3 onions, cut into wedges
- Kosher salt and freshly ground black pepper, taste

DIRECTIONS:

1. Mix the liquid smoke sauce, chipotle powder, Au Jus gravy seasoning packet, salt and pepper. Rub the spice mixture into the pork on all sides.
2. Wrap in plastic wrap and let it marinate in your refrigerator for 3 hours.
3. Prepare your grill for indirect heat. Place the pork butt roast on the grate over a drip pan and top with onions; cover the grill and cook for about 6 hours.
4. Transfer the pork to a cutting board. Now, shred the meat into bite-sized pieces using two forks.
Storing
1. Divide the pork between four airtight containers or Ziploc bags; keep in your refrigerator for up to 3 to 5 days.

2.For freezing, place the pork in airtight containers or heavy-duty freezer bags. Freeze up to 4 months. Defrost in the refrigerator. 3.Enjoy!

NUTRITION:

calories: 350 | fat: 11g |protein: 53.6g | carbs: 5g | fiber: 2.2g | sodium: 0mg

410. Brie-stuffed Meatballs

Prep time: 0 minutes | Cook time: 25 minutes | Serves: 4

INGREDIENTS:

1 2/3 eggs, beaten	3/4 teaspoon dried rosemary
3/4 pound ground pork	8 (1-inch) cubes of brie cheese
1/4 cup double cream	1 2/3 tablespoons scallions, minced
3/4 tablespoon fresh parsley	1 2/3 cloves garlic, minced
Kosher salt and ground black pepper	

DIRECTIONS:

1.Mix all Shopping List items, except for the brie cheese, until everything is well incorporated.
2.Roll the mixture into 10 patties; place a piece of cheese in the center of each patty and roll into a ball.
3.Roast in the preheated oven at 300 degrees F for about 20 minutes. Storing
1.Place the meatballs in airtight containers or Ziploc bags; keep in your refrigerator for up to 3 to 4 days.
2.Freeze the meatballs in airtight containers or heavy-duty freezer bags. Freeze up to 3 to 4 months. To defrost, slowly reheat in a saucepan.
3.Enjoy!

NUTRITION:

calories: 302 | fat: 13g |protein: 33.4g | carbs: 1.9g | fiber: 0.3g | sodium: 0mg

411. Pork in Cheese Sauce

Prep time: 0 minutes | Cook time: 30 minutes | Serves: 4

INGREDIENTS:

1 1/3 pounds pork center cut loin roast, boneless and cut into 6 pieces	2/3 teaspoon dried hot Chile flakes
2/3 tablespoon coconut aminos	2/3 teaspoon dried rosemary
4 ounces blue cheese	2/3 tablespoon lard
1/4 cup heavy cream	1/3 shallot, chopped
1/4 cup port wine	1 1/3 garlic cloves, chopped
1/4 cup roasted vegetable broth, preferably homemade	Salt and freshly cracked black peppercorns, to taste

DIRECTIONS:

1.Rub each piece of the pork with salt, black peppercorns, and rosemary.
2.Melt the lard in a saucepan over a moderately high flame. Sear the pork on all sides about 15 minutes; set aside.
3.Cook the shallot and garlic until they've softened. Add in port wine to scrape up any brown bits from the bottom.
4.Reduce the heat to medium-low and add in the remaining Shopping List items; continue to simmer until the sauce has thickened and reduced. Storing
1.Divide the pork and sauce into six portions; place each portion in a separate airtight container or Ziploc bag; keep in your refrigerator for 3 to 4 days.
2.Freeze the pork and sauce in airtight containers or heavy-duty freezer bags. Freeze up to 4 months. Defrost in the refrigerator. 3.Enjoy!

NUTRITION:

calories: 340 | fat: 18.9g |protein: 40.3g | carbs: 1.9g | fiber: 0.3g | sodium: 0mg

412. Lamb Koftas

Prep time: 30 minutes | Cook time: 15 minutes | Serves: 6

INGREDIENTS:

1 1/2-pound (454 g) ground lamb	3/4 teaspoon ground nutmeg
3/4 cup finely chopped fresh mint, plus 2 tablespoons	3/4 teaspoon freshly ground black pepper
1/3 cup almond or coconut flour	1 1/2 cup plain whole-milk Greek yogurt
1/3 cup finely chopped red onion	
1/3 cup toasted pine nuts	3 tablespoons extra-virgin olive oil
3 teaspoons ground cumin	Zest and juice of 1 lime
2 1/4 teaspoons salt, divided	
1 1/2 teaspoon ground cinnamon	
1 1/2 teaspoon ground ginger	

DIRECTIONS:

1.Heat the oven broiler to the low setting. You can also bake these at high heat (450 to 475°F / 235 to 245°C) if you happen to have a very hot broiler. Submerge four wooden skewers in water and let soak at least 10 minutes to prevent them from burning.
2.In a large bowl, combine the lamb, ½ cup mint, almond flour, red onion, pine nuts, cumin, 1 teaspoon salt, cinnamon, ginger, nutmeg, and pepper and, using your hands, incorporate all the Shopping List items together well.
3.Form the mixture into 12 egg-shaped patties and let sit for 10 minutes.
4.Remove the skewers from the water, thread 3 patties onto each skewer, and place on a broiling pan or wire rack on top of a baking sheet lined with aluminum foil. Broil on the top rack until golden and cooked through, 8 to 12 minutes, flipping once halfway through cooking.
5.While the meat cooks, in a small bowl, combine the yogurt, olive oil, remaining 2 tablespoons chopped mint, remaining ½ teaspoon salt, and lime zest and juice and whisk to combine well. Keep cool until ready to use.
6.Serve the skewers with yogurt sauce.
7.Enjoy!

NUTRITION:

calories: 500 | fat: 42g |protein: 23g | carbs: 9g | fiber: 2g | sodium: 969mg

413. Lamb Burgers with Spicy Mayo

Prep time: 15 minutes | Cook time: 13 minutes | Serves: 4

INGREDIENTS:

1 small onion, minced	1/2 teaspoon coriander
2 garlic clove, minced	16 ounces (227 g) lean ground lamb
4 teaspoons minced fresh parsley	4 tablespoons olive oil mayonnaise
4 teaspoons minced fresh mint	1 teaspoon harissa paste, plus more or less to taste
1/2 teaspoon salt	
Pinch freshly ground black pepper	4 hamburger buns or pitas, fresh greens, tomato slices (optional, for serving)
2 teaspoon cumin	
2 teaspoon smoked paprika	

DIRECTIONS:

1.Preheat the grill to medium-high, to 350°F | 180°C | Fan 160°C. to 400°F | 200°C | Fan 180°C and oil the grill grate. Alternatively, you can cook these in a heavy pan (cast iron is best) on the stovetop.
2.In a large bowl, combine the onion, garlic, parsley, mint, salt, pepper, cumin, paprika, and coriander. Add the lamb and, using your hands, combine the meat with the spices so they are evenly distributed. Form meat mixture into 2 patties.
3.Grill the burgers for 4 minutes per side, or until the internal temperature registers 160°F (71°C) for medium.
4.If cooking on the stovetop, heat the pan to medium-high and oil the pan. Cook the burgers for 5 to 6 minutes per side, or until the internal temperature registers 160°F (71°C).
5.While the burgers are cooking, combine the mayonnaise and harissa in a small bowl.
6.Serve the burgers with the harissa mayonnaise and slices of tomato and fresh greens on a bun or pita—or skip the bun altogether.
7.Enjoy!

NUTRITION:

calories: 381 | fat: 20g |protein: 22g | carbs: 27g | fiber: 2g | sodium: 653mg

414. Filet Mignon

Prep time: 15 minutes | Cook time: 16 minutes | Serves: 4

INGREDIENTS:

4 (3-ounce / 85-g) pieces filet mignon	2 cup low-sodium chicken stock
4 tablespoons olive oil, divided	1 teaspoon dried thyme
16 ounces (227 g) baby bella (cremini) mushrooms, quartered	2 sprig fresh rosemary
	2 teaspoon herbes de Provence
1/3 cup large shallot, minced	1/2 teaspoon salt
4 teaspoons flour	1/2 teaspoon garlic powder
4 teaspoons tomato paste	1/2 teaspoon onion powder
1 cup red wine	Pinch freshly ground black pepper

DIRECTIONS:

1.Preheat oven to 400°F | 200°C | Fan 180°C and set the oven rack to the middle position.
2.Remove the filets from the refrigerator about 30 minutes before you're ready to cook them. Pat them dry with a paper towel and let them rest while you prepare the mushroom sauce.
3.In a sauté pan, heat 1 tablespoon of olive oil over medium-high heat. Add

the mushrooms and shallot and sauté for 10 minutes.
4. Add the flour and tomato paste and cook for another 30 seconds. Add the wine and scrape up any browned bits from the sauté pan. Add the chicken stock, thyme, and rosemary.
5. Stir the sauce so the flour doesn't form lumps and bring it to a boil. Once the sauce thickens, reduce the heat to the lowest setting and cover the pan to keep the sauce warm.
6. In a small bowl, combine the herbes de Provence, salt, garlic powder, onion powder, and pepper.
7. Rub the beef with the remaining 1 tablespoon of olive oil and season it on both sides with the herb mixture.
8. Heat an oven-safe sauté pan over medium-high heat. Add the beef and sear for 2½ minutes on each side. Then, transfer the pan to the oven for 5 more minutes to finish cooking. Use a meat thermometer to check the internal temperature and remove it at 130°F for medium-rare.
9. Tent the meat with foil and let it rest for 5 minutes before serving topped with the mushroom sauce.
10. Enjoy!

NUTRITION:

calories: 385 | fat: 20g | protein: 25g | carbs: 15g | fiber: 0g | sodium: 330mg

415. Pork Souvlaki with Oregano

Prep time: 10 minutes | Cook time: 10 minutes | Serves: 6

INGREDIENTS:

1 1/2 (1 1/2-pound / 680-g) pork loin	1 1/2 tablespoon dried oregano
3 tablespoons garlic, minced	1 1/2 teaspoon salt
1/3 cup extra-virgin olive oil	Pita bread and tzatziki, for serving (optional)
1/3 cup lemon juice	

DIRECTIONS:

1. Cut the pork into 1-inch cubes and put them into a bowl or plastic zip-top bag.
2. In a large bowl, mix together the garlic, olive oil, lemon juice, oregano, and salt.
3. Pour the marinade over the pork and let it marinate for at least 1 hour.
4. Preheat a grill, grill pan, or lightly oiled skillet to high heat. Using wood or metal skewers, thread the pork onto the skewers.
5. Cook the skewers for 3 minutes on each side, for 12 minutes in total.
6. Serve with pita bread and tzatziki sauce, if desired.
7. Enjoy!

NUTRITION:

calories: 416 | fat: 30g | protein: 32g | carbs: 5g | fiber: 1g | sodium: 1184mg

416. Cheesy Pork Loin

Prep time: 0 minutes | Cook time: 25 minutes | Serves: 6

INGREDIENTS:

1 1/2-pound pork loin, cut into 1-inch-thick pieces 1 teaspoon Mediterranean seasoning mix	sliced
	3 tablespoons balsamic vinegar
	3/4 cup Romano cheese, grated
Salt and pepper, to taste	3 tablespoons butter, room temperature
1 1/2 onion, sliced	1 1/2 tablespoon curry paste
1 1/2 teaspoon fresh garlic, smashed	1 1/2 cup roasted vegetable broth
3 tablespoons black olives, pitted and	1 1/2 tablespoon oyster sauce

DIRECTIONS:

1. In a frying pan, melt the butter over a moderately high heat. Once hot, cook the pork until browned on all sides; season with salt and black pepper and set aside.
2. In the pan drippings, cook the onion and garlic for 4 to 5 minutes or until they've softened.
3. Add in the Mediterranean seasoning mix, curry paste, and vegetable broth. Continue to cook until the sauce has thickened and reduced slightly or about 10 minutes. Add in the remaining Shopping List items along with the reserved pork.
4. Top with cheese and cook for 10 minutes longer or until cooked through.
Storing
1. Divide the pork loin between four airtight containers; keep in your refrigerator for 3 to 5 days.
2. For freezing, place the pork loin in airtight containers or heavy-duty freezer bags. Freeze up to 4 to 6 months. Defrost in the refrigerator.
3. Enjoy!

NUTRITION:

calories: 476 | fat: 35.3g | protein: 31.1g | carbs: 6.2g | fiber: 1.4g | sodium: 0mg

417. Pork Tenderloin with Apple Sauce

Prep time: 10 minutes | Cook time: 20 minutes | Serves: 6

INGREDIENTS:

1 1/8 tablespoons extra-virgin olive oil	1/4 cup apple jelly
3/4 (12-ounce / 340-g) pork tenderloin	1/4 cup apple juice
1/4 teaspoon kosher salt	1 1/2 to 3 tablespoons Dijon mustard
1/4 teaspoon freshly ground black pepper	1/3 tablespoon cornstarch
	1/3 tablespoon cream

DIRECTIONS:

1. Preheat oven to 325°F. | 170°C | Fan 150°C
2. In a large sauté pan or skillet, heat the olive oil over medium heat.
3. Add the pork to the skillet, using tongs to turn and sear the pork on all sides. Once seared, sprinkle pork with salt and pepper, and set it on a small baking sheet.
4. In the same skillet, with the juices from the pork, mix the apple jelly, juice, and mustard into the pan juices. Heat thoroughly over low heat, stirring consistently for 5 minutes. Spoon over the pork.
5. Put the pork in the oven and roast for 15 to 17 minutes, or 20 minutes per pound. Every 10 to 15 minutes, baste the pork with the apple-mustard sauce.
6. Once the pork tenderloin is done, remove it from the oven and let it rest for 15 minutes. Then, cut it into 1-inch slices.
7. In a small pot, blend the cornstarch with cream. Heat over low heat. Add the pan juices into the pot, stirring for 2 minutes, until thickened. Serve the sauce over the pork.
8. Enjoy!

NUTRITION:

calories: 146 | fat: 7g | protein: 13g | carbs: 8g | fiber: 0g | sodium: 192mg

418. Easy Fall-off-the-bone Ribs

Prep time: 0 minutes | Cook time: 8 hours | Serves: 6

INGREDIENTS:

1 1/2-pound baby back ribs	1 1/2 teaspoon Italian herb mix
6 tablespoons coconut aminos	1 1/2 tablespoon butter
1/3 cup dry red wine	1 1/2 teaspoon Serrano pepper, minced
3/4 teaspoon cayenne pepper	1 1/2 Italian pepper, thinly sliced
1 1/2 garlic clove, crushed	3 teaspoon grated lemon zest

DIRECTIONS:

1. Butter the sides and bottom of your Crock pot. Place the pork and peppers on the bottom.
2. Add in the remaining Shopping List items.
3. Slow cook for 8 hours on Low heat setting.
Storing
1. Divide the baby back ribs into four portions. Place each portion of the ribs along with the peppers in an airtight container; keep in your refrigerator for 3 to days.
2. For freezing, place the ribs in airtight containers or heavy-duty freezer bags. Freeze up to 4 to months. Defrost in the refrigerator. 3. Reheat in your oven at 250° F until heated through.
4. Enjoy!

NUTRITION:

calories: 192 | fat: 6.9g | protein: 29.8g | carbs: 0.9g | fiber: 0.5g | sodium: 0mg

419. Flank Steak with Artichokes

Prep time: 15 minutes | Cook time: 1 hour | Serves: 6

INGREDIENTS:

6 tablespoons grapeseed oil, divided	tomatoes, drained
3 pounds (907 g) flank steak	1 1/2 cup tomato sauce
1 1/2 (14-ounce / 397-g) can artichoke hearts, drained and roughly chopped	3 tablespoons tomato paste
	1 1/2 teaspoon dried oregano
1 1/2 onion, diced	1 1/2 teaspoon dried parsley
12 garlic cloves, chopped	1 1/2 teaspoon dried basil
1 1/2 (32-ounce / 907-g) container low-sodium beef broth	3/4 teaspoon ground cumin
	4 1/2 bay leaves
1 1/2 (14 1/2-ounce / 411-g) can diced	3 to 3 cups cooked couscous (optional)

DIRECTIONS:

1. Preheat oven to 450°F. | 230°C | Fan 210°C
2. In an oven-safe sauté pan or skillet, heat 3 tablespoons of oil on medium heat. Sear the steak for 2 minutes per side on both sides. 3. Transfer the

steak to the oven for 30 minutes, or until desired tenderness.
4. Meanwhile, in a large pot, combine the remaining 1 tablespoon of oil, artichoke hearts, onion, and garlic. Pour in the beef broth, tomatoes, tomato sauce, and tomato paste. Stir in oregano, parsley, basil, cumin, and bay leaves.
5. Cook the vegetables, covered, for 30 minutes. Remove bay leaf and serve with flank steak and ½ cup of couscous per plate, if using.
6. Enjoy!

NUTRITION:

calories: 577 | fat: 28g | protein: 55g | carbs: 22g | fiber: 6g | sodium: 1405mg

420. Moroccan Pot Roast

Prep time: 15 minutes | Cook time: 50 minutes | Serves: 6

INGREDIENTS:

12 ounces (227 g) mushrooms, sliced	1 1/2 small eggplant, peeled and diced
6 tablespoons extra-virgin olive oil	2 cups low-sodium beef broth
4 1/2 small onions, cut into 2-inch pieces	3/4 cup halved apricots
3 tablespoons paprika	1/3 cup golden raisins
2 1/4 tablespoons garam masala	4 1/2 pounds (1.4 kg) beef chuck roast
3 teaspoons salt	3 tablespoons honey
1/3 teaspoon ground white pepper	1 1/2 tablespoon dried mint
3 tablespoons tomato paste	3 cups cooked brown rice

DIRECTIONS:

1. Set an electric pressure cooker to Sauté and put the mushrooms and oil in the cooker. Sauté for 5 minutes, then add the onions, paprika, garam masala, salt, and white pepper. Stir in the tomato paste and continue to sauté.
2. Add the eggplant and sauté for 5 more minutes, until softened. Pour in the broth. Add the apricots and raisins. Sear the meat for 2 minutes on each side.
3. Close and lock the lid and set the pressure cooker to high for 50 minutes.
4. When cooking is complete, quick release the pressure. Carefully remove the lid, then remove the meat from the sauce and break it into pieces. While the meat is removed, stir honey and mint into the sauce.
5. Assemble plates with ½ cup of brown rice, ½ cup of pot roast sauce, and 3 to 5 pieces of pot roast.
6. Serve when ready.

NUTRITION:

calories: 829 | fat: 34g | protein: 69g | carbs: 70g | fiber: 11g | sodium: 1556mg

421. Lemon-Rosemary Lamb Chops

Prep time: 10 minutes | Cook time: 10 minutes | Serves: 4

INGREDIENTS:

1/3 cup fresh rosemary	1 teaspoons salt
2/3 cup extra-virgin olive oil	2/3 teaspoon freshly ground black pepper
2 2/3 large cloves garlic	
2/3 cup lemon juice	4 (1-inch-thick) lamb chops

DIRECTIONS:

1. In a food processor or blender, blend the garlic, lemon juice, rosemary, olive oil, salt, and black pepper for 15 seconds. Put it aside.
2. Place the lamb chops in a large zip-up plastic bag or container. Cover the lamb with two-thirds of the rosemary dressing, making sure all lamb chops are coated with the dressing. Leave the lamb to marinate in the refrigerator for 1 hour.
3. When you are almost ready to eat, remove the lamb chops from the fridge and let them rest on the counter for 20 minutes. Preheat a grill, grill, or lightly oiled skillet over high heat.
4. Cook the lamb chops for 3 minutes per side. To serve, toss the lamb with the remaining seasoning.
5. Serve when ready.

NUTRITION:

calories: 484 | fat: 42g | protein: 24g | carbs: 5g | fiber: 1g | sodium: 655mg

422. Herbed Lamb Burgers

Prep time: 15 minutes | Cook time: 15 minutes | Serves: 6

INGREDIENTS:

1 1/2 teaspoon ground cumin	3/4 teaspoon dried mint
1 1/2 teaspoon garlic powder	1/3 teaspoon paprika
1 1/2-pound (454 g) ground lamb	pepper
3/4 small red onion, grated	Extra-virgin olive oil
1 1/2 tablespoon dried parsley	6 pita breads, for serving (optional)
1 1/2 teaspoon dried oregano	Tzatziki sauce, for serving (optional)
1/3 teaspoon kosher salt	Pickled onions, for serving (optional)
1/4 teaspoon freshly ground black	

DIRECTIONS:

1. In a bowl, combine the lamb, onion, parsley, oregano, cumin, garlic powder, mint, paprika, salt and pepper. Divide the meat into 4 balls and work into smooth discs.
2. In a large skillet or skillet, heat a drizzle of olive oil over medium heat or brush a grill with oil and set it to medium. Cook the meatballs for 4 to 5 minutes on each side, until they are well cooked and the sauce is transparent.
3. Enjoy lamb burgers in pitas, topped with tzatziki sauce and pickled onions (if using).
4. Serve when ready.

NUTRITION:

calories: 328 | fat: 27g | protein: 19g | carbs: 2g | fiber: 1g | sodium: 215mg

423. Greek-Style Lamb Burgers

Prep time: 10 minutes | Cook time: 10 minutes | Serves: 6

INGREDIENTS:

1 1/2-pound (454 g) ground lamb
6 tablespoons feta cheese, crumbled
3/4 teaspoon salt
3/4 teaspoon freshly ground black pepper
Buns, toppings, and tzatziki, for serving (optional)

DIRECTIONS:

1. Preheat a grill, grill pan or lightly oiled skillet over high heat.
2. In a large bowl, using your hands, combine the lamb with the salt and pepper.
3. Divide the meat into 4 portions. Divide each portion in half to make a top and bottom. Flatten each half into a 3-inch circle. Make a dent in the centre of one of the halves and place 1 tablespoon of feta cheese in the centre. Place the second half of the patty on top of the feta cheese and press down to close the 2 halves together, making it look like a round burger.
4. Cook the stuffed patty for 3 minutes on each side over medium heat. Serve on a bun with your favourite toppings and tzatziki sauce if desired.
5. Serve when ready.

NUTRITION:

calories: 345 | fat: 29g | Protein: 20g | Carbs: 1g | Fiber: 0g | Sodium: 462mg

424. Mediterranean Grilled Skirt Steak

Prep time: 10 minutes | Cook time: 10 minutes | Serves: 6

INGREDIENTS:

3/4 teaspoon freshly ground black pepper	1 1/2-pound (454 g) skirt steak
3 cups prepared hummus	1 1/2 teaspoon salt
1 1/2 tablespoon extra-virgin olive oil	3/4 cup pine nuts

DIRECTIONS:

1. Preheat a grill, grill pan, or lightly oiled skillet over medium heat.
2. Season both sides of the steak with salt and pepper.
3. Cook the meat on each side for 3-5 minutes; 3 minutes for medium and 5 minutes per side for well done. Leave the meat to rest for 5 minutes.
4. Cut the meat into thin strips.
5. Spread the hummus on a serving plate and distribute the meat evenly over the hummus.
6. In a saucepan, over low heat, add the olive oil and pine nuts. Toast them for 3 minutes, stirring constantly with a spoon so that they do not burn.
7. Spread the pine nuts on the meat and serve.
8. Serve when ready.

NUTRITION:

calories: 602 | fat: 41g | protein: 42g | carbs: 20g | fiber: 8g | sodium: 1141mg

425. Braised Veal Shanks

Prep time: 10 minutes | Cook time: 2 hours | Serves: 6

INGREDIENTS:

1 1/2 large onion, chopped
7 1/2 cloves garlic, sliced
3 teaspoons salt
1 1/2 tablespoon fresh thyme
6 veal shanks, bone in
3/4 cup flour
6 tablespoons extra-virgin olive oil
4 1/2 tablespoons tomato paste
9 cups water
Cooked noodles, for serving (optional)

DIRECTIONS:
1. Preheat oven to 350°F | 180°C | Fan 160°C.
2. Flour the veal shanks.
3. Pour the olive oil into a large pot or skillet over medium heat; add the veal shanks. Brown the veal on both sides, about 4 minutes per side. Remove the veal from the pot and set aside.
4. Add the onion, garlic, salt, thyme and tomato paste to the pan and cook for 3 to 4 minutes. Add the water and mix to combine.
5. Return the veal to the pan and bring to a boil. Cover the pan with a lid or foil and cook for 1 hour and 50 minutes. Remove from the oven and serve with cooked pasta if desired.
6. Serve when ready.

NUTRITION:
calories: 400 | fat: 19g | protein: 39g | carbs: 18g | fiber: 2g | sodium: 1368mg

426. Lamb Burgers with Harissa Mayo
Prep time: 10 minutes | Cook time: 13 minutes | Serves: 4

INGREDIENTS:

2 teaspoons smoked paprika
1/2 teaspoon coriander
16 ounces (227 g) lean ground lamb
1 small onion, minced
1/2 teaspoon salt
Pinch freshly ground black pepper
2 teaspoon cumin
2 garlic cloves, minced
4 teaspoons minced fresh parsley
4 teaspoons minced fresh mint
4 tablespoons olive oil mayonnaise
1 teaspoon harissa paste, plus more or less to taste
4 hamburger buns or pitas, fresh greens, tomato slices (optional, for serving)

DIRECTIONS:
1. Preheat the grill to a medium-high temperature from 180°C (350°F) to 205°C (400°F) and oil the grill. Alternatively, you can cook them in a heavy skillet (cast iron is best) on the stovetop.
2. In a large bowl, combine the onion, garlic, parsley, mint, salt, pepper, cumin, paprika, and cilantro. Add the lamb and, using your hands, add the meat to the spices so that they are evenly distributed. Form 2 meatballs with the meat mixture.
3. Grill the burgers for 4 minutes on each side or until the internal temperature reaches 71°C (160°F) for an average value.
4. If you are cooking on the stove, heat the pan to medium-high heat and grease it. Cook the burgers for 5-6 minutes on each side, or until the core temperature reaches 71°C.
5. While the burgers are cooking, combine the mayonnaise and harissa in a small bowl.
6. Serve the burgers with the harissa mayonnaise and tomato slices and fresh vegetables on a bun or pita, or skip the bun altogether.
7. Serve when ready.

NUTRITION:
calories: 381 | fat: 20g | protein: 22g | carbs: 27g | fiber: 2g | sodium: 653mg

427. Rosemary Pork Chops
Prep time: 10 minutes | Cook time: 35 minutes | Serves: 6

INGREDIENTS:

6 pork loin chops, boneless
Salt and black pepper to the taste 4 garlic cloves, minced
1 1/2 tablespoon rosemary, chopped 1 tablespoon olive oil

DIRECTIONS:
1. In a baking dish, combine the pork chops with the rest of the ingredients, mix and bake at 425° F for 10 minutes.
2. Reduce heat to 350° F and cook the ribs for another 25 minutes.
3. Divide the ribs on plates and serve with a side salad.
4. Serve when ready.

NUTRITION:
calories: 161 | fat: 5g | protein: 25g | carbs: 27g | fiber: 1g | sodium: 653mg

428. Pork Chops and Relish
Prep time: 10 minutes | Cook time: 14 minutes | Serves: 4

INGREDIENTS:

4 pork chops, boneless
2 ounces marinated artichoke hearts, chopped and their liquid reserved A pinch of salt and black pepper
2/3 teaspoon hot pepper sauce 1 and 1/2 cups tomatoes, cubed 1 jalapeno pepper, chopped
1/3 cup roasted bell peppers, chopped
1/3 cup black olives, pitted and sliced

DIRECTIONS:
1. In a bowl, mix the chops with the pepper sauce, the liquid reserved for the artichokes, cover and refrigerate for 15 minutes.
2. Heat a grill over medium-high heat, add the pork chops and cook 7 minutes per side.
3. In a bowl, combine the artichokes with the peppers and other ingredients, mix, divide over the chops and serve.
4. Serve when ready.

NUTRITION:
calories: 215 | fat: 6g | protein: 35g | carbs: 6g | fiber: 1g | sodium: 653mg

429. Pork Chops and Peach Chutney
Prep time: 10 minutes | Cook time: 30 minutes | Serves: 6

INGREDIENTS:

6 pork loin chops, boneless
Salt and black pepper to the taste
3/4 teaspoon garlic powder
1/3 teaspoon cumin, ground
3/4 teaspoon sage, dried cooking spray
1 1/2 teaspoon chili powder
1 1/2 teaspoon oregano, dried
For the chutney:
1/3 cup shallot, minced
1 1/2 teaspoon olive oil
3 cups peaches, peeled and chopped
3/4 cup red sweet pepper, chopped
3 tablespoons jalapeno chili pepper, minced
1 1/2 tablespoon balsamic vinegar
3/4 teaspoon cinnamon powder
3 tablespoons cilantro, chopped

DIRECTIONS:
1. Heat a pan with olive oil over medium heat, add the shallot and sauté for 5 minutes.
2. Add the sweet pepper, peaches, chili, vinegar, cinnamon and coriander, mix, simmer for 10 minutes and remove from heat.
3. Meanwhile, in a bowl, combine the pork chops with the cooking spray, salt, pepper, garlic powder, cumin, sage, oregano and chilli powder and scrub well.
4. Heat the grill over medium-high heat, add the pork chops, cook for 6-7 minutes per side, divide into plates and serve with the chutney on top.
5. Enjoy!

NUTRITION:
calories: 297 | fat: 10g | protein: 38g | carbs: 13g | fiber: 2g | sodium: 653mg

430. Glazed Pork Chops
Prep time: 10 minutes | Cook time: 20 minutes | Serves: 6

INGREDIENTS:

1/3 cup apricot preserves
6 pork chops, boneless
1 1/2 tablespoon thyme, chopped
3/4 teaspoon cinnamon powder 2 tablespoons olive oil

DIRECTIONS:
1. Heat a skillet with oil over medium-high heat, add the apricot preserves and cinnamon. Blend, bring to a boil, cook for 10 minutes and remove from heat.
2. Heat the grill over medium-high heat. Brush the pork chops with a little apricot glaze, place them on the grill and cook for 10 minutes.
3. Flip the chops, brush them with more apricot glaze, cook for another 10 minutes and divide into plates.
4. Sprinkle with thyme and serve.
5. Enjoy!

NUTRITION:
calories: 225 | fat: 11g | protein: 23g | carbs: 6g | fiber: 0g | sodium: 653mg

431. Pork Chops and Cherries Mix
Prep time: 10 minutes | Cook time: 12 minutes | Serves: 6

INGREDIENTS:

6 pork chops, boneless
Salt and black pepper to the taste
3/4 cup cranberry juice
1 1/2 and 1/2 teaspoons spicy mustard
3/4 cup dark cherries, pitted and halved cooking spray

DIRECTIONS:
1. Heat a pan greased with cooking spray over medium-high heat, add the pork chops, cook 5 minutes per side and divide them into plates.
2. Heat the same pan over medium heat, add the cranberry juice and the rest of the ingredients, whisk, bring to a boil, cook for 2 minutes, drizzle with the pork chops and serve.
3. Enjoy!

NUTRITION:
calories: 262 | fat: 8g | protein: 30g | carbs: 16g | fiber: 1g | sodium: 653mg

432. Baked Pork Chops
Prep time: 10 minutes | Cook time: 30 minutes | Serves: 6

INGREDIENTS:
6 pork loin chops, boneless
A pinch of salt and black pepper 1 tablespoon sweet paprika
3 tablespoons Dijon mustard
1 Cooking spray

DIRECTIONS:
1. In a bowl, mix the pork chops with salt, pepper, paprika and mustard and rub well.
2. Grease a baking sheet with cooking spray, add pork chops, cover with aluminium foil, place in the oven and bake at 400° F for 30 minutes.
3. Divide the pork chops on plates and serve with a side salad.
4. Enjoy!

NUTRITION:
calories: 167 | fat: 5g | protein: 25g | carbs: 2g | fiber: 1g | sodium: 653mg

433. Pork Chops with Veggies
Prep time: 10 minutes | Cook time: 30 minutes | Serves: 6

INGREDIENTS:
6 pork loin chops, boneless
1 1/2 teaspoon Italian seasoning 1 zucchini, sliced
1 1/2 yellow squash, cubed
1 1/2 cup cherry tomatoes, halved
3/4 teaspoon oregano, dried
Salt and black pepper to the taste
1 1/2 tablespoon olive oil
3 garlic cloves, minced
1/3 cup kalamata olives, pitted and halved
Juice of 1 lime
1/3 cup feta cheese, crumbled

DIRECTIONS:
1. In a baking dish, combine the pork chops with salt, pepper, seasoning and the rest of the ingredients except the cheese, mix a little, put the lid on and bake at 360° F for 30 minutes.
2. Divide the mixture into plates, sprinkle with cheese and serve.
3. Enjoy!

NUTRITION:
calories: 230 | fat: 9g | protein: 28g | carbs: 2g | fiber: 1g | sodium: 653mg

434. Pork Chops and Herbed Tomato Sauce
Prep time: 10 minutes | Cook time: 10 minutes | Serves: 6

INGREDIENTS:
6 pork loin chops, boneless
9 tomatoes, peeled and crushed
3 tablespoons parsley, chopped 2 tablespoons olive oil
1/3 cup kalamata olives, pitted and halved
1 1/2 yellow onion, chopped
1 1/2 garlic clove, minced

DIRECTIONS:
1. Heat a pan with oil over medium heat, add the pork chops, cook for 3 minutes per side and divide them into plates.
2. Heat the same pan over medium heat, add the tomatoes, parsley and the rest of the ingredients, blend, simmer for 4 minutes, drizzle with the ribs and serve.
3. Enjoy!

NUTRITION:
calories: 334 | fat: 17g | protein: 34g | carbs: 12g | fiber: 2g | sodium: 653mg

435. Roasted Lamb Chops
Prep time: 10 minutes | Cook time: 27 minutes | Serves: 6

INGREDIENTS:
6 lamb chops
3/4 cup basil leaves, chopped
3/4 cup mint leaves, chopped
tablespoon rosemary, chopped 2 garlic cloves, minced
tablespoons olive oil
1 1/2 eggplant, cubed
3 zucchinis, cubed
1 1/2 yellow bell pepper, roughly chopped
3 ounces feta cheese, crumbled
12 ounces cherry tomatoes, halved

DIRECTIONS:
1. In a baking dish, combine the pork chops with basil, mint, rosemary and the rest of the ingredients, cover with aluminum foil, bake and cook at 200°F for 27 minutes.
2. Divide the mix on plates and serve.
3. Enjoy!

NUTRITION:
calories: 334 | fat: 17g | protein: 24g | carbs: 18g | fiber: 7g | sodium: 653mg

436. Lemon Leg of Lamb Mix
Prep time: 10 minutes | Cook time: 40 minutes | Serves: 6

INGREDIENTS:
4 1/2-pound leg of lamb, boneless 2 cups goat cheese, crumbled 2 garlic cloves, minced
3 teaspoons lemon zest, grated 1
tablespoon olive oil
3/4 teaspoon thyme, chopped 1 bunch watercress
1 1/2 tablespoon lemon juice

DIRECTIONS:
1. Grease a pan with oil, add the leg of lamb, add the rest of the ingredients except the goat cheese, bake and cook at 425° F for 30 minutes.
2. Add the cheese, mix, cook for another 10 minutes, cool, slice and serve.
3. Enjoy!

NUTRITION:
calories: 680 | fat: 55g | protein: 43g | carbs: 4g | fiber: 1g | sodium: 653mg

437. Pork and Chestnuts Mix
Prep time: 10 minutes | Cook time: 0 minutes | Serves: 6

INGREDIENTS:
2 1/4 cups brown rice, already cooked
9 cups pork roast, already cooked and shredded
4 1/2 ounces water chestnuts, drained
and sliced
3/4 cup sour cream
A pinch of salt and white pepper

DIRECTIONS:
1. In a bowl mix the rice with the roast and the other ingredients, mix and refrigerate for 2 hours before serving.
2. Enjoy!

NUTRITION:
calories: 294 | fat: 17g | protein: 23g | carbs: 16g | fiber: 8g | sodium: 653mg

438. Pork and Sour Cream Mix
Prep time: 10 minutes | Cook time: 40 minutes | Serves: 6

INGREDIENTS:
1 1/2- and 1/2-pounds pork meat, boneless and cubed 1 red onion, chopped
1 1/2 tablespoon avocado oil 1 garlic clove, minced
3/4 cup chicken stock
3 tablespoons hot paprika
Salt and black pepper to the taste
1 1/2 and 1/2 cups sour cream
1 1/2 tablespoon cilantro, chopped

DIRECTIONS:
1. Heat a saucepan with oil over medium heat, add the pork and brown it for 5 minutes.
2. Add the onion and garlic and cook for another 5 minutes.
3. Add the rest of the ingredients except the cilantro, bring to a boil and cook over medium heat for 30 minutes.
4. Add the cilantro, mix, divide into plates and serve.
5. Enjoy!

NUTRITION:
calories: 300 | fat: 9g | protein: 23g | carbs: 15g | fiber: 4g | sodium: 653mg

439. Grilled Pork Chops and Mango Mix
Prep time: 10 minutes | Cook time: 22 minutes | Serves: 6

INGREDIENTS:

6 pork loin chops, boneless
2 tablespoons olive oil
3 spring onions, chopped
2 garlic cloves, minced
3 mangos, peeled and cubed
1 teaspoon sweet paprika
Salt and black pepper to the taste
3/4 teaspoon oregano, dried

DIRECTIONS:

1. Heat a skillet with oil over medium-high heat, add pork chops and sauté for 2 minutes per side.
2. Add the onions and garlic and sauté for another 3 minutes.
3. Add the rest of the ingredients and cook for 15 minutes, stirring occasionally.
4. Divide the mix on plates and serve.
5. Enjoy!

NUTRITION:

calories: 304 | fat: 14g | protein: 23g | carbs: 12g | fiber: 5g | sodium: 653mg

440. Pork and Peas

Prep time: 10 minutes | Cook time: 20 minutes | Serves: 6

INGREDIENTS:

6 ounces snow peas
3 tablespoons avocado oil
1 1/2-pound pork loin, boneless and cubed
1 1/8 cup beef stock
3/4 cup red onion, chopped
Salt and white pepper to the taste

DIRECTIONS:

1. Heat a skillet with oil over medium-high heat, add the pork and sauté for 5 minutes.
2. Add the peas and the rest of the ingredients, mix, bring to a boil and cook over medium heat for 15 minutes.
3. Divide the mix on plates and serve immediately.
4. Enjoy!

NUTRITION:

calories: 332 | fat: 16g | protein: 26g | carbs: 20g | fiber: 10g | sodium: 653mg

441. Lime Cumin Pork

Prep time: 10 minutes | Cook time: 45 minutes | Serves: 6

INGREDIENTS:

1 1/2 red onion, chopped
1 1/2 tablespoon olive oil
1 1/2 and 1/2 teaspoons ginger, grated
3 garlic cloves, chopped
Salt and black pepper to the taste
2 teaspoons cumin, ground
and 1/2 pounds pork meat, roughly cubed
3 cups chicken stock
3 tablespoons lime juice

DIRECTIONS:

1. Heat a saucepan with oil over medium heat, add the meat and sauté for 5 minutes.
2. Add the onion and garlic and cook for another 5 minutes.
3. Add the rest of the ingredients, bring to a boil and cook over medium heat for 35 minutes.
4. Divide into plates and serve.
5. Enjoy!

NUTRITION:

calories: 292 | fat: 16g | protein: 16g | carbs: 10g | fiber: 9g | sodium: 653mg

442. Thyme Pork and Pearl Onions

Prep time: 10 minutes | Cook time: 45 minutes | Serves: 6

INGREDIENTS:

3 pounds pork loin roast, boneless and cubed
3 tablespoons olive oil
Salt and black pepper to the taste
1 1/2 cup tomato sauce
3 garlic cloves, minced
1 1/2 teaspoon thyme, chopped
1 1/8-pound pearl onions, peeled

DIRECTIONS:

1. In a pan, combine the pork with the oil and the rest of the ingredients, mix, put in the oven and cook at 180° F for 45 minutes.
2. Divide the mix on plates and serve.
3. Enjoy!

NUTRITION:

calories: 273 | fat: 15g | protein: 18g | carbs: 16g | fiber: 11g | sodium: 653mg

443. Tomatoes and Carrots Pork Mix

Prep time: 10 minutes | Cook time: 7 hours | Serves: 6

INGREDIENTS:

3 tablespoons olive oil
3/4 cup chicken stock
1 1/2 tablespoon ginger, grated
Salt and black pepper to the taste
1 1/2- and 1/2-pounds pork stew meat, roughly cubed
3 cups tomatoes, chopped
6 ounces carrots, chopped
1 1/2 tablespoon cilantro, chopped

DIRECTIONS:

1. In your slow cooker, combine the oil with the stock, ginger and the rest of the ingredients, cover and cook over low heat for 7 hours.
2. Divide the mix on plates and serve.
3. Enjoy!

NUTRITION:

calories: 303 | fat: 15g | protein: 10g | carbs: 14g | fiber: 8g | sodium: 653mg

444. Pork, Greens and Corn

Prep time: 10 minutes | Cook time: 0 minutes | Serves: 6

INGREDIENTS:

3 red chili, chopped
3 tablespoons balsamic vinegar
1 tablespoon lime juice
1 1/2 teaspoon olive oil
6 ounces mixed salad greens
3 ounces corn
1 1/2 green bell pepper, cut into strips
6 ounces pork stew meat, cooked and cut in thin strips

DIRECTIONS:

1. In a bowl, combine the pork with the pepper and the rest of the ingredients, mix and refrigerate for 10 minutes before serving.
2. Divide the mix on plates and serve.
3. Enjoy!

NUTRITION:

calories: 285 | fat: 14g | protein: 13g | carbs: 23g | fiber: 10g | sodium: 653mg

445. Balsamic Ground Lamb

Prep time: 10 minutes | Cook time: 12 minutes | Serves: 6

INGREDIENTS:

Salt and black pepper to the taste
3 tablespoons olive oil
9 scallions, chopped
3 tablespoons ginger, grated
2 garlic cloves, minced
1 1/2-pound lamb stew, ground
1 tablespoon chili paste
3 tablespoons balsamic vinegar
1/3 cup chicken stock
1/3 cup dill, chopped

DIRECTIONS:

1. Heat a pan with the oil over medium-high heat, add the shallot, stir and sauté for 3 minutes.
2. Add the meat and sauté for another 3 minutes.
3. Add the rest of the ingredients, mix, cook for another 6 minutes, divide into bowls and serve.
4. Enjoy!

NUTRITION:

calories: 303 | fat: 13g | protein: 19g | carbs: 15g | fiber: 9g | sodium: 653mg

446. Oregano and Pesto Lamb

Prep time: 10 minutes | Cook time: 25 minutes | Serves: 6

INGREDIENTS:

3 pounds pork shoulder, boneless and cubed
1/3 cup olive oil
3 teaspoons oregano, dried
1/3 cup lemon juice
6 garlic cloves, minced
3 teaspoons basil pesto
Salt and black pepper to the taste

DIRECTIONS:

1. Heat up a pan with the oil over medium-high heat, add the pork and brown for 5 minutes.
2. Add the rest of the ingredients, cook for 20 minutes more, tossing the mix from time to time, divide between plates and serve.
3. Enjoy!

NUTRITION:
calories: 297 | fat: 14g | protein: 22g | carbs: 16g | fiber: 9g | sodium: 653mg

447. Orange Lamb and Potatoes
Prep time: 10 minutes | Cook time: 7 hours | Serves: 6
INGREDIENTS:

1 1/2-pound small potatoes, peeled and cubed
3 cups stewed tomatoes, drained
Zest and juice of 1 orange 4 garlic cloves, minced
4 1/2- and 1/2-pounds leg of lamb, boneless and cubed
Salt and black pepper to the taste
3/4 cup basil, chopped

DIRECTIONS:

1. In the slow cooker, combine the lamb with the potatoes and the rest of the ingredients, mix, cover and cook on low for 7 hours.
2. Divide the mix on plates and serve hot.
3. Enjoy!

NUTRITION:
calories: 287 | fat: 9g | protein: 18g | carbs: 14g | fiber: 7g | sodium: 653mg

448. Lamb and Zucchini Mix
Prep time: 10 minutes | Cook time: 4 hours | Serves: 6
INGREDIENTS:

3 pounds lamb stew meat, cubed
1 1/2 and 1/2 tablespoons avocado oil
4 1/2 zucchinis, sliced
1 1/2 brown onion, chopped 3 garlic cloves, minced
1 1/2 tablespoon thyme, dried 2 teaspoons sage, dried
1 1/2 cup chicken stock
3 tablespoons tomato paste

DIRECTIONS:

1. In a slow cooker, combine the lamb with the oil, the courgettes and the rest of the ingredients, mix, cover and cook over high heat for 4 hours.
2. Divide the mix on plates and serve immediately.
3. Enjoy!

NUTRITION:
calories: 272 | fat: 14g | protein: 13g | carbs: 14g | fiber: 10g | sodium: 653mg

449. Pork and Sage Couscous
Prep time: 10 minutes | Cook time: 7 hours | Serves: 6
INGREDIENTS:

3 pounds pork loin boneless and sliced
1 1/8 cup veggie stock
3 tablespoons olive oil
3/4 tablespoon chili powder 2 teaspoon
sage, dried
3/4 tablespoon garlic powder
Salt and black pepper to the taste
3 cups couscous, cooked

DIRECTIONS:

1. In a slow cooker, combine the pork with the broth, oil and other ingredients except the couscous, cover and cook over low heat for 7 hours.
2. Divide the mixture into plates, add the couscous aside, sprinkle with the sage and serve.
3. Enjoy!

NUTRITION:
calories: 272 | fat: 14g | protein: 9g | carbs: 16g | fiber: 10g | sodium: 653mg

450. Roasted Basil Pork
Prep time: 10 minutes | Cook time: 3 hours | Serves: 4
INGREDIENTS:

1 1/3 tablespoons garlic, minced 1 tablespoon sweet paprika 1 tablespoon basil, chopped 3 tablespoons olive oil
1 1/3 pounds pork shoulder
Salt and black pepper to the taste

DIRECTIONS:

1. In a baking dish, combine the pork with the garlic and other ingredients, mix and bake at 365° F and cook for 3 hours.
2. Remove the pork shoulder from the oven, slice it, divide it into plates and serve with a side of salad.
3. Enjoy!

NUTRITION:
calories: 303 | fat: 14g | protein: 17g | carbs: 20g | fiber: 14g | sodium: 653mg

451. Fennel Pork
Prep time: 10 minutes | Cook time: 2 hours | Serves: 6
INGREDIENTS:

6 pork loin roasts, trimmed, and boneless
Salt and black pepper to the taste
6 garlic cloves, minced
3 teaspoons fennel, ground 1 tablespoon fennel seeds
3 teaspoons red pepper, crushed
1/3 cup olive oil

DIRECTIONS:

1. In a pan, combine the pork with salt, pepper and the rest of the ingredients, mix, put in the oven and cook at 180° F for 2 hours.
2. Slice the roast, divide it into plates and serve with a side salad.
3. Enjoy!

NUTRITION:
calories: 300 | fat: 4g | protein: 15g | carbs: 6g | fiber: 2g | sodium: 653mg

452. Lamb and Sweet Onion Sauce
Prep time: 10 minutes | Cook time: 40 minutes | Serves: 6
INGREDIENTS:

3 pounds lamb meat, cubed
1 1/2 tablespoon sweet paprika
Salt and black pepper to the taste 1 and 1/2 cups veggie stock
6 garlic cloves, minced
3 tablespoons olive oil
1 1/2-pound sweet onion, chopped 1 cup balsamic vinegar

DIRECTIONS:

1. Heat a saucepan with oil over medium heat, add onion, vinegar, salt and pepper, mix and cook for 10 minutes.
2. Add the meat and the rest of the ingredients, mix, bring to a boil and cook over medium heat for 30 minutes.
3. Divide the mix between plates and serve.
4. Enjoy!

NUTRITION:
calories: 303 | fat: 12g | protein: 17g | carbs: 15g | fiber: 7g | sodium: 653mg

453. Cheddar Lamb and Zucchinis
Prep time: 10 minutes | Cook time: 30 minutes | Serves: 6
INGREDIENTS:

1 1/2-pound lamb meat, cubed 1 tablespoon avocado oil
3 cups zucchinis, chopped
3/4 cup red onion, chopped
Salt and black pepper to the taste
22 1/2 ounces canned roasted 2 tomatoes, crushed
1 1/8 cup cheddar cheese, shredded

DIRECTIONS:

1. Heat a pan with oil over medium-high heat, add the meat and onion and sauté for 5 minutes.
2. Add the rest of the ingredients except the cheese, bring to a boil and cook over medium heat for 20 minutes.
3. Add the cheese, cook for another 5 minutes, divide into plates and serve.
4. Enjoy!

NUTRITION:
calories: 306 | fat: 16g | protein: 18g | carbs: 15g | fiber: 13g | sodium: 653mg

454. Pork and Mustard Shallots Mix
Prep time: 10 minutes | Cook time: 25 minutes | Serves: 6
INGREDIENTS:

4 1/2 shallots, chopped
1 1/2-pound pork loin, cut into strips
3/4 cup veggie stock
3 tablespoons olive oil
A pinch of salt and black pepper
3 teaspoons mustard
1 1/2 tablespoon parsley, chopped

DIRECTIONS:

1. Heat a pan with the oil over medium-high heat, add the shallot and sauté for 5 minutes.
2. Add the meat and cook for 10 minutes, turning it often.

3. Add the rest of the ingredients, mix, cook for another 10 minutes, divide into plates and serve immediately.
4. Enjoy!

NUTRITION:

calories: 296 | fat: 16g | protein: 22g | carbs: 13g | fiber: 12g | sodium: 653mg

455. Creamy Pork and Turnips Mix

Prep time: 10 minutes | Cook time: 1 hour and 20 minutes | Serves: 6

INGREDIENTS:

3 pounds pork loin, sliced 2 tablespoons olive oil
3 turnips, chopped
1 1/2 teaspoon black
3 peppercorns, crushed
3 red onions, chopped
3 cups Greek yogurt
1 1/2 teaspoon mustard
Salt and black pepper to the taste

DIRECTIONS:

1. Heat a skillet with oil over medium-high heat, add the meat, sauté for 4 minutes on each side and transfer to a bowl.
2. Reheat the pan over medium heat, add the onions, turnips and peppercorns and sauté for 5 minutes.
3. Put the meat back, add the rest of the ingredients, mix, place the pan in the oven and cook at 180° F for 1 hour.
4. Divide everything into plates and serve.
5. Enjoy!

NUTRITION:

calories: 217 | fat: 7g | protein: 15g | carbs: 20g | fiber: 10g | sodium: 653mg

456. Ground Lamb Pan

Prep time: 10 minutes | Cook time: 20 minutes | Serves: 6

INGREDIENTS:

Zest and juice of 2 limes
1 1/2- and 1/2-pounds lamb, ground 2 garlic cloves, minced
3 tablespoons olive oil
Salt and black pepper to the taste 1 pint
cherry tomatoes, halved
1 1/2 small red onion, chopped
3 tablespoons tomato paste
1 1/2 tablespoon rosemary, chopped

DIRECTIONS:

1. Heat a skillet with oil over medium-high heat, add the meat and garlic and sauté for 5 minutes.
2. Add the rest of the ingredients, mix, cook for another 15 minutes, divide into bowls and serve.
3. Enjoy!

NUTRITION:

calories: 287 | fat: 9g | protein: 15g | carbs: 20g | fiber: 10g | sodium: 653mg

457. Pork Salad

Prep time: 10 minutes | Cook time: 10 minutes | Serves: 6

INGREDIENTS:

1 1/2-pound pork loin, cut into strips
4 1/2 scallions, chopped
1 1/2 cucumber, sliced
1 1/2 red chili, sliced
1 1/2 tablespoon coriander leaves, chopped
3 ounces walnuts, chopped
3 tablespoons olive oil
Salt and black pepper to the taste
Juice of 1 lime
1 1/2 garlic clove, minced

DIRECTIONS:

1. Heat a skillet with half the oil over medium-high heat, add the meat, cook for 5 minutes on each side and transfer to a bowl.
2. Add the rest of the ingredients to the bowl, mix and serve.
3. Enjoy!

NUTRITION:

calories: 267 | fat: 13g | protein: 17g | carbs: 20g | fiber: 10g | sodium: 653mg

458. Nutmeg Lamb Mix

Prep time: 10 minutes | Cook time: 30 minutes | Serves: 6

INGREDIENTS:

2/3 red onion, chopped
2/3 tablespoon olive oil
1/2 cup celery, chopped
Salt and black pepper to the taste
19 1/3 ounces canned tomatoes, drained and chopped
2/3 garlic clove, minced
2/3-pound lamb meat, cubed
2/3 cup veggie stock
1/3 teaspoon nutmeg, ground
1 1/3 teaspoons parsley, chopped

DIRECTIONS:

1. Heat up a pan with the oil over medium heat, add the onion and the garlic and sauté for 5 minutes.
2. Add the meat and brown for 5 minutes more.
3. Add the rest of the ingredients, bring to a simmer and cook over medium heat for 20 minutes.
4. Divide everything between plates and serve.
5. Enjoy!

NUTRITION:

calories: 284 | fat: 13g | protein: 17g | carbs: 14g | fiber: 8g | sodium: 653mg

459. Turmeric Pork and Parsnips

Prep time: 10 minutes | Cook time: 1 hour and 40 minutes | Serves: 6

INGREDIENTS:

3/4-pound pork loin, sliced 2 tablespoons olive oil
2 1/4 parsnips, sliced
1 1/2 red onion, chopped
Salt and black pepper to the taste
2 1/4 garlic cloves, chopped
1 1/2 cups veggie stock
1 1/2 tablespoons tomato paste
1 1/2 teaspoons turmeric powder 1 teaspoon oregano, dried
1 1/2 tablespoons parsley, chopped

DIRECTIONS:

1. Heat a saucepan with oil over medium-high heat, add the meat, onion and garlic and sauté for 8 minutes.
2. Add the rest of the ingredients, place the pan in the oven and bake at 180° F for 1 hour and 20 minutes.
3. Divide everything into plates and serve.
4. Enjoy!

NUTRITION:

calories: 303 | fat: 23g | protein: 19g | carbs: 22g | fiber: 9g | sodium: 653mg

460. Lamb and Wine Sauce

Prep time: 10 minutes | Cook time: 2 hour and 40 minutes | Serves: 6

INGREDIENTS:

3 tablespoons olive oil
3 pounds leg of lamb, trimmed and sliced
4 1/2 garlic cloves, chopped
3 yellow onions, chopped 3 cups veggie stock
3 cups dry red wine
3 tablespoons tomato paste
6 tablespoons avocado oil
1 1/2 teaspoon thyme, chopped
Salt and black pepper to the taste

DIRECTIONS:

1. Heat a skillet with oil over medium-high heat, add the meat, brown for 5 minutes on each side and transfer to a pan.
2. Heat the skillet over medium heat, add the avocado oil, add the onions and garlic and sauté for 5 minutes.
3. Add the remaining ingredients, mix, bring to a boil and cook for 10 minutes.
4. Pour the sauce over the meat, place the pan in the oven and cook at 180° F for 2 hours and 20 minutes.
5. Divide everything into plates and serve.
6. Enjoy!

NUTRITION:

calories: 273 | fat: 21g | protein: 18g | carbs: 16g | fiber: 11g | sodium: 653mg

461. Sweet Chili Lamb

Prep time: 10 minutes | Cook time: 25 minutes | Serves: 6

INGREDIENTS:

1 1/2 tablespoon olive oil
1 1/2-pound lamb stew meat, cubed
3/4 cup sweet chili sauce
1 1/2 cup carrot, chopped
3/4 cup veggie stock
1 1/2 tablespoon cilantro, chopped Salt and black pepper to the taste

DIRECTIONS:

1. Heat a skillet with oil over medium-high heat, add the lamb and sauté for 5 minutes.

2. Add the rest of the ingredients, bring to a boil and cook over medium heat for another 20 minutes.
3. Divide everything into plates and serve.
4. Enjoy!

NUTRITION:
calories: 287 | fat: 21g | protein: 18g | carbs: 25g | fiber: 11g | sodium: 653mg

462. Italian Pork and Mushrooms
Prep time: 10 minutes | Cook time: 7 hours | Serves: 6

INGREDIENTS:
1 1/2 pounds pork stew meat, cubed Salt and black pepper to the taste
3 cups veggie stock
3 tablespoons olive oil
1 1/2 yellow onion, chopped
3 tablespoons thyme, chopped 4 garlic cloves, minced
1 1/2-pound white mushrooms, chopped
3 cups tomatoes, crushed
3/4 cup parsley, chopped

DIRECTIONS:
1. In your slow cooker, combine the meat with salt, pepper, broth and the rest of the ingredients, cover and cook over low heat for 7 hours.
2. Divide the mix on plates and serve immediately.
3. Enjoy!

NUTRITION:
calories: 328 | fat: 16g | protein: 15g | carbs: 11g | fiber: 9g | sodium: 653mg

463. Lamb and Dill Apples
Prep time: 10 minutes | Cook time: 25 minutes | Serves: 6

INGREDIENTS:
4 1/2 green apples, cored, peeled and cubed
Juice of 1 lemon
1 1/2-pound lamb stew meat, cubed 1 small bunch dill, chopped
3 ounces heavy cream
3 tablespoon olive oil
Salt and black pepper to the taste

DIRECTIONS:
1. Heat a skillet with oil over medium-high heat, add the lamb and sauté for 5 minutes.
2. Add the rest of the ingredients, bring to a boil and cook over medium heat for 20 minutes.
3. Divide the mix on plates and serve.
4. Enjoy!

NUTRITION:
calories: 328 | fat: 16g | protein: 14g | carbs: 21g | fiber: 10g | sodium: 653mg

464. Pork Chops and Tarragon Sauce
Prep time: 10 minutes | Cook time: 28 minutes | Serves: 6

INGREDIENTS:
6 pork chops
Salt and black pepper to the taste 2 tablespoons avocado oil
3/4 cup tomato puree
1 1/2 tablespoon Italian seasoning
1 1/2 tablespoon tarragon, chopped

DIRECTIONS:
1. Heat a skillet with the avocado oil over medium-high heat, add the pork chops and sauté for 4 minutes on each side.
2. Add the rest of the ingredients, place the pan in the oven and bake at 400° F for 20 minutes.
3. Divide everything into plates and serve.
4. Enjoy!

NUTRITION:
calories: 219 | fat: 18g | protein: 12g | carbs: 11g | fiber: 10g | sodium: 653mg

465. Chili Pork Meatballs
Prep time: 10 minutes | Cook time: 20 minutes | Serves: 6

INGREDIENTS:
1 1/2-pound pork meat, ground
3/4 cup parsley, chopped
1 1/2 cup yellow onion, chopped 4 garlic cloves, minced
1 1/2 tablespoon ginger, grated 1 Thai chili, chopped
3 tablespoons olive oil 1 cup veggie stock
3 tablespoons sweet paprika

DIRECTIONS:
1. In a bowl, mix the pork with the other ingredients except the oil, the broth and the paprika, mix well and form medium balls with this mixture.
2. Heat a skillet with oil over medium-high heat, add the meatballs and cook 4 minutes per side.
3. Add the broth and paprika, mix gently, simmer over medium heat for another 12 minutes, divide into bowls and serve.
4. Enjoy!

NUTRITION:
calories: 224 | fat: 18g | protein: 14g | carbs: 11g | fiber: 10g | sodium: 653mg

466. Lamb and Peanuts Mix
Prep time: 10 minutes | Cook time: 20 minutes | Serves: 6

INGREDIENTS:
3 tablespoons lime juice
1 1/2 tablespoon balsamic vinegar 5 garlic cloves, minced
3 tablespoons olive oil
Salt and black pepper to the taste 1- and
1/2-pound lamb meat, cubed
3 tablespoons peanuts, toasted and chopped
3 scallions, chopped

DIRECTIONS:
1. Heat a skillet with oil over medium-high heat, add the meat and cook for 4 minutes on each side.
2. Add the shallot and garlic and sauté for another 2 minutes.
3. Add the rest of the ingredients, skip cooking for another 10 minutes, divide into plates and serve immediately.
4. Enjoy!

NUTRITION:
calories: 300 | fat: 14g | protein: 17g | carbs: 15g | fiber: 9g | sodium: 653mg

467. Lamb and Green Onions Mix
Prep time: 10 minutes | Cook time: 25 minutes | Serves: 6

INGREDIENTS:
1 1/2- and 1/2-pounds lamb, cubed 2 garlic cloves, minced
3 tablespoons olive oil
Salt and black pepper to the taste
3/4 cup veggie stock
3/4 teaspoon saffron powder
1/3 teaspoon cumin, ground 4 green onions, sliced

DIRECTIONS:
1. Heat a pan with the oil over medium-high heat, add the garlic, spring onions, saffron and cumin, stir and sauté for 5 minutes.
2. Add the meat and brown it for another 5 minutes.
3. Add salt, pepper and broth, mix, bring to a boil and cook over medium heat for another 15 minutes.
4. Divide everything into plates and serve immediately.
5. Enjoy!

NUTRITION:
calories: 292 | fat: 13g | protein: 14g | carbs: 13g | fiber: 9g | sodium: 653mg

468. Pork Chops and Peppercorns Mix
Prep time: 10 minutes | Cook time: 20 minutes | Serves: 6

INGREDIENTS:
1 1/2 cup red onion, sliced
1 1/2 tablespoon black
3 peppercorns, crushed
1/3 cup veggie stock
7 1/2 garlic cloves, minced
A pinch of salt and black pepper
3 tablespoons olive oil
6 pork chops

DIRECTIONS:
1. Heat a skillet with oil over medium-high heat, add the pork chops and sauté for 4 minutes per side.
2. Add the onion and garlic and cook for another 2 minutes.
3. Add the rest of the ingredients, cook for 10 minutes, stirring occasionally, divide into plates and serve.
4. Enjoy!

NUTRITION:
calories: 232 | fat: 9g | protein: 24g | carbs: 13g | fiber: 5g | sodium: 653mg

469. Lamb and Barley Mix

Prep time: 10 minutes | Cook time: 8 hours and 10 minutes | Serves: 6

INGREDIENTS:

3 tablespoons olive oil
1 1/2 cup barley soaked overnight, drained and rinsed
1 1/2-pound lamb meat, cubed
1 1/2 red onion, chopped
6 garlic cloves, minced 3 carrots, chopped
9 tablespoons dill, chopped 2 tablespoons tomato paste 3 cups veggie stock
A pinch of salt and black pepper

DIRECTIONS:

1. Heat a pan with oil over medium-high heat, add the meat, brown it for 5 minutes on each side and transfer to the slow cooker.
2. Add the barley and the rest of the ingredients, cover and cook over low heat for 8 hours.
3. Divide everything into plates and serve.
4. Enjoy!

NUTRITION:

calories: 292 | fat: 12g | protein: 7g | carbs: 16g | fiber: 5g | sodium: 653mg

470. Pork and Cabbage Mix

Prep time: 10 minutes | Cook time: 8 hours and 10 minutes | Serves: 6

INGREDIENTS:

3 pounds pork stew meat, roughly cubed
1 1/2 and 1/2 cups veggie stock
3 red onions, sliced
3 tablespoons olive oil
3 garlic cloves, minced
1 1/2 tablespoon sweet paprika
1 1/2 green cabbage head, shredded
3/4 cup tomato sauce
Salt and black pepper to the taste
1/3 cup dill, chopped

DIRECTIONS:

1. Heat a skillet with oil over medium-high heat, add the meat, sauté for 5 minutes on each side and transfer to a slow cooker.
2. Add the onions, broth and the rest of the ingredients, cover and cook over low heat for 8 hours.
3. Divide the mix on plates and serve immediately.
4. Enjoy!

NUTRITION:

calories: 299 | fat: 14g | protein: 15g | carbs: 16g | fiber: 10g | sodium: 653mg

471. Lamb and Rice

Prep time: 10 minutes | Cook time: 1 hours and 10 minutes | Serves: 6

INGREDIENTS:

1 1/2 tablespoon lime juice
1 1/2 yellow onion, chopped 1 pound lamb, cubed
3-ounce avocado oil
3 garlic cloves, minced
Salt and black pepper to the taste
3 cups veggie stock
1 1/2 cup brown rice
A handful parsley, chopped

DIRECTIONS:

1. Heat a pan with the avocado oil over medium-high heat, add the onion, stir and sauté for 5 minutes.
2. Add the meat and sauté for another 5 minutes.
3. Add the rest of the ingredients except the parsley, bring to a boil and cook over medium heat for 1 hour.
4. Add the parsley, mix, divide everything into plates and serve.
5. Enjoy!

NUTRITION:

calories: 302 | fat: 13g | protein: 14g | carbs: 15g | fiber: 10g | sodium: 653mg

472. Lamb and Raisins

Prep time: 10 minutes | Cook time: 30 minutes | Serves: 6

INGREDIENTS:

1 1/2 cup raisins
1 1/2- and 1/2-pounds lamb, cubed 1 tablespoon olive oil
1 1/2 garlic clove, minced
1 1/2 yellow onion, grated
1 1/2 tablespoon ginger, grated
3 tablespoons orange juice
A pinch of salt and black pepper
1 1/2 cup veggie stock

DIRECTIONS:

1. Heat a pan with the oil over medium-high heat, add the garlic and onion and sauté for 5 minutes.
2. Add the lamb and sauté for another 5 minutes.
3. Add the rest of the ingredients, bring to a boil and cook over medium heat for 20 minutes.
4. Divide the mix on plates and serve.
5. Enjoy!

NUTRITION:

calories: 292 | fat: 13g | protein: 16g | carbs: 17g | fiber: 9g | sodium: 653mg

473. Sour Cream Lamb Mix

Prep time: 10 minutes | Cook time: 2 hours and 15 minutes | Serves: 6

INGREDIENTS:

3 pounds leg of lamb, boneless 2 tablespoons mustard
3/4 cup avocado oil
3 tablespoons basil, chopped 2 tablespoons tomato paste 2 garlic cloves, minced
Salt and black pepper to the taste
1 1/2 cup white wine
3/4 cup sour cream

DIRECTIONS:

1. Heat a skillet with avocado oil over medium-high heat, add the meat and sauté for 6 minutes on each side.
2. Add the rest of the ingredients, place the pan in the oven and bake at 180° F for 2 hours.
3. Divide the mix on plates and serve.
4. Enjoy!

NUTRITION:

calories: 312 | fat: 12g | protein: 16g | carbs: 21g | fiber: 16g | sodium: 653mg

474. Garlic Lamb and Peppers

Prep time: 10 minutes | Cook time: 1 hours and 30 minutes | Serves: 6

INGREDIENTS:

1 1/2 red bell pepper, sliced
1 1/2 green bell pepper, sliced 1 yellow bell pepper, sliced 2 tablespoons olive oil
1/2 cup mint, chopped
6 garlic cloves, minced
3/4 cup veggie stock
and 1/2 tablespoon lemon juice
6 lamb chops
Salt and black pepper to the taste

DIRECTIONS:

1. Heat a skillet with oil over medium-high heat, add the lamb chops and sauté for 4 minutes per side.
2. Add the rest of the ingredients, place the pan in the oven and bake at 180° F for 1 hour and 20 minutes.
3. Divide the mix on plates and serve.
4. Enjoy!

NUTRITION:

calories: 300 | fat: 14g | protein: 24g | carbs: 15g | fiber: 9g | sodium: 653mg

475. Lamb and Cauliflower Mix

Prep time: 10 minutes | Cook time: 1 hour | Serves: 6

INGREDIENTS:

1 1/2 pounds lamb meat, roughly cubed
3 tablespoons olive oil
1 1/2 teaspoon garlic, minced
1 1/2 yellow onion, chopped
1 1/2 teaspoon rosemary, chopped 1 cup veggie stock
3 cups cauliflower florets
3 tablespoons sweet paprika Salt and pepper to the taste

DIRECTIONS:

1. Heat a saucepan with the oil over medium-high heat, add the onion and garlic and fry for 5 minutes.
2. Add the meat and sauté for another 5-6 minutes.
3. Add the rest of the ingredients, bring to a boil and cook over medium heat for 50 minutes.
4. Divide the mix on plates and serve.
5. Enjoy!

NUTRITION:

calories: 336 | fat: 14g | protein: 24g | carbs: 21g | fiber: 10g | sodium: 653mg

476. Allspice Pork Mix

Prep time: 10 minutes | Cook time: 8 hours | Serves: 6

INGREDIENTS:

3 pounds pork loin, sliced 1 tablespoon olive oil
Salt and white pepper to the taste
3 shallots, chopped
3 teaspoons whole allspice, ground
1 1/2 cup veggie stock
1 1/2 tablespoon tomato paste
3 bay leaves

DIRECTIONS:

1. In your slow cooker, combine the pork with the oil, salt, pepper and the rest of the ingredients, cover and cook over low heat for 8 hours.
2. Divide the mix on plates and serve immediately.
3. Enjoy!

NUTRITION:

calories: 329 | fat: 14g | protein: 24g | carbs: 18g | fiber: 11g | sodium: 653mg

477. Minty Balsamic Lamb

Prep time: 10 minutes | Cook time: 11 minutes | Serves: 6

INGREDIENTS:

3 red chilies, chopped
3 tablespoons balsamic vinegar 1 cup mint leaves, chopped
Salt and black pepper to the taste
3 tablespoons olive oil
6 lamb fillets
1 1/2 tablespoon sweet paprika

DIRECTIONS:

1. Heat a skillet with half the oil over medium-high heat, add the chilies, vinegar and the rest of the ingredients except the lamb, blend and cook over medium heat for 5 minutes.
2. Brush the lamb with the rest of the oil, season with salt and black pepper, place on the preheated grill and cook over medium heat for 3 minutes per side.
3. Divide the lamb on plates, drizzle with the mint vinaigrette and serve.
4. Enjoy!

NUTRITION:

calories: 312 | fat: 12g | protein: 17g | carbs: 17g | fiber: 9g | sodium: 653mg

478. Tasty Lamb Ribs

Prep time: 10 minutes | Cook time: 2 hours | Serves: 6

INGREDIENTS:

3 garlic cloves, minced
1/3 cup shallot, chopped
3 tablespoons fish sauce
3/4 cup veggie stock
3 tablespoons olive oil
1 1/2 and 1/2 tablespoons lemon juice
1 1/2 tablespoon coriander seeds, ground
1 1/2 tablespoon ginger, grated
Salt and black pepper to the taste
3 pounds lamb ribs

DIRECTIONS:

1. In a pan, combine the lamb with the garlic, the shallot and the rest of the ingredients, mix, bake at 300° F and cook for 2 hours.
2. Divide the lamb on plates and serve with a side salad.
3. Enjoy!

NUTRITION:

calories: 293 | fat: 9g | protein: 24g | carbs: 17g | fiber: 9g | sodium: 653mg

479. Cinnamon and Coriander Lamb

Prep time: 10 minutes | Cook time: 6 hours | Serves: 6

INGREDIENTS:

1 1/2- and 1/2-pounds lamb shoulder, cubed
3 tomatoes, chopped
1 1/2 garlic clove, minced
1 1/2 tablespoon cinnamon powder Salt and black pepper to the taste
3/4 cup veggie stock
1 1/2 bunch coriander, chopped

DIRECTIONS:

1. In your slow cooker, combine the lamb with the tomatoes and the rest of the ingredients, cover and cook over low heat for 6 hours.
2. Divide everything into plates and serve.
3. Enjoy!

NUTRITION:

calories: 352 | fat: 15g | protein: 15g | carbs: 18g | fiber: 10g | sodium: 653mg

480. Lamb and Plums Mix

Prep time: 10 minutes | Cook time: 6 hours and 10 minutes | Serves: 6

INGREDIENTS:

6 lamb shanks
1 1/2 red onion, chopped
3 tablespoons olive oil
1 1/2 cup plums, pitted and halved 1
tablespoon sweet paprika
3 cups chicken stock
Salt and pepper to the taste

DIRECTIONS:

1. Heat a skillet with oil over medium-high heat, add lamb, sauté for 5 minutes on each side and transfer to slow cooker.
2. Add the rest of the ingredients, cover and cook on High for 6 hours.
3. Divide the mix on plates and serve immediately.
4. Enjoy!

NUTRITION:

calories: 293 | fat: 13g | protein: 15g | carbs: 15g | fiber: 9g | sodium: 653mg

481. Rosemary Lamb

Prep time: 10 minutes | Cook time: 6 hours | Serves: 6

INGREDIENTS:

3 pounds lamb shoulder, cubed 1 tablespoon rosemary, chopped
3 garlic cloves, minced
3/4 cup lamb stock
6 bay leaves
Salt and black pepper to the taste

DIRECTIONS:

1. In your slow cooker, combine the lamb with the rosemary and the rest of the ingredients, cover and cook over high heat for 6 hours.
2. Divide the mix between the plates and serve.
3. Enjoy!

NUTRITION:

calories: 292 | fat: 13g | protein: 15g | carbs: 18g | fiber: 11g | sodium: 653mg

482. Lemony Lamb and Potatoes

Prep time: 10 minutes | Cook time: 2 hours and 10 minutes | Serves: 6

INGREDIENTS:

3-pound lamb meat, cubed 2 tablespoons olive oil
3 springs rosemary, chopped
3 tablespoons parsley, chopped 1 tablespoon lemon rind, grated 3 garlic cloves, minced
3 tablespoons lemon juice
3 pounds baby potatoes, scrubbed and halved
1 1/2 cup veggie stock

DIRECTIONS:

1. In a pan, combine the meat with the oil and the rest of the ingredients, put it in the oven and cook at 200° F for 2 hours and 10 minutes.
2. Divide the mix on plates and serve.
3. Enjoy!

NUTRITION:

calories: 302 | fat: 15g | protein: 15g | carbs: 23g | fiber: 10g | sodium: 653mg

483. Lamb and Feta Artichokes

Prep time: 10 minutes | Cook time: 8 hours and 5 minutes | Serves: 6

INGREDIENTS:

3 pounds lamb shoulder, boneless and roughly cubed 2 spring onions, chopped
1 1/2 tablespoon olive oil
4 1/2 garlic cloves, minced
1 1/2 tablespoon lemon juice
Salt and black pepper to the taste 1 and
1/2 cups veggie stock
9 ounces canned artichoke hearts, drained and quartered
3/4 cup feta cheese, crumbled
3 tablespoons parsley, chopped

DIRECTIONS:

1. Heat a skillet with oil over medium-high heat, add lamb, sauté 5 minutes and transfer to slow cooker.
2. Add the rest of the ingredients except the parsley and cheese, cover and cook over low heat for 8 hours.
3. Add the cheese and parsley, divide the mixture into plates and serve.
4. Enjoy!

NUTRITION:

calories: 330 | fat: 15g | protein: 17g | carbs: 21g | fiber: 14g | sodium: 653mg

484. Lamb and Mango Sauce

Prep time: 10 minutes | Cook time: 1 hour | Serves: 6

INGREDIENTS:

3 cups Greek yogurt
1 1/2 cup mango, peeled and cubed 1 yellow onion, chopped
1/2 cup parsley, chopped 1 pound lamb, cubed
3/4 teaspoon red pepper flakes
Salt and black pepper to the taste
3 tablespoons olive oil
1/3 teaspoon cinnamon powder

DIRECTIONS:

1. Heat a skillet with oil over medium-high heat, add the meat and sauté for 5 minutes.
2. Add the onion and sauté for another 5 minutes.
3. Add the rest of the ingredients, mix, bring to a boil and cook over medium heat for 45 minutes.
4. Divide everything into plates and serve.
5. Enjoy!

NUTRITION:

calories: 300 | fat: 15g | protein: 17g | carbs: 15g | fiber: 9g | sodium: 653mg

485. Pork Chops with Sweet Peppers and Cabbage

Prep time: 10 minutes | Cook time: 23 minutes | Serves: 6

INGREDIENTS:

6 pork chops
1 1/2 teaspoon rosemary, dried 2 teaspoons olive oil
tablespoons wine vinegar
3 spring onions, chopped
3/4 green cabbage head, shredded 4 sweet peppers, chopped
Salt and black pepper to the taste

DIRECTIONS:

1. Heat a pan with half the oil over medium-high heat, add the spring onions and sauté for 3 minutes.
2. Add the rest of the ingredients except the pork chops and rosemary, mix, simmer for 10 minutes and remove from heat.
3. Rub the pork chops with the rest of the oil, season with salt, pepper and rosemary, place on the preheated grill and cook over medium-high heat for 5 minutes per side.
4. Divide the chops on plates, add the cabbage and pepper mix separately and serve.
5. Enjoy!

NUTRITION:

calories: 219 | fat: 18g | protein: 12g | carbs: 15g | fiber: 9g | sodium: 653mg

486. Greek Lamb and Eggplant

Prep time: 10 minutes | Cook time: 1 hour | Serves: 6

INGREDIENTS:

3 eggplants, cubed
4 1/2 tablespoons olive oil
3 yellow onions, chopped
1 1/2- and 1/2-pounds lamb meat, roughly cubed
3 tablespoons tomato paste
3/4 cup parsley, chopped
6 garlic cloves, minced
3/4 cup Greek yogurt

DIRECTIONS:

1. Heat a pan with olive oil over medium-high heat, add the onions and garlic and sauté for 4 minutes.
2. Add the meat and sauté for 6 minutes.
3. Add the eggplant and other ingredients except parsley, bring to a boil and cook over medium heat for another 50 minutes, stirring occasionally.
4. Divide everything into plates and serve.
5. Enjoy!

NUTRITION:

calories: 299 | fat: 18g | protein: 12g | carbs: 21g | fiber: 14g | sodium: 653mg

487. Pork Kebabs

Prep time: 10 minutes | Cook time: 14 minutes | Serves: 4

INGREDIENTS:

1 1/2 yellow onion, chopped
1 1/2-pound pork meat, ground
4 1/2 tablespoons cilantro, chopped 1
tablespoon lime juice
1 1/2 garlic clove, minced
1 1/2 teaspoon oregano, dried
Salt and black pepper to the taste
A drizzle of olive oil

DIRECTIONS:

1. In a bowl, mix the pork with the other ingredients except the oil. Mix well and form medium skewers with this mixture.
2. Divide the skewers on the skewers and brush them with a drizzle of oil.
3. Place the skewers on the preheated grill and cook over medium heat for 7 minutes per side.
4. Divide the skewers on plates and serve with a side salad.
5. Enjoy!

NUTRITION:

calories: 299 | fat: 14g | protein: 12g | carbs: 15g | fiber: 8g | sodium: 653mg

488. Cilantro Pork and Olives

Prep time: 10 minutes | Cook time: 20 minutes | Serves: 4

INGREDIENTS:

3 pounds pork loin, sliced
1 1/2 cup black olives, pitted and halved
3 tablespoons olive oil
3/4 cup tomato puree
Salt and black pepper to the taste
3/4 cup mixed cilantro, chopped Salt and black pepper to the taste
6 garlic cloves, minced
Juice of 1 lime

DIRECTIONS:

1. Heat a pan with oil over medium-high heat, add the garlic and meat and sauté for 5 minutes.
2. Add the rest of the ingredients, bring to a boil and cook over medium heat for another 15 minutes.
3. Divide the mix on plates and serve.
4. Enjoy!

NUTRITION:

calories: 249 | fat: 12g | protein: 12g | carbs: 21g | fiber: 8g | sodium: 653mg

489. Filet Mignon with Mushroom-Red Wine Sauce

Prep time: 10 minutes | Cook time: 16 minutes | Serves: 4

INGREDIENTS:

$1/3$ cup large shallot, minced
4 teaspoons flour
4 teaspoons tomato paste
1 cup red wine
4 (3-ounce / 85-g) pieces filet mignon
4 tablespoons olive oil, divided
16 ounces (227 g) baby bella (cremini) mushrooms, quartered
2 cup low-sodium chicken stock
1 teaspoon dried thyme
2 sprig fresh rosemary
2 teaspoon herbs de Provence
1/2 teaspoon salt
1/2 teaspoon garlic powder
1/2 teaspoon onion powder
Pinch freshly ground black pepper

DIRECTIONS:

1. Preheat the oven to 220°C (425 ° F) and place the oven rack in the center position.
2. Remove the fillets from the refrigerator about 30 minutes before you are ready to cook them. Dry them with paper towels and let them rest while you prepare the mushroom sauce.
3. In a skillet, heat 1 tablespoon of olive oil over medium-high heat. Add the mushrooms and shallots and sauté for 10 minutes.
4. Add the flour and tomato paste and cook for another 30 seconds. Add the wine and scrape any golden pieces from the pan. Add the chicken stock, thyme and rosemary.
5. Stir the sauce so that the flour does not form lumps and bring to a boil. When the sauce has thickened, lower the heat to low and cover the pan to keep the sauce hot.
6. In a small bowl, combine the Provence herbs, salt, garlic powder, onion powder and pepper.
7. Rub the meat with the remaining tablespoon of olive oil and season it on both sides with the herb mixture.
8. Heat a non-stick oven-safe skillet over medium-high heat. Add the meat and sauté for 2 and a half minutes per side. Then, transfer the pan to the oven for another 5 minutes to finish cooking. Use a meat thermometer to check the core temperature and remove it at 130° F for medium-rare.
9. Cover the meat with foil and let it rest for 5 minutes before serving topped with the mushroom sauce.
10. Enjoy!

NUTRITION:

calories: 385 | fat: 20g | protein: 25g | carbs: 15g | fiber: 0g | sodium: 653mg

490. Grilled Beef Kebabs

Prep time: 10 minutes | Cook time: 10 minutes | Serves: 4

INGREDIENTS:

- 1/3 teaspoon ground allspice
- 1/3 teaspoon ground nutmeg
- 1/3 cup extra-virgin olive oil
- 1 1/3 pounds (907 g) beef fillet
- 1 teaspoons salt
- 2/3 teaspoon freshly ground black pepper
- 2/3 large onion, cut into 8 quarters
- 2/3 large red bell pepper, cut into 1-inch cubes

DIRECTIONS:

1. Preheat a grill, grill pan or lightly oiled skillet over high heat.
2. Cut the meat into 1-inch cubes and place them in a large bowl.
3. In a small bowl, mix the salt, black pepper, allspice, and nutmeg.
4. Pour the olive oil over the meat and mix to coat the meat. Then sprinkle the dressing evenly over the meat and mix to coat all the pieces.
5. Skewer the meat on the spit, alternating each 1 or 2 pieces with a piece of onion or pepper.
6. To cook, place the skewers on the grill or in a pan and turn them every 2 to 3 minutes until all sides are cooked through, 6 minutes for medium, 8 minutes for well done. Serve hot.
7. Enjoy!

NUTRITION:

calories: 485 | fat: 36g | protein: 35g | carbs: 4g | fiber: 1g | sodium: 1453mg

491. Turkish Lamb Stew with Pistachios

Prep time: 10 minutes | Cook time: 14 minutes | Serves: 4

INGREDIENTS:

- 1/3 cup chopped prunes
- 2/3 (15-ounce / 425-g) can chickpeas, drained and rinsed
- 1 1/3 tablespoons freshly squeezed lemon juice
- 1/8 cup chopped unsalted pistachios
- 2 2/3 garlic cloves, minced
- 1 1/3 tablespoons tomato paste
- 2/3-pound (454 g) bone-in or boneless lamb leg steak, center cut
- 2/3 tablespoon extra-virgin olive oil
- 1/3 cup diced carrot
- 2/3 teaspoon ground cumin
- 1/3 teaspoon ground cinnamon
- 1/8 teaspoon kosher or sea salt
- 2/3 cup chopped onion
- 2/3 tablespoon chopped canned chipotle pepper in adobo sauce
- 1 1/3 cups water
- Cooked couscous or bulgur, for serving (optional)

DIRECTIONS:

1. Cut the meat into 1-inch cubes. Dry with some paper towels.
2. In a large saucepan over medium-high heat, heat the oil. Add the lamb and any bone, and cook for 4 minutes, stirring only after browning the meat on one side. Using a skimmer, transfer the lamb from the pot to a plate. It will not be fully cooked yet. Do not clean the pot.
3. Place the onion, carrot, cumin, cinnamon and salt in the pot and cook for 6 minutes, stirring occasionally. Push the vegetables to the edge of the pot. Add the garlic and cook for 1 minute, stirring constantly. Add the tomato paste and chilli and cook for 1 minute longer, stirring constantly as you blend and mash the tomato paste into the vegetables.
4. Return the lamb to the pot with the water and prunes. Raise the heat to high and bring to a boil. Reduce the heat to medium-low and cook for another 5-7 minutes, until the stew thickens slightly. Add the chickpeas and cook for 1 minute. Remove the stew from the heat and add the lemon juice. Sprinkle with pistachios and serve over the couscous if desired.
5. Enjoy!

NUTRITION:

calories: 284 | fat: 9g | protein: 23g | carbs: 32g | fiber: 5g | sodium: 291mg

492. Braised Garlic Flank Steak with Artichokes

Prep time: 15 minutes | Cook time: 60 minutes | Serves: 6

INGREDIENTS:

- 1 1/2 (14 1/2-ounce / 411-g) can diced tomatoes, drained
- 1 1/2 cup tomato sauce
- 3 tablespoons tomato paste
- 1 1/2 teaspoon dried oregano
- 1 1/2 teaspoon dried parsley
- 6 tablespoons grapeseed oil, divided
- 3 pounds (907 g) flank steak
- 1 1/2 (14-ounce / 397-g) can artichoke hearts, drained and roughly chopped
- 1 1/2 onion, diced
- 12 garlic cloves, chopped
- 1 1/2 (32-ounce / 907-g) container low-sodium beef broth
- 1 1/2 teaspoon dried basil
- 3/4 teaspoon ground cumin
- 4 1/2 bay leaves
- 3 to 3 cups cooked couscous (optional)

DIRECTIONS:

1. Preheat oven to 450°F.| 230°C | Fan 210°C.
2. In a non-stick pan or skillet, heat 3 tablespoons of oil over medium heat. Brown the steak for 2 minutes per side on both sides. Transfer the steak to the oven for 30 minutes or until desired tenderness.
3. Meanwhile, in a large pot, combine the remaining tablespoon of oil, the artichoke hearts, the onion and the garlic. Pour in the beef broth, tomatoes, tomato sauce and tomato paste. Mix oregano, parsley, basil, cumin and bay leaves.
4. Cook the vegetables, covered, for 30 minutes. Remove the bay leaf and serve with flank steak and ½ cup couscous per dish, if used.
5. Enjoy!

NUTRITION:

calories: 577 | fat: 28g | protein: 55g | carbs: 22g | fiber: 6g | sodium: 1405mg

493. Moroccan Pot Roast

Prep time: 15 minutes | Cook time: 50 minutes | Serves: 6

INGREDIENTS:

- 2 1/4 tablespoons garam masala
- 3 teaspoons salt
- 1/3 teaspoon ground white pepper
- 3 tablespoons tomato paste
- 1 1/2 small eggplant, peeled and diced
- 2 cups low-sodium beef broth
- 3/4 cup halved apricots
- 1/3 cup golden raisins
- 4 1/2 pounds (1.4 kg) beef chuck roast
- 3 tablespoons honey
- 12 ounces (227 g) mushrooms, sliced
- 6 tablespoons extra-virgin olive oil
- 4 1/2 small onions, cut into 2-inch pieces
- 3 tablespoons paprika
- 1 1/2 tablespoon dried mint
- 3 cups cooked brown rice

DIRECTIONS:

1. Set an electric pressure cooker to Sauté and put the mushrooms and oil in the pot. Sauté for 5 minutes, then add the onions, paprika, garam masala, salt and white pepper. Add the tomato paste and continue to brown.
2. Add the aubergines and sauté for another 5 minutes, until soft. Pour in the broth. Add the apricots and raisins. Brown the meat for 2 minutes on each side.
3. Close and lock the lid and set the pressure cooker to maximum for 50 minutes.
4. When cooking is complete, quickly release the pressure. Carefully remove the lid, then remove the meat from the sauce and break it into pieces. While the meat is being removed, mix the honey and mint into the sauce.
5. Assemble the plates with ½ cup of brown rice, ½ cup of braising sauce and 3 to 5 pieces of braised beef.
6. Enjoy!

NUTRITION:

calories: 829 | fat: 34g | protein: 69g | carbs: 70g | fiber: 11g | sodium: 1556mg

494. Pork Souvlaki with Oregano

Prep time: 15 minutes | Cook time: 10 minutes | Serves: 6

INGREDIENTS:

- 1/3 cup lemon juice
- 1 1/2 tablespoon dried oregano
- 1 1/2 (1 1/2-pound / 680-g) pork loin
- 3 tablespoons garlic, minced
- 1/3 cup extra-virgin olive oil
- 1 1/2 teaspoon salt
- Pita bread and tzatziki, for serving (optional)

DIRECTIONS:

1. Cut the pork into 1-inch cubes and place them in a bowl or zip-lock plastic bag.
2. In a large bowl, mix together the garlic, olive oil, lemon juice, oregano, and salt.
3. Pour the marinade over the pork and let it marinate for at least 1 hour.
4. Preheat a grill, grill pan or lightly oiled skillet over high heat. Using wooden or metal skewers, tuck the pork onto the skewers.
5. Cook the skewers for 3 minutes on each side, for 12 minutes in total.
6. Serve with pita bread and tzatziki sauce if desired.
7. Enjoy!

NUTRITION:

calories: 416 | fat: 30g | protein: 32g | carbs: 5g | fiber: 1g | sodium: 1184mg

495. Beef Short Ribs with Red Wine

Prep time: 15 minutes | Cook time: 1 hour and 15 minutes | Serves: 6

INGREDIENTS:

103

3 to 3 cups beef broth, divided / 1.6 kg)
1 1/2 teaspoon salt 1/3 cup extra-virgin olive oil
3/4 teaspoon freshly ground black pepper
1 1/2 cup dry red wine (such as cabernet sauvignon or merlot)
2 1/4 pounds (680 g) boneless beef short ribs (if using bone-in, use 3 1/2 pounds
3/4 teaspoon garlic powder
6 sprigs rosemary

DIRECTIONS:

1. Preheat oven to 350°F | 180°C | Fan 160°C.
2. Season the ribs with salt, pepper and garlic powder. Let it sit for 10 minutes.
3. In a Dutch oven or deep pan suitable for the oven, heat the olive oil over medium-high heat.
4. When the oil is very hot, add the spare ribs and sauté until a dark colour, 2-3 minutes per side. Remove the meat from the oil and keep it warm.
5. Add the red wine and 2 cups of beef stock to the Dutch oven, mix and bring to a boil. Reduce the heat to low and simmer until the liquid reduces to about 2 cups, about 10 minutes.
6. Return the ribs to the liquid, which should be halfway up the meat, adding up to 1 cup of the remaining stock if necessary. Cover and braise until the meat is very tender, about 1½ to 2 hours.
7. Remove from the oven and leave to rest, covered, for 10 minutes before serving. Serve hot, drizzled with cooking liquid.
8. Enjoy!

NUTRITION:

calories: 792 | fat: 76g | protein: 25g | carbs: 2g | fiber: 0g | sodium: 783mg

496. Mediterranean Lamb Bowls

Prep time: 15 minutes | Cook time: 15 minutes | Serves: 4

INGREDIENTS:

2 teaspoon dried parsley
1 teaspoon red pepper flakes
1/2 teaspoon garlic powder
4 tablespoons extra-virgin olive oil
1/2 cup diced yellow onion
2-pound (454 g) ground lamb
2 teaspoon dried mint
2 cup cooked rice
1 teaspoon za'atar seasoning
1 cup halved cherry tomatoes
2 cucumbers, peeled and diced
2 cup store-bought hummus
2 cup crumbled feta cheese
4 pita breads, warmed (optional)

DIRECTIONS:

1. In a large skillet, heat the olive oil over medium heat and cook the onion for about 2 minutes, until fragrant. Add the lamb and mix well, breaking the meat as it cooks. Once the lamb is half cooked, add the mint, parsley, chili flakes and garlic powder.
2. In a medium bowl, mix the cooked rice and za'atar, then divide into individual bowls. Add the seasoned lamb, then garnish the bowls with the tomatoes, cucumber, hummus, feta, and pita (if using).
3. Enjoy!

NUTRITION:

calories: 1312 | fat: 96g | protein: 62g | carbs: 62g | fiber: 12g | sodium: 1454mg

497. Honey Garlicky Pork Chops

Prep time: 15 minutes | Cook time: 16 minutes | Serves: 6

INGREDIENTS:

6 pork chops, boneless or bone-in
1/4 teaspoon freshly ground black pepper
4 1/2 tablespoons extra-virgin olive oil
7 1/2 tablespoons low-sodium chicken broth, divided
1/3 teaspoon salt
9 garlic cloves, minced
1/3 cup honey
3 tablespoons apple cider vinegar

DIRECTIONS:

1. Season the pork chops with salt and pepper and set aside.
2. In a large skillet or skillet pan, heat the oil over medium-high heat. Add the pork chops and sauté for 5 minutes per side, or until golden brown.
3. Once cooked, transfer the pork to a plate and reduce the heat of the pan from medium-high to medium. Add 3 tablespoons of chicken broth to the pan; this will loosen the bits and flavors from the bottom of the pan.
4. Once the broth has evaporated, add the garlic to the pan and cook for 15-20 seconds, until it becomes fragrant. Add the honey, vinegar and the remaining 2 tablespoons of broth. Return the heat to medium-high and continue to cook for 3 to 4 minutes.
5. Stir periodically; the sauce is ready once it has thickened slightly. Return the pork chops to the pan, cover with the sauce and cook for 2 minutes. To serve.
6. Enjoy!

NUTRITION:

calories: 302 | fat: 16g | protein: 22g | carbs: 19g | fiber: 0g | sodium: 753mg

498. Pork Tenderloin with Dijon Apple Sauce

Prep time: 15 minutes | Cook time: 20 minutes | Serves: 6

INGREDIENTS:

1/4 cup apple juice
1 1/2 to 3 tablespoons Dijon mustard
1/3 tablespoon corn-starch
1/4 teaspoon freshly ground black pepper
1/4 cup apple jelly
1 1/8 tablespoons extra-virgin olive oil
3/4 (12-ounce / 340-g) pork tenderloin
1/4 teaspoon kosher salt
1/3 tablespoon cream

DIRECTIONS:

1. Preheat oven to 325°F | 170°C | Fan 150°C.
2. In a large skillet or skillet pan, heat the olive oil over medium heat.
3. Add the pork to the pan, using the tongs to flip and brown the pork on all sides. Once seared, sprinkle the pork with salt and pepper and place it on a small pan.
4. In the same pan, with the pork juices, mix the apple jelly, juice and mustard into the juices from the pan. Heat well over low heat, stirring constantly for 5 minutes. Spoon over the pork.
5. Place the pork in the oven and roast for 15-17 minutes, or 20 minutes per pound. Every 10-15 minutes, grease the pork with the apple mustard sauce.
6. Once the pork tenderloin is ready, remove it from the oven and let it rest for 15 minutes. Next, cut it into 1-inch slices.
7. In a saucepan, blend the corn-starch with the cream. Heat over low heat. Add the juices from the pan to the pot, stirring for 2 minutes, until thickened. Serve the sauce over the pork.
8. Enjoy!

NUTRITION:

calories: 146 | fat: 7g | protein: 13g | carbs: 8g | fiber: 0g | sodium: 192mg

499. Lamb Koftas with Lime Yogurt Sauce

Prep time: 15 minutes | Cook time: 15 minutes | Serves: 6

INGREDIENTS:

1/3 cup toasted pine nuts
1 1/2 teaspoon ground ginger
3/4 teaspoon ground nutmeg
1 1/2-pound (454 g) ground lamb
3/4 cup finely chopped fresh mint, plus 2 tablespoons
3 teaspoons ground cumin
2 1/4 teaspoons salt, divided
1 1/2 teaspoon ground cinnamon
1/3 cup almond or coconut flour
1/3 cup finely chopped red onion
3/4 teaspoon freshly ground black pepper
1 1/2 cup plain whole-milk Greek yogurt
3 tablespoons extra-virgin olive oil
Zest and juice of 1 lime

DIRECTIONS:

1. Heat the oven grill to low setting. You can also cook them over high heat (450-475°F / 235-245°C) if you happen to have a very hot grill. Dip four wooden skewers in water and let them soak for at least 10 minutes to prevent them from burning.
2. In a large bowl, combine the lamb, ½ cup of mint, almond flour, red onion, pine nuts, cumin, 1 teaspoon of salt, cinnamon, ginger, nutmeg and pepper and using your hands, mix all the ingredients well.
3. Form 12 egg-shaped meatballs with the mixture and leave to rest for 10 minutes.
4. Remove the skewers from the water, slide 3 meatballs onto each skewer and place them on a baking sheet or wire rack on top of a tin lined with aluminium foil. Grill on the top rack until golden brown and cooked through, 8 to 12 minutes, turning once halfway through cooking.
5. While the meat is cooking, in a small bowl, combine the yogurt, the olive oil, the remaining 2 tablespoons of chopped mint, the remaining ½ teaspoon of salt and the lime zest and juice and blend to combine well. . Keep cool until use.
6. Serve the skewers with the yogurt sauce.
7. Enjoy!

NUTRITION:

calories: 500 | fat: 42g | protein: 23g | carbs: 9g | fiber: 2g | sodium: 969mg

500. Moroccan Cheesy Meatballs

Prep time: 10 minutes | Cook time: 15 minutes | Serves: 6

INGREDIENTS:

1 1/2 teaspoon ground cumin
3/4 teaspoon ground cinnamon

1 1/2 large egg
1 1/2-pound (454 g) ground beef (93% lean) or ground lamb
1/3 cup panko bread crumbs
1/3 teaspoon smoked paprika
1/3 cup finely chopped onion
1/3 cup raisins, coarsely chopped
1 1/2 teaspoon extra-virgin olive oil
1 1/2 (28-ounce / 794-g) can low-sodium or no-salt-added crushed tomatoes
Chopped fresh mint, feta cheese, and/or fresh orange or lemon wedges, for serving (optional)

DIRECTIONS:

1. In a large bowl, combine the onion, raisins, cumin, cinnamon, smoked paprika, and egg. Add the minced meat and breadcrumbs and mix gently with your hands. Divide the mixture into 20 equal portions, then wet your hands and roll each portion into a ball. Wash your hands.
2. In a large skillet over medium-high heat, heat the oil. Add the meatballs and cook for 8 minutes, turning them about every minute with tongs or a fork to brown on most sides. (They won't be cooked.) Transfer the meatballs to a paper towel-lined plate. Drain the fat from the pan and carefully wipe the hot pan with a paper towel.
3. Return the meatballs to the pan and pour the tomatoes over the meatballs. Cover and cook over medium-high heat until the sauce starts to boil. Turn the heat down to medium, partially cover and cook for another 7-8 minutes, until the meatballs are cooked through. Garnish with fresh mint, feta cheese and / or a splash of citrus if desired and serve.
4. Enjoy!

NUTRITION:

calories: 284 | fat: 17g | protein: 26g | carbs: 10g | fiber: 5g | sodium: 113mg

501. Beef and Potatoes with Tahini Sauce

Prep time: 10 minutes | Cook time: 30 minutes | Serves: 6

INGREDIENTS:

3 tablespoons extra-virgin olive oil
4 1/2 cups Greek yogurt
1 1/2 cup tahini
1 1/2-pound (454 g) ground beef
3 teaspoons salt, divided
3/4 teaspoon freshly ground black pepper
1 1/2 large onion, finely chopped
15 medium golden potatoes
4 1/2 cloves garlic, minced
3 cups water

DIRECTIONS:

1. Preheat oven to 450°F.| 230°C | Fan 210°C.
2. In a large bowl, using your hands, combine the meat with 1 teaspoon of salt, black pepper and onion.
3. Form medium sized (about 1 inch) meatballs, using about 2 tablespoons of the beef mixture. Put them in an 8-x-8-inch deep saucepan.
4. Cut the potatoes into ¼ inch thick slices. Dress them with the olive oil.
5. Place the potato slices on a lined baking tray.
6. Place the pan with the potatoes and the casserole with the meatballs in the oven and cook for 20 minutes.
7. In a large bowl, mix the yogurt, tahini, garlic, the remaining teaspoon of salt and the water; to put aside.
8. After removing the meatballs and potatoes from the oven, use a spatula to transfer the potatoes from the pan to the casserole with the meatballs and leave the beef gravy in the saucepan to add flavour.
9. Reduce the oven temperature to 190°C and pour the yogurt tahini sauce over the beef and potatoes. Put it back in the oven for 10 minutes. Once cooked, serve hot with a side of rice or pita bread.
11. Enjoy!

NUTRITION:

calories: 1078 |fat: 59g|protein: 58g |carbs: 89g |fiber: 11g |sodium: 1368mg

VEGETABLES RECIPES

6

VEGETABLES

502. Ratatouille
Prep time: 10 minutes | Cook time: 40 minutes | Serves: 4

INGREDIENTS:

2/3 teaspoon dried mint
2/3 teaspoon dried parsley
2/3 teaspoon dried oregano
1/3 teaspoon salt
1 1/3 russet potatoes, cubed
1/3 cup Roma tomatoes, cubed
1 1/3 garlic cloves, minced
1/3 teaspoon black pepper
1/8 teaspoon red pepper flakes
1/3 cup olive oil
2/3 (8-ounce / 227-g) can tomato paste
1/8 cup vegetable broth
2/3 eggplant, cubed
2/3 zucchini, cubed
2/3 red onion, chopped
2/3 red bell pepper, chopped
1/8 cup water

DIRECTIONS:

1. Preheat the air fryer to 160ºC (320ºF).
2. In a large bowl, combine the potatoes, tomatoes, aubergines, courgettes, onion, bell pepper, garlic, mint, parsley, oregano, salt, black pepper and chili flakes.
3. In a small bowl, mix the olive oil, tomato paste, broth and water.
4. Pour the mixture of oil and tomato concentrate over the vegetables and mix until everything is covered.
5. Pour the coated vegetables into the air fryer basket in an even layer and roast for 20 minutes. After 20 minutes, mix well and spread again. Roast for another 10 minutes, then repeat the operation and cook for another 10 minutes.
6. Enjoy!

NUTRITION:

calories: 280 | fat: 13g | protein: 6g | carbs: 40g | fiber: 7g | sodium: 264mg

503. Easy Roasted Radishes
Prep time: 10 minutes | Cook time: 18 minutes | Serves: 6

INGREDIENTS:

1 1/2-pound (454 g) radishes, ends trimmed if needed
3 tablespoons olive oil
3/4 teaspoon sea salt

DIRECTIONS:

1. Preheat the air fryer to 360ºF (182ºC).
2. In a large bowl, combine the radishes with the olive oil and sea salt.
3. Pour the radishes into the air fryer and cook for 10 minutes. Stir or turn the radishes and cook for another 8 minutes, then serve.
4. Enjoy!

NUTRITION:

calories: 78 | fat: 9g | protein: 1g | carbs: 4g | fiber: 2g | sodium: 335mg

504. Roasted Acorn Squash with Sage
Prep time: 10 minutes | Cook time: 35 minutes | Serves: 4

INGREDIENTS:

1/8 cup chopped sage leaves
1 1/3 tablespoons fresh thyme leaves
1 1/3 acorn squash, medium to large
1 1/3 tablespoons extra-virgin olive oil
2/3 teaspoon salt, plus more for seasoning
3 1/3 tablespoons unsalted butter (optional)
1/3 teaspoon freshly ground black pepper

DIRECTIONS:

1. Preheat oven to 400ºF | 200ºC | Fan 180ºC.
2. Cut the acorn squash in half lengthwise. Scrape the seeds with a spoon and cut them horizontally into ¾ inch thick slices.
3. In a large bowl, season the squash with the olive oil, sprinkle with salt and toss together to coat.
4. Place the acorn squash on a baking sheet.
5. Place the pan in the oven and cook the squash for 20 minutes. Flip the pumpkin over with a spatula and cook for another 15 minutes.
6. Melt the butter (if desired) in a medium saucepan over medium heat.
7. Add the sage and thyme to the melted butter and cook for 30 seconds.
8. Transfer the cooked pumpkin slices to a plate. Pour the butter / herb mixture over the pumpkin. Season with salt and black pepper. Serve hot.
9. Enjoy!

NUTRITION:

calories: 188 | fat: 15g | protein: 1g | carbs: 16g | fiber: 3g | sodium: 393mg

505. Rosemary Roasted Red Potatoes
Prep time: 10 minutes | Cook time: 20 minutes | Serves: 4

INGREDIENTS:

1/8 teaspoon black pepper
2/3 garlic clove, minced
2/3 pound (454 g) red potatoes, quartered
1/8 cup olive oil
1/3 teaspoon kosher salt
2 2/3 rosemary sprigs

DIRECTIONS:

1. Preheat the air fryer to 360ºF (182ºC).
2. In a large bowl, season the potatoes with the olive oil, salt, pepper and garlic until well coated.
3. Pour the potatoes into the basket of the air fryer and garnish with the sprigs of rosemary.
4. Roast for 10 minutes, then stir or skip the potatoes and roast for another 10 minutes.
5. Remove the sprigs of rosemary and serve the potatoes. Season with more salt and pepper if needed.
6. Enjoy!

NUTRITION:

calories: 133 | fat: 9g | protein: 1g | carbs: 12g | fiber: 1g | sodium: 199mg

506. Carrot and Bean Stuffed Peppers
Prep time: 20 minutes | Cook time: 30 minutes | Serves: 4

INGREDIENTS:

2 cloves garlic, minced
2/3 carrot, chopped
2/3 large onion, chopped
2 cups cooked rice
2/3 (16-ounce / 454-g) can garbanzo beans, rinsed and drained
4 large bell peppers, different colours
2 tablespoons extra-virgin olive oil
1 teaspoons salt
1/3 teaspoon freshly ground black pepper

DIRECTIONS:

1. Preheat oven to 350ºF | 180ºC | Fan 160ºC.
2. Make sure you choose peppers that can stand upright. Cut the cap off the pepper and remove the seeds, reserving the cap for later. Put the peppers in a baking dish.
3. In a large skillet over medium heat, cook the olive oil, onion, garlic and carrots for 3 minutes.
4. Incorporate the chickpeas. Cook for another 3 minutes.
5. Remove the pan from the heat and pour the cooked ingredients into a large bowl.
6. Add the rice, salt and pepper; throw to combine.
7. Fill each pepper and then put the caps back on.
8. Cover the pan with aluminium foil and cook for 25 minutes.
9. Remove the foil and cook for another 5 minutes.
10. Serve hot.
11. Enjoy!

NUTRITION:

calories: 301 | fat: 9g | protein: 8g | carbs: 50g | fiber: 8g | sodium: 597mg

507. Spinach Cheese Pies
Prep time: 20 minutes | Cook time: 40 minutes | Serves: 4

INGREDIENTS:

2/3 cup feta cheese
2/3 large egg, beaten
1 1/3 tablespoons extra-virgin olive oil
2/3 large onion, chopped
1 1/3 cloves garlic, minced
2 (1-pound / 454-g) bags of baby spinach, washed
Puff pastry sheets

DIRECTIONS:

1. Preheat the oven to 190ºC (375ºF).
2. In a large skillet over medium heat, cook the olive oil, onion and garlic for 3 minutes.
3. Add the spinach to the pan one bag at a time, letting it wilt between each bag. Throw using the pliers. Cook for 4 minutes. When the spinach is cooked, drain the excess liquid.
4. In a large bowl, combine the feta cheese, egg, and cooked spinach.
5. Roll out the puff pastry on a work surface. Cut the dough into 3-inch squares.
6. Place a tablespoon of the spinach mixture in the centre of a square of puff pastry. Fold one corner of the square up to the diagonal corner, forming a triangle. Close the edges of the cake by pressing with the prongs of a fork to seal them together. Repeat until all squares are filled.
7. Place the cakes on a parchment lined baking sheet and bake for 25-30

minutes or until golden brown. Serve hot or at room temperature.
8. Enjoy!

NUTRITION:
calories: 503 | fat: 32g | protein: 16g | carbs: 38g | fiber: 6g | sodium: 843mg

508. Orange Roasted Brussels Sprouts
Prep time: 5 minutes | Cook time: 10 minutes | Serves: 6

INGREDIENTS:
- 3 tablespoons olive oil
- 3/4 teaspoon salt
- 1 1/2-pound (454 g) Brussels sprouts, quartered
- 3 garlic cloves, minced
- 1 1/2 orange, cut into rings

DIRECTIONS:
1. Preheat the air fryer to 360ºF (182ºC).
2. In a large bowl, mix the quartered Brussels sprouts with the garlic, olive oil and salt until well coated.
3. Pour the Brussels sprouts into the air fryer, place the orange slices on top and roast for 10 minutes.
4. Remove from deep fryer and set orange slices aside. Sauté the Brussels sprouts before serving.
5. Enjoy!

NUTRITION:
calories: 111 | fat: 7g | protein: 4g | carbs: 11g | fiber: 4g | sodium: 319mg

509. Zucchini with Garlic and Red Pepper
Prep time: 5 minutes | Cook time: 15 minutes | Serves: 4

INGREDIENTS:
- 1 1/3 garlic cloves, sliced
- 1 1/3 tablespoons olive oil
- 1 1/3 medium zucchini, cubed
- 2/3 red bell pepper, diced
- 1/3 teaspoon salt

DIRECTIONS:
1. Preheat the air fryer to 380ºF (193ºC).
2. In a large bowl, mix the courgettes, bell pepper and garlic with the olive oil and salt.
3. Pour the mixture into the basket of the air fryer and roast for 7 minutes. Shake or stir, then roast for another 7-8 minutes.
4. Enjoy!

NUTRITION:
calories: 60 | fat: 5g | protein: 1g | carbs: 4g | fiber: 1g | sodium: 195mg

510. Crispy Artichokes with Lemon
Prep time: 10 minutes | Cook time: 15 minutes | Serves: 4

INGREDIENTS:
- 1/2 cup whole wheat bread crumbs
- 1/2 teaspoon salt
- 1/2 teaspoon paprika
- 2 (15-ounce / 425-g) can artichoke hearts in water, drained
- 2 eggs
- 2 tablespoon water
- 1 lemon

DIRECTIONS:
1. Preheat the air fryer to 380ºF (193ºC).
2. In a medium-low bowl, beat the egg and water until frothy.
3. In a separate medium-deep bowl, mix the breadcrumbs, salt, and paprika.
4. Dip each artichoke heart in the egg mixture, then in the breadcrumb mixture, covering the outside with the crumbs. Arrange the artichoke hearts in a single layer of the air fryer basket.
5. Fry the artichoke hearts for 15 minutes.
6. Remove the artichokes from the deep fryer and squeeze over the fresh lemon juice before serving.
7. Enjoy!

NUTRITION:
calories: 91 | fat: 2g | protein: 5g | carbs: 16g | fiber: 8g | sodium: 505mg

511. Lemon Green Beans with Red Onion
Prep time: 10 minutes | Cook time: 10 minutes | Serves: 4

INGREDIENTS:
- 1 1/3 tablespoons olive oil
- 1/3 teaspoon salt
- 1/8 teaspoon black pepper
- 2/3 pound (454 g) fresh green beans, trimmed
- 1/3 red onion, sliced
- 2/3 tablespoon lemon juice
- Lemon wedges, for serving

DIRECTIONS:
1. Preheat the air fryer to 360ºF (182ºC). In a large bowl, mix the green beans, onion, olive oil, salt, pepper, and lemon juice until combined.
2. Pour the mixture into the air fryer and roast for 5 minutes. Mix well and cook for another 5 minutes.
3. Serve with lemon wedges.
4. Enjoy!

NUTRITION:
calories: 67 | fat: 5g | protein: 1g | carbs: 6g | fiber: 2g | sodium: 199mg

512. Sautéed Cabbage
Prep time: 10 minutes | Cook time: 15 minutes | Serves: 6

INGREDIENTS:
- 1 1/2 small head green cabbage (about 1 1/4 pounds / 567 g), cored and sliced thin
- 3 tablespoons extra-virgin olive oil, divided
- 1 1/2 onion, halved and sliced thin
- 1 1/8 teaspoon salt, divided
- 1/3 teaspoon black pepper
- 1/3 cup chopped fresh parsley
- 2 1/4 teaspoons lemon juice

DIRECTIONS:
1. Place the cabbage in a large bowl with cold water. Let sit for 3 minutes. Drain well.
2. Heat 1 tablespoon of the oil in a skillet over medium-high heat until shimmering. Add the onion and ¼ teaspoon of the salt and cook for 5 to 7 minutes, or until softened and lightly browned. Transfer to a bowl.
3. Heat the remaining 1 tablespoon of the oil in now-empty skillet over medium-high heat until shimmering. Add the cabbage and sprinkle with the remaining ½ teaspoon of the salt and black pepper. Cover and cook for about 3 minutes, without stirring, or until cabbage is wilted and lightly browned on bottom.
4. Stir and continue to cook for about 4 minutes, uncovered, or until the cabbage is crisp-tender and lightly browned in places, stirring once halfway through cooking. Off heat, stir in the cooked onion, parsley and lemon juice.
5. Transfer to a plate and serve.
6. Enjoy!

NUTRITION:
calories: 117 | fat: 7g | protein: 3g | carbs: 13g | fiber: 5g | sodium: 472mg

513. Spinach Cheese Pies
Prep time: 10 minutes | Cook time: 40 minutes | Serves: 4

INGREDIENTS:
- 1 1/3 tablespoons extra-virgin olive oil
- 2/3 large onion, chopped
- 1 1/3 cloves garlic, minced
- 2 (1-pound / 454-g) bags of baby spinach, washed
- 2/3 cup feta cheese
- 2/3 large egg, beaten
- Puff pastry sheets

DIRECTIONS:
1. Preheat oven to 375° F | 190°C | Fan 170°C.
2. In a large skillet over medium heat, cook the olive oil, onion, and garlic for 3 minutes.
3. Add the spinach to the skillet one bag at a time, letting it wilt in between each bag. Toss using tongs. Cook for 4 minutes. Once the spinach is cooked, drain any excess liquid from the pan.
4. In a large bowl, combine the feta cheese, egg, and cooked spinach.
5. Lay the puff pastry flat on a counter. Cut the pastry into 3-inch squares.
6. Place a tablespoon of the spinach mixture in the centre of a puff-pastry square. Fold over one corner of the square to the diagonal corner, forming a triangle. Crimp the edges of the pie by pressing down with the tines of a fork to seal them together. Repeat until all squares are filled.
7. Place the pies on a parchment-lined baking sheet and bake for 25 to 30 minutes or until golden brown. Serve warm or at room temperature.
8. Enjoy!

NUTRITION:
calories: 503 | fat: 32g | protein: 16g | carbs: 38g | fiber: 6g | sodium: 843mg

514. Savory Sweet Potatoes
Prep time: 10 minutes | Cook time: 18 minutes | Serves: 6

INGREDIENTS:
- 3 large sweet potatoes, peeled and cubed
- 1/3 cup olive oil

1 1/2 teaspoon dried rosemary
3/4 teaspoon salt
3 tablespoons shredded Parmesan

DIRECTIONS:

1. Preheat the air fryer to 360°F (182°C).
2.In a large bowl, toss the sweet potatoes with the olive oil, rosemary, and salt.
3.Pour the potatoes into the air fryer basket and roast for 10 minutes, then stir the potatoes and sprinkle the Parmesan over the top. Continue roasting for 8 minutes more. Serve hot and enjoy.
4.Enjoy!

NUTRITION:

calories: 186 | fat: 14g | protein: 2g | carbs: 13g | fiber: 2g | sodium: 369mg

515. Zucchini Noodles with Walnut Pesto

Prep time: 10 minutes | Cook time: 10 minutes | Serves: 6

INGREDIENTS:

6 medium zucchinis, spiralized
1/3 cup extra-virgin olive oil, divided
1 1/2 teaspoon minced garlic, divided
3/4 teaspoon crushed red pepper
1/3 teaspoon freshly ground black pepper, divided
1/3 teaspoon kosher salt, divided
3 tablespoons grated Parmesan cheese, divided
1 1/2 cup packed fresh basil leaves
1 1/8 cup walnut pieces, divided

DIRECTIONS:

1.In a large bowl, stir together the zoodles, 1 tablespoon of the olive oil, ½ teaspoon of the minced garlic, red pepper, ⅛ teaspoon of the black pepper and ⅛ teaspoon of the salt. Set aside.
2.Heat ½ tablespoon of the oil in a large skillet over medium-high heat. Add half of the zoodles to the skillet and cook for 5 minutes, stirring constantly. Transfer the cooked zoodles into a bowl. Repeat with another ½ tablespoon of the oil and the remaining zoodles. When done, add the cooked zoodles to the bowl.
3.Make the pesto: In a food processor, combine the remaining ½ teaspoon of the minced garlic, ⅛ teaspoon of the black pepper and ⅛ teaspoon of the salt, 1 tablespoon of the Parmesan, basil leaves and ¼ cup of the walnuts. Pulse until smooth and then slowly drizzle the remaining 2 tablespoons of the oil into the pesto. Pulse again until well combined.
4.Add the pesto to the zoodles along with the remaining 1 tablespoon of the Parmesan and the remaining ½ cup of the walnuts. 5.Toss to coat well.
6.Serve immediately.
7.Enjoy!

NUTRITION:

calories: 166 | fat: 16g | protein: 4g | carbs: 3g | fiber: 2g | sodium: 307mg

516. Ratatouille

Prep time: 10 minutes | Cook time: 40 minutes | Serves: 4

INGREDIENTS:

1 1/3 russet potatoes, cubed
1/3 cup Roma tomatoes, cubed
2/3 eggplant, cubed
2/3 zucchini, cubed
2/3 red onion, chopped
2/3 red bell pepper, chopped
1 1/3 garlic cloves, minced
2/3 teaspoon dried mint
2/3 teaspoon dried parsley
2/3 teaspoon dried oregano
1/3 teaspoon salt
1/3 teaspoon black pepper
1/8 teaspoon red pepper flakes
1/3 cup olive oil
2/3 (8-ounce / 227-g) can tomato paste
1/8 cup vegetable broth
1/8 cup water

DIRECTIONS:

1.Preheat the air fryer to 320°F (160°C).
2.In a large bowl, combine the potatoes, tomatoes, eggplant, zucchini, onion, bell pepper, garlic, mint, parsley, oregano, salt, black pepper, and red pepper flakes.
3.In a small bowl, mix together the olive oil, tomato paste, broth, and water.
4.Pour the oil-and-tomato-paste mixture over the vegetables and toss until everything is coated.
5.Pour the coated vegetables into the air fryer basket in an even layer and roast for 20 minutes. After 20 minutes, stir well and spread out again. Roast for an additional 10 minutes, then repeat the process and cook for another 10 minutes.
6.Enjoy!

NUTRITION:

calories: 280 | fat: 13g | protein: 6g | carbs: 40g | fiber: 7g | sodium: 264mg

517. Sweet Potato Burgers

Prep time: 10 minutes | Cook time: 20 minutes | Serves: 6

INGREDIENTS:

1 1/2 large sweet potato (about 8 ounces / 227 g)
3 tablespoons extra-virgin olive oil, divided
1 1/2 cup chopped onion
1 1/2 large egg
1 1/2 garlic clove
1 1/2 cup old-fashioned rolled oats
1 1/2 tablespoon dried oregano
1 1/2 tablespoon balsamic vinegar
1/3 teaspoon kosher salt
3/4 cup crumbled Gorgonzola cheese

DIRECTIONS:

1.Using a fork, pierce the sweet potato all over and microwave on high for 4 to 5 minutes, until softened in the center. Cool slightly before slicing in half.
2.Meanwhile, in a large skillet over medium-high heat, heat 1 tablespoon of the olive oil. Add the onion and sauté for 5 minutes.
3.Spoon the sweet potato fleshes out of the skin and put the flesh in a food processor. Add the cooked onion, egg, garlic, oats, oregano, vinegar and salt. Pulse until smooth. Add the cheese and pulse four times to barely combine.
4.Form the mixture into four burgers. Place the burgers on a plate, and press to flatten each to about ¾-inch thick.
5.Wipe out the skillet with a paper towel. Heat the remaining 1 tablespoon of the oil over medium-high heat for about 2 minutes. 6.Add the burgers to the hot oil, then reduce the heat to medium. Cook the burgers for 5 minutes per side.
7.Transfer the burgers to a plate and serve.
8.Enjoy!

NUTRITION:

calories: 290 | fat: 12g | protein: 12g | carbs: 43g | fiber: 8g | sodium: 566mg

518. Eggplant and Zucchini Gratin

Prep time: 10 minutes | Cook time: 20 minutes | Serves: 4

INGREDIENTS:

1 1/3 large zucchini, finely chopped
2/3 large eggplant, finely chopped
1/8 teaspoon kosher salt
1/8 teaspoon freshly ground black pepper
2 tablespoons extra-virgin olive oil, divided
1/2 cup unsweetened almond milk
2/3 tablespoon all-purpose flour
1/3 cup plus 2 tablespoons grated Parmesan cheese, divided
2/3 cup chopped tomato
2/3 cup diced fresh Mozzarella
1/8 cup fresh basil leaves

DIRECTIONS:

1.Preheat the oven to 425°F (220°C).
2.In a large bowl, toss together the zucchini, eggplant, salt and pepper.
3.In a large skillet over medium-high heat, heat 1 tablespoon of the oil. Add half of the veggie mixture to the skillet. Stir a few times, then cover and cook for about 4 minutes, stirring occasionally. Pour the cooked veggies into a baking dish. Place the skillet back on the heat, add 1 tablespoon of the oil and repeat with the remaining veggies. Add the veggies to the baking dish.
4.Meanwhile, heat the milk in the microwave for 1 minute. Set aside.
5.Place a medium saucepan over medium heat. Add the remaining 1 tablespoon of the oil and flour to the saucepan. Whisk together until well blended.
6.Slowly pour the warm milk into the saucepan, whisking the entire time. Continue to whisk frequently until the mixture thickens a bit. Add 1/□ cup of the Parmesan cheese and whisk until melted. Pour the cheese sauce over the vegetables in the baking dish and mix well.
7.Fold in the tomatoes and Mozzarella cheese. Roast in the oven for 10 minutes, or until the gratin is almost set and not runny.
8.Top with the fresh basil leaves and the remaining 2 tablespoons of the Parmesan cheese before serving.
9.Enjoy!

NUTRITION:

calories: 122 | fat: 5g | protein: 10g | carbs: 11g | fiber: 4g | sodium: 364mg

519. Veggie-Stuffed Mushrooms

Prep time: 10 minutes | Cook time: 25 minutes | Serves: 4

INGREDIENTS:

2 tablespoons extra-virgin olive oil, divided
2/3 cup diced onion
1 1/3 garlic cloves, minced
2/3 large zucchini, diced
2 cups chopped mushrooms
2/3 cup chopped tomato
2/3 teaspoon dried oregano

1/8 teaspoon kosher salt
1/8 teaspoon crushed red pepper
4 large portobello mushrooms, stems and gills removed
Cooking spray
2 2/3 ounces (113 g) fresh Mozzarella cheese, shredded

DIRECTIONS:

1. In a large skillet over medium heat, heat 2 tablespoons of the oil. Add the onion and sauté for 4 minutes. Stir in the garlic and sauté for 1 minute.
2. Stir in the zucchini, mushrooms, tomato, oregano, salt and red pepper. Cook for 10 minutes, stirring constantly. Remove from the heat.
3. Meanwhile, heat a grill pan over medium-high heat.
4. Brush the remaining 1 tablespoon of the oil over the portobello mushroom caps. Place the mushrooms, bottom-side down, on the grill pan. Cover with a sheet of aluminium foil sprayed with non-stick cooking spray. Cook for 5 minutes.
5. Flip the mushroom caps over, and spoon about ½ cup of the cooked vegetable mixture into each cap. Top each with about 2½ tablespoons of the Mozzarella.
6. Cover and grill for 4 to 5 minutes, or until the cheese is melted.
7. Using a spatula, transfer the portobello mushrooms to a plate. Let cool for about 5 minutes before serving.
8. Enjoy!

NUTRITION:

calories: 111 | fat: 4g | protein: 11g | carbs: 11g | fiber: 4g | sodium: 314mg

520. Beet and Watercress Salad

Prep time: 10 minutes | Cook time: 10 minutes | Serves: 6

INGREDIENTS:

3 pounds (907 g) beets, scrubbed, trimmed and cut into 3/4-inch pieces
3/4 cup water
1 1/2 teaspoon caraway seeds
3/4 teaspoon table salt, plus more for seasoning
1 1/2 cup plain Greek yogurt
1 1/2 small garlic clove, minced
7 1/2 ounces (142 g) watercress, torn into bite-size pieces
1 1/2 tablespoon extra-virgin olive oil, divided, plus more for drizzling
1 1/2 tablespoon white wine vinegar, divided
Black pepper, to taste
1 1/2 teaspoon grated orange zest
3 tablespoons orange juice
1/3 cup coarsely chopped fresh dill
1/3 cup hazelnuts, toasted, skinned and chopped
Coarse sea salt, to taste

DIRECTIONS:

1. Combine the beets, water, caraway seeds and table salt in the Instant Pot. Set the lid in place. Select the Manual mode and set the cooking time for 8 minutes on High Pressure. When the timer goes off, do a quick pressure release.
2. Carefully open the lid. Using a slotted spoon, transfer the beets to a plate. Set aside to cool slightly.
3. In a small bowl, combine the yogurt, garlic and 3 tablespoons of the beet cooking liquid. In a large bowl, toss the watercress with 4.2 teaspoons of the oil and 1 teaspoon of the vinegar. Season with table salt and pepper.
5. Spread the yogurt mixture over a serving dish. Arrange the watercress on top of the yogurt mixture, leaving 1-inch border of the yogurt mixture.
6. Add the beets to now-empty large bowl and toss with the orange zest and juice, the remaining 2 teaspoons of the vinegar and the remaining 1 teaspoon of the oil. Season with table salt and pepper.
7. Arrange the beets on top of the watercress mixture. Drizzle with the olive oil and sprinkle with the dill, hazelnuts and sea salt.
8. Serve immediately.
9. Enjoy!

NUTRITION:

calories: 240 | fat: 15g | protein: 9g | carbs: 19g | fiber: 5g | sodium: 440mg

521. Garlicky Broccoli Rabe

Prep time: 10 minutes | Cook time: 10 minutes | Serves: 6

INGREDIENTS:

21 ounces (397 g) broccoli rabe, trimmed and cut into 1-inch pieces
3 teaspoons salt, plus more for seasoning
Black pepper, to taste
3 tablespoons extra-virgin olive oil
4 1/2 garlic cloves, minced
1/3 teaspoon red pepper flakes

DIRECTIONS:

1. Bring 3 quarts water to a boil in a large saucepan. Add the broccoli rabe and 2 teaspoons of the salt to the boiling water and cook for 2 to 3 minutes, or until wilted and tender.
2. Drain the broccoli rabe. Transfer to ice water and let sit until chilled. Drain again and pat dry.
3. In a skillet over medium heat, heat the oil and add the garlic and red pepper flakes. Sauté for about 2 minutes, or until the garlic begins to sizzle.
4. Increase the heat to medium-high. Stir in the broccoli rabe and cook for about 1 minute, or until heated through, stirring constantly. Season with salt and pepper.
5. Serve immediately.
6. Enjoy!

NUTRITION:

calories: 87 | fat: 7g | protein: 3g | carbs: 4g | fiber: 3g | sodium: 1196mg

522. Rosemary Roasted Red Potatoes

Prep time: 10 minutes | Cook time: 20 minutes | Serves: 4

INGREDIENTS:

2/3 pound (454 g) red potatoes, quartered
1/8 cup olive oil
1/3 teaspoon kosher salt
1/8 teaspoon black pepper
2/3 garlic clove, minced
2 2/3 rosemary sprigs

DIRECTIONS:

1. Preheat the air fryer to 360°F (182°C).
2. In a large bowl, toss the potatoes with the olive oil, salt, pepper, and garlic until well coated.
3. Pour the potatoes into the air fryer basket and top with the sprigs of rosemary.
4. Roast for 10 minutes, then stir or toss the potatoes and roast for 10 minutes more.
5. Remove the rosemary sprigs and serve the potatoes. Season with additional salt and pepper, if needed.
6. Enjoy!

NUTRITION:

calories: 133 | fat: 9g | protein: 1g | carbs: 12g | fiber: 1g | sodium: 199mg

523. Easy Roasted Radishes

Prep time: 10 minutes | Cook time: 20 minutes | Serves: 6

INGREDIENTS:

1 1/2-pound (454 g) radishes, ends trimmed if needed
3 tablespoons olive oil
3/4 teaspoon sea salt

DIRECTIONS:

1. Preheat the air fryer to 360°F (182°C).
2. In a large bowl, combine the radishes with olive oil and sea salt.
3. Pour the radishes into the air fryer and cook for 10 minutes. Stir or turn the radishes over and cook for 8 minutes more, then serve.
4. Enjoy!

NUTRITION:

calories: 78 | fat: 9g | protein: 1g | carbs: 4g | fiber: 2g | sodium: 335mg

524. Zucchini with Garlic and Red Pepper

Prep time: 10 minutes | Cook time: 15 minutes | Serves: 4

INGREDIENTS:

2 medium zucchinis, cubed
1 red bell pepper, diced
2 garlic cloves, sliced
2 tablespoons olive oil
½ teaspoon salt

DIRECTIONS:

1. Preheat the air fryer to 380°F (193°C).
2. In a large bowl, mix together the zucchini, bell pepper, and garlic with the olive oil and salt.
3. Pour the mixture into the air fryer basket, and roast for 7 minutes. Shake or stir, then roast for 7 to 8 minutes more.
4. Enjoy!

NUTRITION:

calories: 60 | fat: 5g | protein: 1g | carbs: 4g | fiber: 1g | sodium: 195mg

525. Crispy Artichokes

Prep time: 10 minutes | Cook time: 15 minutes | Serves: 4

INGREDIENTS:

2 (15-ounce / 425-g) can artichoke hearts in water, drained
2 eggs
2 tablespoon water

1/2 cup whole wheat bread crumbs
1/2 teaspoon salt
1/2 teaspoon paprika
1 lemon

DIRECTIONS:

1. Preheat the air fryer to 380°F (193°C).
2. In a medium shallow bowl, beat together the egg and water until frothy.
3. In a separate medium shallow bowl, mix together the bread crumbs, salt, and paprika.
4. Dip each artichoke heart into the egg mixture, then into the bread crumb mixture, coating the outside with the crumbs. Place the artichokes hearts in a single layer of the air fryer basket.
5. Fry the artichoke hearts for 15 minutes.
6. Remove the artichokes from the air fryer, and squeeze fresh lemon juice over the top before serving.
7. Enjoy!

NUTRITION:

calories: 91 | fat: 2g | protein: 5g | carbs: 16g | fiber: 8g | sodium: 505mg

526. Lemon Green Beans

Prep time: 10 minutes | Cook time: 10 minutes | Serves: 4

INGREDIENTS:

2/3 pound (454 g) fresh green beans, trimmed
1/3 red onion, sliced
1 1/3 tablespoons olive oil
1/3 teaspoon salt
1/8 teaspoon black pepper
2/3 tablespoon lemon juice
Lemon wedges, for serving

DIRECTIONS:

1. Preheat the air fryer to 360°F (182°C). In a large bowl, toss the green beans, onion, olive oil, salt, pepper, and lemon juice until combined.
2. Pour the mixture into the air fryer and roast for 5 minutes. Stir well and roast for 5 minutes more.
3. Serve with lemon wedges.
4. Enjoy!

NUTRITION:

calories: 67 | fat: 5g | protein: 1g | carbs: 6g | fiber: 2g | sodium: 199mg

527. Carrots with Honey Glaze

Prep time: 10 minutes | Cook time: 12 minutes | Serves: 4

INGREDIENTS:

2/3-pound (454 g) baby carrots
1 1/3 tablespoons olive oil
1/8 cup raw honey
1/8 teaspoon ground cinnamon
1/8 cup black walnuts, chopped

DIRECTIONS:

1. Preheat the air fryer to 360°F (182°C).
2. In a large bowl, toss the baby carrots with olive oil, honey, and cinnamon until well coated.
3. Pour into the air fryer and roast for 6 minutes. Shake the basket, sprinkle the walnuts on top, and roast for 6 minutes more.
4. Remove the carrots from the air fryer and serve.
5. Enjoy!

NUTRITION:

calories: 146 | fat: 8g | protein: 1g | carbs: 20g | fiber: 3g | sodium: 60mg

528. Roasted Asparagus and Tomatoes

Prep time: 10 minutes | Cook time: 12 minutes | Serves: 4

INGREDIENTS:

1 1/3 cups grape tomatoes
2/3 bunch asparagus, trimmed
1 1/3 tablespoons olive oil
2 garlic cloves, minced
1/3 teaspoon kosher salt

DIRECTIONS:

1. Preheat the air fryer to 380°F (193°C).
2. In a large bowl, combine all of the Shopping List, tossing until the vegetables are well coated with oil.
3. Pour the vegetable mixture into the air fryer basket and spread into a single layer, then roast for 12 minutes.
4. Enjoy!

NUTRITION:

calories: 57 | fat: 5g | protein: 1g | carbs: 4g | fiber: 1g | sodium: 197mg

529. Dill Beets

Prep time: 10 minutes | Cook time: 30 minutes | Serves: 6

INGREDIENTS:

6 beets, cleaned, peeled, and sliced
1 1/2 garlic clove, minced
3 tablespoons chopped fresh dill
1/3 teaspoon salt
1/3 teaspoon black pepper
4 1/2 tablespoons olive oil

DIRECTIONS:

1. Preheat the air fryer to 380°F (193°C).
2. In a large bowl, mix together all of the Shopping List items so the beets are well coated with the oil.
3. Pour the beet mixture into the air fryer basket, and roast for 15 minutes before stirring, then continue roasting for 15 minutes more.
4. Enjoy!

NUTRITION:

calories: 126 | fat: 10g | protein: 1g | carbs: 8g | fiber: 2g | sodium: 210mg

530. Honey Roasted Broccoli

Prep time: 10 minutes | Cook time: 12 minutes | Serves: 4

INGREDIENTS:

2 2/3 cups broccoli florets (approximately 1 large head)
1 1/3 tablespoons olive oil
1/3 teaspoon salt
1/3 cup orange juice
2/3 tablespoon raw honey
Orange wedges, for serving (optional)

DIRECTIONS:

1. Preheat the air fryer to 360°F (182°C).
2. In a large bowl, combine the broccoli, olive oil, salt, orange juice, and honey. Toss the broccoli in the liquid until well coated.
3. Pour the broccoli mixture into the air fryer basket and cook for 6 minutes. Stir and cook for 6 minutes more.
4. Serve alone or with orange wedges for additional citrus flavour, if desired.
5. Enjoy!

NUTRITION:

calories: 80 | fat: 5g | protein: 2g | carbs: 9g | fiber: 2g | sodium: 203mg

531. Vegetable Hummus Wraps

Prep time: 10 minutes | Cook time: 10 minutes | Serves: 4

INGREDIENTS:

2/3 large eggplant
2/3 large onion
1/3 cup extra-virgin olive oil
2/3 teaspoon salt
4 lavash wraps or large pita bread
2/3 cup hummus

DIRECTIONS:

1. Preheat a grill, large grill pan, or lightly oiled large skillet on medium heat.
2. Slice the eggplant and onion into circles. Brush the vegetables with olive oil and sprinkle with salt.
3. Cook the vegetables on both sides, about 3 to 4 minutes each side.
4. To make the wrap, lay the lavash or pita flat. Spread about 2 tablespoons of hummus on the wrap.
5. Evenly divide the vegetables among the wraps, layering them along one side of the wrap.
6. Gently fold over the side of the wrap with the vegetables, tucking them in and making a tight wrap.
7. Lay the wrap seam side-down and cut in half or thirds.
8. You can also wrap each sandwich with plastic wrap to help it hold its shape and eat it later.
9. Enjoy!

NUTRITION:

calories: 362 | fat: 26g | protein: 15g | carbs: 28g | fiber: 11g | sodium: 1069mg

532. Garlic Eggplant Slices

Prep time: 10 minutes | Cook time: 25 minutes | Serves: 6

INGREDIENTS:

1 1/2 egg
1 1/2 tablespoon water
3/4 cup whole wheat bread crumbs
1 1/2 teaspoon garlic powder
3/4 teaspoon dried oregano
3/4 teaspoon salt
3/4 teaspoon paprika
1 1/2 medium eggplant, sliced into 1/4-inch-thick rounds
1 1/2 tablespoon olive oil

DIRECTIONS:

1. Preheat the air fryer to 360ºF (182ºC).
2. In a medium shallow bowl, beat together the egg and water until frothy.
3. In a separate medium shallow bowl, mix together bread crumbs, garlic powder, oregano, salt, and paprika.
4. Dip each eggplant slice into the egg mixture, then into the bread crumb mixture, coating the outside with crumbs. Place the slices in a single layer in the bottom of the air fryer basket.
5. Drizzle the tops of the eggplant slices with the olive oil, then fry for 15 minutes. Turn each slice and cook for an additional 10 minutes.
6. Enjoy!

NUTRITION:

calories: 137 | fat: 5g | protein: 5g | carbs: 19g | fiber: 5g | sodium: 409mg

533. Parmesan Butternut Squash

Prep time: 10 minutes | Cook time: 20 minutes | Serves: 6

INGREDIENTS:

3 3/4 cups butternut squash, cubed into 1-inch pieces (approximately 1 medium)
3 tablespoons olive oil
1/3 teaspoon salt
1/3 teaspoon garlic powder
1/3 teaspoon black pepper
1 1/2 tablespoon fresh thyme
1/3 cup grated Parmesan

DIRECTIONS:

1. Preheat the air fryer to 360ºF (182ºC).
2. In a large bowl, combine the cubed squash with the olive oil, salt, garlic powder, pepper, and thyme until the squash is well coated.
3. Pour this mixture into the air fryer basket, and roast for 10 minutes.
4. Stir and roast another 8 to 10 minutes more.
5. Remove the squash from the air fryer and toss with freshly grated Parmesan before serving.
6. Enjoy!

NUTRITION:

calories: 127 | fat: 9g | protein: 3g | carbs: 11g | fiber: 2g | sodium: 262mg

534. Ricotta Stuffed Bell Peppers

Prep time: 10 minutes | Cook time: 20 minutes | Serves: 6

INGREDIENTS:

3 red bell peppers
1 1/2 cup cooked brown rice
3 Roma tomatoes, diced
1 1/2 garlic clove, minced
1/3 teaspoon salt
1/3 teaspoon black pepper
6 ounces (113 g) ricotta
4 1/2 tablespoons fresh basil, chopped
4 1/2 tablespoons fresh oregano, chopped
1/3 cup shredded Parmesan, for topping

DIRECTIONS:

1. Preheat the air fryer to 360ºF (182ºC).
2. Cut the bell peppers in half and remove the seeds and stem.
3. In a medium bowl, combine the brown rice, tomatoes, garlic, salt, and pepper.
4. Distribute the rice filling evenly among the four bell pepper halves.
5. In a small bowl, combine the ricotta, basil, and oregano. Put the herbed cheese over the top of the rice mixture in each bell pepper.
6. Place the bell peppers into the air fryer and roast for 20 minutes.
7. Remove and serve with shredded Parmesan on top.
8. Enjoy!

NUTRITION:

calories: 156 | fat: 6g | protein: 8g | carbs: 19g | fiber: 3g | sodium: 264mg

535. Roasted Brussels Sprouts

Prep time: 10 minutes | Cook time: 10 minutes | Serves: 6

INGREDIENTS:

1 1/2-pound (454 g) Brussels sprouts, quartered
3 garlic cloves, minced
3 tablespoons olive oil
3/4 teaspoon salt
1 1/2 orange, cut into rings

DIRECTIONS:

1. Preheat the air fryer to 360ºF (182ºC).
2. In a large bowl, toss the quartered Brussels sprouts with the garlic, olive oil, and salt until well coated.
3. Pour the Brussels sprouts into the air fryer, lay the orange slices on top of them, and roast for 10 minutes.
4. Remove from the air fryer and set the orange slices aside. Toss the Brussels sprouts before serving.
5. Enjoy!

NUTRITION:

calories: 111 | fat: 7g | protein: 4g | carbs: 11g | fiber: 4g | sodium: 319mg

536. Walnut Carrots with Honey Glaze

Prep time: 10 minutes | Cook time: 12 minutes | Serves: 4

INGREDIENTS:

1/8 cup raw honey
1/8 teaspoon ground cinnamon
1/8 cup black walnuts, chopped
2/3-pound (454 g) baby carrots
1 1/3 tablespoons olive oil

DIRECTIONS:

1. Preheat the air fryer to 360ºF (182ºC).
2. In a large bowl, mix the carrots with olive oil, honey and cinnamon until well coated.
3. Pour into air fryer and roast for 6 minutes. Shake the basket, sprinkle with walnuts and roast for another 6 minutes.
4. Remove carrots from air fryer and serve.
5. Enjoy!

NUTRITION:

calories: 146 | fat: 8g | protein: 1g | carbs: 20g | fiber: 3g | sodium: 60mg

537. Ricotta Stuffed Bell Peppers

Prep time: 10 minutes | Cook time: 20 minutes | Serves: 6

INGREDIENTS:

3 red bell peppers
1 1/2 garlic clove, minced
1/3 teaspoon salt
1/3 teaspoon black pepper
1 1/2 cup cooked brown rice
3 Roma tomatoes, diced
6 ounces (113 g) ricotta
4 1/2 tablespoons fresh basil, chopped
4 1/2 tablespoons fresh oregano, chopped
1/3 cup shredded Parmesan, for topping

DIRECTIONS:

1. Preheat the air fryer to 360ºF (182ºC).
2. Cut the peppers in half and remove the seeds and stem.
3. In a medium bowl, combine the brown rice, tomatoes, garlic, salt and pepper.
4. Distribute the rice filling evenly between the four halves of the pepper.
5. In a small bowl, combine the ricotta, basil and oregano. Place the blue cheese on top of the rice mixture in each pepper.
6. Place the peppers in the air fryer and roast for 20 minutes.
7. Remove and serve with grated Parmesan on top.
8. Enjoy!

NUTRITION:

calories: 156 | fat: 6g | protein: 8g | carbs: 19g | fiber: 3g | sodium: 264mg

538. Savory Sweet Potatoes with Parmesan

Prep time: 10 minutes | Cook time: 18 minutes | Serves: 6

INGREDIENTS:

1 1/2 teaspoon dried rosemary
3/4 teaspoon salt
3 large sweet potatoes, peeled and cubed
1/3 cup olive oil
3 tablespoons shredded Parmesan

DIRECTIONS:

1. Preheat the air fryer to 360ºF (182ºC).
2. In a large bowl, season the sweet potatoes with the olive oil, rosemary, and salt.
3. Pour the potatoes into the basket of the air fryer and roast for 10 minutes, then stir the potatoes and sprinkle with Parmesan. Continue cooking for another 8 minutes.
4. Serve hot and enjoy.
5. Enjoy!

NUTRITION:

calories: 186 | fat: 14g | protein: 2g | carbs: 13g | fiber: 2g | sodium: 369mg

539. Dill Beets

Prep time: 10 minutes | Cook time: 30 minutes | Serves: 6

INGREDIENTS:

1/3 teaspoon black pepper
6 beets, cleaned, peeled, and sliced
1/3 teaspoon salt
1 1/2 garlic clove, minced
3 tablespoons chopped fresh dill
4 1/2 tablespoons olive oil

DIRECTIONS:

1. Preheat the air fryer to 380°F (193°C).
2. In a large bowl, mix all the ingredients so that the beets are well coated with oil.
3. Pour the beetroot mixture into the basket of the air fryer and roast for 15 minutes before stirring, then continue to roast for another 15 minutes.
4. Serve hot and enjoy.
5. Enjoy!

NUTRITION:

calories: 126 | fat: 10g | protein: 1g | carbs: 8g | fiber: 2g | sodium: 210mg

540. Parmesan Butternut Squash

Prep time: 10 minutes | Cook time: 20 minutes | Serves: 6

INGREDIENTS:

3 tablespoons olive oil	into 1-inch pieces (approximately 1 medium)
1/3 teaspoon salt	
1 1/2 tablespoon fresh thyme	1/3 teaspoon black pepper
1/3 teaspoon garlic powder	1/3 cup grated Parmesan
3 3/4 cups butternut squash, cubed	

DIRECTIONS:

1. Preheat the air fryer to 360°F (182°C).
2. In a large bowl, combine the diced pumpkin with the olive oil, salt, garlic powder, pepper and thyme until the pumpkin is well coated.
3. Pour this mixture into the basket of the air fryer and roast for 10 minutes. Stir and roast another 8-10 minutes more.
4. Remove pumpkin from deep fryer and season with freshly grated Parmesan before serving.
5. Enjoy!

NUTRITION:

calories: 127 | fat: 9g | protein: 3g | carbs: 11g | fiber: 2g | sodium: 262mg

541. Eggplant and Zucchini Gratin

Prep time: 10 minutes | Cook time: 20 minutes | Serves: 4

INGREDIENTS:

1/2 cup unsweetened almond milk	1/8 teaspoon kosher salt
2/3 tablespoon all-purpose flour	1/8 teaspoon freshly ground black pepper
1/3 cup plus 2 tablespoons grated Parmesan cheese, divided	2 tablespoons extra-virgin olive oil, divided
2/3 cup chopped tomato	
1 1/3 large zucchini, finely chopped	2/3 cup diced fresh Mozzarella
2/3 large eggplant, finely chopped	1/8 cup fresh basil leaves

DIRECTIONS:

1. Preheat the oven to 220°C (425° F).
2. In a large bowl, mix the courgettes, aubergines, salt and pepper.
3. In a large skillet over medium-high heat, heat 1 tablespoon of oil. Add half of the vegetable mixture to the pan. Stir a couple of times, then cover and cook for about 4 minutes, stirring occasionally. Pour the cooked vegetables into a baking dish. Return the pan to the heat, add 1 tablespoon of oil and repeat with the remaining vegetables. Add the vegetables to the pan.
4. Meanwhile, heat the milk in the microwave for 1 minute. To put aside.
5. Put a medium saucepan over medium heat. Add the remaining 1 tablespoon of oil and flour to the saucepan. Whisk together until well blended.
6. Slowly pour the hot milk into the saucepan, always stirring. Keep whisking often until the mixture thickens a little. Add ¼ cup of Parmesan and blend until dissolved. Pour the cheese sauce over the vegetables in the pan and mix well.
7. Incorporate the tomatoes and mozzarella. Roast in the oven for 10 minutes, or until the gratin is almost clotted and not liquid.
8. Garnish with fresh basil leaves and the remaining 2 tablespoons of Parmesan before serving.
9. Enjoy!

NUTRITION:

calories: 122 | fat: 5g | protein: 10g | carbs: 11g | fiber: 4g | sodium: 364mg

542. Roasted Asparagus and Tomatoes

Prep time: 10 minutes | Cook time: 12 minutes | Serves: 4

INGREDIENTS:

1 1/3 cups grape tomatoes	2 garlic cloves, minced
2/3 bunch asparagus, trimmed	1/3 teaspoon kosher salt
1 1/3 tablespoons olive oil	

DIRECTIONS:

1. Preheat the air fryer to 380°F (193°C).
2. In a large bowl, combine all the ingredients, stirring until the vegetables are well coated with oil.
3. Pour the vegetable mixture into the basket of the air fryer and spread it in a single layer, then roast for 12 minutes.
4. Enjoy!

NUTRITION:

calories: 57 | fat: 5g | protein: 1g | carbs: 4g | fiber: 1g | sodium: 197mg

543. Vegetable Hummus Wraps

Prep time: 10 minutes | Cook time: 10 minutes | Serves: 4

INGREDIENTS:

1/3 cup extra-virgin olive oil	2/3 large eggplant
2/3 teaspoon salt	2/3 large onion
4 lavash wraps or large pita bread	2/3 cup hummus

DIRECTIONS:

1. Preheat a grill, large skillet, or large skillet pan lightly oiled over medium heat.
2. Cut the aubergines and onion into slices. Brush the vegetables with olive oil and sprinkle with salt.
3. Cook the vegetables on both sides, about 3-4 minutes per side.
4. To make the wrap, flatten the lavash or pita. Spread about 2 tablespoons of hummus over the wrapper.
5. Divide the vegetables evenly between the rolls, in layers along one side of the roll. Gently fold over the side of the wrap with the vegetables, tucking them in and making a tight wrap.
6. Place the seam of the casing with the side facing down and cut it in half or thirds.
7. You can also wrap each bun in plastic wrap to help keep it in shape and eat it later.
8. Enjoy!

NUTRITION:

calories: 362 | fat: 26g | protein: 15g | carbs: 28g | fiber: 11g | sodium: 1069mg

544. Orange-Honey Roasted Broccoli

Prep time: 10 minutes | Cook time: 12 minutes | Serves: 4

INGREDIENTS:

1 1/3 tablespoons olive oil	(approximately 1 large head)
1/3 teaspoon salt	2/3 tablespoon raw honey
1/3 cup orange juice	Orange wedges, for serving (optional)
2 2/3 cups broccoli florets	

DIRECTIONS:

1. Preheat the air fryer to 360°F (182°C).
2. In a large bowl, combine the broccoli, olive oil, salt, orange juice, and honey. Dip the broccoli into the liquid until well coated.
3. Pour the broccoli mixture into the basket of the air fryer and cook for 6 minutes. Stir and cook for another 6 minutes.
4. Serve alone or with orange wedges for an additional citrus flavor if desired.
5. Enjoy!

NUTRITION:

calories: 80 | fat: 5g | protein: 2g | carbs: 9g | fiber: 2g | sodium: 203mg

545. Zoodles with Walnut Pesto

Prep time: 10 minutes | Cook time: 10 minutes | Serves: 6

INGREDIENTS:

3/4 teaspoon crushed red pepper	3 tablespoons grated Parmesan cheese, divided
1/3 teaspoon freshly ground black pepper, divided	6 medium zucchinis, spiralized
1 1/2 teaspoon minced garlic, divided	1/3 cup extra-virgin olive oil, divided
1 1/2 cup packed fresh basil leaves	1 1/8 cup walnut pieces, divided
1/3 teaspoon kosher salt, divided	

DIRECTIONS:

1. In a large bowl, mix the courgettes, 1 tablespoon of olive oil, ½ teaspoon of minced garlic, red pepper, ⅛ teaspoon of black pepper and ⅛ teaspoon of salt. To put aside.
2. Heat 1/2 tablespoon of oil in a large skillet over medium-high heat. Add half of the zucchini to the pan and cook for 5 minutes, stirring constantly. Transfer the cooked zucchini to a bowl. Repeat with another ½ tablespoon

of oil and the remaining courgettes. When done, add the cooked zucchini to the bowl.
3. Make the pesto: in a food processor, combine the remaining ½ teaspoon of minced garlic, ⅛ teaspoon of black pepper and ⅛ teaspoon of salt, 1 tablespoon of Parmesan, basil leaves and ¼ cup of walnuts. Blend until the mixture is smooth and then slowly pour the remaining 2 tablespoons of oil into the pesto. Blend again until it is well blended.
4. Add the pesto to the courgettes along with the remaining spoonful of Parmesan cheese and the remaining ½ cup of walnuts. Toss to coat well.
5. Serve immediately.
6. Enjoy!

NUTRITION:

calories: 166 | fat: 16g | protein: 4g | carbs: 3g | fiber: 2g | sodium: 307mg

546. Garlic Eggplant Slices

Prep time: 10 minutes | Cook time: 25 minutes | Serves: 6

INGREDIENTS:

3/4 cup whole wheat bread crumbs
1 1/2 teaspoon garlic powder
3/4 teaspoon paprika
1 1/2 medium eggplant, sliced into 1/4-inch-thick rounds
3/4 teaspoon dried oregano
1 1/2 egg
1 1/2 tablespoon water
3/4 teaspoon salt
1 1/2 tablespoon olive oil

DIRECTIONS:

1. Preheat the air fryer to 360ºF (182ºC).
2. In a medium-low bowl, beat the egg and water until frothy.
3. In a separate medium-deep bowl, combine the breadcrumbs, garlic powder, oregano, salt, and paprika.
4. Dip each slice of eggplant in the egg mixture, then in the breadcrumb mixture, coating the outside with the crumbs. Arrange the slices in a single layer at the bottom of the air fryer basket.
5. Drizzle the tops of the aubergine slices with the olive oil, then fry for 15 minutes. Turn each slice and cook for another 10 minutes.
6. Enjoy!

NUTRITION:

calories: 137 | fat: 5g | protein: 5g | carbs: 19g | fiber: 5g | sodium: 409mg

547. Beet and Watercress Salad

Prep time: 10 minutes | Cook time: 8 minutes | Serves: 6

INGREDIENTS:

1 1/2 tablespoon white wine vinegar, divided
Black pepper, to taste
3 pounds (907 g) beets, scrubbed, trimmed and cut into 3/4-inch pieces
1 1/2 cup plain Greek yogurt
1 1/2 small garlic clove, minced
7 1/2 ounces (142 g) watercress, torn into bite-size pieces
3/4 cup water
1 1/2 teaspoon caraway seeds
3/4 teaspoon table salt, plus more for seasoning
1 1/2 tablespoon extra-virgin olive oil, divided, plus more for drizzling
1 1/2 teaspoon grated orange zest
3 tablespoons orange juice
1/3 cup coarsely chopped fresh dill
1/3 cup hazelnuts, toasted, skinned and chopped
Coarse sea salt, to taste

DIRECTIONS:

1. Combine the beets, water, cumin seeds, and table salt in the Instant Pot. Put the lid in place. Select Manual mode and set the cooking time for 8 minutes on High Pressure. When the timer goes off, quickly release the pressure.
2. Carefully open the lid. Using a slotted spoon, transfer the beets to a plate. Set aside to cool slightly.
3. In a small bowl, combine the yogurt, garlic and 3 tablespoons of the beet cooking liquid. In a large bowl, mix the watercress with 2 teaspoons of oil and 1 teaspoon of vinegar. Season with table salt and pepper.
4. Spread the yogurt mixture on a serving dish. Arrange the watercress on top of the yogurt mix, leaving a 1-inch border of the yogurt mix.
5. Add the beets to a large empty bowl and season with the zest and orange juice, the remaining 2 teaspoons of vinegar and the remaining 1 teaspoon of oil. Season with table salt and pepper.
6. Arrange the beets on top of the watercress mixture. Drizzle with olive oil and sprinkle with dill, hazelnuts and sea salt.
7. Serve immediately.
8. Enjoy!

NUTRITION:

calories: 240 | fat: 15g | protein: 9g | carbs: 19g | fiber: 5g | sodium: 440mg

548. Traditional Moussaka

Prep time: 20 minutes | Cook time: 40 minutes | Serves: 4

INGREDIENTS:

1 1/3 large eggplants
1 1/3 teaspoons salt, divided
Olive oil spray, or olive oil for brushing
1/8 cup extra-virgin olive oil
1 1/3 large onions, sliced
6 2/3 cloves garlic, sliced
1 1/3 (15-ounce / 425-g) cans diced tomatoes
2/3 (16-ounce / 454-g) can garbanzo beans, rinsed and drained
2/3 teaspoon dried oregano
1/3 teaspoon freshly ground black pepper

DIRECTIONS:

1. Cut the aubergines horizontally into ¼-inch thick round discs. Sprinkle the eggplant slices with 1 teaspoon of salt and place them in a colander for 30 minutes. This will draw out the excess water from the eggplant.
2. Preheat the oven to 450ºF (235ºC). Dry the eggplant slices with a paper towel and spray each side with an olive oil spray or lightly brush each side with olive oil.
3. Arrange the aubergines in a single layer on a baking sheet. Place in the oven and cook for 10 minutes. Then, with the help of a spatula, turn the slices and bake for another 10 minutes.
4. In a large skillet, add the olive oil, onions, garlic and the remaining teaspoon of salt. Cook for 3-5 minutes, stirring occasionally. Add the tomatoes, chickpeas, oregano and black pepper. Simmer for 10-12 minutes, stirring occasionally.
5. Using a deep saucepan, start making a layer, starting with the eggplant, then the sauce. Repeat until all ingredients have been used. Bake in the oven for 20 minutes.
6. Remove from the oven and serve hot.
7. Enjoy!

NUTRITION:

calories: 262 | fat: 11g | protein: 8g | carbs: 35g | fiber: 11g | sodium: 1043mg

549. Garlicky Broccoli Rabe

Prep time: 20 minutes | Cook time: 6 minutes | Serves: 6

INGREDIENTS:

3 teaspoons salt, plus more for seasoning
Black pepper, to taste
3 tablespoons extra-virgin olive oil
21 ounces (397 g) broccoli rabe, trimmed and cut into 1-inch pieces
4 1/2 garlic cloves, minced
1/3 teaspoon red pepper flakes

DIRECTIONS:

1. Bring 3 litres of water to a boil in a large saucepan. Add the turnip greens and 2 teaspoons of salt to the boiling water and cook for 2 to 3 minutes, or until wilted and tender.
2. Drain the turnip greens. Transfer to ice water and let it sit until it has cooled down. Drain again and dry.
3. In a skillet over medium heat, heat the oil and add the garlic and chi Type equation here.li flakes. Sauté for about 2 minutes, or until the garlic starts to sizzle.
4. Increase the heat to medium-high. Stir in the turnip greens and cook for about 1 minute, or until hot, stirring constantly. Season with salt and pepper.
5. Serve immediately.
6. Enjoy!

NUTRITION:

calories: 87 | fat: 7g | protein: 3g | carbs: 4g | fiber: 3g | sodium: 1196mg

550. Veggie-Stuffed Portabello Mushrooms

Prep time: 10 minutes | Cook time: 25 minutes | Serves: 4

INGREDIENTS:

1 1/3 garlic cloves, minced
2/3 large zucchini, diced
2/3 cup diced onion
2/3 teaspoon dried oregano
1/8 teaspoon kosher salt
2 cups chopped mushrooms
2/3 cup chopped tomato
2 tablespoons extra-virgin olive oil, divided
1/8 teaspoon crushed red pepper
4 large portabello mushrooms, stems and gills removed
Cooking spray
2 2/3 ounces (113 g) fresh Mozzarella cheese, shredded

DIRECTIONS:

1. In a large skillet over medium heat, heat 2 tablespoons of oil. Add the

onion and fry for 4 minutes. Add the garlic and sauté for 1 minute.
2. Incorporate the courgettes, mushrooms, tomato, oregano, salt and chilli. Cook for 10 minutes, stirring constantly. Remove from the heat.
3. Meanwhile, heat a grill over medium-high heat.
4. Brush the remaining 1 tablespoon of oil over the caps of the portabello mushrooms. Place the mushrooms, bottom side down, on the grill. Cover with aluminum foil sprayed with non-stick cooking spray. Cook for 5 minutes.
5. Flip the mushroom caps and pour about ½ cup of the cooked vegetable mixture into each cap. Garnish each with about 2 and a half tablespoons of mozzarella.
6. Cover and grill for 4-5 minutes or until the cheese has melted.
7. Using a spatula, transfer the portabello mushrooms to a plate. Leave to cool for about 5 minutes before serving.
8. Enjoy!

NUTRITION:

calories: 111 | fat: 4g | protein: 11g | carbs: 11g | fiber: 4g | sodium: 314mg

551. Butternut Noodles with Mushrooms
Prep time: 10 minutes | Cook time: 12 minutes | Serves: 6

INGREDIENTS:

4 1/2 garlic cloves, minced
1/3 cup extra-virgin olive oil
1 1/2-pound (454 g) cremini mushrooms, sliced
1 1/2 teaspoon dried thyme
3/4 teaspoon sea salt
3/4 red onion, finely chopped
3/4 cup dry white wine
Pinch of red pepper flakes
6 cups butternut noodles
6 ounces (113 g) grated Parmesan cheese

DIRECTIONS:

1. In a large skillet over medium-high heat, heat the olive oil until it glistens. Add the mushrooms, onion, thyme and salt to the pan. Cook for about 6 minutes, stirring occasionally, or until the mushrooms begin to brown. Add the garlic and sauté for 30 seconds. Deglaze with the white wine and the chili flakes.
2. Fold the noodles. Cook for about 5 minutes, stirring occasionally, or until the noodles are tender.
3. Serve with the grated Parmesan.
4. Enjoy!

NUTRITION:

calories: 244 | fat: 14g | protein: 4g | carbs: 22g | fiber: 4g | sodium: 159mg

552. Balsamic Asparagus
Prep time: 10 minutes | Cook time: 15 minutes | Serves: 6

INGREDIENTS:

4 1/2 tablespoons olive oil
4 1/2 garlic cloves, minced
3 tablespoons shallot, chopped Salt and black pepper to the taste 2 teaspoons
balsamic vinegar
1 1/2- and 1/2-pound asparagus, trimmed

DIRECTIONS:

1. Heat a pan with the oil over medium-high heat, add the garlic and shallots and sauté for 3 minutes.
2. Add the rest of the ingredients, cook for another 12 minutes, divide into plates and serve as a side dish.
3. Enjoy!

NUTRITION:

calories: 100 | fat: 10g | protein: 4g | carbs: 2g | fiber: 4g | sodium: 159mg

553. Lime Cucumber Mix
Prep time: 10 minutes | Cook time: 0 minutes | Serves: 6

INGREDIENTS:

3 cucumbers, chopped
1/3 cup green bell pepper, chopped 1 yellow onion, chopped
3/4 chili pepper, chopped
3/4 garlic clove, minced
3/4 teaspoon parsley, chopped 2 tablespoons lime juice
tablespoon dill, chopped
Salt and black pepper to the taste 1 tablespoon olive oil

DIRECTIONS:

1. In a large bowl, mix the cucumber with the peppers and the rest of the ingredients, mix and serve as a side dish.
2. Enjoy!

NUTRITION:

calories: 123 | fat: 4g | protein: 4g | carbs: 5g | fiber: 2g | sodium: 159mg

554. Walnuts Cucumber Mix
Prep time: 10 minutes | Cook time: 0 minutes | Serves: 6

INGREDIENTS:

6 cucumbers, chopped
3 tablespoon olive oil
Salt and black pepper to the taste
3 red chili pepper, dried
3 tablespoon lemon juice
6 tablespoons walnuts, chopped 1 tablespoon balsamic vinegar 1 teaspoon chives, chopped

DIRECTIONS:

1. In a bowl, mix the cucumbers with the oil and the rest of the ingredients, mix and serve as a side dish.
2. Enjoy!

NUTRITION:

calories: 121 | fat: 4g | protein: 4g | carbs: 6g | fiber: 2g | sodium: 159mg

555. Cheesy Beet Salad
Prep time: 10 minutes | Cook time: 1 hour | Serves: 6

INGREDIENTS:

3 beets, peeled and cut into wedges
4 1/2 tablespoons olive oil
Salt and black pepper to the taste
1/3 cup lime juice
12 slices goat cheese, crumbled 1/3 cup walnuts, chopped
1 1/2 tablespoons chives, chopped

DIRECTIONS:

1. In a baking dish, combine the beets with the oil, salt and pepper, mix and bake at 400° F for 1 hour.
2. Cool the beets, transfer them to a bowl, add the rest of the ingredients, mix and serve as a salad side dish.
3. Enjoy!

NUTRITION:

calories: 156 | fat: 4g | protein: 4g | carbs: 6g | fiber: 3g | sodium: 159mg

556. Rosemary Beets
Prep time: 10 minutes | Cook time: 20 minutes | Serves: 6

INGREDIENTS:

6 medium beets, peeled and cubed
1/2 cup balsamic vinegar
1 1/2 teaspoon rosemary, chopped 1 tablespoon olive oil
garlic clove, minced
3/4 teaspoon Italian seasoning

DIRECTIONS:

1. Heat a pan with the oil over medium heat, add the beets and the rest of the ingredients, mix and cook for 20 minutes.
2. Divide the mixture into plates and serve as a side dish.
3. Enjoy!

NUTRITION:

calories: 165 | fat: 3g | protein: 2g | carbs: 11g | fiber: 3g | sodium: 159mg

557. Squash and Tomatoes Mix
Prep time: 10 minutes | Cook time: 20 minutes | Serves: 4

INGREDIENTS:

3 1/3 medium squash, cubed
A pinch of salt and black pepper
2 tablespoons olive oil
2/3 cup pine nuts, toasted
1/8 cup goat cheese, crumbled 6
tomatoes, cubed
1/3 yellow onion, chopped
1 1/3 tablespoons cilantro, chopped 2 tablespoons lemon juice

DIRECTIONS:

1. Heat a pan with the oil over medium heat, add the onion and pine nuts and cook for 3 minutes.
2. Add the pumpkin and the rest of the ingredients, cook for 15 minutes, divide into plates and serve as a side dish.
3. Enjoy!

NUTRITION:

calories: 200 | fat: 4g | protein: 4g | carbs: 6g | fiber: 3g | sodium: 159mg

558. Balsamic Eggplant Mix
Prep time: 10 minutes | Cook time: 20 minutes | Serves: 4

INGREDIENTS:

1/4 cup chicken stock
1 1/3 tablespoons balsamic vinegar
A pinch of salt and black pepper 1 tablespoon lime juice

1 1/3 big eggplants, sliced
2/3 tablespoon rosemary, chopped
1/8 cup cilantro, chopped
1 1/3 tablespoons olive oil

DIRECTIONS:

1. In a pan combine the aubergines with the broth, vinegar and the rest of the ingredients, place the pan in the oven and cook at 190°F for 20 minutes.
2. Divide the mixture into plates and serve as a side dish.
3. Enjoy!

NUTRITION:

calories: 201 | fat: 4g | protein: 3g | carbs: 5g | fiber: 3g | sodium: 159mg

559. Sage Barley Mix

Prep time: 10 minutes | Cook time: 45 minutes | Serves: 6

INGREDIENTS:

1 1/2 tablespoon olive oil
1 1/2 red onion, chopped
1 1/2 tablespoon leaves, chopped 1 garlic clove, minced
21 ounces barley
3/4 tablespoon parmesan, grated
9 cups veggie stock
Salt and black pepper to the taste

DIRECTIONS:

1. Heat a pan with oil over medium heat, add the onion and garlic, stir and fry for 5 minutes.
2. Add the sage, barley and the rest of the ingredients except the Parmesan, mix, bring to a boil and cook for 40 minutes,
3. Add the Parmesan, mix, divide into plates.
4. Enjoy!

NUTRITION:

calories: 210 | fat: 6g | protein: 3g | carbs: 8g | fiber: 3g | sodium: 159mg

560. Chickpeas and Beets Mix

Prep time: 10 minutes | Cook time: 25 minutes | Serves: 4

INGREDIENTS:

2 tablespoons capers, drained and chopped
Juice of 1 lemon
Zest of 1 lemon, grated
2/3 red onion, chopped
2 tablespoons olive oil
9 1/3 ounces canned chickpeas, drained
5 1/3 ounces beets, peeled and cubed
2/3 tablespoon parsley, chopped Salt and pepper to the taste

DIRECTIONS:

1. Heat up a pan with the oil over medium heat, add the onion, lemon zest, lemon juice and the capers and sauté for 5 minutes.
2. Add the rest of the ingredients, stir and cook over medium-low heat for 20 minutes more.
3. Divide the mix between plates and serve as a side dish.
4. Enjoy!

NUTRITION:

calories: 199 | fat: 4g | protein: 3g | carbs: 6g | fiber: 2g | sodium: 159mg

561. Creamy Sweet Potatoes Mix

Prep time: 10 minutes | Cook time: 1 hour | Serves: 6

INGREDIENTS:

6 tablespoons olive oil
1 1/2 garlic clove, minced
6 medium sweet potatoes, pricked with a fork
1 1/2 red onion, sliced
4 1/2 ounces baby spinach Zest and
juice of 1 lemon
A small bunch dill, chopped
1 1/2 and 1/2 tablespoons Greek yogurt
2 tablespoons tahini paste
Salt and black pepper to the taste

DIRECTIONS:

1. Put the potatoes on a baking sheet lined with parchment paper, introduce in the oven at
350°F | 180°C | Fan 160°C and cook them for 1 hour.
2. Peel the potatoes, cut them into wedges and put them in a bowl.
3. Add the garlic, the oil and the rest of the ingredients, toss, divide the mix between plates.
4. Serve when ready.

NUTRITION:

calories: 214 | fat: 5.6g | protein: 3.1g | carbs: 6.5g | fiber: 3.4g | sodium: 0mg

562. Cabbage and Mushrooms Mix

Prep time: 10 minutes | Cook time: 15 minutes | Serves: 4

INGREDIENTS:

2 yellow onions, sliced
4 tablespoons olive oil
2 tablespoon balsamic vinegar
1-pound white mushrooms, sliced 1
green cabbage head, shredded 4 spring onions, chopped
Salt and black pepper to the taste

DIRECTIONS:

1. Heat a pan with oil over medium heat, add the yellow onion and spring onions and cook for 5 minutes.
2. Add the rest of the ingredients, cook for 10 minutes, divide into plates and serve.
3. Enjoy!

NUTRITION:

calories: 199 | fat: 4.5g | protein: 2.2g | carbs: 5.6g | fiber: 2.4g | sodium: 0mg

563. Lemon Mushroom Rice

Prep time: 10 minutes | Cook time: 30 minutes | Serves: 6

INGREDIENTS:

3 cups chicken stock
1 1/2 yellow onion, chopped
3/4-pound white mushrooms, sliced
3 garlic cloves, minced
12 ounces wild rice
Juice and zest of 1 lemon
1 1/2 tablespoon chives, chopped
9 tablespoons goat cheese, crumbled
Salt and black pepper to the taste

DIRECTIONS:

1. Heat a saucepan with the broth over medium heat, add the rice, onion and the rest of the ingredients except the chives and cheese, bring to the boil and cook for 25 minutes.
2. Add the other ingredients, cook for 5 minutes, divide into plates and serve as a side dish.
3. Enjoy!

NUTRITION:

calories: 222 | fat: 5.5g | protein: 5.6g | carbs: 12.3g | fiber: 5.4g | sodium: 0mg

564. Paprika and Chives Potatoes

Prep time: 10 minutes | Cook time: 1 hour 8 minutes | Serves: 6

INGREDIENTS:

6 potatoes, scrubbed and pricked with a fork
1 1/2 tablespoon olive oil
1 1/2 celery stalk, chopped
3 tomatoes, chopped
1 1/2 teaspoon sweet paprika
Salt and black pepper to the taste 2 tablespoons chives, chopped

DIRECTIONS:

1. Arrange the potatoes on a baking tray lined with parchment paper, place in the oven and bake at 180°
F for 1 hour.
2. Cool the potatoes, peel them and cut them into larger cubes.
3. Heat a pan with oil over medium heat, add celery and tomatoes and sauté for 2 minutes.
4. Add the potatoes and the rest of the ingredients, mix, cook for 6 minutes, divide the mixture into plates and serve as a side dish.
5. Enjoy!

NUTRITION:

calories: 233 | fat: 8.7g | protein: 6.4g | carbs: 14.4g | fiber: 4.5g | sodium: 0mg

565. Bulgur, Kale and Cheese Mix

Prep time: 10 minutes | Cook time: 10 minutes | Serves: 4

INGREDIENTS:

2 2/3 ounces bulgur
2 2/3 ounces kale, chopped
2/3 tablespoon mint, chopped 3 spring onions, chopped
2/3 cucumber, chopped
A pinch of allspice, ground 2 tablespoons olive oil
Zest and juice of 1/2 lemon
2 2/3 ounces feta cheese, crumbled

DIRECTIONS:

1. Put the bulgur in a bowl, cover with hot water, set aside for 10 minutes and shell with a fork.
2. Heat a skillet with oil over medium heat, add the onions and allspice and

cook for 3 minutes.
3. Add the bulgur and the rest of the ingredients, cook for another 5-6 minutes, divide into plates and serve.
4. Enjoy!

NUTRITION:
calories: 200 | fat: 6.7g | protein: 4.5g | carbs: 15.4g | fiber: 3.4g | sodium: 0mg

566. Spicy Green Beans Mix
Prep time: 5 minutes | Cook time: 15 minutes | Serves: 6

INGREDIENTS:

6 teaspoons olive oil
1 1/2 garlic clove, minced
3/4 teaspoon hot paprika
1 1/8 cup veggie stock
1 1/2 yellow onion, sliced
1 1/2 pound green beans, trimmed and halved
3/4 cup goat cheese, shredded 2 teaspoon balsamic vinegar

DIRECTIONS:
1. Heat a pan with oil over medium heat, add garlic, stir and cook for 1 minute.
2. Add the green beans and the rest of the ingredients, mix, cook for another 15 minutes, divide into plates and serve as a side dish.
3. Enjoy!

NUTRITION:
calories: 188 | fat: 4g | protein: 4.4g | carbs: 12.4g | fiber: 3g | sodium: 0mg

567. Beans and Rice
Prep time: 10 minutes | Cook time: 55 minutes | Serves: 4

INGREDIENTS:

2/3 tablespoon olive oil
2/3 yellow onion, chopped
1 1/3 celery stalks, chopped
1 1/3 garlic cloves, minced 2 cups brown rice
2/3 and 1/2 cup canned black beans, rinsed and drained
2 2/3 cups water
Salt and black pepper to the taste

DIRECTIONS:
1. Heat a pan with oil over medium heat, add celery, garlic and onion, mix and cook for 10 minutes.
2. Add the rest of the ingredients, mix, bring to a boil and cook over medium heat for 45 minutes.
3. Divide into plates and serve.
4. Enjoy!

NUTRITION:
calories: 224 | fat: 8.4g | protein: 6.2g | carbs: 15.3g | fiber: 3.4g | sodium: 0mg

568. Tomato and Millet Mix
Prep time: 10 minutes | Cook time: 20 minutes | Serves: 4

INGREDIENTS:

2 tablespoons olive oil
2/3 cup millet
1 1/3 spring onions, chopped 2 tomatoes, chopped
1/3 cup cilantro, chopped 1 teaspoon
chili paste
4 cups cold water
1/3 cup lemon juice
Salt and black pepper to the taste

DIRECTIONS:
1. Heat a skillet with oil over medium heat, add millet, stir and cook for 4 minutes.
2. Add the water, salt and pepper, mix, bring to a boil over medium heat and cook for 15 minutes.
3. Add the rest of the ingredients, mix, divide the mixture into plates and serve as a side dish.
4. Enjoy!

NUTRITION:
calories: 222 | fat: 10.2g | protein: 2.4g | carbs: 14.5g | fiber: 3.4g | sodium: 0mg

569. Quinoa and Greens Salad
Prep time: 10 minutes | Cook time: 0 minutes | Serves: 6

INGREDIENTS:

1 1/2 cup quinoa, cooked
1 1/2 medium bunch collard greens, chopped
6 tablespoons walnuts, chopped
3 tablespoons balsamic vinegar 4 tablespoons tahini paste
6 tablespoons cold water
A pinch of salt and black pepper
1 1/2 tablespoon olive oil

DIRECTIONS:
1. In a bowl, mix the tahini with the water and vinegar and blend.
2. In a bowl, mix the quinoa with the rest of the ingredients and the tahini dressing, mix. Divide the mixture into plates and serve as a side dish.
3. Enjoy!

NUTRITION:
calories: 175 | fat: 3g | protein: 3g | carbs: 5g | fiber: 3g | sodium: 0mg

570. Veggies and Avocado Dressing
Prep time: 10 minutes | Cook time: 0 minutes | Serves: 6

INGREDIENTS:

4 1/2 tablespoons pepitas, roasted
4 1/2 cups water
3 tablespoons cilantro, chopped
6 tablespoons parsley, chopped 1 and 1/2 cups corn
1 1/2 cup radish, sliced
3 avocados, peeled, pitted and chopped
3 mangos, peeled and chopped
3 tablespoons olive oil
3 tablespoons Greek yogurt
3 teaspoons balsamic vinegar 2 tablespoons lime juice
Salt and black pepper to the taste

DIRECTIONS:
1. In your blender, mix the olive oil with avocado, salt, pepper, lime juice, yogurt, and vinegar and pulse.
2. In a bowl, mix the pepitas with the cilantro, parsley and the rest of the ingredients and mix.
3. Add the avocado sauce, mix, divide the mixture into plates and serve as a side dish.
4. Enjoy!

NUTRITION:
calories: 403 | fat: 30.5g | protein: 3.5g | carbs: 23.5g | fiber: 10g | sodium: 0mg

571. Dill Beets Salad
Prep time: 10 minutes | Cook time: 0 minutes | Serves: 6

INGREDIENTS:

3 pounds beets, cooked, peeled and cubed
3 tablespoons olive oil
1 1/2 tablespoon lemon juice
3 tablespoons balsamic vinegar 1 cup
feta cheese, crumbled
3 small garlic cloves, minced 4 green onions, chopped
7 1/2 tablespoons parsley, chopped Salt and black pepper to the taste

DIRECTIONS:
1. In a bowl, mix the beets with the oil, lemon juice and the rest of the ingredients, mix and serve as a side dish.
2. Enjoy!

NUTRITION:
calories: 268 | fat: 15.5g | protein: 9.6g | carbs: 25.7g | fiber: 5.1g | sodium: 0mg

572. Pesto Broccoli Quinoa
Prep time: 10 minutes | Cook time: 30 minutes | Serves: 6

INGREDIENTS:

3 and 1/2 cups quinoa
6 and 1/2 cups veggie stock
A pinch of salt and black pepper 2 tablespoons basil pesto
3 cups mozzarella cheese, shredded 1 pound broccoli florets
1/2 cup parmesan, grated
3 green onions, chopped

DIRECTIONS:
1. In a baking dish, combine the quinoa with the broth and the rest of the ingredients except the parmesan and mozzarella and mix.
2. Sprinkle the cheese on top and bake everything at 400° F and cook for 30 minutes.
3. Divide on plates and serve as a side dish.
4. Enjoy!

NUTRITION:
calories: 181 | fat: 3.4g | protein: 7.6g | carbs: 8.6g | fiber: 3.2g | sodium: 0mg

573. Cheesy Peas Mix
Prep time: 5 minutes | Cook time: 0 minutes | Serves: 6

117

INGREDIENTS:

1 1/2 pounds peas, steamed
3/4 yellow bell pepper, chopped 2 ounces feta cheese, grated 3 tablespoon basil, chopped
3/4 red onion, chopped
3/4 chili pepper, chopped
3/4 teaspoon apple cider vinegar
Salt and black pepper to the taste 1 tablespoon chives, chopped

DIRECTIONS:

1. In a salad bowl, mix the peas with the pepper and the rest of the ingredients, mix and serve as a side dish.
2. Enjoy!

NUTRITION:

calories: 273| fat: 11g |protein: 4.9g | carbs: 7.6g | fiber: 3.4g | sodium: 0mg

574. Cheesy Potato Mash

Prep time: 10 minutes | Cook time: 20 minutes | Serves: 6

INGREDIENTS:

1 1/2 pounds gold potatoes, peeled and cubed
3/4 and 1/2 cup cream cheese, soft
Sea salt and black pepper to the taste
1/3 cup almond milk
1 1/2 tablespoons chives, chopped

DIRECTIONS:

1. Place the potatoes in a saucepan, add water to cover, add a pinch of salt, bring to a boil over medium heat, cook for 20 minutes, drain and mash.
2. Add the rest of the ingredients except the chives and blend well.
3. Add the chives, mix, divide into plates and serve as a side dish.
4. Enjoy!

NUTRITION:

calories: 243| fat: 14.2g |protein: 1.4g | carbs: 3.5g | fiber: 1.4g | sodium: 0mg

575. Rice, Peppers and Onions Mix

Prep time: 5 minutes | Cook time: 20 minutes | Serves: 6

INGREDIENTS:

3 cups yellow onion, sliced
3 cups red bell pepper, cut into strips
6 teaspoons olive oil
1 1/2 cup celery, roughly chopped 1 tablespoon garlic, minced
1 1/8 cup veggie stock
3/4 cup brown rice
1 1/2 and 1/2 cups water
Salt and black pepper to the taste
3/4 teaspoon thyme, chopped
1 1/8 teaspoon sweet paprika
6 teaspoons green onions, chopped

DIRECTIONS:

1. Heat a pan with the oil over medium-high heat, add the onion, garlic, celery and pepper, stir and cook for 10 minutes.
2. Add the rice and the rest of the ingredients, mix, bring to the boil and cook for 12 minutes.
3. Divide on plates and serve as a side dish.
4. Enjoy!

NUTRITION:

calories: 312| fat: 4.5g |protein: 4.5g | carbs: 22.4g | fiber: 8.4g | sodium: 0mg

576. Lemony Barley and Yogurt

Prep time: 10 minutes | Cook time: 30 minutes | Serves: 6

INGREDIENTS:

3/4 cup barley
1 1/2 and 1/2 cup veggie stock
3/4 cup Greek yogurt
Salt and black pepper to the taste
3 tablespoons olive oil
1 1/2 tablespoon lemon juice
1/3 cup mint, chopped
1 1/2 apple, cored and chopped

DIRECTIONS:

1. Put the barley in a pot, add the broth and salt, bring to the boil and simmer for 30 minutes.
2. Drain, transfer the barley to a bowl, add the rest of the ingredients, mix, divide into plates and serve as a side dish.
3. Enjoy!

NUTRITION:

calories:263 | fat: 9g |protein: 6.5g | carbs: 17.4g | fiber: 11.4g | sodium: 0mg

577. Chard and Couscous

Prep time: 10 minutes | Cook time: 10 minutes | Serves: 6

INGREDIENTS:

15 ounces couscous and 1/2 cup hot water
3 garlic cloves, minced
3 tablespoons olive oil
3/4 cup raisins bunches
Swiss chard, chopped
Salt and black pepper to the taste

DIRECTIONS:

1. Put the couscous in a bowl, add the water, mix, cover, set aside for 10 minutes and shell with a fork.
2. Heat a pan with the oil over medium heat, add the garlic and fry for 1 minute.
3. Add the couscous and the rest of the ingredients, mix, divide into plates and serve.
4. Enjoy!

NUTRITION:

calories:300 | fat: 6.9g |protein: 6g | carbs: 17.4g | fiber: 11.4g | sodium: 0mg

578. Chili Cabbage and Coconut

Prep time: 5 minutes | Cook time: 20 minutes | Serves: 6

INGREDIENTS:

3 tablespoons olive oil
1 1/2 spring curry leaves, chopped
1 1/2 teaspoon mustard seeds, crushed 1 green cabbage head, shredded
6 green chili peppers, chopped
3/4 cup coconut flesh, grated
Salt and black pepper to the taste

DIRECTIONS:

1. Heat a pan with the oil over medium heat, add the curry leaves, mustard seeds and chili and cook for 5 minutes.
2. Add the rest of the ingredients, mix and cook for another 15 minutes.
3. Divide the mixture into plates and serve as a side dish.
4. Enjoy!

NUTRITION:

calories:221 | fat: 5.5g | protein: 6.7g | carbs: 22.1g | fiber: 11.1g | sodium: 0mg

579. Chickpeas, Figs and Couscous

Prep time: 10 minutes | Cook time: 20 minutes | Serves: 6

INGREDIENTS:

1 1/2 red onion, chopped
3 tablespoons olive oil
3 garlic cloves, minced
42 ounces canned chickpeas, drained and rinsed
3 cups veggie stock
3 cups couscous, cooked
3 tablespoons coriander, chopped
3/4 cup figs, dried and chopped
Salt and black pepper to the taste

DIRECTIONS:

1. Heat a pan with the oil over medium heat, add the onion and garlic, stir and sauté for 5 minutes.
2. Add the chickpeas and the rest of the ingredients except the couscous and cook over medium heat for 15 minutes, stirring often.
3. Divide the couscous into plates, spread the chickpea mixture over the top and serve.
4. Enjoy!

NUTRITION:

calories:263 | fat: 11.5g |protein: 7.3g | carbs: 22.4 | fiber: 11.5g |sodium: 0mg

580. Cheesy Tomato Salad

Prep time: 5 minutes | Cook time: 0 minutes | Serves: 6

INGREDIENTS:

3 pounds tomatoes, sliced 1 red onion, chopped
Sea salt and black pepper to the taste
6 ounces feta cheese, crumbled
3 tablespoons mint, chopped A drizzle of olive oil

DIRECTIONS:

1. In a salad bowl, mix the tomatoes with the onion and the rest of the ingredients, mix and serve as a salad side dish.
2. Enjoy!

NUTRITION:

calories:190 | fat: 4.5g |protein: 3.3g | carbs: 8.7 | fiber: 3.4g | sodium: 0mg

581. Balsamic Tomato Mix
Prep time: 6 minutes | Cook time: 0 minutes | Serves: 6

INGREDIENTS:

3 pounds cherry tomatoes, halved
3 tablespoons olive oil
3 tablespoons balsamic vinegar 1 garlic clove, minced
1 1/2 cup basil, chopped
1 1/2 tablespoon chives, chopped
Salt and black pepper to the taste

DIRECTIONS:

1. In a bowl, combine the tomatoes with the garlic, basil and the rest of the ingredients, mix and serve as a salad side dish.
2. Enjoy!

NUTRITION:

calories:200 | fat: 5.6g |protein: 4.3g |carbs: 15.1 | fiber: 4.5g | sodium: 0mg

582. Vinegar Cucumber Mix
Prep time: 5 minutes | Cook time: 0 minutes | Serves: 4

INGREDIENTS:

2/3 tablespoon olive oil
2 2/3 cucumbers, sliced
Salt and black pepper to the taste
2/3 red onion, chopped
2 tablespoons red wine vinegar 1 bunch basil, chopped
2/3 teaspoon honey

DIRECTIONS:

1. In a bowl, mix the vinegar with the basil, salt, pepper, oil and honey and mix well.
2. In a bowl, mix the cucumber with the onion and vinaigrette, mix and serve as a salad side dish.
3. Enjoy!

NUTRITION:

calories:182 | fat: 7.8g |protein: 4.1g | carbs: 4.3 | fiber: 2.1g | sodium: 0mg

583. Avocado and Onion Mix
Prep time: 10 minutes | Cook time: 0 minutes | Serves: 6

INGREDIENTS:

6 avocados, pitted, peeled and sliced
1 1/2 red onion, sliced
3 tablespoons olive oil
3 tablespoons lime juice
1/3 cup dill, chopped
Sea salt and black pepper to the taste

DIRECTIONS:

1. In a salad bowl, mix the avocados with the onion and the rest of the ingredients, mix and serve as a side dish.
2. Enjoy!

NUTRITION:

calories:465 | fat: 23.5g |protein: 5.4g | carbs: 21.4 | fiber: 14.3g | sodium: 0mg

584. Eggplant and Bell Pepper Mix
Prep time: 10 minutes | Cook time:45 minutes | Serves: 6

INGREDIENTS:

3 green bell peppers, cut into strips
3 eggplants, sliced
3 tablespoons tomato paste
Salt and black pepper to the taste
6 garlic cloves, minced
1/3 cup olive oil
1 1/2 tablespoon cilantro, chopped 1 tablespoon chives, chopped

DIRECTIONS:

1. In a baking dish, add the peppers to the aubergines and the rest of the ingredients, bake and cook at 180° F for 45 minutes.
2. Divide the mixture into plates and serve as a side dish.
3. Enjoy!

NUTRITION:

calories:207 | fat: 13.3g |protein: 3.8g | carbs: 23.4 | fiber: 13.3g | sodium: 0mg

585. Basil and Sun-dried Tomatoes Rice
Prep time: 10 minutes | Cook time:25 minutes | Serves: 6

INGREDIENTS:

7 1/2 cups chicken stock
1 1/2 yellow onion, chopped
15 ounces sun dried tomatoes in olive oil, drained and chopped
3 cups Arborio rice
Salt and black pepper to the taste 1 and 1/2 cup parmesan, grated
3 tablespoons olive oil
1/3 cup basil leaves, chopped

DIRECTIONS:

1. Heat a pan with oil over medium heat, add the onion and tomatoes and sauté for 5 minutes.
2. Add the rice, broth and the rest of the ingredients except the Parmesan, bring to a boil and cook over medium heat for 20 minutes.
3. Add the Parmesan, mix, divide the mixture into plates and serve as a side dish.
4. Enjoy!

NUTRITION:

calories:426 | fat: 8.4g |protein: 7.5g | carbs: 56.3 | fiber: 3.2g | sodium: 0mg

586. Dill Cucumber Salad
Prep time: 1 hour | Cook time: 0 minutes | Serves: 6

INGREDIENTS:

3 cucumbers, sliced
3/4 cup white wine vinegar 2 white onions, sliced
3/4 tablespoon dill, chopped

DIRECTIONS:

1. In a bowl, mix the cucumber with the onions, vinegar and dill, mix well and refrigerate for 1 hour before serving as a side salad.
2. Enjoy!

NUTRITION:

calories:182 | fat: 3.5g | protein: 4.5g | carbs: 8.5 | fiber: 4.5g | sodium: 0mg

587. Herbed Cucumber and Avocado Mix
Prep time: 10 minutes | Cook time: 0 minutes | Serves: 6

INGREDIENTS:

3 cucumbers, sliced
3 avocados, pitted, peeled and cubed
1 1/2 tablespoon lemon juice
3 tablespoons olive oil
3 teaspoons balsamic vinegar 1
teaspoon dill, dried
1 1/2 tablespoon cilantro, chopped
1 tablespoon chives, chopped 1 tablespoon basil, chopped
1 1/2 tablespoon oregano, chopped

DIRECTIONS:

1. In a bowl, mix the cucumbers with the avocados with the rest of the ingredients, mix and serve as a side dish.
2. Enjoy!

NUTRITION:

calories:343 | fat: 9.6g |protein: 7.4g | carbs: 16.5 | fiber: 2.5g | sodium: 0mg

588. Basil Bell Peppers and Cucumber Mix
Prep time: 5 minutes | Cook time: 0 minutes | Serves: 4

INGREDIENTS:

2/3 red bell pepper, cut into strips
2/3 green bell pepper, cut into strips
1 1/3 cucumbers, sliced
1/3 cup balsamic vinegar
1 1/3 tablespoons olive oil
2/3 tablespoon sesame seeds, toasted 1 tablespoon basil, chopped

DIRECTIONS:

1. In a bowl, combine the peppers with the cucumber and the rest of the ingredients except the sesame seeds and mix.
2. Sprinkle with sesame seeds, divide the mixture into plates and serve as a side dish.
3. Enjoy!

NUTRITION:

calories:226 | fat: 8.7g |protein: 5.6g | carbs: 14.4 | fiber: 3.4g | sodium: 0mg

589. Fennel and Walnuts Salad
Prep time: 5 minutes | Cook time: 0 minutes | Serves: 6

INGREDIENTS:

12 dates, pitted and sliced 2 fennel bulbs, sliced

3 tablespoons chives, chopped
3/4 cup walnuts, chopped
3 tablespoons lime juice
3 tablespoons olive oil
Salt and black pepper to the taste

DIRECTIONS:

1. In a salad bowl, combine the fennel with the dates and the rest of the ingredients, mix, divide into plates and serve as a side of salad.
2. Enjoy!

NUTRITION:

calories:200 | fat: 7.6g | protein: 4.3g | carbs: 14.5 | fiber: 2.4g | sodium: 0mg

590. Tomatoes and Black Beans Mix

Prep time: 10 minutes | Cook time: 0 minutes | Serves: 6

INGREDIENTS:

22 1/2 ounces canned black beans, drained and rinsed
1 1/2 cup cherry tomatoes, halved
3 spring onions, chopped 3 tablespoons olive oil
1 1/2 and 1/2 teaspoons orange zest,
grated
1 1/2 teaspoon honey
Salt and black pepper to the taste
3/4 teaspoon cumin, ground 1 tablespoon lime juice

DIRECTIONS:

1. In a bowl, combine the beans with the cherry tomatoes, onions and the rest of the ingredients, mix and refrigerate for 10 minutes before serving as a side dish.
2. Enjoy!

NUTRITION:

calories:284 | fat: 7.5g | protein: 12.4g | carbs: 25.5 | fiber: 15.3g | sodium: 0mg

591. Herbed Beets and Scallions Salad

Prep time: 10 minutes | Cook time: 0 minutes | Serves: 6

INGREDIENTS:

3 red beets, cooked, peeled and sliced
4 1/2 scallions, chopped
Zest of 1 lemon, grated
1 1/2 cups mixed basil with mint, parsley and cilantro, chopped
1/4 cup balsamic vinegar
1 1/2 teaspoons poppy seeds
3/4 and 1/2 tablespoons olive oil
Salt and black pepper to the taste

DIRECTIONS:

1. In a salad bowl, combine the beets with the shallot, lemon zest and the rest of the ingredients, mix, refrigerate for 10 minutes and serve as a side salad.
2. Enjoy!

NUTRITION:

calories:283 | fat: 11.4g | protein: 6.5g | carbs: 13.5 | fiber: 3.5g | sodium: 0mg

592. Tomatoes and Endives Mix

Prep time: 10 minutes | Cook time: 20 minutes | Serves: 6

INGREDIENTS:

6 endives, shredded
21 ounces canned
3 tomatoes, chopped
Salt and black pepper to the taste
3 garlic cloves, minced
3/4 teaspoon red pepper, crushed 3 tablespoons olive oil
1 1/2 tablespoon oregano, chopped
3 tablespoons parmesan, grated 1 tablespoon cilantro, chopped

DIRECTIONS:

1. Heat a pan with the oil over medium heat, add the garlic and chilli and cook for 2-3 minutes.
2. Add the endives, tomatoes, salt, pepper and oregano, mix and sauté for another 15 minutes.
3. Add the remaining ingredients, mix, cook for 2 minutes, divide the mixture into plates and serve as a side dish.
4. Enjoy!

NUTRITION:

calories:232 | fat: 7.5g | protein: 4.5g | carbs: 14.3 | fiber: 3.5g | sodium: 0mg

593. Yogurt Peppers Mix

Prep time: 10 minutes | Cook time: 15 minutes | Serves: 6

INGREDIENTS:

3 red bell peppers, cut into thick strips
3 tablespoons olive oil
shallots, chopped
4 1/2 garlic cloves, minced
Salt and black pepper to the taste
3/4 cup Greek yogurt
1 1/2 tablespoon cilantro, chopped

DIRECTIONS:

1. Heat a pan with the oil over medium heat, add the shallot and garlic, mix and cook for 5 minutes.
2. Add the rest of the ingredients, mix, cook for another 10 minutes, divide the mixture into plates and serve as a side dish.
3. Enjoy!

NUTRITION:

calories:274 | fat: 11g | protein: 13.3g | carbs: 6.5 | fiber: 3.5g | sodium: 0mg

594. Basil Artichokes

Prep time: 10 minutes | Cook time: 12 minutes | Serves: 6

INGREDIENTS:

1 1/2 red onion, chopped
3 garlic cloves, minced
Salt and black pepper to the taste
3/4 cup veggie stock
15 ounces canned artichoke hearts,
drained
1 1/2 tablespoon olive oil
1 1/2 teaspoon lemon juice
3 tablespoons basil, chopped

DIRECTIONS:

1. Heat a pan with the oil over medium-high heat, add the onion and garlic, stir and fry for 2 minutes.
2. Add the artichokes and the rest of the ingredients, mix, cook for another 10 minutes, divide into plates and serve as a side dish.
3. Enjoy!

NUTRITION:

calories:105 | fat: 7.6g | protein: 2.5g | carbs: 6.7 | fiber: 3g | sodium: 0mg

595. Broccoli and Roasted Peppers

Prep time: 10 minutes | Cook time: 10 minutes | Serves: 6

INGREDIENTS:

1 1/2-pound broccoli florets
3 garlic cloves, minced
1 1/2 tablespoon olive oil
1/3 cup roasted peppers, chopped 2
tablespoons balsamic vinegar Salt and black pepper to the taste 1 tablespoon cilantro, chopped

DIRECTIONS:

1. Heat a skillet with oil over medium-high heat, add the garlic and peppers and cook for 2 minutes.
2. Add the broccoli and the rest of the ingredients, mix, cook over medium heat for another 8 minutes, divide into plates and serve as a side dish.
3. Enjoy!

NUTRITION:

calories:193 | fat: 5.6g | protein: 4.5g | carbs: 8.6 | fiber: 3.45g | sodium: 0mg

596. Cauliflower Quinoa

Prep time: 5 minutes | Cook time: 10 minutes | Serves: 6

INGREDIENTS:

1 1/2 and 1/2 cups quinoa, coked 3 tablespoons olive oil
4 1/2 cups cauliflower florets
3 spring onions, chopped
Salt and pepper to the taste
1 1/2 tablespoon red wine vinegar
1 tablespoon parsley, chopped 1 tablespoon chives, chopped

DIRECTIONS:

1. Heat a skillet with oil over medium-high heat, add the spring onions and cook for 2 minutes.
2. Add the cauliflower, quinoa and the rest of the ingredients, mix, cook over medium heat for 8-9 minutes, divide into plates and serve as a side dish.
3. Enjoy!

NUTRITION:

calories:220 | fat: 16.7g | protein: 5.4g | carbs: 6.8 | fiber: 5.6g | sodium: 0mg

597. Mixed Veggies and Chard

Prep time: 10 minutes | Cook time: 20 minutes | Serves: 6

INGREDIENTS:

- 3/4 cup celery, chopped
- 3/4 cup carrot, chopped
- 3/4 cup red onion, chopped
- 3/4 cup red bell pepper, chopped
- 1 tablespoon olive oil
- 1 1/2 cup veggie stock
- 3/4 cup black olives, pitted and chopped
- 15 ounces ruby chard, torn
- Salt and black pepper to the taste
- 1 teaspoon balsamic vinegar

DIRECTIONS:

1. Heat a pan with the oil over medium-high heat, add the celery, carrot, onion, pepper, salt and pepper, mix and sauté for 5 minutes.
2. Add the rest of the ingredients, mix, cook over medium heat for another 15 minutes, divide into plates and serve as a side dish.
3. Enjoy!

NUTRITION:

calories:150 | fat: 6.7g | protein: 5.4g | carbs: 6.8 | fiber: 2.6g | sodium: 0mg

598. Spicy Broccoli and Almonds

Prep time: 10 minutes | Cook time: 30 minutes | Serves: 6

INGREDIENTS:

- 1 1/2 broccoli head, florets separated
- 2 garlic cloves, minced
- 1 1/2 tablespoon olive oil
- 1 1/2 tablespoon chili powder
- Salt and black pepper to the taste
- 1 tablespoon mint, chopped
- 3 tablespoons almonds, toasted and chopped

DIRECTIONS:

1. In a pan, combine the broccoli with the garlic, oil and the rest of the ingredients, mix, put in the oven and cook at 180° F for 30 minutes.
2. Divide the mixture into plates and serve as a side dish.
3. Enjoy!

NUTRITION:

calories:156 | fat: 5.4g | protein: 2g | carbs: 4.3 | fiber: 2g | sodium: 0mg

599. Lemony Carrots

Prep time: 10 minutes | Cook time: 40 minutes | Serves: 6

INGREDIENTS:

- 3 tablespoons olive oil
- 3 pounds baby carrots, trimmed
- Salt and black pepper to the taste
- 3/4 teaspoon lemon zest, grated
- 1 tablespoon lemon juice
- 1/2 cup Greek yogurt
- 1 1/2 garlic clove, minced
- 1 1/2 teaspoon cumin, ground
- 1 1/2 tablespoon dill, chopped

DIRECTIONS:

1. In a baking dish, combine the carrots with the oil, salt, pepper and the rest of the ingredients except the dill, mix and cook at 200° F for 20 minutes.
2. Reduce the temperature to 375° F and cook for another 20 minutes.
3. Divide the mixture into plates, sprinkle with dill and serve.
4. Enjoy!

NUTRITION:

calories:192 | fat: 5.4g | protein: 5.6g | carbs: 7.3 | fiber: 3.4g | sodium: 0mg

600. Oregano Potatoes

Prep time: 10 minutes | Cook time: 40 minutes | Serves: 6

INGREDIENTS:

- 9 red potatoes, peeled and cut into wedges
- Salt and black pepper to the taste
- 3 tablespoons olive oil
- 1 1/2 teaspoon lemon zest, grated
- 1 teaspoon oregano, dried
- 1 1/2 tablespoon chives, chopped
- 3/4 cup chicken stock

DIRECTIONS:

1. In a pan, combine the potatoes with salt, pepper, oil and the rest of the ingredients except the chives, mix, put in the oven and cook at 425° F for 40 minutes.
2. Divide the mixture into plates, sprinkle with chives and serve as a side dish.
3. Enjoy!

NUTRITION:

calories:245 | fat: 4.5g | protein: 6.4g | carbs: 7.1 | fiber: 2.8g | sodium: 0mg

601. Baby Squash and Lentils Mix

Prep time: 10 minutes | Cook time: 10 minutes | Serves: 6

INGREDIENTS:

- 3 tablespoons olive oil
- 3/4 teaspoon sweet paprika
- 15 ounces baby squash, sliced
- 1 1/2 tablespoon balsamic vinegar
- 22 1/2 ounces canned lentils, drained and rinsed
- Salt and black pepper to the taste
- 1 1/2 tablespoon dill, chopped

DIRECTIONS:

1. Heat a pan with the oil over medium heat, add the pumpkin, lentils and the rest of the ingredients, mix and cook over medium heat for 10 minutes.
2. Divide the mixture into plates and serve as a side dish.
3. Enjoy!

NUTRITION:

calories:438 | fat: 8.4g | protein: 22.4g | carbs: 65.5 | fiber: 32.4g | sodium: 0mg

602. Parmesan Quinoa and Mushrooms

Prep time: 10 minutes | Cook time: 20 minutes | Serves: 6

INGREDIENTS:

- 1 1/2 cup quinoa, cooked
- 3/4 cup chicken stock
- 3 tablespoons olive oil
- 9 ounces white mushrooms, sliced
- 1 1/2 teaspoon garlic, minced
- Salt and black pepper to the taste
- 3/4 cup parmesan, grated
- 3 tablespoons cilantro, chopped

DIRECTIONS:

1. Heat a pan with the oil over medium heat, add the garlic and mushrooms, mix and sauté for 10 minutes.
2. Add the quinoa and the rest of the ingredients, mix, cook over medium heat for another 10 minutes, divide into plates and serve as a side dish.
3. Enjoy!

NUTRITION:

calories:233 | fat: 9.5g | protein: 12.5g | carbs: 27.4 | fiber: 6.4g | sodium: 0mg

603. Chives Rice Mix

Prep time: 5 minutes | Cook time: 5 minutes | Serves: 6

INGREDIENTS:

- 3 tablespoons avocado oil
- 1 1/2 cup Arborio rice, cooked
- 3 tablespoons chives, chopped
- Salt and black pepper to the taste
- 3 teaspoons lemon juice

DIRECTIONS:

1. Heat a pan with the avocado oil over medium high heat, add the rice and the rest of the ingredients, mix, cook for 5 minutes, divide the mixture into plates and serve as a side dish.
2. Enjoy!

NUTRITION:

calories:236 | fat: 9g | protein: 4.5g | carbs: 17.5 | fiber: 12.4g | sodium: 0mg

604. Green Beans and Peppers Mix

Prep time: 10 minutes | Cook time: 10 minutes | Serves: 6

INGREDIENTS:

- 3 tablespoons olive oil
- 1 1/2- and 1/2-pounds green beans, trimmed and halved
- Salt and black pepper to the taste
- 3 red bell peppers, cut into strips
- 1 1/2 tablespoon lime juice
- 3 tablespoons rosemary, chopped
- 1 tablespoon dill, chopped

DIRECTIONS:

1. Heat a pan with oil over medium heat, add the peppers and green beans, mix and cook for 5 minutes.
2. Add the rest of the ingredients, mix, cook for another 5 minutes, divide into plates and serve as a side dish.
3. Enjoy!

NUTRITION:

calories:222 | fat: 8.6g | protein: 3.4g | carbs: 8.6 | fiber: 3.4g | sodium: 0mg

605. Garlic Snap Peas Mix

Prep time: 10 minutes | Cook time: 10 minutes | Serves: 6

INGREDIENTS:

3/4 cup walnuts, chopped 2 teaspoons lime juice
1/3 cup olive oil
1 1/2 and 1/2 teaspoons garlic, minced
3/4 cup veggie stock
1 1/2-pound sugar snap peas
Salt and black pepper to the taste 1 tablespoon chives, chopped

DIRECTIONS:

1. Heat a pan with the broth over medium heat, add the peas and cook for 5 minutes.
2. Add the rest of the ingredients except the chives, cook for another 5 minutes and divide into plates.
3. Sprinkle with chives and serve as a side dish.
4. Enjoy!

NUTRITION:

calories:200 | fat: 7.6g | protein: 4.3g | carbs: 8.5 | fiber: 3.5g | sodium: 0mg

606. Corn and Olives

Prep time: 5 minutes | Cook time: 0 minutes | Serves: 6

INGREDIENTS:

3 cups corn
6 ounces green olives, pitted and halved
3/4 teaspoon balsamic vinegar
1 1/2 tablespoon oregano, chopped 1 teaspoon thyme, chopped
Salt and black pepper to the taste
3 tablespoons extra virgin olive oil

DIRECTIONS:

1. In a bowl, combine the corn with the olives and the rest of the ingredients, mix and serve as a side dish..
2. Enjoy!

NUTRITION

calories:154 | fat: 10g | protein: 9.3g | carbs: 17 | fiber: 3.4g | sodium: 0mg

607. Rosemary Red Quinoa

Prep time: 10 minutes | Cook time: 25 minutes | Serves: 4

INGREDIENTS:

2 2/3 cups chicken stock
1 1/3 cups red quinoa, rinsed 1 red onion, chopped
1 1/3 tablespoons olive oil
2/3 tablespoon garlic, minced
2/3 teaspoon lemon zest, grated 2 tablespoons lemon juice
Salt and black pepper to the taste 2 tablespoons rosemary, chopped

DIRECTIONS:

1. Heat a pan with the oil over medium heat, add the onion and garlic and fry for 5 minutes.
2. Add the quinoa, broth and the rest of the ingredients, bring to a boil and cook for 20 minutes, stirring occasionally.
3. Divide the mix on plates and serve.
4. Enjoy!

NUTRITION

calories:193 | fat: 7.9g | protein: 1.3g | carbs: 5.4 | fiber: 1.4g | sodium: 0mg

608. Thyme Corn and Cheese Mix

Prep time: 5 minutes | Cook time: 0 minutes | Serves: 6

INGREDIENTS:

1 1/2 tablespoon olive oil
1 1/2 teaspoon thyme, chopped 1 cup scallions, sliced
3 cups corn
Salt and black pepper to the taste
3 tablespoons blue cheese, crumbled 1 tablespoon chives, chopped

DIRECTIONS:

1. In a salad bowl, combine the corn with the shallot, thyme and the rest of the ingredients, mix, divide into plates and serve.
2. Enjoy!

NUTRITION

calories:183 | fat: 5.5g | protein: 0g | carbs: 14.5 | fiber: 7.5g | sodium: 0mg

609. Olives and Carrots Sauté

Prep time: 10 minutes | Cook time: 20 minutes | Serves: 6

INGREDIENTS:

1 1/2 tablespoon green olives, pitted and sliced
4 1/2 tablespoons olive oil
3 teaspoons capers, drained and chopped
3/4 teaspoon lemon zest, grated
1 1/2 and 1/2 teaspoons balsamic vinegar
1/3 teaspoon rosemary, dried
1/3 cup veggie stock
Salt and black pepper to the taste
3 pounds carrots, sliced
3 spring onions, chopped
1 1/2 tablespoon parsley, chopped

DIRECTIONS:

1. Heat a pan with oil over medium heat, add carrots and sauté for 5 minutes.
2. Add the green olives, capers and the rest of the ingredients except parsley and chives, mix and cook over medium heat for 15 minutes.
3. Add the chives and parsley, mix, divide the mixture into plates and serve as a side dish.
4. Enjoy!

NUTRITION

calories:244 | fat: 11g | protein: 6.3g | carbs: 5.6 | fiber: 3.5g | sodium: 0mg

610. Lemon Endives

Prep time: 10 minutes | Cook time: 35 minutes | Serves: 6

INGREDIENTS:

Juice of 1 and 1/2 lemons
Salt and black pepper to the taste
4 1/2 tablespoons olive oil
1/3 cup veggie stock
6 endives, halved lengthwise 1 tablespoon dill, chopped

DIRECTIONS:

1. In a baking dish, combine the endives with the rest of the ingredients, bake and cook at 180° F for 35 minutes.
2. Divide the endives on plates and serve as a side dish.
3. Enjoy!

NUTRITION

calories:221 | fat: 5.4g | protein: 14.3g | carbs: 15.4 | fiber: 6.4g | sodium: 0mg

611. Leeks Sauté

Prep time: 10 minutes | Cook time: 15 minutes | Serves: 6

INGREDIENTS:

3 pounds leeks, sliced
3 tablespoons chicken stock 2 tablespoons tomato paste 1 tablespoon olive oil
3 tablespoons thyme, chopped Salt and black pepper to the taste

DIRECTIONS:

1. Heat a pan with oil over medium heat, add the leeks and brown them for 5 minutes.
2. Add the rest of the ingredients, mix, increase the heat to medium-high and cook for another 10 minutes.
3. Divide everything into plates and serve as a side dish.
4. Enjoy!

NUTRITION:

calories:200 | fat: 11g | protein: 3g | carbs: 16g | fiber: 5g | sodium: 0mg

612. Braised Cauliflower with White Wine

Prep time: 10 minutes | Cook time: 15 minutes | Serves: 6

INGREDIENTS:

1/4 teaspoon red pepper flakes
1 1/2 head cauliflower (2 pounds / 907 g), cored and cut into 1 1/2-inch florets
4 1/2 tablespoons plus 1 teaspoon extra-virgin olive oil, divided
4 1/2 garlic cloves, minced
1/3 teaspoon salt, plus more for seasoning
Black pepper, to taste
⅓ cup vegetable broth
⅓ cup dry white wine
3 tablespoons minced fresh parsley

DIRECTIONS:

1. Combine 1 teaspoon of oil, garlic and chili in a small bowl.
2. Heat the remaining 3 tablespoons of oil in a skillet over medium-high heat until they glisten. Add the cauliflower and ¼ teaspoon of salt and cook for 7-9 minutes, stirring occasionally, or until the florets are golden.
3. Push the cauliflower to the sides of the pan. Add the garlic mixture to the centre of the pan. Cook for about 30 seconds, or until fragrant. Stir the garlic mixture into the cauliflower.
4. Pour in the broth and wine and bring to a boil. Reduce the heat to medium-low. Cover and cook for 4-6 minutes or until the cauliflower is tender and crisp. With the fire off, add the parsley and season with salt and

pepper.
5. Serve immediately.
6. Enjoy!

NUTRITION:

calories: 143 | fat: 11g | protein: 3g | carbs: 8g | fiber: 3g | sodium: 263mg

613. Cheesy Sweet Potato Burgers

Prep time: 10 minutes | Cook time: 20 minutes | Serves: 6

INGREDIENTS:

1 1/2 cup chopped onion	1 1/2 garlic clove
3 tablespoons extra-virgin olive oil, divided	1 1/2 cup old-fashioned rolled oats
	1 1/2 tablespoon dried oregano
1 1/2 tablespoon balsamic vinegar	1 1/2 large sweet potato (about 8 ounces / 227 g)
1/3 teaspoon kosher salt	
1 1/2 large egg	3/4 cup crumbled Gorgonzola cheese

DIRECTIONS:

1. Using a fork, pierce the whole sweet potato and microwave on high for 4-5 minutes, until soft in the centre. Cool slightly before cutting in half.
2. Meanwhile, in a large skillet over medium-high heat, heat 1 tablespoon of olive oil. Add the onion and sauté for 5 minutes.
3. Spoon the sweet potato pulp off the skin and place the pulp in a food processor. Add the cooked onion, egg, garlic, oats, oregano, vinegar and salt. Blend until smooth. Add the cheese and whisk four times to barely mix.
4. Form four burgers with the mixture. Place the burgers on a plate and press to flatten each to a thickness of about inch by inch.
5. Clean the pan with a paper towel. Heat the remaining tablespoon of oil over medium-high heat for about 2 minutes. Add the burgers to the hot oil, then reduce the heat to medium. Cook the burgers for 5 minutes on each side.
6. Transfer the burgers to a plate and serve.
7. Enjoy!

NUTRITION:

calories: 290 | fat: 12g | protein: 12g | carbs: 43g | fiber: 8g | sodium: 566mg

614. Sautéed Cabbage with Parsley

Prep time: 10 minutes | Cook time: 15 minutes | Serves: 6

INGREDIENTS:

1/3 teaspoon black pepper	3 tablespoons extra-virgin olive oil, divided
1/3 cup chopped fresh parsley	
1 1/2 small head green cabbage (about 1 1/4 pounds / 567 g), cored and sliced thin	1 1/2 onion, halved and sliced thin
	1 1/8 teaspoon salt, divided
	2 1/4 teaspoons lemon juice

DIRECTIONS:

1. Put the cabbage in a large bowl with cold water. Let it rest for 3 minutes. Drain well.
2. Heat 1 tablespoon of oil in a skillet over medium-high heat until it glistens. Add the onion and ¼ teaspoon of salt and cook for 5-7 minutes, or until soft and lightly browned. Transfer to a bowl.
3. Heat the remaining tablespoon of oil in an empty skillet over medium-high heat until it glistens. Add the cabbage and sprinkle with the remaining ½ teaspoon of salt and black pepper. Cover and cook for about 3 minutes, without stirring, or until the cabbage is wilted and lightly browned on the bottom.
4. Stir and continue to cook for about 4 minutes, uncovered, or until the cabbage is tender and crisp and lightly browned in places, stirring once halfway through cooking. With the heat off, add the cooked onion, parsley and lemon juice.
5. Transfer to a plate and serve.
6. Enjoy!

NUTRITION:

calories: 117 | fat: 7g | protein: 3g | carbs: 13g | fiber: 5g | sodium: 472mg

615. Cauliflower Steaks with Arugula

Prep time: 10 minutes | Cook time: 20 minutes | Serves: 6

INGREDIENTS:

Cauliflower:	Dressing:
1 1/2 head cauliflower	2 1/4 tablespoons extra-virgin olive oil
Cooking spray	2 1/4 tablespoons honey mustard
3/4 teaspoon garlic powder	1 1/2 teaspoon freshly squeezed lemon juice
6 cups arugula	

DIRECTIONS:

1. Preheat the oven to 220ºC (425 ° F).
2. Remove the leaves from the head of the cauliflower and cut it in half lengthwise. Cut from each half of the steaks 2.5 cm thick.
3. Spray both sides of each steak with cooking spray and season both sides with the garlic powder.
4. Place the cauliflower steaks on a baking sheet, cover with foil and roast in the oven for 10 minutes.
5. Remove the pan from the oven and gently pull the foil to avoid steam. Turn the steaks, then roast uncovered for another 10 minutes.
6. Meanwhile, prepare the dressing: whisk together the olive oil, honey mustard and lemon juice in a small bowl.
7. When the cauliflower steaks are ready, divide them into four equal parts. Garnish each portion with a quarter of rocket and seasoning.
8. Serve immediately.
9. Enjoy!

NUTRITION:

calories: 115 | fat: 6g | protein: 5g | carbs: 14g | fiber: 4g | sodium: 97mg

616. Parmesan Stuffed Zucchini Boats

Prep time: 10 minutes | Cook time: 15 minutes | Serves: 6

INGREDIENTS:

3 zucchinis	1 1/2 cup no-sugar-added spaghetti sauce
1 1/2 cup canned low-sodium chickpeas, drained and rinsed	
	1/3 cup shredded Parmesan cheese

DIRECTIONS:

1. Preheat the oven to 220ºC (425° F).
2. In a medium bowl, mix together the chickpeas and spaghetti sauce.
3. Cut the courgettes in half lengthwise and gently scrape a long spoon each half to remove the seeds.
4. Stuff each courgette half with the chickpea sauce and garnish with a quarter of Parmesan cheese.
5. Place the zucchini halves on a baking sheet and roast in the oven for 15 minutes.
6. Transfer to a plate. Leave to rest for 5 minutes before serving.
7. Enjoy!

NUTRITION:

calories: 139 | fat: 4g | protein: 8g | carbs: 20g | fiber: 5g | sodium: 344mg

SIDES RECIPES

7

SIDES

617. Spicy Wilted Greens

Prep time: 10 minutes | Cook time: 5 minutes | Serves: 4

INGREDIENTS:

- Pinch salt
- 2 tablespoon olive oil
- 4 garlic cloves, minced
- 6 cups sliced greens (kale, spinach, chard, beet greens, dandelion greens, or a combination)
- Pinch red pepper flakes (or more to taste)

DIRECTIONS:

1. Heat the olive oil in a skillet over medium-high heat. Add the garlic and sauté for 30 seconds, or just until it becomes fragrant.
2. Add the vegetables, salt and pepper flakes and stir to combine. Let the vegetables wilt, but don't overcook. Remove the pan from the heat and serve.
3. Enjoy!

NUTRITION:

calories: 91 | fat: 7g | protein: 1g | carbs: 7g | fiber: 3g | sodium: 111mg

618. Mediterranean Bruschetta Hummus Platter

Prep time: 10 minutes | Cook time: 0 minutes | Serves: 4

INGREDIENTS:

- 2/3 (10-ounce / 283-g) container plain hummus
- 1 1/3 tablespoons balsamic glaze
- 1/3 cup finely diced fresh tomato
- 1/3 cup finely diced seedless English cucumber
- 2/3 teaspoon extra-virgin olive oil
- 1/8 cup Herbed Olive Oil
- 2 2/3 warmed pitas, cut into wedges, for serving
- Carrot sticks, for serving
- 1 1/3 tablespoons crumbled feta cheese
- 2/3 tablespoon fresh chopped parsley or basil
- Celery sticks, for serving
- Sliced bell peppers, for serving
- Broccoli, for serving
- Purple cauliflower, for serving

DIRECTIONS:

1. In a small bowl, mix the tomato and cucumber and drizzle with the olive oil. Stack the cucumber mixture on a new hummus container.
2. Season the hummus and vegetables with the balsamic glaze. Complete with crumbled feta and fresh parsley.
3. Place the hummus on a large cutting board.
4. Pour the herb olive oil into a small bowl and place it on the cutting board. Surround the bowls with the pita slices and cut the carrot sticks, celery sticks, sliced peppers, broccoli and cauliflower.
5. Enjoy!

NUTRITION:

calories: 345 | fat: 19g | protein: 9g | carbs: 32g | fiber: 3g | sodium: 473mg

619. Garlic Broccoli with Artichoke Hearts

Prep time: 10 minutes | Cook time: 10 minutes | Serves: 6

INGREDIENTS:

- 1 1/2 (13 3/4-ounce / 390-g) can artichoke hearts, drained and quartered
- 1 1/2 tablespoon water
- 3 pounds (907 g) fresh broccoli rabe
- 1 1/2 teaspoon red pepper flakes
- 3 tablespoons red wine vinegar
- 3/4 cup extra-virgin olive oil, divided
- 4 1/2 garlic cloves, finely minced
- 1 1/2 teaspoon salt
- Freshly ground black pepper, to taste

DIRECTIONS:

1. Remove the thick lower stems and yellow leaves from the turnip greens and discard them. Cut into individual florets with a couple of inches of thin stem attached.
2. In a large skillet, heat ¼ cup of olive oil over medium-high heat. Add the chopped broccoli, garlic, salt and red pepper flakes and sauté for 5 minutes, until the broccoli begins to soften. Add the artichoke hearts and sauté for another 2 minutes.
3. Add water and reduce heat to low. Cover and simmer until broccoli stems are tender, 3 to 5 minutes.
4. In a small bowl, whisk together the remaining ¼ cup olive oil and vinegar. Season the broccoli and artichokes. Season with ground black pepper if desired.
5. Enjoy!

NUTRITION:

calories: 358 | fat: 35g | protein: 11g | carbs: 18g | fiber: 10g | sodium: 918mg

620. Garlicky Roasted Grape Tomatoes

Prep time: 10 minutes | Cook time: 45 minutes | Serves: 4

INGREDIENTS:

- 1/2 cup olive oil
- 1 teaspoon salt
- 2 fresh rosemary sprigs
- 2-pint grape tomatoes
- 20 whole garlic cloves, skins removed
- 2 fresh thyme sprigs

DIRECTIONS:

1. Preheat oven to 350°F | 180°C | Fan 160°C.
2. Mix the tomatoes, garlic cloves, oil, salt and herb sprigs in a baking dish.
3. Roast the tomatoes until soft and just starting to caramelize, about 45 minutes.
4. Remove herbs before serving.
5. Enjoy!

NUTRITION:

calories: 271 | fat: 26g | protein: 3g | carbs: 12g | fiber: 3g | sodium: 593mg

621. Lemon and Thyme Roasted Vegetables

Prep time: 10 minutes | Cook time: 50 minutes | Serves: 4

INGREDIENTS:

- 4 tablespoons olive oil, divided
- 4 medium carrots
- 1/2-pound (113 g) asparagus
- 1 fresh lemon, sliced
- Salt and freshly ground black pepper, to taste
- 2 head garlic, cloves split apart, unpeeled
- 12 Brussels sprouts
- 4 cups cauliflower florets
- 1 pint cherry or grape tomatoes
- 6 sprigs fresh thyme or 1/2 teaspoon dried thyme
- Freshly squeezed lemon juice

DIRECTIONS:

1. Preheat the oven to 190°C (375°F) and set the rack in the centre position. Line a baking sheet with parchment paper or aluminum foil.
2. Place the garlic cloves in a small aluminium foil and wrap them lightly to enclose them, but do not seal the package. Drizzle with 1 teaspoon of olive oil. Place the foil packet on the baking sheet and roast for 30 minutes while preparing the remaining vegetables.
3. While the garlic is roasting, clean, peel and cut the vegetables: cut the carrots into half-inch wide and 3-4-inch-long strips; detach the hard tips from the asparagus; remove the hard ends of the Brussels sprouts and cut them in half if they are large; cut the cauliflower into 2-inch florets; keep the tomatoes whole. Vegetables should be cut into similar sized pieces for even roasting.
4. Put all the vegetables and lemon slices in a large bowl. Season with the remaining 5 teaspoons of olive oil and season generously with salt and pepper.
5. Raise the oven temperature to 400°F (205 ° C).
6. Arrange the vegetables on the pan in a single layer, leaving the packet of garlic cloves on the pan. Roast for 20 minutes, turning occasionally, until tender.
7. When the vegetables are tender, remove from the oven and sprinkle with thyme leaves. Let the garlic cloves sit until they cool enough to handle, then remove the skin. Leave them whole or gently mash them.
8. Mix the garlic with the vegetables and an additional squeeze of fresh lemon juice.
9. Enjoy!

NUTRITION:

calories: 256 | fat: 15g | protein: 7g | carbs: 31g | fiber: 9g | sodium: 168mg

622. Roasted Parmesan Rosemary Potatoes

Prep time: 10 minutes | Cook time: 55 minutes | Serves: 4

INGREDIENTS:

- 2 tablespoon olive oil
- 1 teaspoon garlic powder
- 1/2 teaspoon salt
- 24 ounces (340 g) red potatoes (3 to 4 small potatoes)
- 2 tablespoon grated Parmesan cheese
- 2 teaspoon minced fresh rosemary (from 1 sprig)

DIRECTIONS:

1. Preheat the oven to 220°C (425° F) and set the rack in the lower position. Line a baking sheet with parchment paper. (Don't use foil, as the potatoes will stick.)
2. Rub the potatoes and dry them well. Cut into 1-inch cubes.

3. In a bowl, combine the potatoes, olive oil, garlic powder, and salt. Mix well to coat.
4. Place the potatoes on the parchment paper and roast for 10 minutes. Flip the potatoes over and put them back in the oven for another 10 minutes.
5. Check the potatoes to make sure they are golden brown on the top and bottom. Throw them again, lower the heat to 180ºC and roast for another 30 minutes.
6. When the potatoes are golden, crisp and cooked, sprinkle with Parmesan and mix again. Return to the oven for 3 minutes to let the cheese melt a little.
7. Remove from the oven and sprinkle with fresh rosemary.
8. Enjoy!

NUTRITION:

calories: 193 | fat: 8g | protein: 5g | carbs: 28g | fiber: 3g | sodium: 334mg

623. Artichoke Olive Pasta

Prep time: 10 minutes | Cook time: 25 minutes | Serves: 6

INGREDIENTS:

- salt pepper
- 3 tablespoons olive oil, divided
- 3 garlic cloves, thinly sliced
- 1 1/2 can artichoke hearts, drained, rinsed, and quartered lengthwise
- 1-pint grape tomatoes, halved lengthwise, divided
- 3/4 cup fresh basil leaves, torn apart
- 18 ounces whole-wheat spaghetti
- 3/4 medium onion, thinly sliced
- 3/4 cup dry white wine
- 1/2 cup pitted Kalamata olives, quartered lengthwise
- 1/3 cup grated Parmesan cheese, plus extra for serving

DIRECTIONS:

1. Fill a large pot with salted water.
2. Pour the water to a boil and cook your pasta according to package instructions until al dente.
3. Drain the pasta and reserve 1 cup of the cooking water.
4. Return the pasta to the pot and set aside.
5. Heat 1 tablespoon of olive oil in a large skillet over medium-high heat.
6. Add onion and garlic, season with pepper and salt, and cook well for about 3-4 minutes until nicely browned.
7. Add wine and cook for 2 minutes until evaporated.
8. Stir in artichokes and keep cooking 2-3 minutes until brown.
9. Add olives and half of your tomatoes.
10. Cook well for 1-2 minutes until the tomatoes start to break down.
11. Add pasta to the skillet.
12. Stir in the rest of the tomatoes, cheese, basil, and remaining oil.
13. Thin the mixture with the reserved pasta water if needed.
14. Place in containers and sprinkle with extra cheese.
15. Enjoy!

NUTRITION:

calories: 1340 | fat: 11g | protein: 22g | carbs: 35g | fiber: 7g | sodium: 334mg

624. Kidney Bean, Veggie, And Grape Salad

Prep time: 10 minutes | Cook time: 25 minutes | Serves: 6

INGREDIENTS:

- 2 1/4 cups red grapes, halved
- 1 1/2 (15-ounce) can red kidney beans, drained and rinsed
- 15 ounces cherry tomatoes, halved (quartered if tomatoes are large)
- 6 (6-inch) Persian cucumbers, quartered vertically and chopped
- 3/4 cup green pumpkin seeds (pepitas)
- 3/4 cup feta cheese
- 3 3/4 ounces baby spinach leaves (about 4 cups)
- 3/4 cup Dijon Red Wine Vinaigrette

DIRECTIONS:

1. Place the grapes, kidney beans, cherry tomatoes, cucumbers, pumpkin seeds, and feta in a large mixing bowl and mix to combine.
2. Place cups of the salad mixture in each of 4 containers. Then place 1 cup of spinach leaves on top of each salad. Pour 2 tablespoons of vinaigrette into each of 4 sauce containers. Refrigerate all the containers.
3. Store covered containers in the refrigerator for up to 5 days.
4. Enjoy!

NUTRITION:

calories: 322 | fat: 25g | protein: 16g | carbs: 37g | fiber: 10g | sodium: 435mg

625. Veggie Mediterranean Pasta

Prep time: 10 minutes | Cook time: 2 hours | Serves: 6

INGREDIENTS:

- 1 1/2 tablespoon olive oil
- 1 1/2 small onion, finely chopped
- 3 small garlic cloves, finely chopped
- 3 14-ounce cans diced tomatoes
- 1 1/2 tablespoon sun-dried tomato paste 1 bay leaf
- 1 1/2 teaspoon dried thyme
- 1 1/2 teaspoon dried basil
- 1 1/2 teaspoon oregano
- 1 1/2 teaspoon dried parsley
- 3/4 teaspoon salt
- 3/4 teaspoon brown sugar freshly
- ground black pepper
- 1 1/2-piece aubergine
- 3 pieces courgettes
- 3 pieces red peppers, de-seeded 2 garlic cloves, peeled
- 2-3 tablespoons olive oil
- 18 small vine-ripened tomatoes
- 24 ounces of pasta of your preferred shape, such as Gigli, conchiglie, etc. 3 1/2 ounces parmesan cheese
- bread of your choice

DIRECTIONS:

1. Heat oil in a pan over medium heat.
2. Add onions and fry them until tender.
3. Add garlic and stir-fry for 1 minute.
4. Add the remaining Shopping List listed under the sauce and bring to a boil.
5. Reduce the heat, cover, and simmer for 60 minutes.
6. Season with black pepper and salt as needed. Set aside.
7. Preheat oven to 350° F.
8. Chop up courgettes, aubergine and red peppers into 1-inch pieces.
9. Place them on a roasting pan along with whole garlic cloves.
10 Drizzle with olive oil and season with salt and black pepper.
11. Mix the veggies well and roast in the oven for 45 minutes until they are tender.
12. Add tomatoes just before 20 minutes to end time.
13. Cook your pasta according to package instructions.
14. Drain well and stir into the sauce.
15. Divide the pasta sauce between 4 containers and top with vegetables.
16. Grate some parmesan cheese on top and serve with bread.
17. Enjoy!

NUTRITION:

calories: 211 | fat: 14g | protein: 4g | carbs: 0g | fiber: 5g | sodium: 317mg

626. Fried Green Beans

Prep time: 10 minutes | Cook time: 15 Minutes | Serves: 4

INGREDIENTS:

- 1-pound green beans, trimmed
- 2 eggs
- 4 tablespoons olive oil
- 2 1/2 tablespoons almond flour
- 4 tablespoons parmesan cheese
- 1 teaspoon garlic powder sea salt or plain salt
- freshly ground black pepper

DIRECTIONS:

1. Start by beating the egg and olive oil in a bowl.
2. Then, mix the remaining Ingredients in a separate bowl and set aside.
3. Now, dip the green beans in the egg mixture and then coat with the dry mix.
4. Finally, grease a baking pan, then transfer the beans to the pan and bake at 250 degrees F for about 12-15 minutes or until crisp.
5. Serve warm. Enjoy!

NUTRITION:

calories: 334 | fat: 23g | protein: 4g | carbs: 109g | fiber: 5g | sodium: 397mg Total Sugars: 1.9 g, Protein:18g

627. Garlic Shrimp Pasta

Prep time: 10 minutes | Cook time: 15 Minutes | Serves: 6

INGREDIENTS:

- 9 ounces whole-wheat spaghetti, your favourite
- 18 ounces raw shrimp, peeled, deveined, and cut into 1-inch pieces
- 1 1/2 bunch asparagus, trimmed and thinly sliced
- 1 1/2 large bell pepper, thinly sliced
- 4 1/2 cloves garlic, chopped
- 2 teaspoon kosher salt
- 2 1/4 cups non-fat plain yogurt
- 1/3 cup flat-leaf parsley, chopped
- 4 1/2 tablespoons lemon juice
- 1 1/2 tablespoon extra-virgin olive oil
- 3/4 teaspoon fresh ground black pepper
- 1/3 cup toasted pine nuts

DIRECTIONS:

1. Bring water to a boil in a large pot.
2. Add spaghetti and cook for about minutes less than called for by the package instructions.
3. Add shrimp, bell pepper, asparagus and cook for about 2-4 minutes until the shrimp are tender.

4. Drain the pasta.
5. In a large bowl, mash the garlic until paste forms.
6. Whisk yogurt, parsley, oil, pepper, and lemon juice into the garlic paste.
7. Add pasta mixture and toss well.
8. Cool and spread over the containers.
9. Sprinkle with pine nuts.
10. Enjoy!

NUTRITION:

calories: 504 | fat: 15g | protein: 15g | carbs: 199g | fiber: 5g | sodium: 2052mg

628. Mushroom Fettuccine

Prep time: 10 minutes | Cook time: 15 Minutes | Serves: 6

INGREDIENTS:

- 18 ounces whole-wheat fettuccine (or any other)
- 1 1/2 tablespoon extra-virgin olive oil
- 6 cups mixed mushrooms, such as oyster, cremini, etc., sliced
- 6 cups broccoli, divided
- 1 1/2 tablespoon minced garlic
- 3/4 cup dry sherry
- 3 cups low-fat milk
- 3 tablespoons all-purpose flour
- 3/4 teaspoon salt
- 3/4 teaspoon freshly ground pepper
- 1 1/2 cup finely shredded Asiago cheese, plus some for topping

DIRECTIONS:

1. Cook pasta in a large pot of boiling water for about 8- minutes.
2. Drain pasta and set it to the side.
3. Add oil to large skillet and heat over medium heat.
4. Add mushrooms and broccoli, and cook for about 8-10 minutes until the mushrooms have released the liquid.
5. Add garlic and cook for about 1 minute until fragrant.
6. Add sherry, making sure to scrape up any brown bits.
7. Bring the mix to a boil and cook for about 1 minute until evaporated.
8. In a separate bowl, whisk flour and milk.
9. Add the mix to your skillet, and season with salt and pepper.
10. Cook well for about 2 minutes until the sauce begins to bubble and is thickened.
11. Stir in Asiago cheese until it has fully melted.
12. Add the sauce to your pasta and give it a gentle toss.
13. Spread over the containers. Serve with extra cheese.
14. Enjoy!

NUTRITION:

calories: 503 | fat: 19g | protein: 17g | carbs: 59g | fiber: 12g | sodium: 1136mg

629. Lemon Garlic Sardine

Prep time: 10 minutes | Cook time: 15 Minutes | Serves: 6

INGREDIENTS:

- 12 ounces whole-wheat fettuccine
- 6 tablespoons extra-virgin olive oil, divided
- 6 cloves garlic, minced
- 1 1/2 cup fresh breadcrumbs
- 1/3 cup lemon juice
- 3 teaspoon freshly ground pepper
- 3/4 teaspoon of salt
- 4-ounce cans boneless and skinless sardines, dipped in tomato sauce
- 3/4 cup fresh parsley, chopped
- 1/3 cup finely shredded parmesan cheese

DIRECTIONS:

1. Fill a large pot with water and bring to a boil.
2. Cook pasta according to package instructions until tender (about 10 minutes).
3. In a small skillet, heat 2 tablespoons of oil over medium heat.
4. Add garlic and cook for about 20 seconds, until sizzling and fragrant.
5. Transfer the garlic to a large bowl.
6. Add the remaining 2 tablespoons of oil to skillet and heat over medium heat.
7. Add breadcrumbs and cook for 5-6 minutes until golden and crispy.
8. Whisk lemon juice, salt, and pepper into the garlic bowl.
9. Add pasta to the garlic bowl, along with garlic, sardines, parmesan, and parsley; give it a gentle stir.
10. Cool and spread over the containers.
11. Before eating, sprinkle with breadcrumbs.
12. Enjoy!

NUTRITION:

calories: 633 | fat: 27g | protein: 17g | carbs: 59g | fiber: 7g | sodium: 771mg

630. Spinach Almond Stir-fry

Prep time: 10 minutes | Cook time: 10 Minutes | Serves: 4

INGREDIENTS:

- 4 ounces spinach
- 2 tablespoon coconut oil
- 6 tablespoons almond, slices sea salt or
- plain salt
- freshly ground black pepper

DIRECTIONS:

1. Start by heating a skillet with coconut oil; add spinach and let it cook.
2. Then, add salt and pepper as the spinach is cooking.
3. Finally, add in the almond slices.
4. Serve warm.
5. Enjoy!

NUTRITION:

calories: 117 | fat: 11g | protein: 3g | carbs: 59g | fiber: 7g | sodium: 23mg

631. BBQ Carrots

Prep time: 10 minutes | Cook time: 30 Minutes | Serves: 6

INGREDIENTS:

- 1 1/2 pounds baby carrots (organic) 1 tablespoon olive oil
- 3/4 tablespoon garlic powder 1 tablespoon onion powder sea salt or plain salt
- freshly ground black pepper

DIRECTIONS:

1. Mix all the Shopping List in a plastic bag so that the carrots are well coated with the mixture.
2. Then, on the BBQ grill place a piece of aluminium foil and spread the carrots in a single layer.
3. Finally, grill for 30 minutes or until tender.
4. Serve warm.
5. Enjoy!

NUTRITION:

calories: 388 | fat: 1g | protein: 1g | carbs: 59g | fiber: 4g | sodium: 89mg

632. Baked Zucchini Sticks

Prep time: 10 minutes | Cook time: 20 Minutes | Serves: 6

INGREDIENTS:

- 1/4 cup feta cheese, crumbled
- 3 zucchinis
- 1/4 cup parsley, chopped
- 1/3 cup tomatoes, minced
- 1/3 cup kalamata olives, pitted and minced
- 3/4 cup red bell pepper, minced
- 3/4 tablespoon oregano
- 1/4 cup garlic, minced
- 3/4 tablespoon basil sea salt or plain salt
- freshly ground black pepper

DIRECTIONS:

1. Start by cutting zucchini in half (lengthwise) and scoop out the middle.
2. Then, combine garlic, black pepper, bell pepper, oregano, basil, tomatoes, and olives in a bowl.
3. Now, fill in the middle of each zucchini with this mixture. Place these on a prepared baking dish and bake the dish at 250° F for about 15 minutes.
4. Finally, top with feta cheese and broil on high for 3 minutes or until done. Garnish with parsley.
5. Serve warm.
6. Enjoy!

NUTRITION:

calories: 53 | fat: 2g | protein: 2g | carbs: 59g | fiber: 4g | sodium: 138mg

633. Mint Tabbouleh

Prep time: 10 minutes | Cook time: 15 Minutes | Serves: 4

INGREDIENTS:

- 1/8 cup fine bulgur
- 1/4 cup water, boiling
- 2 tablespoons lemon juice
- 1/8 teaspoon honey
- 1 cups pistachio, finely chopped
- 2/3 cup curly parsley, finely chopped
- 2/3 small cucumber, finely chopped
- 2/3 medium tomato, finely chopped
- 2 2/3 green onions, finely chopped
- 1/4 cup fresh mint, finely chopped
- 2 tablespoons olive oil

DIRECTIONS:

1. Take a large bowl and add bulgur and 1/3 cup of boiling water.
2. Allow it to stand for about 5 minutes.
3. Stir in honey and lemon juice and allow it to stand for 5 minutes more.

4. Fluff up the bulgur with a fork and stir in the rest of the Shopping List.
5. Season with salt and pepper.
6. Enjoy!

NUTRITION:

calories: 150 | fat: 13g | protein: 4g | carbs: 59g | fiber: 2g | sodium: 78mg

634. Red Onion Kale Pasta

Prep time: 10 minutes | Cook time: 25 Minutes | Serves: 6

INGREDIENTS:

- 3 3/4 cups vegetable broth
- 1 1/8 cup dry lentils
- 3/4 teaspoon of salt
- 1 1/2 bay leaf
- 1/3 cup olive oil
- 1 1/2 large red onion, chopped
- 1 1/2 teaspoon fresh thyme, chopped
- 3/4 teaspoon fresh oregano, chopped
- 1 1/2 teaspoon salt, divided
- 3/4 teaspoon black pepper
- 12 ounces vegan sausage, sliced into 1/4-inch slices
- 1 1/2 bunch kale, stems removed and coarsely chopped
- 1 1/2 pack rotini

DIRECTIONS:

1. Add vegetable broth, ½ teaspoons of salt, bay leaf, and lentils to a saucepan over high heat and bring to a boil.
2. Reduce the heat to medium-low and allow to cook for about minutes until tender.
3. Discard the bay leaf.
4. Take another skillet and heat olive oil over medium-high heat.
5. Stir in thyme, onions, oregano, ½ a teaspoon of salt, and pepper; cook for 1 minute.
6. Add sausage and reduce heat to medium-low.
7. Cook for 10 minutes until the onions are tender.
8. Bring water to a boil in a large pot, and then add rotini pasta and kale.
9. Cook for about 8 minutes until al dente.
10. Remove a bit of the cooking water and put it to the side.
11. Drain the pasta and kale and return to the pot.
12. Stir in both the lentils mixture and the onions mixture.
13. Add the reserved cooking liquid to add just a bit of moistness.
14. Spread over containers.
15. Enjoy!

NUTRITION:

calories: 508 | fat: 17g | protein: 30g | carbs: 59g | fiber: 2g | sodium: 2431mg

635. Olive Tuna Pasta

Prep time: 10 minutes | Cook time: 20 Minutes | Serves: 6

INGREDIENTS:

- 12 ounces of tuna steak, cut into 3 pieces
- 1/3 cup green olives, chopped
- 4 1/2 cloves garlic, minced
- 3 cups grape tomatoes, halved
- 3/4 cup white wine
- 3 tablespoons lemon juice
- 9 ounces pasta - whole wheat Goretti, rotini, or penne
- 10-ounce package frozen artichoke hearts, thawed and squeezed dry
- 6 tablespoons extra-virgin olive oil, divided
- 3 teaspoons fresh grated lemon zest
- 3 teaspoons fresh rosemary, chopped, divided
- 3/4 teaspoon salt, divided
- 1/3 teaspoon fresh ground pepper
- 1/3 cup fresh basil, chopped

DIRECTIONS:

1. Preheat grill to medium-high heat.
2. Take a large pot of water and put it on to boil.
3. Place the tuna pieces in a bowl and add 1 tablespoon of oil, 1 teaspoon of rosemary, lemon zest, ¼ teaspoon of salt, and pepper.
4. Grill the tuna for about 3 minutes per side.
5. Transfer tuna to a plate and allow it to cool.
6. Place the pasta in boiling water and cook according to package instructions.
7. Drain the pasta.
8. Flake the tuna into bite-sized pieces.
9. In a large skillet, heat remaining oil over medium heat.
10. Add artichoke hearts, garlic, olives, and remaining rosemary.
11. Cook for about 3-4 minutes until slightly browned.
12. Add tomatoes, wine, and bring the mixture to a boil.
13. Cook for about 3 minutes until the tomatoes are broken down.
14. Stir in pasta, lemon juice, tuna, and remaining salt.
15. Cook for 1-2 minutes until nicely heated.
16. Spread over the containers.
17. Before eating, garnish with some basil and enjoy!
18. Enjoy!

NUTRITION:

calories: 455 | fat: 21g | protein: 22g | carbs: 59g | fiber: 6g | sodium: 685mg

636. Sumac Chickpea Bowl

Prep time: 10 minutes | Cook time: 25 Minutes | Serves: 6

INGREDIENTS:

- 1 cup uncooked bulgur 1 1/3 cups water
- 1/4 teaspoon kosher salt
- 1 1/2 teaspoon olive oil
- 3 tablespoons olive oil
- 3 (15.5-ounce) cans low-sodium chickpeas, drained and rinsed
- 4 1/2 tablespoons sumac
- 1/3 teaspoon kosher salt
- 6 Persian cucumbers, quartered lengthwise and chopped (about 2 cups)
- 15 ounces cherry tomatoes, quartered
- 1/3 cup chopped fresh mint
- cup chopped fresh parsley
- 6 teaspoons olive oil
- 3 tablespoons plus
- 3 teaspoons freshly squeezed lemon juice
- 1/3 teaspoon kosher salt
- 3 tablespoons unsalted tahini
- 1/3 teaspoon garlic powder
- 7 1/2 tablespoons water

DIRECTIONS:

1. Place the bulgur, water, and salt in a saucepan, and bring to a boil. Once it boils, cover the pot with a lid and turn off the heat. 2. Let the covered pot stand for minutes. Stir the oil into the cooked bulgur. Cool.
3. Place ½ cup of bulgur in each of 4 microwaveable containers.
4. Heat the oil in a 12-inch skillet over medium-high heat. Once the oil is shimmering, add the chickpeas, sumac, and salt, and stir to coat. Cook for 2 minutes without stirring. Give the chickpeas a stir and cook for another 2 minutes without stirring. Stir and cook for 2 more minutes.
5. Place ¾ cup of cooled chickpeas in each of the 4 bulgur containers.
6. Combine all the Shopping List for the salad in a medium mixing bowl. Taste for salt and lemon, and add more if you need it.
7. Place 1¼ cup of salad in each of 4 containers. These containers will not be reheated.
8. Combine the tahini and garlic powder in a small bowl. Whisk in 1 tablespoon of water at a time until all 5 tablespoons have been incorporated and a thin sauce has formed. It will thicken as it sits.
9. Place 1 tablespoon of tahini sauce in each of 4 small sauce containers.
10. Store covered containers in the refrigerator for up to 5 days. When serving, reheat the bulgur and chickpeas, add them to the salad, and drizzle the tahini sauce over the top.

NUTRITION:

calories: 485 | fat: 19g | protein: 16g | carbs: 67g | fiber: 19g | sodium: 361mg

637. Basil Pasta

Prep time: 10 minutes | Cook time: 40 minutes | Serves: 6

INGREDIENTS:

- 3 red peppers, de-seeded and cut into chunks
- 3 red onions cut into wedges
- 3 mild red chilies, de-seeded and diced
- 4 1/2 garlic cloves, coarsely chopped
- 1 1/2 teaspoon golden caster sugar
- 3 tablespoons olive oil, plus extra for serving
- 3 pounds small ripe tomatoes, quartered
- 18 ounces pasta
- a handful of basil leaves, torn
- 3 tablespoons grated parmesan salt pepper

DIRECTIONS:

1. Preheat oven to 375° F | 190°C | Fan 170°C.
2. On a large roasting pan, spread peppers, red onion, garlic, and chilies.
3. Sprinkle sugar on top.
4. Drizzle olive oil and season with salt and pepper.
5. Roast the veggies for 1minutes.
6. Add tomatoes and roast for another 15 minutes.
7. In a large pot, cook your pasta in salted boiling water according to instructions.
8. Once ready, drain pasta.
9. Remove the veggies from the oven and carefully add pasta.
10. Toss everything well and let it cool.
11. Spread over the containers.
12. Before eating, place torn basil leaves on top, and sprinkle with parmesan.
13. Enjoy!

NUTRITION:

calories: 384 | fat: 10g | protein: 1g | carbs: 59g | fiber: 2g | sodium: 361mg

638. Scallops Pea Fettuccine

Prep time: 10 minutes | Cook time: 15 minutes | Serves: 6

INGREDIENTS:

12 ounces whole-wheat fettuccine (pasta, macaroni) 1-pound large sea scallops
1/3 teaspoon salt, divided
1 1/2 tablespoon extra-virgin olive oil
1 1/2 8-ounce bottle of clam juice
1cup low-fat milk
1/3 teaspoon ground white pepper
4 1/2 cups frozen peas, thawed
1 1/8 cup finely shredded Romano cheese, divided
1/2 cup fresh chives, chopped
3/4 teaspoon freshly grated lemon zest
1 1/2 teaspoon lemon juice

DIRECTIONS:

1. Boil water in a large pot and cook fettuccine according to package instructions.
2. Drain well and put it to the side.
3. Heat oil in a large, non-stick skillet over medium-high heat.
4. Pat the scallops dry and sprinkle them with 1/8 teaspoon of salt.
5. Add the scallops to the skillet and cook for about 2-3 minutes per side until golden brown. Remove scallops from pan.
6. Add clam juice to the pan you removed the scallops from.
7. In another bowl, whisk in milk, white pepper, flour, and remaining 1/8 teaspoon of salt.
8. Once the mixture is smooth, whisk into the pan with the clam juice.
9. Bring the entire mix to a simmer and keep stirring for about 1-2 minutes until the sauce is thick.
10. Return the scallops to the pan and add peas. Bring it to a simmer.
11. Stir in fettuccine, chives, ½ cup of Romano cheese, lemon zest, and lemon juice.
12. Mix well until thoroughly combined.
13. Cool and spread over containers.
14. Before eating, serve with remaining cheese sprinkled on top.
15. Enjoy!

NUTRITION:

calories: 388 | fat: 9g | protein: 24g | carbs: 50g | fiber: 2g | sodium: 645mg

639. Baked Tilapia with Roasted Red Potatoes

Prep time: 10 minutes | Cook time: 35 minutes | Serves: 4

INGREDIENTS:

6 teaspoons olive oil, divided
2 small yellow onion, very thinly sliced (about 2 1/2 cups) 1 large red bell pepper, thinly sliced (about 2 cups)
20 ounces baby red potatoes, quartered (about 1-inch pieces)
3/4 teaspoon kosher salt, divided
2 teaspoon chopped garlic
2 tablespoon capers, drained, rinsed, and roughly chopped
1/2 cup golden raisins
2 (1/2-ounce) pack fresh basil, roughly chopped
5 ounces baby spinach, large leaves torn in half (about 4 cups) 2 teaspoons freshly squeezed lemon juice
16 ounces tilapia or other thin white fish (see tip)

DIRECTIONS:

1. Preheat the oven to 450°F. Line a sheet pan with a silicone baking mat or parchment paper.
2. Heat teaspoons of oil in a 12-inch skillet over medium heat. When the oil is shimmering, add the onions and peppers. Cook for 12 minutes, stirring occasionally. The onions should be very soft.
3. While the onions and peppers are cooking, place the potatoes on the sheet pan and toss with ⅛ teaspoon of salt and the remaining 1 teaspoon of oil. Spread the potatoes out evenly across half of the pan. Roast in the oven for 10 minutes.
4. Once the onions are soft, add the garlic, capers, raisins, basil, ⅛ teaspoon of salt, and the spinach. Stir to combine and cook for 3 more minutes to wilt the spinach.
5. Carefully remove the sheet pan from the oven after 10 minutes. Add half of the onion mixture to the empty side of the pan to form a nest for the fish. Place the fish on top and season with the remaining ⅛ teaspoon of salt and the lemon juice. Spread the rest of the onion mixture evenly across the top of the fish.
6. Place the pan back in the oven and cook for 10 minutes. The fish should be flaky.
7. When the fish and potatoes have cooled, place 1 piece of fish plus half of the potatoes and half of the onion mixture in each of 2 containers. Refrigerate.
8. Enjoy!

NUTRITION:

calories: 427 | fat: 2g | protein: 31g | carbs: 59g | fiber: 10g | sodium: 952mg

640. Mediterranean Focaccia

Prep time: 10 minutes | Cook time: 30 minutes | Serves: 6

INGREDIENTS:

5 1/3 2 cups flour
1 3/4 2 cups warm water
3 tablespoons olive oil
4 1/2 teaspoons dry yeast
2 1/4 teaspoons salt
1 1/2 cup black olives, pitted and coarsely chopped sea salt
olive oil

DIRECTIONS:

1. Place flour and yeast in a large bowl.
2. Make a well and pour in water, salt, and oil.
3. Gradually keep mixing until everything is incorporated well.
4. Knead for about 20 minutes.
5. Add black olives and mix well.
6. Form a ball and allow it to rise for about 45 minutes (in a bowl covered with a towel).
7. Once the dough is ready, push air out of it by crushing it using your palm.
8. Roll out the dough onto a floured surface to a thickness of about ½ an inch.
9. Place it on a baking sheet covered with parchment paper, and allow the dough to rise for another 45 minutes.
10. Preheat oven to 425° F.
11. Press fingers into the dough at regular intervals to pierce the dough.
12. When ready to bake, pour a bit of olive oil into the holes and sprinkle with salt.
13. Bake for 20-30 minutes.
14. Enjoy!

NUTRITION:

calories: 523 | fat: 11g | protein: 13g | carbs: 89g | fiber: 4g | sodium: 3495mg

641. Cheesy Olive Bread

Prep time: 10 minutes | Cook time: 15 minutes | Serves: 6

INGREDIENTS:

1/3 cup softened butter
1/4 cup mayo
3/4 teaspoon garlic powder
3/4 teaspoon onion powder
1 1/2 cups shredded mozzarella cheese
1/3 cup chopped black olives
3/4 loaf of French Bread, halved longways

DIRECTIONS:

1. Preheat oven to 350°F | 180°C | Fan 160°C.
2. Stir butter and mayo together in a bowl until it is smooth and creamy.
3. Add onion powder, garlic powder, olives, and cheese and stir.
4. Spread the mixture over French bread.
5. Place bread on a baking sheet and bake for 10-12 minutes.
6. Increase the heat to broil and cook until the cheese has melted and the bread is golden brown.
7. Cool and chill.
8. Pre-heat before eating.
9. Enjoy!

NUTRITION:

calories: 307 | fat: 17g | protein: 8g | carbs: 30g | fiber: 1g | sodium: 482mg

642. Red Wine–marinated Flank Steak

Prep time: 10 minutes | Cook time: 10 minutes | Serves: 6

INGREDIENTS:

12 ounces flank steak, trimmed of visible fat
3/4 cup red wine
3 tablespoons low-sodium soy sauce
1 1/2 tablespoon olive oil
3/4 teaspoon garlic powder
12 ounces Brussels sprouts, stemmed, halved, and very thinly sliced
4 1/2 tablespoons unsalted sunflower seeds
4 1/2 tablespoons freshly squeezed lemon juice
1 1/2 tablespoon plus
1 1/2 teaspoon olive oil
3 tablespoons dried cranberries
1/4 teaspoon kosher salt
1 cup Artichoke-Olive Compote

DIRECTIONS:

1. Place all the Shopping List ingredients for the steak in a gallon-size resealable bag. Allow the steak to marinate overnight or up to 2 hours.
2. Place the oven rack about 6 inches from the heating element. Preheat the oven to the broil setting (use the high setting if you have multiple settings).
3. Cover a sheet pan with foil. Lift the steak out of the marinade and place on top of the foil-lined sheet pan. Place the pan in the oven and cook for

to 6 minutes on one side. Flip the steak over to the other side and broil for 4 to 6 minutes more.
4. Remove from the oven and allow to rest for to 10 minutes. Medium-rare will be about 135°F when an instant-read meat thermometer is inserted.
5. On a cutting board, slice the steak thinly against the grain and divide the steak between 2 containers.
6. Combine the Brussels sprouts, sunflower seeds, lemon juice, olive oil, cranberries, and salt in a medium bowl.
7. Place 1 cup of Brussels sprout slaw and □ cup of artichoke-olive compote in each of 2 containers. The slaw and compote are meant to be eaten at room temperature, while the steak can be eaten warm. However, if you want to eat the steak at room temperature as well, all the items can be put in the same container.
8. Store covered containers in the refrigerator for up to 5 days.
9. Enjoy!

NUTRITION:

calories: 601 | fat: 31g | protein: 29g | carbs: 26g | fiber: 1g | sodium: 1098mg

643. Spanish Chicken Sausage

Prep time: 10 minutes | Cook time: 30 minutes | Serves: 6

INGREDIENTS:

6 teaspoons olive oil, divided
(12-ounce) package cooked chicken sausage, sliced
9 ounces uncooked peeled, deveined medium shrimp
1 1/2 large green bell pepper, chopped (about 1 1/2 cups)
1 1/2 small yellow onion, chopped (about 2 cups)
3 teaspoons chopped garlic
3 teaspoons smoked paprika
1 1/2 teaspoon dried thyme leaves
1 1/2 teaspoon dried oregano
3/4 teaspoon kosher salt
3/4 cup quick-cooking or instant brown rice
1 1/2 (14.5-ounce) can no-salt-added diced tomatoes in juice
1 1/2 cup low-sodium chicken broth
1 1/2 medium zucchini, halved vertically and sliced into half-moons

DIRECTIONS:

1. Heat 2 teaspoons of oil in a soup pot over medium-high heat. When the oil is shimmering, add the sausage and brown for 5 minutes. Add the shrimp and cook for 2 more minute. Remove the sausage and shrimp, and place them on a plate.
2. Add the remaining teaspoons of oil to the pot, and when the oil is shimmering, add the bell pepper, onion, and garlic. Sauté until soft, about 5 minutes.
3. Add the sausage, shrimp, paprika, thyme, oregano, salt, rice, tomatoes, and broth to the pot, and stir to combine. Bring to a boil, then cover the pot and turn the heat down to low. Simmer for 15 minutes.
4. After 15 minutes, add the zucchini, return the cover to the pot, and continue to simmer for 5 or 10 more minutes, until the zucchini is crisp-tender and the rice has absorbed most of the liquid.
5. Place about 2 cups of the rice mixture in each of 4 containers.
6. Store covered containers in the refrigerator for up to 5 days.
7. Enjoy!

NUTRITION:

calories: 333 | fat: 14g | protein: 29g | carbs: 29g | fiber: 6g | sodium: 954mg

644. Smoked Salmon

Prep time: 10 minutes | Cook time: 10 minutes | Serves: 6

INGREDIENTS:

1 1/2 (16-ounce) container whole-milk ricotta cheese
1 1/2 teaspoon finely grated lemon zest
4 1/2 tablespoons chopped fresh dill
12 ounces smoked salmon
6 (6-inch) Persian cucumbers or 2 small European cucumbers, sliced
3 cups sugar snap peas
6 whole-wheat pitas, each cut into 4 pieces

DIRECTIONS:

1. Mix all the Shopping List for the lemon-dill ricotta in a medium bowl.
2. Divide the salmon, cucumbers, and snap peas among 4 containers.
3. Place 1 pita in each of 4 resealable bags.
4. Place ½ cup of ricotta spread in each of separate small containers, since it may release some liquid after a couple of days.
5. Store covered containers in the refrigerator for up to 4 days. Store the pita at room temperature or in the refrigerator.
6. Enjoy!

NUTRITION:

calories: 400 | fat: 20g | protein: 32g | carbs: 40g | fiber: 8g | sodium: 1388mg

645. Braised Artichokes

Prep time: 10 minutes | Cook time: 30 minutes | Serves: 4

INGREDIENTS:

4 tablespoons olive oil
1 1/3 pounds baby artichokes, trimmed
1/3 cup lemon juice
2 2/3 garlic cloves, thinly sliced
1/3 teaspoon salt
1 pound's tomatoes, seeded and diced
1/3 cup almonds, toasted and sliced

DIRECTIONS:

1. Heat oil in a skillet over medium heat.
2. Add artichokes, garlic, and lemon juice, and allow the garlic to sizzle.
3. Season with salt.
4. Reduce heat to medium-low, cover, and simmer for about 15 minutes.
5. Uncover, add tomatoes, and simmer for another 10 minutes until the tomato liquid has mostly evaporated.
6. Season with more salt and pepper.
7. Sprinkle with toasted almonds.
8. Enjoy!

NUTRITION:

calories: 265 | fat: 1g | protein: 7g | carbs: 23g | fiber: 8g | sodium: 265mg

646. Baked Mushrooms

Prep time: 10 minutes | Cook time: 20 minutes | Serves: 4

INGREDIENTS:

1-pound mushrooms (sliced)
4 tablespoons olive oil (onion and garlic flavoured)
2 can tomatoes
2 cup Parmesan cheese
1 teaspoon oregano
2 tablespoon basil sea salt or plain salt
freshly ground black pepper

DIRECTIONS:

1. Heat the olive oil in the pan and add the mushrooms, salt, and pepper. Cook for about 2 minutes.
2. Then, transfer the mushrooms into a baking dish.
3. Now, in a separate bowl mix the tomatoes, basil, oregano, salt, and pepper, and layer it on the mushrooms. Top it with Parmesan cheese.
4. Finally, bake the dish at 0° F 2 for about 18-22 minutes or until done.
5. Serve warm.
6. Enjoy!

NUTRITION:

calories: 358 | fat: 27g | protein: 24g | carbs: 13g | fiber: 3g | sodium: 535mg

647. Romano Broccolini

Prep time: 5 minutes | Cook time: 10 minutes | Serves: 4

INGREDIENTS:

2 bunch broccolini (about 5 ounces / 142 g)
1/2 teaspoon salt
4 tablespoons grated Romano cheese
2 tablespoon olive oil
1 teaspoon garlic powder

DIRECTIONS:

1. Preheat the oven to 400°F | 200°C | Fan 180°C and set the oven rack in the centre position. Line a baking sheet with parchment paper or aluminium foil.
2. Cut the hard ends of the broccolini and place them in a medium bowl. Add the olive oil, garlic powder, and salt and stir to combine. Arrange the broccolini on the lined pan.
3. Roast for 7 minutes, turning pieces halfway through cooking time.
4. Remove the pan from the oven and sprinkle the cheese on the broccolini. With a pair of tongs, carefully flip the pieces over to cover all sides. Return to the oven for another 2 to 3 minutes, or until the cheese melts and starts to turn golden.
5. Enjoy!

NUTRITION:

calories: 114 | fat: 9g | protein: 4g | carbs: 5g | fiber: 2g | sodium: 400mg

648. Sautéed Riced Cauliflower

Prep time: 5 minutes | Cook time: 10 minutes | Serves: 4

INGREDIENTS:

1/8 cup extra-virgin olive oil
1 1/3 garlic cloves, finely minced
2/3 small head cauliflower, broken into florets

1 teaspoons salt
pepper
1/3 teaspoon freshly ground black

DIRECTIONS:

1. Place the florets in a food processor and blend several times until the cauliflower is the consistency of rice or couscous.
2. In a large skillet, heat the olive oil over medium-high heat. Add the cauliflower, garlic, salt and pepper and sauté for 5 minutes, just to remove the crunchiness but not enough to soak the cauliflower.
3. Remove the cauliflower from the pan and place it in a bowl until ready to use. Drizzle with chopped herbs and additional olive oil for a simple side dish, drizzle with sautéed veggies and protein, or use in your favourite recipe.
4. Enjoy!

NUTRITION:

calories: 92 | fat: 8g | protein: 1g | carbs: 3g | fiber: 0g | sodium: 595mg

649. Balsamic Brussels Sprouts and Delicate Squash

Prep time: 10 minutes | Cook time: 30 minutes | Serves: 4

INGREDIENTS:

2 cup fresh cranberries
4 teaspoons olive oil
Salt and freshly ground black pepper, to taste
4 tablespoons roasted pumpkin seeds
1 pound (227 g) Brussels sprouts, ends trimmed and outer leaves removed
2 medium delicate squash, halved lengthwise, seeded, and cut into 1-inch pieces
1 cup balsamic vinegar
4 tablespoons fresh pomegranate arils (seeds)

DIRECTIONS:

1. Preheat the oven to 400°F | 200°C | Fan 180°C and set the rack in the centre position. Line a baking sheet with parchment paper.
2. Combine the Brussels sprouts, pumpkin and cranberries in a large bowl. Drizzle with olive oil and season generously with salt and pepper. Mix well to coat and arrange in a single layer on the pan.
3. Roast for 30 minutes, turning the vegetables in half or until the Brussels sprouts are brown and crispy in spots and the squash has golden flecks.
4. While the vegetables are cooking, make the balsamic glaze by simmering the vinegar for 10-12 minutes, or until the mixture has reduced to about ¼ cup and takes on a syrupy consistency.
5. Remove the vegetables from the oven, drizzle with balsamic syrup and sprinkle with pumpkin seeds and pomegranate arils before serving.
6. Enjoy!

NUTRITION:

calories: 201 | fat: 7g | protein: 6g | carbs: 21g | fiber: 8g | sodium: 34mg

650. Roasted Lemon Tahini Cauliflower

Prep time: 10 minutes | Cook time: 20 minutes | Serves: 4

INGREDIENTS:

4 tablespoons freshly squeezed lemon juice
2 tablespoon olive oil
1 large head cauliflower, stemmed and broken into florets (about 3 cups)
4 tablespoons tahini
2 teaspoon harissa paste
Pinch salt

DIRECTIONS:

1. Preheat the oven to 400°F | 200°C | Fan 180°C and set the rack in the lowest position. Line a baking sheet with parchment paper or aluminium foil.
2. Mix the cauliflower florets with the olive oil in a large bowl and transfer them to the pan. Reserve the bowl to make the tahini sauce.
3. Roast the cauliflower for 15 minutes, turning it once or twice, until it begins to brown.
4. In the same bowl, combine the tahini, lemon juice, harissa and salt.
5. When the cauliflower is tender, remove it from the oven and toss with the tahini sauce. Return to the pan and cook for another 5 minutes.
6. Enjoy!

NUTRITION:

calories: 205 | fat: 15g | protein: 7g | carbs: 15g | fiber: 7g | sodium: 161mg

651. Herb-Roasted Vegetables

Prep time: 10 minutes | Cook time: 45 minutes | Serves: 4

INGREDIENTS:

2/3 tablespoon garlic powder
1 1/3 eggplants, peeled and sliced 1/8 inch thick
2/3 zucchini, sliced 1/4 inch thick
2/3 yellow summer squash, sliced 1/4 inch thick
1/8 teaspoon dried oregano
1/8 teaspoon dried basil
non-stick cooking spray
1 1/3 Roma tomatoes, sliced 1/8 inch thick
1/8 cup, plus 2 tablespoons extra-virgin olive oil, divided
1/8 teaspoon salt
Freshly ground black pepper, to taste

DIRECTIONS:

1. Preheat the oven to 400°F | 200°C | Fan 180°C.
2. Spray a 9x13 inch pan with cooking spray. On the plate, season the aubergines, courgettes, squash and tomatoes with 2 tablespoons of oil, garlic powder, oregano, basil, salt and pepper.
3. Raising the vegetables alternate layers of eggplant, courgette, pumpkin and Roma tomato.
4. Sprinkle the top with the remaining ¼ cup of olive oil.
5. Cook, uncovered, for 40-45 minutes or until vegetables are golden brown.
6. Enjoy!

NUTRITION:

calories: 186 | fat: 14g | protein: 3g | carbs: 15g | fiber: 5g | sodium: 110mg

652. Pistachio Citrus Asparagus

Prep time: 10 minutes | Cook time: 15 minutes | Serves: 6

INGREDIENTS:

1 1/2 tablespoon red wine vinegar
1 1/2 teaspoon salt, divided
Zest and juice of 1 lemon
3/4 cup shelled pistachios
1/3 teaspoon freshly ground black pepper
7 1/2 tablespoons extra-virgin olive oil, divided
Zest and juice of 2 clementine's or 1 orange (about 1/4 cup juice and 1 tablespoon zest)
1 1/2 pound (454 g) fresh asparagus
1 1/2 tablespoon water

DIRECTIONS:

1. In a small bowl, whisk together 4 tablespoons of olive oil, the juice and zest of clementine and lemon, vinegar, ½ teaspoon of salt and pepper. Put aside.
2. In a medium dry skillet, toast the pistachios over medium-high heat until lightly browned, 2-3 minutes, being careful not to let them burn. Transfer to a cutting board and chop coarsely. Put aside.
3. Trim the rough ends of the asparagus, usually the last 1 or 2 inches of each spear. In a skillet, heat the remaining tablespoon of olive oil over medium-high heat. Add the asparagus and sauté for 2 to 3 minutes. Sprinkle with the remaining ½ teaspoon of salt and add the water. Reduce the heat to medium-low, cover and cook until tender, another 2-4 minutes, depending on the thickness of the spears.
4. Transfer the cooked asparagus to a serving dish. Add the pistachios to the dressing and blend to combine. Pour the dressing over the hot asparagus and toss to coat.
5. Enjoy!

NUTRITION:

calories: 284 | fat: 24g | protein: 6g | carbs: 11g | fiber: 4g | sodium: 594mg

653. Honey Roasted Rainbow Carrots

Prep time: 10 minutes | Cook time: 20 minutes | Serves: 4

INGREDIENTS:

4 tablespoons fresh orange juice
2 tablespoon honey
1 pound (227 g) rainbow carrots (about 4)
1 teaspoon coriander
Pinch salt

DIRECTIONS:

1. Preheat oven to 400°F | 200°C | Fan 180°C and set the oven rack in the centre position.
2. Peel the carrots and cut them lengthwise into evenly thick slices. Put them in a large bowl.
3. In a small bowl, mix together the orange juice, honey, coriander, and salt.
4. Pour the orange juice mixture over the carrots and mix well to coat.
5. Spread the carrots on a baking sheet in a single layer.
6. Roast for 15-20 minutes or until fork is tender.
7. Enjoy!

NUTRITION:

calories: 85 | fat: 0g | protein: 1g | carbs: 21g | fiber: 3g | sodium: 156mg

654. Spinach and Zucchini Lasagne

Prep time: 10 minutes | Cook time: 1 hour | Serves: 4

INGREDIENTS:

1 cup whole-milk ricotta cheese
1/8 cup chopped fresh basil or 2 teaspoons dried basil
4 ounces (227 g) frozen spinach, thawed and well drained (about 1 cup)
1/4 teaspoon freshly ground black pepper
1 cup shredded fresh whole-milk Mozzarella cheese
1/2 teaspoon garlic powder
1/4 cup extra-virgin olive oil, divided
2 to 5 medium zucchini squash
1/2 teaspoon salt
1 cup shredded Parmesan cheese
1/4 (24-ounce / 680-g) jar low-sugar marinara sauce (less than 5 grams sugar)

DIRECTIONS:

1. Preheat the oven to 220ºC (425 ° F).
2. Line two baking sheets with parchment paper or aluminium foil and drizzle each with 2 tablespoons of olive oil, distributing it evenly.
3. Cut the courgettes lengthwise into ¼-inch long slices and arrange them on the prepared baking sheet in a single layer. Sprinkle with ½ teaspoon of sales per sheet. Cook until soft, but not soft, 15 to 18 minutes. Remove from the oven and allow the lasagne to cool slightly before assembling.
4. Reduce the oven temperature to 190ºC (375ºF).
5. While the courgettes are cooking, prepare the filling. In a large bowl, combine the spinach, ricotta, basil, garlic powder, and pepper. In a small bowl, combine the mozzarella and parmesan. In a medium bowl, combine the marinara sauce and the remaining olive oil cup and mix to fully incorporate the oil into the sauce.
6. To assemble the lasagne, assemble one-third of the sea sauce mixture on the bottom of a 9x13 inch glass pan and spread evenly. Arrange 1 layer of softened courgette slices to cover the sauce completely, then add a third of the ricotta and spinach mixture and spread evenly over the courgettes. Sprinkle a third of the Mozzarella-Parmesan mixture over the ricotta. Repeat with 2 more cycles of these layers: marinara, zucchini, ricotta-spinach, then blend the cheese.
7. Cook until the cheese is bubbly and melted, 30 to 35 minutes. Lower the grill and cook until the top is golden brown, about 5 minutes. Remove from the oven and allow to cool slightly before slicing.
8. Enjoy!

NUTRITION:

calories: 521 | fat: 41g | protein: 25g | carbs: 13g | fiber: 3g | sodium: 712mg

8

BEANS RECIPES

BEANS

655. White Bean Lettuce Wraps

Prep time: 10 minutes | Cook time: 9 minutes | Serves: 6

INGREDIENTS:

- 1/3 teaspoon freshly ground black pepper
- 1 1/2 (15-ounce / 425-g) can cannellini or great northern beans, drained and rinsed
- 1 1/2 tablespoon extra-virgin olive oil
- 1/3 cup finely chopped fresh curly parsley
- 3/4 cup diced red onion
- 1 1/8 cup chopped fresh tomatoes
- 3/4 cup lemony garlic hummus or 1/2 cup prepared hummus
- 12 romaine lettuce leaves

DIRECTIONS:

1. In a large skillet over medium heat, heat the oil. Add the onion and cook for 3 minutes, stirring occasionally. Add the tomatoes and pepper and cook for another 3 minutes, stirring occasionally. Add the beans and cook for another 3 minutes, stirring occasionally. Remove from the heat and add the parsley.
2. Spread 1 tablespoon of hummus on each lettuce leaf. Evenly distribute the hot bean mixture in the centre of each leaf. Fold one side of the lettuce leaf over the filling lengthwise, then fold on the other side to form a wrap and serve.
3. Enjoy!

NUTRITION:

calories: 188 | fat: 5g | protein: 10g | carbs: 28g | fiber: 9g | sodium: 115mg

656. Baked Sweet Potato Black Bean Burgers

Prep time: 10 minutes | Cook time: 10 minutes | Serves: 6

INGREDIENTS:

- 1 1/2 (15-ounce / 425-g) can black beans, drained and rinsed
- 1/3 teaspoon black pepper
- 1 1/2 tablespoon lemon juice
- 1 1/2 cup cooked brown rice
- 1/3 to 1/2 cup whole wheat bread crumbs
- 1 1/2 cup mashed sweet potato
- 1/3 teaspoon dried marjoram
- 1 1/2 garlic clove, minced
- 3/4 teaspoon dried oregano
- 1/3 teaspoon dried thyme
- 1/3 teaspoon salt
- 1 1/2 tablespoon olive oil
- For Serving:
- Whole wheat buns or whole wheat pitas
- Plain Greek yogurt
- Avocado
- Lettuce
- Tomato
- Red onion

DIRECTIONS:

1. Preheat the air fryer to 380°F (193°C).
2. In a large bowl, mash the black beans with the back of a fork until large pieces remain.
3. Add the sweet potato mash, oregano, thyme, marjoram, garlic, salt, pepper and lemon juice and mix until well blended.
4. Incorporate the cooked rice.
5. Add 1 cup of wholemeal breadcrumbs and mix. Check if the mixture is dry enough to make meatballs. If it feels too moist and melted, add another cup of breadcrumbs and mix.
6. Form 4 meatballs with the dough. Place them in the basket of the air fryer in a single layer, making sure they don't touch each other.
7. Brush half the olive oil over the meatballs and cook for 5 minutes.
8. Flip the meatballs, brush the other side with the remaining oil and cook for another 4-5 minutes.
9. Serve on toasted wholemeal sandwiches or wholemeal pita bread with a tablespoon of yogurt and avocado, lettuce, tomato and red onion to taste.
10. Enjoy!

NUTRITION:

calories: 263 | fat: 5g | protein: 9g | carbs: 47g | fiber: 8g | sodium: 247mg

657. Garbanzo and Fava Bean Ful

Prep time: 10 minutes | Cook time: 10 minutes | Serves: 4

INGREDIENTS:

- 2 cloves garlic, peeled and minced
- 2/3 teaspoon salt
- 2 tablespoons extra-virgin olive oil
- 2/3 (16-ounce / 454-g) can garbanzo beans, rinsed and drained
- 2/3 (15-ounce / 425-g) can fava beans, rinsed and drained
- 2 cups water
- 1/3 cup lemon juice

DIRECTIONS:

1. In a 3-quart saucepan over medium heat, cook the chickpeas, broad beans and water for 10 minutes.
2. Reserving 1 cup of the liquid from the cooked beans, drain and place them in a bowl.
3. Mix together the reserved liquid, lemon juice, minced garlic and salt and add to the beans in the bowl. Using a potato masher, mash about half of the beans in the bowl.
4. After mashing half of the beans, stir again to make sure the beans are well blended.
5. Pour over the olive oil.
6. Serve hot or cold with pita bread.
7. Enjoy!

NUTRITION:

calories: 199 | fat: 9g | protein: 10g | carbs: 25g | fiber: 9g | sodium: 395mg

658. Lentil Stuffed Tomatoes

Prep time: 10 minutes | Cook time: 15 minutes | Serves: 6

INGREDIENTS:

- 1/3 teaspoon black pepper
- 6 ounces (113 g) goat cheese
- 3 tablespoons shredded Parmesan cheese
- 1 1/2 tablespoon minced red onion
- 6 basil leaves, minced
- 1/3 teaspoon salt
- 6 tomatoes
- 3/4 cup cooked red lentils
- 1 1/2 garlic clove, minced

DIRECTIONS:

1. Preheat the air fryer to 380°F (193°C).
2. Cut off the top of each tomato.
3. Using a knife and spoon, cut and hollow out half of the pulp inside the tomato. Put it in a medium bowl.
4. In the bowl with the tomato, add the cooked lentils, garlic, onion, basil, salt, pepper and goat cheese. Mix until well combined.
5. Pour the filling into the hollowed cavity of each of the tomatoes, then garnish each with ½ tablespoon of grated Parmesan cheese.
6. Place the tomatoes in a single layer in the basket of the air fryer and cook for 15 minutes.
7. Enjoy!

NUTRITION:

calories: 138 | fat: 7g | protein: 9g | carbs: 11g | fiber: 4g | sodium: 317mg

659. Herb Lentil-Rice Balls

Base
Prep time: 5 minutes | Cook time: 11 minutes | Serves: 4

INGREDIENTS:

- 2/3 cup cooked brown rice
- 2/3 tablespoon lemon juice
- 2/3 tablespoon olive oil
- 1/8 white onion, minced
- 1/8 cup parsley leaves
- 3 1/3 basil leaves
- 1/3 cup cooked green lentils
- 1 1/3 garlic cloves, minced
- 1/3 teaspoon salt

DIRECTIONS:

1. Preheat the air fryer to 380°F (193°C).
2. In a food processor, blend the cooked lentils with the garlic, onion, parsley and basil until smooth. (You will need a few bits of lentils in the mixture.)
3. Pour the lentil mixture into a large bowl and add the brown rice, lemon juice, olive oil and salt. Mix until well combined.
4. Form the rice mixture into 1-inch balls. Arrange the rice balls in a single layer in the basket of the air fryer, making sure they do not touch each other.
5. Fry for 6 minutes. Turn the rice balls and fry them for another 4-5 minutes or until golden brown on all sides.
6. Enjoy!

NUTRITION:

calories: 80 | fat: 3g | protein: 2g | carbs: 12g | fiber: 2g | sodium: 198mg

660. Black-Eyed Peas Salad with Walnuts

Prep time: 10 minutes | Cook time: 0 minutes | Serves: 6

INGREDIENTS:

- 3 tablespoons lemon juice
- 3 tablespoons pomegranate molasses

3 (15-ounce / 425-g) cans black-eyed peas, rinsed
3/4 cup pomegranate seeds
3/4 cup minced fresh parsley
1/3 teaspoon salt, or more to taste
1/4 teaspoon pepper, or more to taste
4 1/2 tablespoons extra-virgin olive oil
4 1/2 tablespoons dukkha, divided
3/4 cup walnuts, toasted and chopped
6 scallions, sliced thinly

DIRECTIONS:

1. In a large bowl, whisk together the olive oil, 2 tablespoons of dukkha, lemon juice, pomegranate molasses, salt and pepper.
2. Incorporate the other ingredients. Season with salt and pepper.
3. Sprinkle with the remaining spoonful of dukkha before serving.
4. Enjoy!

NUTRITION:

calories: 155 | fat: 11g | protein: 2g | carbs: 12g | fiber: 2g | sodium: 105mg

661. Oregano Lentil and Carrot Patties

Prep time: 15 minutes | Cook time: 10 minutes | Serves: 6

INGREDIENTS:

1 1/2 jalapeño, seeded and minced
3/4 teaspoon smoked paprika
3/4 teaspoon dried oregano
1/3 teaspoon salt
1 1/2 cup cooked brown lentils
1/3 cup fresh parsley leaves
3/4 cup shredded carrots
1/3 red onion, minced
1/3 red bell pepper, minced
1/3 teaspoon black pepper
3 garlic cloves, minced
1 1/2 egg
3 tablespoons lemon juice
3 tablespoons olive oil, divided
3/4 teaspoon onion powder
3/4 cup whole wheat bread crumbs
For Serving:
Whole wheat buns or whole wheat pitas
Plain Greek yogurt
Tomato
Lettuce
Red Onion

DIRECTIONS:

1. Preheat the air fryer to 380ºF (193ºC).
2. In a food processor, blend the mostly smooth lentils and parsley. (You will need a few bits of lentils in the mixture.)
3. Pour the lentils into a large bowl and combine the carrots, onion, pepper, jalapeño, garlic, egg, lemon juice and 1 tablespoon of olive oil.
4. Add the onion powder, paprika, oregano, salt, pepper and breadcrumbs. Mix everything until the seasonings and breadcrumbs are well distributed.
5. Form 4 meatballs with the dough. Place them in the air fryer basket in a single layer, making sure they don't touch each other. Brush the meatballs with the remaining 1 tablespoon of olive oil.
6. Cook for 5 minutes. Flip the meatballs over and cook for another 5 minutes.
7. Serve on toasted whole meal sandwiches or whole meal pitas with a tablespoon of yogurt and lettuce, tomato and red onion to taste.
8. Enjoy!

NUTRITION:

calories: 206 | fat: 9g | protein: 8g | carbs: 25g | fiber: 6g | sodium: 384mg

662. Green Bean and Halloumi Cheese Salad

Prep time: 15 minutes | Cook time: 6 minutes | Serves: 4

INGREDIENTS:

For the Dressing:
1/2 cup plain kefir or buttermilk
1/2 teaspoon garlic powder
Pinch salt
2 tablespoon olive oil
4 teaspoons freshly squeezed lemon juice
1/2 teaspoon onion powder
Pinch freshly ground black pepper
For the Salad:
1 pound (227 g) very fresh green beans, trimmed
4 ounces (57 g) Halloumi cheese, sliced into 2 (1/2-inch-thick) slices
1 cup cherry or grape tomatoes, halved
1/2 cup very thinly sliced sweet onion
4 ounces (57 g) prosciutto, cooked crisp and crumbled

DIRECTIONS:

Make the Dressing
1. Combine the kefir or buttermilk, olive oil, lemon juice, onion powder, garlic powder, salt, and pepper in a small bowl and whisk well. Set the dressing aside.
Make the Salad
1. Fill a medium-sized saucepan with about 1 inch of water and add the green beans. Cover and steam for about 3 to 4 minutes, or until the beans are tender. Don't overcook. Drain the beans, rinse them immediately with cold water and set them aside to cool.
2. Heat a non-stick skillet over medium-high heat and place the halloumi slices in the hot skillet. After about 2 minutes, check if the cheese is golden on the bottom. If it is, flip the slices and cook for another minute or until the second side is golden brown.
3. Remove the cheese from the pan and cut each piece into cubes (about 1 square inch)
4. Place the green beans, halloumi, tomatoes and sliced onion in a large bowl and toss to combine.
5. Pour the dressing over the salad and mix well to combine. Sprinkle the ham on top.
6. Enjoy!

NUTRITION:

calories: 273 | fat: 18g | protein: 15g | carbs: 16g | fiber: 5g | sodium: 506mg

663. Italian-Style Baked Beans

Prep time: 10 minutes | Cook time: 15 minutes | Serves: 4

INGREDIENTS:

1 1/3 teaspoons extra-virgin olive oil
1/8 cup red wine vinegar
1 1/3 tablespoons honey
1/8 teaspoon ground cinnamon
1/3 cup minced onion
2/3 (12-ounce / 340-g) can low-sodium tomato paste
1/3 cup water
1 1/3 (15-ounce / 425-g) cans cannellini or great northern beans, undrained

DIRECTIONS:

1. In a medium saucepan over medium heat, heat the oil. Add the onion and cook for 5 minutes, stirring often. Add the tomato paste, vinegar, honey, cinnamon and water and mix well. Turn down the heat.
2. Drain and rinse a can of beans in a colander and add them to the saucepan. Pour the entire second can of beans (including the liquid) into the saucepan. Cook for 10 minutes, stirring occasionally, and serve.
3. Enjoy!

NUTRITION:

calories: 290 | fat: 2g | protein: 15g | carbs: 53g | fiber: 11g | sodium: 647mg

664. Garlic and Parsley Chickpeas

Prep time: 10 minutes | Cook time: 20 minutes | Serves: 6

INGREDIENTS:

1 1/2 onion, chopped finely
1/3 teaspoon salt, plus more to taste
Black pepper, to taste
3 (15-ounce / 425-g) cans chickpeas, rinsed
1 1/2 cup vegetable broth
1/3 cup extra-virgin olive oil, divided
6 garlic cloves, sliced thinly
1/4 teaspoon red pepper flakes
3 tablespoons minced fresh parsley
3 teaspoons lemon juice

DIRECTIONS:

1. Add 3 tablespoons of olive oil, garlic and red pepper to a skillet over medium heat. Cook for about 3 minutes, stirring constantly, or until the garlic turns golden but not brown.
2. Stir in the onion and teaspoon of salt and cook for 5-7 minutes, or until soft and lightly browned.
3. Add the chickpeas and stock to the pan and bring to a boil. Reduce the heat to medium-low, cover and cook for about 7 minutes, or until the chickpeas are cooked through and the flavors blend.
4. Uncover, raise the heat and continue cooking for about 3 more minutes, or until most of the liquid has evaporated.
5. Turn off the heat, add the parsley and lemon juice. Season to taste with salt and pepper and season with the remaining spoonful of olive oil.
6. Serve hot.
7. Enjoy!

NUTRITION:

calories: 220 | fat: 11g | protein: 6g | carbs: 24g | fiber: 6g | sodium: 467mg

665. French Green Lentils with Chard

Prep time: 15 minutes | Cook time: 20 minutes | Serves: 4

INGREDIENTS:

1 1/3 garlic cloves, minced
2/3 teaspoon minced fresh thyme or 1/4 teaspoon dried
1 2/3 cups water
1/3 teaspoon table salt
2 tablespoons whole-grain mustard
1/3 teaspoon grated lemon zest plus 1 teaspoon juice
2/3 cup French green lentils, picked over and rinsed
1 1/3 tablespoons extra-virgin olive oil, plus extra for drizzling
8 ounces (340 g) Swiss chard, stems chopped fine, leaves sliced into 1/2-inch-wide strips
2/3 onion, chopped fine
2 tablespoons sliced almonds, toasted
1 1/3 tablespoons chopped fresh parsley

DIRECTIONS:

1. Using the highest sauté function, heat the oil in the Instant Pot until it glistens. Add the chard stalks, onion and salt and cook until the vegetables soften, about 5 minutes. Stir in the garlic and thyme and cook until fragrant, about 30 seconds. Combine the water and lentils.
2. Lock the lid in place and close the pressure release valve. Select the high pressure cooking function and cook for 11 minutes. Turn off the Instant Pot and let the pressure naturally release for 15 minutes. Quickly release the residual pressure, then carefully remove the lid, allowing the steam to escape away from you.
3. Mix the chard leaves with the lentils, 1 handful at a time, and cook over a residual heat until wilted, about 5 minutes. Mix the mustard and lemon zest and juice. Season with salt and pepper to taste. Transfer to a serving dish, drizzle with extra oil and sprinkle with almonds and parsley. To serve.
4. Enjoy!

NUTRITION:

calories: 190 | fat: 8g | protein: 9g | carbs: 23g | fiber: 6g | sodium: 470mg

666. Mashed Beans with Cumin

Prep time: 10 minutes | Cook time: 12 minutes | Serves: 6

INGREDIENTS:

- 1 1/2 teaspoon ground cumin
- 3 (15-ounce / 425-g) cans fava beans
- 4 1/2 tablespoons tahini
- 1 1/2 tomato, cored and cut into 1/2-inch pieces
- 1 1/2 small onion, chopped finely
- 3 tablespoons lemon juice, plus lemon wedges for serving
- 1 1/2 tablespoon extra-virgin olive oil, plus extra for serving
- 6 garlic cloves, minced
- Salt and pepper, to taste
- 3 hard-cooked large eggs, chopped
- 3 tablespoons minced fresh parsley

DIRECTIONS:

1. Add the olive oil, garlic and cumin to a medium saucepan over medium heat. Cook for about 2 minutes, or until fragrant.
2. Incorporate the beans with their liquid and tahini. Bring to a boil and cook for 8-10 minutes, or until the liquid thickens slightly.
3. Turn off the heat, mash the beans to a coarse consistency with a potato masher. Mix the lemon juice and 1 teaspoon of pepper. Season with salt and pepper.
4. Transfer the mashed beans to a serving dish. Complete with the tomato, onion, eggs and parsley. Drizzle with extra olive oil.
5. Serve with the lemon wedges.
6. Enjoy!

NUTRITION:

calories: 125 | fat: 8g | protein: 5g | carbs: 9g | fiber: 3g | sodium: 131mg

667. White Cannellini Bean Stew

Prep time: 10 minutes | Cook time: 30 minutes | Serves: 6

INGREDIENTS:

- 4 1/2 tablespoons extra-virgin olive oil
- 1 1/2 cup carrots, chopped
- 6 cups vegetable broth
- 1 1/2 large onion, chopped
- 1 1/2 (15-ounce / 425-g) can diced tomatoes
- 3 (15-ounce / 425-g) cans white cannellini beans
- 1 1/2 teaspoon salt
- 1 1/2 (1-pound / 454-g) bag baby spinach, washed

DIRECTIONS:

1. In a large saucepan over medium heat, cook the olive oil and onion for 5 minutes.
2. Add the tomatoes, beans, carrots, broth and salt. Stir and cook for 20 minutes.
3. Add the spinach, a handful at a time, and cook for 5 minutes, until the spinach has wilted.
4. Serve hot.
5. Enjoy!

NUTRITION:

calories: 356 | fat: 12g | protein: 15g | carbs: 47g | fiber: 16g | sodium: 1832mg

GRAINS & RICE RECIPES

9

GRAINS AND RICE

668. Creamy Parmesan Garlic Polenta
Prep time: 5 minutes | Cook time: 30 minutes | Serves: 6

INGREDIENTS:

- 1 1/2 teaspoon salt
- 1 1/2 cup polenta
- 6 tablespoons (1/2 stick) unsalted butter, divided (optional)
- 1 1/2 tablespoon garlic, finely chopped
- 6 cups water
- 1 1/8 cup Parmesan cheese, divided

DIRECTIONS:

1. In a large saucepan over medium heat, cook 3 tablespoons of butter (if desired) and garlic for 2 minutes.
2. Add the water and salt and bring to a boil. Add the polenta and whisk immediately until it begins to thicken, about 3 minutes. Lower the heat, cover and cook for 25 minutes, stirring every 5 minutes.
3. Using a wooden spoon, add ½ cup of Parmesan.
4. To serve, pour the polenta into a large bowl. Sprinkle the top with the remaining spoonful of butter (if desired) and ¼ cup of the remaining Parmesan. Serve hot.
5. Enjoy!

NUTRITION:

calories: 297 | fat: 16g | protein: 9g | carbs: 28g | fiber: 2g | sodium: 838mg

669. Lentil Bulgur Pilaf
Prep time: 10 minutes | Cook time: 50 minutes | Serves: 4

INGREDIENTS:

- 4 cups water
- 1 1/3 cups brown lentils, picked over and rinsed
- 1/3 cup extra-virgin olive oil
- 2 2/3 large onions, chopped
- 1 1/3 teaspoons salt, divided
- 2/3 teaspoon freshly ground black pepper
- 2/3 cup bulgur wheat

DIRECTIONS:

1. In a large saucepan over medium heat, cook and mix the olive oil, onions and 1 teaspoon of salt for 12-15 minutes, until the onions turn a medium brown / golden color.
2. Place half of the cooked onions in a bowl.
3. Add the water, the remaining teaspoon of salt and the lentils to the remaining onions. Shake. Cover and cook for 30 minutes.
4. Incorporate the black pepper and bulgur, cover and cook for 5 minutes. Shell with a fork, cover and leave to rest for another 5 minutes.
5. Arrange the lentils and bulgur on a serving plate and garnish with the set aside onions. Serve hot.
6. Enjoy!

NUTRITION:

calories: 479 | fat: 20g | protein: 20g | carbs: 60g | fiber: 24g | sodium: 789mg

670. Mushroom Parmesan Risotto
Prep time: 10 minutes | Cook time: 30 minutes | Serves: 6

INGREDIENTS:

- 9 cups vegetable broth
- 4 1/2 tablespoons extra-virgin olive oil, divided
- 3 cloves garlic, minced
- 2 1/4 cups Arborio rice
- 1 1/2 teaspoon salt
- 1 1/2-pound (454 g) cremini mushrooms, cleaned and sliced
- 1 1/2 medium onion, finely chopped
- 3/4 cup freshly grated Parmesan cheese
- 3/4 teaspoon freshly ground black pepper

DIRECTIONS:

1. In a saucepan over medium heat, bring the broth over low heat.
2. In a large skillet over medium heat, cook 1 tablespoon of olive oil and the sliced mushrooms for 5-7 minutes. Set the cooked mushrooms aside.
3. In the same pan over medium heat, add the remaining 2 tablespoons of olive oil, onion and garlic. Cook for 3 minutes.
4. Add the rice, salt, and 1 cup of broth to the pan. Mix the ingredients and cook over low heat until most of the liquid is absorbed. Continue adding ½ cup of broth at a time, stirring until absorbed. Repeat until all the broth is used up.
5. With the last addition of broth, add the cooked mushrooms, Parmesan and black pepper. Cook for another 2 minutes. Serve immediately.
6. Enjoy!

NUTRITION:

calories: 410 | fat: 12g | protein: 11g | carbs: 65g | fiber: 3g | sodium: 2086mg

671. Mushroom Barley Pilaf
Prep time: 5 minutes | Cook time: 37 minutes | Serves: 6

INGREDIENTS:

- 3/4 teaspoon salt
- 1/3 teaspoon smoked paprika
- 12 ounces (227 g) button mushrooms, diced
- 3/4 yellow onion, diced
- 3 garlic cloves, minced
- 1 1/2 tablespoon fresh thyme, chopped
- Olive oil cooking spray
- 3 tablespoons olive oil
- 1 1/2 cup pearl barley
- 3 cups vegetable broth
- Fresh parsley, for garnish

DIRECTIONS:

1. Preheat the air fryer to 380ºF (193ºC). Lightly coat the inside of a 5-cup saucepan with cooking spray olive oil. (The shape of the saucepan will depend on the size of the air fryer, but it must be able to hold at least 5 cups.)
2. In a large skillet, heat the olive oil over medium heat. Add the mushrooms and onion and cook, stirring occasionally, for 5 minutes or until the mushrooms begin to brown.
3. Add the garlic and cook for another 2 minutes. Transfer the vegetables to a large bowl.
4. Add the barley, stock, thyme, salt and paprika.
5. Pour the barley and vegetable mixture into the prepared saucepan and place the dish in the air fryer. Bake for 15 minutes.
6. Stir in the barley mixture. Reduce the heat to 360ºF (182ºC), then return the barley to the air fryer and bake for another 15 minutes.
7. Remove from deep fryer and let stand for 5 minutes before shelling with a fork and garnish with fresh parsley.
8. Enjoy!

NUTRITION:

calories: 263 | fat: 8g | protein: 7g | carbs: 44g | fiber: 9g | sodium: 576mg

672. Couscous Confetti Salad
Prep time: 5 minutes | Cook time: 20 minutes | Serves: 6

INGREDIENTS:

- 3 carrots, chopped
- 1 1/2 cup fresh peas
- 3/4 cup golden raisins
- 4 1/2 tablespoons extra-virgin olive oil
- 1 1/2 large onion, chopped
- 1 1/2 teaspoon salt
- 3 cups vegetable broth
- 3 cups couscous

DIRECTIONS:

1. In a medium saucepan over medium heat, gently mix the olive oil, onions, carrots, peas, and raisins and cook for 5 minutes.
2. Add the salt and broth and mix to combine. Bring to a boil and boil the ingredients for 5 minutes.
3. Add the couscous. Stir, lower the heat, cover and cook for 10 minutes. Shell with a fork and serve.
4. Enjoy!

NUTRITION:

calories: 511 | fat: 12g | protein: 14g | carbs: 92g | fiber: 7g | sodium: 504mg

673. Toasted Barley and Almond Pilaf
Prep time: 10 minutes | Cook time: 5 minutes | Serves: 6

INGREDIENTS:

- 4 ounces (57 g) mushrooms, sliced
- 1/2 cup sliced almonds
- 2 tablespoon olive oil
- 1 cup uncooked pearled barley
- 3 cups low-sodium chicken stock
- 1 teaspoon dried thyme
- 2 garlic cloves, minced
- 6 scallions, minced
- 2 tablespoon fresh minced parsley
- Salt, to taste

DIRECTIONS:

1. Heat the oil in a saucepan over medium-high heat. Add the garlic, shallots, mushrooms and almonds and sauté for 3 minutes.
2. Add the barley and cook, stirring, for 1 minute to toast.
3. Add the chicken stock and thyme and bring to a boil.
4. Cover and reduce heat to low. Simmer the barley for 30 minutes, or until the liquid is absorbed and the barley is tender.
5. Sprinkle with fresh parsley and season with salt before serving.
6. Enjoy!

NUTRITION:

calories: 333 | fat: 13g | protein: 10g | carbs: 46g | fiber: 9g | sodium:

141mg

674. Rustic Lentil-Rice Pilaf
Prep time: 5 minutes | Cook time: 50 minutes | Serves: 4

INGREDIENTS:
4 cups water	2/3 large onion, chopped
2/3 teaspoon ground cumin	1 1/3 cups brown lentils, picked over and rinsed
2/3 teaspoon salt	
1/8 cup extra-virgin olive oil	2/3 cup basmati rice

DIRECTIONS:
1. In a medium saucepan over medium heat, cook the olive oil and onions for 7-10 minutes until the edges are browned.
2. Raise the heat, add the water, cumin and salt and bring to a boil, boiling for about 3 minutes.
3. Add the lentils and reduce the heat. Cover the pot and cook for 20 minutes, stirring occasionally.
4. Incorporate the rice and cover; cook for another 20 minutes.
5. Shell the rice with a fork and serve hot.
6. Enjoy!

NUTRITION:
calories: 397 | fat: 11g | protein: 18g | carbs: 60g | fiber: 18g | sodium: 396mg

675. Bulgur Pilaf with Garbanzos
Prep time: 5 minutes | Cook time: 20 minutes | Serves: 6

INGREDIENTS:
3 cups bulgur wheat, rinsed and drained	1 1/2 (16-ounce / 454-g) can garbanzo beans, rinsed and drained
2 1/4 teaspoons salt	
4 1/2 tablespoons extra-virgin olive oil	3/4 teaspoon cinnamon
1 1/2 large onion, chopped	6 cups water

DIRECTIONS:
1. In a large saucepan over medium heat, cook the olive oil and onion for 5 minutes.
2. Add the chickpeas and cook for another 5 minutes.
3. Add the bulgur, salt, cinnamon and water and stir to combine. Cover the pot, lower the heat and cook for 10 minutes.
4. When cooked, shell the pilaf with a fork. Cover and let it rest for another 5 minutes.
5. Enjoy!

NUTRITION:
calories: 462 | fat: 13g | protein: 15g | carbs: 76g | fiber: 19g | sodium: 890mg

676. Farro Risotto with Fresh Sage
Prep time: 10 minutes | Cook time: 35 minutes | Serves: 4

INGREDIENTS:
Olive oil cooking spray	1 cup uncooked farro
2/3 tablespoon fresh sage, chopped	1 2/3 cups chicken broth
1/3 teaspoon salt	2/3 cup tomato sauce
1 1/3 tablespoons olive oil	2/3 yellow onion, diced
2/3 cup Parmesan cheese, grated, divided	2 garlic cloves, minced

DIRECTIONS:
1. Preheat the air fryer to 380ºF (193ºC). Lightly coat the inside of a 5-cup saucepan with cooking spray olive oil. (The shape of the saucepan will depend on the size of the air fryer, but it must be able to hold at least 5 cups.)
2. In a large bowl, combine the farro, broth, tomato sauce, onion, garlic, sage, salt, olive oil and ½ cup of Parmesan.
3. Pour the spelled mixture into the prepared saucepan and cover with aluminum foil.
4. Cook for 20 minutes, then uncover and mix. Sprinkle the remaining ½ cup of Parmesan on top and cook for another 15 minutes.
5. Stir well before serving.
6. Enjoy!

NUTRITION:
calories: 284 | fat: 9g | protein: 12g | carbs: 40g | fiber: 3g | sodium: 564mg

677. Wild Mushroom Farrotto with Parmesan
Prep time: 15 minutes | Cook time: 7 minutes | Serves: 6

INGREDIENTS:
1/3 ounce (7 g) dried porcini mushrooms, rinsed and chopped fine	18 ounces (340 g) cremini or white mushrooms, trimmed and sliced thin
3 teaspoons minced fresh thyme or 1/2 teaspoon dried	3/4 onion, chopped fine
3/4 teaspoon table salt	1/3 cup dry white wine
1/3 teaspoon pepper	3 3/4 cups chicken or vegetable broth, plus extra as needed
1 1/2 garlic clove, minced	
2 1/4 cups whole farro	3 ounces (57 g) Parmesan cheese, grated, plus extra for serving
4 1/2 tablespoons extra-virgin olive oil, divided, plus extra for drizzling	3 teaspoons lemon juice
	3/4 cup chopped fresh parsley

DIRECTIONS:
1. Blend the spelled in the blender until about half of the kernels are broken into smaller pieces, about 6 pulses.
2. Using the highest sauté function, heat 2 tablespoons of oil in the Instant Pot until it glistens. Add the cremini mushrooms, onion, salt and pepper, partially cover and cook until the mushrooms have softened and released their liquid, about 5 minutes. Stir in the spelled, garlic, porcini mushrooms and thyme and cook until fragrant, about 1 minute. Deglaze with the wine and cook until almost evaporated, about 30 seconds. Stir in the broth.
3. Lock the lid in place and close the pressure release valve. Select the high-pressure cooking function and cook for 12 minutes. Turn off Instant Pot and quick release pressure. Carefully remove the lid, allowing the steam to escape from you.
4. If necessary, adjust the consistency with more hot broth, or continue to cook the farrotto, using the highest sauté function, stirring often, until the right consistency is obtained. (The farrotto should be slightly thick and the spoon dragged along the bottom of the multicooker should leave a trail that fills quickly.) Add the Parmesan and the remaining spoonful of oil and mix vigorously until the farrotto is creamy. Add the lemon juice and season with salt and pepper to taste. Sprinkle individual portions with extra parsley and Parmesan and drizzle with extra oil before serving.
5. Enjoy!

NUTRITION:
calories: 280 | fat: 9g | protein: 13g | carbs: 35g | fiber: 3g | sodium: 630mg

678. Pearl Barley Risotto with Parmesan Cheese
Prep time: 5 minutes | Cook time: 20 minutes | Serves: 4

INGREDIENTS:
1/3 cup dry white wine	2/3 cup chopped yellow onion
2/3 cup freshly grated Parmesan cheese, divided	1 1/3 cups uncooked pearl barley
1/8 teaspoon kosher or sea salt	1/8 teaspoon freshly ground black pepper
2 2/3 cups low-sodium or no-salt-added vegetable broth	Fresh chopped chives and lemon wedges, for serving (optional)
2/3 tablespoon extra-virgin olive oil	

DIRECTIONS:
1. Pour the broth into a medium saucepan and bring to a boil.
2. Heat the olive oil in a large saucepan over medium-high heat. Add the onion and cook for about 4 minutes, stirring occasionally.
3. Add the barley and cook for 2 minutes, stirring, or until the barley is toasted. Deglaze with the wine and cook for about 1 minute, or until most of the liquid evaporates. Add 1 cup of hot broth to the pot and cook, stirring, for about 2 minutes or until most of the liquid is absorbed.
4. Add the remaining stock, 1 cup at a time, cooking until each cup is absorbed (about 2 minutes each time) before adding the next. The last addition of broth will take a little longer to absorb, about 4 minutes.
5. Remove the pot from the heat and add ½ cup of cheese, salt and pepper.
6. Serve with the remaining ½ cup of cheese on the side, along with the chives and lemon wedges (if desired).
7. Enjoy!

NUTRITION:
calories: 421 | fat: 11g | protein: 15g | carbs: 67g | fiber: 11g | sodium: 641mg

679. Bow Ties with Zucchini
Prep time: 10 minutes | Cook time: 32 minutes | Serves: 6

INGREDIENTS:
1/3 teaspoon kosher or sea salt	3 garlic cloves, minced
3/4 cup 2% milk	4 1/2 large or 4 medium zucchinis, diced
1/3 teaspoon ground nutmeg	3/4 teaspoon freshly ground black pepper
4 1/2 tablespoons extra-virgin olive oil	

139

12 ounces (227 g) uncooked farfalle (bow ties) or other small pasta shape
3/4 cup grated Parmesan or Romano cheese
1 1/2 tablespoon freshly squeezed lemon juice

DIRECTIONS:

1. In a large skillet over medium heat, heat the oil. Add the garlic and cook for 1 minute, stirring often. Add the courgettes, pepper and salt. Mix well, cover and cook for 15 minutes, stirring once or twice.
2. In a small microwave-safe bowl, heat the milk in the microwave on full power for 30 seconds. Mix the milk and nutmeg in the pan and cook uncovered for another 5 minutes, stirring occasionally.
3. While the courgettes are cooking, in a large pot, cook the pasta according to package directions.
4. Drain the pasta in a colander, keeping about 2 tablespoons of the pasta water. Add the pasta and pasta water to the pan. Mix everything and remove from the heat. Add the cheese and lemon juice and serve.
5. Enjoy!

NUTRITION:

calories: 190 | fat: 9g | protein: 7g | carbs: 20g | fiber: 2g | sodium: 475mg

680. Dinner Meaty Baked Penne

Prep time: 5 minutes | Cook time: 50 minutes | Serves: 6

INGREDIENTS:

3/4 teaspoon salt
3/4 (25-ounce / 709-g) jar marinara sauce
3/4 (1-pound / 454-g) bag baby spinach, washed
3/4-pound (454 g) penne pasta
3/4-pound (454 g) ground beef
2 1/4 cups shredded Mozzarella cheese, divided

DIRECTIONS:

1. Bring plenty of salted water to a boil, add the penne and cook for 7 minutes. Keep 2 cups of pasta water and drain the pasta.
2. Preheat oven to 350°F | 180°C | Fan 160°C
3. In a large saucepan over medium heat, cook the ground beef and salt. Brown the minced meat for about 5 minutes.
4. Mix the marinara sauce and 2 cups of pasta water. Cook for 5 minutes.
5. Add a handful of spinach at a time to the sauce and cook for another 3 minutes.
6. To assemble, in a 9x13 inch pan, add the pasta and pour the pasta sauce over it. Stir in 1½ cups of mozzarella. Cover the dish with foil and cook for 20 minutes.
7. After 20 minutes, remove the foil, cover with the rest of the mozzarella and cook for another 10 minutes. Serve hot.
8. Enjoy!

NUTRITION:

calories: 497 | fat: 17g | protein: 31g | carbs: 54g | fiber: 4g | sodium: 619mg

681. Quinoa with Baby Potatoes and Broccoli

Prep time: 5 minutes | Cook time: 10 minutes | Serves: 6

INGREDIENTS:

3 cups cooked quinoa
Zest of 1 lemon
3 tablespoons olive oil
1 1/2 cup baby potatoes, cut in half
1 1/2 cup broccoli florets
Sea salt and freshly ground pepper, to taste

DIRECTIONS:

1. Heat the olive oil in a large skillet over medium heat until it glistens.
2. Add the potatoes and cook for about 6-7 minutes, or until soft and golden. Add the broccoli and cook for about 3 minutes, or until tender.
3. Remove from the heat and add the quinoa and lemon zest. Season with salt and pepper to taste, then serve.
4. Enjoy!

NUTRITION:

calories: 205 | fat: 8g | protein: 5g | carbs: 27g | fiber: 3g | sodium: 158mg

682. Fusilli with Chickpea Sauce

Prep time: 15 minutes | Cook time: 15 minutes | Serves: 6

INGREDIENTS:

1/3 cup extra-virgin olive oil
3/4 large shallot, chopped
7 1/2 garlic cloves, thinly sliced
1 1/2 (15-ounce / 425-g) can chickpeas, drained and rinsed, reserving 1/2 cup canning liquid
Pinch red pepper flakes
1 1/2 cup whole-grain fusilli pasta
1/3 teaspoon salt
1/4 teaspoon freshly ground black pepper
1/3 cup shaved fresh Parmesan cheese
1/3 cup chopped fresh basil
3 teaspoons dried parsley
1 1/2 teaspoon dried oregano
Red pepper flakes

DIRECTIONS:

1. In a medium pan, heat the oil over medium heat, and sauté the shallot and garlic for 3 to 5 minutes, until the garlic is golden. Add ¾ of the chickpeas plus 2 tablespoons of liquid from the can, and bring to a simmer.
2. Remove from the heat, transfer into a standard blender, and blend until smooth. At this point, add the remaining chickpeas. Add more reserved chickpea liquid if it becomes thick.
3. Bring a large pot of salted water to a boil and cook pasta until al dente, about 8 minutes. Reserve ½ cup of the pasta water, drain the pasta, and return it to the pot.
4. Add the chickpea sauce to the hot pasta and add up to ¼ cup of the pasta water. You may need to add more pasta water to reach your desired consistency.
5. Place the pasta pot over medium heat and mix occasionally until the sauce thickens. Season with salt and pepper.
Serve, garnished with Parmesan, basil, parsley, oregano, and red pepper flakes.
6. Enjoy!

NUTRITION:

calories: 310 | fat: 16g | protein: 10g | carbs: 33g | fiber: 6g | sodium: 243mg

683. Quinoa

Prep time: 5 minutes | Cook time: 10 minutes | Serves: 6

INGREDIENTS:

3 tablespoons olive oil
1 1/2 cup baby potatoes, cut in half
1 1/2 cup broccoli florets
3 cups cooked quinoa
Zest of 1 lemon
Sea salt and freshly ground pepper, to taste

DIRECTIONS:

1. Heat the olive oil in a large skillet over medium heat until shimmering.
2. Add the potatoes and cook for about 6 to 7 minutes, or until softened and golden brown. Add the broccoli and cook for about 3 minutes, or until tender.
3. Remove from the heat and add the quinoa and lemon zest. Season with salt and pepper to taste, then serve.
4. Enjoy!

NUTRITION:

calories: 205 | fat: 8g | protein: 5g | carbs: 27g | fiber: 3g | sodium: 158mg

684. Prosciutto with Beans

Prep time: 0 minutes | Cook time: 15 minutes | Serves: 6

INGREDIENTS:

18 oz pasta, cooked and drained Pepper and salt to taste
4 1/2 tbsp snipped fresh chives
3 cups arugula or watercress leaves, loosely packed
3/4 cup chicken broth, warm
1 1/2 tbsp Herbed garlic butter
3/4 cup shredded pecorino Toscano
3 oz prosciutto, cut into bite sizes 2 cups cherry tomatoes, halved
1 1/2 can of 19oz white kidney beans, rinsed and drained

DIRECTIONS:

1. Heat over medium low fire herbed garlic butter, cheese, prosciutto, tomatoes and beans in a big saucepan for 2 minutes.
2. Once mixture is simmering, stir constantly to melt cheese while gradually stirring in the broth.
3. Once cheese is fully melted and incorporated, add chives, arugula, pepper and salt.
4. Turn off the fire and toss in the cooked pasta. Serve and enjoy.
5. Enjoy!

NUTRITION:

calories: 452 | fat: 11.7g | protein: 30.64g | carbs: 57.9g | fiber: 0g | sodium: 0mg

685. Couscous with Asparagus

Prep time: 5 minutes | Cook time: 25 minutes | Serves: 4

INGREDIENTS:

1 pounds (680 g) asparagus spears, ends trimmed and stalks chopped into 1-inch pieces
2/3 garlic clove, minced
2/3 tablespoon extra-virgin olive oil
1/8 teaspoon freshly ground black pepper
1 1/8 cups water
2/3 (8-ounce / 227-g) box uncooked whole-wheat or regular Israeli couscous

(about 1 1/3 cups)
1/8 teaspoon kosher salt
2/3 cup garlic-and-herb goat cheese, at room temperature

DIRECTIONS:
1. Preheat the oven to 400°F | 200°C | Fan 180°C
2. In a large bowl, stir together the asparagus, garlic, oil, and pepper. Spread the asparagus on a large, rimmed baking sheet and roast for 10 minutes, stirring a few times. Remove the pan from the oven, and spoon the asparagus into a large serving bowl. Set aside.
3. While the asparagus is roasting, bring the water to a boil in a medium saucepan. Add the couscous and season with salt, stirring well.
4. Reduce the heat to medium-low. Cover and cook for 12 minutes, or until the water is absorbed.
5. Pour the hot couscous into the bowl with the asparagus. Add the goat cheese and mix thoroughly until completely melted.
6. Serve immediately.
7. Enjoy!

NUTRITION:
calories: 103 | fat: 2g | protein: 6g | carbs: 18g | fiber: 5g | sodium: 343mg

686. Bow Ties with Zucchini

Prep time: 10 minutes | Cook time: 32 minutes | Serves: 6

INGREDIENTS:

4 1/2 tablespoons extra-virgin olive oil
3 garlic cloves, minced
4 1/2 large or 4 medium zucchinis, diced
3/4 teaspoon freshly ground black pepper
1/3 teaspoon kosher or sea salt
3/4 cup 2% milk
1/3 teaspoon ground nutmeg
12 ounces (227 g) uncooked farfalle (bow ties) or other small pasta shape
3/4 cup grated Parmesan or Romano cheese
1 1/2 tablespoon freshly squeezed lemon juice

DIRECTIONS:
1. In a large skillet over medium heat, heat the oil. Add the garlic and cook for 1 minute, stirring frequently. Add the zucchini, pepper, and salt. Stir well, cover, and cook for 15 minutes, stirring once or twice.
2. In a small, microwave-safe bowl, warm the milk in the microwave on high for 30 seconds. Stir the milk and nutmeg into the skillet and cook uncovered for another 5 minutes, stirring occasionally.
3. While the zucchini is cooking, in a large stockpot, cook the pasta according to the package instructions.
4. Drain the pasta in a colander, saving about 2 tablespoons of pasta water. Add the pasta and pasta water to the skillet. Mix everything together and remove from the heat. Stir in the cheese and lemon juice and serve.
5. Enjoy!

NUTRITION:
calories: 190 | fat: 9g | protein: 7g | carbs: 20g | fiber: 2g | sodium: 475mg

687. Pasta with Parmesan

Prep time: 10 minutes | Cook time: 14 minutes | Serves: 6

INGREDIENTS:

12 ounces (227 g) uncooked penne
1 1/2 tablespoon extra-virgin olive oil
3 garlic cloves, minced
1/3 teaspoon crushed red pepper
3 cups chopped fresh flat-leaf (Italian) parsley, including stems
7 1/2 cups loosely packed baby spinach
1/3 teaspoon ground nutmeg
1/3 teaspoon freshly ground black pepper
1/3 teaspoon kosher or sea salt
1/3 cup Castelvetrano olives, pitted and sliced
1/3 cup grated Pecorino Romano or Parmesan cheese

DIRECTIONS:
1. In a large stockpot, cook the pasta according to the package instructions, but boil 1 minute less than instructed. Drain the pasta, and save ¼ cup of the cooking water.
2. While the pasta is cooking, in a large skillet over medium heat, heat the oil. Add the garlic and crushed red pepper, and cook for 30 seconds, stirring constantly. Add the parsley and cook for 1 minute, stirring constantly. Add the spinach, nutmeg, pepper, and salt, and cook for 3 minutes, stirring occasionally, until the spinach is wilted.
3. Add the pasta and the reserved ¼ cup pasta water to the skillet. Stir in the olives, and cook for about 2 minutes, until most of the pasta water has been absorbed. Remove from the heat, stir in the cheese, and serve.
4. Enjoy!

NUTRITION:
calories: 262 | fat: 3g | protein: 15g | carbs: 51g | fiber: 12g | sodium: 1180mg

688. Dinner Meaty Baked Penne

Prep time: 5 minutes | Cook time: 50 minutes | Serves: 6

INGREDIENTS:

3/4-pound (454 g) penne pasta
3/4-pound (454 g) ground beef
3/4 teaspoon salt
3/4 (25-ounce / 709-g) jar marinara sauce
3/4 (1-pound / 454-g) bag baby spinach, washed
2 1/4 cups shredded Mozzarella cheese, divided

DIRECTIONS:
1. Bring a large pot of salted water to a boil, add the penne, and cook for 7 minutes. Reserve 2 cups of the pasta water and drain the pasta.
2. Preheat oven to 350°F | 180°C | Fan 160°C
3. In a large saucepan over medium heat, cook the ground beef and salt. Brown the ground beef for about 5 minutes.
4. Stir in marinara sauce, and 2 cups of pasta water. Let simmer for 5 minutes.
5. Add a handful of spinach at a time into the sauce, and cook for another 3 minutes.
6. To assemble, in a 9-by-13-inch baking dish, add the pasta and pour the pasta sauce over it. Stir in 1½ cups of the Mozzarella cheese. Cover the dish with foil and bake for 20 minutes.
7. After 20 minutes, remove the foil, top with the rest of the Mozzarella, and bake for another 10 minutes. Serve warm.
8. Enjoy!

NUTRITION:
calories: 497 | fat: 17g | protein: 31g | carbs: 54g | fiber: 4g | sodium: 619mg

689. Easy Pasta with Pesto

Prep time: 10 minutes | Cook time: 8 minutes | Serves: 6

INGREDIENTS:

1 1/2-pound (454 g) spaghetti
6 cups fresh basil leaves, stems removed
4 1/2 cloves garlic
1 1/2 teaspoon salt
3/4 teaspoon freshly ground black
pepper
3/4 cup toasted pine nuts
1/3 cup lemon juice
3/4 cup grated Parmesan cheese
1 1/2 cup extra-virgin olive oil

DIRECTIONS:
1. Bring a large pot of salted water to a boil. Add the spaghetti to the pot and cook for 8 minutes.
2. In a food processor, place the remaining Shopping List ingredients, except for the olive oil, and pulse.
3. While the processor is running, slowly drizzle the olive oil through the top opening. Process until all the olive oil has been added.
4. Reserve ½ cup of the cooking liquid. Drain the pasta and put it into a large bowl. Add the pesto and cooking liquid to the bowl of pasta and toss everything together.
5. Serve immediately.
6. Enjoy!

NUTRITION:
calories: 1067 | fat: 72g | protein: 23g | carbs: 91g | fiber: 6g | sodium: 817mg

690. Chicken Rice

Prep time: 10 minutes | Cook time: 16 minutes | Serves: 6

INGREDIENTS:

1 1/3 lb. chicken breast, skinless, boneless, and cut into chunks
9 2/3 oz can cannellini beans 4 cups chicken broth
1 1/3 cups wild rice
2/3 tbsp Italian seasoning
2/3 small onion, chopped
2/3 tbsp garlic, chopped 1 tbsp olive oil
Pepper Salt

DIRECTIONS:
1. Add oil into the inner pot of instant pot and set the pot on sauté mode. Add garlic and onion and sauté for 2 minutes.
2. Add chicken and cook for 2 minutes. Add remaining Shopping List ingredients and stir well.
3. Seal pot with lid and cook on high for 12 minutes.
4. Once done, release pressure using quick release. Remove lid. Stir well and serve.
5. Enjoy!

NUTRITION:

calories: 399 | fat: 6.4g | protein: 31.6g | carbs: 53.4g | fiber: 6g | sodium: 817mg

691. Asparagus & Grape Tomato Pasta

Prep time: 10 minutes | Cook time: 25 minutes | Serves: 4

INGREDIENTS:

5 1/3 ounces (227 g) uncooked small pasta, like orecchiette (little ears) or farfalle (bow ties)
1 pounds (680 g) fresh asparagus, ends trimmed and stalks chopped into 1-inch pieces
1 cup grape tomato, halved
1 1/3 tablespoons extra-virgin olive oil
1/8 teaspoon freshly ground black pepper
1/8 teaspoon kosher or sea salt
1 1/3 cups fresh Mozzarella, drained and cut into bite-size pieces
1/3 cup torn fresh basil leaves
1 1/3 tablespoons balsamic vinegar

DIRECTIONS:

1. Preheat the oven to 400°F | 200°C | Fan 180°C
2. In a large stockpot, cook the pasta according to the package instructions. Drain, reserving about ¼ cup of the pasta water.
3. While the pasta is cooking, in a large bowl, toss the asparagus, tomatoes, oil, pepper, and salt together. Spread the mixture onto a large, rimmed baking sheet and bake for 15 minutes, stirring twice as it cooks.
4. Remove the vegetables from the oven, and add the cooked pasta to the baking sheet. Mix with a few tablespoons of pasta water to help the sauce become smoother and the saucy vegetables stick to the pasta.
5. Gently mix in the Mozzarella and basil. Drizzle with the balsamic vinegar. Serve from the baking sheet or pour the pasta into a large bowl.
6. If you want to make this dish ahead of time or to serve it cold, follow the recipe up to step 4, then refrigerate the pasta and vegetables. When you are ready to serve, follow step 5 either with the cold pasta or with warm pasta that's been gently reheated in a pot on the stove.
7. Enjoy!

NUTRITION:

calories: 147 | fat: 2g | protein: 16g | carbs: 17g | fiber: 4g | sodium: 420mg

692. Pasta With Pesto

Prep time: 10 minutes | Cook time: 10 minutes | Serves: 6

INGREDIENTS:

12 oz whole-grain pasta
1/2 cup mozzarella cheese, grated
1/2 cup pesto
7 1/2 oz fresh spinach
2 2/3 cup water
12 oz mushrooms, chopped
1 tbsp olive oil
Pepper Salt

DIRECTIONS:

1. Add oil into the inner pot of instant pot and set the pot on sauté mode.
2. Add mushrooms and sauté for 5 minutes.
3. Add water and pasta and stir well.
4. Seal pot with lid and cook on high for 5 minutes.
5. Once done, release pressure using quick release. Remove lid.
6. Stir in remaining Shopping List ingredients and serve.
7. Enjoy!

NUTRITION:

calories: 213 | fat: 17.3g | protein: 7.4g | carbs: 9.5g | fiber: 4g | sodium: 420mg

693. Shrimp Fettuccine

Prep time: 10 minutes | Cook time: 15 minutes | Serves: 6

INGREDIENTS:

12 ounces (227 g) fettuccine pasta
1/3 cup extra-virgin olive oil
4 1/2 tablespoons garlic, minced
1 1/2 pound (454 g) large shrimp, peeled and deveined
1/3 cup lemon juice
1 1/2 tablespoon lemon zest
3/4 teaspoon salt
3/4 teaspoon freshly ground black pepper

DIRECTIONS:

1. Bring a large pot of salted water to a boil. Add the fettuccine and cook for 8 minutes. Reserve ½ cup of the cooking liquid and drain the pasta.
2. In a large saucepan over medium heat, heat the olive oil. Add the garlic and sauté for 1 minute.
3. Add the shrimp to the saucepan and cook each side for 3 minutes. Remove the shrimp from the pan and set aside.
4. Add the remaining Shopping List ingredients to the saucepan. Stir in the cooking liquid. Add the pasta and toss together to evenly coat the pasta.
5. Transfer the pasta to a serving dish and serve topped with the cooked shrimp.
6. Enjoy!

NUTRITION:

calories: 485 | fat: 17g | protein: 33g | carbs: 50g | fiber: 4g | sodium: 407mg

694. Spaghetti with Pine Nuts and Cheese

Prep time: 10 minutes | Cook time: 11 minutes | Serves: 6

INGREDIENTS:

12 ounces (227 g) spaghetti
6 tablespoons almond butter
1 1/2 teaspoon freshly ground black pepper
3/4 cup pine nuts
1 1/2 cup fresh grated Parmesan cheese, divided

DIRECTIONS:

1. Bring a large pot of salted water to a boil. Add the pasta and cook for 8 minutes.
2. In a large saucepan over medium heat, combine the butter, black pepper, and pine nuts. Cook for 2 to 3 minutes, or until the pine nuts are lightly toasted.
3. Reserve ½ cup of the pasta water. Drain the pasta and place it into the pan with the pine nuts.
4. Add ¾ cup of the Parmesan cheese and the reserved pasta water to the pasta and toss everything together to evenly coat the pasta.
5. Transfer the pasta to a serving dish and top with the remaining ¼ cup of the Parmesan cheese. Serve immediately.
6. Enjoy!

NUTRITION:

calories: 542 | fat: 32g | protein: 20g | carbs: 46g | fiber: 2g | sodium: 552mg

695. Risotto with Parmesan Cheese

Prep time: 5 minutes | Cook time: 20 minutes | Serves: 4

INGREDIENTS:

2 2/3 cups low-sodium or no-salt-added vegetable broth
2/3 tablespoon extra-virgin olive oil
2/3 cup chopped yellow onion
1 1/3 cups uncooked pearl barley
1/3 cup dry white wine
2/3 cup freshly grated Parmesan cheese, divided
1/8 teaspoon kosher or sea salt
1/8 teaspoon freshly ground black pepper
Fresh chopped chives and lemon wedges, for serving (optional)

DIRECTIONS:

1. Pour the broth into a medium saucepan and bring to a simmer.
2. Heat the olive oil in a large stockpot over medium-high heat. Add the onion and cook for about 4 minutes, stirring occasionally.
3. Add the barley and cook for 2 minutes, stirring, or until the barley is toasted. Pour in the wine and cook for about 1 minute, or until most of the liquid evaporates. Add 1 cup of the warm broth into the pot and cook, stirring, for about 2 minutes, or until most of the liquid is absorbed.
4. Add the remaining broth, 1 cup at a time, cooking until each cup is absorbed (about 2 minutes each time) before adding the next. 5. The last addition of broth will take a bit longer to absorb, about 4 minutes.
6. Remove the pot from the heat, and stir in ½ cup of the cheese, and the salt and pepper.
7. Serve with the remaining ½ cup of the cheese on the side, along with the chives and lemon wedges (if desired).
8. Enjoy!

NUTRITION:

calories: 421 | fat: 11g | protein: 15g | carbs: 67g | fiber: 11g | sodium: 641mg

696. Freekeh Pilaf

Prep time: 10 minutes | Cook time: 10 minutes | Serves: 6

INGREDIENTS:

3 tablespoons extra-virgin olive oil, plus extra for drizzling
1 1/2 shallot, minced
2 1/4 teaspoons grated fresh ginger
1/3 teaspoon ground coriander
1/3 teaspoon ground cumin
Salt and pepper, to taste
2 2/3 cups water
2 1/4 cups cracked freekeh, rinsed
4 1/2 ounces (85 g) pitted dates, chopped
1/3 cup shelled pistachios, toasted and coarsely chopped
2 1/4 tablespoons lemon juice
1/3 cup chopped fresh mint

DIRECTIONS:

1. Set the Instant Pot to Sauté mode and heat the olive oil until shimmering.
2. Add the shallot, ginger, coriander, cumin, salt, and pepper to the pot and cook for about 2 minutes, or until the shallot is softened. 3.Stir in the water and freekeh.
4. Secure the lid. Select the Manual mode and set the cooking time for 4 minutes at High Pressure. Once cooking is complete, do a quick pressure release. Carefully open the lid.
5. Add the dates, pistachios and lemon juice and gently fluff the freekeh with a fork to combine. Season to taste with salt and pepper.
6. Transfer to a serving dish and sprinkle with the mint. Serve drizzled with extra olive oil.
7. Enjoy!

NUTRITION:

calories: 280| fat: 8g | protein: 8g | carbs: 46g | fiber: 9g | sodium: 200mg

697. Greek Rice

Prep time: 10 minutes | Cook time: 10 minutes | Serves: 4

INGREDIENTS:

1-3/4 cup brown rice, rinsed and drained
1/2 cup roasted red peppers, chopped
2/3 cup olives, chopped
2/3 tsp dried oregano
2/3 tsp Greek seasoning
1/2 cup vegetable broth 2 tbsp olive oil
Salt

DIRECTIONS:

1. Add oil into the inner pot of instant pot and set the pot on sauté mode.
2. Add rice and cook for 5 minutes.
3. Add remaining Shopping List ingredients except for red peppers and olives and stir well.
4. Seal pot with lid and cook on high for 5 minutes.
5. Once done, allow to release pressure naturally for 10 minutes then release remaining using quick release. Remove lid.
6. Add red peppers and olives and stir well. Serve when ready.
7. Enjoy!

NUTRITION:

calories: 285| fat: 9.1g | protein: 6g | carbs: 45.7g | fiber: 9g | sodium: 200mg

698. Quinoa Buffalo Bites

Prep time: 0 minutes | Cook time: 15 minutes | Serves: 6

INGREDIENTS:

3 cups cooked quinoa
1 1/2 cup shredded mozzarella
3/4 cup buffalo sauce
1/3 cup +1 Tbsp flour
1 1/2 egg
1/3 cup chopped cilantro 1 small onion, diced

DIRECTIONS:

1. Preheat oven to 350°F | 180°C | Fan 160°C
2. Mix all Shopping List ingredients in large bowl.
3. Press mixture into greased mini muffin tins.
4. Bake for approximately 15 minutes or until bites are golden.
5. Enjoy on its own or with blue cheese or ranch dip.
6. Enjoy!

NUTRITION:

calories: 212| fat: 3g | protein: 15.9g | carbs: 30.6g | fiber: 0g | sodium: 0mg

699. Bucatini-Puttanesca Style-

Prep time: 0 minutes | Cook time: 40 minutes | Serves: 6

INGREDIENTS:

1 1/2 tbsp capers, rinsed
3 tsp coarsely chopped fresh oregano
1 1/2 tsp finely chopped garlic
1/4 tsp salt
12-oz bucatini pasta
3 cups coarsely chopped canned no-salt-added whole peeled tomatoes with their juice
4 1/2 tbsp extra virgin olive oil, divided
6 anchovy fillets, chopped
12 black Kalamata olives, pitted and sliced into slivers

DIRECTIONS:

1. Cook bucatini pasta according to package instructions. Drain, keep warm, and set aside.
2. On medium heat, place a large nonstick saucepan and heat 2 tbsp oil.
3. Sauté anchovies until it starts to disintegrate.
4. Add garlic and sauté for 15 seconds.
5. Add tomatoes, sauté for 15 to 20 minutes or until no longer watery. Season with 1/8 tsp salt.
6. Add oregano, capers, and olives.
7. Add pasta, sautéing until heated through.
8. To serve, drizzle pasta with remaining olive oil.
9. Enjoy!

NUTRITION:

calories: 207| fat: 7g | protein: 5.1g | carbs: 31.1g | fiber: 0g | sodium: 0mg

700. Herb Rice

Prep time: 0 minutes | Cook time: 40 minutes | Serves: 6

INGREDIENTS:

1 1/2 cup brown rice, rinsed 1 tbsp olive oil
2 1/4 cups water
3/4 cup fresh mix herbs, chopped 1 tsp salt

DIRECTIONS:

1. Add all Shopping List ingredients into the inner pot of instant pot and stir well.
2. Seal pot with lid and cook on high for 4 minutes.
3. Once done, allow to release pressure naturally for 10 minutes then release remaining using quick release. Remove lid.
4. Stir well and serve
5. Enjoy!

NUTRITION:

calories: 264| fat: 9.9g | protein: 7.3g | carbs: 36.7g | fiber: 0g | sodium: 0mg

701. Bulgur Salad

Prep time: 10 minutes | Cook time: 1 minute | Serves: 4

INGREDIENTS:

1 cup bulgur wheat
1/2 cup fresh parsley, chopped 1 tbsp fresh mint, chopped
2/3 cup feta cheese, crumbled 2 tbsp fresh lemon juice
4 tbsp olives, chopped 1/4 cup olive oil
1 cup tomatoes, chopped 1/3 cup cucumber, chopped
1 cup water
Salt

DIRECTIONS:

1. Add the bulgur wheat, water, and salt into the instant pot.
2. Seal pot with lid and cook on high for 1 minute.
3. Once done, release pressure using quick release. Remove lid.
4. Transfer bulgur wheat to the mixing bowl. Add remaining Shopping List ingredients to the bowl
and mix well. Serve when ready.
5. Enjoy!

NUTRITION:

calories: 430| fat: 32.2g | protein: 8.9g | carbs: 31.5g | fiber: 0g | sodium: 0mg

702. Pesto Pasta and Shrimps

Prep time: 0 minutes | Cook time: 15 minutes | Serves: 6

INGREDIENTS:

1/3 cup pesto, divided
1/3 cup shaved Parmesan Cheese
2 lbs. large shrimp, peeled and deveined
1 1/2 cup halved grape tomatoes
4-oz angel hair pasta, cooked, rinsed and drained

DIRECTIONS:

1. On medium high heat, place a nonstick large fry pan and grease with cooking spray.
2. Add tomatoes, pesto and shrimp. Cook for 15 minutes or until shrimps are opaque, while covered.
3. Stir in cooked pasta and cook until heated through.
4. Transfer to a serving plate and garnish with Parmesan cheese.
5. Enjoy!

NUTRITION:

calories: 319| fat: 11g | protein: 31.4g | carbs: 23.6g | fiber: 0g | sodium: 0mg

703. Herb Polenta

Prep time: 10 minutes | Cook time: 12 minutes | Serves: 4

INGREDIENTS:

2/3 cup polenta
1/8 tsp nutmeg
2 tbsp fresh parsley, chopped
1/8 cup milk
1/3 cup parmesan cheese, grated
2 2/3 cups vegetable broth
1 1/3 tsp thyme, chopped
1 1/3 tsp rosemary, chopped 2 tsp sage, chopped
2/3 small onion, chopped 2 tbsp olive oil
Salt

DIRECTIONS:

1. Add oil into the inner pot of instant pot and set the pot on sauté mode.
2. Add onion and herbs and sauté for 4 minutes.
3. Add polenta, broth, and salt and stir well.
4. Seal pot with lid and cook on high for 8 minutes.
5. Once done, allow to release pressure naturally. Remove lid.
6. Stir in remaining Shopping List ingredients and serve.
7. Enjoy!

NUTRITION:

calories: 196 | fat: 7.8g | protein: 8.5g | carbs: 23.5g | fiber: 0g | sodium: 0mg

704. Quinoa and Three Beans Recipe

Prep time: 0 minutes | Cook time: 35 minutes | Serves: 6

INGREDIENTS:

3/4 cup grape tomatoes, sliced in half
3/4 cup quinoa
3/4 cup seedless cucumber, chopped
3/4 red bell pepper, seeds removed and chopped
3/4 tablespoon balsamic vinegar
3/4 yellow bell pepper, seeds removed and chopped
1/2-pound green beans, trimmed and snapped into 2-inch pieces
1/4 cup pitted kalamata olives, cut in half
1/4 cup chopped fresh basil
1/4 cup diced red onion
1/4 cup feta cheese crumbles 1/4 cup olive oil
1/4 teaspoon dried basil
1/4 teaspoon dried oregano
11 1/4 ounces garbanzo beans, drained and rinsed 15 ounces white beans, drained and rinsed
1 1/2 cups water
1 1/2 garlic cloves, smashed
kosher salt and freshly ground black pepper to taste

DIRECTIONS:

1. Bring water and quinoa to a boil in a medium saucepan. Cover, reduce heat to low, and cook until quinoa is tender, around 15 minutes.
2. Remove from heat and let stand for 5 minutes, covered.
3. Remove lid and fluff with a fork. Transfer to a large salad bowl.
4. Meanwhile, bring a large pot of salted water to a boil and blanch the green beans for two minutes. Drain and place in a bowl of ice water. Drain well.
5. Add the fresh basil, olives, feta cheese, red onion, tomatoes, cucumbers, peppers, white beans, garbanzo beans, and green beans in bowl of quinoa.
6. In a small bowl, whisk together the pepper, salt, oregano, dried basil, balsamic, and olive oil. Pour dressing over the salad and gently toss salad until coated with dressing.
7. Season with additional salt and pepper if needed. Serve when ready.
8. Enjoy!

NUTRITION:

calories: 249 | fat: 10g | protein: 8g | carbs: 31g | fiber: 0g | sodium: 0mg

705. Raisins, Nuts and Beef on Hashweh Rice

Prep time: 0 minutes | Cook time: 50 minutes | Serves: 6

INGREDIENTS:

1/3 cup dark raisins, soaked in 2 cups water for an hour
1/4 cup slivered almonds, toasted and soaked in 2 cups water overnight
1/4 cup pine nuts, toasted and soaked in 2 cups water overnight
1/3 cup fresh parsley leaves, roughly chopped
Pepper and salt to taste
1/2 tsp ground cinnamon, divided
1/2 tsp cloves, divided
3/4 tsp garlic powder
1 1/3 tsp allspice, divided
3/4 lb. lean ground beef or lean ground lamb
3/4 small red onion, finely chopped
Olive oil
1/3 cups medium grain rice

DIRECTIONS:

1. For 15 to 20 minutes, soak rice in cold water. You will know that soaking is enough when you can snap a grain of rice easily between your thumb and index finger. Once soaking is done, drain rice well.
2. Meanwhile, drain pine nuts, almonds and raisins for at least a minute and transfer to one bowl. Set aside.
3. On a heavy cooking pot on medium high heat, heat 1 tbsp olive oil.
4. Once oil is hot, add red onions. Sauté for a minute before adding ground meat and sauté for another minute.
5. Season ground meat with pepper, salt, ½ tsp ground cinnamon, ½ tsp ground cloves, 1 tsp garlic powder, and 1 ¼ tsp allspice.
6. Sauté ground meat for 10 minutes or until browned and cooked fully. Drain fat.
7. In same pot with cooked ground meat, add rice on top of meat.
8. Season with a bit of pepper and salt. Add remaining cinnamon, ground cloves, and allspice. Do not mix.
9. Add 1 tbsp olive oil and 2 ½ cups of water. Bring to a boil and once boiling, lower fire to a simmer. Cook while covered until liquid is fully absorbed, around 20 to 25 minutes.
10. Turn of fire.
11. To serve, place a large serving platter that fully covers the mouth of the pot. Place platter upside down on mouth of pot, and invert pot. The inside of the pot should now rest on the platter with the rice on bottom of plate and ground meat on top of it.
12. Garnish the top of the meat with raisins, almonds, pine nuts, and parsley. Serve when ready.
13. Enjoy!

NUTRITION:

calories: 357 | fat: 15.9g | protein: 16.7g | carbs: 39g | fiber: 0g | sodium: 0mg

706. Shrimp Paella Made with Quinoa

Prep time: 0 minutes | Cook time: 40 minutes | Serves: 6

INGREDIENTS:

3/4 lb. large shrimp, peeled, deveined and thawed
3/4 tsp seafood seasoning
3/4 cup frozen green peas
3/4 red bell pepper, cored, seeded & membrane removed, sliced into 1/2-inch strips
1/2 cup sliced sun-dried tomatoes, packed in olive oil Salt to taste
1/2 tsp black pepper
1/2 tsp Spanish paprika
1/2 tsp saffron threads (optional turmeric) 1 bay leaf
1/4 tsp crushed red pepper flakes
2 1/2 cups chicken broth, fat free, low sodium
1 1/4 cups dry quinoa, rinse well
1 3/4 tbsp olive oil
1 3/4 cloves garlic, minced
3/4 yellow onion, diced

DIRECTIONS:

1. Season shrimp with seafood seasoning and a pinch of salt. Toss to mix well and refrigerate until ready to use.
2. Prepare and wash quinoa. Set aside.
3. On medium low heat, place a large nonstick skillet and heat oil. Add onions and for 5 minutes sauté until soft and tender.
4. Add paprika, saffron (or turmeric), bay leaves, red pepper flakes, chicken broth and quinoa. Season with salt and pepper.
5. Cover skillet and bring to a boil. Once boiling, lower fire to a simmer and cook until all liquid is absorbed, around ten minutes.
6. Add shrimp, peas and sun-dried tomatoes. For 5 minutes, cover and cook.
7. Once done, turn off fire and for ten minutes allow paella to set while still covered.
8. To serve, remove bay leaf and enjoy with a squeeze of lemon if desired.
9. Enjoy!

NUTRITION:

calories: 324 | fat: 11.6g | protein: 22g | carbs: 33g | fiber: 0g | sodium: 0mg

707. Pasta with Fresh Tomato

Prep time: 0 minutes | Cook time: 20 minutes | Serves: 6

INGREDIENTS:

1/3 cup torn fresh basil leaves 1/8 tsp black pepper
1/3 tsp salt
9 tbsp grated fresh pecorino Romano cheese, divided
2 lbs. tomatoes, chopped
3 tsp minced garlic
1 1/2 cup vertically sliced onions
3 tsp olive oil
12 oz sweet Italian sausage
12 oz uncooked penne, cooked and drained

DIRECTIONS:

1. On medium high heat, place a nonstick fry pan with oil and cook for five minutes onion and sausage. Stir
constantly to break sausage into pieces.
2. Stir in garlic and continue cooking for two minutes more.
3. Add tomatoes and cook for another two minutes.
4. Remove pan from fire, season with pepper and salt. Mix well.
5. Stir in 2 tbsp cheese and pasta. Toss well.
6. Transfer to a serving dish, garnish with basil and remaining cheese before serving.
7. Enjoy!

NUTRITION:

calories: 376| fat: 11g | protein: 17g | carbs: 50g | fiber: 0g | sodium: 0mg

708. Linguine with Tomato Sauce
Prep time: 0 minutes | Cook time: 12 minutes | Serves: 6

INGREDIENTS:

- 1/3 cup grated low-fat Parmesan cheese
- 3/4 cup loosely packed fresh basil leaves, torn 12 oz whole wheat linguine
- 3 cups loosely packed baby arugula
- 3 green onions, green parts only, sliced thinly
- 3 tbsp balsamic vinegar
- 3 tbsp extra virgin olive oil
- 3 large vine-ripened tomatoes
- 4 1/2 oz low-fat Brie cheese, cubed, rind removed and discarded 3 tbsp toasted pine nuts
- Pepper and salt to taste

DIRECTIONS:

1. Toss together pepper, salt, vinegar, oil, onions, Parmesan, basil, arugula, Brie and tomatoes in a large bowl and set aside.
2. Cook linguine following package instructions. Reserve 1 cup of pasta cooking water after linguine is cooked. Drain and discard the rest of the pasta. Do not run under cold water, instead immediately add into bowl of salad. Let it stand for a minute without mixing.
3. Add ¼ cup of reserved pasta water into bowl to make a creamy sauce. Add more pasta water if desired. Toss to mix well.
4. Enjoy!

NUTRITION:

calories: 274| fat: 10g | protein: 47g | carbs: 30g | fiber: 0g | sodium: 0mg

709. Red Quinoa Peach Porridge
Prep time: 10 minutes | Cook time: 12 minutes | Serves: 4

INGREDIENTS:

- 1 cup old fashioned rolled oats
- 1 cup red quinoa
- 2 cup milk
- 2 cups water
- 8 peaches, peeled and sliced

DIRECTIONS:

1. In a small saucepan, place the peaches and quinoa. Add water and cook for 30 minutes.
2. Add the oatmeal and milk last and cook until the oats become tender.
3. Stir occasionally to avoid the porridge sticking on the bottom of the pan.
4. Enjoy!

NUTRITION:

calories: 456| fat: 9g | protein: 16g | carbs: 77g | fiber: 0g | sodium: 0mg

710. Red Wine Risotto
Prep time: 10 minutes | Cook time: 25 minutes | Serves: 4

INGREDIENTS:

- Pepper to taste
- 1/2 cup finely shredded Parmigiana-Reggiano cheese, divided
- 1 tsp tomato paste
- 1 cup dry red wine
- 1/8 tsp salt
- 3/4 cups Italian 'risotto' rice 2 cloves garlic, minced
- 1/2 medium onion, freshly chopped 2 tbsp extra-virgin olive oil
- 2 1/4 cups reduced sodium beef broth

DIRECTIONS:

1. On medium high heat, bring to a simmer broth in a medium fry pan. Lower fire so broth is steaming but not simmering.
2. On medium low heat, place a Dutch oven and heat oil.
3. Sauté onions for 5 minutes. Add garlic and cook for 2 minutes.
4. Add rice, mix well, and season with salt.
5. Into rice, add a generous splash of wine and ½ cup of broth.
6. Lower fire to a gentle simmer, cook until liquid is fully absorbed while stirring rice every once in a while.
7. Add another splash of wine and ½ cup of broth. Stirring once in a while.
8. Add tomato paste and stir to mix well.
9. Continue cooking and adding wine and broth until broth is used up.
10. Once done cooking, turn off fire and stir in pepper and ¾ cup cheese.
11. To serve, sprinkle with remaining cheese.
12. Enjoy!

NUTRITION:

calories: 231| fat: 9g | protein: 7g | carbs: 33g | fiber: 8g | sodium: 100mg

711. Rice & Salad
Prep time: 10 minutes | Cook time: 50 minutes | Serves: 6

INGREDIENTS:

- 3 cup basmati rice salt
- 3/4 Tablespoons lemon juice
- 1 1/2 teaspoon grated orange zest
- 3 Tablespoons fresh orange juice
- 1/3 cup olive oil
- 3/4 teaspoon cinnamon
- Salt and pepper to taste
- 6 chopped green onions 1/2 cup dried currants
- 1 1/8 cup shelled pistachios or almonds
- 1/3 cup chopped fresh parsley

DIRECTIONS:

1. Place a nonstick pot on medium high heat and add rice. Toast rice until opaque and starts to smell, around 10 minutes.
2. Add 4 quarts of boiling water to pot and 2 tsp salt. Boil until tender, around 8 minutes uncovered.
3. Drain the rice and spread out on a lined cookie sheet to cool completely.
4. In a large salad bowl, whisk well the oil, juices and spices. Add salt and pepper to taste.
5. Add half of the green onions, half of parsley, currants, and nuts.
6. Toss with the cooled rice and let stand for at least 20 minutes.
7. If needed adjust seasoning with pepper and salt.
8. Garnish with remaining parsley and green onions.
9. Enjoy!

NUTRITION:

calories: 450| fat: 24g | protein: 9g | carbs: 50g | fiber: 8g | sodium: 100mg

712. Stuffed Tomatoes with Chili
Prep time: 10 minutes | Cook time: 55 minutes | Serves: 4

INGREDIENTS:

- 2 2/3 oz Colby-Jack shredded cheese
- 1/8 cup water
- 2/3 cup uncooked quinoa
- 4 large ripe tomatoes
- 1/8 tsp freshly ground black pepper
- 1/2 tsp ground cumin
- 2/3 tsp salt, divided
- 2/3 tbsp fresh lime juice 1 tbsp olive oil
- 1 1/3 tbsp chopped fresh oregano 1 cup chopped onion
- 1 1/3 cups fresh corn kernels
- 1 1/3 poblano chilies

DIRECTIONS:

1. Preheat broiler to high.
2. Slice lengthwise the chilies and press on a baking sheet lined with foil. Broil for 8 minutes. Remove from oven and let cool for 10 minutes. Peel the chilies and chop coarsely and place in medium sized bowl.
2. Place onion and corn in baking sheet and broil for ten minutes. Stir two times while broiling. Remove from oven and mix in with chopped chilies.
3. Add black pepper, cumin, ¼ tsp salt, lime juice, oil and oregano. Mix well.
4. Cut off the tops of tomatoes and set aside. Leave the tomato shell intact as you scoop out the tomato pulp.
5. Drain tomato pulp as you press down with a spoon. Reserve 1¼ cups of tomato pulp liquid and discard the rest. Invert the tomato shells on a wire rack for 30 mins and then wipe the insides dry with a paper towel.
6. Season with ½ tsp salt the tomato pulp.
7. On a sieve over a bowl, place quinoa. Add water until it covers quinoa. Rub quinoa grains for 30 seconds together with hands; rinse and drain. Repeat this procedure two times and drain well at the end.
8. In medium saucepan bring to a boil remaining salt, ¼ cup water, quinoa and tomato liquid.
9. Once boiling, reduce heat and simmer for 15 minutes or until liquid is fully absorbed. Remove from heat and fluff quinoa with fork. Transfer and mix well the quinoa with the corn mixture.
10. Spoon ¾ cup of the quinoa-corn mixture into the tomato shells, top with cheese and cover with the tomato top. Bake in a preheated 350°F oven for 15 minutes and then broil high for another 1.5 minutes.
11. Enjoy!

NUTRITION:

calories: 276| fat: 14g | protein: 13g | carbs: 46g | fiber: 8g | sodium: 100mg

713. Quinoa & Black Bean
Prep time: 10 minutes | Cook time: 60 minutes | Serves: 4

INGREDIENTS:

- 2 sweet potatoes
- 1/4 onion, diced
- 1/2 garlic glove, crushed and diced
- 1/4 large bell pepper diced (about 2/3
- cups) Handful of diced cilantros
- 1/4 cup cooked quinoa
- 1/4 cup black beans
- 1/2 tbsp olive oil

1/2 tbsp chili powder
1/4 tbsp cumin
1/4 tbsp paprika
1/4 tbsp oregano
1 tbsp lime juice
1 tbsp honey Sprinkle salt
1/2 cup shredded cheddar cheese

DIRECTIONS:

1. Preheat oven to 400°F | 200°C | Fan 180°C.
2. Wash and scrub outside of potatoes. Poke with fork a few times and then place on parchment paper on cookie sheet. Bake for 40-45 minutes or until it is cooked.
3. While potatoes are baking, sauté onions, garlic, olive oil and spices in a pan on the stove until onions are translucent and soft.
4. In the last 10 minutes while the potatoes are cooking, in a large bowl combine the onion mixture with the beans, quinoa, honey, lime juice, cilantro and ½ cup cheese. Mix well.
5. When potatoes are cooked, remove from oven and let cool slightly. When cool to touch, cut in half and scoop out most of the insides. Leave a thin ring of potato so that it will hold its shape. You can save the sweet potato guts for another recipe, such as my veggie burgers.
6. Fill with bean and quinoa mixture. Top with remaining cheddar cheese.
7. (If making this a freezer meal, stop here. Individually wrap potato skins in plastic wrap and place on flat surface to freeze. Once frozen, place all potatoes in large zip lock container or Tupperware.) Return to oven for an additional 10 minutes or until cheese is melted.
8. Enjoy!

NUTRITION:

calories: 243 | fat: 8g | protein: 9g | carbs: 37g | fiber: 8g | sodium: 100mg

714. Ricotta and Spinach Ravioli

Prep time: 10 minutes | Cook time: 15 minutes | Serves: 4

INGREDIENTS:

2 cup chicken stock
2 cup frozen spinach, thawed 1 batch pasta dough
Shopping List Filling
6 tbsp heavy cream
2 cup ricotta
3 1/2 cups baby spinach
2 small onions, finely chopped
4 tbsp butter

DIRECTIONS:

1. Create the filling: In a fry pan, sauté onion and butter around five minutes. Add the baby spinach leaves and continue simmering for another four minutes. Remove from heat, drain liquid and mince the onion and leaves. Then combine with 2 tbsp cream and the ricotta ensuring that it is well combined. Add pepper and salt to taste.
2. With your pasta dough, divide it into four balls. Roll out one ball to ¼ inch thick rectangular spread. Cut a 1½ inch by 3-inch rectangles. Place filling on the middle of the rectangles, around 1 tablespoonful and brush filling with cold water. Fold the rectangles in half, ensuring that no air is trapped within and seal using a cookie cutter. Use up all the filling.
3. Create Pasta Sauce: Until smooth, puree chicken stock and spinach. Pour into heated fry pan and for two minutes cook it. Add 1 tbsp cream and season with pepper and salt. Continue cooking for a minute and turn of fire.
4. Cook the raviolis by submerging in a boiling pot of water with salt. Cook until al dente then drains. Then quickly transfer the cooked ravioli into the fry pan of pasta sauce, toss to mix and serve.
5. Enjoy!

NUTRITION:

calories: 443 | fat: 36g | protein: 18g | carbs: 12g | fiber: 8g | sodium: 100mg

715. Seafood and Veggie Pasta

Prep time: 10 minutes | Cook time: 20 minutes | Serves: 6

INGREDIENTS:

1/3 tsp pepper
1/3 tsp salt
1 1/2 lb raw shelled shrimp
1 1/2 lemon, cut into wedges
1 1/2 tbsp butter
3 tbsp olive oil
5-oz cans chopped clams, drained
(reserve 2 tbsp clam juice)
3 tbsp dry white wine
6 cloves garlic, minced
6 cups zucchini, spiralled (use a veggie spiralizer)
6 tbsp Parmesan Cheese
Chopped fresh parsley to garnish

DIRECTIONS:

1. Ready the zucchini and spiralize with a veggie spiralizer. Arrange 1 cup of zucchini noodle per bowl, for a total of 4 bowls.
2. On medium heat, place a large nonstick saucepan and heat oil and butter.
3. For a minute, sauté garlic. Add shrimp and cook for 3 minutes until opaque or cooked.
4. Add white wine, reserved clam juice and clams. Bring to a simmer and continue simmering for 2 minutes or until half of liquid has evaporated. Stir constantly.
5. Season with pepper and salt. And if needed add more to taste.
6. Remove from fire and evenly distribute seafood sauce to 4 bowls.
7. Top with a tablespoonful of Parmesan cheese per bowl, serve and enjoy.
8. Enjoy!

NUTRITION:

calories: 324 | fat: 11g | protein: 43g | carbs: 12g | fiber: 8g | sodium: 100mg

716. Seafood Paella with Couscous

Prep time: 10 minutes | Cook time: 15 minutes | Serves: 6

INGREDIENTS:

3/4 cup whole wheat couscous
6 oz small shrimp, peeled and deveined
6 oz bay scallops, tough muscle removed
1/3 cup vegetable broth
1 1/2 cup freshly diced tomatoes and juice Pinch of crumbled saffron threads
1/3 tsp freshly ground pepper
1/3 tsp salt
3/4 tsp fennel seed
3/4 tsp dried thyme
1 1/2 clove garlic, minced
1 1/2 medium onion, chopped
3 tsp extra virgin olive oil

DIRECTIONS:

1. Put on medium fire a large saucepan and add oil. Stir in the onion and sauté for three minutes before adding: saffron, pepper, salt, fennel seed, thyme, and garlic. Continue to sauté for another minute.
2. Then add the broth and tomatoes and let boil. Once boiling, reduce the fire, cover and continue to cook for another 2 minutes.
3. Add the scallops and increase heat to medium and stir occasionally and cook for 2 minutes. Add the shrimp and wait for 2 minutes more before adding the couscous. Then remove from heat, cover and set aside for five minutes before carefully mixing.
4. Enjoy!

NUTRITION:

calories: 117 | fat: 11g | protein: 11g | carbs: 12g | fiber: 8g | sodium: 100mg

717. Shrimp, Lemon and Basil Pasta

Prep time: 10 minutes | Cook time: 25 minutes | Serves: 6

INGREDIENTS:

3 cups baby spinach
3/4 tsp salt
3 tbsp fresh lemon juice
3 tbsp extra virgin olive oil
4 1/2 tbsp drained capers
1/3 cup chopped fresh basil
1 1/2 lb. peeled and deveined large shrimp
12 oz uncooked spaghetti
4 1/2 quarts water

DIRECTIONS:

1. In a pot, bring to boil 3 quarts water. Add the pasta and allow to boil for another eight minutes before adding the shrimp and boiling for another three minutes or until pasta is cooked.
2. Drain the pasta and transfer to a bowl. Add salt, lemon juice, olive oil, capers and basil while mixing well.
3. To serve, place baby spinach on plate around ½ cup and topped with ½ cup of pasta.
4. Enjoy!

NUTRITION:

calories: 151 | fat: 7g | protein: 4g | carbs: 18g | fiber: 8g | sodium: 100mg

718. Spaghetti in Avocado Sauce

Prep time: 10 minutes | Cook time: 30 minutes | Serves: 4

INGREDIENTS:

Freshly ground black pepper Zest and juice of 1 lemon
2/3 avocado, pitted and peeled 1-pound spaghetti
Salt
2/3 tbsp Olive oil
5 1/3 oz small shrimp, shelled and deveined
1/8 cup dry white wine
2/3 large onion, finely sliced

DIRECTIONS:

1. Let a big pot of water boil. Once boiling, add the spaghetti or pasta and cook following package instructions until al dente. Drain and set aside.
2. In a large fry pan, over medium heat, sauté wine and onions for ten minutes or until onions are translucent and soft.
3. Add the shrimp into the fry pan and increase heat to high while constantly

sautéing until shrimp is cooked around 5 minutes. 4.Turn the heat off. Season with salt and add the oil right away. Then quickly toss in the cooked pasta, mix well.
5.In a blender, until smooth, puree the lemon juice and avocado. Pour into the fry pan of pasta, combine well. Garnish with pepper and lemon zest then serve.
6.Enjoy!

NUTRITION:

calories: 206 | fat: 7g | protein: 10g | carbs: 26g | fiber: 8g | sodium: 100mg

719. Shrimp Pasta

Prep time: 10 minutes | Cook time: 10 minutes | Serves: 4

INGREDIENTS:

8 oz pasta, cooked and drained	1/8 tsp crushed red pepper 6 cloves garlic, minced
2/3 cup finely shredded Parmesan Cheese	1/4 cup finely chopped onion
1/8 cup snipped fresh basil	1 1/3 tbsp olive oil
1/3 cup whipping cream	1/8 cup butter
1/3 cup dry white wine	1 lbs. fresh, peeled, deveined, rinsed and drained medium shrimps
2/3 12oz jar roasted red sweet peppers, drained and chopped	

DIRECTIONS:

1.On medium high heat, heat butter in a big fry pan and add garlic and onions. Stir fry until onions are soft, around 2 minutes. Add crushed red pepper and shrimps, sauté for another 2 minutes before adding wine and roasted peppers.
2.Allow mixture to boil before lowering heat to low and for 2 minutes, let the mixture simmer uncovered. Stirring occasionally, add cream once shrimp is cooked and simmer for a minute.
3.Add basil and remove from fire. Toss in the pasta and mix gently. Transfer to serving plates and top with cheese.
4.Enjoy!

NUTRITION:

calories: 418 | fat: 18g | protein: 37g | carbs: 26g | fiber: 8g | sodium: 100mg

720. Squash and Eggplant Casserole

Prep time: 10 minutes | Cook time: 45 minutes | Serves: 4

INGREDIENTS:

1 cup dry white wine	Salt and pepper to taste
2 eggplants, halved and cut to 1-inch slices	Polenta Ingredients:
2 large onions, cut into wedges	1/2 cup parmesan cheese, grated
2 red bell pepper, seeded and cut to julienned strips	2 cup instant polenta
2 small butternut squash, cut into 1-inch slices	4 tbsp fresh oregano, chopped
4 tbsp olive oil	Topping Shopping List
24 baby corn	2 garlic cloves, chopped
2 cups low sodium vegetable broth	4 tbsp slivered almonds
	10 tbsp parsley, chopped Grated zest of 1 lemon

DIRECTIONS:

1. Preheat oven to 350°F | 180°C | Fan 160°C.
2.In a casserole, heat the oil and add the onion wedges and baby corn. Sauté over medium high heat for 5 minutes. Stir occasionally to prevent the onions and baby corn from sticking to the bottom of the pan.
3.Add the butternut squash to the casserole and toss the vegetables. Add the eggplants and the red pepper.
4.Cover the vegetables and cook over low to medium heat.
5.Cook for about 10 minutes before adding the wine. Let the wine sizzle before stirring in the broth. Bring to a boil and cook in the oven for 30 minutes.
6.While the casserole is cooking inside the oven, make the topping by spreading the slivered almonds on a baking tray and toasting under the grill until they are lightly browned.
7.Place the toasted almonds in a small bowl and mix the remaining Shopping List ingredients for the toppings.
8.Prepare the polenta. In a large saucepan, bring 3 cups of water to boil over high heat.
9.Add the polenta and continue whisking until it absorbs all the water.
10.Reduce the heat to medium until the polenta is thick. Add the parmesan cheese and oregano.
11.Serve the polenta on plates and add the casserole on top. Sprinkle the toppings on top.
12.Enjoy!

NUTRITION:

calories: 579 | fat: 19g | protein: 22g | carbs: 79g | fiber: 8g | sodium: 100mg

721. Simple Penne Anti-Pasto

Prep time: 10 minutes | Cook time: 15 minutes | Serves: 6

INGREDIENTS:

1/3 cup pine nuts, toasted	dried tomato halves packed in oil 3 oz chopped prosciutto
3/4 cup grated Parmigiano-Reggiano cheese, divided 8oz penne pasta, cooked and drained	1/2 cup pesto
1 1/2 6oz jar drained, sliced, marinated and quartered artichoke hearts	3/4 cup pitted and chopped Kalamata olives
1 1/2 7 oz jar drained and chopped sun-	1 1/2 medium red bell pepper

DIRECTIONS:

1.Slice bell pepper; discard membranes, seeds and stem. On a foil lined baking sheet, place bell pepper halves, press down by hand and broil in oven for 8 minutes. Remove from oven, put in a sealed bag for 5 minutes before peeling and chopping.
2.Place chopped bell pepper in a bowl and mix in artichokes, tomatoes, prosciutto, pesto and olives.
3.Toss in ¼ cup cheese and pasta. Transfer to a serving dish and garnish with ¼ cup cheese and pine nuts.
4.Enjoy!

NUTRITION:

calories: 606 | fat: 27g | protein: 27g | carbs: 70g | fiber: 8g | sodium: 100mg

722. Lasagne Rolls

Prep time: 10 minutes | Cook time: 20 minutes | Serves: 4

INGREDIENTS:

1/8 tsp crushed red pepper	sauce
1/8 tsp salt	2/3 tbsp extra virgin olive oil
1/3 cup shredded mozzarella cheese	8 whole wheat lasagne noodles 2 tbsp Kalamata olives, chopped 3 cloves minced garlic
1/3 cups parmesan cheese, shredded 1 14-oz package tofu, cubed	
2/3 25-oz can of low-sodium marinara	2 cups spinach, chopped

DIRECTIONS:

1.Put enough water on a large pot and cook the lasagne noodles according to package instructions. Drain, rinse and set aside until ready to use.
2.In a large skillet, sauté garlic over medium heat for 20 seconds. Add the tofu and spinach and cook until the spinach wilts. 3.Transfer this mixture in a bowl and add parmesan olives, salt, red pepper and 2/3 cup of the marinara sauce.
4.In a pan, spread a cup of marinara sauce on the bottom. To make the rolls, place noodle on a surface and spread ¼ cup of the tofu filling. Roll up and place it on the pan with the marinara sauce. Do this procedure until all lasagne noodles are rolled.
5.Place the pan over high heat and bring to a simmer. Reduce the heat to medium and let it cook for 3 more minutes. Sprinkle mozzarella cheese and let the cheese melt for 2 minutes. Serve hot.
6.Enjoy!

NUTRITION:

calories: 304 | fat: 19g | protein: 23g | carbs: 39g | fiber: 8g | sodium: 100mg

723. Mushroom Bolognese

Prep time: 10 minutes | Cook time: 65 minutes | Serves: 4

INGREDIENTS:

1/8 cup chopped fresh parsley	5 1/3 cups finely chopped cremini mushrooms
1 1/3 oz Parmigiano-Reggiano cheese, grated	1/3 lb. ground pork
2/3 tbsp kosher salt	1/3 tsp freshly ground black pepper, divided
10-oz whole wheat spaghetti, cooked and drained	1/2 tsp kosher salt, divided 2 1/2 cups chopped onion
1/8 cup milk	
14-oz can whole peeled tomatoes	2/3 tbsp olive oil
1/3 cup white wine	2/3 cup boiling water
2/3 tbsp tomato paste	1 1/3 1/2-oz dried porcini mushrooms
2/3 tbsp minced garlic	

DIRECTIONS:

1. Let porcini stand in a boiling bowl of water for 20 minutes, drain (reserve liquid), rinse and chop. Set aside.
2. On medium high heat, place a Dutch oven with olive oil and cook pork, ¼ tsp pepper, ¼ tsp salt and onions for 10 minutes. Constantly mix to break ground pork pieces.
3. Stir in ¼ tsp pepper, ¼ tsp salt, garlic and cremini mushrooms. Continue cooking until liquid has evaporated, around 15 minutes.
4. Stirring constantly, add porcini and sauté for a minute.
5. Stir in wine, porcini liquid, tomatoes and tomato paste. Let it simmer for 40 minutes. Stir occasionally. Pour milk and cook for another two minutes before removing from heat.
6. Stir in pasta and transfer to a serving dish. Garnish with parsley and cheese before serving.
7. Enjoy!

NUTRITION:

calories: 358 | fat: 15g | protein: 21g | carbs: 32g | fiber: 8g | sodium: 100mg

724. Spanish Rice

Prep time: 10 minutes | Cook time: 20 minutes | Serves: 6

INGREDIENTS:

- 3 tablespoons extra-virgin olive oil
- 1 1/2 medium onion, finely chopped
- 1 1/2 large tomato, finely diced
- 3 tablespoons tomato paste
- 1 1/2 teaspoon smoked paprika
- 1 1/2 teaspoon salt
- 2 1/4 cups basmati rice
- 4 1/2 cups water

DIRECTIONS:

1. In a medium pot over medium heat, cook the olive oil, onion, and tomato for 3 minutes.
2. Stir in the tomato paste, paprika, salt, and rice. Cook for 1 minute.
3. Add the water, cover the pot, and turn the heat to low. Cook for 12 minutes.
4. Gently toss the rice, cover, and cook for another 3 minutes.
5. Enjoy!

NUTRITION:

calories: 328 | fat: 7g | protein: 6g | carbs: 60g | fiber: 2g | sodium: 651mg

725. Rice Casserole with Cheesy Beef

Prep time: 10 minutes | Cook time: 32 minutes | Serves: 4

INGREDIENTS:

- 2 tablespoons chopped green bell pepper
- 1/2 teaspoon Worcestershire sauce
- 1/2 teaspoon ground cumin
- 1/2 cup shredded Cheddar cheese
- 1/2 cup finely chopped onion
- 1/2 cup chili sauce
- 2/3 cup uncooked long grain rice
- 1/2-pound lean ground beef
- 1 teaspoon salt
- 1 teaspoon brown sugar
- 1 pinch ground black pepper
- 1 cup water
- 1 (14.5 ounce) can canned tomatoes
- 2 tablespoon chopped fresh cilantro

DIRECTIONS:

1. Place a non-stick saucepan on medium heat and brown beef for 10 minutes while crumbling beef. Discard fat.
2. Stir in pepper, Worcestershire sauce, cumin, brown sugar, salt, chili sauce, rice, water, tomatoes, green bell pepper, and onion. 3. Mix well and cook for 10 minutes until blended and a bit tender.
4. Transfer to an ovenproof casserole and press down firmly. Sprinkle cheese on top and cook for 7 minutes at 400°F preheated oven. Broil for 3 minutes until top is lightly browned.
5. Serve and enjoy with chopped cilantro.
6. Enjoy!

NUTRITION:

calories: 460 | fat: 7g | protein: 37g | carbs: 35g | fiber: 2g | sodium: 651mg

726. Turkey and Quinoa

Prep time: 10 minutes | Cook time: 55 minutes | Serves: 4

INGREDIENTS:

- 2 large red bell peppers
- 1 1/3 tsp chopped fresh rosemary
- 1 1/3 tbsp chopped fresh parsley
- tbsp chopped pecans, toasted
- 1/8 cup extra virgin olive oil
- 1/3 cup chicken stock
- 1/3 lb. fully cooked smoked turkey sausage, diced
- 1/3 tsp salt
- 1 1/3 cups water
- 2/3 cup uncooked quinoa

DIRECTIONS:

1. On high heat, place a large saucepan and add salt, water and quinoa. Bring to a boil.
2. Once boiling, reduce fire to a simmer, cover and cook until all water is absorbed around 15 minutes.
3. Uncover quinoa, turn off fire and let it stand for another 5 minutes.
4. Add rosemary, parsley, pecans, olive oil, chicken stock and turkey sausage into pan of quinoa. Mix well.
5. Slice peppers lengthwise in half and discard membranes and seeds. In another boiling pot of water, add peppers, boil for 5 minutes, drain and discard water.
6. Grease a 13 x 9 baking dish and preheat oven to 350°F.
7. Place boiled bell pepper onto prepared baking dish, evenly fill with the quinoa mixture and pop into oven.
8. Bake for 15 minutes.
9. Enjoy!

NUTRITION:

calories: 255 | fat: 12g | protein: 14g | carbs: 21g | fiber: 2g | sodium: 651mg

727. Vegetables and Sun-Dried Tomato

Prep time: 10 minutes | Cook time: 30 minutes | Serves: 6

INGREDIENTS:

- 1 1/2 tsp finely shredded lemon peel
- 3/4 cup finely shredded Parmesan cheese 1 1/4 cups milk
- 3 tbsp all-purpose flour
- 12 fresh mushrooms, sliced
- 2 1/4 cups fresh broccoli florets
- 6 oz fresh trimmed and quartered
- Brussels sprouts
- 6 oz trimmed fresh asparagus spears
- 1 1/2 tbsp olive oil
- 6 tbsp butter
- 3/4 cup chopped dried tomatoes 8 oz dried fettuccine

DIRECTIONS:

1. In a boiling pot of water, add fettuccine and cook following manufacturer's instructions. Two minutes before the pasta is cooked, add the dried tomatoes. Drain pasta and tomatoes and return to pot to keep warm. Set aside.
2. On medium high heat, in a big fry pan with 1 tbsp butter, fry mushrooms, broccoli, Brussels sprouts and asparagus. Cook for eight minutes while covered, transfer to a plate and put aside.
3. Using same fry pan, add remaining butter and flour. Stirring vigorously, cook for a minute or until thickened. Add Parmesan cheese, milk and mix until cheese is melted around five minutes.
4. Toss in the pasta and mix. Transfer to serving dish. Garnish with Parmesan cheese and lemon peel before serving.
5. Enjoy!

NUTRITION:

calories: 439 | fat: 19g | protein: 16g | carbs: 52g | fiber: 2g | sodium: 651mg

728. Fried Rice

Prep time: 10 minutes | Cook time: 20 minutes | Serves: 6

INGREDIENTS:

- 6 cups cold cooked rice
- 3/4 cup peas
- 1 1/2 medium yellow onion, diced 5 tbsp olive oil
- 6 oz frozen medium shrimp, thawed,
- shelled, deveined and chopped finely
- 9 oz roast pork
- 3 large eggs
- Salt and freshly ground black pepper
- 3/4 tsp corn-starch

DIRECTIONS:

1. Combine the salt and ground black pepper and 1/2 tsp corn-starch, coat the shrimp with it. Chop the roasted pork. Beat the eggs and set aside.
2. Stir-fry the shrimp in a wok on high heat with 1 tbsp heated oil until pink, around 3 minutes. Set the shrimp aside and stir fry the roasted pork briefly. Remove both from the pan.
3. In the same pan, stir-fry the onion until soft, Stir the peas and cook until bright green. Remove both from pan.
4. Add 2 tbsp oil in the same pan, add the cooked rice. Stir and separate the individual grains. Add the beaten eggs, toss the rice. 5. Add the roasted pork, shrimp, vegetables and onion. Toss everything together. Season with salt and pepper to taste.
6. Enjoy!

NUTRITION:

calories: 556 | fat: 25g | protein: 20g | carbs: 60g | fiber: 2g | sodium: 651mg

729. Tortellini Salad

Prep time: 10 minutes | Cook time: 20 minutes | Serves: 6

INGREDIENTS:

- 1/2 red onion, chopped finely
- 1/2 cup sunflower seeds
- 1/2 cup raisins
- 1 1/2 heads fresh broccoli, cut into florets
- 1 tsp cider vinegar
- 1/4 cup white sugar
- 1/4 cup mayonnaise
- 20-oz fresh cheese filled tortellini

DIRECTIONS:

1. In a large pot of boiling water, cook tortellini according to package instructions. Drain and rinse with cold water and set aside.
2. Whisk vinegar, sugar and mayonnaise to create your salad dressing.
3. Mix together in a large bowl red onion, sunflower seeds, raisins, tortellini and broccoli. Pour dressing and toss to coat.
4. Enjoy!

NUTRITION:

calories: 272 | fat: 8g | protein: 20g | carbs: 38g | fiber: 2g | sodium: 651mg

730. Lentil-Rice Pilaf

Prep time: 10 minutes | Cook time: 50 minutes | Serves: 4

INGREDIENTS:

- 1/8 cup extra-virgin olive oil
- 2/3 large onion, chopped
- 4 cups water
- 2/3 teaspoon ground cumin
- 2/3 teaspoon salt
- 1 1/3 cups brown lentils, picked over and rinsed
- 2/3 cup basmati rice

DIRECTIONS:

1. In a medium pot over medium heat, cook the olive oil and onions for 7 to 10 minutes until the edges are browned.
2. Turn the heat to high, add the water, cumin, and salt, and bring this mixture to a boil, boiling for about 3 minutes.
3. Add the lentils and turn the heat to medium-low. Cover the pot and cook for 20 minutes, stirring occasionally.
4. Stir in the rice and cover; cook for an additional 20 minutes.
5. Fluff the rice with a fork and serve warm.
6. Enjoy!

NUTRITION:

calories: 397 | fat: 11g | protein: 18g | carbs: 60g | fiber: 18g | sodium: 396mg

731. Bulgur Pilaf with Garbanzos

Prep time: 10 minutes | Cook time: 20 minutes | Serves: 6

INGREDIENTS:

- 4 1/2 tablespoons extra-virgin olive oil
- 1 1/2 large onion, chopped
- 1 1/2 (16-ounce / 454-g) can garbanzo beans, rinsed and drained
- 3 cups bulgur wheat, rinsed and drained
- 2 1/4 teaspoons salt
- 3/4 teaspoon cinnamon
- 6 cups water

DIRECTIONS:

1. In a large pot over medium heat, cook the olive oil and onion for 5 minutes.
2. Add the garbanzo beans and cook for another 5 minutes.
3. Add the bulgur, salt, cinnamon, and water and stir to combine. Cover the pot, turn the heat to low, and cook for 10 minutes.
4. When the cooking is done, fluff the pilaf with a fork. Cover and let sit for another 5 minutes.
5. Enjoy!

NUTRITION:

calories: 462 | fat: 13g | protein: 15g | carbs: 76g | fiber: 19g | sodium: 890mg

732. Lentil Bulgur Pilaf

Prep time: 10 minutes | Cook time: 50 minutes | Serves: 4

INGREDIENTS:

- 1/3 cup extra-virgin olive oil
- 2 2/3 large onions, chopped
- 1 1/3 teaspoons salt, divided
- 4 cups water
- 1 1/3 cups brown lentils, picked over and rinsed
- 2/3 teaspoon freshly ground black pepper
- 2/3 cup bulgur wheat

DIRECTIONS:

1. In a large pot over medium heat, cook and stir the olive oil, onions, and 1 teaspoon of salt for 12 to 15 minutes, until the onions are a medium brown/golden colour.
2. Put half of the cooked onions in a bowl.
3. Add the water, remaining 1 teaspoon of salt, and lentils to the remaining onions. Stir. Cover and cook for 30 minutes.
4. Stir in the black pepper and bulgur, cover, and cook for 5 minutes. Fluff with a fork, cover, and let stand for another 5 minutes.
5. Spoon the lentils and bulgur onto a serving plate and top with the reserved onions. Serve warm.
6. Enjoy!

NUTRITION:

calories: 479 | fat: 20g | protein: 20g | carbs: 60g | fiber: 24g | sodium: 789mg

733. Spanish Chicken and Rice

Prep time: 10 minutes | Cook time: 50 minutes | Serves: 4

INGREDIENTS:

- 4 teaspoons smoked paprika
- 4 teaspoons ground cumin
- 3 teaspoons garlic salt
- 1 1/2 teaspoon chili powder
- 1/2 teaspoon dried oregano
- 2 lemons
- 4 boneless, skinless chicken breasts
- 6 tablespoons extra-virgin olive oil, divided
- 4 large shallots, diced
- 2 cup uncooked white rice
- 4 cups vegetable stock
- 2 cup broccoli florets
- 1/3 cup chopped parsley

DIRECTIONS:

1. In a small bowl, whisk together the paprika, cumin, garlic salt, chili powder, and oregano. Divide in half and set aside. Into another small bowl, juice the lemon and set aside.
2. Put the chicken in a medium bowl. Coat the chicken with 2 tablespoons of olive oil and rub with half of the seasoning mix.
3. In a large pan, heat the remaining 1 tablespoon of olive oil and cook the chicken for 2 to 3 minutes on each side, until just browned but not cooked through.
4. Add shallots to the same pan and cook until translucent, then add the rice and cook for 1 more minute to toast. Add the vegetable stock, lemon juice, and the remaining seasoning mix and stir to combine. Return the chicken to the pan on top of the rice. Cover and cook for 15 minutes.
5. Uncover and add the broccoli florets. Cover and cook an additional 5 minutes, until the liquid is absorbed, rice is tender, and chicken is cooked through.
6. Top with freshly chopped parsley and serve immediately.
7. Enjoy!

NUTRITION:

calories: 750 | fat: 25g | protein: 36g | carbs: 101g | fiber: 7g | sodium: 1823mg

734. Toasted Barley and Almond Pilaf

Prep time: 10 minutes | Cook time: 5 minutes | Serves: 4

INGREDIENTS:

- 2 tablespoon olive oil
- 2 garlic cloves, minced
- 6 scallions, minced
- 4 ounces (57 g) mushrooms, sliced
- 1/2 cup sliced almonds
- 1 cup uncooked pearled barley
- 3 cups low-sodium chicken stock
- 1 teaspoon dried thyme
- 2 tablespoon fresh minced parsley
- Salt, to taste

DIRECTIONS:

1. Heat the oil in a saucepan over medium-high heat. Add the garlic, scallions, mushrooms, and almonds, and sauté for 3 minutes.
2. Add the barley and cook, stirring, for 1 minute to toast it.
3. Add the chicken stock and thyme and bring the mixture to a boil.
4. Cover and reduce the heat to low. Simmer the barley for 30 minutes, or until the liquid is absorbed and the barley is tender.
5. Sprinkle with fresh parsley and season with salt before serving.
6. Enjoy!

NUTRITION:

calories: 333 | fat: 13g | protein: 10g | carbs: 46g | fiber: 9g | sodium: 141mg

735. Brown Rice Bowls with Roasted Vegetables

Prep time: 10 minutes | Cook time: 20 minutes | Serves: 6

INGREDIENTS:

non-stick cooking spray
3 cups broccoli florets
3 cups cauliflower florets
1 1/2 (15-ounce / 425-g) can chickpeas, drained and rinsed
1 1/2 cup carrots sliced 1 inch thick
3 to 3 tablespoons extra-virgin olive oil, divided
Salt and freshly ground black pepper, to taste
3 to 3 tablespoons sesame seeds, for garnish
3 cups cooked brown rice
Dressing:
4 1/2 to 4 tablespoons tahini
3 tablespoons honey
1 1/2 lemon, juiced
1 1/2 garlic clove, minced
Salt and freshly ground black pepper, to taste

DIRECTIONS:

1. Preheat the oven to 400°F | 200°C | Fan 180°C. Spray two baking sheets with cooking spray.
2. Cover the first baking sheet with the broccoli and cauliflower and the second with the chickpeas and carrots. Toss each sheet with half of the oil and season with salt and pepper before placing in oven.
3. Cook the carrots and chickpeas for 10 minutes, leaving the carrots still just crisp, and the broccoli and cauliflower for 20 minutes, until tender. Stir each halfway through cooking.
4. To make the dressing, in a small bowl, mix the tahini, honey, lemon juice, and garlic. Season with salt and pepper and set aside.
5. Divide the rice into individual bowls, then layer with vegetables and drizzle dressing over the dish.
6. Enjoy!

NUTRITION:

calories: 454 | fat: 18g | protein: 12g | carbs: 62g | fiber: 11g | sodium: 61mg

736. Lentils and Brown Rice

Prep time: 10 minutes | Cook time: 23 minutes | Serves: 6

INGREDIENTS:

3 1/3 cups low-sodium or no-salt-added vegetable broth
3/4 cup uncooked brown or green lentils
3/4 cup uncooked instant brown rice
3/4 cup diced carrots
3/4 cup diced celery
1 1/2 (2 1/4-ounce / 64-g) can sliced olives, drained
1/3 cup diced red onion
1/3 cup chopped fresh curly-leaf parsley
2 1/4 tablespoons extra-virgin olive oil
1 1/2 tablespoon freshly squeezed lemon juice
1 1/2 garlic clove, minced
1/3 teaspoon kosher or sea salt
1/3 teaspoon freshly ground black pepper

DIRECTIONS:

1. In a medium saucepan over high heat, bring the broth and lentils to a boil, cover, and lower the heat to medium-low. Cook for 8 minutes.
2. Raise the heat to medium, and stir in the rice. Cover the pot and cook the mixture for 15 minutes, or until the liquid is absorbed. 3. Remove the pot from the heat and let it sit, covered, for 1 minute, then stir.
4. While the lentils and rice are cooking, mix together the carrots, celery, olives, onion, and parsley in a large serving bowl.
5. In a small bowl, whisk together the oil, lemon juice, garlic, salt, and pepper. Set aside.
6. When the lentils and rice are cooked, add them to the serving bowl. Pour the dressing on top, and mix everything together. Serve warm or cold, or store in a sealed container in the refrigerator for up to 7 days.
7. Enjoy!

NUTRITION:

calories: 170 | fat: 5g | protein: 5g | carbs: 25g | fiber: 2g | sodium: 566mg

737. Wild Mushroom Farro

Prep time: 10 minutes | Cook time: 7 minutes | Serves: 6

INGREDIENTS:

2 1/4 cups whole farro
4 1/2 tablespoons extra-virgin olive oil, divided, plus extra for drizzling
18 ounces (340 g) cremini or white mushrooms, trimmed and sliced thin
3/4 onion, chopped fine
3/4 teaspoon table salt
1/3 teaspoon pepper
1 1/2 garlic clove, minced
1/3 ounce (7 g) dried porcini mushrooms, rinsed and chopped fine
3 teaspoons minced fresh thyme or 1/2 teaspoon dried
1/3 cup dry white wine
3 3/4 cups chicken or vegetable broth, plus extra as needed
3 ounces (57 g) Parmesan cheese, grated, plus extra for serving
3 teaspoons lemon juice
3/4 cup chopped fresh parsley

DIRECTIONS:

1. Pulse farro in blender until about half of grains are broken into smaller pieces, about 6 pulses.
2. Using highest sauté function, heat 2 tablespoons oil in Instant Pot until shimmering. Add cremini mushrooms, onion, salt, and pepper, partially cover, and cook until mushrooms are softened and have released their liquid, about 5 minutes. Stir in farro, garlic, porcini mushrooms, and thyme and cook until fragrant, about 1 minute. Stir in wine and cook until nearly evaporated, about 30 seconds. Stir in broth.
3. Lock lid in place and close pressure release valve. Select high pressure cook function and cook for 12 minutes. Turn off Instant 4. Pot and quick-release pressure. Carefully remove lid, allowing steam to escape away from you.
5. If necessary, adjust consistency with extra hot broth, or continue to cook Frerotte, using highest sauté function, stirring frequently, until proper consistency is achieved. (Frerotte should be slightly thickened, and spoon dragged along bottom of multicooker should leave trail that quickly fills in.) Add Parmesan and remaining 1 tablespoon oil and stir vigorously until Frerotte becomes creamy. 6. Stir in lemon juice and season with salt and pepper to taste. Sprinkle individual portions with parsley and extra Parmesan, and drizzle with extra oil before serving.
7. Enjoy!

NUTRITION:

calories: 280 | fat: 9g | protein: 13g | carbs: 35g | fiber: 3g | sodium: 630mg

738. Brown Rice and Chickpea

Prep time: 10 minutes | Cook time: 45 minutes | Serves: 4

INGREDIENTS:

Olive oil cooking spray
2/3 cup long-grain brown rice
1 1/2 cups chicken stock
2/3 (15 1/2-ounce / 439-g) can chickpeas, drained and rinsed
1/3 cup diced carrot
1/3 cup green peas
2/3 teaspoon ground cumin
1/3 teaspoon ground turmeric
1/3 teaspoon ground ginger
1/3 teaspoon onion powder
1/3 teaspoon salt
1/8 teaspoon ground cinnamon
1/8 teaspoon garlic powder
1/8 teaspoon black pepper
Fresh parsley, for garnish

DIRECTIONS:

1. Preheat the air fryer to 380°F (193°C). Lightly coat the inside of a 5-cup capacity casserole dish with olive oil cooking spray.
2. In the casserole dish, combine the rice, stock, chickpeas, carrot, peas, cumin, turmeric, ginger, onion powder, salt, cinnamon, garlic powder, and black pepper. Stir well to combine.
3. Cover loosely with aluminium foil.
4. Place the covered casserole dish into the air fryer and bake for 20 minutes. Remove from the air fryer and stir well.
5. Place the casserole back into the air fryer, uncovered, and bake for 25 minutes more.
6. Fluff with a spoon and sprinkle with fresh chopped parsley before serving.
7. Enjoy!

NUTRITION:

calories: 204 | fat: 1g | protein: 7g | carbs: 40g | fiber: 4g | sodium: 623mg

739. Mushroom Parmesan Risotto

Prep time: 10 minutes | Cook time: 30 minutes | Serves: 6

INGREDIENTS:

9 cups vegetable broth
4 1/2 tablespoons extra-virgin olive oil, divided
1 1/2-pound (454 g) cremini mushrooms, cleaned and sliced
1 1/2 medium onion, finely chopped
3 cloves garlic, minced
2 1/4 cups Arborio rice
1 1/2 teaspoon salt
3/4 cup freshly grated Parmesan cheese
3/4 teaspoon freshly ground black pepper

DIRECTIONS:

1. In a saucepan over medium heat, bring the broth to a low simmer.
2. In a large skillet over medium heat, cook 1 tablespoon olive oil and the sliced mushrooms for 5 to 7 minutes. Set cooked mushrooms aside.
3. In the same skillet over medium heat, add the 2 remaining tablespoons of olive oil, onion, and garlic. Cook for 3 minutes.

4. Add the rice, salt, and 1 cup of broth to the skillet. Stir the Shopping List ingredients together and cook over low heat until most of the liquid is absorbed. Continue adding ½ cup of broth at a time, stirring until it is absorbed. Repeat until all of the broth is used up.
5. With the final addition of broth, add the cooked mushrooms, Parmesan cheese, and black pepper. Cook for 2 more minutes. 6.Serve immediately.
7. Enjoy!

NUTRITION:

calories: 410 | fat: 12g | protein: 11g | carbs: 65g | fiber: 3g | sodium: 2086mg

740. Parmesan Garlic Polenta

Prep time: 10 minutes | Cook time: 30 minutes | Serves: 6

INGREDIENTS:

6 tablespoons (1/2 stick) unsalted butter, divided (optional)
1 1/2 tablespoon garlic, finely chopped
6 cups water
1 1/2 teaspoon salt
1 1/2 cup polenta
1 1/8 cup Parmesan cheese, divided

DIRECTIONS:

1. In a large pot over medium heat, cook 3 tablespoons of butter (if desired) and the garlic for 2 minutes.
2. Add the water and salt, and bring to a boil. Add the polenta and immediately whisk until it starts to thicken, about 3 minutes. 3.Turn the heat to low, cover, and cook for 25 minutes, whisking every 5 minutes.
4. Using a wooden spoon, stir in ½ cup of the Parmesan cheese.
5. To serve, pour the polenta into a large serving bowl. Sprinkle the top with the remaining 1 tablespoon butter (if desired) and ¼ cup of remaining Parmesan cheese. Serve warm.
6. Enjoy!

NUTRITION:

calories: 297 | fat: 16g | protein: 9g | carbs: 28g | fiber: 2g | sodium: 838mg

741. Mushroom Barley Pilaf

Prep time: 10 minutes | Cook time: 37 minutes | Serves: 6

INGREDIENTS:

Olive oil cooking spray
3 tablespoons olive oil
12 ounces (227 g) button mushrooms, diced
3/4 yellow onion, diced
3 garlic cloves, minced
1 1/2 cup pearl barley
3 cups vegetable broth
1 1/2 tablespoon fresh thyme, chopped
3/4 teaspoon salt
1/3 teaspoon smoked paprika
Fresh parsley, for garnish

DIRECTIONS:

1. Preheat the air fryer to 380ºF (193ºC). Lightly coat the inside of a 5-cup capacity casserole dish with olive oil cooking spray. (The shape of the casserole dish will depend upon the size of the air fryer, but it needs to be able to hold at least 5 cups.)
2. In a large skillet, heat the olive oil over medium heat. Add the mushrooms and onion and cook, stirring occasionally, for 5 minutes, or until the mushrooms begin to brown.
3. Add the garlic and cook for an additional 2 minutes. Transfer the vegetables to a large bowl.
4. Add the barley, broth, thyme, salt, and paprika.
5. Pour the barley-and-vegetable mixture into the prepared casserole dish, and place the dish into the air fryer. Bake for 15 minutes.
6. Stir the barley mixture. Reduce the heat to 360ºF (182ºC), then return the barley to the air fryer and bake for 15 minutes more.
7. Remove from the air fryer and let sit for 5 minutes before fluffing with a fork and topping with fresh parsley.
8. Enjoy!

NUTRITION:

calories: 263 | fat: 8g | protein: 7g | carbs: 44g | fiber: 9g | sodium: 576mg

742. Moroccan-Style Brown Rice and Chickpea

Prep time: 10 minutes | Cook time: 45 minutes | Serves: 4

INGREDIENTS:

1/2 (15 1/2-ounce / 439-g) can chickpeas, drained and rinsed
1/4 cup diced carrot
1/4 cup green peas
1/4 teaspoon onion powder
1/2 teaspoon ground cumin
Olive oil cooking spray
1/4 teaspoon salt
1/2 cup long-grain brown rice
1 cups chicken stock
1/4 teaspoon ground turmeric
1/4 teaspoon ground ginger
1/8 teaspoon ground cinnamon
1/8 teaspoon garlic powder
1/8 teaspoon black pepper
Fresh parsley, for garnish

DIRECTIONS:

1. Preheat the air fryer to 380ºF (193ºC). Lightly coat the inside of a 5-cup saucepan with cooking spray olive oil.
2. In the saucepan, combine the rice, broth, chickpeas, carrot, peas, cumin, turmeric, ginger, onion powder, salt, cinnamon, garlic powder and black pepper. Mix well to combine.
3. Cover loosely with aluminium foil.
4. Place the covered saucepan in the air fryer and cook for 20 minutes. Remove from air fryer and mix well.
5. Return the saucepan to the air fryer, uncovered, and cook for another 25 minutes.
6. Shell with a spoon and sprinkle with chopped fresh parsley before serving.
7. Enjoy!

NUTRITION:

calories: 204 | fat: 1g | protein: 7g | carbs: 40g | fiber: 4g | sodium: 623mg

743. Mediterranean Lentils and Brown Rice

Prep time: 10 minutes | Cook time: 23 minutes | Serves: 6

INGREDIENTS:

1/3 cup chopped fresh curly-leaf parsley
2 1/4 tablespoons extra-virgin olive oil
3 1/3 cups low-sodium or no-salt-added vegetable broth
1/3 cup diced red onion
1 1/2 tablespoon freshly squeezed lemon juice
1 1/2 garlic clove, minced
3/4 cup uncooked brown or green lentils
3/4 cup uncooked instant brown rice
3/4 cup diced carrots
3/4 cup diced celery
1 1/2 (2 1/4-ounce / 64-g) can sliced olives, drained
1/3 teaspoon kosher or sea salt
1/3 teaspoon freshly ground black pepper

DIRECTIONS:

1. In a medium saucepan over high heat, bring the broth and lentils to a boil, cover and lower the heat to medium-low. Cook for 8 minutes.
2. Raise the heat to medium and add the rice. Cover the pot and cook theAmixture for 15 minutes, or until the liquid has absorbed. Remove the pot from the heat and let it sit, covered, for 1 minute, then stir.
3. While the lentils and rice are cooking, mix together the carrots, celery, olives, onion and parsley in a large serving bowl.
4. In a small bowl, whisk together the oil, lemon juice, garlic, salt and pepper. To put aside.
5. When the lentils and rice are cooked, pour them into the serving bowl. Pour over the dressing and mix everything. Serve hot or cold, or store in a sealed container in the refrigerator for up to 7 days.
6. Enjoy!

NUTRITION:

calories: 170 | fat: 5g | protein: 5g | carbs: 25g | fiber: 2g | sodium: 566mg

744. Simple Spanish Rice

Prep time: 10 minutes | Cook time: 20 minutes | Serves: 6

INGREDIENTS:

3 tablespoons tomato paste
1 1/2 teaspoon smoked paprika
3 tablespoons extra-virgin olive oil
1 1/2 medium onion, finely chopped
1 1/2 large tomato, finely diced
1 1/2 teaspoon salt
2 1/4 cups basmati rice
4 1/2 cups water

DIRECTIONS:

1. In a medium saucepan over medium heat, cook the olive oil, onion and tomato for 3 minutes.
2. Incorporate the tomato paste, paprika, salt and rice. Cook for 1 minute.
3. Add the water, cover the pot and turn the heat down. Cook for 12 minutes.
4. Gently stir the rice, cover and cook for another 3 minutes.
5. Enjoy!

NUTRITION:

calories: 328 | fat: 7g | protein: 6g | carbs: 60g | fiber: 2g | sodium: 651mg

745. Spanish Chicken and Rice

Prep time: 10 minutes | Cook time: 30 minutes | Serves: 4

INGREDIENTS:

6 tablespoons extra-virgin olive oil, divided

4 large shallots, diced
4 teaspoons smoked paprika
2 lemons
4 boneless, skinless chicken breasts
4 teaspoons ground cumin
3 teaspoons garlic salt
1 1/2 teaspoon chili powder
1/2 teaspoon dried oregano
2 cup uncooked white rice
4 cups vegetable stock
2 cup broccoli florets
1/3 cup chopped parsley

DIRECTIONS:

1. In a small bowl, whisk together the paprika, cumin, garlic salt, chili powder, and oregano. Divide in half and set aside. In another small bowl, squeeze the lemon and set aside.
2. Place the chicken in a medium bowl. Brush the chicken with 2 tablespoons of olive oil and scrub with half of the seasoning mix.
3. In a large skillet, heat the remaining tablespoon of olive oil and cook the chicken for 2 to 3 minutes on each side, until just browned but not completely cooked.
4. Add the shallots to the same pan and cook until translucent, then add the rice and cook for 1 minute more to toast. Add the vegetable stock, lemon juice, and remaining seasoning mix and mix to combine. Return the chicken to the pan on top of the rice. 5.Cover and cook for 15 minutes.
6. Uncover and add the broccoli florets. Cover and cook for another 5 minutes, until the liquid is absorbed, the rice is tender, and the chicken is cooked through.
7. Top with chopped fresh parsley and serve immediately.
8. Enjoy!

NUTRITION:

calories: 750 | fat: 25g | protein: 36g | carbs: 101g | fiber: 7g | sodium: 1823mg

746. Spaghetti with Pine Nuts and Cheese

Prep time: 10 minutes | Cook time: 11 minutes | Serves: 6

INGREDIENTS:

1 1/2 teaspoon freshly ground black pepper
3/4 cup pine nuts
12 ounces (227 g) spaghetti
6 tablespoons almond butter
1 1/2 cup fresh grated Parmesan cheese, divided

DIRECTIONS:

1. Bring a large pot of salted water to a boil. Add the pasta and cook for 8 minutes.
2. In a large saucepan over medium heat, combine the butter, black pepper, and pine nuts. Cook for 2 to 3 minutes, or until the pine nuts are lightly toasted.
3. Reserve ½ cup of pasta water. Drain the pasta and put it in the pan with the pine nuts.
4. Add a cup of Parmesan and the pasta water reserved for the pasta and mix everything to season the pasta evenly.
5. Transfer the pasta to a serving dish and garnish with the remaining ¼ cup of Parmesan. Serve immediately.
6. Enjoy!

NUTRITION:

calories: 542 | fat: 32g | protein: 20g | carbs: 46g | fiber: 2g | sodium: 552mg

747. Whole-Wheat Fusilli with Chickpea Sauce

Prep time: 10 minutes | Cook time: 15 minutes | Serves: 6

INGREDIENTS:

7 1/2 garlic cloves, thinly sliced
1 1/2 (15-ounce / 425-g) can chickpeas, drained and rinsed, reserving 1/2 cup canning liquid
Pinch red pepper flakes
1/3 teaspoon salt
1/4 teaspoon freshly ground black pepper
1 1/2 cup whole-grain fusilli pasta
1/3 cup extra-virgin olive oil
3/4 large shallot, chopped
1/3 cup shaved fresh Parmesan cheese
1/3 cup chopped fresh basil
3 teaspoons dried parsley
1 1/2 teaspoon dried oregano
Red pepper flakes

DIRECTIONS:

1. In a medium skillet, heat the oil over medium heat and sauté the shallots and garlic for 3-5 minutes, until the garlic is golden. Add ¾ of the chickpeas plus 2 tablespoons of liquid from the pan and bring to a boil.
2. Remove from heat, transfer to a standard blender and blend until smooth. Now add the remaining chickpeas. Add more reserved chickpea liquid if it becomes thick.
3. Bring a large pot of salted water to a boil and cook the pasta until al dente, about 8 minutes. Save 1/2 cup of pasta water, drain the pasta and put it back in the pot.
4. Add the chickpea sauce to the hot pasta and add up to ¼ cup of the pasta water. You may need to add more water to the pasta to achieve the desired consistency.
5. Put the pasta on medium heat and stir occasionally until the sauce thickens. Season with salt and pepper.
6. Serve, garnished with Parmesan, basil, parsley, oregano and chilli flakes.
7. Enjoy!

NUTRITION:

calories: 310 | fat: 16g | protein: 10g | carbs: 33g | fiber: 6g | sodium: 243mg

748. Israeli Couscous with Asparagus

Prep time: 10 minutes | Cook time: 25 minutes | Serves: 4

INGREDIENTS:

1/8 teaspoon freshly ground black pepper
1 1/8 cups water
1 pounds (680 g) asparagus spears, ends trimmed and stalks chopped into 1-inch pieces
2/3 garlic clove, minced
2/3 tablespoon extra-virgin olive oil
2/3 (8-ounce / 227-g) box uncooked whole-wheat or regular Israeli couscous (about 1⅓ cups)
1/8 teaspoon kosher salt
2/3 cup garlic-and-herb goat cheese, at room temperature

DIRECTIONS:

1. Preheat the oven to 220°C (425° F).
2. In a large bowl, mix together the asparagus, garlic, oil and pepper. Spread the asparagus on a large rimmed baking sheet and cook for 10 minutes, stirring a couple of times. Remove the pan from the oven and pour the asparagus into a large serving bowl. Put aside.
3. While the asparagus is cooking, bring the water to a boil in a medium saucepan. Add the couscous and season with salt, mixing well.
4. Reduce the heat to medium-low. Cover and cook for 12 minutes, or until the water is absorbed.
5. Pour the hot couscous into the bowl with the asparagus. Add the goat cheese and mix thoroughly until completely dissolved.
6. Serve immediately.
7. Enjoy!

NUTRITION:

calories: 103 | fat: 2g | protein: 6g | carbs: 18g | fiber: 5g | sodium: 343mg

749. Triple-Green Pasta with Parmesan

Prep time: 10 minutes | Cook time: 15 minutes | Serves: 6

INGREDIENTS:

3 cups chopped fresh flat-leaf (Italian) parsley, including stems
7 1/2 cups loosely packed baby spinach
1/3 teaspoon ground nutmeg
1/3 teaspoon kosher or sea salt
⅓ cup Castelvetrano olives, pitted and sliced
⅓ cup grated Pecorino Romano or Parmesan cheese
12 ounces (227 g) uncooked penne
1 1/2 tablespoon extra-virgin olive oil
3 garlic cloves, minced
1/3 teaspoon crushed red pepper
1/3 teaspoon freshly ground black pepper

DIRECTIONS:

1. In a large saucepan, cook pasta according to package directions, but boil 1 minute less than instructions. Drain the pasta and keep ¼ cup of the cooking water.
2. While the pasta is cooking, in a large skillet over medium heat, heat the oil. Add the garlic and chopped red pepper and cook for 30 seconds, stirring constantly. Add the parsley and cook for 1 minute, stirring constantly. Add the spinach, nutmeg, pepper and salt and cook for 3 minutes, stirring occasionally, until the spinach is wilted.
3. Add the pasta and the water of the pasta set aside from the cup into the pan. Add the olives and cook for about 2 minutes, until most of the water in the pasta has been absorbed. Remove from the heat, stir in the cheese and serve.
4. Enjoy!

NUTRITION:

calories: 262 | fat: 3g | protein: 15g | carbs: 51g | fiber: 12g | sodium: 1180mg

750. Creamy Garlic Parmesan Chicken Pasta

Prep time: 10 minutes | Cook time: 15 minutes | Serves: 6

INGREDIENTS:

3 cups chopped fresh flat-leaf (Italian) parsley, including stems
7 1/2 cups loosely packed baby spinach
1/3 teaspoon ground nutmeg

1/3 teaspoon kosher or sea salt
⅓ cup Castelvetrano olives, pitted and sliced
⅓ cup grated Pecorino Romano or Parmesan cheese
12 ounces (227 g) uncooked penne
1 1/2 tablespoon extra-virgin olive oil
3 garlic cloves, minced
1/3 teaspoon crushed red pepper
1/3 teaspoon freshly ground black pepper

DIRECTIONS:

1. In a large skillet over medium heat, heat the olive oil. Add the chicken and cook for 3 minutes.
2. Add the onion, garlic and salt to the pan. Cook for 7 minutes, stirring occasionally.
3. In the meantime, bring plenty of salted water to a boil and add the pasta, then cook for 7 minutes.
4. While the pasta is cooking, add the cream, ½ cup of Parmesan cheese and black pepper to the chicken. Simmer for 3 minutes.
5. Reserve ½ cup of pasta water. Drain the pasta and add it to the chicken cream sauce.
6. Add the pasta water reserved for the pasta and mix. Simmer for 2 minutes. Garnish with the remaining ¼ cup of Parmesan and serve hot.
7. Enjoy!

NUTRITION:

calories: 879 | fat: 42g | protein: 35g | carbs: 90g | fiber: 5g | sodium: 1283mg

751. Buckwheat Groats with Root Vegetables

Prep time: 10 minutes | Cook time: 40 minutes | Serves: 4

INGREDIENTS:

1/8 cup plus 1 tablespoon olive oil, divided
1 1/3 rosemary sprigs
2/3 cup buckwheat groats
1 1/3 cups vegetable broth
1 1/3 garlic cloves, minced
1 1/3 large potatoes, cubed
2/3 teaspoon salt
1 1/3 carrots, sliced
2/3 small rutabaga, cubed
Olive oil cooking spray
1 1/3 celery stalks, chopped
1/3 teaspoon smoked paprika
1/3 yellow onion, chopped

DIRECTIONS:

1. Preheat the air fryer to 380°F (193°C). Lightly coat the inside of a 5-cup saucepan with cooking spray olive oil.
2. In a large bowl, mix the potatoes, carrots, turnip and celery with the paprika and 1 cup of olive oil.
3. Pour the vegetable mixture into the prepared saucepan and garnish with the rosemary sprigs. Place the saucepan in the air fryer and cook for 15 minutes.
4. While the vegetables are cooking, rinse and drain the buckwheat groats.
5. In a medium saucepan over medium-high heat, combine the groats, vegetable broth, garlic, onion and salt with the remaining tablespoon of olive oil. Bring the mixture to a boil, then reduce the heat to low, cover and cook for 10-12 minutes.
6. Remove the saucepan from the air fryer. Remove the sprigs of rosemary and discard. Pour the cooked buckwheat into the dish with the vegetables and mix to combine. Cover with aluminium foil and cook for another 15 minutes.
7. Stir before serving.
8. Enjoy!

NUTRITION:

calories: 344 | fat: 12g | protein: 8g | carbs: 50g | fiber: 7g | sodium: 876mg

752. Brown Rice Bowls with Roasted Vegetables

Prep time: 10 minutes | Cook time: 20 minutes | Serves: 6

INGREDIENTS:

Salt and freshly ground black pepper, to taste
3 to 3 tablespoons sesame seeds, for garnish
non-stick cooking spray
3 cups broccoli florets
1 1/2 cup carrots sliced 1 inch thick
3 cups cauliflower florets
1 1/2 (15-ounce / 425-g) can chickpeas, drained and rinsed
3 to 3 tablespoons extra-virgin olive oil, divided
3 cups cooked brown rice
Dressing:
4 1/2 to 4 tablespoons tahini
3 tablespoons honey
1 1/2 lemon, juiced
1 1/2 garlic clove, minced
Salt and freshly ground black pepper, to taste

DIRECTIONS:

1. Preheat the oven to 400°F | 200°C. Fan 180°C. Spray two baking sheets with cooking spray.
2. Cover the first pan with the broccoli and cauliflower and the second with the chickpeas and carrots. Season each sheet with half the oil and season with salt and pepper before baking.
3. Cook the carrots and chickpeas for 10 minutes, leaving the carrots still just crisp, and the broccoli and cauliflower for 20 minutes, until tender. Stir each halfway through cooking.
4. To make the dressing, in a small bowl, mix the tahini, honey, lemon juice, and garlic. Season with salt and pepper and set aside.
5. Divide the rice into individual bowls, then cover with the vegetables and pour the dressing onto the plate.
6. Enjoy!

NUTRITION:

calories: 454 | fat: 18g | protein: 12g | carbs: 62g | fiber: 11g | sodium: 61mg

753. Garlic Shrimp Fettuccine

Prep time: 10 minutes | Cook time: 15 minutes | Serves: 6

INGREDIENTS:

3/4 teaspoon salt
3/4 teaspoon freshly ground black pepper
12 ounces (227 g) fettuccine pasta
⅓ cup lemon juice
1 1/2 tablespoon lemon zest
1/3 cup extra-virgin olive oil
4 1/2 tablespoons garlic, minced
1 1/2 pound (454 g) large shrimp, peeled and deveined

DIRECTIONS:

1. Bring a large pot of salted water to a boil. Add the fettuccine and cook for 8 minutes. Keep ½ cup of the cooking liquid and drain the pasta.
2. In a large saucepan over medium heat, heat the olive oil. Add the garlic and sauté for 1 minute.
3. Add the shrimp to the saucepan and cook for 3 minutes on each side. Remove the shrimp from the pan and set aside.
4. Add the other ingredients to the saucepan. Incorporate the cooking liquid. Add the pasta and mix to evenly season the pasta.
5. Transfer the pasta to a serving dish and serve topped with the cooked prawns.
6. Enjoy!

NUTRITION:

calories: 485 | fat: 17g | protein: 33g | carbs: 50g | fiber: 4g | sodium: 407mg

754. Freekeh Pilaf with Dates and Pistachios

Prep time: 10 minutes | Cook time: 10 minutes | Serves: 6

INGREDIENTS:

1/3 teaspoon ground coriander
2 1/4 cups cracked freekeh, rinsed
4 1/2 ounces (85 g) pitted dates, chopped
1/3 cup shelled pistachios, toasted and coarsely chopped
1/3 teaspoon ground cumin
Salt and pepper, to taste
3 tablespoons extra-virgin olive oil, plus extra for drizzling
1 1/2 shallot, minced
2 1/4 teaspoons grated fresh ginger
2 2/3 cups water
2 1/4 tablespoons lemon juice
1/3 cup chopped fresh mint

DIRECTIONS:

1. Set the Instant Pot to Sauté mode and heat the olive oil until it glistens.
2. Add the shallot, ginger, coriander, cumin, salt and pepper to the pot and cook for about 2 minutes, or until the shallot softens. Incorporate the water and freekeh.
3. Attach the cover. Select Manual mode and set the cooking time to 4 minutes at High Pressure. Once cooking is complete, make a quick pressure release. Open the lid carefully.
4. Add dates, pistachios and lemon juice and gently shell the freekeh with a fork to mix.
Season with salt and pepper.
5. Transfer to a serving dish and sprinkle with mint. Serve seasoned with extra olive oil.
6. Enjoy!

NUTRITION:

calories: 280 | fat: 8g | protein: 8g | carbs: 46g | fiber: 9g | sodium: 200mg

755. Simple Pesto Pasta

Prep time: 10 minutes | Cook time: 10 minutes | Serves: 6

INGREDIENTS:

6 cups fresh basil leaves, stems removed
4 1/2 cloves garlic
1 1/2 teaspoon salt
1/3 cup lemon juice
1 1/2-pound (454 g) spaghetti
3/4 teaspoon freshly ground black pepper
3/4 cup toasted pine nuts
3/4 cup grated Parmesan cheese
1 1/2 cup extra-virgin olive oil

DIRECTIONS:

1. Bring a large pot of salted water to a boil. Add the spaghetti to the pot and cook for 8 minutes.
2. In a food processor, put the other ingredients, except the olive oil, and pulse.
3. While the food processor is running, slowly pour the olive oil through the top opening. Work until all the olive oil has been added.
4. Save ½ cup of the cooking liquid. Drain the pasta and put it in a large bowl. Add the pesto and cooking liquid to the pasta bowl and mix everything together.
5. Serve immediately.
6. Enjoy!

NUTRITION:

calories: 1067 | fat: 72g | protein: 23g | carbs: 91g | fiber: 6g | sodium: 817mg

756. Asparagus and Grape Tomato Pasta

Prep time: 10 minutes | Cook time: 25 minutes | Serves: 4

INGREDIENTS:

1 1/3 tablespoons extra-virgin olive oil
1/8 teaspoon freshly ground black pepper
1/8 teaspoon kosher or sea salt
1 1/3 cups fresh Mozzarella, drained and cut into bite-size pieces
5 1/3 ounces (227 g) uncooked small pasta, like orecchiette (little ears) or farfalle (bow ties)
1 pounds (680 g) fresh asparagus, ends trimmed and stalks chopped into 1-inch pieces
1 cup grape tomato, halved
1/3 cup torn fresh basil leaves
1 1/3 tablespoons balsamic vinegar

DIRECTIONS:

1. Preheat the oven to 400°F | 200°C | Fan 180°C.
2. In a large saucepan, cook the pasta according to package directions. Drain, reserving about ¼ cup of pasta water.
3. While the pasta is cooking, in a large bowl, mix the asparagus, tomatoes, oil, pepper and salt. Spread the mixture onto a large, rimmed baking sheet and cook for 15 minutes, stirring twice during cooking.
4. Remove the vegetables from the oven and add the cooked pasta to the pan. Mix the pasta with a few tablespoons of water to help the sauce become smoother and the saucy vegetables stick to the pasta.
5. Gently incorporate the mozzarella and basil. Season with the balsamic vinegar. Serve from the pan or pour the pasta into a large bowl.
6. If you want to prepare this dish in advance or serve it cold, follow the recipe up to step 4, then refrigerate the pasta and vegetables. When you are ready to serve, follow step 5 with either the cold pasta or the hot pasta that has been gently heated in a pot on the stove.
7. Enjoy!

NUTRITION:

calories: 147 | fat: 2g | protein: 16g | carbs: 17g | fiber: 4g | sodium: 420mg

10

SOUP & SALAD RECIPES

SOUP & SALADS

757. Authentic Greek Salad
Prep time: 10 minutes | Cook time: 0 minutes | Serves: 6

INGREDIENTS:

- 6 ounces (113 g) pitted Kalamata olives
- 1/3 cup extra-virgin olive oil
- 1 1/2 green bell pepper, cut into 1- to 1 1/2-inch chunks
- 1/3 small red onion, thinly sliced
- 1 1/2 tablespoon red wine vinegar
- 1 1/2 tablespoon chopped fresh oregano or 1 teaspoon dried oregano
- 3 tablespoons freshly squeezed lemon juice
- 3 large English cucumbers
- 6 Roma tomatoes, quartered
- 1/3 teaspoon freshly ground black pepper
- 6 ounces (113 g) crumbled traditional feta cheese

DIRECTIONS:

1. Cut the cucumbers in half lengthwise and then into half-inch thick half-moons. Put in a large bowl.
2. Add the quartered tomatoes, pepper, red onion and olives.
3. In a small bowl, whisk together the olive oil, lemon juice, vinegar, oregano and pepper. Sprinkle the vegetables and mix to coat.
4. Divide between salad plates and garnish each with 28g of feta.
5. Enjoy!

NUTRITION:

calories: 278 | fat: 22g | protein: 8g | carbs: 12g | fiber: 4g | sodium: 572mg

758. Beet Summer Salad
Prep time: 10 minutes | Cook time: 40 minutes | Serves: 6

INGREDIENTS:

- 6 heads of Treviso radicchio
- 1/3 cup lemon juice
- 9 medium to large fresh red or yellow beets
- 1/3 cup plus 1 tablespoon extra-virgin olive oil, divided
- 3 shallots, peeled and sliced
- 3/4 teaspoon salt
- 9 ounces (170 g) feta cheese, crumbled

DIRECTIONS:

1. Preheat the oven to 400°F | 200°C | Fan 180°C.
2. Cut the stalks and roots of the beets. Wash the beets well and dry them with a paper towel.
3. Peel the beets using a peeler. Cut them into half-centimetre pieces and place them in a large bowl.
4. Add 1 tablespoon of olive oil to the bowl and mix to coat, then pour the beets onto a baking sheet. Distribute the beets so that they are evenly distributed.
5. Cook for 35-40 minutes until the beets are tender, turning them once or twice with a spatula.
6. When the beets are cooked, set them aside and let cool for 10 minutes.
7. While the beets cool, cut the radicchio into 1-inch pieces and arrange on a serving plate.
8. Once the beets have cooled, pour them over the radicchio, then spread the shallots evenly over the beets.
9. In a small bowl, whisk the remaining cup of olive oil, lemon juice, and salt together. Dress the salad in layers with the dressing. Complete the salad with the feta cheese on top.
10. Enjoy!

NUTRITION:

calories: 389 | fat: 31g | protein: 10g | carbs: 22g | fiber: 5g | sodium: 893mg

759. Quinoa and Garbanzo Salad
Prep time: 10 minutes | Cook time: 30 minutes | Serves: 4

INGREDIENTS:

- 1 teaspoons salt, divided
- 1/2 cup thinly sliced onions (red or white)
- 2 cups water
- 1/8 cup lemon juice
- 1 cup red or yellow quinoa
- 1/2 (16-ounce / 454-g) can garbanzo beans, rinsed and drained
- 1/3 cup extra-virgin olive oil
- 1/2 teaspoon freshly ground black pepper

DIRECTIONS:

1. In a 3-liter saucepan over medium heat, bring the water to a boil.
2. Add quinoa and 1 teaspoon of salt to the pot. Stir, cover and cook over low heat for 15-20 minutes.
3. Turn off the heat, shell the quinoa with a fork, cover again and let it rest for another 5-10 minutes.
4. Put the quinoa, onions and cooked chickpeas in a large bowl.
5. In a separate small bowl, whisk together the olive oil, lemon juice, remaining teaspoon of salt and black pepper.
6. Add the dressing to the quinoa mixture and mix everything gently. Serve warm or cold.
7. Enjoy!

NUTRITION:

calories: 318 | fat: 6g | protein: 9g | carbs: 43g | fiber: 13g | sodium: 585mg

760. Israeli Salad
Prep time: 10 minutes | Cook time: 6 minutes | Serves: 6

INGREDIENTS:

- 1/3 cup shelled pumpkin seeds
- 1/3 cup shelled sunflower seeds
- 3 large English cucumbers, unpeeled and finely chopped
- 1/3 cup pine nuts
- 3/4 small red onion, finely chopped
- 3/4 cup finely chopped fresh flat-leaf Italian parsley
- 1/3 cup extra-virgin olive oil
- 3 to 3 tablespoons freshly squeezed lemon juice (from 1 lemon)
- 1 1/2 teaspoon salt
- 1/3 cup shelled pistachios
- 1/3 cup coarsely chopped walnuts
- 1 1/2-pint cherry tomatoes, finely chopped
- 1/3 teaspoon freshly ground black pepper
- 6 cups baby arugula

DIRECTIONS:

1. In a large, dry skillet, toast the pine nuts, pistachios, walnuts, pumpkin seeds and sunflower seeds over medium-low heat until golden and fragrant, 5 to 6 minutes, being careful not to burn them. Remove from the heat and set aside.
2. In a large bowl, combine the cucumber, tomatoes, red onion and parsley.
3. In a small bowl, whisk together the olive oil, lemon juice, salt and pepper. Pour over the chopped vegetables and mix to coat.
4. Add the toasted nuts and seeds and the rocket and mix with the salad to mix well. Serve at room temperature or cold.
5. Enjoy!

NUTRITION:

calories: 414 | fat: 34g | protein: 10g | carbs: 17g | fiber: 6g | sodium: 642mg

761. Winter Salad with Red Wine Vinaigrette
Prep time: 10 minutes | Cook time: 0 minutes | Serves: 6

INGREDIENTS:

- 1/3 cup peeled, julienned carrots
- 3 celery stalks, thinly sliced
- 9 stalks kale, stems removed and greens roughly chopped
- 3/4 cup chopped pitted Kalamata olives
- 3/4 cup thinly sliced radicchio
- 1 1/2 small green apple, thinly sliced
- 3/4 cup crumbled feta cheese
- 3/4 cup dried currants
- 3 scallions, both green and white parts, thinly sliced
- 1/3 cup Red Wine Vinaigrette
- Salt and freshly ground black pepper, to taste (optional)

DIRECTIONS:

1. In a large bowl, combine the apple, kale, feta, currants, olives, radicchio, shallots, carrots and celery and mix well. Season with the vinaigrette. Season with salt and pepper (if used), then serve.
2. Enjoy!

NUTRITION:

calories: 253 | fat: 15g | protein: 6g | carbs: 29g | fiber: 4g | sodium: 480mg

762. Tomato and Lentil Salad with Feta
Prep time: 10 minutes | Cook time: 30 minutes | Serves: 6

INGREDIENTS:

- 2 1/4 teaspoons salt, divided
- 3 large ripe tomatoes
- 1/3 cup lemon juice
- 3 Persian cucumbers
- 4 1/2 cups water
- 1 1/2 cup brown or green lentils, picked over and rinsed
- 3/4 cup extra-virgin olive oil
- 1 1/2 cup crumbled feta cheese

DIRECTIONS:

1. In a large saucepan over medium heat, bring the water, lentils, and 1 teaspoon of salt to a boil, then reduce the heat to low. Cover the pot and

continue cooking, stirring occasionally, for 30 minutes. (Lentils should be cooked so they no longer have a crunchiness, but still hold their shape. You should be able to smooth the lentils between your two fingers when pinched.)
2. Once the lentils are cooked, drain them to remove excess water and place them in a large bowl. Let it cool down.
3. Dice the tomatoes and cucumbers, then add them to the lentils.
4. In a small bowl, whisk together the lemon juice, olive oil and the remaining ½ teaspoon of salt.
5. Pour the dressing over the lentils and vegetables. Add the feta cheese to the bowl and gently mix all the ingredients together.
6. Enjoy!

NUTRITION:

calories: 521 | fat: 36g | protein: 18g | carbs: 35g | fiber: 15g | sodium: 1304mg

763. Orange Avocado and Almond Salad

Prep time: 10 minutes | Cook time: 0 minutes | Serves: 4

INGREDIENTS:

- 1/3 cup sliced almonds
- 1/3 cup honey
- 2/3 tablespoon extra-virgin olive oil
- 1 1/3 large Gala apples, chopped
- 1 1/3 oranges, segmented and chopped
- 1/3 teaspoon grated orange zest
- 2/3 large avocado, semi-ripened, medium diced

DIRECTIONS:

1. In a large bowl, combine the apples, oranges and almonds. Gently mix.
2. In a small bowl, whisk the honey, oil and orange zest. Put aside.
3. Pour the orange zest mix over the fruit salad and mix. Add the avocado and mix gently once more.
4. Enjoy!

NUTRITION:

calories: 296 | fat: 12g | protein: 3g | carbs: 50g | fiber: 7g | sodium: 4mg

764. Cauliflower Tabbouleh Salad

Prep time: 10 minutes | Cook time: 5 minutes | Serves: 4

INGREDIENTS:

- 1/3 cup chopped Italian parsley
- 1/3 cup chopped pitted Kalamata olives
- 1 1/3 tablespoons minced red onion
- Juice of 1 lemon (about 2 tablespoons)
- 4 tablespoons extra-virgin olive oil, divided
- 2 2/3 cups riced cauliflower
- 1/3 large cucumber, peeled, seeded, and chopped
- 1/3 cup chopped mint leaves
- 2 garlic cloves, finely minced
- 1 teaspoons salt
- 1/3 teaspoon freshly ground black pepper
- 1 1/3 cups baby arugula or spinach leaves
- 1 1/3 medium avocados, peeled, pitted, and diced
- 2/3 cup quartered cherry tomatoes

DIRECTIONS:

1. In a large skillet, heat 2 tablespoons of olive oil over medium-high heat. Add the cauliflower, garlic, salt and pepper and sauté until tender but not soft, 3 to 4 minutes. Remove from the heat and place in a large bowl.
2. Add the cucumber, mint, parsley, olives, red onion, lemon juice and the remaining 4 tablespoons of olive oil and mix well. Refrigerate, uncovered, for at least 30 minutes or up to 2 hours.
3. Before serving, add the rocket, avocado and tomatoes and mix to combine well. Season to taste with salt and pepper and serve cold or at room temperature.
4. Enjoy!

NUTRITION:

calories: 235 | fat: 21g | protein: 4g | carbs: 12g | fiber: 6g | sodium: 623mg

765. Tabouli Salad

Prep time: 10 minutes | Cook time: 5 minutes | Serves: 4

INGREDIENTS:

- 1/2 cup bulgur wheat, grind
- 1/4 cup extra-virgin olive oil
- 2 cups Italian parsley, finely chopped
- 1/4 cup lemon juice
- 1 cup ripe tomato, finely diced
- 1/2 cup green onion, finely chopped
- 3/4 teaspoons salt
- 1/2 teaspoon dried mint

DIRECTIONS:

1. Before chopping the vegetables, put the bulgur in a small bowl. Rinse with water, drain and let it sit in the bowl while you prepare the other ingredients.
2. Put the parsley, tomatoes, green onion and bulgur in a large bowl.
3. In a small bowl, whisk together the lemon juice, olive oil, salt and mint.
4. Pour the dressing over the tomato, onion and bulgur mixture, mixing everything together. Add more salt to taste. Serve immediately or refrigerate for up to 2 days.
5. Enjoy!

NUTRITION:

calories: 207 | fat: 14g | protein: 4g | carbs: 19g | fiber: 5g | sodium: 462mg

766. Arugula, Watermelon, and Feta Salad

Prep time: 10 minutes | Cook time: 0 minutes | Serves: 4

INGREDIENTS:

- 5 cups watermelon, cut into bite-size cubes
- 4 ounces (57 g) feta cheese, crumbled
- 6 cups packed arugula
- 4 tablespoons balsamic glaze

DIRECTIONS:

1. Divide the rocket between two plates.
2. Divide the watermelon cubes between the rocket beds.
3. Sprinkle 1 ounce (28 g) of feta cheese on each salad.
4. Sprinkle about 1 tablespoon of frosting (or more if desired) on each salad.
5. Enjoy!

NUTRITION:

calories: 159 | fat: 7g | protein: 6g | carbs: 21g | fiber: 1g | sodium: 327mg

767. Tahini Barley Salad

Prep time: 10 minutes | Cook time: 8 minutes | Serves: 4

INGREDIENTS:

- 1 teaspoons table salt, for cooking barley
- 1/8 cup tahini
- 2/3 teaspoon grated lemon zest plus 1/4 cup juice (2 lemons)
- 1/2 teaspoon table salt
- 2/3 English cucumber, cut into 1/2-inch pieces
- 2/3 carrot, peeled and shredded
- 2/3 red bell pepper, stemmed, seeded, and chopped
- 2 2/3 scallions, thinly sliced
- 1 1/3 tablespoons finely chopped jarred hot cherry peppers
- 2/3 tablespoon sumac, divided
- 2/3 garlic clove, minced
- 1 cups pearl barley
- 3 1/3 tablespoons extra-virgin olive oil, divided
- 1/8 cup coarsely chopped fresh mint

DIRECTIONS:

1. Combine 6 cups of water, barley, 1 tablespoon of oil and 1½ teaspoon of salt in the Instant Pot. Lock the lid in place and close the pressure release valve. Select the high-pressure cooking function and cook for 8 minutes. Turn off the Instant Pot and let the pressure naturally release for 15 minutes. Quickly release the residual pressure, then carefully remove the lid, allowing the steam to escape away from you. Drain the barley, spread it on a rimmed baking sheet and allow to cool completely, about 15 minutes.
2. Meanwhile, whisk the remaining ¼ cup of oil, tahini, 2 tablespoons of water, lemon zest and juice, 1 teaspoon sumac, garlic and ¾ teaspoon of salt in a large bowl until combined; let it rest for 15 minutes.
3. Measure and reserve ½ cup of seasoning for serving. Add the barley, cucumber, carrot, bell pepper, shallot and cherry peppers to the bowl with the dressing and toss gently to combine. Season with salt and pepper to taste. Transfer the salad to a serving dish and sprinkle with mint and the remaining 2 teaspoons of sumac. Serve, passing the reserved dressing aside.
4. Enjoy!

NUTRITION:

calories: 370 | fat: 18g | protein: 8g | carbs: 47g | fiber: 10g | sodium: 510mg

768. Avocado and Hearts of Palm Salad

Prep time: 10 minutes | Cook time: 0 minutes | Serves: 6

INGREDIENTS:

- 1 1/2 avocado, cut into 1/2-inch pieces
- 1 1/2 cup halved yellow cherry tomatoes
- 1/3 cup coarsely chopped flat-leaf parsley
- 3 tablespoons low-fat mayonnaise
- 3 tablespoons extra-virgin olive oil
- 3/4 small shallot, thinly sliced
- 3 (14-ounce / 397-g) cans hearts of palm, drained and cut into 1/2-inch-thick slices
- 1/3 teaspoon salt
- 1/4 teaspoon freshly ground black pepper

DIRECTIONS:

1. In a large bowl, mix the hearts of palm, avocado, tomatoes, scallions,

and parsley.
2. In a small bowl, whisk the mayonnaise, olive oil, salt and pepper, then mix in the large bowl.
3.Enjoy!

NUTRITION:

calories: 192 | fat: 15g | protein: 5g | carbs: 14g | fiber: 7g | sodium: 841mg

769. Greek Vegetable Salad
Prep time: 10 minutes | Cook time: 0 minutes | Serves: 6

INGREDIENTS:

1 1/2 head iceberg lettuce
3 cups cherry tomatoes
1 1/2 large cucumber
1 1/2 medium onion
3/4 cup extra-virgin olive oil
1/3 cup lemon juice
1 1/2 teaspoon salt
1 1/2 clove garlic, minced
1 1/2 cup Kalamata olives, pitted
1 1/2 (6-ounce / 170-g) package feta cheese, crumbled

DIRECTIONS:

1.Cut the lettuce into 1-inch pieces and place them in a large salad bowl.
2.Cut the tomatoes in half and add them to the salad bowl.
3.Cut the cucumber into bite-sized pieces and add them to the salad bowl.
4.Thinly slice the onion and add it to the salad bowl.
5.In another small bowl, whisk together the olive oil, lemon juice, salt and garlic. Pour the dressing over the salad and mix gently to coat evenly.
6.Enjoy!

NUTRITION:

calories: 539 | fat: 50g | protein: 9g | carbs: 17g | fiber: 4g | sodium: 1758mg

770. Pistachio-Parmesan Kale and Arugula Salad
Prep time: 10 minutes | Cook time: 0 minutes | Serves: 4

INGREDIENTS:

1 1/3 tablespoons freshly squeezed lemon juice
1/3 teaspoon smoked paprika
1 1/3 cups arugula
4 cups raw kale, centre ribs removed
and discarded, leaves coarsely chopped
1/8 cup extra-virgin olive oil
1/3 cup unsalted shelled pistachios
4 tablespoons grated Parmesan or Pecorino Romano cheese

DIRECTIONS:

1.In a large salad bowl, combine the kale, oil, lemon juice and smoked paprika. With your hands, gently massage the leaves for about 15 seconds or so, until they are all completely covered. Let the cabbage rest for 10 minutes.
2.When ready to serve, gently mix the rocket and pistachios. Divide the salad into six serving bowls, sprinkle 1 tablespoon of grated cheese on top
3.Enjoy!

NUTRITION:

calories: 105 | fat: 9g | protein: 4g | carbs: 3g | fiber: 2g | sodium: 176mg

771. Tuna Salad
Prep time: 10 minutes | Cook time: 0 minutes | Serves: 6

INGREDIENTS:

3/4 cup thinly sliced sun-dried tomatoes
1/3 cup sliced pitted Kalamata olives
3 (5-ounce / 142-g) cans water-packed, white albacore tuna, drained
2/3 cup crumbled feta cheese
4 1/2 tablespoons extra-virgin olive oil
3/4 teaspoon dried cilantro
1/3 cup thinly sliced scallions, both green and white parts
6 cups spring mix greens
1 1/2 (15-ounce / 425-g) can cannellini beans, drained
3 or 3 leaves thinly chopped fresh sweet basil
1 1/2 lime, zested and juiced
Kosher salt and freshly ground black pepper, to taste

DIRECTIONS:

1.In a large bowl, combine the vegetables, beans, tuna, feta, tomatoes, olives, scallions, olive oil, coriander, basil, and lime juice and zest. Season with salt and pepper, mix and enjoy!
2.Enjoy!

NUTRITION:

calories: 355 | fat: 19g | protein: 22g | carbs: 25g | fiber: 8g | sodium: 744mg

772. Balsamic Baby Spinach Salad
Prep time: 10 minutes | Cook time: 0 minutes | Serves: 6

INGREDIENTS:

3/4 teaspoon fresh lemon zest
4 1/2 tablespoons balsamic vinegar
1 1/2 large ripe tomato
1 1/2 medium red onion
1/3 cup extra-virgin olive oil
3/4 teaspoon salt
1 1/2-pound (454 g) baby spinach, washed, stems removed

DIRECTIONS:

1.Cut the tomato into ¼-inch cubes and slice the onion into long slices.
2.In a small bowl, whisk together the lemon zest, balsamic vinegar, olive oil and salt.
3.Put the spinach, tomatoes and onions in a large bowl. Pour the dressing over
4.Enjoy!

NUTRITION:

calories: 172 | fat: 14g | protein: 4g | carbs: 9g | fiber: 4g | sodium: 389mg

773. Citrus Fennel and Pecan Salad
Prep time: 10 minutes | Cook time: 0 minutes | Serves: 4

INGREDIENTS:

2 tablespoon blood orange vinegar, other orange vinegar, or cider vinegar
2 tablespoon honey
Salt, to taste
Freshly ground black pepper, to taste
4 tablespoons fresh orange juice
6 tablespoons olive oil
4 cups packed baby kale
2 medium navel or blood orange, segmented
1 small fennel bulb, stems and leaves removed, sliced into matchsticks
6 tablespoons toasted pecans, chopped
4 ounces (57 g) goat cheese, crumbled

DIRECTIONS:

1.Make the Dressing
2.Combine the orange juice, olive oil, vinegar, and honey in a small bowl and whisk to combine. Season with salt and pepper. Set the dressing aside.
3.Make the Salad
4.Divide the baby kale, orange segments, fennel, pecans, and goat cheese evenly between two plates.
5.Enjoy!

NUTRITION:

calories: 502 | fat: 39g | protein: 13g | carbs: 30g | fiber: 6g | sodium: 158mg

774. Kale Salad with Anchovy Dressing
Prep time: 10 minutes | Cook time: 0 minutes | Serves: 6

INGREDIENTS:

12 anchovy fillets, roughly chopped
1 1/2 large bunch lacinato or dinosaur kale
1/3 cup extra-virgin olive oil
1/3 cup toasted pine nuts
1 1/2 cup shaved or coarsely shredded fresh Parmesan cheese
3 to 3 tablespoons freshly squeezed lemon juice (from 1 large lemon)
3 teaspoons red pepper flakes (optional)

DIRECTIONS:

1.Remove the rough centre stems from the cabbage leaves and coarsely tear each leaf into strips approximately 4 x 1 inch. Put the black cabbage in a large bowl and add the pine nuts and cheese.
2.In a small bowl, whisk together the olive oil, anchovies, lemon juice, and red pepper flakes (if using). Sprinkle the salad and mix to coat well. Leave to rest at room temperature for 30 minutes before serving, turning again just before serving.
3.Enjoy!

NUTRITION:

calories: 337 | fat: 25g | protein: 16g | carbs: 12g | fiber: 2g | sodium: 603mg

775. Cantaloupe Caprese Salad
Prep time: 10 minutes | Cook time: 0 minutes | Serves: 4

INGREDIENTS:

2/3 cup grape tomatoes
1 1/3 cups fresh Mozzarella balls
1 1/3 tablespoons extra-virgin olive oil
2/3 tablespoon balsamic vinegar
2/3 cantaloupe, quartered and seeded
1/3 small seedless watermelon
1/3 cup fresh basil or mint leaves, torn into small pieces
1/8 teaspoon freshly ground black pepper

1/8 teaspoon kosher or sea salt

DIRECTIONS:

1. Using a melon digger or a teaspoon-sized metal measuring cup, pick the balls out of the melon. You should get 2½ to 3 cups from a cantaloupe. (If you prefer, cut the melon into bite-sized pieces instead of making balls.) Place them in a large colander over a large serving bowl.
2. Using the same method, ball or cut the watermelon into bite-sized pieces; you should take about 2 cups. Place the watermelon balls in the colander with the melon.
3. Let the fruit drain for 10 minutes. Pour the juice from the bowl into a container to refrigerate and store for drinking or adding to smoothies. Dry the bowl and insert the cut fruit.
4. Add the tomatoes, mozzarella, basil, oil, vinegar, pepper and salt to the fruit mixture. Gently mix until everything is incorporated and serve.
5. Enjoy!

NUTRITION:

calories: 58 | fat: 2g | protein: 1g | carbs: 8g | fiber: 1g | sodium: 156mg

776. Zesty Spanish Potato Salad

Prep time: 10 minutes | Cook time: 7 minutes | Serves: 4

INGREDIENTS:

1/3 teaspoon freshly ground black pepper
1/3 teaspoon dried mustard seed
1/3 tablespoon freshly squeezed lemon juice
2 large hard-boiled eggs, chopped
2 2/3 russet potatoes, peeled and chopped
2/3 cup frozen mixed vegetables, thawed
1/3 cup plain, unsweetened, full-fat Greek yogurt
3 1/3 tablespoons pitted Spanish olives
1/3 teaspoon dried dill
Salt, to taste

DIRECTIONS:

1. Place the potatoes in a large pot of water and boil for 5-7 minutes, until they are just tender, periodically checking their cooking. You don't have to overcook them.
2. Meanwhile, in a large bowl, combine the eggs, vegetables, yogurt, olives, pepper, mustard, lemon juice, and dill. Season with salt to taste. When the potatoes have cooled a little, add them to a large bowl, then mix well and serve.
3. Enjoy!

NUTRITION:

calories: 192 | fat: 5g | protein: 9g | carbs: 30g | fiber: 2g | sodium: 59mg

777. Tricolor Summer Salad

Prep time: 10 minutes | Cook time: 0 minutes | Serves: 6

INGREDIENTS:

2 1/4 cups chopped orange, yellow, and red tomatoes
3/4 cucumber, peeled and diced
1/3 cup while balsamic vinegar
1/3 cup extra-virgin olive oil
3 tablespoons Dijon mustard
1 1/2 tablespoon sugar
3/4 teaspoon garlic salt
3/4 teaspoon freshly ground black pepper
1 1/2 small red onion, thinly sliced
1/3 cup crumbled feta (optional)

DIRECTIONS:

1. In a small bowl, whisk the vinegar, mustard, sugar, pepper, and garlic salt. Then slowly blend the olive oil
2. In a large bowl, add the tomatoes, cucumber and red onion. Add the dressing. Stir once or twice and serve with the feta crumbs (if desired) sprinkled on top.
3. Enjoy!

NUTRITION:

calories: 246 | fat: 18g | protein: 1g | carbs: 19g | fiber: 2g | sodium: 483mg

778. Arugula and Walnut Salad

Prep time: 10 minutes | Cook time: 0 minutes | Serves: 6

INGREDIENTS:

1 1/2 tablespoon red wine vinegar
3/4 teaspoon salt
1/3 teaspoon freshly ground black pepper
1 1/2 cup coarsely chopped walnuts
1 1/2 cup crumbled goat cheese
12 cups baby arugula
6 tablespoons extra-virgin olive oil
Zest and juice of 2 clementine's or 1 orange (2 to 3 tablespoons)
3/4 cup pomegranate seeds

DIRECTIONS:

1. In a small bowl, whisk together the olive oil, zest and juice, vinegar, salt and pepper and set aside.
2. To assemble the salad to serve, in a large bowl, combine the rocket, walnuts, goat cheese and pomegranate seeds. Drizzle with the dressing and toss to coat.
3. Enjoy!

NUTRITION:

calories: 444 | fat: 40g | protein: 10g | carbs: 11g | fiber: 3g | sodium: 412mg

779. Fig, Prosciutto and Arugula Salad

Prep time: 10 minutes | Cook time: 1 minutes | Serves: 4

INGREDIENTS:

6 very thin slices prosciutto, trimmed of any fat and sliced lengthwise into 1-inch strips
1/2 cup pecan halves, lightly toasted
4 tablespoons crumbled blue cheese
6 cups arugula
8 fresh, ripe figs (or 4 to 6 dried figs), stemmed and sliced
4 tablespoons olive oil
2 to 2 tablespoons balsamic glaze

DIRECTIONS:

1. In a large bowl, season the rocket and figs with the olive oil.
2. Place the ham on a microwave-safe plate and heat it at full power in the microwave for 60 seconds or until it starts to crisp.
3. Add the crispy ham, pecans and blue cheese to the bowl. Skip the salad lightly.
4. Season with the balsamic glaze.
5. Enjoy!

NUTRITION:

calories: 519 | fat: 38g | protein: 20g | carbs: 29g | fiber: 6g | sodium: 482mg

780. Italian Celery and Orange Salad

Prep time: 10 minutes | Cook time: 0 minutes | Serves: 4

INGREDIENTS:

1/8 cup sliced red onion
2/3 tablespoon extra-virgin olive oil
2 celery stalks, including leaves, sliced diagonally into 1/2-inch slices
2/3 tablespoon olive brine
1 1/3 large oranges, peeled and sliced into rounds
1/3 cup green olives (or any variety)
2/3 tablespoon freshly squeezed lemon or orange juice
1/8 teaspoon kosher or sea salt
1/8 teaspoon freshly ground black pepper

DIRECTIONS:

1. Place the celery, oranges, olives and onion on a large serving dish or in a large, shallow bowl.
2. In a small bowl, whisk together the oil, olive brine, and lemon juice. Pour over the salad, sprinkle with salt and pepper and serve.
3. Enjoy!

NUTRITION:

calories: 21 | fat: 1g | protein: 1g | carbs: 1g | fiber: 1g | sodium: 138mg

781. Tomato Hummus Soup

Prep time: 10 minutes | Cook time: 10 minutes | Serves: 4

INGREDIENTS:

Salt, to taste
1/2 cup fresh basil leaves, thinly sliced (optional, for garnish)
2 (14 1/2-ounce / 411-g) can crushed tomatoes with basil
2 cup roasted red pepper hummus
4 cups low-sodium chicken stock
Garlic croutons (optional, for garnish)

DIRECTIONS:

1. Combine canned tomatoes, hummus and chicken stock in a blender and blend until smooth. Pour the mixture into a saucepan and bring to a boil.
2. Season with salt and fresh basil if desired. Serve with garlic croutons as a garnish if desired.
3. Enjoy!

NUTRITION:

calories: 148 | fat: 6g | protein: 5g | carbs: 19g | fiber: 4g | sodium: 680mg

782. Greek Chicken Artichoke Soup

Prep time: 10 minutes | Cook time: 15 minutes | Serves: 6

INGREDIENTS:

1/3 cup freshly squeezed lemon juice (about 2 lemons)

1 1/8 cup extra-virgin olive oil, divided
12 ounces (227 g) cooked chicken, coarsely chopped
6 cups chicken stock
3 cups riced cauliflower, divided
3 large egg yolks
1 1/2 (13 3/4-ounce / 390-g) can artichoke hearts, drained and quartered
1/3 cup chopped fresh dill

DIRECTIONS:

1. In a large saucepan, bring the broth to a boil. Reduce heat to low and simmer, covered.
2. Transfer 1 cup of hot broth to a blender or food processor. Add ½ cup of raw cauliflower, egg yolks, lemon juice and puree. While the robot or blender is running, pour in ½ cup of olive oil and blend until smooth.
3. Stirring constantly, pour the puree into the boiling broth until it is well blended and homogeneous. Add the chicken and artichokes and simmer until thickened slightly, 8 to 10 minutes. Stir in the dill and the remaining 1½ cups of the rice cauliflower. Serve hot, topped with the remaining ¼ cup of olive oil.
4. Enjoy!

NUTRITION:

calories: 566 | fat: 46g | protein: 24g | carbs: 14g | fiber: 7g | sodium: 754mg

783. Pasta Bean Soup

Prep time: 10 minutes | Cook time: 25 minutes | Serves: 4

INGREDIENTS:

2 2/3 cups low-sodium or no-salt-added vegetable broth
1 1/3 (15 1/2-ounce / 439-g) cans cannellini, great northern, or light kidney beans, undrained
1 1/3 tablespoons extra-virgin olive oil
1/8 teaspoon crushed red pepper
1/3 cup chopped onion (about 1/4 onion)
2 garlic cloves, minced (about 1 1/2 teaspoons)
2/3 tablespoon minced fresh rosemary or 1 teaspoon dried rosemary
2/3 (28-ounce / 794-g) can low-sodium or no-salt-added crushed tomatoes
1 1/3 tablespoons tomato paste
5 1/3 ounces (227 g) uncooked short pasta, such as ditalini, tubetti, or elbows
4 tablespoons grated Parmesan cheese (about 1 1/2 ounces / 43 g)

DIRECTIONS:

1. In a large saucepan over medium heat, heat the oil. Add the onion and cook for 4 minutes, stirring often. Add the garlic, rosemary and chopped chilli. Cook for 1 minute, stirring often. Add the broth, canned beans with their liquid, tomatoes and tomato paste. Simmer for 5 minutes.
2. To thicken the soup, carefully transfer 2 cups to a blender. Blend, then stir in the pot.
3. Bring the soup to a boil over high heat. Add the pasta and lower the heat to low heat. Cook the pasta for the time recommended on the package, stirring every few minutes to prevent the pasta from sticking to the pot. Taste the pasta to make sure it is well cooked (it may take a few minutes longer than the recommended cooking time, as it cooks with other ingredients).
4. Pour the soup into bowls, garnish each with 1 tablespoon of grated cheese and serve.
5. Enjoy!

NUTRITION:

calories: 583 | fat: 6g | protein: 32g | carbs: 103g | fiber: 29g | sodium: 234mg

784. Lentil Soup

Prep time: 10 minutes | Cook time: 1 hour 20 minutes | Serves: 4

INGREDIENTS:

1/8 cup long-grain rice, rinsed
2 tablespoons extra-virgin olive oil
6 2/3 cups water
1 1/3 cups brown lentils, picked over and rinsed
1 1/3 medium potatoes, peeled
1 1/3 teaspoons salt, divided
2/3 large onion, chopped
2/3 teaspoon ground cumin
1/3 teaspoon freshly ground black pepper

DIRECTIONS:

1. In a large saucepan over medium heat, bring the water, lentils and 1 teaspoon of salt to a boil and continue to cook, stirring occasionally, for 30 minutes.
2. After 30 minutes, add the rice to the lentils. Cover and continue to simmer, stirring occasionally, for another 30 minutes.
3. Remove the pan from the heat and, using an immersion blender, blend the lentils and rice for 1 or 2 minutes until smooth.
4. Put the pot back on the stove over low heat.
5. In a small skillet over medium heat, cook the olive oil and onions for 5 minutes until the onions are golden. Add the onions to the soup.
6. Cut the potatoes into ¼-inch pieces and add them to the soup.
7. Add the remaining teaspoon of salt, cumin and black pepper to the soup. Stir and continue to cook for 10-15 minutes, or until the potatoes are cooked through. Serve hot.
8. Enjoy!

NUTRITION:

calories: 348 | fat: 9g | protein: 18g | carbs: 53g | fiber: 20g | sodium: 795mg

785. Lemon Chicken Orzo Soup

Prep time: 10 minutes | Cook time: 20 minutes | Serves: 4

INGREDIENTS:

1/4 cup chopped carrots
1 1/2 garlic cloves, minced
4 1/2 cups low-sodium chicken broth
1 cup shredded cooked chicken breast
1/4 cup freshly squeezed lemon juice
1/4 cup chopped celery
1/2 tablespoon extra-virgin olive oil
1/2 cup chopped onion
Zest of 1 lemon, grated
1/2 to 2 teaspoons dried oregano
4 ounces (227 g) cooked orzo pasta

DIRECTIONS:

1. In a large saucepan, heat the oil over medium heat and add the onion, carrots, celery and garlic and cook for about 5 minutes, until the onions are translucent. Add the broth and bring to the boil.
2. Reduce to a simmer, cover and cook for another 10 minutes, until the flavours blend. Then add the shredded chicken, the lemon juice and zest, and the oregano.
3. Serve the barley in the bowls first, then add the chicken stock.
4. Enjoy!

NUTRITION:

calories: 215 | fat: 5g | protein: 16g | carbs: 27g | fiber: 2g | sodium: 114mg

786. Thyme Carrot Soup with Parmesan

Prep time: 10 minutes | Cook time: 20 minutes | Serves: 6

INGREDIENTS:

3 3/4 cups water
1 1/2 teaspoon dried thyme
3 pounds (907 g) carrots, unpeeled, cut into 1/2-inch slices (about 6 cups)
3 tablespoons extra-virgin olive oil, divided
1 1/2 cup chopped onion (about 1/2 medium onion)
3 cups low-sodium or no-salt-added vegetable (or chicken) broth
1/3 teaspoon crushed red pepper
1/3 teaspoon kosher or sea salt
6 thin slices whole-grain bread
1/3 cup freshly grated Parmesan cheese (about 1 ounce / 28 g)

DIRECTIONS:

1. Place an oven rack about four inches below the grill element. Place two large, rimmed baking sheets in the oven on any oven rack. Preheat the oven to 450°F | 230°C | Fan 210°C.
2. In a large bowl, season the carrots with 1 tablespoon of oil to coat them. With oven mitts, carefully remove the pans from the oven and evenly distribute the carrots on both pans. Cook for 20 minutes, until the carrots are just tender, stirring halfway through. Carrots will still be a little firm. Remove the carrots from the oven and turn the oven on high.
3. While the carrots are roasting, in a large saucepan over medium-high heat, heat 1 tablespoon of oil. Add the onion and cook for 5 minutes, stirring occasionally. Add the broth, water, thyme, chopped chilli and salt. Bring to a boil, cover, then remove the pan from the heat until the carrots are done roasting.
4. Add the roasted carrots to the pot and blend with a hand blender (or use a regular blender: carefully pour the hot soup in batches, then return the soup to the pot). Heat the soup for about 1 minute over medium-high heat, until it is hot.
5. Turn the oven on to high heat. Put the bread on the baking sheet. Sprinkle the cheese evenly over the slices of bread. Bake the bread 4 inches under the heating element for 1 to 2 minutes, or until the cheese melts, watching carefully to prevent burning.
6. Cut the bread into small croutons. Divide the soup evenly into four bowls, garnish each with the parmesan croutons and serve.
5. Enjoy!

NUTRITION:

calories: 312 | fat: 6g | protein: 6g | carbs: 53g | fiber: 10g | sodium: 650mg

787. Pastina Chicken Soup

Prep time: 10 minutes | Cook time: 25 minutes | Serves: 4

INGREDIENTS:

1/8 teaspoon kosher or sea salt	acini de pepe or pastina pasta
1 1/3 garlic cloves, minced (about 1 teaspoon)	2/3 tablespoon extra-virgin olive oil
2 cups packed chopped kale (center ribs removed)	2/3 cup minced carrots (about 2 carrots)
	5 1/3 cups low-sodium or no-salt-added chicken (or vegetable) broth
1/8 teaspoon freshly ground black pepper	1 1/3 cups shredded cooked chicken (about 12 ounces / 340 g)
1/2 cup (6 ounces / 170 g) uncooked	2 tablespoons grated Parmesan cheese

DIRECTIONS:

1. In a large saucepan over medium heat, heat the oil. Add the garlic and cook for 30 seconds, stirring often. Add the cabbage and carrots and cook for 5 minutes, stirring occasionally.
2. Add the broth, salt and pepper and raise the heat. Bring the broth to the boil and add the pasta. Lower the heat to medium and cook for 10 minutes, or until the pasta is cooked, stirring every few minutes so the pasta doesn't stick to the bottom. Add the chicken and cook for another 2 minutes to heat it up.
3. Pour the soup into six bowls, cover each with ½ tablespoon of cheese and serve.
4. Enjoy!

NUTRITION:

calories: 275 | fat: 19g | protein: 16g | carbs: 11g | fiber: 2g | sodium: 298mg

788. Cabbage Salad

Prep time: 10 minutes | Cook time: 25 minutes | Serves: 6

INGREDIENTS:

Mint - 1 tbsp., chopped	Carrot - 1, grated
Ground coriander - 1/2 tsp. Savoy cabbage - 1, shredded	Red onion – 1, sliced
	Honey - 1 tsp.
Greek yogurt - 1/2 cup	Lemon zest - 1 tsp.
Cumin seeds - 1/4 tsp.	Lemon juice - 2 tbsp.
Extra virgin olive oil - 2 tbsp.	Salt and pepper - to taste

DIRECTIONS:

1. In a salad bowl, mix all Shopping List ingredients.
2. You can add salt and pepper to suit your taste and then mix again.
3. This salad is best when cool and freshly made.
4. Enjoy!

NUTRITION:

calories: 276 | fat: 15g | protein: 22g | carbs: 11g | fiber: 2g | sodium: 298mg

789. Balela Salad

Prep time: 10 minutes | Cook time: 0 minutes | Serves: 4

INGREDIENTS:

2/3 jalapeno, finely chopped (optional)	parts, chopped
1/3 green bell pepper, cored and chopped	Dressing Shopping List
	2/3 garlic clove, minced
1 2/3 cups grape tomatoes, slice in halves	2/3 tsp ground sumac
	1/3 tsp Aleppo pepper
1/3 cup sun-dried tomatoes	1/8 cup Early Harvest Greek extra virgin olive oil
1/3 cup freshly chopped parsley leaves	
1/3 cup freshly chopped mint or basil leaves	1/8 to 1/2 tsp crushed red pepper (optional)
1/4 cup pitted Kalamata olives	2/3 tbsp lemon juice
1/8 cup pitted green olives	1 1/3 tbsp white wine vinegar
2 1/3 cups cooked chickpeas, drained and rinsed	Salt and black pepper, a generous pinch to your taste
3–5 green onions, both white and green	

DIRECTIONS:

1. Mix together the salad Shopping List ingredients in a large salad bowl.
2. In a separate smaller bowl or jar, mix together the dressing Shopping List ingredients.
3. Drizzle the dressing over the salad and gently toss to coat.
4. Set aside for 30 minutes to allow the flavours to mix.
5. Enjoy!

NUTRITION:

calories: 257 | fat: 12g | protein: 8g | carbs: 30g | fiber: 2g | sodium: 298mg

790. Charred Tomato and Broccoli Salad

Prep time: 10 minutes | Cook time: 2 minutes | Serves: 4

INGREDIENTS:

1/8 cup lemon juice	2/3 tsp salt
1/3 tsp chili powder	1 1/3 cups broccoli florets
1 lbs. boneless chicken breast	2/3 tbsp extra virgin olive oil, divided to 2 and 3 tablespoons 2
1 lbs. medium tomato	
2/3 tsp freshly ground pepper	

DIRECTIONS:

1. Place the chicken in a skillet and add just enough water to cover the chicken. Bring to a simmer over high heat. Reduce the heat once the liquid boils and cook the chicken thoroughly for 12 minutes. Once cooked, shred the chicken into bite-sized pieces.
2. On a large pot, bring water to a boil and add the broccoli. Cook for 5 minutes until slightly tender. Drain and rinse the broccoli with cold water. Set aside.
3. Core the tomatoes and cut them crosswise. Discard the seeds and set the tomatoes cut side down on paper towels. Pat them dry.
4. In a heavy skillet, heat the pan over high heat until very hot. Brush the cut sides of the tomatoes with olive oil and place them on the pan. Cook the tomatoes until the sides are charred. Set aside.
5. In the same pan, heat the remaining 3 tablespoon olive oil over medium heat. Stir the salt, chili powder and pepper and stir for 45 seconds. Pour over the lemon juice and remove the pan from the heat.
6. Plate the broccoli, shredded chicken and chili powder mixture dressing.
7. Enjoy!

NUTRITION:

calories: 210 | fat: 12g | protein: 27g | carbs: 7g | fiber: 8g | sodium: 298mg

791. Grilled Salmon Summer Salad

Prep time: 10 minutes | Cook time: 30 minutes | Serves: 6

INGREDIENTS:

Salmon fillets - 2	Lemon - 1, juiced
Salt and pepper - to taste Vegetable stock - 2 cups	Green olives - 1/2 cup, sliced Cucumber - 1, cubed
Bulgur - 1/2 cup	Green onion - 1, chopped red pepper - 1, chopped
Cherry tomatoes - 1 cup, halved	
Sweet corn - 1/2 cup	Red bell pepper - 1, cored and diced

DIRECTIONS:

1. Heat a grill pan on medium and then place salmon on, seasoning with salt and pepper. Grill both sides of salmon until brown and set aside.
2. Heat stock in sauce pan until hot and then add in bulgur and cook until liquid is completely soaked into bulgur.
3. Mix salmon, bulgur and all other Shopping List in a salad bowl and again add salt and pepper, if desired, to suit your taste.
4. Serve salad as soon as completed.
5. Enjoy!

NUTRITION:

calories: 168 | fat: 6g | protein: 5g | carbs: 19g | fiber: 4g | sodium: 680mg

792. Peppy Pepper Tomato Salad

Prep time: 10 minutes | Cook time: 20 minutes | Serves: 6

INGREDIENTS:

Yellow bell pepper - 1, cored and diced	Tomatoes - 4, diced
Cucumbers - 4, diced	Red bell peppers - 2, cored and diced
Red onion - 1, chopped Balsamic vinegar – 1 tbsp. Extra virgin olive oil – 2 tbsp.	Chili flakes - 1 pinch
	Salt and pepper - to taste

DIRECTIONS:

1. Mix all above Shopping List ingredients in a salad bowl, except salt and pepper.
2. Season with salt and pepper to suit your taste and mix well.
3. Eat while fresh.
4. Enjoy!

NUTRITION:

calories: 160 | fat: 6g | protein:12g | carbs: 19g | fiber: 4g | sodium: 680mg

793. Bulgur Salad

Prep time: 10 minutes | Cook time: 30 minutes | Serves: 6

INGREDIENTS:

Vegetable stock - 2 cups Bulgur - 2/3 cup
Garlic clove - 1, minced
Cherry tomatoes - 1 cup, halved
Almonds - 2 tbsp., sliced
Dates - 1 4 cup, pitted and chopped
Lemon juice - 1 tbsp.
Baby spinach - 8 oz.
Cucumber - 1, diced
Balsamic vinegar - 1 tbsp. Salt and pepper - to taste Mixed seeds - 2 tbsp.

DIRECTIONS:

1. Pour stock into sauce pan and heat until hot, then stir in bulgur and cook until bulgur has absorbed all stock.
2. Put in salad bowl and add remaining Shopping List ingredients, stir well.
3. Add salt and pepper to suit your taste.
4. Serve and eat immediately.
5. Enjoy!

NUTRITION:

calories: 178 | fat: 7g | protein: 5g | carbs: 19g | fiber: 4g | sodium: 680mg

794. Tuna Salad

Prep time: 10 minutes | Cook time: 15 minutes | Serves: 6

INGREDIENTS:

Green olives - 1/4 cup, sliced Tuna in water - 1 can, drained
Pine nuts - 2 tbsp.
Artichoke hearts – 1 jar, drained and chopped
Extra virgin olive oil: 2 tbsp.
Lemon:1, juiced
Arugula - 2 leaves
Dijon mustard - 1 tbsp.
Salt and pepper - to taste

DIRECTIONS:

1. Mix mustard, oil and lemon juice in a bowl to make a dressing. Combine the artichoke hearts, tuna, green olives, arugula and pine nuts in a salad bowl.
2. In a separate salad bowl, mix tuna, arugula, pine nuts, artichoke hearts and tuna.
3. Pour dressing mix onto salad and serve fresh.
4. Enjoy!

NUTRITION:

calories: 208 | fat: 6g | protein: 9g | carbs: 19g | fiber: 4g | sodium: 680mg

795. Sweet and Sour Spinach Salad

Prep time: 10 minutes | Cook time: 15 minutes | Serves: 6

INGREDIENTS:

Red onions - 2, sliced
Baby spinach leaves - 4
Sesame oil - 1 2 tsp.
Apple cider vinegar - 2 tbsp.
Honey - 1 tsp.
Sesame seeds - 2 tbsp.
Salt and pepper - to taste

DIRECTIONS:

1. Mix together honey, sesame oil, vinegar and sesame seeds in a small bowl to make a dressing. Add in salt and pepper to suit your taste.
2. Add red onions and spinach together in a salad bowl.
3. Pour dressing over the salad and serve while cool and fresh.
4. Enjoy!

NUTRITION:

calories: 177 | fat: 8g | protein: 13g | carbs: 22g | fiber: 4g | sodium: 622mg

796. Easy Eggplant Salad

Prep time: 10 minutes | Cook time: 30 minutes | Serves: 6

INGREDIENTS:

Salt and pepper - to taste
Eggplant - 2, sliced
Smoked paprika - 1 tsp.
Extra virgin olive oil - 2 tbsp.
Garlic cloves - 2, minced Mixed greens - 2 cups Sherry vinegar - 2 tbsp.

DIRECTIONS:

1. Mix together garlic, paprika and oil in a small bowl.
2. Place eggplant on a plate and sprinkle with salt and pepper to suit your taste. Next, brush oil mixture onto the eggplant.
3. Cook eggplant on a medium heated grill pan until brown on both sides. Once cooked, put eggplant into a salad bowl.
4. Top with greens and vinegar, serve and eat.
5. Enjoy!

NUTRITION:

calories: 172 | fat: 8g | protein: 13g | carbs: 22g | fiber: 4g | sodium: 680mg

797. Yogurt Lettuce Salad Recipe

Prep time: 10 minutes | Cook time: 20 minutes | Serves: 6

INGREDIENTS:

Shredded Romaine lettuce: 1 head
Sliced cucumbers: 2
2 minced garlic cloves
Greek yogurt: 1/2 cup
Dijon mustard: 1 teaspoon
Chili powder: 1 pinch
Extra virgin olive oil: 2 tablespoon
Lemon juice: 1 tablespoon Chopped dill: 2 tablespoons
4 chopped mint leaves Pepper and salt to taste

DIRECTIONS:

1. In a salad bowl, combine the lettuce with the cucumbers.
2. Add the yogurt, chili, mustard, lemon juice, dill, mint, garlic and oil in a mortar with pepper and salt as desired. Then, mix well into paste; this is the dressing for the salad.
3. Top the Salad with the dressing, then serve fresh.
4. Enjoy!

NUTRITION:

calories: 172 | fat: 8g | protein: 13g | carbs: 22g | fiber: 4g | sodium: 456mg

798. Grapy Fennel salad

Prep time: 10 minutes | Cook time: 15 minutes | Serves: 4

INGREDIENTS:

Grape seed oil: 1 tablespoon
Chopped dill: 1 tablespoon
1 finely sliced fennel bulb
Toasted almond slices: 2 tablespoons
Chopped mint: 1 teaspoon
1 grapefruit already cut into segments
1 orange already cut into segments
Pepper and salt as desired

DIRECTIONS:

1. Using a platter, mix the grapefruit and orange segments with the fennel bulb
2. Add the mint, almond slices and dill, top with the oil and add pepper and salt as desired.
3. You can now serve the Salad fresh.
4. Enjoy!

NUTRITION:

calories: 155 | fat: 8g | protein: 23g | carbs: 22g | fiber: 4g | sodium: 456mg

799. Greenie salad recipe

Prep time: 10 minutes | Cook time: 15 minutes | Serves: 6

INGREDIENTS:

Extra virgin olive oil: 2 tablespoons
Mixed greens: 12 oz.
Pitted black olives: 1/2 cup
Pitted green olives: 1/4 cup
Sherry vinegar: 2 tablespoons
Pitted Kalamata olives: 1/2 cup
Almond slices: 2 tablespoons
Parmesan shavings: 2 oz.
Sliced Parma ham: 2 oz.
Pepper and salt as desired

DIRECTIONS:

1. Stir the almonds, olives and mixed greens together in a salad bowl
2. Drizzle the oil and vinegar then sprinkle pepper and salt as you want.
3. Top with the Parma ham and Parmesan shavings before serving.
4. You can now serve fresh.
5. Enjoy!

NUTRITION:

calories: 166 | fat: 6g | protein: 5g | carbs: 19g | fiber: 12g | sodium: 456mg

800. Broccoli Salad with Caramelized Onions

Prep time: 10 minutes | Cook time: 25 minutes | Serves: 6

INGREDIENTS:

Extra virgin olive oil - 3 tbsp. red onions - 2, sliced
Dried thyme - 1 tsp.
Balsamic vinegar - 2 tbsp. vinegar
Broccoli - 1 lb., cut into florets salt and pepper - to taste

DIRECTIONS:

1. Heat extra virgin olive oil in a pan over high heat and add in sliced onions. Cook for approximately 10 minutes or until the onions are caramelized. Stir in vinegar and thyme and then remove from stove.
2. Mix together the broccoli and onion mixture in a bowl, adding salt and pepper if desired. Serve and eat salad as soon as possible.
3. Enjoy!

NUTRITION:

calories: 188 | fat: 12g | protein: 21g | carbs: 24g | fiber: 4g | sodium: 633mg

801. Sweet Potato Salad

Prep time: 10 minutes | Cook time: 30 minutes | Serves: 6

INGREDIENTS:

Honey - 2 tbsp.
Sumac spice - 1 tsp.
Sweet potato - 2, finely sliced Extra virgin olive oil - 3 tbsp.
Dried mint - 1 tsp.
Balsamic vinegar – 1 tbsp.
Salt and pepper - to taste
Pomegranate - 1, seeded
Mixed greens - 3 cups

DIRECTIONS:

1. Place sweet potato slices on a plate and add sumac, mint, salt and pepper on both sides. Next, drizzle oil and honey over both sides.
2. Add oil to a grill pan and heat. Grill sweet potatoes on medium heat until brown on both sides.
3. Put sweet potatoes in a salad bowl and top with pomegranate and mixed greens.
4. Stir and eat right away.
5. Enjoy!

NUTRITION:

calories: 144 | fat: 8g | protein: 13g | carbs: 18g | fiber: 4g | sodium: 680mg

802. Chickpea Salad

Prep time: 10 minutes | Cook time: 15 minutes | Serves: 6

INGREDIENTS:

Chickpeas - 1 can, drained
Cherry tomatoes - 1 cup, quartered
Parsley - 1 2 cup, chopped
Red seedless grapes - 1 2 cup, halved
Feta cheese - 4 oz., cubed
Salt and pepper - to taste
Lemon juice - 1 tbsp.
Greek yogurt - 1 4 cup
Extra virgin olive oil - 2 tbsp.

DIRECTIONS:

1. In a salad bowl, mix together parsley, chickpeas, grapes, feta cheese and tomatoes.
2. Add in remaining Shopping List ingredients, seasoning with salt and pepper to suit your taste.
3. This fresh salad is best when served right away.
4. Enjoy!

NUTRITION:

calories: 132 | fat: 10g | protein: 13g | carbs: 22g | fiber: 4g | sodium: 680mg

803. Couscous Arugula Salad

Prep time: 10 minutes | Cook time: 20 minutes | Serves: 6

INGREDIENTS:

Couscous - 1 2 cup
Vegetable stock - 1 cup
Asparagus - 1 bunch, peeled
Lemon - 1, juiced
Dried tarragon - 1 tsp.
Arugula - 2 cups
Salt and pepper - to taste

DIRECTIONS:

1. Heat vegetable stock in a pot until hot. Remove from heat and add in couscous. Cover until couscous has absorbed all the stock.
2. Pour in a bowl and fluff with a fork and then set aside to cool.
3. Peel asparagus with a vegetable peeler, making them into ribbons and put into a bowl with couscous.
4. Add remaining Shopping List ingredients and add salt and pepper to suit your taste.
5. Serve the salad immediately.
6. Enjoy!

NUTRITION:

calories: 182 | fat: 8g | protein: 25g | carbs: 22g | fiber: 4g | sodium: 679mg

804. Spinach and Grilled Feta Salad

Prep time: 10 minutes | Cook time: 20 minutes | Serves: 4

INGREDIENTS:

Feta cheese - 8 oz., sliced
Black olives - 1/4 cup, sliced green olives - 1/4 cup, sliced Baby spinach - 4 cups
Garlic cloves - 2, minced
Capers - 1 tsp., chopped
Extra virgin olive oil - 2 tbsp. red wine vinegar - 1 tbsp.

DIRECTIONS:

1. Grill feta cheese slices over medium to high flame until brown on both sides.
2. In a salad bowl, mix green olives, black olives and spinach.
3. In a separate bowl, mix vinegar, capers and oil together to make a dressing.
4. Top salad with the dressing and cheese and it's ready to serve.
5. Enjoy!

NUTRITION:

calories: 172 | fat: 6g | protein: 17g | carbs: 22g | fiber: 4g | sodium: 680mg

805. Orange salad

Prep time: 10 minutes | Cook time: 15 minutes | Serves: 6

INGREDIENTS:

6 sliced endives
3 sliced red onion
3 oranges already cut into segments
Extra virgin olive oil: 2 tablespoons
Pepper and salt to taste

DIRECTIONS:

1. Mix all the Shopping List ingredients in a salad bowl
2. Sprinkle pepper and salt to taste.
3. You can now serve the salad fresh.
4. Enjoy!

NUTRITION:

calories: 194 | fat: 11g | protein: 13g | carbs: 15g | fiber: 8g | sodium: 680mg

806. Baked Cauliflower Mixed Salad

Prep time: 10 minutes | Cook time: 30 minutes | Serves: 6

INGREDIENTS:

Cauliflower - 1 lb., cut into florets Extra virgin olive oil - 2 tbsp.
Dried mint - 1 tsp.
Dried oregano - 1 tsp.
Parsley - 2 tbsp., chopped
Red pepper - 1, chopped Lemon - 1, juiced
Green onion - 1, chopped Cilantro - 2 tbsp., chopped Salt and pepper to taste

DIRECTIONS:

1. Preheat oven to 350°F | 180°C | Fan 160°C.
2. In a deep baking pan, combine olive oil, mint, cauliflower and oregano and bake for 15 minutes.
3. Once cooked, pour into a salad bowl and add remaining Shopping List ingredients, stirring together.
4. Plate the salad and eat fresh and warm.
5. Enjoy!

NUTRITION:

calories: 122 | fat: 8g | protein: 25g | carbs: 22g | fiber: 7g | sodium: 680mg

807. Cool Salad

Prep time: 10 minutes | Cook time: 15 minutes | Serves: 6

INGREDIENTS:

Greek yogurt - 1/2 cup
Dill - 2 tbsp., chopped Lemon juice - 1 tsp.
Cucumbers - 4, diced
Garlic cloves - 2, minced Salt and pepper - to taste

DIRECTIONS:

1. Mix all Shopping List ingredients in a salad bowl.
2. Add salt and pepper to suit your taste and eat.
3. Enjoy!

NUTRITION:

calories: 172 | fat: 8g | protein: 13g | carbs: 22g | fiber: 4g | sodium: 680mg

808. Bell Pepper and Tomato Salad

Prep time: 10 minutes | Cook time: 15 minutes | Serves: 6

INGREDIENTS:

Roasted red bell pepper - 8, sliced Extra virgin olive oil - 2 tbsp.
Chili flakes - 1 pinch
Garlic cloves - 4, minced Pine nuts - 2 tbsp.
Shallot - 1, sliced
Cherry tomatoes - 1 cup, halved Parsley - 2 tbsp., chopped Balsamic vinegar - 1 tbsp.
Salt and pepper - to taste

DIRECTIONS:

1. Mix all Shopping List ingredients: except salt and pepper in a salad bowl.
2. Season with salt and pepper if you want, to suit your taste.
3. Eat once freshly made.
4. Enjoy!

NUTRITION:

calories: 202 | fat: 8g | protein: 13g | carbs: 22g | fiber: 9g | sodium: 680mg

809. Spinach Salad

Prep time: 10 minutes | Cook time: 20 minutes | Serves: 6

INGREDIENTS:

Red beets - 2, cooked and diced Apple cider vinegar - 1 tbsp.
Baby spinach - 3 cups
Greek yogurt - 1/4 cup
Horseradish - 1 tbsp.
Salt and pepper - to taste

DIRECTIONS:

1. Mix beets and spinach in a salad bowl.
2. Add in yogurt, horseradish, and vinegar. You can also add salt and pepper if you wish.
3. Serve salad as soon as mixed.
4. Enjoy!

NUTRITION:

calories: 179 | fat: 5g | protein: 18g | carbs: 22g | fiber: 4g | sodium: 580mg

810. Olive and Red Bean Salad

Prep time: 10 minutes | Cook time: 20 minutes | Serves: 6

INGREDIENTS:

Red onions - 2, sliced
Garlic cloves - 2, minced Balsamic vinegar - 2 tbsp.
Green olives - 1/4 cup, sliced Salt and pepper - to taste Mixed greens - 2 cups
Red beans - 1 can, drained Chili flakes - 1 pinch
Extra virgin olive oil - 2 tbsp. Parsley - 2 tbsp., chopped

DIRECTIONS:

1. In a salad bowl, mix all Shopping List ingredients.
2. Add salt and pepper, if desired, and serve right away.
3. Enjoy!

NUTRITION:

calories: 166 | fat: 9g | protein: 10g | carbs: 16g | fiber: 7g | sodium: 434mg

811. Blue Cheese and Portobello Salad

Prep time: 10 minutes | Cook time: 15 minutes | Serves: 4

INGREDIENTS:

1 cup croutons
2 tbsp merlot wine
2 tbsp water
2 tsp minced garlic
2 tsp olive oil
2 large Portobello mushrooms, stemmed, wiped clean and cut into bite sized pieces
4 pieces roasted red peppers (canned), sliced
4 tbsp balsamic vinegar
4 tbsp crumbled blue cheese 4 slices red onion
12 asparagus stalks cut into 1-inch sections
12 cups lettuce, chopped Ground pepper to taste

DIRECTIONS:

1. On medium heat, place a small pan and heat oil. Once hot, add onions and mushrooms. For 4 to 6 minutes, sauté until tender.
2. Add garlic and for a minute continue sautéing.
3. Pour in wine and cook for a minute.
4. Bring an inch of water to a boil in a pot with steamer basket. Once boiling, add asparagus, steam for 2 to 3 minutes or until crisp and tender, while covered. Once cooked, remove basket from pot and set aside.
5. In a small bowl whisk thoroughly black pepper, water, balsamic vinegar, and blue cheese.
6. To serve, place 3 cups of lettuce on each plate.
7. Add 1 roasted pepper, ½ of asparagus, ½ of mushroom mixture, whisk blue cheese dressing before drizzling equally on to plates.
8. Garnish with croutons
9. Enjoy!

NUTRITION:

calories: 660 | fat: 9g | protein: 38g | carbs: 30g | fiber:42g | sodium: 434mg

812. Arugula Salad

Prep time: 10 minutes | Cook time: 15 minutes | Serves: 6

INGREDIENTS:

Roasted red bell peppers - 6, sliced
Pine nuts - 2 tbsp.
Dried raisins - 2 tbsp.
Red onion - 1, sliced
Arugula - 3 cups
Balsamic vinegar - 2 tbsp
Feta cheese - 4 oz., crumbled
Extra virgin olive oil – 2 tbsp
Feta cheese - 4 oz., crumbled
Salt and pepper to taste

DIRECTIONS:

1. Using a salad bowl, combine vinegar, olive oil, pine nuts, raisins, peppers and onions.
2. Add arugula and feta cheese to the mix and serve.
3. Enjoy!

NUTRITION:

calories: 189 | fat: 8g | protein: 18g | carbs: 22g | fiber: 4g | sodium: 556mg

813. Anchovy and Orange Salad

Prep time: 10 minutes | Cook time: 0 minutes | Serves: 6

INGREDIENTS:

1 small red onion, sliced into thin rounds
1 tbsp fresh lemon juice
1/8 tsp pepper or more to taste
16 oil cure Kalamata olives
1 tsp finely minced fennel
l fronds for garnish
3 tbsp extra virgin olive oil
4 small oranges, preferably blood oranges
6 anchovy fillets

DIRECTIONS:

1. With a paring knife, peel oranges including the membrane that surrounds it.
2. In a plate, slice oranges into thin circles and allow plate to catch the orange juices.
3. On serving plate, arrange orange slices on a layer.
4. Sprinkle oranges with onion, followed by olives and then anchovy fillets.
5. Drizzle with oil, lemon juice and orange juice.
6. Sprinkle with pepper.
7. Allow salad to stand for 30 minutes at room temperature to allow the flavours to develop.
8. To serve, garnish with fennel fronds and enjoy.
9. Enjoy!

NUTRITION:

calories: 133 | fat: 8g | protein: 4g | carbs: 14g | fiber: 4g | sodium: 556mg

814. Cucumber Greek yoghurt Salad

Prep time: 10 minutes | Cook time: 0 minutes | Serves: 4

INGREDIENTS:

2 2/3 tbsp Greek yogurt
2 2/3 large cucumbers peeled seeded and sliced
2/3 tbsp dried dill
2/3 tbsp apple cider vinegar 1/4 tsp
garlic powder
1/8 tsp ground black pepper
1/3 tsp sugar
1/3 tsp salt

DIRECTIONS:

1. Place all the Shopping List ingredients, except the cucumber, into a bowl and whisk this until all is incorporated. Add your cucumber slices and toss until all is well mixed.
2. Let the salad chill 10 minutes in the refrigerator and then serve.
3. Enjoy!

NUTRITION:

calories: 152 | fat: 5g | protein: 17g | carbs: 22g | fiber: 4g | sodium: 456mg

815. Chickpea Salad Recipe

Prep time: 10 minutes | Cook time: 15 minutes | Serves: 6

INGREDIENTS:

Drained chickpeas: 1 can
Halved cherry tomatoes: 1 cup
Sun-dried chopped tomatoes: 1/2 cups
Arugula: 2 cups
Cubed pita bread: 1
Pitted black olives: 1/2 cups
1 sliced shallot
Cumin seeds: 1/2 teaspoon
Coriander seeds: 1/2 teaspoon
Chili powder: 1/4 teaspoon Chopped mint: 1 teaspoon Pepper and salt to taste
Crumbled goat cheese: 4 oz.

DIRECTIONS:

1. In a salad bowl, mix the tomatoes, chickpeas, pita bread, arugula, olives, shallot, spices and mint.
2. Stir in pepper and salt as desired to the cheese and stir.
3. You can now serve the fresh Salad.
4. Enjoy!

NUTRITION:

calories: 132 | fat: 5g | protein: 11g | carbs: 24g | fiber: 7g | sodium: 621mg

816. Lentil Salmon Salad

Prep time: 10 minutes | Cook time: 25 minutes | Serves: 6

INGREDIENTS:

Vegetable stock - 2 cups
Green lentils - 1, rinsed
Red onion - 1, chopped Parsley - 1/2 cup, chopped
Smoked salmon - 4 oz., shredded
Cilantro - 2 tbsp., chopped
Red pepper - 1, chopped Lemon - 1, juiced
Salt and pepper - to taste

DIRECTIONS:

1. Cook vegetable stock and lentils in a sauce pan for 15 to 20 minutes, on low heat. Ensure all liquid has been absorbed and then remove from heat.
2. Pour into a salad bowl and top with red pepper, parsley, cilantro and salt and pepper (to suit your taste) and mix.
3. Mix in lemon juice and shredded salmon.
4. This salad should be served fresh.
5. Enjoy!

NUTRITION:

calories: 172 | fat: 8g | protein: 13g | carbs: 22g | fiber: 4g | sodium: 680mg

817. Detox Salad

Prep time: 10 minutes | Cook time: 0 minutes | Serves: 6

INGREDIENTS:

1 1/2 large apple, diced
1 1/2 large beet, coarsely grated
1 1/2 large carrot, coarsely grated
1 1/2 tbsp chia seeds
1 1/2 tbsp almonds, chopped 2 tbsp lemon juice
3 tbsp pumpkin seed oil 4 cups mixed greens

DIRECTIONS:

1. In a medium salad bowl, except for mixed greens, combine all Shopping List ingredients thoroughly.
2. Divide the mixed greens into 4 salad plates.
3. Evenly top mixed greens with the salad bowl mixture.
4. Enjoy!

NUTRITION:

calories: 136 | fat: 8g | protein: 19g | carbs: 14g | fiber: 4g | sodium: 680mg

818. Carrot Salad

Prep time: 10 minutes | Cook time: 0 minutes | Serves: 6

INGREDIENTS:

1/3 tsp chipotle powder
1 1/2 bunch scallions, sliced
1 1/2 cup cherry tomatoes, halved 1 large avocado, diced
1 1/2 tbsp chili powder
1 1/2 tbsp lemon juice
3 tbsp olive oil
1 1/2 tbsp lime juice
3 cups carrots, spiralized
Salt to taste

DIRECTIONS:

1. In a salad bowl, mix and arrange avocado, cherry tomatoes, scallions and spiralized carrots. Set aside.
2. In a small bowl, whisk salt, chipotle powder, chili powder, olive oil, lemon juice and lime juice thoroughly.
3. Pour dressing over noodle salad. Toss to coat well.
4. Enjoy!

NUTRITION:

calories: 243 | fat: 14g | protein: 3g | carbs: 24g | fiber: 4g | sodium: 680mg

819. Vegetable Patch Salad

Prep time: 10 minutes | Cook time: 30 minutes | Serves: 4

INGREDIENTS:

Cauliflower - 1 bunch, cut into florets
Zucchini - 1, sliced
Sweet potato - 1, peeled and cubed
Baby carrots - 1/2 lb.
Salt and pepper - to taste Dried basil - 1 tsp.
Red onions - 2, sliced
Eggplant - 2, cubed Endive - 1, sliced
Extra virgin olive oil - 3 tbsp.
Lemon – 1, juiced
Balsamic vinegar - 1 tbsp.

DIRECTIONS:

1. Preheat oven to 350°F | 180°C | Fan 160°C. Mix together all vegetables, basil, salt, pepper and oil in a baking dish and cook for 25 – 30 minutes.
2. After cooked, pour into salad bowl and stir in vinegar and lemon juice.
3. Dish up and serve.
4. Enjoy!

NUTRITION:

calories: 155 | fat: 4g | protein: 12g | carbs: 22g | fiber: 9g | sodium: 680mg

820. Asian Salad with pistachios

Prep time: 10 minutes | Cook time: 0 minutes | Serves: 4

INGREDIENTS:

1/8 cup chopped pistachios
1/8 cup green onions, sliced
2/3 bunch watercress, trimmed
2/3 cup red bell pepper, diced
1 1/3 cups medium sized fennel bulb, thinly sliced
2/3 tbsp vegetable oil
1 1/3 cups Asian pears, cut into matchstick size
2 tbsp fresh lime juice

DIRECTIONS:

1. In a large salad bowl, mix pistachios, green onions, bell pepper, fennel, watercress and pears.
2. In a small bowl, mix vegetable oil and lime juice. Season with pepper and salt to taste.
3. Pour dressing to salad and gently mix before serving.
4. Enjoy!

NUTRITION:

calories: 160 | fat: 1g | protein: 1g | carbs: 16g | fiber: 9g | sodium: 680mg

821. Noodle Salad

Prep time: 10 minutes | Cook time: 0 minutes | Serves: 6

INGREDIENTS:

1 1/2 cup shredded green cabbage 1 cup shredded red cabbage 1/4 cup chopped cilantro
1/3 cup chopped peanuts 1/4 cup chopped scallions
4 1/2 cups shiitake noodles (drained and rinsed)
Asian Peanut Sauce Shopping List
1/3 cup sugar free peanut butter
1/3 teaspoon cayenne pepper
3/4 cup filtered water
3/4 teaspoon kosher salt
1 1/2 tablespoon fish sauce (or coconut aminos for vegan)
1 1/2 tablespoon granulated erythritol sweetener
1 1/2 tablespoon lime juice
1 1/2 tablespoon toasted sesame oil
1 1/2 tablespoon wheat-free soy sauce
1 1/2 teaspoon minced garlic
3 tablespoons minced ginger

DIRECTIONS:

1. In a large salad bowl, combine all noodle salad Shopping List ingredients and toss well to mix.
2. In a blender, mix all sauce Shopping List ingredients and pulse until smooth and creamy.
3. Pour sauce over the salad and toss well to coat.
4. Enjoy!

NUTRITION:

calories: 104 | fat: 16g | protein: 7g | carbs: 12g | fiber: 9g | sodium: 680mg

822. Arugula with Blueberries

Prep time: 10 minutes | Cook time: 0 minutes | Serves: 4

INGREDIENTS:

- 1 cup slivered almonds
- 1 cup blueberries, fresh 1 ripe red pear, sliced
- 2 shallots, minced
- 2 tsp minced garlic
- 2 tsp whole grain mustard 2 tbsp fresh lemon juice
- 6 tbsp extra virgin olive oil
- 12 cups arugula

DIRECTIONS:

1. In a big mixing bowl, mix garlic, olive oil, lemon juice and mustard.
2. Once thoroughly mixed, add remaining Shopping List ingredients.
3. Toss to coat.
4. Enjoy!

NUTRITION:

calories: 530 | fat: 38g | protein: 6g | carbs: 12g | fiber: 9g | sodium: 680mg

823. Blue Cheese and Arugula Salad

Prep time: 10 minutes | Cook time: 0 minutes | Serves: 6

INGREDIENTS:

- 1/3 cup crumbled blue cheese 1 tsp Dijon mustard
- 1-pint fresh figs, quartered 2 bags arugula
- 4 1/2 tbsp Balsamic Vinegar 3 tbsp olive oil
- Pepper and salt to taste

DIRECTIONS:

1. Whisk thoroughly together pepper, salt, olive oil, Dijon mustard, and balsamic vinegar to make the dressing. Set aside in the refrigerator for at least 30 minutes to marinate and allow the spices to combine.
2. On four serving plates, evenly arrange arugula and top with blue cheese and figs.
3. Drizzle each plate of salad with 1 1/2 tbsp of prepared dressing.
4. Enjoy!

NUTRITION:

calories: 202 | fat: 10g | protein: 2g | carbs: 25g | fiber: 9g | sodium: 680mg

824. Broccoli Salad

Prep time: 10 minutes | Cook time: 0 minutes | Serves: 6

INGREDIENTS:

- 1/3 tsp sea salt
- 1/3 tsp ground cinnamon
- 3/4 tsp ground turmeric
- 1 1/8 tsp ground ginger
- 3/4 tbsp extra virgin olive oil
- 3/4 tbsp apple cider vinegar
- 3 tbsp chopped green onion
- 1/2 cup coconut cream
- 3/4 cup carrots, shredded
- 1 1/2 small head of broccoli, chopped

DIRECTIONS:

1. In a large salad bowl, mix well salt, cinnamon, turmeric, ginger, olive oil, and vinegar.
2. Add remaining Shopping List ingredients, tossing well to coat.
3. Pop in the refrigerator for at least 30 to 60 minutes before serving.
4. Enjoy!

NUTRITION:

calories: 90 | fat: 10g | protein: 1g | carbs: 4g | fiber: 7g | sodium: 680mg

825. Greek Salad

Prep time: 10 minutes | Cook time: 0 minutes | Serves: 6

INGREDIENTS:

- 1/3 tsp pepper
- 1/3 tsp salt
- 3/4 cup crumbled feta cheese
- 3/4 cup finely chopped red onion
- 3/4 cup sliced ripe black olives
- 1 1/2 medium cucumber, peeled, seeded and chopped
- 1 1/2 tbsp chopped fresh dill
- 1 1/2 tsp garlic powder
- 1/2 cup red wine vinegar
- 3/4 cups chopped cooked chicken
- 3 medium tomatoes, chopped
- 3 tbsp extra virgin olive oil
- 9 cups chopped romaine lettuce

DIRECTIONS:

1. In a large bowl, whisk well pepper, salt, garlic powder, dill, oil and vinegar.
2. Add feta, olives, onion, cucumber, tomatoes, chicken, and lettuce.
3. Toss well to combine.
4. Enjoy!

NUTRITION:

calories: 461 | fat: 37g | protein: 19g | carbs: 10g | fiber: 7g | sodium: 680mg

826. Classic Greek Salad

Prep time: 10 minutes | Cook time: 0 minutes | Serves: 6

INGREDIENTS:

- 1/3 cup extra virgin olive oil, plus more for drizzling
- 1/3 cup red wine vinegar
- 1 1/2 4-oz block Greek feta cheese packed in brine
- 1 1/2 cup Kalamata olives, halved and pitted
- 1 1/2 lemon, juiced and zested
- 1 1/2 small red onion, halved and thinly sliced
- 1 1/2 tsp dried oregano
- 1 1/2 tsp honey
- 21 small vine-ripened tomatoes, quartered
- 7 1/2 Persian cucumbers
- Fresh oregano leaves for topping, optional
- Pepper to taste
- Salt to taste

DIRECTIONS:

1. In a bowl of ice water, soak red onions with 2 tbsp salt.
2. In a large bowl, whisk well ¼ tsp pepper, ½ tsp salt, dried oregano, honey, lemon zest, lemon juice, and vinegar. Slowly pour olive oil in a steady stream as you briskly whisk mixture. Continue whisking until emulsified.
3. Add olives and tomatoes, toss to coat with dressing.
4. Alternately peel cucumber leaving strips of skin on. Trim ends slice lengthwise and chop in ½-inch thick cubes. Add into bowl of tomatoes.
5. Drain onions and add into bowl of tomatoes. Toss well to coat and mix.
6. Drain feta and slice into four equal rectangles.
7. Divide Greek salad into serving plates, top each with oregano and feta.
8. Enjoy!

NUTRITION:

calories: 365 | fat: 24g | protein: 9g | carbs: 26g | fiber: 7g | sodium: 680mg

827. Zucchini Noodle Bowl

Prep time: 10 minutes | Cook time: 20 minutes | Serves: 6

INGREDIENTS:

- 1/3 cup basil leaves, roughly chopped
- 1/3 cup olive oil
- 1/3 tsp sea salt
- 3/4 tsp salt 1 tsp garlic powder
- 1 1/2 lb. peeled and uncooked shrimp
- 1 1/2 tsp lemon zest
- 1 1/2 tsp lime zest
- 3 tbsp butter
- 3 tbsp lemon juice
- 3 tbsp lime juice
- 1 1/2 clementine, peeled and separated
- 6 cups zucchini, spirals or noodles
- pinch of black pepper

DIRECTIONS:

1. Make zucchini noodles and set aside.
2. On medium heat, place a large non-stick saucepan and heat butter.
3. Meanwhile, pat dry shrimp and season with salt and garlic. Add into hot saucepan and sauté for 6 minutes or until opaque and cooked.
4. Remove from pan, transfer to a bowl and put aside.
5. Right away, add zucchini noodles to still hot pan and stir fry for a minute. Leave noodles on pan as you prepare the dressing.
6. Blend well salt, olive oil, juice and zest in a small bowl.
7. Then place noodles into salad bowl, top with shrimp, pour oil mixture, basil and clementine. Toss to mix well.
8. Refrigerate for an hour before serving.
9. Enjoy!

NUTRITION:

calories: 353 | fat: 21g | protein: 9g | carbs: 14g | fiber: 7g | sodium: 680mg

828. Coleslaw

Prep time: 10 minutes | Cook time: 0 minutes | Serves: 6

INGREDIENTS:

- 1/3 cup chopped fresh cilantro 1 1/2 tbsp minced garlic
- 1 1/4 carrots, julienned
- 1 1/4 cups shredded napa cabbage 2 cups thinly sliced red cabbage 2 red bell peppers, thinly sliced
- 1 1/4 tbsp minced fresh ginger root
- 1 3/4 tbsp brown sugar
- 2/3 tbsp soy sauce
- 1 1/4 cups thinly sliced green cabbage
- 3 tbsp creamy peanut butter
- 2/3 green onions, chopped
- 3 2/3 tbsp rice wine vinegar
- 3 2/3 tbsp vegetable oil

DIRECTIONS:
1. Mix thoroughly the following in a medium bowl: garlic, ginger, brown sugar, soy sauce, peanut butter, oil and rice vinegar.
2. In a separate bowl, blend well cilantro, green onions, carrots, bell pepper, Napa cabbage, red cabbage and green cabbage. Pour in the peanut sauce above and toss to mix well.
3. Enjoy!

NUTRITION:

calories: 193 | fat: 12g | protein: 4g | carbs: 16g | fiber: 7g | sodium: 680mg

829. Cucumber and Tomato Salad
Prep time: 10 minutes | Cook time: 0 minutes | Serves: 6

INGREDIENTS:

Ground pepper to taste
Salt to taste
1 1/2 tbsp fresh lemon juice 1 onion, chopped
1 1/2 cucumber, peeled and diced 2 tomatoes, chopped
6 cups spinach

DIRECTIONS:
1. In a salad bowl, mix onions, cucumbers and tomatoes.
2. Season with pepper and salt to taste.
3. Add lemon juice and mix well.
4. Add spinach, toss to coat.
5. Enjoy!

NUTRITION:

calories: 70 | fat: 3g | protein: 4g | carbs: 7g | fiber: 7g | sodium: 680mg

830. Cucumber Salad Japanese Style
Prep time: 10 minutes | Cook time: 0 minutes | Serves: 6

INGREDIENTS:

2/3 tsp minced fresh ginger root
1 1/4 tsp salt
1/3 cup rice vinegar
1 1/4 large cucumber, ribbon cut
4 3/4 tsp white sugar

DIRECTIONS:
1. Mix well ginger, salt, sugar and vinegar in a small bowl.
2. Add ribbon cut cucumbers and mix well.
3. Let stand for at least one hour in the refrigerator before serving.
4. Enjoy!

NUTRITION:

calories: 29 | fat: 2g | protein: 7g | carbs: 6g | fiber: 7g | sodium: 680mg

831. Easy Garden Salad with Arugula
Prep time: 10 minutes | Cook time: 0 minutes | Serves: 4

INGREDIENTS:

1/2 cup grated parmesan cheese
1/2 cup pine nuts
2 cup cherry tomatoes, halved
2 large avocados, sliced into 1/2-inch cubes
2 tbsp rice vinegar
2 tbsp olive oil or grapeseed oil
8 cups young arugula leaves, rinsed and dried
Black pepper, freshly ground
Salt to taste

DIRECTIONS:
1. Get a bowl with cover, big enough to hold the salad and mix together the parmesan cheese, vinegar, oil, pine nuts, cherry tomatoes and arugula.
2. Season with pepper and salt according to your preference. Place the lid and jiggle the covered bowl to combine the salad.
3. Serve the salad topped with sliced avocadoes.
4. Enjoy!

NUTRITION:

calories: 490 | fat: 43g | protein: 9g | carbs: 15g | fiber: 7g | sodium: 680mg

832. Easy Quinoa & Pear Salad
Prep time: 10 minutes | Cook time: 0 minutes | Serves: 4

INGREDIENTS:

1/8 cup chopped parsley
1/8 cup chopped scallions
1/8 cup lime juice
1/3 cup diced cucumber
1/3 cup diced red pepper
1/3 cup dried wild blueberries
1/3 cup olive oil
1/3 cup spicy pecans, chopped
1/8 cup red onion, diced
1/3 cup diced carrots
1/3 cup diced celery
2/3 tbsp chopped parsley
2/3 tsp honey
2/3 tsp sea salt
2/3 fresh pears, cut into chunks
1 1/3 cups cooked quinoa

DIRECTIONS:
1. In a small bowl mix well olive oil, salt, lime juice, honey, and parsley. Set aside.
2. In large salad bowl, add remaining Shopping List ingredients and toss to mix well.
3. Pour dressing and toss well to coat.
4. Enjoy!

NUTRITION:

calories: 382 | fat: 43g | protein: 5g | carbs: 31g | fiber: 7g | sodium: 680mg

833. Easy-Peasy Club Salad
Prep time: 10 minutes | Cook time: 0 minutes | Serves: 4

INGREDIENTS:

2/3 cup cherry tomatoes, halved
2/3 teaspoon garlic powder
2/3 teaspoon onion powder
1 1/3 cup diced cucumber
1 1/3 tablespoon Dijon mustard
1 1/3 tablespoon milk
1 1/3 teaspoon dried parsley
2 2/3 tablespoons mayonnaise
2 2/3 tablespoons sour cream
2 2/3 cups romaine lettuce, torn into pieces
4 large hard-boiled eggs, sliced
2/3 ounces cheddar cheese, cubed

DIRECTIONS:
1. Make the dressing by mixing garlic powder, onion powder, dried parsley, mayonnaise, and sour cream in a small bowl. Add a tablespoon of milk and mix well. If you want the dressing thinner, you can add more milk.
2. In a salad platter, layer salad Shopping List ingredients with Dijon mustard in the middle.
3. Evenly drizzle with dressing and toss well to coat.
4. Enjoy!

NUTRITION:

calories: 335 | fat: 26g | protein: 16g | carbs: 7g | fiber: 7g | sodium: 680mg

834. Fruity Asparagus-Quinoa Salad
Prep time: 10 minutes | Cook time: 25 minutes | Serves: 6

INGREDIENTS:

1/4 cup chopped pecans, toasted
1/3 cup finely chopped white onion
1/3 jalapeno pepper, diced
1/3 lb. asparagus, sliced to 2-inch lengths, steamed and chilled
1/3 tsp kosher salt
3/4 cup fresh orange sections 1 cup uncooked quinoa
3/4 tsp olive oil 2 cups water
3/4 tbsp minced red onion
3 3/4 dates, pitted and chopped
Dressing Ingredients:
1/4 tsp ground black pepper
1/4 tsp kosher salt
3/4 garlic clove, minced 1 tbsp olive oil
1 1/2 tbsp chopped fresh mint
1 1/2 tbsp fresh lemon juice Mint sprigs – optional

DIRECTIONS:
1. Wash and rub with your hands the quinoa in a bowl at least three times, discarding water each and every time.
2. On medium high heat, place a large non-stick fry pan and heat 1 tsp olive oil. For two minutes, sauté onions before adding quinoa and sautéing for another five minutes.
3. Add ½ tsp salt and 2 cups water and bring to a boil. Lower heat to simmer, cover and cook for 15 minutes. Turn off heat and let stand until water is absorbed.
4. Add pepper, asparagus, dates, pecans and orange sections into a salad bowl. Add cooked quinoa, toss to mix well.
5. In a small bowl, whisk mint, garlic, black pepper, salt, olive oil and lemon juice to create the dressing.
6. Pour dressing over salad.
7. Enjoy!

NUTRITION:

calories: 173 | fat: 6g | protein: 5g | carbs: 24g | fiber: 7g | sodium: 680mg

835. Garden Salad with Oranges and Olives

Prep time: 10 minutes | Cook time: 15 minutes | Serves: 6

INGREDIENTS:

- 3/4 cup red wine vinegar
- 1 1/2 tbsp extra virgin olive oil
- 1 1/2 tbsp finely chopped celery
- 3 tbsp finely chopped red onion
- 24 large ripe black olives
- 1 1/2 garlic cloves
- 3 navel oranges, peeled and segmented
- 6 boneless, skinless chicken breasts, 4-oz each
- 6 garlic cloves, minced
- 12 cups leaf lettuce, washed and dried
- Cracked black pepper to taste

DIRECTIONS:

1. Prepare the dressing by mixing pepper, celery, onion, olive oil, garlic and vinegar in a small bowl. Whisk well to combine.
2. Lightly grease grate and preheat grill to high.
3. Rub chicken with the garlic cloves and discard garlic.
4. Grill chicken for 5 minutes per side or until cooked through.
5. Remove from grill and let it stand for 5 minutes before cutting into ½-inch strips.
6. In 4 serving plates, evenly arrange two cups lettuce, ¼ of the sliced oranges and 4 olives per plate. Top each plate with ¼ serving of grilled chicken, evenly drizzle with dressing.
7. Enjoy!

NUTRITION:

calories: 259 | fat: 2g | protein: 48g | carbs: 12g | fiber: 7g | sodium: 680mg

836. Garden Salad with Grapes

Prep time: 10 minutes | Cook time: 0 minutes | Serves: 4

INGREDIENTS:

- 1/8 tsp black pepper
- 1/8 tsp salt
- 1/3 tsp stone-ground mustard
- 2/3 tsp chopped fresh thyme
- 2/3 tsp honey
- 2/3 tsp maple syrup
- 1 1/3 cups red grapes, halved
- 1 1/3 tbsp toasted sunflower seed kernels
- 1 1/3 tsp grapeseed oil
- 1 1/3 tbsp red wine vinegar
- 4 2/3 cups loosely packed baby arugula

DIRECTIONS:

1. In a small bowl whisk together mustard, syrup, honey and vinegar. Whisking continuously, slowly add oil.
2. In a large salad bowl, mix thyme, seeds, grapes and arugula.
3. Drizzle with the oil dressing, season with pepper and salt.
4. Gently toss to coat salad with the dressing.
5. Enjoy!

NUTRITION:

calories: 85 | fat: 3g | protein: 48g | carbs: 12g | fiber: 7g | sodium: 680mg

837. Ginger Yogurt Dressed Citrus Salad

Prep time: 10 minutes | Cook time: 2 minutes | Serves: 4

INGREDIENTS:

- 1/2 cup minced crystallized ginger
- 2/3 16-oz Greek yogurt
- 1/8 tsp ground cinnamon
- 1 1/3 tbsp honey
- 1/3 cup dried cranberries 3 navel oranges
- 1 1/3 large tangerines, peeled
- 2/3 pink grapefruit, peeled

DIRECTIONS:

1. Into sections, break tangerines and grapefruit.
2. Cut tangerine sections in half.
3. Slice grapefruit sections into thirds.
4. Cut orange pith and peel in half and slice oranges into ¼-inch thick rounds, then quartered.
5. In a medium bowl, mix oranges, grapefruit, tangerines and its juices.
6. Add cinnamon, honey and ½ cup of cranberries.
7. Cover and place in the refrigerator for an hour.
8. In a small bowl, mix ginger and yogurt.
9. To serve, add a dollop of yogurt dressing onto a serving of fruit and sprinkle with cranberries.
10. Enjoy!

NUTRITION:

calories: 190 | fat: 12g | protein: 3g | carbs: 16g | fiber: 7g | sodium: 680mg

838. Garden Salad with Balsamic Vinegar

Prep time: 10 minutes | Cook time: 0 minutes | Serves: 4

INGREDIENTS:

- 4 cup baby arugula
- 4 cup spinach
- 4 tbsp raisins
- 4 tbsp almonds, shaved or chopped
- 4 tbsp balsamic vinegar
- 2 tbsp extra virgin olive oil

DIRECTIONS:

1. In a plate, mix arugula and spinach.
2. Top with raisins and almonds.
3. Drizzle olive oil and balsamic vinegar.
4. Enjoy!

NUTRITION:

calories: 206 | fat: 15g | protein: 5g | carbs: 14g | fiber: 7g | sodium: 680mg

839. Goat Cheese and Oregano Dressing Salad

Prep time: 10 minutes | Cook time: 0 minutes | Serves: 6

INGREDIENTS:

- 1 1/8 cup crumbled soft fresh goat cheese
- 2 1/4 cups diced celery
- 2 1/4 large red bell peppers, diced
- 3 tbsp chopped fresh oregano
- 1/2 cup chopped red onion
- 3 tbsp extra virgin olive oil
- 3 tbsp fresh lemon juice
- 6 cups baby spinach leaves, coarsely chopped

DIRECTIONS:

1. In a large salad bowl, mix oregano, lemon juice and oil.
2. Add pepper and salt to taste.
3. Mix in red onion, goat cheese, celery, bell peppers and spinach.
4. Toss to coat well.
5. Enjoy!

NUTRITION:

calories: 110 | fat: 4g | protein: 6g | carbs: 10g | fiber: 7g | sodium: 680mg

840. Grape and Walnut Garden Salad

Prep time: 10 minutes | Cook time: 0 minutes | Serves: 4

INGREDIENTS:

- 2 cup chopped walnuts, toasted
- 4 ripe persimmons
- 2 cup red grapes, halved lengthwise
- 4 shallots, minced
- 4 tsp minced garlic
- 4 tsp whole grain mustard
- 8 tbsp fresh lemon juice
- 12 tbsp extra virgin olive oil
- 24 cups baby spinach

DIRECTIONS:

1. Cut persimmon and red pear into ½-inch cubes. Discard seeds.
2. In a medium bowl, whisk garlic, shallot, olive oil, lemon juice and mustard to make the dressing.
3. In a medium salad bowl, toss to mix spinach, pear and persimmon.
4. Pour in dressing and toss to coat well.
5. Garnish with pecans.
6. Enjoy!

NUTRITION:

calories: 440 | fat: 28g | protein: 6g | carbs: 39g | fiber: 7g | sodium: 680mg

841. Greek Antipasto Salad

Prep time: 10 minutes | Cook time: 0 minutes | Serves: 6

INGREDIENTS:

- 3/4 cup artichoke hearts, chipped
- 3/4 cup olives, sliced
- 3/4 cup sweet peppers, roasted
- 1 1/2 large head romaine lettuce, chopped
- 6 ounces cooked prosciutto, cut into thin strips
- 6 ounces cooked salami, cubed Italian dressing to taste

DIRECTIONS:

1. In a large mixing bowl, add all the Shopping List ingredients, except the Italian dressing. Mix everything until the vegetables are evenly distributed.
2. Add the Italian dressing and toss to combine.
3. Enjoy!

NUTRITION:

calories: 425 | fat: 38g | protein: 39g | carbs: 12g | fiber: 7g | sodium: 680mg

842. Grilled Halloumi Cheese Salad

Prep time: 10 minutes | Cook time: 0 minutes | Serves: 4

INGREDIENTS:

2 oz chopped walnuts
4 handful baby arugulas
4 Persian cucumber, sliced into circles about 1/2-inch thick
12 oz halloumi cheese
20 grape tomatoes, sliced in half
balsamic vinegar
olive oil
salt

DIRECTIONS:

1. Cut the cheese into 1/3 slices. For 3 to 5 minutes each side, grill the kinds of cheese until you can see grill marks.
2. In a salad bowl, add arugula, cucumber, and tomatoes. Drizzle with olive oil and balsamic vinegar. Season with salt and toss well coat.
3. Sprinkle walnuts and add grilled halloumi.
4. Enjoy!

NUTRITION:

calories: 543 | fat: 47g | protein: 21g | carbs: 9g | fiber: 7g | sodium: 680mg

843. Grilled Eggplant Salad

Prep time: 10 minutes | Cook time: 18 minutes | Serves: 6

INGREDIENTS:

1 1/2 avocado, halved, pitted, peeled and cubed
1 1/2 Italian eggplant, cut into 1-inch-thick slices
1 1/2 large red onion, cut into rounds
1 1/2 lemon, zested
1 1/2 tbsp coarsely chopped oregano leaves
1 1/2 tbsp red wine vinegar
1 1/2 tsp Dijon mustard
Canola oil
Freshly ground black pepper
1 1/2 tsp Honey
1 1/2 tbsp Olive oil
Parsley sprigs for garnish
Salt

DIRECTIONS:

1. With canola oil, brush onions and eggplant and place on grill.
2. Grill on high until onions are slightly charred and eggplants are soft; around 5 minutes for onions and 8 to 12 minutes for eggplant.
3. Remove from grill and let cool for 5 minutes.
4. Roughly chop eggplants and onions and place in salad bowl.
5. Add avocado and toss to mix.
6. Whisk oregano, mustard and red wine vinegar in a small bowl.
7. Whisk in olive oil and honey to taste. Season with pepper and salt to taste.
8. Pour dressing to eggplant mixture, toss to mix well.
9. Garnish with parsley sprigs and lemon zest before serving.
10. Enjoy!

NUTRITION:

calories: 190 | fat: 12g | protein: 2g | carbs: 16g | fiber: 7g | sodium: 680mg

844. Thai Chicken Soup

Prep time: 10 minutes | Cook time: 8 hours 25 mins | Serves: 6

INGREDIENTS:

1/2 lemongrass stalk, cut into large chunks
2 1/2 thick slices of fresh ginger
1/2 whole chicken
10 fresh basil leaves
1/2 lime, juiced
1/2 tablespoon salt

DIRECTIONS:

1. Place the chicken, 10 basil leaves, lemongrass, ginger, salt and water into the slow cooker.
2. Cook for about 8 hours on low and dish out into a bowl.
3. Stir in fresh lime juice and basil leaves to serve. Enjoy!

NUTRITION:

calories: 255 | fat: 17g | protein: 25g | carbs: 2g | fiber: 7g | sodium: 680mg

845. Grilled Vegetable Salad

Prep time: 10 minutes | Cook time: 7 minutes | Serves: 4

INGREDIENTS:

1/3 cup extra virgin olive oil, for brushing
1/3 cup fresh basil leaves
1/3 lb. feta cheese
2/3 bunch asparagus, trimmed and cut into bite-size pieces
1 1/3 medium onion, cut into 1/2-inch rings
1-pint cherry tomatoes
1 1/3 red bell pepper, quartered, seeds and ribs removed
1 1/3 yellow bell pepper, quartered, seeds and ribs removed Pepper and salt to taste

DIRECTIONS:

1. Toss olive oil and vegetables in a large bowl. Season with salt and pepper.
2. Frill vegetables in a preheated griller for 5-7 minutes or until charred and tender. Transfer veggies to a platter, add feta and basil.
3. In a separate small bowl, mix olive oil, balsamic vinegar, garlic seasoned with pepper and salt.
4. Drizzle dressing over vegetables and serve.
5. Enjoy!

NUTRITION:

calories: 147 | fat: 19g | protein: 3g | carbs: 12g | fiber: 7g | sodium: 680mg

846. Detox Salad

Prep time: 10 minutes | Cook time: 0 minutes | Serves: 6

INGREDIENTS:

6 cups mixed greens
3 tbsp lemon juice
3 tbsp pumpkin seed oil 1 tbsp chia seeds
3 tbsp almonds, chopped 1 large apple, diced
large carrot, coarsely grated
1 1/2 large beet, coarsely grated

DIRECTIONS:

1. In a medium salad bowl, except for mixed greens, combine all Shopping List ingredients thoroughly.
2. Divide the mixed greens into 4 salad plates.
3. Evenly top mixed greens with the salad bowl mixture.
4. Enjoy!

NUTRITION:

calories: 141 | fat: 9g | protein: 3g | carbs: 14g | fiber: 7g | sodium: 680mg

847. Herbed Calamari Salad

Prep time: 10 minutes | Cook time: 25 minutes | Serves: 4

INGREDIENTS:

1/8 cup finely chopped cilantro leaves
1/8 cup finely chopped mint leaves
1/8 tsp freshly ground black pepper
1/3 cup finely chopped flat leaf parsley leaves
1/2 tsp kosher salt
1/3 lbs. cleaned and trimmed uncooked
calamari rings and tentacles, defrosted
2 medium garlic cloves, smashed and minced
1 1/3 tbsp extra virgin olive oil
A pinch of crushed red pepper flakes
Juice of 1 large lemon
Peel of 1 lemon, thinly sliced into strips

DIRECTIONS:

1. On a non-stick large fry pan, heat 1½ tbsp olive oil. Once hot, sauté garlic until fragrant; around a minute.
2. Add calamari, making sure that they are in one layer, if pan is too small then cook in batches.
3. Season with pepper and salt; after 2 to 4 minutes of searing, remove calamari from pan with a slotted spoon and transfer to a large bowl. Continue cooking remainder of calamari.
4. Season cooked calamari with herbs, lemon rind, lemon juice, red pepper flakes, pepper, salt, and remaining olive oil.
5. Toss well to coat.
6. Enjoy!

NUTRITION:

calories: 551 | fat: 9g | protein: 7g | carbs: 121g | fiber: 7g | sodium: 680mg

848. Cauliflower, Leek & Bacon Soup

Prep time: 10 minutes | Cook time: 10 minutes | Serves: 6

INGREDIENTS:

6 cups chicken broth
3/4 cauliflower head, chopped 1 leek, chopped
Salt and black pepper, to taste
7 1/2 bacon strips

DIRECTIONS:

1. Put the cauliflower, leek and chicken broth into the pot and cook for about 1 hour on medium heat.
2. Transfer into an immersion blender and pulse until smooth.
3. Return the soup into the pot and microwave the bacon strips for 1 minute.
4. Cut the bacon into small pieces and put into the soup.
5. Cook on for about 30 minutes on low heat.

6. Season with salt and pepper and serve.
7. Enjoy!

NUTRITION:

calories: 185 | fat: 9g | protein: 10g | carbs: 6g | fiber: 7g | sodium: 1153mg

849. Zucchini Soup

Base
Prep time: 10 minutes | Cook time: 20 minutes | Serves: 4

INGREDIENTS:

1 medium onion, peeled and chopped	black pepper
2 cup bone broth	1 tablespoon parsley, chopped, for garnish
2 tablespoon coconut oil	
3 zucchinis, cut into chunks	1 tablespoon coconut cream, for garnish
1 tablespoon nutritional yeast Dash of	

DIRECTIONS:

1. Melt the coconut oil in a large pan over medium heat and add onions.
2. Sauté for about 3 minutes and add zucchinis and bone broth.
3. Reduce the heat to simmer for about 15 minutes and cover the pan.
4. Add nutritional yeast and transfer to an immersion blender.
5. Blend until smooth and season with black pepper.
6. Top with coconut cream and parsley to serve.
7. Enjoy!

NUTRITION:

calories: 154 | fat: 9g | protein: 13g | carbs: 8g | fiber: 7g | sodium: 93mg

850. Herbed Chicken Salad Greek Style

Prep time: 10 minutes | Cook time: 0 minutes | Serves: 4

INGREDIENTS:

1/8 cup or 1 oz crumbled feta cheese	2/3-pound skinless, boneless chicken breast, cut into 1-inch cubes
1/3 tsp garlic powder	
1/3 tsp salt	1 1/3 tsp bottled minced garlic 1 tsp ground oregano
1/2 tsp black pepper, divided	
2/3 cup grape tomatoes, halved	1 1/3 tsp sesame seed paste or tahini 5 tsp fresh lemon juice, divided
2/3 cup peeled and chopped English cucumbers	
2/3 cup plain fat-free yogurt	4 pitted kalamata olives, halved 8 cups chopped romaine lettuce cooking spray

DIRECTIONS:

1. In a bowl, mix together ¼ tsp salt, ½ tsp pepper, garlic powder and oregano. Then on medium high heat, place a skillet and coat with cooking spray and sauté together the spice mixture and chicken until chicken is cooked. Before transferring to bowl, drizzle with juice.
2. In a small bowl, mix thoroughly the following: garlic, tahini, yogurt, ¼ tsp pepper, ¼ tsp salt, and 2 tsp juice.
3. In another bowl, mix together olives, tomatoes, cucumber and lettuce.
4. To Serve salad, place 2½ cups of lettuce mixture on plate, topped with ½ cup chicken mixture, 3 tbsp yogurt mixture and 1 tbsp of cheese.
5. Enjoy!

NUTRITION:

calories: 170 | fat: 9g | protein: 20g | carbs: 13g | fiber: 7g | sodium: 93mg

851. Spring Soup with Poached Egg

Prep time: 10 minutes | Cook time: 20 minutes | Serves: 4

INGREDIENTS:

64 oz vegetable broth	head romaine lettuce, chopped
4 eggs	Salt, to taste

DIRECTIONS:

1. Bring the vegetable broth to a boil and reduce the heat.
2. Poach the eggs for 5 minutes in the broth and remove them into 2 bowls.
3. Stir in romaine lettuce into the broth and cook for 4 minutes.
4. Dish out in a bowl and serve hot.
5. Enjoy!

NUTRITION:

calories: 158 | fat: 8g | protein: 15g | carbs: 6g | fiber: 7g | sodium: 93mg

852. Mint Avocado Chilled Soup

Prep time: 10 minutes | Cook time: 15 minutes | Serves: 4

INGREDIENTS:

Romaine lettuce leaves	2 medium ripe avocados
2 Tablespoon lime juice	2 cup coconut milk, chilled 20 fresh mint leaves
Salt to taste	

DIRECTIONS:

1. Put all the Shopping List ingredients in a blender and blend until smooth.
2. Refrigerate for about 10 minutes and serve chilled.
3. Enjoy!

NUTRITION:

calories: 432 | fat: 42g | protein: 5g | carbs: 16g | fiber: 7g | sodium: 93mg

853. Butternut Squash Soup

Prep time: 10 minutes | Cook time: 1 hour 45 minutes | Serves: 6

INGREDIENTS:

1 1/2 small onion, chopped	4 1/2 tablespoons coconut oil
6 cups chicken broth	Salt, to taste
1 1/2 butternut squash	Nutmeg and pepper, to taste

DIRECTIONS:

1. Put oil and onions in a large pot. Sauté for about 3 minutes and add chicken broth and butternut squash.
2. Simmer for about 1 hour on medium heat and transfer into an immersion blender.
3. Pulse until smooth and season with salt, pepper and nutmeg.
4. Return to the pot and cook for about 30 minutes.
5. Dish out and serve hot.
6. Enjoy!

NUTRITION:

calories: 149 | fat: 11g | protein: 5g | carbs: 16g | fiber: 7g | sodium: 765mg

854. Spring Soup with Poached Egg

Prep time: 10 minutes | Cook time: 20 minutes | Serves: 4

INGREDIENTS:

4 eggs	2 head of romaine lettuce, chopped
4 tablespoons butter	Salt, to taste
8 cups chicken broth	

DIRECTIONS:

1. Boil the chicken broth and lower heat.
2. Poach the eggs in the broth for about 5 minutes and remove the eggs.
3. Place each egg into a bowl and add chopped romaine lettuce into the broth.
4. Cook for about 10 minutes and ladle the broth with the lettuce into the bowls.
5. Enjoy!

NUTRITION:

calories: 264 | fat: 18g | protein: 16g | carbs: 7g | fiber: 7g | sodium: 765mg

855. Egg Drop Soup

Prep time: 10 minutes | Cook time: 20 minutes | Serves: 6

INGREDIENTS:

4 1/2 cups bone broth	3 cups Swiss chard, chopped
3 eggs, whisked	3 tablespoons coconut aminos
1 1/2 teaspoon ground oregano	1 1/2 teaspoon ginger, grated
4 1/2 tablespoons butter	Salt and black pepper, to taste

DIRECTIONS:

1. Heat the bone broth in a saucepan and add whisked eggs while stirring slowly.
2. Add the Swiss chard, butter, coconut aminos, ginger, oregano and salt and black pepper.
3. Cook for about 3 minutes and serve hot.
4. Enjoy!

NUTRITION:

calories: 185 | fat: 11g | protein: 19g | carbs: 3g | fiber: 7g | sodium: 252mg

856. Mushroom Spinach Soup

Prep time: 10 minutes | Cook time: 25 minutes | Serves: 6

INGREDIENTS:

1 1/2 cup spinach, cleaned and chopped	1 1/2 onion
100g mushrooms, chopped	9 garlic cloves

3/4 teaspoon red chili powder Salt and black pepper, to taste 3 tablespoons buttermilk
1 1/2 teaspoon almond flour 2 cups chicken broth
4 1/2 tablespoons butter
1/3 cup fresh cream for garnish

DIRECTIONS:
1. Heat butter in a pan and add onions and garlic.
2. Sauté for about 3 minutes and add spinach, salt and red chili powder.
3. Sauté for about 4 minutes and add mushrooms.
4. Transfer into a blender and blend to make a puree.
5. Return to the pan and add buttermilk and almond flour for creamy texture.
6. Mix well and simmer for about 2 minutes.
7. Garnish with fresh cream and serve hot.
8. Enjoy!

NUTRITION:
calories: 160 | fat: 13g | protein: 5g | carbs: 7g | fiber: 7g | sodium: 462mg

857. Delicata Squash Soup
Prep time: 10 minutes | Cook time: 45 minutes | Serves: 6

INGREDIENTS:

1 3/4 cups beef bone broth
1 1/4 small onion, peeled and grated.
2/3 teaspoon sea salt
1/3 teaspoon poultry seasoning
2 1/3 small Delicate Squash, chopped
2 1/3 garlic cloves, minced
2 1/3 tablespoons olive oil
1/3 teaspoon black pepper
1 1/4 small lemon, juiced
6 tablespoons sour cream

DIRECTIONS:
1. Heat butter in a pan and add onions and garlic.
2. Sauté for about 3 minutes and add spinach, salt and red chili powder.
3. Sauté for about 4 minutes and add mushrooms.
4. Transfer into a blender and blend to make a puree.
5. Return to the pan and add buttermilk and almond flour for creamy texture.
6. Mix well and simmer for about 2 minutes.
7. Garnish with fresh cream and serve hot.
8. Enjoy!

NUTRITION:
calories: 109 | fat: 9g | protein: 3g | carbs: 5g | fiber: 7g | sodium: 279mg

858. Broccoli Soup
Prep time: 10 minutes | Cook time: 10 minutes | Serves: 4

INGREDIENTS:

2 tablespoons ghee
3 1/3 garlic cloves
2/3 teaspoon sage
1/8 teaspoon ginger
1 1/3 cups broccoli
2/3 small onion
2/3 teaspoon oregano
1/3 teaspoon parsley
Salt and black pepper, to taste
4 cups vegetable broth
2 2/3 tablespoons butter

DIRECTIONS:
1. Put ghee, onions, spices and garlic in a pot and cook for 3 minutes.
2. Add broccoli and cook for about 4 minutes.
3. Add vegetable broth, cover and allow it to simmer for about 30 minutes.
4. Transfer into a blender and blend until smooth.
5. Add the butter to give it a creamy delicious texture and flavour.
6. Enjoy!

NUTRITION:
calories: 183 | fat: 9g | protein: 7g | carbs: 6g | fiber: 7g | sodium: 829mg

859. Chicken Soup
Prep time: 10 minutes | Cook time: 40 minutes | Serves: 6

INGREDIENTS:

2 tablespoons parsley
2 celery stalks, chopped
6 tablespoons butter
1 cup heavy whipping cream
4 cups chicken, cooked and shredded
4 tablespoons ranch dressing
¼ cup yellow onions, chopped
8 oz cream cheese
8 cups chicken broth
7 hearty bacon slices, crumbled

DIRECTIONS:
1. Heat butter in a pan and add chicken.
2. Cook for about 5 minutes and add 1½ cups water.
3. Cover and cook for about 10 minutes.
4. Put the chicken and rest of the Shopping List ingredients into the saucepan except parsley and cook for about 10 minutes.
5. Top with parsley and serve hot.
6. Enjoy!

NUTRITION:
calories: 444 | fat: 34g | protein: 28g | carbs: 6g | fiber: 7g | sodium: 1572mg

860. Chicken Veggie Soup
Prep time: 10 minutes | Cook time: 20 minutes | Serves: 4

INGREDIENTS:

1 1/3 chicken thighs
8 cups water
2/3 tablespoon adobo seasoning
2 2/3 celery ribs
2/3 yellow onion
1 teaspoon whole black peppercorn
4 sprigs fresh parsley
2/3 teaspoons coarse sea salt
1 1/3 carrots
4 mushrooms, sliced
1 1/3 garlic cloves
2/3 bay leaf
2 sprigs fresh thyme

DIRECTIONS:
1. Put water, chicken thighs, carrots, celery ribs, onion, garlic cloves and herbs in a large pot.
2. Bring to a boil and reduce the heat to low.
3. Cover the pot and simmer for about 30 minutes.
4. Dish out the chicken and shred it, removing the bones.
5. Put the bones back into the pot and simmer for about 20 minutes.
6. Strain the broth, discarding the chunks and put the liquid back into the pot.
7. Bring it to a boil and simmer for about 30 minutes.
8. Put the mushrooms in the broth and simmer for about 10 minutes.
9. Dish out to serve hot.
10. Enjoy!

NUTRITION:
calories: 250 | fat: 9g | protein: 35g | carbs: 7g | fiber: 7g | sodium: 852mg

861. Apple Pumpkin Soup
Prep time: 10 minutes | Cook time: 10 minutes | Serves: 4

INGREDIENTS:

1/2 apple, chopped
1/2 whole kabocha pumpkin, peeled, seeded and cubed
1/2 cup almond flour
1/8 cup ghee
1/2 pinch cardamom powder
1 quart's water
1/8 cup coconut cream
1/2 pinch ground black pepper

DIRECTIONS:
1. Heat ghee in the bottom of a heavy pot and add apples.
2. Cook for about 5 minutes on a medium flame and add pumpkin.
3. Sauté for about 3 minutes and add almond flour.
4. Sauté for about 1 minute and add water.
5. Lower the flame and cook for about 30 minutes.
6. Transfer the soup into an immersion blender and blend until smooth.
7. Top with coconut cream and serve. Enjoy!

NUTRITION:
calories: 186 | fat: 14g | protein: 3g | carbs: 10g | fiber: 7g | sodium: 8mg

862. French Onion Soup
Prep time: 10 minutes | Cook time: 40 minutes | Serves: 4

INGREDIENTS:

2 1/2 tablespoons butter
250 g brown onion medium 4 drops
liquid stevia
2 tablespoons olive oil 3 cups beef stock

DIRECTIONS:
1. Put the butter and olive oil in a large pot over medium low heat and add onions and salt.
2. Cook for about 5 minutes and stir in stevia.
3. Cook for another 5 minutes and add beef stock.
4. Reduce the heat to low and simmer for about 25 minutes.
5. Dish out into soup bowls and serve hot.
6. Enjoy!

NUTRITION:
calories: 198 | fat: 20g | protein: 3g | carbs: 6g | fiber: 7g | sodium: 883mg

863. Kale Salad Recipe

Prep time: 10 minutes | Cook time: 7 minutes | Serves: 6

INGREDIENTS:

- 1/3 cup Kalamata olives
- 3/4 of a lemon
- 2 1/4 tbsp flaxseeds
- 1 1/2 garlic clove, minced
- 1 1/2 small cucumber, sliced thinly
- 1 1/2 tbsp extra virgin olive oil
- 3 tbsp green onion, chopped
- 3 tbsp red onion, minced
- 9 cups dinosaur kale, chopped a pinch of dried basil
- a pinch of salt

DIRECTIONS:

1. Bring a medium pot, half-filled with water to a boil.
2. Rinse kale and cut into small strips. Place in a steamer and put on top of boiling water and steam for 5 – 7 minutes.
3. Transfer steamed kale to a salad bowl.
4. Season kale with oil, salt, basil and lemon. Toss to coat well.
5. Add remaining Shopping List into salad bowl, toss to mix.
6. Enjoy!

NUTRITION:

calories: 92 | fat: 6g | protein: 3g | carbs: 6g | fiber: 7g | sodium: 883mg

864. Cauliflower and Thyme Soup

Prep time: 10 minutes | Cook time: 30 minutes | Serves: 4

INGREDIENTS:

- 1 1/3 teaspoons thyme powder
- 2/3 head cauliflower
- 2 cups vegetable stock
- 1/3 teaspoon matcha green tea powder
- 2 tablespoons olive oil
- Salt and black pepper, to taste
- 3 1/3 garlic cloves, chopped

DIRECTIONS:

1. Put the vegetable stock, thyme and matcha powder in a large pot over medium-high heat and bring to a boil.
2. Add cauliflower and cook for about 10 minutes.
3. Meanwhile, put the olive oil and garlic in a small sauce pan and cook for about 1 minute.
4. Add the garlic, salt and black pepper and cook for about 2 minutes.
5. Transfer into an immersion blender and blend until smooth.
6. Dish out and serve immediately.
7. Enjoy!

NUTRITION:

calories: 79 | fat: 6g | protein: 3g | carbs: 3g | fiber: 7g | sodium: 39mg

865. Chicken Noodle Soup

Prep time: 10 minutes | Cook time: 30 minutes | Serves: 4

INGREDIENTS:

- 2/3 onion, minced
- 2/3 rib celery, sliced
- 2 cups chicken, shredded
- 2 eggs, lightly beaten
- 2/3 green onion, for garnish
- 1 1/3 tablespoons coconut oil
- 2/3 carrot, peeled and thinly sliced
- 1 1/3 teaspoons dried thyme
- 1 2/3 quarts homemade bone broth
- 1/8 cup fresh parsley, minced
- Salt and black pepper, to taste

DIRECTIONS:

1. Heat coconut oil over medium-high heat in a large pot and add onions, carrots, and celery.
2. Cook for about 4 minutes and stir in the bone broth, thyme and chicken.
3. Simmer for about 15 minutes and stir in parsley.
4. Pour beaten eggs into the soup in a slow steady stream.
5. Remove soup from heat and let it stand for about 2 minutes.
6. Season with salt and black pepper and dish out to serve.
7. Enjoy!

NUTRITION:

calories: 226 | fat: 8g | protein: 31g | carbs: 3g | fiber: 7g | sodium: 152mg

866. Green Chicken Enchilada Soup

Prep time: 10 minutes | Cook time: 30 minutes | Serves: 4

INGREDIENTS:

- 2/3 onion, minced
- 2/3 rib celery, sliced
- 2 cups chicken, shredded
- 2 eggs, lightly beaten
- 2/3 green onion, for garnish
- 1 1/3 tablespoons coconut oil
- 2/3 carrot, peeled and thinly sliced
- 1 1/3 teaspoons dried thyme
- 1 2/3 quarts homemade bone broth
- 1/8 cup fresh parsley, minced
- Salt and black pepper, to taste

DIRECTIONS:

1. Heat coconut oil over medium-high heat in a large pot and add onions, carrots, and celery.
2. Cook for about 4 minutes and stir in the bone broth, thyme and chicken.
3. Simmer for about 15 minutes and stir in parsley.
4. Pour beaten eggs into the soup in a slow steady stream.
5. Remove soup from heat and let it stand for about 2 minutes.
6. Season with salt and black pepper and dish out to serve.
7. Enjoy!

NUTRITION:

calories: 226 | fat: 8g | protein: 31g | carbs: 3g | fiber: 7g | sodium: 152mg

867. BBQ Chicken Pizza Soup

Base
Prep time: 10 minutes | Cook time: 1 hour 30 minutes | Serves: 4

INGREDIENTS:

- 4 chicken legs
- 2/3 medium red onion, diced
- 2 2/3 garlic cloves
- 2/3 large tomato, unsweetened
- 2 2/3 cups green beans
- 1/2 cup BBQ Sauce
- 1 cups mozzarella cheese, shredded
- 1/8 cup ghee
- 1 1/3 quarts water
- 1 1/3 quarts chicken stock
- Salt and black pepper, to taste
- Fresh cilantro, for garnishing

DIRECTIONS:

1. Put chicken, water and salt in a large pot and bring to a boil.
2. Reduce the heat to medium-low and cook for about 75 minutes.
3. Shred the meat off the bones using a fork and keep aside.
4. Put ghee, red onions and garlic in a large soup and cook over a medium heat.
5. Add chicken stock and bring to a boil over a high heat.
6. Add green beans and tomato to the pot and cook for about 15 minutes.
7. Add BBQ Sauce, shredded chicken, salt and black pepper to the pot.
8. Ladle the soup into serving bowls and top with shredded mozzarella cheese and cilantro to serve.
9. Enjoy!

NUTRITION:

calories: 449 | fat: 32g | protein: 30g | carbs: 7g | fiber: 7g | sodium: 252mg

868. Salmon Stew Soup

Prep time: 10 minutes | Cook time: 25 minutes | Serves: 4

INGREDIENTS:

- 3 1/4 cups chicken broth
- 2 1/3 salmon fillets, chunked
- 1 2/3 tablespoons butter
- 3/4 cup parsley, chopped
- 2 1/3 cups Swiss chard, roughly chopped
- 1 2/3 Italian squash, chopped
- 3/4 garlic clove, crushed
- 1/3 lemon, juiced
- Salt and black pepper, to taste
- 1 2/3 eggs

DIRECTIONS:

1. Put the chicken broth and garlic in a pot and bring to a boil.
2. Add salmon, lemon juice and butter in the pot and cook for about 10 minutes on medium heat.
3. Add Swiss chard, Italian squash, salt and pepper and cook for about 10 minutes.
4. Whisk eggs and add to the pot, stirring continuously.
5. Garnish with parsley and serve.
6. Enjoy!

NUTRITION:

calories: 262 | fat: 14g | protein: 27g | carbs: 7g | fiber: 7g | sodium: 1021mg

869. Spicy Halibut Tomato Soup

Prep time: 10 minutes | Cook time: 1 hour 5 minutes | Serves: 4

INGREDIENTS:

- 1 garlic clove, minced
- 1/2 tablespoon olive oil
- 1/8 cup fresh parsley, chopped
- 5 anchovies canned in oil, minced
- 3 cups vegetable broth
- 1/2 teaspoon black pepper
- 1/2-pound halibut fillets, chopped 3 tomatoes, peeled and diced
- 1/2 teaspoon salt
- 1/2 teaspoon red chili flakes

DIRECTIONS:

1. Heat olive oil in a large stockpot over medium heat and add garlic and

half of the parsley.
2. Add anchovies, tomatoes, vegetable broth, red chili flakes, salt and black pepper and bring to a boil.
3. Reduce the heat to medium-low and simmer for about 20 minutes.
4. Add halibut fillets and cook for about 10 minutes.
5. Dish out the halibut and shred into small pieces.
6. Mix back with the soup and garnish with the remaining fresh parsley to serve.
7. Enjoy!

NUTRITION:

calories: 170 | fat: 6g | protein: 23g | carbs: 7g | fiber: 7g | sodium: 2103mg

870. Traditional Chicken Soup

Prep time: 10 minutes | Cook time: 1 hour 45 minutes | Serves: 4

INGREDIENTS:

1 1/3 pounds chicken	2 garlic cloves
1 1/3 quarts water	1 1/3 thyme sprigs
2 2/3 stalks celery	1 1/3 rosemary sprigs
1/4 large red onion	Salt and black pepper, to taste
2/3 large carrot	

DIRECTIONS:

1. Put water and chicken in the stock pot on medium high heat.
2. Bring to a boil and allow it to simmer for about 10 minutes.
3. Add onion, garlic, celery, salt and pepper and simmer on medium low heat for 30 minutes.
4. Add thyme and carrots and simmer on low for another 30 minutes.
5. Dish out the chicken and shred the pieces, removing the bones.
6. Return the chicken pieces to the pot and add rosemary sprigs.
7. Simmer for about 20 minutes at low heat and dish out to serve.
8. Enjoy!

NUTRITION:

calories: 357 | fat: 7g | protein: 66g | carbs: 3g | fiber: 7g | sodium: 175mg

871. Chicken Cabbage Soup

Prep time: 10 minutes | Cook time: 35 minutes | Serves: 4

INGREDIENTS:

1 celery stalks	4 cups chicken broth
1 garlic clove, minced	1/2 medium carrot
2 oz. butter	1 cup green cabbage, sliced into strips
3 oz. mushrooms, sliced	1 teaspoon dried parsley
1 tablespoons onion, dried and minced	1/8 teaspoon black pepper
1/2 teaspoon salt	3/4 rotisserie chickens, shredded

DIRECTIONS:

1. Melt butter in a large pot and add celery, mushrooms, onions and garlic into the pot.
2. Cook for about 4 minutes and add broth, parsley, carrot, salt and black pepper.
3. Simmer for about 10 minutes and add cooked chicken and cabbage.
4. Simmer for an additional 12 minutes until the cabbage is tender.
5. Dish out and serve hot.
6. Enjoy!

NUTRITION:

calories: 184 | fat: 13g | protein: 12g | carbs: 4g | fiber: 7g | sodium: 1244mg

872. Chicken Mulligatawny Soup

Prep time: 10 minutes | Cook time: 30 minutes | Serves: 4

INGREDIENTS:

2/3 tablespoons curry powder	1/8 cup apple cider
1 1/4 cups celery root, diced	1/4 cup sour cream
3/4 tablespoons Swerve	1/8 cup fresh parsley, chopped
4 cups chicken broth	3/4 tablespoons butter
2 cups chicken, chopped and cooked	Salt and black pepper, to taste

DIRECTIONS:

1. Combine the broth, butter, chicken, curry powder, celery root and apple cider in a large soup pot.
2. Bring to a boil and simmer for about 30 minutes.
3. Stir in Swerve, sour cream, fresh parsley, salt and black pepper.
4. Dish out and serve hot.
5. Enjoy!

NUTRITION:

calories: 215 | fat: 8g | protein: 26g | carbs: 7g | fiber: 7g | sodium: 878mg

873. Chicken Kale Soup

Prep time: 10 minutes | Cook time: 6 hours 10 minutes | Serves: 4

INGREDIENTS:

1 1/3 pounds chicken breast, skinless	2/3 cups chicken stock
1/4 cup onion	1/8 cup lemon juice
2/3 tablespoon olive oil	3 1/3 ounces baby kale leaves
9 1/3 ounces chicken bone broth	Salt, to taste
1/3 cup olive oil	

DIRECTIONS:

1. Season chicken with salt and black pepper.
2. Heat olive oil over medium heat in a large skillet and add seasoned chicken.
3. Reduce the temperature and cook for about 15 minutes.
4. Shred the chicken and place in the crock pot.
5. Process the chicken broth and onions in a blender and blend until smooth.
6. Pour into crock pot and stir in the remaining Shopping List ingredients.
7. Cook on low for about 6 hours, stirring once while cooking.
8. Enjoy!

NUTRITION:

calories: 261 | fat: 21g | protein: 14g | carbs: 2g | fiber: 7g | sodium: 264mg

874. Paella Soup

Prep time: 10 minutes | Cook time: 25 minutes | Serves: 4

INGREDIENTS:

2/3 teaspoon ground turmeric	2/3 cup frozen green peas
2/3 teaspoon dried thyme	1 1/3 tablespoons extra-virgin olive oil
1 cup coarsely chopped red bell pepper (about 1 large pepper)	2/3 cup chopped onion (about 1/2 medium onion)
1 cup coarsely chopped green bell pepper (about 1 large pepper)	1 2/3 cups water
1 1/3 garlic cloves, chopped (about 1 teaspoon)	2/3 (28-ounce / 794-g) can low-sodium or no-salt-added crushed tomatoes
1 1/3 teaspoons smoked paprika	2/3 pound (454 g) fresh raw medium shrimp (or frozen raw shrimp completely thawed), shells and tails removed
1 2/3 cups uncooked instant brown rice	
1 1/3 cups low-sodium or no-salt-added chicken broth	

DIRECTIONS:

1. Place the frozen peas on the counter to partially thaw them while making the soup.
2. In a large saucepan over medium-high heat, heat the oil. Add the onion, red and green peppers and garlic. Cook for 8 minutes, stirring occasionally. Add the turmeric, thyme and smoked paprika and cook for another 2 minutes, stirring often. Add the rice, broth and water. Bring to a boil over high heat. Cover, reduce the heat to medium-low and cook for 10 minutes.
3. Stir the peas, tomatoes and shrimp into the soup. Cook for 4-6 minutes, until the shrimp are cooked through, going from gray to pink and white. The soup will be very thick, almost like a stew, when it is time to serve.
4. Enjoy!

NUTRITION:

calories: 275 | fat: 5g | protein: 18g | carbs: 41g | fiber: 6g | sodium: 644mg

875. Chicken Provençal Soup

Prep time: 20 minutes | Cook time: 30 minutes | Serves: 4

INGREDIENTS:

1 1/3 tablespoons tomato paste	minced, stalks discarded, bulbs halved, cored, and cut into 1/2-inch pieces
2 2/3 garlic cloves, minced	2/3 onion, chopped
4 2/3 cups water, divided	1 1/8 teaspoons table salt
2/3 (14 1/2-ounce / 411-g) can diced tomatoes, drained	1 1/3 (12-ounce / 340-g) bone-in split chicken breasts, trimmed
1 1/3 carrots, peeled, halved lengthwise, and sliced 1/2 inch thick	2 2/3 (5- to 7-ounce / 142- to 198-g) bone-in chicken thighs, trimmed
2/3 tablespoon minced fresh thyme or 1 teaspoon dried	1/3 cup pitted brine-cured green olives, chopped
1 1/3 anchovy fillets, minced	2/3 teaspoon grated orange zest
2/3 tablespoon extra-virgin olive oil	
1 1/3 fennel bulbs, 2 tablespoons fronds	

DIRECTIONS:

1. Using the highest sauté function, heat the oil in the Instant Pot until it glistens. Add the fennel pieces, onion and salt and cook until the vegetables

have softened, about 5 minutes. Mix the tomato paste, garlic, thyme and anchovies and cook until fragrant, about 30 seconds. Stir in 5 cups of water, scraping off any browned pieces, then add the tomatoes and carrots. Place the chicken breasts and thighs in a saucepan.
2. Lock the lid in place and close the pressure release valve. Select the high-pressure cooking function and cook for 20 minutes. Turn off Instant Pot and quick release pressure. Carefully remove the lid, allowing the steam to escape from you.
3. Transfer the chicken to a cutting board, allow to cool slightly, then chop into bite-sized pieces using 2 forks; discard the skin and bones.
4. Using a wide, shallow spoon, skim the excess fat from the surface of the soup. Stir the chicken and any accumulated juices, olives and remaining 2 cups of water into the soup and let it sit until warm, about 3 minutes. Incorporate the fennel leaves and orange zest and season with salt and pepper to taste. To serve.
5. Enjoy!

NUTRITION:

calories: 170 | fat: 5g | protein: 19g | carbs: 11g | fiber: 3g | sodium: 870mg

876. White Bean and Carrot Soup

Prep time: 10 minutes | Cook time: 20 minutes | Serves: 4

INGREDIENTS:

1 1/3 cups celery, diced
1 1/3 (15-ounce / 425-g) cans white beans, rinsed and drained
1 1/3 cups carrots, diced
5 1/3 cups vegetable broth
2 tablespoons extra-virgin olive oil
2/3 large onion, finely chopped
2 large garlic cloves, minced
2/3 teaspoon salt
1/3 teaspoon freshly ground black pepper

DIRECTIONS:

1. In a large saucepan over medium heat, cook the olive oil, onion and garlic for 2-3 minutes.
2. Add the carrots and celery and cook for another 3-5 minutes, stirring occasionally.
3. Add the beans, broth, salt and pepper. Stir and simmer for 15-17 minutes, stirring occasionally. Serve hot.
4. Enjoy!

NUTRITION:

calories: 244 | fat: 7g | protein: 9g | carbs: 36g | fiber: 10g | sodium: 1160mg

877. White Bean Soup with Kale

Prep time: 25 minutes | Cook time: 30 minutes | Serves: 6

INGREDIENTS:

1 1/2 celery stalk, chopped
1 1/2 cup chopped baby kale
1 1/2 teaspoon salt (optional)
3/4 teaspoon freshly ground black pepper (optional)
1 1/2 teaspoon garlic powder
4 1/2 cups low-sodium vegetable broth
1 1/2 to 2 tablespoons extra-virgin olive oil
1 1/2 large shallot, minced
1 1/2 large purple carrot, chopped
1 1/2 (15-ounce / 425-g) can cannellini beans
1 1/2 lemon, juiced and zested
2 1/4 tablespoons chopped fresh thyme (optional)
4 1/2 tablespoons chopped fresh oregano (optional)

DIRECTIONS:

1. In a large, deep saucepan, heat the oil. Add the shallot, carrot, celery and garlic powder and sauté over medium-low heat for 3-5 minutes, until the vegetables are golden.
2. Add the vegetable stock and beans and bring to the boil. Cook for 15 minutes.
3. Add the kale, salt and pepper. Cook for another 5-10 minutes, until the cabbage is soft. Just before serving, add the lemon juice and zest, thyme and oregano.
4. Enjoy!

NUTRITION:

calories: 165 | fat: 4g | protein: 7g | carbs: 26g | fiber: 7g | sodium: 135mg

878. Tomato Basil Soup

Prep time: 10 minutes | Cook time: 10 minutes | Serves: 4

INGREDIENTS:

4 garlic cloves, minced
2 (14 1/2-ounce / 411-g) can plum tomatoes, whole or diced
1/2 cup extra-virgin olive oil
2 cup vegetable broth
1/2 cup chopped fresh basil

DIRECTIONS:

1. In a medium saucepan, heat the oil over medium heat, then add the garlic and cook for 2 minutes, until fragrant.
2. Meanwhile, in a bowl with a hand blender or blender, blend the tomatoes and their juices.
3. Add the tomato puree and stock to the pot and mix well. Simmer for 10-15 minutes and serve, garnished with basil.
4. Enjoy!

NUTRITION:

calories: 307 | fat: 27g | protein: 3g | carbs: 11g | fiber: 4g | sodium: 661mg

879. Vegetable Gazpacho Soup

Prep time: 10 minutes | Cook time: 0 minutes | Serves: 4

INGREDIENTS:

1/3 cup extra-virgin olive oil, plus more for garnish
1 1/3 tablespoons red wine vinegar
1/3 cup water
2/3 clove garlic, finely chopped
1 1/3 slices white bread, crust removed
1 1/3 pounds (907 g) ripe tomatoes
2/3 Persian cucumber, peeled and chopped
2/3 teaspoon salt
1/3 teaspoon freshly ground black pepper

DIRECTIONS:

1. Soak the bread in water for 5 minutes; discard the water when done.
2. Blend the bread, tomatoes, cucumber, garlic, olive oil, vinegar, salt and black pepper in a food processor or blender until smooth.
3. Pour the soup into a glass container and refrigerate until completely cooled.
4. When ready to serve, pour the soup into a bowl and drizzle with a drizzle of olive oil.
5. Enjoy!

NUTRITION:

calories: 163 | fat: 13g | protein: 2g | carbs: 12g | fiber: 2g | sodium: 442mg

880. Beans and Kale Fagioli

Prep time: 15 minutes | Cook time: 45 minutes | Serves: 4

INGREDIENTS:

2 large garlic cloves, minced
6 tablespoons tomato paste
8 cups low-sodium vegetable broth
1 medium onion, diced
2 cup packed kale, stemmed and chopped
2 (15-ounce / 425-g) can red kidney beans, drained and rinsed
2 tablespoon olive oil
4 medium carrots, diced
4 medium celery stalks, diced
2 (15-ounce / 425-g) can cannellini beans, drained and rinsed
1 cup fresh basil, chopped
Salt, to taste
Freshly ground black pepper, to taste

DIRECTIONS:

1. Heat the olive oil in a stockpot over medium-high heat. Add the carrots, celery, onion, and garlic and sauté for 10 minutes, or until the vegetables start to turn golden.
2. Stir in the tomato paste and cook for about 30 seconds.
3. Add the vegetable broth and bring the soup to a boil. Cover, and reduce the heat to low. Cook the soup for 45 minutes, or until the carrots are tender.
3. Using an immersion blender, purée the soup so that it's partly smooth, but with some chunks of vegetables. If you don't have an immersion blender, scoop out about ½ of the soup and blend it in a blender, then add it back to the pot.
4. Add the kale, beans, and basil. Season with salt and pepper.
5. Enjoy!

NUTRITION:

calories: 215 | fat: 4g | protein: 11g | carbs: 35g | fiber: 11g | sodium: 486mg

881. Farro, Pancetta, and Leek Soup

Prep time: 10 minutes | Cook time: 15 minutes | Serves: 4

INGREDIENTS:

2/3 celery rib, chopped
2/3 tablespoon extra-virgin olive oil, plus extra for drizzling
2 ounces (85 g) pancetta, chopped fine
2/3-pound (454 g) leeks, ends trimmed,
chopped, and washed thoroughly
2/3 cup whole farro
1 1/3 carrots, peeled and chopped
5 1/3 cups chicken broth, plus extra as needed

1/3 cup minced fresh parsley

Grated Parmesan cheese

DIRECTIONS:

1. Blend the spelled in the blender until about half of the beans are broken into smaller pieces, about 6 pulses; to put aside.
2. Using the highest sauté function, heat the oil in the Instant Pot until it glistens. Add the bacon and cook until lightly browned, 3 to 5 minutes. Stir in the leeks, carrots and celery and cook until softened, about 5 minutes. Incorporate the broth, scraping off any golden pieces, then add the spelled.
3. Lock the lid in place and close the pressure release valve. Select the high-pressure cooking function and cook for 8 minutes. Turn off Instant Pot and quick release pressure. Carefully remove the lid, allowing the steam to escape from you.
4. Adjust the consistency with extra hot broth if needed. Stir in the parsley and season with salt and pepper to taste. Drizzle individual portions with extra oil and garnish with Parmesan before serving.
5. Enjoy!

NUTRITION:

calories: 180 | fat: 6g | protein: 22g | carbs: 24g | fiber: 1g | sodium: 950mg

882. Lentil and Chorizo Sausage Soup

Prep time: 15 minutes | Cook time: 18 minutes | Serves: 4

INGREDIENTS:

- 2/3 tablespoon extra-virgin olive oil, plus extra for drizzling
- 5 1/3 ounces (227 g) Spanish-style chorizo sausage, quartered lengthwise and sliced thin
- 2 2/3 garlic cloves, minced
- 1 teaspoon smoked paprika
- 3 1/3 cups water
- 2/3 pound (454 g) French green lentils, picked over and rinsed
- 2 2/3 cups chicken broth
- 2/3 tablespoon sherry vinegar, plus extra for seasoning
- 1 1/3 bay leaves
- 2/3 teaspoon table salt
- 2/3 large onion, peeled
- 1 1/3 carrots, peeled and halved crosswise
- 1/3 cup slivered almonds, toasted
- 1/3 cup minced fresh parsley

DIRECTIONS:

1. Using highest sauté function, heat oil in Instant Pot until shimmering. Add chorizo and cook until lightly browned, 3 to 5 minutes. 2. Stir in garlic and paprika and cook until fragrant, about 30 seconds. Stir in water, scraping up any browned bits, then stir in lentils, broth, vinegar, bay leaves, and salt. Nestle onion and carrots into pot.
3. Lock lid in place and close pressure release valve. Select high pressure cook function and cook for 14 minutes. Turn off Instant 4. Pot and quick-release pressure. Carefully remove lid, allowing steam to escape away from you.
5. Discard Bay leaves. Using slotted spoon, transfer onion and carrots to food processor and process until smooth, about 1 minute, scraping down sides of bowl as needed. Stir vegetable mixture into lentils and season with salt, pepper, and extra vinegar to taste. 6. Drizzle individual portions with extra oil, and sprinkle with almonds and parsley before serving.
7. Enjoy!

NUTRITION:

calories: 360 | fat: 16g | protein: 21g | carbs: 29g | fiber: 7g | sodium: 950mg

883. Mushroom Barley Soup

Prep time: 5 minutes | Cook time: 25 minutes | Serves: 4

INGREDIENTS:

- 4 cups low-sodium or no-salt-added vegetable broth
- 2/3 cup chopped onion (about 1/2 medium onion)
- 2/3 cup chopped carrots (about 2 carrots)
- 3 2/3 cups chopped mushrooms (about 12 ounces / 340 g)
- 2/3 cup uncooked pearled barley
- 1 1/3 tablespoons extra-virgin olive oil
- 1/8 cup red wine
- 1 1/3 tablespoons tomato paste
- 2 2/3 sprigs fresh thyme or 1/2 teaspoon dried thyme
- 2/3 dried bay leaf
- 4 tablespoons grated Parmesan cheese

DIRECTIONS:

1. In a large saucepan over medium heat, heat the oil. Add the onion and carrots and cook for 5 minutes, stirring often. Turn up the heat to medium-high and add the mushrooms. Cook for 3 minutes, stirring often.
2. Add the broth, barley, wine, tomato paste, thyme and bay leaf. Stir, cover the pot and bring the soup to a boil. Once it boils, stir a couple of times, reduce the heat to medium-low, cover and cook for another 12-15 minutes, until the barley is completely cooked.
3. Remove Bay leaf and serve in bowls with 1 tablespoon of cheese sprinkled on top of each.
7. Enjoy!

NUTRITION:

calories: 195 | fat: 4g | protein: 7g | carbs: 34g | fiber: 6g | sodium: 173mg

884. Moroccan Lamb Lentil Soup

Prep time: 15 minutes | Cook time: 25 minutes | Serves: 4

INGREDIENTS:

- 2/3 cup French green lentils, picked over and rinsed
- 2/3 (15-ounce / 425-g) can chickpeas, rinsed
- 2/3 onion, chopped fine
- 1/8 cup harissa, plus extra for serving
- 2/3 tablespoon all-purpose flour
- 5 1/3 cups chicken broth
- 2/3-pound (454 g) lamb shoulder chops (blade or round bone), 1 to 1 1/2 inches thick, trimmed and halved
- 1/2 teaspoon table salt, divided
- 1/8 teaspoon pepper
- 2/3 tablespoon extra-virgin olive oil
- 1 1/3 tomatoes, cored and cut into 1/4-inch pieces
- 1/3 cup chopped fresh cilantro

DIRECTIONS:

1. Dry the lamb with paper towels and sprinkle with ¼ teaspoon of salt and pepper. Using the highest sauté function, heat the oil in the Instant Pot for 5 minutes (or until it smokes). Place the lamb in a pot and cook until well browned on the first side, about 4 minutes; transfer to plate.
2. Add the onion and the remaining ½ teaspoon of salt to the remaining fat in the pan and cook, using the highest sauté setting, until softened, about 5 minutes. Mix the harissa and flour and cook until fragrant, about 30 seconds. Slowly incorporate the broth, scraping off any golden pieces and levelling any lumps. Stir in the lentils, then place the lamb in the multicooker and add the accumulated juices.
3. Lock the lid in place and close the pressure release valve. Select the high-pressure cooking function and cook for 10 minutes. Turn off Instant Pot and quick release pressure. Carefully remove the lid, allowing the steam to escape from you.
4. Transfer the lamb to a cutting board, allow it to cool slightly, then chop it into bite-sized pieces using 2 forks; discard excess fat and bones. Stir the lamb and chickpeas into the soup and let it sit until warm, about 3 minutes. Season with salt and pepper to taste. Garnish individual portions with tomatoes and sprinkle with cilantro. Serve, passing the extra harissa separately.
5. Enjoy!

NUTRITION:

calories: 300 | fat: 13g | protein: 22g | carbs: 24g | fiber: 6g | sodium: 940mg

885. Avocado and Tomato Gazpacho

Prep time: 15 minutes | Cook time: 0 minutes | Serves: 6

INGREDIENTS:

- 1/3 cup chopped fresh cilantro
- 1/3 cup chopped scallions, green part only
- 1 1/2 medium bell pepper (red, orange or yellow), chopped
- 1 1/2 cup plain whole-milk Greek yogurt
- 1/3 cup extra-virgin olive oil
- 3 tablespoons red wine vinegar
- 3 cups chopped tomatoes
- 3 large ripe avocados, halved and pitted
- 1 1/2 large cucumber, peeled and seeded
- Juice of 2 limes or 1 lemon
- 3/4 to 1 teaspoon salt
- 1/3 teaspoon freshly ground black pepper

DIRECTIONS:

1. In a blender or in a large bowl, if using an immersion blender, combine the tomatoes, avocados, cucumber, bell pepper, yogurt, olive oil, cilantro, scallions, vinegar, and lime juice. Blend until smooth. If using a stand blender, you may need to blend in two or three batches.
2. Season with salt and pepper and blend to combine the flavours.
3. Chill in the refrigerator for 1 to 2 hours before serving. Serve cold.
4. Enjoy!

NUTRITION:

calories: 392 | fat: 32g | protein: 6g | carbs: 20g | fiber: 9g | sodium: 335mg

DESSERT RECIPES

DESSERTS

886. Cranberry Orange Loaf
Prep time: 20 minutes | Cook time: 45 minutes | Makes 1 loaf

INGREDIENTS:
- ⅛ teaspoon ground cinnamon
- ⅛ teaspoon ground cardamom
- ½ cup water
- 3 cups all-purpose flour
- 1 (¼-ounce / 7-g) package quick-rise yeast
- ½ teaspoon salt
- ½ cup almond milk
- ⅓ cup butter, cubed (optional)
- ½ cup chopped walnuts
- 2 tablespoons grated orange zest
- 1 (12-ounce / 340-g) can cranberry sauce
- 2 tablespoons orange juice

DIRECTIONS:
1. In a large bowl, combine the flour, baking powder, salt, cinnamon and cardamom.
2. In a small saucepan, heat the water, almond milk, and butter (if desired) over medium-high heat. Once it boils, reduce the heat to medium-low. Cook for 10-15 minutes, until the liquid thickens.
3. Pour the liquid ingredients into the dry ingredients and, using a wooden spoon or spatula, mix the dough until it forms a ball in the bowl.
4. Place the dough in a greased bowl, cover tightly with a tea towel and set aside for 1 hour.
5. To make the cranberry filling: In a medium bowl, mix the cranberry sauce with the walnuts, orange zest and orange juice in a large bowl.
6. Roll the dough into a rectangle approximately 1 inch thick and 10 x 7 inches wide.
7. Spread the cranberry filling evenly over the surface of the rolled-out dough, leaving a 1-inch border around the edges. Starting from the long side, tuck the dough under with your fingertips and roll the dough well. Put the rolled dough in an "S" shape in a baking dish.
8. Let the bread rise again, for about 30-40 minutes.
9. Preheat the oven to 350°F (180°C).
10. Bake in a preheated oven, 45 minutes.

NUTRITION:
calories: 483 | fat: 15g | protein: 8g | carbs: 79g | fiber: 4g | sodium: 232mg

887. Crepes
Prep time: 15 minutes | Cook time: 30 minutes | Serves: 6

INGREDIENTS:
- 1 1/2 cup. flour
- 6 eggs
- 2 cups. milk
- 3 tbsp. butter
- 3 tbsp. sugar
- 3/4 tsp. salt

DIRECTIONS:
1. In a mixing bowl, while stirring add the eggs, milk, and melted butter,
2. Then add flour, sugar, and salt continuing to stir.
3. Heat a pan over the medium heat and oil with butter.
4. Now pour the batter into the pan and tilt the pan till the bottom surface is well coated.
5. Cook over the medium heat for 1-2 minutes.
6. Enjoy!

NUTRITION:
calories: 221 | fat: 10g | protein: 5g | carbs: 31g | fiber: 3g | sodium: 335mg

888. Banana Nut Chocolate Chip Muffins
Prep time: 10 minutes | Cook time: 40 minutes | Serves: 6

INGREDIENTS:
- 2 1/4 oz. chocolate chips
- 5 1/4 oz. banana
- 1 1/2 large egg
- 273 ml milk
- 13 1/8 oz. pastry
- 4 oz. granulated sugar
- 3 tsp. baking powder
- 93 ml. olive oil

DIRECTIONS:
1. Preheat oven to 450°F | 230°C | Fan 210°C
2. In a large bowl, combine flour, sugar, baking powder and cinnamon.
3. Mash a banana, add to the bowl and stir or walnuts if preferred.
4. Then make a well in the centre of the bowl then add olive oil, milk, then add the eggs.
5. Mix the flour mixture with this newly prepared mixture but do not over mix.
6. Now add the mixture into a muffin tray.
7. Bake for about 10-15 minutes, let them cool them before serving.
8. Enjoy!

NUTRITION:
calories: 271 | fat: 16g | protein: 4g | carbs: 29g | fiber: 4g | sodium: 51mg

889. Fig and Yogurt Bruschetta
Prep time: 10 minutes | Cook time: 15 minutes | Serves: 6

INGREDIENTS:
- 6 small figs
- 195 ml. yogurt
- 4 1/2 slices bread
- 6 tbsp. fig preserves
- 3 tbsp. pecans
- Fresh mint

DIRECTIONS:
1. Toast your bread under a grill for about 1-2 minutes per side, until golden brown.
2. Cut the bread pieces in half.
3. Then spread the yogurt on each piece.
4. Top the bread and yogurt with fig preserves and chopped nuts. (You may use fresh figs, and if preferred), you can also use sliced mint too.
5. Enjoy!

NUTRITION:
calories: 245 | fat: 10g | protein: 8g | carbs: 31g | fiber: 3g | sodium: 51mg

890. Sesame Seed Cookies
Prep time: 10 minutes | Cook time: 15 minutes | Makes 14 to 16 cookies

INGREDIENTS:
- 1 cup sesame seeds, hulled
- 1 cup sugar
- 8 tablespoons (1 stick) salted butter, softened (optional)
- 2 large eggs
- 1¼ cups flour

DIRECTIONS:
1. Preheat the oven to 350°F | 180°C | Fan 160°C. Toast the sesame seeds on a baking sheet for 3 minutes. Set aside and let cool.
2. Using a mixer, whisk together the sugar and butter (if desired).
3. Add the eggs one at a time until they are well blended.
4. Add the flour and toasted sesame seeds and mix until well blended.
5. Pour tablespoons of cookie dough onto a baking sheet and form into round balls, about 1 inch in diameter, similar to a walnut.
6. Place in the oven and cook for 5-7 minutes or until golden brown.
7. Enjoy!

NUTRITION:
calories: 218 | fat: 12g | protein: 4g | carbs: 25g | fiber: 2g | sodium: 58mg

891. Honey Walnut Baklava
Prep time: 30 minutes | Cook time: 1 hour | Serves: 4

INGREDIENTS:
- 1 cup (2 sticks) unsalted butter, melted (optional)
- 2 cups very finely chopped walnuts or pecans
- 1 teaspoon cinnamon
- 1 (16-ounce / 454-g) package phyllo dough, thawed
- 1 (12-ounce / 340-g) jar honey

DIRECTIONS:
1. Preheat the oven to 350°F | 180°C | Fan 160°C.
2. In a bowl, combine the chopped walnuts and cinnamon.
3. Using a paintbrush, grease the sides and bottom of a 9-by-13-inch pan.
4. Take the phyllo dough out of the package and cut it to the size of the pan with a sharp knife.
5. Put a sheet of phyllo dough on the bottom of the plate, brush with butter and repeat until you have 8 layers.
6. Sprinkle 1 cup of nut mixture onto the layers of phyllo dough. Cover with a sheet of phyllo dough, butter that sheet and repeat until you have 4 buttered sheets of phyllo dough.
7. Sprinkle 1/4 cup of nut mixture for another layer of nuts. Repeat the layering of walnuts and 4 sheets of buttered phyllo dough until all the walnut mixture is gone. The last layer should be 8 sheets of buttered phyllo dough.
8. Before baking, cut the baklava into the desired shapes; traditionally these are diamonds, triangles or squares.
9. Bake the baklava for 1 hour or until the top layer is golden brown.
10. While the baklava is cooking, heat the honey in a pan until hot and easy to pour.
11. Once the baklava is cooked, immediately pour the honey evenly over the baklava and let it absorb, about 20 minutes. Serve hot or at room temperature.
12. Enjoy!

NUTRITION:

calories: 754 | fat: 46g | protein: 8g | carbs: 77g | fiber: 3g | sodium: 33mg

892. Chocolate Brownies

Prep time: 30 minutes | Cook time: 1 hour | Serves: 6

INGREDIENTS:

- 3 tbsp. cocoa
- 6 oz. chocolate
- 6 oz. butter
- 6 large eggs
- 1 1/2 tsp. vanilla extract
- 6 3/4 oz. flour
- 21 3/4 oz. granulated sugar
- Non-stick cooking spray

DIRECTIONS:

1. Preheat. oven to 325°F.| 170°C | Fan 150°C
2. In a saucepan, melt butter constantly stir until everything fully melts then add chocolate and cocoa.
3. Now beat the eggs using a hand mixture, add sugar and vanilla.
4. Now combine both mixtures.
5. Now use a baking pan and coat with oil, then add the prepared mixture.
6. Bake for about 20-25 minutes.
7. Leave to rest for cooling, and serve.
8. Enjoy!

NUTRITION:

calories: 287 | fat: 14g | protein: 6g | carbs: 41g | fiber: 2g | sodium: 33mg

893. Zuppa Inglese

Prep time: 20 minutes | Cook time: 1 hour | Serves: 6

INGREDIENTS:

- 1 cup. coffee (espresso)
- 735 ml. milk
- 1 1/2 tbsp. butter
- 8 1/4 oz. ladyfingers
- 1 1/2 large egg
- 4 1/2 oz. rice flour
- 2 1/4 tbsp. corn starch
- 1 1/2 tsp. lemon extract
- 4 1/2 oz. granulated sugar
- 120 ml. brandy

DIRECTIONS:

1. In a large pan on medium heat, whisk the eggs and add the sugar.
2. Stir in the flour and corn-starch, milk and mix well until combined.
3. Once the mixture becomes thick, remove it from the heat and allow it to cool.
4. Meanwhile, make the espresso and also allow to cool.
5. Dip each ladyfinger's top into the espresso, then dip it into the pan.
6. Now allow to cool and place in refrigerator.
7. Serve when ready.
8. Enjoy!

NUTRITION:

calories: 302 | fat: 17g | protein: 6g | carbs: 43g | fiber: 7g | sodium: 33mg

894. Easy Crema Catalano

Prep time: 20 minutes | Cook time: 55 Minutes | Serves: 6

INGREDIENTS:

- 9 eggs yolks
- 1290 ml. milk
- 11 1/4 oz. caster sugar
- 4 1/2 tbsps. corn flour
- 1 1/2 lemon, zested
- 1 1/2 cinnamon stick

DIRECTIONS:

1. Inside a medium-size bowl start beating the egg yolks along with sugar until fully mixed.
2. Next, grab a heavy bottom saucepan and add the milk, lemon zest followed by a cinnamon stick, while bringing it to a simmer.
3. Remove the pan from the heat, then crack the eggs in this mixture while whisking them constantly.
4. Add the corn flour and milk then, mix the custard mixture in it.
5. Now heat this mixture in the pan over medium heat for about 10-15 minutes.
7. After refrigerator for about 1-2 hours, then serve.
8. Enjoy!

NUTRITION:

calories: 262 | fat: 15g | protein: 6g | carbs: 34g | fiber: 7g | sodium: 33mg

895. Spanish Yogurt Cake

Prep time: 20 minutes | Cook time: 70 Minutes | Serves: 4

INGREDIENTS:

- 5 oz. yogurt
- 1/3 lemon juice
- 1 2/3 tsp. yeast
- 2 eggs
- 2 2/3 yogurt containers

DIRECTIONS:

1. Preheat the oven to 300°F.| 150°C |130°C
2. In a mixing bowl crack the eggs and beat until fluffy.
3. Mix all the ingredients in until you get a smooth batter.
4. Oil a pan and fill it with the batter, (if your oven is extra hot, loosely cover the pan with tinfoil).
5. Now bake for 45-60 minutes, or until a knife inserted into the centre comes out dry.
6. Allow to cool and serve.
7. Enjoy!

NUTRITION:

calories: 345 | fat: 21g | protein: 6g | carbs: 41g | fiber: 5g| sodium: 33mg

896. Fig Crostini with Mascarpone

Prep time: 10 minutes | Cook time: 10 Minutes | Serves: 4

INGREDIENTS:

- 2/3 long French baguette
- 2 2/3 tablespoons (1/2 stick) salted butter, melted (optional)
- 2/3 (8-ounce / 227-g) tub mascarpone cheese
- 2/3 (12-ounce / 340-g) jar fig jam or preserves

DIRECTIONS:

1. Preheat the oven to 350°F | 180°C | Fan 160°C.
2. Cut the bread into ¼ inch thick slices.
3. Arrange the slices of bread on a baking sheet and brush each slice with melted butter (if desired).
4. Place the pan in the oven and toast the bread for 5-7 minutes, until golden.
5. Let the bread cool slightly. Spread about a teaspoon of mascarpone on each slice of bread.
6. Garnish with a teaspoon of jam. Serve immediately.
7. Enjoy!

NUTRITION:

calories: 445 | fat: 24g | protein: 3g | carbs: 48g | fiber: 5g | sodium: 314mg

897. Cream Cheese and Ricotta Cheesecake

Prep time: 5 minutes | Cook time: 60 Minutes | Serves: 4

INGREDIENTS:

- 1/2 tablespoon lemon zest
- 1 (8-ounce / 227-g) packages full-fat cream cheese
- 1/2 (16-ounce / 454-g) container full-fat ricotta cheese
- 3/4 cups granulated sugar
- 2 1/2 large eggs
- non-stick cooking spray

DIRECTIONS:

1. Preheat the oven to 350°F | 180°C | Fan 160°C.
2. Using a mixer, blend the cream cheese and ricotta together.
3. Incorporate the sugar and lemon zest.
4. Incorporate the eggs; pour 1 egg at a time, blend for 10 seconds and repeat.
5. Line a 9-inch springform pan with parchment paper and non-stick spray. Wrap the bottom of the pan with foil. Pour the cheesecake mixture into the pan.
6. To make a double boiler, take a pan or pan larger than the cheesecake pan. Fill the pan about ½ high with lukewarm water. Put the pan in a double boiler. Put everything back in the oven and let the cheesecake cook for 1 hour.
7. After cooking, remove the pan from the water bath and remove the foil. Let the cheesecake cool for 1 hour on the counter. Then put in the fridge to cool for at least 3 hours before serving.
8. Enjoy!

NUTRITION:

calories: 489 | fat: 31g | protein: 15g | carbs: 42g | fiber: 0g | sodium: 264mg

898. Cretan Pancakes

Prep time: 10 minutes | Cook time: 21 Minutes | Serves: 4

INGREDIENTS:

- 12 tbsp. flour
- 3 glass lukewarm water
- 2 tsp. salt
- 2 cups. olive oil

DIRECTIONS:

1. Whisk all ingredients (except the oil) until you have no lumps then let the mixture "sit" for 1/2 hour.

2. In a pan over medium heat, heat the oil and add 1 tbsp of dough.
3. Cook for 30 seconds on each side, until golden.
4. Enjoy it served with honey and cinnamon.
5. Enjoy!

NUTRITION:

calories: 245 | fat: 23g | protein: 5g | carbs: 22g | fiber: 6g | sodium: 264mg

899. Blackberry Lemon Panna Cotta

Prep time: 20 minutes | Cook time: 10 Minutes | Serves: 4

INGREDIENTS:

- 6 tablespoons sugar
- 2 teaspoon lemon zest
- 2 teaspoon unflavoured powdered gelatine
- 2 tablespoons freshly squeezed lemon juice
- 1 1/2 cup half-and-half, divided
- 1 cup heavy cream
- 2 teaspoon lemon extract
- 1 cup fresh blackberries
- Lemon peels to garnish (optional)

DIRECTIONS:

1. Put half cup in a small bowl.
2. Sprinkle the gelatine powder evenly over the half and half and set aside for 10 minutes to hydrate.
3. In a saucepan, combine the remaining ½ cup of half and half, cream, sugar, lemon zest, lemon juice and lemon extract. Heat the mixture over medium heat for 4 minutes, or until it barely boils, don't let it come to a full boil. Remove from the heat.
4. When the gelatine is hydrated, add it to the hot cream mixture, stirring as the gelatine melts.
5. If lumps of gelatine remain, strain the liquid or remove the lumps with a spoon.
6. Pour the mixture into 2 dessert glasses or stemless wine glasses and refrigerate for at least 6 hours, or overnight.
7. Serve with fresh berries and garnish with a few strips of fresh lemon zest if desired.
8. Enjoy!

NUTRITION:

calories: 422 | fat: 33g | protein: 6g | carbs: 28g | fiber: 2g | sodium: 64mg

900. Chocolate Dessert Hummus

Prep time: 15 minutes | Cook time: 0 Minutes | Serves: 4

INGREDIENTS:

- 2 tablespoon maple syrup
- 2 tablespoon almond butter
- 4 tablespoons coconut oil
- Pinch salt
- 1 cup chickpeas, drained and rinsed
- 4 tablespoons unsweetened cocoa powder
- 2 tablespoon maple syrup, plus more to taste
- 4 tablespoons almond milk, or more as needed, to thin
- Pinch salt
- 4 tablespoons pecans

DIRECTIONS:

1. To make the caramel, put the coconut oil in a small microwave-safe bowl. If it's solid, heat it in the microwave for about 15 seconds to melt it.
2. Incorporate the maple syrup, almond butter and salt.
3. Put the caramel in the refrigerator for 5-10 minutes to thicken.
4. In a food processor, combine the chickpeas, cocoa powder, maple syrup, almond milk and a pinch of salt and work until smooth. Scrape the sides to make sure everything is incorporated.
5. If the hummus seems too thick, add another tablespoon of almond milk.
6. Add pecans and blend 6 times to coarsely chop.
7. Transfer the hummus to a serving bowl and when the caramel has thickened, mix it into the hummus. Gently fold it, but don't mix it completely.
8. Serve with fresh fruit or pretzels.
9. Enjoy!

NUTRITION:

calories: 321 | fat: 22g | protein: 7g | carbs: 30g | fiber: 6g | sodium: 100mg

901. Panna Cotta

Prep time: 10 minutes | Cook time: 35 Minutes | Serves: 6

INGREDIENTS:

- 3/4 cup of heavy cream
- 3 3/4 cups of milk
- 1 1/2 package frozen strawberries, thawed
- 3/4 tsp. vanilla extract
- 2 1/4 envelopes of unflavoured gelatine
- 2 1/4 cup of sugar

DIRECTIONS:

1. In a saucepan mix 2 cups of milk, 3/2 cup of sugar, and heavy cream.
2. Bring to a low simmer.
3. In a bowl pour the leftover 1/2 cup of milk over the unflavoured gelatine.
4. Now remove the pan from the heat and toss in the dissolved gelatine with the vanilla extract.
5. Pour into pudding cups and chill for about two hours.
6. Combine the berries and sugar into a bowl remembering to sieve to remove any seeds.
7. Now boil over a medium heat, reduce the heat, and continue to cook for 5 minutes.
8. For serving, run a knife all around the edges of each custard cup to loosen it.
9. Dribble the coulis over the top and serve.
10. Enjoy!

NUTRITION:

calories: 204 | fat: 12g | protein: 6g | carbs: 35g | fiber: 4g | sodium: 100mg

902. Strawberry Shortbread Cookies

Prep time: 20 minutes | Cook time: 10 Minutes | Makes 2 dozen cookies

INGREDIENTS:

- 1 1/3 teaspoons baking powder
- 2/3 teaspoon baking soda
- 1 1/3 tablespoons brandy
- 2/3 teaspoon vanilla extract
- 1/3 teaspoon salt
- 1 1/3 cups strawberry preserves
- 1 1/3 cups corn-starch
- 1 cup all-purpose flour
- 2/3 cup (2 sticks) cold butter, cut into 1-inch cubes (optional)
- 2/3 cup sugar
- 2 2/3 large egg yolks
- Confectioners' sugar, for sprinkling

DIRECTIONS:

1. In a bowl, combine the corn-starch, flour, baking powder and baking soda and mix. Using your hands or 2 forks, mix the butter (if desired) and sugar until combined, with small pieces of butter remaining.
2. Add the egg yolks, brandy, vanilla and salt, stirring slowly until all ingredients are combined. If you have a stand mixer, you can mix these ingredients together with the leaf whisk and then finish kneading by hand, but it is not necessary.
3. Wrap the dough in plastic wrap and place it in a resealable plastic bag for at least 1 hour.
4. Preheat the oven to 350°F | 180°C | Fan 160°C.
5. Roll out the dough to a ¼ inch thickness and cut, placing 12 cookies on a sheet. Bake the sheets one at a time on the top shelf of the oven for 12-14 minutes.
6. Let the cookies cool completely and garnish with about 1 tablespoon of strawberry jam.
7. Sprinkle with powdered sugar.
8. Enjoy!

NUTRITION:

calories: 157 | fat: 6g | protein: 1g | carbs: 26g | fiber: 0g | sodium: 132mg

903. Fig's cake

Prep time: 10 minutes | Cook time: 60 Minutes | Serves: 6

INGREDIENTS:

- 1/3 cup of stevia
- 4 1/2 figs, cut in quarters
- 1/3 teaspoon vanilla extract
- 3/4 cup almond flour
- 3 eggs, beaten

DIRECTIONS:

1. Spread the figs in the bottom of a springform pan lined with baking paper.
2. In a bowl, combine remaining Shopping List ingredients, whisk and pour over figs.
3. Bake at 375° F for 1 hour, flip the cake when done and serve.
4. Enjoy!

NUTRITION:

calories: 200 | fat: 4g | protein: 8g | carbs: 8g | fiber: 0g | sodium: 132mg

904. Cinnamon chickpea cookies

Prep time: 10 minutes | Cook time: 60 Minutes | Serves: 6

INGREDIENTS:

1/2 cup canned chickpeas, drained, rinsed and mashed

1 cup almond flour
1/2 teaspoon cinnamon powder
1/2 teaspoon baking powder
1/2 cup avocado oil
1/4 cup of stevia

1 egg, beaten
1 teaspoons of almond extract
1/2 cup of raisins
1/2 cup coconut, unsweetened and shredded

DIRECTIONS:

1. In a bowl, combine the chickpeas with the flour, cinnamon and other Shopping List ingredients, and whisk well until combined.
2. Scoop spoonsful of dough onto a baking sheet lined with baking paper, place in 350° F oven and bake for 20 minutes.
3. Let them cool for a few minutes and serve.
4. Enjoy!

NUTRITION:

calories: 200 | fat: 4g | protein: 8g | carbs: 9g | fiber: 3g | sodium: 132mg

905. Grape Stew

Prep time: 10 minutes | Cook time: 10 minutes | Serves: 6

INGREDIENTS:

1 cup of stevia
1 1/2 tablespoon olive oil
1/2 cup coconut water

1 1/2 teaspoon of vanilla extract
1 1/2 teaspoon lemon zest, grated
3 cups red grapes, halved

DIRECTIONS:

1. Heat a skillet with water over medium heat, add the oil, stevia and the rest of the Shopping List ingredients, stir, simmer for 10 minutes, divide into cups and serve.
2. Enjoy!

NUTRITION:

calories: 122 | fat: 3g | protein: 8g | carbs: 9g | fiber: 3g | sodium: 132mg

906. Cocoa Yogurt Mixture

Prep time: 10 minutes | Cook time: 0 minutes | Serves: 4

INGREDIENTS:

4 tablespoons of cocoa powder
1/2 cup strawberries, chopped

1 1/2 cup Greek yogurt
10 drops vanilla stevia

DIRECTIONS:

1. In a bowl, mix the yogurt with the cocoa, strawberries and stevia and whisk well.
2. Divide mixture among bowls and serve.
3. Enjoy!

NUTRITION:

calories: 200 | fat: 8g | protein: 8g | carbs: 9g | fiber: 3g | sodium: 132mg

907. Papaya cream

Prep time: 10 minutes | Cook time: 0 minutes | Serves: 4

INGREDIENTS:

2 cup papaya, peeled and chopped
2 cup heavy cream

2 tablespoons of stevia
1 teaspoon of vanilla extract

DIRECTIONS:

1. In a blender, combine the cream with the papaya and other ingredients, pulse well, divide into cups and serve cold.
2. Enjoy!

NUTRITION:

calories: 182 | fat: 3g | protein: 2g | carbs: 3g | fiber: 3g | sodium: 132mg

908. Blackberry and Apple Tart

Prep time: 10 minutes | Cook time: 30 minutes | Serves: 4

INGREDIENTS:

1/2 cup of stevia
4 cups of blackberries
1/8 cup apples, core and cubes
1/8 teaspoon baking powder
2/3 tablespoon lime juice

1/3 cup of almond flour
1/3 cup of water
2 1/3 tablespoon avocado oil cooking spray

DIRECTIONS:

1. In a bowl, mix berries with half the stevia and lemon juice, sprinkle with flour, whisk and pour into a baking dish greased with cooking spray.
2. In another bowl, mix the flour with the rest of the sugar, yeast, water and oil, and mix everything together with your hands.
3. Spread over berries, place in 375° F oven and bake for 30 minutes.
4. Serve hot.
5. Enjoy!

NUTRITION:

calories: 221 | fat: 6g | protein: 9g | carbs: 6g | fiber: 3g | sodium: 132mg

909. Green Tea and Vanilla Cream

Prep time: 2 hours | Cook time: 0 minutes | Serves: 6

INGREDIENTS:

21 ounces of almond milk, warm
3 tablespoons of green tea powder
21 ounces of heavy cream

3 tablespoons of stevia
1 1/2 teaspoon vanilla extract
1 1/2 teaspoon powdered gelatine

DIRECTIONS:

1. I In a bowl, combine the almond milk with the green tea powder and the rest of the Shopping List ingredients, whisk well, chill, divide into cups and keep in the fridge for 2 hours before serving.
2. Enjoy!

NUTRITION:

calories: 120 | fat: 3g | protein: 4g | carbs: 7g | fiber: 3g | sodium: 132mg

910. Cinnamon and banana cupcakes

Prep time: 2 hours | Cook time: 20 minutes | Serves: 6

INGREDIENTS:

6 tablespoons avocado oil
6 eggs
3/4 cup of orange juice
3 teaspoons of cinnamon powder
1 1/2 teaspoon of vanilla extract

3 bananas, peeled and chopped
1 1/8 cup almond flour
3/4 teaspoon baking powder
Cooking spray

DIRECTIONS:

1. In a bowl, combine oil with eggs, orange juice and remaining ingredients except cooking spray, whisk well, pour into cupcake pan greased with cooking spray, place in 350° F oven and bake for 20 minutes.
2. Cool the cupcakes and serve.
3. Enjoy!

NUTRITION:

calories: 142 | fat: 5g | protein: 4g | carbs: 5g | fiber: 4g | sodium: 132mg

911. Mixed Berry Stew

Prep time: 10 minutes | Cook time: 15 minutes | Serves: 4

INGREDIENTS:

Peel of 1 lemon, grated Juice of 1 lemon
1/3 pint of blueberries
1 1/3 pint of strawberries, halved

1 1/3 cups of water
1 1/3 tablespoons of stevia

DIRECTIONS:

1 In a skillet, combine the berries with the water, stevia and other ingredients, bring to a boil, cook over medium heat for 15 minutes, divide into bowls and serve cold.
2. Enjoy!

NUTRITION:

calories: 172 | fat: 7g | protein: 4g | carbs: 8g | fiber: 3g | sodium: 132mg

912. Sweet cherry cream with cocoa

Prep time: 10 minutes | Cook time: 0 minutes | Serves: 6

INGREDIENTS:

3/4 cup of cocoa powder
1 1/8 cup of red cherry jam
1/3 cup of stevia

3 cups of water
1 1/2 pound of cherries, pitted and halved

DIRECTIONS:

1. In a blender, blend cherries with water and the rest of the ingredients, press well, divide into cups and refrigerate for 2 hours before serving.
2. Enjoy!

NUTRITION:

calories: 162 | fat: 3g | protein: 1g | carbs: 5g | fiber: 3g | sodium: 132mg

913. Oranges and apricots cake

Prep time: 10 minutes | Cook time: 20 minutes | Serves: 6

INGREDIENTS:

1/2 cup of stevia
1 1/2 cups of almond flour
1/4 cup olive oil
1/3 cup of almond milk
3/4 teaspoon of baking powder
1 1/2 eggs
1/3 teaspoon vanilla extract Juice and zest of 2 oranges
1 1/2 cups apricots, chopped

DIRECTIONS:

1. In a bowl, mix the stevia with the flour and the rest of the Shopping List ingredients, whisk and pour into a cake pan lined with baking paper.
2. Place in 375° F oven, bake for 20 minutes, cool, slice and serve.
3. Enjoy!

NUTRITION:

calories: 221 | fat: 8g | protein: 5g | carbs: 14g | fiber: 3g | sodium: 132mg

914. Cherry Cream

Prep time: 10 minutes | Cook time: 0 minutes | Serves: 6

INGREDIENTS:

3 cups cherries, pitted and chopped
1 1/2 cup almond milk
3/4 cup whipping cream
4 1/2 eggs, beaten
1/2 cup of stevia
3 teaspoon of lemon juice
3/4 teaspoon of vanilla extract

DIRECTIONS:

1. In your food processor, combine the cherries with the milk and the rest of the ingredients, pulse well, divide into cups and keep in the fridge for 2 hours before serving.
2. Enjoy!

NUTRITION:

calories: 220 | fat: 4g | protein: 5g | carbs: 5g | fiber: 3g | sodium: 132mg

915. Lemon cream

Prep time: 10 minutes | Cook time: 10 minutes | Serves: 4

INGREDIENTS:

1 1/3 eggs, beaten
3/4 cup of stevia
6 2/3 tablespoons avocado oil
2/3 cup heavy cream
Juice of 2 lemons
Peel of 2 lemons, grated

DIRECTIONS:

1. In a skillet, combine cream with lemon juice and remaining ingredients, whisk well, cook for 10 minutes, divide into cups and refrigerate for 1 hour before serving.
2. Enjoy!

NUTRITION:

calories: 200 | fat: 8g | protein: 4g | carbs: 8g | fiber: 4g | sodium: 132mg

916. Chocolate Cups

Prep time: 10 minutes | Cook time: 0 minutes | Serves: 4

INGREDIENTS:

1/3 cup avocado oil
2/3 cup melted chocolate
2/3 teaspoon of matcha powder
2 tablespoons of stevia

DIRECTIONS:

1. In a bowl, mix the chocolate with the oil and the rest of the ingredients, whisk very well, divide into cups and keep in the freezer for 2 hours before serving.
2. Enjoy!

NUTRITION:

calories: 174 | fat: 9g | protein: 2g | carbs: 3g | fiber: 2g | sodium: 132mg

917. Apple Couscous Pudding

Prep time: 10 minutes | Cook time: 25 minutes | Serves: 6

INGREDIENTS:

3/4 cup of couscous
2 1/4 cups of milk
1/3 cup apple, pitted and chopped
4 1/2 tablespoons stevia
3/4 teaspoon of rose water
1 1/2 tablespoon of orange zest, grated

DIRECTIONS:

1. Heat a skillet with milk over medium heat, add couscous and the rest of the ingredients, whisk, simmer for 25 minutes, divide into bowls and serve.
2. Enjoy!

NUTRITION:

calories: 150 | fat: 4g | protein: 4g | carbs: 7g | fiber: 5g | sodium: 132mg

918. Tangerine Cream

Prep time: 20 minutes | Cook time: 0 minutes | Serves: 4

INGREDIENTS:

1 mandarin, peeled and cut into wedges
Juice of 2 mandarins
1 tablespoons of stevia
2 eggs, beaten
1/3 cup of stevia
1/3 cup almonds, ground

DIRECTIONS:

1. In a blender, combine mandarins with mandarin juice and other ingredients, whisk well, divide into cups and refrigerate for 20 minutes before serving.
2. Enjoy!

NUTRITION:

calories: 106 | fat: 3g | protein: 4g | carbs: 72g | fiber: 0g | sodium: 132mg

919. Cold Lemon Squares

Prep time: 30 minutes | Cook time: 0 minutes | Serves: 6

INGREDIENTS:

3 cups of avocado oil + a thread
3 bananas, peeled and chopped 1 tablespoon honey
1/3 cup of lemon juice
A pinch of lemon zest, grated

DIRECTIONS:

1. In your food processor, blend the bananas with the rest of the ingredients, give it a good pulse, and spread over the bottom of a pan greased with a drizzle of oil.
2. Place in the refrigerator for 30 minutes, cut into slices and serve.
3. Enjoy!

NUTRITION:

calories: 136 | fat: 11g | protein: 1g | carbs: 7g | fiber: 0g | sodium: 132mg

920. Apple and Plum Cake

Prep time: 10 minutes | Cook time: 40 minutes | Serves: 6

INGREDIENTS:

10 1/2 ounces of almond flour
1 1/2 beaten egg
7 1/2 tablespoons of stevia
4 1/2 ounces of hot almond milk
3 pounds of plums, pitted and cut into quarters
3 apples, pitted and chopped
Peel of 1 lemon, grated
1 1/2 teaspoon baking powder

DIRECTIONS:

1. In a bowl, mix the almond milk with the egg, stevia and the rest of the Shopping List ingredients, except the cooking spray, and whisk well.
2. Grease a cake pans with oil, pour cake mix inside, place in oven and bake at 350° F for 40 minutes.
3. Cool, slice and serve.
4. Enjoy!

NUTRITION:

calories: 206 | fat: 6g | protein: 6g | carbs: 8g | fiber: 6g | sodium: 132mg

921. Cocoa Brownies

Prep time: 10 minutes | Cook time: 20 minutes | Serves: 4

INGREDIENTS:

15 ounces canned lentils, rinsed and drained
1/2 tablespoon honey
1/2 banana, peeled and chopped
1/4 teaspoon of baking soda
2 tablespoons almond butter
1 tablespoons cocoa powder cooking spray

DIRECTIONS:

1. In a food processor, combine the lentils with the honey and other Shopping List ingredients, except the cooking spray, and give it a good pulse.
2. Pour into a baking dish greased with cooking spray, spread evenly, place in 375° F oven and bake for 20 minutes.
3. Cut the brownies and serve them cold.
4. Enjoy!

NUTRITION:

calories: 200 | fat: 4g | protein: 4g | carbs: 8g | fiber: 2g | sodium: 132mg

922. Black Tea Cake

Prep time: 10 minutes | Cook time: 35 minutes | Serves: 4

INGREDIENTS:

- 3 tablespoons black tea powder
- 1 cup almond milk, warmed
- 1/2 cup avocado oil
- 1 cups of stevia
- 2 eggs
- 1 teaspoons of vanilla extract 3 1/2 cups of almond flour
- 1/2 teaspoon of baking soda
- 1 teaspoons of baking powder

DIRECTIONS:

1. In a bowl, combine the almond milk with the oil, stevia and the rest of the ingredients and whisk well.
2. Pour into a cake pan lined with parchment paper, place in 350° F oven and bake for 35 minutes.
3. Allow the cake to cool, cut into slices and serve.
4. Enjoy!

NUTRITION:

calories: 200 | fat: 6g | protein: 4g | carbs: 6g | fiber: 4g | sodium: 132mg

923. Creamy Mint and Strawberry Blend

Prep time: 10 minutes | Cook time: 30 minutes | Serves: 4

INGREDIENTS:

- 1/8 cup of stevia
- 1 cup almond flour
- 2/3 teaspoon baking powder
- 2/3 cup almond milk
- 2/3 egg, beaten
- 1 1/3 cups strawberries, sliced
- 2/3 tablespoon mint, chopped
- 2/3 teaspoon lime zest, grated
- 1/3 cup of whipping cream

DIRECTIONS:

1. In a bowl, combine the almond with the strawberries, mint and the other ingredients, except the cooking spray, and whisk well.
2. Grease 6 ramekins with cooking spray, pour strawberry mix inside, place in oven and bake at 350° F for 30 minutes.
3. Cool and serve.
4. Enjoy!

NUTRITION:

calories: 200 | fat: 6g | protein: 4g | carbs: 6g | fiber: 4g | sodium: 132mg

924. Almond cream with cardamom

Prep time: 30 minutes | Cook time: 0 minutes | Serves: 6

INGREDIENTS:

- Juice of 1 lime
- 3/4 cup of stevia
- 3 and 1/2 cups of water
- 4 1/2 cups of almond milk
- 3/4 cup of honey
- 3 teaspoons of cardamom, ground
- 1 1/2 teaspoon of rosewater
- 1 1/2 teaspoon of vanilla extract

DIRECTIONS:

1. In a blender, combine the almond milk with the cardamom and the rest of the Shopping List ingredients, pulse well, divide into cups and refrigerate for 30 minutes before serving.
2. Enjoy!

NUTRITION:

calories: 283 | fat: 11g | protein: 7g | carbs: 4g | fiber: 4g | sodium: 132mg

925. Strawberry Cream

Prep time: 10 minutes | Cook time: 20 minutes | Serves: 6

INGREDIENTS:

- 3/4 cup of stevia
- 3 pounds of strawberries, chopped
- 1 1/2 cup almond milk
- Peel of 1 lemon, grated
- 3/4 cup heavy cream
- 4 1/2 egg yolks, beaten

DIRECTIONS:

1. Heat a saucepan with the milk over medium-high heat, add the stevia and the rest of the ingredients, whisk well, simmer for 20 minutes, divide into cups and serve cold.
2. Enjoy!

NUTRITION:

calories: 152 | fat: 4g | protein: 7g | carbs: 5g | fiber: 5g | sodium: 132mg

926. Banana and Semolina Pudding with Cinnamon

Prep time: 5 minutes | Cook time: 7 minutes | Serves: 4

INGREDIENTS:

- 1 1/3 cups semolina, ground
- 2/3 cup olive oil
- 2 2/3 cups of hot water
- 1 1/3 bananas, peeled and chopped
- 2/3 teaspoon cinnamon powder
- 2 2/3 tablespoons of stevia

DIRECTIONS:

1. Heat a skillet with the oil over medium-high heat, add the semolina and sauté for 3 minutes, stirring often.
2. Add the water and the rest of the ingredients, except the cinnamon, stir and simmer for another 4 minutes.
3. Divide into bowls, sprinkle with cinnamon and serve.
4. Enjoy!

NUTRITION:

calories: 162 | fat: 8g | protein: 8g | carbs: 5g | fiber: 4g | sodium: 132mg

927. Apple pudding with lime

Prep time: 10 minutes | Cook time: 15 minutes | Serves: 6

INGREDIENTS:

- 1 1/8 cup of stevia
- 3 3/4 cups almond milk
- 4 1/2 egg yolks, beaten
- Juice of 2 limes
- 1 1/2 cup apples, core and cubes Zest of 2 limes, grated

DIRECTIONS:

1. In a bowl, mix the stevia with the milk and other ingredients and whisk well.
2. Divide into ramekins, place in oven and bake at 380° F for 15 minutes.
3. Serve the pudding cold.
4. Enjoy!

NUTRITION:

calories: 199 | fat: 5g | protein: 5g | carbs: 11g | fiber: 3g | sodium: 132mg

928. Greek Raisins and Vanilla Cream

Prep time: 10 minutes | Cook time: 0 minutes | Serves: 6

INGREDIENTS:

- 1 1/2 cup of heavy cream
- 3 cups of Greek yogurt
- 4 1/2 tablespoons of stevia
- 3 tablespoons of raisins
- 3 tablespoons of lime juice

DIRECTIONS:

1. In a blender, combine the cream with the yogurt and the rest of the ingredients, pulse well, divide into cups and refrigerate for 2 hours before serving.
2. Enjoy!

NUTRITION:

calories: 192 | fat: 6g | protein: 5g | carbs: 9g | fiber: 3g | sodium: 132mg

929. Lemon Pudding with Nutmeg

Prep time: 10 minutes | Cook time: 20 minutes | Serves: 4

INGREDIENTS:

- 1 1/3 tablespoons of lemon marmalade
- 2 2/3 eggs, beaten
- 1 1/3 tablespoons of stevia
- 2 cups of almond milk
- 2 2/3 allspice berries, crushed
- 1/8 teaspoon nutmeg, grated

DIRECTIONS:

1. In a bowl, mix the lemon marmalade with the eggs and other ingredients and whisk well.
2. Divide mixture among ramekins, place in oven and bake at 350° F for 20 minutes.
3. Serve cold.
4. Enjoy!

NUTRITION:

calories: 220 | fat: 6g | protein: 5g | carbs: 3g | fiber: 3g | sodium: 132mg

930. Rhubarb and apple cream

Prep time: 10 minutes | Cook time: 0 minutes | Serves: 4

INGREDIENTS:

1 1/3 cups rhubarb, chopped
1 cups stevia
1 1/3 eggs, beaten
1/3 teaspoon nutmeg, ground
2/3 tablespoon avocado oil
1/4 cup of almond milk

DIRECTIONS:

1. In a blender, combine rhubarb with stevia and the rest of the ingredients, pulse well, divide into cups and serve cold.
2. Serve cold.
3. Enjoy!

NUTRITION:

calories: 200 | fat: 6g | protein: 7g | carbs: 3g | fiber: 3g | sodium: 132mg

931. Almond rice dessert

Prep time: 10 minutes | Cook time: 20 minutes | Serves: 6

INGREDIENTS:

1 1/2 cup of white rice
3 cups of almond milk
1 1/2 cup almonds, chopped
3/4 cup of stevia
1 1/2 tablespoon of cinnamon powder
3/4 cup pomegranate seeds

DIRECTIONS:

1. In a saucepan, mix the rice with the milk and stevia, bring to a boil and cook for 20 minutes, stirring often.
2. Add the rest of the ingredients, mix, divide into bowls and serve.
3. Enjoy!

NUTRITION:

calories: 234 | fat: 9g | protein: 6g | carbs: 12g | fiber: 3g | sodium: 132mg

932. Watermelon cream

Prep time: 15 minutes | Cook time: 0 minutes | Serves: 4

INGREDIENTS:

2-pound watermelon, peeled and chopped
2 teaspoon vanilla extract
2 cup heavy cream
2 teaspoon lime juice
4 tablespoons stevia

DIRECTIONS:

1. In a blender, combine watermelon with cream and the rest of the ingredients, pulse well, divide into cups and refrigerate for 15 minutes before serving.
2. Enjoy!

NUTRITION:

calories: 122 | fat: 5g | protein: 6g | carbs: 5g | fiber: 3g | sodium: 132mg

933. Vanilla Cake

Prep time: 10 minutes | Cook time: 25 minutes | Serves: 4

INGREDIENTS:

3/4 cups of almond flour
1 1/4 teaspoons baking powder
1/3 cup olive oil
1/4 cup of almond milk
1-2/3 cup of stevia
1/3 cups of water
1/3 tablespoon of lime juice
3/4 teaspoons of vanilla extract
Cooking spray

DIRECTIONS:

1. In a bowl, mix the almond flour with the baking powder, oil and the rest of the ingredients, except the cooking spray, and whisk well.
2. Pour the mixture into a cake pan greased with cooking spray, place in the oven and bake at 370° F for 25 minutes.
3. Allow the cake to cool, cut and serve!
4. Enjoy!

NUTRITION:

calories: 200 | fat: 7g | protein: 6g | carbs: 5g | fiber: 3g | sodium: 132mg

934. Walnut cake

Prep time: 10 minutes | Cook time: 40 minutes | Serves: 6

INGREDIENTS:

3/4-pound walnuts, chopped Zest of 1 orange, grated
2 cups stevia
3 eggs, beaten
1 1/2 teaspoon almond extract
2 1/4 cup almond flour
1 1/2 teaspoon baking soda

DIRECTIONS:

1. In a bowl, combine walnuts with orange zest and other ingredients, whisk well and pour into a cake pan lined with baking paper.
2. Place in 350° F oven, bake for 40 minutes, cool, slice and serve.
3. Enjoy!

NUTRITION:

calories: 205 | fat: 14g | protein: 3g | carbs: 9g | fiber: 7g | sodium: 132mg

935. Bowl of Chia and Berry Smoothie

Prep time: 10 minutes | Cook time: 0 minutes | Serves: 4

INGREDIENTS:

3 cup almond milk
2 cup blackberries
1/2 cup strawberries, chopped
3 tablespoons chia seeds
2 teaspoon cinnamon powder

DIRECTIONS:

1. In a blender, combine blackberries with strawberries and the rest of the ingredients, pulse well, divide into small bowls and serve cold.
2. Enjoy!

NUTRITION:

calories: 182 | fat: 3g | protein: 3g | carbs: 8g | fiber: 3g | sodium: 132mg

936. Coconut Cream with Mint

Prep time: 10 minutes | Cook time: 0 minutes | Serves: 4

INGREDIENTS:

2 bananas, peeled
4 cups coconut pulp, shredded
6 tablespoons mint, chopped
3 cups coconut water
4 tablespoons stevia
1 avocado, pitted and peeled

DIRECTIONS:

1. In a blender, combine the coconut with the banana and the rest of the ingredients, pulse well, divide into cups and serve cold.
2. Enjoy!

NUTRITION:

calories: 193 | fat: 5g | protein: 3g | carbs: 7g | fiber: 3g | sodium: 132mg

937. Pineapple Pudding

Prep time: 10 minutes | Cook time: 40 minutes | Serves: 6

INGREDIENTS:

3 cups of almond flour
1/3 cup olive oil
1 1/2 teaspoon of vanilla extract
3 1/3 cups of stevia
4 1/2 eggs, beaten
2 cups natural applesauce
3 teaspoons baking powder
2 cups almond milk
3 cups pineapple, chopped
Cooking spray

DIRECTIONS:

1. In a bowl, combine the almond flour with the oil and the rest of the ingredients, except the cooking spray, and mix well.
2. Grease a cake pans with cooking spray, pour the pudding mix inside, place in the oven and bake at 370° F for 40 minutes.
3. Serve the pudding cold.
4. Enjoy!

NUTRITION:

calories: 223 | fat: 8g | protein: 3g | carbs: 7g | fiber: 3g | sodium: 132mg

938. Cocoa and pear cream

Prep time: 10 minutes | Cook time: 0 minutes | Serves: 6

INGREDIENTS:

1/2 cup heavy cream
1/2 cup stevia
1 1/8 cup of cocoa powder
9 ounces dark chocolate, chopped
Zest of 1 lemon
1-1/2 pears, chopped

DIRECTIONS:

1. In a blender, combine the cream with stevia and the rest of the ingredients, pulse well, divide into cups and serve cold.
2. Enjoy!

NUTRITION:

calories: 172 | fat: 5g | protein: 3g | carbs: 7g | fiber: 3g | sodium: 132mg

939. Blueberry stew

Prep time: 10 minutes | Cook time: 10 minutes | Serves: 6

INGREDIENTS:

3 cups of blueberries	3/4 cups pure apple juice
3 tablespoons of stevia	1 1/2 teaspoon vanilla extract

DIRECTIONS:

1. In a skillet, combine blueberries with stevia and other ingredients, bring to a boil and cook over medium-low heat for 10 minutes.
2. Divide into cups and serve cold.
3. Enjoy!

NUTRITION:

calories: 192 | fat: 5g | protein: 4g | carbs: 9g | fiber: 3g | sodium: 132mg

940. Hazelnut pudding

Prep time: 10 minutes | Cook time: 40 minutes | Serves: 6

INGREDIENTS:

1/4 cup of almond flour	1-1/3 cup Greek yogurt
1 1/2 tablespoons hazelnuts, chopped	3/4 teaspoon baking powder
3 3/4 eggs, beaten	3/4 teaspoon of vanilla extract
3/4 cup of stevia	

DIRECTIONS:

1. In a bowl, combine the flour with the hazelnuts and other ingredients, whisk well and pour into a cake pan lined with baking paper,
2. Place in 350° F oven, bake for 30 minutes, cool, slice and serve.
3. Enjoy!

NUTRITION:

calories: 178 | fat: 8g | protein: 4g | carbs: 11g | fiber: 3g | sodium: 132mg

941. Vanilla and lime caramel

Prep time: 10 minutes | Cook time: 0 minutes | Serves: 4

INGREDIENTS:

1/4 cup cashew butter	1/3 teaspoon lime zest, grated
3 1/3 tablespoons of lime juice	1 tablespoon stevia

DIRECTIONS:

1. In a bowl, mix cashew butter with remaining ingredients and whisk well.
2. Line a muffin tray with baking paper, pour 1 tablespoon lime fudge mixture into each of the muffin cups and keep in the freezer for 3 hours before serving.
3. Enjoy!

NUTRITION:

calories: 200 | fat: 4g | protein: 5g | carbs: 13g | fiber: 3g | sodium: 132mg

942. Almond and Oat Pudding

Prep time: 10 minutes | Cook time: 15 minutes | Serves: 6

INGREDIENTS:

1 1/2 tablespoon lemon juice Zest of 1 lime	3/4 cup of oats
3/4 cups of almond milk	3 tablespoons of stevia
1 1/2 teaspoon of almond extract	3/4 cup silver almonds, chopped

DIRECTIONS:

1. In a skillet, combine almond milk with lime zest and remaining ingredients, whisk, bring to a boil and cook over medium heat for 15 minutes.
2. Divide the mix into bowls and serve cold.
3. Enjoy!

NUTRITION:

calories: 174 | fat: 12g | protein: 5g | carbs: 13g | fiber: 3g | sodium: 132mg

943. Baked Pears with Mascarpone Cheese

Prep time: 10 minutes | Cook time: 20 minutes | Serves: 4

INGREDIENTS:

2 teaspoon vanilla, divided	1/2 teaspoon ground coriander
1/2 teaspoon ginger	4 ripe pears, peeled
2 tablespoon plus	1/2 cup mascarpone cheese
4 teaspoons honey, divided	Pinch salt
1/2 cup minced walnuts	

DIRECTIONS:

1. Preheat the oven to 350°F | 180°C | Fan 160°C and set the rack in the centre position. Grease a small pan.
2. Cut the pears in half lengthwise. Using a spoon, core each piece. Place the pears cut side up in the pan.
3. Combine 1 tablespoon of honey, ½ teaspoon of vanilla, ginger and coriander in a small bowl. Pour this mixture evenly over the halves of the pears.
4. Sprinkle the walnuts on the pear halves.
5. Bake for 20 minutes, or until the pears are golden and you can easily skewer them with a knife.
6. While the pears are cooking, mix the mascarpone with the remaining 2 teaspoons of honey, ½ teaspoon of vanilla and a pinch of salt. Mix well to combine.
7. Divide the mascarpone between the halves of the hot pears and serve.
8. Enjoy!

NUTRITION:

calories: 307 | fat: 16g | protein: 4g | carbs: 43g | fiber: 6g | sodium: 89mg

944. Vanilla Cake Bites

Prep time: 10 minutes | Cook time: 45 minutes | Makes 24 bites

INGREDIENTS:

1 (8-ounce / 227-g) cream cheese	3 large eggs, divided
1 (12-ounce / 340-g) box butter cake mix	1 cup sugar
½ cup (1 stick) butter, melted (optional)	1 teaspoon vanilla extract

DIRECTIONS:

1. Preheat the oven to 350°F | 180°C | Fan 160°C.
2. To make the first layer, in a medium bowl, whisk the cake mixture, butter (if desired) and 1 egg. Then, pour the mixture into the prepared pan.
3. In a separate bowl, to make layer 2, mix the sugar, cream cheese, remaining 2 eggs and vanilla and gently pour over the first layer. Cook for 45-50 minutes and allow to cool.
4. Cut the cake into 24 squares.
5. Enjoy!

NUTRITION:

calories: 160 | fat: 8g | protein: 2g | carbs: 20g | fiber: 0g | sodium: 156mg

945. Berry and Honey Compote

Prep time: 5 minutes | Cook time: 2 to 5 minutes | Serves 2 to 3

INGREDIENTS:

¼ cup fresh berries	½ cup honey
2 tablespoons grated orange zest	

DIRECTIONS:

1. In a small saucepan, heat the honey, berries, and orange zest over medium-low heat for 2-5 minutes, until the sauce thickens, or heat for 15 seconds in the microwave. Serve the sprinkled compote on pancakes, muffins or French toast.
2. Enjoy!

NUTRITION:

calories: 272 | fat: 0g | protein: 1g | carbs: 74g | fiber: 1g | sodium: 4mg

946. Creamy Rice Pudding

Prep time: 5 minutes | Cook time: 45 minutes | Serves 4

INGREDIENTS:

2/3 tablespoon rose water or orange blossom water	3 1/3 cups unsweetened almond milk
3/4 cups long-grain rice	2/3 cup sugar
	2/3 teaspoon cinnamon

DIRECTIONS:

1. Rinse the rice under cold water for 30 seconds.
2. Put the rice, milk and sugar in a large pot. Bring to a light boil while continuing to mix.
3. Lower the heat and simmer for 40-45 minutes, stirring every 3-4 minutes so that the rice does not stick to the bottom of the pan.
4. Add rose water at the end and simmer for 5 minutes.
5. Divide the pudding into 6 bowls. Sprinkle the top with cinnamon. Cool for at least 1 hour before serving. Store in the fridge.
6. Enjoy!

NUTRITION:

calories: 323 | fat: 7g | protein: 9g | carbs: 56g | fiber: 1g | sodium: 102mg

947. Fruit and Nut Dark Chocolate Bark

Prep time: 15 minutes | Cook time: 5 minutes | Serves 4

INGREDIENTS:

4 tablespoons chopped nuts (almonds, pecans, walnuts, hazelnuts, pistachios, or any combination of those)
6 ounces (85 g) good-quality dark chocolate chips (about ⅔ cup)
1/2 cup chopped dried fruit (apricots, blueberries, figs, prunes, or any combination of those)

DIRECTIONS:

1. Line a baking sheet with parchment paper.
2. Place the walnuts in a skillet over medium-high heat and toast for 60 seconds, or just until fragrant.
3. Put the chocolate in a glass bowl suitable for microwave or in a measuring cup and microwave on maximum power for 1 minute. Stir in the chocolate and let the undissolved flakes warm up and melt. If needed, heat for another 20-30 seconds, but keep an eye on it to make sure it doesn't burn.
4. Pour the chocolate onto the pan. Sprinkle the dried fruit and nuts evenly over the chocolate and tap gently so that they stick together.
5. Transfer the pan to the refrigerator for at least 1 hour to harden the chocolate.
6. When solid, break into pieces. Store leftover chocolate in the refrigerator or freezer.
7. Enjoy!

NUTRITION:

calories: 284 | fat: 16g | protein: 4g | carbs: 39g | fiber: 2g | sodium: 2mg

948. Pound Cake with Citrus Glaze

Prep time: 10 minutes | Cook time: 45 minutes | Serves 4

INGREDIENTS:

⅓ cup extra-virgin olive oil
1/2 cup unsweetened almond milk
non-stick cooking spray
1/2 cup sugar
1/2 lemon, zested and juiced
1 cup all-purpose flour
1/2 teaspoon baking soda
1/2 teaspoon salt
1/2 to 2 tablespoons freshly squeezed lemon juice
1/2 cup powdered sugar
1/4 teaspoon vanilla extract

DIRECTIONS:

1. Preheat the oven to 350°F | 180°C | Fan 160°C. Line a 9-inch baking sheet with parchment paper and coat the paper with non-stick cooking spray.
2. In a large bowl, whisk the sugar and olive oil together until creamy. Add the milk and the lemon juice and zest. Let it sit for 5-7 minutes.
3. In a medium bowl, combine the flour, baking soda, and salt. Add the dry ingredients to the milk mixture and mix until incorporated.
4. Pour the batter into the prepared pan and level the top. Cook until a toothpick or toothpick inserted in the middle comes out clean with a few crumbs attached, about 45 minutes.
5. Remove the cake from the oven and let it cool for at least 10 minutes in the pan. Transfer to a wire rack placed on a baking sheet and allow to cool completely.
Make the Glaze
6. In a small bowl, whisk together the powdered sugar, lemon juice and vanilla until smooth. Pour the icing over the cooled cake, letting the excess from the cake drip onto the baking sheet below.
7. Enjoy!

NUTRITION:

calories: 347 | fat: 9g | protein: 4g | carbs: 64g | fiber: 1g | sodium: 481mg

949. Grilled Fruit Skewers

Prep time: 10 minutes | Cook time: 10 minutes | Serves 4

INGREDIENTS:

2 teaspoon vanilla extract
Pinch salt
⅔ cup prepared labneh, or, if making your own, ⅔ cup full-fat plain Greek yogurt
4 tablespoons honey
6 cups fresh fruit cut into 2-inch chunks (pineapple, cantaloupe, nectarines, strawberries, plums, or mango)

DIRECTIONS:

1. If you are making your own labneh, place a colander over a bowl and line it with cheesecloth. Put the Greek yogurt in the cheesecloth and wrap it. Place the bowl in the refrigerator and let it rest for at least 12-24 hours, until it is as thick as a soft cheese.
2. Mix honey, vanilla and salt in labneh. Stir well to mix and set aside.
3. Heat the grill to medium temperature (about 300°F / 150°C) and oil the grill. Alternatively, you can cook them on the stovetop in a heavy skillet (cast iron is fine).
4. Place the fruit on the skewers and grill for 4 minutes on each side, or until the fruit is soft and has grill marks on each side.
5. Serve the fruit with labneh to soak.
6. Enjoy!

NUTRITION:

calories: 292 | fat: 6g | protein: 5g | carbs: 60g | fiber: 4g | sodium: 131mg

950. Buttery Almond Cookies

Prep time: 5 minutes | Cook time: 10 minutes | Serves 4

INGREDIENTS:

5 ⅓ tablespoons (1 stick) room temperature salted butter (optional)
⅔ large egg
⅓ cup sugar
1 cup all-purpose flour
2/3 cup ground almonds or almond flour

DIRECTIONS:

1. Preheat the oven to 190°C (375°F).
2. Using a mixer, whisk together the sugar and butter (if desired).
3. Add the egg and mix until blended.
4. Alternately add the flour and ground almonds, ½ cup at a time, while the mixer is slow.
5. Once everything is combined, line a baking sheet with parchment paper. Place a tablespoon of dough on the baking sheet, keeping the cookies at least 2 inches apart.
6. Place the pan in the oven and bake until the cookies begin to brown around the edges, about 5-7 minutes.
7. Enjoy!

NUTRITION:

calories: 604 | fat: 36g | protein: 11g | carbs: 63g | fiber: 4g | sodium: 181mg

951. Apple Pie Pockets

Prep time: 5 minutes | Cook time: 15 minutes | Serves 4

INGREDIENTS:

1/8 cup brown sugar
1/8 teaspoon ground cinnamon
2/3 organic puff pastry, rolled out, at room temperature
2/3 Gala apple, peeled and sliced
1/8 teaspoon ground cardamom
non-stick cooking spray
Honey, for topping

DIRECTIONS:

1. Preheat the oven to 350°F | 180°C | Fan 160°C.
2. Cut the shortcrust pastry into 4 uniform discs. Peel and slice the apple. In a small bowl, mix the slices with brown sugar, cinnamon, and cardamom.
3. Spray a muffin pans very well with non-stick cooking spray. Make sure you spray only the muffin stands you intend to use.
4. Once sprinkled, line the bottom of the muffin mold with the batter and place 1 or 2 broken apple slices on top. Fold the remaining dough over the apple and sprinkle with honey.
5. Cook for 15 minutes or until golden and bubbly.
6. Enjoy!

NUTRITION:

calories: 250 | fat: 15g | protein: 3g | carbs: 30g | fiber: 1g | sodium: 98mg

952. Orange Mug Cake

Prep time: 10 minutes | Cook time: 2 minutes | Serves 4

INGREDIENTS:

2 teaspoon orange zest
2 eggs
1 teaspoon orange extract
1 teaspoon vanilla extract
1 teaspoon baking powder
Pinch salt
12 tablespoons flour
4 tablespoons sugar
4 tablespoons olive oil
4 tablespoons freshly squeezed orange juice
4 tablespoons unsweetened almond milk

DIRECTIONS:

1. In a small bowl, combine the flour, sugar, baking powder, salt and orange zest.
2. In a separate bowl, whisk together the egg, olive oil, orange juice, milk, orange extract and vanilla extract.
3. Pour the dry ingredients into the wet ingredients and mix to combine.

The batter will be thick.
4. Divide the mixture into two small cups that hold at least 6 oz / 170g each, or 1 (12 oz / 340g).
5. Microwave each cup separately. Small ones should take around 60 seconds and a large cup should take around 90 seconds, but microwaves can vary. The cake will be cooked when it comes off the sides of the cup.
6. Enjoy!

NUTRITION:

calories: 302 | fat: 17g | protein: 6g | carbs: 33g | fiber: 1g | sodium: 117mg

953. Pomegranate Blueberry Granita

Prep time: 10 minutes | Cook time: 10 minutes | Serves 4

INGREDIENTS:

- 1/2 cup sugar
- 1/2 cup water
- 2 cup frozen wild blueberries
- 2 cup pomegranate or pomegranate blueberry juice

DIRECTIONS:

1. Combine the frozen blueberries and pomegranate juice in a saucepan and bring to a boil. Reduce the heat and simmer for 5 minutes, or until the blueberries begin to crack.
2. While the juice and berries are cooking, combine the sugar and water in a small microwave-safe bowl. Microwave for 60 seconds, or until it comes to a boil. Stir to dissolve all the sugar and set the syrup aside.
3. Combine the blueberry mixture and sugar syrup in a blender and blend for 1 minute, or until the fruit is completely pureed.
4. Pour the mixture into a 20x8 inch pan or similar sized bowl. The liquid should be about ½ inch on the sides. Let the mixture cool for 30 minutes and then place it in the freezer.
5. Every 30 minutes for the next 2 hours, scrape the granita with a fork to prevent it from solidifying.
6. Serve after 2 hours, or store in a covered container in the freezer.
7. Enjoy!

NUTRITION:

calories: 214 | fat: 0g | protein: 1g | carbs: 54g | fiber: 2g | sodium: 15mg

12

APPETIZERS
&
SNACKS

APPETIZERS AND SNACKS

954. Greek-Style Potato Skins
Prep time: 10 minutes | Cook time: 45 minutes | Serves 6

INGREDIENTS:
- 1/3 teaspoon black pepper
- 3 tablespoons fresh cilantro, chopped, plus more for serving
- 1/3 cup Kalamata olives, diced
- 3 russet potatoes
- 4 1/2 tablespoons olive oil, divided, plus more for drizzling (optional)
- 1 1/2 teaspoon kosher salt, divided
- 1/3 cup crumbled feta
- Chopped fresh parsley, for garnish (optional)

DIRECTIONS:
1. Preheat the air fryer to 380°F (193°C).
2. Using a fork, make 2 or 3 holes in the potatoes, then cover them with about ½ tablespoon of olive oil and ½ teaspoon of salt.
3. Place the potatoes in the basket of the air fryer and cook for 30 minutes.
4. Remove the potatoes from the deep fryer and cut them in half. Using a spoon, scoop out the pulp from the potatoes, leaving a ½ inch layer of potatoes inside the skins and set the skins aside.
5. In a medium bowl, combine the harvested whole potatoes with the remaining 2 tablespoons of olive oil, ½ teaspoon of salt, black pepper and coriander. Mix until well combined.
6. Divide the potato filling into the now empty skins, distributing it evenly over them. Garnish each potato with a tablespoon of olives and feta.
7. Return the potato skins to the air fryer and cook for 15 minutes.
8. Serve with more chopped cilantro or parsley and a drizzle of olive oil, if desired.
9. Enjoy!

NUTRITION:
calories: 270 | fat: 13g | protein: 5g | carbs: 34g | fiber: 3g | sodium: 748mg

955. Creamy Hummus
Prep time: 10 minutes | Cook time: 0 minutes | Serves 4

INGREDIENTS:
- 1/4 cup tahini paste
- 1 tablespoon extra-virgin olive oil, divided
- 1 cloves garlic, peeled
- 1/8 cup lemon juice
- 1/2 (15-ounce / 425-g) can garbanzo beans, rinsed and drained
- 1/2 teaspoon salt
- 1/8 cup plain Greek yogurt

DIRECTIONS:
1. Add the chickpeas, garlic cloves, lemon juice and salt to a food processor equipped with a chopping blade. Blend for 1 minute, until smooth.
2. Scrape the sides of the processor. Add the Greek yogurt, tahini pastes and 1 tablespoon of olive oil and blend for another minute, until creamy and well blended.
3. Pour the hummus into a serving bowl. Pour over the remaining spoonful of olive oil.
4. Enjoy!

NUTRITION:
calories: 189 | fat: 13g | protein: 7g | carbs: 14g | fiber: 4g | sodium: 313mg

956. Citrus Garlic Marinated Olives
Prep time: 10 minutes | Cook time: 0 minutes | makes 2 cups

INGREDIENTS:
- ¼ cup extra-virgin olive oil
- ¼ cup red wine vinegar
- Zest and juice of 2 clementine's or 1 large orange
- 1 teaspoon red pepper flakes
- 4 garlic cloves, finely minced
- 2 cups mixed green olives with pits
- 2 bay leaves
- ½ teaspoon ground cumin
- ½ teaspoon ground allspice

DIRECTIONS:
1. In a large glass bowl or jar, combine the olives, vinegar, oil, garlic, orange zest and juice, red pepper flakes, bay leaves, cumin, and allspice and mix well. Cover and refrigerate for at least
2. 4 hours or up to a week to allow the olives to marinate, tossing again before serving.
3. Enjoy!

NUTRITION:
calories: 133 | fat: 14g | protein: 1g | carbs: 3g | fiber: 2g | sodium: 501mg

957. Fried Green Beans
Prep time: 5 minutes | Cook time: 5 minutes | Serves 6

INGREDIENTS:
- 1 1/2 tablespoon whole wheat flour
- 1/3 teaspoon paprika
- 3/4 teaspoon garlic powder
- 1 1/2 egg
- 3 tablespoons water
- 3/4 teaspoon salt
- 1/3 cup whole wheat bread crumbs
- 3/4 pound (227 g) whole green beans
- Lemon-Yogurt Sauce:
- 1/3 teaspoon salt
- 3/4 cup non-fat plain Greek yogurt
- 1 1/2 tablespoon lemon juice
- 1/4 teaspoon cayenne pepper

DIRECTIONS:
1. Preheat the air fryer to 380°F (193°C).
2. In a medium-low bowl, beat the egg and water until frothy.
3. In a separate medium-deep bowl, whisk together the flour, paprika, garlic powder, and salt, then add the breadcrumbs.
4. Spray cooking spray on the bottom of the air fryer.
5. Dip each bean in the egg mixture, then in the breadcrumb mixture, coating the outside with the crumbs. Arrange the green beans in a single layer at the bottom of the air fryer basket.
6. Fry in the air fryer for 5 minutes or until the breading is golden brown. Make the Lemon-Yogurt Sauce
7. In a small bowl, combine the yogurt, lemon juice, salt, and cayenne pepper.
8. Serve the green bean fried potatoes along with the yogurt and lemon sauce as a snack or appetizer.
9. Enjoy!

NUTRITION:
calories: 88 | fat: 2g | protein: 7g | carbs: 12g | fiber: 2g | sodium: 502mg

958. Quinoa-Feta Stuffed Mushrooms
Prep time: 5 minutes | Cook time: 8 minutes | Serves 4

INGREDIENTS:
- 1/8 teaspoon salt
- 1/8 teaspoon dried oregano
- 16 button mushrooms, stemmed
- 1 1/3 tablespoons finely diced red bell pepper
- 2/3 garlic clove, minced
- 1/8 cup cooked quinoa
- 1 1/3 ounces (57 g) crumbled feta
- 2 tablespoons whole wheat bread crumbs
- Olive oil cooking spray

DIRECTIONS:
1. Preheat the air fryer to 360°F (182°C).
2. In a small bowl, combine the pepper, garlic, quinoa, salt, and oregano.
3. Pour the quinoa filling into the mushroom caps until just filled.
4. Add a small piece of feta cheese on top of each mushroom.
5. Sprinkle a pinch of breadcrumbs over the feta on each mushroom.
6. Spray the fryer basket with cooking spray olive oil, then gently place the mushrooms in the basket, making sure they do not touch each other. (Depending on the size of the air fryer, they may need to be cooked in two batches.)
7. Place the basket in the air fryer and cook for 8 minutes.
8. Remove from air fryer and serve.
9. Enjoy!

NUTRITION:
calories: 97 | fat: 4g | protein: 7g | carbs: 11g | fiber: 2g | sodium: 167mg

959. Tuna and Caper Croquettes
Prep time: 10 minutes | Cook time: 25 minutes | Makes 36 croquettes

INGREDIENTS:
- 2 teaspoons minced capers
- ½ teaspoon dried dill
- ¼ teaspoon freshly ground black pepper
- 2 large eggs
- 6 tablespoons extra-virgin olive oil, plus 1 to 2 cups
- 5 tablespoons almond flour, plus 1 cup, divided
- 1¼ cups heavy cream
- 1 (4-ounce / 113-g) can olive oil-packed yellowfin tuna
- 1 tablespoon chopped red onion
- 1 cup panko bread crumbs (or a gluten-free version)

DIRECTIONS:
1. In a large skillet, heat 6 tablespoons of olive oil over medium-low heat. Add 5 tablespoons of almond flour and cook, stirring constantly, until a smooth paste forms and the flour turns slightly golden, 2 to 3 minutes.

2. Increase the heat to medium-high and gradually add the cream, stirring constantly until completely smooth and thickened, another 4 to 5 minutes.
3. Remove from the heat and stir in the tuna, red onion, capers, dill and pepper.
4. Transfer the mixture to an 8-inch square pan well coated with olive oil and allow to cool to room temperature. Cover and refrigerate until cool, at least 4 hours or overnight.
5. To form the croquettes, arrange three bowls. In one, beat the eggs. In another, add the remaining almond flour. In the third, add the panko. Line a baking sheet with parchment paper.
6. Using a spoon, put about a tablespoon of cold prepared dough into the flour mixture and roll out to coat. Remove the excess and, using your hands, roll into an oval.
7. Dip the croquette in the beaten egg, then lightly coat in the panko. Place on a lined baking sheet and repeat with the remaining dough.
8. In a small saucepan, heat the remaining 1 to 2 cups of olive oil, so that the oil is about 1 inch deep, over medium-high heat. The smaller the pan, the less oil you will need, but you will need more for each batch.
9. Check if the oil is ready by throwing a pinch of panko into the pot. If it sizzles, the oil is ready for frying. If it sinks, it's not ready yet. Once the oil has heated up, fry the croquettes 3 or 4 at a time, depending on the size of your pan, removing them with a skimmer when they are golden. You will need to adjust the oil temperature from time to time to prevent it from burning. If the kibble browns very quickly, lower the temperature.
10. Enjoy!

NUTRITION:

calories: 245 | fat: 22g | protein: 6g | carbs: 7g | fiber: 1g | sodium: 85mg

960. Lemon Marinated Feta and Artichokes
Prep time: 10 minutes | Cook time: 0 minutes | Makes 1½ cups

INGREDIENTS:

2 tablespoons roughly chopped fresh rosemary
4 ounces (113 g) traditional Greek feta, cut into ½-inch cubes
Zest and juice of 1 lemon
4 ounces (113 g) drained artichoke hearts, quartered lengthwise
⅓ cup extra-virgin olive oil
2 tablespoons roughly chopped fresh parsley
½ teaspoon black peppercorns

DIRECTIONS:

1. In a glass bowl or large glass jar, combine the feta and artichoke hearts. Add the olive oil, lemon zest and juice, rosemary, parsley and peppercorns and mix gently to coat, being careful not to crumble the feta.
2. Cover and refrigerate for at least 4 hours or up to 4 days. Take out of the refrigerator 30 minutes before serving.

NUTRITION:

calories: 235 | fat: 23g | protein: 4g | carbs: 3g | fiber: 1g | sodium: 406mg

961. Kalamata Olive Tapenade
Prep time: 10 minutes | Cook time: 0 minutes | Makes 2 cups

INGREDIENTS:

1 teaspoon Dijon mustard
2 cups pitted Kalamata olives or other black olives
1 garlic clove, finely minced
1 cooked egg yolk
2 anchovy fillets, chopped
2 teaspoons chopped capers
¼ cup extra-virgin olive oil
Vegetables, for serving (optional)

DIRECTIONS:

1. In a large bowl or glass jar, combine the olives, vinegar, oil, garlic, orange zest and juice, chili flakes, bay leaves, cumin and allspice and mix well. Cover and refrigerate for at least 4 hours or up to a week to allow the olives to marinate, turning them again before serving.

NUTRITION:

calories: 179 | fat: 19g | protein: 2g | carbs: 3g | fiber: 2g | sodium: 812mg

962. Falafel Balls with Garlic-Yogurt Sauce
Prep time: 5 minutes | Cook time: 15 minutes | Serves 6

INGREDIENTS:

3 garlic cloves, minced
3/4 tablespoon ground cumin
1 1/2 (15-ounce / 425-g) can chickpeas, drained and rinsed
3/4 cup fresh parsley
1 1/2 tablespoon whole wheat flour
Salt, to taste
Garlic-Yogurt Sauce:
1 1/2 tablespoon chopped fresh dill
1 1/2 cup non-fat plain Greek yogurt
1 1/2 garlic clove, minced
3 tablespoons lemon juice

DIRECTIONS:

1. Preheat the air fryer to 360ºF (182ºC).
2. Put the chickpeas in a food processor. Blend until almost chopped, then add the parsley, garlic and cumin and blend for another 1 to 2 minutes, or until the ingredients are blended and turn into a paste.
3. Add the flour. Blend a few more times until they are blended. The dough will have a consistency, but the chickpeas will need to be cut into small pieces.
4. Using clean hands, roll out the dough into 8 equal sized balls, then tap the balls lightly so that they become disks about ½ thick.
5. Spray the fryer basket with cooking spray olive oil, then place the falafel balls in the basket in a single layer, making sure they do not touch each other.
6. Fry in the air fryer for 15 minutes.
Make the Garlic-Yogurt Sauce
7. In a small bowl, combine the yogurt, garlic, dill, and lemon juice.
8. Once the falafels are cooked and browned on all sides, remove them from the air fryer and season with salt.
9. Serve hot with a side of sauce.
10. Enjoy!

NUTRITION:

calories: 151 | fat: 2g | protein: 12g | carbs: 22g | fiber: 5g | sodium: 141mg

963. Sweet Potato Chips
Prep time: 5 minutes | Cook time: 15 minutes | Serves 4

INGREDIENTS:

2 large sweet potato, thinly sliced
1/4 teaspoon salt
4 tablespoons olive oil

DIRECTIONS:

1. Preheat the air fryer to 380ºF (193ºC).
2. In a small bowl, mix together the sweet potatoes, salt, and olive oil until the potatoes are well coated.
3. Place the sweet potato slices in the air fryer and roll them out in a single layer.
4. Fry for 10 minutes. Stir, then air fry for another 3-5 minutes or until the fries reach your preferred crunchiness level.
5. Enjoy!

NUTRITION:

calories: 175 | fat: 14g | protein: 1g | carbs: 13g | fiber: 2g | sodium: 191mg

964. Crunchy Chili Chickpeas
Prep time: 5 minutes | Cook time: 15 minutes | Serves 6

INGREDIENTS:

1/3 teaspoon salt
1/4 teaspoon chili powder
1/4 teaspoon garlic powder
1 1/2 (15-ounce / 425-g) can cooked
chickpeas, drained and rinsed
1 1/2 tablespoon olive oil
1/4 teaspoon paprika

DIRECTIONS:

1. Preheat the air fryer to 380ºF (193ºC).
2. In a medium bowl, mix all ingredients until the chickpeas are well coated.
3. Pour the chickpeas into the air fryer and spread them in a single layer.
4. Roast for 15 minutes, stirring once halfway through the cooking time.
5. Enjoy!

NUTRITION:

calories: 109 | fat: 5g | protein: 4g | carbs: 13g | fiber: 4g | sodium: 283mg

965. Meatballs Platter
Prep time: 5 minutes | Cook time: 15 minutes | Serves 6

INGREDIENTS:

1 1/2-pound beef meat, ground
1/3 cup panko breadcrumbs
A pinch of salt and black pepper 3 tablespoons red onion, grated
1/3 cup parsley, chopped
3 garlic cloves, minced
tablespoons lemon juice Zest of 1
lemon, grated
1 1/2 egg
3/4 teaspoon cumin, ground
3/4 teaspoon coriander, ground
1/3 teaspoon cinnamon powder
3 ounces feta cheese, crumbled
Cooking spray

DIRECTIONS:

1. In a bowl, mix the beef with the breadcrumbs, salt, pepper and the rest of the ingredients except the cooking spray, mix well and form medium

189

balls with this mixture.
2. Arrange the meatballs on a baking sheet lined with parchment paper, grease them with cooking spray and bake at 450° F for 15 minutes.
3. Arrange the meatballs on a serving plate and serve as an appetizer.
4. Enjoy!

NUTRITION:

calories: 300 | fat: 15g | protein: 35g | carbs: 13g | fiber: 4g | sodium: 283mg

966. Yogurt Dip

Prep time: 10 minutes | Cook time: 0 minutes | Serves 4

INGREDIENTS:

- 1 1/3 cups Greek yogurt
- 1 1/3 tablespoons pistachios, toasted and chopped
- A pinch of salt and white pepper
- 1 1/3 tablespoons mint, chopped
- 2/3 tablespoon kalamata olives, pitted and chopped
- 1/8 cup za'atar spice
- 1/8 cup pomegranate seeds 1/3 cup olive oil

DIRECTIONS:

1. In a bowl, combine the yogurt with the pistachios and the rest of the ingredients, blend well, divide into small bowls and serve with the pita chips on the side.
2. Enjoy!

NUTRITION:

calories: 294 | fat: 18g | protein: 10g | carbs: 13g | fiber: 18g | sodium: 283mg

967. Tomato Bruschetta

Prep time: 10 minutes | Cook time: 10 minutes | Serves 4

INGREDIENTS:

- 4 baguettes, sliced
- 1/4 cup basil, chopped 6 tomatoes, cubed
- garlic cloves, minced
- A pinch of salt and black pepper
- 2/3 teaspoon olive oil
- 2/3 tablespoon balsamic vinegar
- 1/3 teaspoon garlic powder cooking spray

DIRECTIONS:

1. Arrange the baguette slices on a baking sheet lined with parchment paper, grease them with cooking spray and bake at 200° C for 10 minutes.
2. In a bowl, mix the tomatoes with the basil and other ingredients, mix well and set aside for 10 minutes.
3. Divide the tomato sauce over each slice of baguette, arrange them all on a serving plate and serve.
4. Enjoy!

NUTRITION:

calories: 162 | fat: 4g | protein: 4g | carbs: 29g | fiber: 18g | sodium: 283mg

968. Artichoke Flatbread

Prep time: 10 minutes | Cook time: 15 minutes | Serves 6

INGREDIENTS:

- 7 1/2 tablespoons olive oil
- 3 garlic cloves, minced
- 3 tablespoons parsley, chopped
- 3 round whole wheat flatbreads 4 tablespoons parmesan, grated
- 3/4 cup mozzarella cheese, grated
- 21 ounces canned artichokes, drained and quartered
- 1 1/2 cup baby spinach, chopped
- 3/4 cup cherry tomatoes, halved
- 3/4 teaspoon basil, dried
- Salt and black pepper to the taste

DIRECTIONS:

1. In a bowl, mix the parsley with the garlic and 4 tablespoons of oil, mix well and distribute it on the wraps.
2. Sprinkle the mozzarella and half of the Parmesan.
3. In a bowl, mix the artichokes with the spinach, tomatoes, basil, salt, pepper and the rest of the oil, mix and also distribute on the wraps.
4. Sprinkle with the rest of the Parmesan, arrange the wraps on a baking tray lined with parchment paper and bake at 425° for 15 minutes.
5. Serve as an appetizer.
6. Enjoy!

NUTRITION:

calories: 223 | fat: 11g | protein: 7g | carbs: 15g | fiber: 18g | sodium: 283mg

969. Red Pepper Tapenade

Prep time: 10 minutes | Cook time: 0 minutes | Serves 6

INGREDIENTS:

- 10 1/2 ounces roasted red peppers, chopped
- 3/4 cup parmesan, grated
- 1/2 cup parsley, chopped
- 21 ounces canned artichokes, drained
- and chopped
- 4 1/2 tablespoons olive oil
- 1/3 cup capers, drained
- 1- 1/2 tablespoons lemon juice 2 garlic cloves, minced

DIRECTIONS:

1. In your blender, combine the red peppers with the Parmesan and the rest of the ingredients and blend well.
2. Divide into cups and serve as a snack.
3. Enjoy!

NUTRITION:

calories: 200 | fat: 5g | protein: 4g | carbs: 12g | fiber: 4g | sodium: 283mg

970. Coriander Falafel

Prep time: 10 minutes | Cook time: 10 minutes | Serves 4

INGREDIENTS:

- 1/2 cup canned garbanzo beans, drained and rinsed 1 bunch parsley leaves
- 1/2 yellow onion, chopped
- 2 1/2 garlic cloves, minced
- 1/2 teaspoon coriander, ground
- A pinch of salt and black pepper
- 1/8 teaspoon cayenne pepper
- 1/8 teaspoon baking soda
- 1/8 teaspoon cumin powder 1 teaspoon lemon juice
- 1 1/2 tablespoons tapioca flour Olive oil for frying

DIRECTIONS:

1. In your food processor, combine the beans with the parsley, onion and the rest of the ingredients, except the oil and flour, and knead well.
2. Transfer the mixture to a bowl, add the flour, mix well, form 16 balls with this mixture and flatten them a little.
3. Heat a pan with a drizzle of oil over medium-high heat, add the falafel, cook for 5 minutes per side, transfer to paper towels, drain the excess oil, arrange them on a serving plate and serve as an appetizer.
4. Enjoy!

NUTRITION:

calories: 112 | fat: 5g | protein: 4g | carbs: 12g | fiber: 4g | sodium: 283mg

971. Red Pepper Hummus

Prep time: 10 minutes | Cook time: 0 minutes | Serves 4

INGREDIENTS:

- 4 ounces roasted red peppers, peeled and chopped
- 10 2/3 ounces canned chickpeas, drained and rinsed
- 1/8 cup Greek yogurt
- 2 tablespoons tahini paste Juice of 1 lemon
- 2 garlic cloves, minced
- 2/3 tablespoon olive oil
- A pinch of salt and black pepper 1 tablespoon parsley, chopped

DIRECTIONS:

1. In your food processor, combine the red peppers with the rest of the ingredients, except the oil and parsley, and blend well.
2. Add the oil, blend again, divide into bowls, sprinkle with parsley and serve as a holiday seasoning.
3. Enjoy!

NUTRITION:

calories: 255 | fat: 11g | protein: 6g | carbs: 12g | fiber: 4g | sodium: 283mg

972. White Bean Dip

Prep time: 10 minutes | Cook time: 0 minutes | Serves 6

INGREDIENTS:

- 22 1/2 ounces canned white beans, drained and rinsed
- 9 ounces canned artichoke hearts, drained and quartered 4 garlic cloves, minced
- 1 1/2 tablespoon basil, chopped 2 tablespoons olive oil
- Juice of 1/2 lemon
- Zest of 1/2 lemon, grated
- Salt and black pepper to the taste

DIRECTIONS:

1. In your food processor, combine the beans with the artichokes and the rest of the ingredients except the oil and blend well.
2. Gradually add the oil, blend the mixture again, divide into cups and serve as a party sauce.
3. Enjoy!

NUTRITION:
calories: 274 | fat: 11g | protein: 6g | carbs: 18g | fiber: 6g | sodium: 283mg

973. Hummus with Ground Lamb
Prep time: 10 minutes | Cook time: 15 minutes | Serves 4
INGREDIENTS:

5 ounces hummus
6 ounces lamb meat, ground
1/4 cup pomegranate seeds
1/8 cup parsley, chopped
1/2 tablespoon olive oil
Pita chips for serving

DIRECTIONS:

1. Heat a skillet with oil over medium-high heat, add the meat and brown it for 15 minutes, stirring often.
2. Spread the hummus on a serving dish, spread the minced lamb over the entire surface, distribute the pomegranate seeds and parsley and season with the pita chips as a snack.
3. Enjoy!

NUTRITION:
calories: 133 | fat: 9g | protein: 6g | carbs: 18g | fiber: 6g | sodium: 283mg

974. Eggplant Dip
Prep time: 10 minutes | Cook time: 40 minutes | Serves 6
INGREDIENTS:

1 1/2 eggplant, poked with a fork 2 tablespoons tahini paste
3 tablespoons lemon juice 2 garlic cloves, minced
1 1/2 tablespoon olive oil
Salt and black pepper to the taste 1 tablespoon parsley, chopped

DIRECTIONS:

1. Place the eggplants in a baking dish, bake at 400° F for 40 minutes, cool, peel and transfer to the food processor.
2. Add the rest of the ingredients except the parsley, blend well, divide into bowls and serve as an appetizer with the parsley sprinkled on top.
3. Enjoy!

NUTRITION:
calories: 121 | fat: 9g | protein: 6g | carbs: 18g | fiber: 6g | sodium: 283mg

975. Veggie Fritters
Prep time: 10 minutes | Cook time: 10 minutes | Serves 4
INGREDIENTS:

garlic cloves, minced
1 yellow onions, chopped 4 scallions, chopped
1 carrot, grated
1 teaspoons cumin, ground
1/4 teaspoon turmeric powder
Salt and black pepper to the taste
1/8 teaspoon coriander, ground 2 tablespoons parsley, chopped
1/8 teaspoon lemon juice
1/4 cup almond flour
1 beet, peeled and grated 2 eggs, whisked
1/8 cup tapioca flour
1 tablespoons olive oil

DIRECTIONS:

1. In a bowl, combine the garlic with the onions, the shallot and the rest of the ingredients except the oil, mix well and form medium pancakes with this mixture.
2. Heat a skillet with oil over medium-high heat, add the pancakes, cook for 5 minutes on each side, arrange on a serving plate and serve.
3. Enjoy!

NUTRITION:
calories: 209 | fat: 11g | protein: 6g | carbs: 18g | fiber: 6g | sodium: 283mg

976. Bulgur Lamb Meatballs
Prep time: 10 minutes | Cook time: 15 minutes | Serves 4
INGREDIENTS:

1 cup Greek yogurt
1/3 teaspoon cumin, ground
2/3 cup cucumber, shredded
1/3 teaspoon garlic, minced
A pinch of salt and black pepper
2/3 cup bulgur
1 1/3 cups water
2/3-pound lamb, ground
1/8 cup parsley, chopped
1/8 cup shallots, chopped
1/3 teaspoon allspice, ground
1/3 teaspoon cinnamon powder 1 tablespoon olive oil

DIRECTIONS:

1. In a bowl, combine the bulgur with the water, cover the bowl, set aside for 10 minutes, drain and transfer to a bowl.
2. Add the meat, yogurt and the rest of the ingredients except the oil, mix well and form medium balls with this mixture.
3. Heat a pan with oil over medium-high heat. Add the meatballs, cook for 7 minutes on each side, arrange them all on a serving dish and serve as an appetizer.
4. Enjoy!

NUTRITION:
calories: 300 | fat: 9g | protein: 6g | carbs: 22g | fiber: 6g | sodium: 283mg

977. Cucumber Bites
Prep time: 10 minutes | Cook time: 0 minutes | Serves 6
INGREDIENTS:

1/2 English cucumber, sliced into 32 rounds
5 ounces hummus
8 cherry tomatoes, halved
1/2 tablespoon parsley, chopped
1/2-ounce feta cheese, crumbled

DIRECTIONS:

1. Spread the hummus on each round cucumber, divide the tomato halves on each, sprinkle the cheese and parsley and serve as an appetizer.
2. Enjoy!

NUTRITION:
calories: 162 | fat: 9g | protein: 6g | carbs: 6g | fiber: 6g | sodium: 283mg

978. Stuffed Avocado
Prep time: 10 minutes | Cook time: 0 minutes | Serves 4
INGREDIENTS:

2 avocados, halved and pitted
20 ounces canned tuna, drained
4 tablespoons sun-dried tomatoes, chopped
3 tablespoon basil pesto
4 tablespoons black olives, pitted and chopped
Salt and black pepper to the taste
4 teaspoons pine nuts, toasted and chopped
2 tablespoon basil, chopped

DIRECTIONS:

1. In a bowl, combine the tuna with the sun-dried tomatoes and the rest of the ingredients, except the avocado, and mix.
2. Stuff the avocado halves with the tuna mix and serve as an appetizer.
3. Enjoy!

NUTRITION:
calories: 233 | fat: 9g | protein: 6g | carbs: 11g | fiber: 6g | sodium: 283mg

979. Wrapped Plums
Prep time: 10 minutes | Cook time: 0 minutes | Serves 4
INGREDIENTS:

1 ounce's prosciutto, cut into 16 pieces
2 plums, quartered
1/2 tablespoon chives, chopped
A pinch of red pepper flakes, crushed

DIRECTIONS:

1. Wrap each quarter of plum in a slice of ham, arrange them all on a serving dish, sprinkle with chives and pepper flakes and serve.
2. Enjoy!

NUTRITION:
calories: 30 | fat: 9g | protein: 1g | carbs: 4g | fiber: 6g | sodium: 283mg

980. Cucumber Sandwich Bites
Prep time: 5 minutes | Cook time: 0 minutes | Serves 6
INGREDIENTS:

1/2 cucumber, sliced
4 slices whole wheat bread
1 tablespoons cream cheese, soft 1 tablespoon chives, chopped
1/8 cup avocado, peeled, pitted and mashed
1/2 teaspoon mustard
Salt and black pepper to the taste

DIRECTIONS:

1. Spread the mashed avocado on each slice of bread, spread the rest of the

ingredients as well, except the cucumber slices.
2. Divide the cucumber slices over the slices of bread, cut each slice into three, arrange them on a serving platter and serve as an appetizer.
3. Enjoy!

NUTRITION:

calories: 187 | fat: 12.4g | protein: 8.2g | carbs: 4.5g | fiber: 2.1g | sodium: 283mg

981. Cucumber Rolls
Prep time: 5 minutes | Cook time: 0 minutes | Serves 4

INGREDIENTS:

2/3 big cucumber, sliced lengthwise 1 mashed
tablespoon parsley, chopped
5 1/3 ounces canned tuna, drained and
Salt and black pepper to the taste
2/3 teaspoon lime juice

DIRECTIONS:

1. Arrange the cucumber slices on a work surface, divide the rest of the ingredients and roll up.
2. Arrange all the rolls on a serving plate and serve as an appetizer.
3. Enjoy!

NUTRITION:

calories: 200 | fat: 6g | protein: 8.2g | carbs: 3.5g | fiber: 3.41g | sodium: 283mg

982. Olives and Cheese Stuffed Tomatoes
Prep time: 10 minutes | Cook time: 0 minutes | Serves 6

INGREDIENTS:

6 cherry tomatoes, top cut off and insides scooped out 2 tablespoons olive oil
1/8 teaspoon red pepper flakes
1/8 cup feta cheese, crumbled
1/2 tablespoons black olive paste
1/8 cup mint, torn

DIRECTIONS:

1. In a bowl, mix the olive paste with the rest of the ingredients, except the cherry tomatoes, and blend well.
2. Stuff the cherry tomatoes with this mixture, arrange them all on a serving dish and serve as an appetizer.
3. Enjoy!

NUTRITION:

calories: 136 | fat: 8.6g | protein: 8.2g | carbs: 5.1g | fiber: 4.8g | sodium: 283mg

Tomato Salsa
Prep time: 10 minutes | Cook time: 0 minutes | Serves 4

INGREDIENTS:

2/3 garlic clove, minced
2 2/3 tablespoons olive oil
3 1/3 tomatoes, cubed
2/3 tablespoon balsamic vinegar
1/8 cup basil, chopped
2/3 tablespoon parsley, chopped 1 tablespoon chives, chopped
Salt and black pepper to the taste
Pita chips for serving

DIRECTIONS:

1. In a bowl, mix the tomatoes with the garlic and the rest of the ingredients, except the pita. Mix, divide into small bowls and serve with the pita on the side.
2. Enjoy!

NUTRITION:

calories: 160 | fat: 13g | protein: 2g | carbs: 10g | fiber: 45g | sodium: 283mg

983. Chili Mango and Watermelon Salsa
Prep time: 10 minutes | Cook time: 0 minutes | Serves 6

INGREDIENTS:

1/2 red tomato, chopped
Salt and black pepper to the taste
1/2 cup watermelon, seedless, peeled and cubed
1/2 red onion, chopped
1 1/2 mangos, peeled and chopped 2 chili peppers, chopped
1/8 cup cilantro, chopped 3 tablespoons lime juice Pita chips for serving

DIRECTIONS:

1. In a bowl, mix the tomato with the watermelon, onion and the rest of the ingredients, except the pita, and mix well.

2. Divide the mixture into bowls and serve with fries on the side.
3. Enjoy!

NUTRITION:

calories: 62 | fat: 4g | protein: 2g | carbs: 3g | fiber: 1g | sodium: 283mg

984. Creamy Spinach and Shallots Dip
Prep time: 10 minutes | Cook time: 0 minutes | Serves 6

INGREDIENTS:

1 1/2-pound spinach, roughly chopped
3 shallots, chopped
3 tablespoons mint, chopped
1 1/8 cup cream cheese, soft
Salt and black pepper to the taste

DIRECTIONS:

1. In a blender, combine the spinach with the shallot and the rest of the ingredients and blend well.
2. Divide into small bowls and serve as a party sauce.
3. Enjoy!

NUTRITION:

calories: 204 | fat: 11g | protein: 5g | carbs: 4g | fiber: 3g | sodium: 283mg

985. Feta Artichoke Dip
Prep time: 10 minutes | Cook time: 30 minutes | Serves 6

INGREDIENTS:

6 ounces artichoke hearts, drained and quartered
1/2 cup basil, chopped
1/2 cup green olives, pitted and chopped
3/4 cup parmesan cheese, grated
3 3/4 ounces feta cheese, crumbled

DIRECTIONS:

1. In the food processor, mix the artichokes with the basil and the rest of the ingredients, blend well and transfer to a pan.
2. Place in the oven, bake at 375° F for 30 minutes and serve as a party sauce.
3. Enjoy!

NUTRITION:

calories: 186 | fat: 12g | protein: 5g | carbs: 2g | fiber: 3g | sodium: 283mg

986. Avocado Dip
Prep time: 10 minutes | Cook time: 0 minutes | Serves 6

INGREDIENTS:

1/3 cup heavy cream
3/4 green chili pepper, chopped Salt and pepper to the taste
3 avocados, pitted, peeled and chopped
3/4 cup cilantro, chopped
1/4 cup lime juice

DIRECTIONS:

1. In a blender, combine the cream with the avocados and the rest of the ingredients and blend well.
2. Divide the mixture into bowls and serve cold as a party sauce.
3. Enjoy!

NUTRITION:

calories: 200 | fat: 14g | protein: 7g | carbs: 2g | fiber: 3g | sodium: 283mg

987. Goat Cheese and Chives Spread
Prep time: 10 minutes | Cook time: 0 minutes | Serves 6

INGREDIENTS:

3 ounces goat cheese, crumbled
1 1/8 cup sour cream
3 tablespoons chives, chopped 1
tablespoon lemon juice
Salt and black pepper to the taste
3 tablespoons extra virgin olive oil

DIRECTIONS:

1. In a bowl, mix the goat cheese with the cream and the rest of the ingredients and mix very well.
2. Refrigerate for 10 minutes and serve as a spreadable feast.
3. Enjoy!

NUTRITION:

calories: 220 | fat: 11g | protein: 5g | carbs: 8g | fiber: 4g | sodium: 283mg

988. Chickpeas Salsa
Prep time: 10 minutes | Cook time: 0 minutes | Serves 4

INGREDIENTS:

2 2/3 spring onions, chopped
2/3 cup baby spinach
10 ounces canned chickpeas, drained and rinsed
Salt and black pepper to the taste
1 1/3 tablespoons olive oil
1 1/3 tablespoons lemon juice
2/3 tablespoon cilantro, chopped

DIRECTIONS:
1. In a bowl, mix the chickpeas with the spinach, spring onions and the rest of the ingredients. Mix, divide into small bowls and serve as a snack.
2. Enjoy!

NUTRITION:
calories: 224 | fat: 5g | protein: 15g | carbs: 8g | fiber: 1g | sodium: 283mg

989. Ginger and Cream Cheese Dip
Prep time: 10 minutes | Cook time: 0 minutes | Serves 4

INGREDIENTS:
1/3 cup ginger, grated
1 1/3 bunches cilantro, chopped
1 1/3 tablespoons balsamic vinegar
1/3 cup olive oil
1 cups cream cheese, soft

DIRECTIONS:
1. In your blender, mix the ginger with the rest of the ingredients and blend well.
2. Divide into small bowls and serve as a party sauce.
3. Enjoy!

NUTRITION:
calories: 213 | fat: 4g | protein: 17g | carbs: 8g | fiber: 4g | sodium: 283mg

990. Walnuts Yogurt Dip
Prep time: 10 minutes | Cook time: 0 minutes | Serves 4

INGREDIENTS:
1 1/2 garlic cloves, minced
1 cup Greek yogurt
1/8 cup dill, chopped
1/2 tablespoon chives, chopped
1/8 cup walnuts, chopped
Salt and black pepper to the taste

DIRECTIONS:
1. In a bowl, mix the garlic with the yogurt and the rest of the ingredients, whisk well, divide into small bowls and serve as a party sauce.
2. Enjoy!

NUTRITION:
calories: 200 | fat: 6g | protein: 8g | carbs: 15g | fiber: 6g | sodium: 283mg

991. Herbed Goat Cheese Dip
Prep time: 10 minutes | Cook time: 0 minutes | Serves 6

INGREDIENTS:
¼ cup mixed parsley, chopped
¼ cup chives, chopped
8 ounces goat cheese, soft
Salt and black pepper to the taste
A drizzle of olive oil

DIRECTIONS:
1. In the food processor, mix the goat cheese with the parsley and the rest of the ingredients and blend well.
2. Divide into small bowls and serve as a party sauce.
3. Enjoy!

NUTRITION:
calories: 245 | fat: 11g | protein: 11g | carbs: 8g | fiber: 4g | sodium: 283mg

992. Scallions Dip
Prep time: 10 minutes | Cook time: 0 minutes | Serves 4

INGREDIENTS:
3 scallions, chopped
1/2 garlic clove, minced
1 1/2 tablespoons olive oil
Salt and black pepper to the taste
1/2 tablespoon lemon juice
3/4 cups cream cheese, soft
ounces prosciutto, cooked and crumbled

DIRECTIONS:
1. In a bowl, mix the shallots with the garlic and the rest of the ingredients, except the ham, and blend well.
2. Divide into bowls, sprinkle the ham and serve as a party sauce.
3. Enjoy!

NUTRITION:
calories: 144 | fat: 7g | protein: 5g | carbs: 6g | fiber: 4g | sodium: 283mg

993. Tomato Cream Cheese Spread
Prep time: 10 minutes | Cook time: 0 minutes | Serves 4

INGREDIENTS:
8 ounces cream cheese, soft
2/3 big tomato, cubed
1/8 cup homemade mayonnaise 2 garlic clove, minced
1 1/3 tablespoons red onion, chopped 2 tablespoons lime juice
Salt and black pepper to the taste

DIRECTIONS:
1. In your blender, mix the cream cheese with the tomato and the rest of the ingredients. Blend well, divide into bowls and serve cold.
2. Enjoy!

NUTRITION:
calories: 204 | fat: 6g | protein: 4g | carbs: 7g | fiber: 1g | sodium: 283mg

994. Pesto Dip
Prep time: 10 minutes | Cook time: 0 minutes | Serves: 4

INGREDIENTS:
2/3 cup cream cheese, soft
2 tablespoons basil pesto
Salt and black pepper to the taste
2/3 cup heavy cream
2/3 tablespoon chives, chopped

DIRECTIONS:
1. In a bowl, mix the cream cheese with the pesto and the rest of the ingredients and mix well.
2. Divide into small cups and serve as a party sauce.
3. Enjoy!

NUTRITION:
calories: 320 | fat: 14g | protein: 5g | carbs: 6g | fiber: 4g | sodium: 100mg

995. Vinegar Beet Bites
Prep time: 10 minutes | Cook time: 30 minutes | Serves: 6

INGREDIENTS:
3 beets, sliced
A pinch of sea salt and black pepper
1/2 cup balsamic vinegar
1 1/2 cup olive oil

DIRECTIONS:
1. In a bowl, mix the cream cheese with the pesto and the rest of the ingredients and mix well.
2. Divide into small cups and serve as a party sauce.
3. Enjoy!

NUTRITION:
calories: 199 | fat: 5g | protein: 5g | carbs: 8g | fiber: 3g | sodium: 100mg

996. Zucchini and Olives Salsa
Prep time: 10 minutes | Cook time: 0 minutes | Serves: 6

INGREDIENTS:
3/4 cup black olives, pitted and sliced 3 zucchinis, cut with a spiralizer
1 1/2 cup cherry tomatoes, halved Salt and black pepper to the taste 1 small red onion, chopped
3/4 cup feta cheese, crumbled
3/4 cup olive oil
1/3 cup apple cider vinegar

DIRECTIONS:
1. In a bowl mix the olives with the courgettes and the rest of the ingredients, mix, divide into small bowls and serve as an appetizer.
2. Enjoy!

NUTRITION:
calories: 140 | fat: 14g | protein: 5g | carbs: 3g | fiber: 3g | sodium: 100mg

997. Strawberry and Carrots Salad
Prep time: 10 minutes | Cook time: 0 minutes | Serves: 6

INGREDIENTS:
9 carrots, peeled and grated 10 strawberries, halved
Salt and black pepper to the taste 2 tablespoons balsamic vinegar
1 1/2 tablespoon Dijon mustard
1/3 cup lemon juice
3 tablespoons olive oil

DIRECTIONS:
1. In a bowl, mix the carrots with the strawberries and the rest of the

ingredients. Mix, divide into appetizer plates and serve.
2.Enjoy!

NUTRITION:

calories: 182 | fat: 4g | protein: 5g | carbs: 7g | fiber: 3g | sodium: 100mg

998. Hot Squash Wedges

Prep time: 10 minutes | Cook time: 25 minutes | Serves: 4

INGREDIENTS:

4 tablespoons olive oil
1 1/3 tablespoons chili paste
2/3 butternut squash, peeled and cut into wedges
1 1/3 tablespoons balsamic vinegar
2/3 tablespoon chives, chopped

DIRECTIONS:

1.In a bowl, mix the pumpkin wedges with the chilli paste and the rest of the ingredients, mix them, spread them on a baking sheet lined with parchment paper and bake at 200° F for 25 minutes, turning them from time to time.
2. Divide the wedges into bowls and serve as a snack.
3.Enjoy!

NUTRITION:

calories: 180 | fat: 4g | protein: 5g | carbs: 6g | fiber: 4g | sodium: 100mg

999. Shrimp and Cucumber Bites

Prep time: 10 minutes | Cook time: 0 minutes | Serves: 4

INGREDIENTS:

1/2 big cucumber, cubed
1/2-pound shrimp, cooked, peeled, deveined and chopped 2 tablespoons heavy cream
Salt and black pepper to the taste
6 whole grain crackers

DIRECTIONS:

1.In a bowl, mix the cucumber with the rest of the ingredients except the crackers and mix well.
2.Arrange the crackers on a serving plate, spread the prawn mix on each and serve.
3.Enjoy!

NUTRITION:

calories: 155 | fat: 8g | protein: 17g | carbs: 11g | fiber: 4g | sodium: 100mg

1000. Salmon Rolls

Prep time: 10 minutes | Cook time: 0 minutes | Serves: 4

INGREDIENTS:

1/3 big long cucumber, thinly sliced lengthwise
2/3 teaspoons lime juice
1 1/3 ounces cream cheese, soft
1/3 teaspoon lemon zest, grated Salt and black pepper to the taste
2/3 teaspoons dill, chopped
1 1/3 ounces smoked salmon, cut into strips

DIRECTIONS:

1. Arrange the cucumber slices on a work surface and cover each with a strip of salmon.
2. In a bowl, mix the rest of the ingredients, mix and spread over the salmon.
3. Roll up the salmon and cucumber strips, arrange them on a serving dish and serve as an appetizer.
4.Enjoy!

NUTRITION:

calories: 245 | fat: 15g | protein: 17g | carbs: 16g | fiber: 4g | sodium: 100mg

1001. Eggplant Bombs

Prep time: 10 minutes | Cook time: 45 minutes | Serves: 4

INGREDIENTS:

2 2/3 cups eggplants, chopped 3 tablespoons olive oil
2 garlic cloves, minced 2 eggs, whisked
Salt and black pepper to the taste
2/3 cup parsley, chopped
1/3 cup parmesan cheese, finely grated
1/2 cups bread crumbs

DIRECTIONS:

1. Heat a pan with the oil over medium high heat, add the garlic and eggplant and cook for 15 minutes, stirring often.
2. In a bowl, combine the eggplant mixture with the rest of the ingredients, mix well and form medium balls with this mixture.
3. Arrange the balls on a baking sheet lined with parchment paper and bake at 350° F for 30 minutes.
4. Serve as a snack.
5.Enjoy!

NUTRITION:

calories: 224 | fat: 10g | protein: 3g | carbs: 5g | fiber: 1g | sodium: 100mg

1002. Eggplant Bites

Prep time: 10 minutes | Cook time: 15 minutes | Serves: 4

INGREDIENTS:

1 eggplant, cut into 20 slices 2 tablespoons olive oil
1/4 cup roasted peppers, chopped
1/4 cup kalamata olives, pitted and chopped
1/2 tablespoon lime juice
1/2 teaspoon red pepper flakes, crushed
Salt and black pepper to the taste
1 tablespoons mint, chopped

DIRECTIONS:

1. In a bowl, mix the roasted peppers with the olives, half of the oil and the rest of the ingredients, except the eggplant slices, and mix well.
2. Brush the aubergine slices with the rest of the olive oil on both sides, place them on the preheated grill over medium-high heat, cook for 7 minutes on each side and transfer to a serving dish.
3. Garnish each eggplant slice with the roasted pepper mix and serve.
4. Enjoy!

NUTRITION:

calories: 214 | fat: 10g | protein: 5g | carbs: 15g | fiber: 5g | sodium: 100mg

1003. Sage Eggplant Chips

Prep time: 10 minutes | Cook time: 45 minutes | Serves: 6

INGREDIENTS:

1 1/2 tablespoon olive oil
3 eggplants, sliced
3/4 tablespoon smoked paprika Salt and black pepper to the taste
3/4 teaspoon turmeric powder
3/4 teaspoon onion powder 2 teaspoons sage, dried

DIRECTIONS:

1. In a bowl, mix the eggplant slices with the rest of the ingredients and mix well.
2. Spread the auberge slices on a baking tray lined with parchment paper, bake at 180°F for 45 minutes and serve cold as a snack.
3. Enjoy!

NUTRITION:

calories: 139 | fat: 7g | protein: 2g | carbs: 11g | fiber: 4g | sodium: 100mg

1004. Tomato Dip

Prep time: 10 minutes | Cook time: 0 minutes | Serves: 6

INGREDIENTS:

1 1/2-pound tomatoes, peeled and chopped
Salt and black pepper to the taste
2 1/4 teaspoons balsamic vinegar
3/4 teaspoon oregano, chopped 3 tablespoons olive oil
1 1/2 garlic cloves, minced
3 tablespoons parsley, chopped

DIRECTIONS:

1.In a blender, combine the tomatoes with oregano, salt, pepper and the rest of the ingredients, whisk well, divide into small bowls and serve as a party sauce.
2.Enjoy!

NUTRITION:

calories: 124 | fat: 4g | protein: 3g | carbs: 3g | fiber: 2g | sodium: 100mg

1005. Oregano Avocado Salad

Prep time: 10 minutes | Cook time: 0 minutes | Serves: 6

INGREDIENTS:

A drizzle of olive oil
3 small avocados, pitted and cubed
1 1/2 teaspoon mustard
1 1/2 tablespoon white vinegar
1 1/2 tablespoon oregano, chopped
1 1/2 teaspoon honey
Salt and black pepper to the taste

DIRECTIONS:

1. In a bowl, combine the avocados with the oil and the rest of the ingredients. Mix, divide into appetizer plates and serve.
2. Enjoy!

NUTRITION:
calories: 244 | fat: 14g | protein: 8g | carbs: 23g | fiber: 12g | sodium: 100mg

1006. Lentils Spread
Prep time: 10 minutes | Cook time: 0 minutes | Serves: 6

INGREDIENTS:

1/2 garlic clove, minced
6 ounces canned lentils, drained and rinsed
1/2 teaspoon oregano, dried
1/8 teaspoon basil, dried
1 1/2 tablespoons olive oil
1/2 tablespoon balsamic vinegar
Salt and black pepper to the taste

DIRECTIONS:

1. In a blender, combine the lentils with the garlic and the rest of the ingredients, blend well, divide in bowls and serve as an appetizer.
2. Enjoy!

NUTRITION:
calories: 287 | fat: 9g | protein: 9g | carbs: 15g | fiber: 3g | sodium: 100mg

1007. Chickpeas and Eggplant Bowls
Prep time: 10 minutes | Cook time: 10 minutes | Serves: 6

INGREDIENTS:

3 eggplants, cut in half lengthwise and cubed
1 1/2 red onion, chopped
Juice of 1 lime
1 1/2 tablespoon olive oil
42 ounces canned chickpeas, drained and rinsed
1 1/2 bunch parsley, chopped
A pinch of salt and black pepper
1 tablespoon balsamic vinegar

DIRECTIONS:

1. Spread the eggplant cubes on a baking sheet lined with baking paper, pour half the oil over them, season with salt and pepper and cook at 170°F for 10 minutes.
2. Cool the aubergines, add the rest of the ingredients, mix, divide into appetizer plates and serve.
3. Enjoy!

NUTRITION:
calories: 263 | fat: 12g | protein: 7g | carbs: 15g | fiber: 9g | sodium: 100mg

1008. Cheese and Egg Salad
Prep time: 10 minutes | Cook time: 0 minutes | Serves: 6

INGREDIENTS:

3 tablespoons olive oil
18 eggs, hard boiled, peeled and chopped
Juice of 1 lime
21 ounces feta cheese, crumbled
Salt and black pepper to the taste
1/3 cup mustard
1 1/8 cup sun-dried tomatoes, chopped
1 1/2 cup walnuts, chopped

DIRECTIONS:

1. In a bowl, combine the eggs with the oil and the rest of the ingredients and mix well.
2. Divide into small bowls and serve cold as an appetizer.
3. Enjoy!

NUTRITION:
calories: 288 | fat: 8g | protein: 7g | carbs: 15g | fiber: 9g | sodium: 100mg

1009. Stuffed Zucchinis
Prep time: 10 minutes | Cook time: 40 minutes | Serves: 4

INGREDIENTS:

4 zucchinis, halved lengthwise and insides scooped out
1 1/3 garlic cloves, minced
1 1/3 tablespoons oregano, chopped
Juice of 2 lemons
Salt and black pepper to the taste
1 1/3 tablespoons olive oil
5 1/3 ounces feta cheese, crumbed

DIRECTIONS:

1. Arrange the zucchini halves on a baking sheet lined with parchment paper, divide the cheese and the rest of the ingredients into each zucchini halves and bake at 450° F for 40 minutes.
2. Arrange the stuffed courgettes on a serving dish and serve as an appetizer.
3. Enjoy!

NUTRITION:
calories: 246 | fat: 8g | protein: 9g | carbs: 10g | fiber: 6g | sodium: 100mg

1010. Pomegranate Dip
Prep time: 10 minutes | Cook time: 0 minutes | Serves: 4

INGREDIENTS:

2/3 tablespoon olive oil
2 garlic cloves, peeled
1/8 teaspoon cumin
4 tablespoons cold water
1/3 cup tahini paste
1/3 cup pomegranate seeds
1/8 cup pistachios, chopped

DIRECTIONS:

1. In a blender, combine the oil with the garlic and the rest of the ingredients, blend well, divide into cups and serve cold as a party sauce.
2. Enjoy!

NUTRITION:
calories: 200 | fat: 8g | protein: 6g | carbs: 8g | fiber: 5g | sodium: 100mg

1011. Lentils and Tomato Dip
Prep time: 10 minutes | Cook time: 0 minutes | Serves: 4

INGREDIENTS:

2/3 cup red lentils, cooked
Salt and black pepper to the taste
2 tablespoons lemon juice
garlic clove, minced
1 1/3 tablespoons tomato paste
1 1/3 tablespoon cilantro, chopped
2 tablespoons olive oil
1 1/3 teaspoons cumin, ground

DIRECTIONS:

1. In your blender, combine the lentils with the lemon juice, salt, pepper and the rest of the ingredients and blend well.
2. Transfer to bowl and refrigerate for 1 hour before serving.
3. Enjoy!

NUTRITION:
calories: 244 | fat: 8g | protein: 8g | carbs: 26g | fiber: 12g | sodium: 100mg

1012. Lentils Stuffed Potato Skins
Prep time: 10 minutes | Cook time: 30 minutes | Serves: 4

INGREDIENTS:

8 red baby potatoes
1/3 cup red lentils, cooked and drained
1 tablespoons olive oil
1 garlic clove, minced
1/2 tablespoon chives, chopped
1/4 teaspoon hot chili sauce
Salt and black pepper to the taste

DIRECTIONS:

1. Place the potatoes in a saucepan, add water to cover, bring to a boil over medium-low heat, cook for 15 minutes, drain, cool, cut them in half, remove the pulp, transfer it to a blender and blend a little.
2. Add the rest of the ingredients to the blender, blend well again and fill the potato skins with this mixture.
3. Arrange the stuffed potatoes on a baking sheet lined with parchment paper, place them in the oven at 375° F and cook for 15 minutes.
4. Arrange on a plate and serve as an appetizer.
5. Enjoy!

NUTRITION:
calories: 300 | fat: 9g | protein: 8g | carbs: 22g | fiber: 14g | sodium: 100mg

HOLIDAY & PIZZA

13

Holiday And Pizza Recipes

1013. Sicilian Cannoli

Prep time: 10 minutes | Cook time: 1 hour 20 minutes | Serves: 10

INGREDIENTS:

- 1 dash of salt
- 1 cup Marsala Wine
- 2 egg white
- 1 1/2 cups all-purpose flour
- 2 tablespoons unsalted butter
- 1/1/2 teaspoon sugar
- Oil for frying
- 1/2 teaspoon vanilla extract
- 2 1/2 cups full fat ricotta cheese
- 1/2 cup powdered sugar
- 1 cup mini chocolate chips
- 5 tablespoons mixed candies fruit peels (optional)
- 5 glaced cherries, finely chopped (optional)

DIRECTIONS:

1. For the cannoli:
2. Mix the butter, flour, salt, and sugar well in a bowl.
3. Then add the wine just enough to form a relatively homogeneous and consistent dough and knead for 2-3 minutes until it becomes smooth.
4. Form a ball, wrap it in plastic wrap and let it rest for about an hour.
5. Cut the dough in half and roll it out to about 1/4 inch thick. Cut into four pieces (squares). Place a metal tube diagonally across each square and wrap the dough. Finally, brush the edges with the beaten egg white.
6. In a large skillet, heat the oil until it reaches 350 degrees F. Dip one or two tubes into the pan and cooks until golden brown.
7. Remove from the pan, cool, and gently slide the cannoli shell out of the tube.
8. Continue cooking the rest of the cannoli following the same process.
9. To make the filling:
10. First, to eliminate excess water, let the ricotta rest in a colander in a small bowl in the refrigerator for about 30 minutes.
11. After that, mix the ricotta with the rest of the ingredients. Put in the fridge and let it cool for another 30 minutes.
12. Carefully fill each cannolo shell and sprinkle with some extra powdered sugar if desired.
13. Let it cool down.
14. Enjoy!

NUTRITION:

calories: 292 | fat: 6g | protein: 5g | carbs: 50g | fiber: 4g | sodium: 100mg

1014. Italian Lasagna

Prep time: 10 minutes | Cook time: 4 hour 10 minutes | Serves: 10

INGREDIENTS:

- 2 bay leaves
- 1 teaspoon of sea salt and pepper flakes
- 1 1/2 glass of red wine
- 2 tablespoons of olive oil
- 1 pound of ground pork
- 2 cups of sifted tomatoes
- 2 1/2 tablespoons of tomato paste
- 5 cups of beef broth
- 1 1/2 cup finely chopped carrot
- 1 cup finely chopped celery stalk
- 1 cup finely chopped white onion
- 1 pound of ground beef
- 1 lb fresh lasagne pasta sheets
- 17 oz. balls mozzarella
- 4 tablespoons of all-purpose flour
- 3 1/2 cups of whole milk
- 1 teaspoon of salt and pepper or to taste
- ½ teaspoon of nutmeg
- 1 1/2 cup freshly grated Parmesan cheese
- 4 tablespoons of butter

DIRECTIONS:

For Ragù:
1. Finely chop the onion, carrot, and celery and brown the vegetables in a large pan with a drizzle of oil. Add the minced pork and beef and cook until golden brown.
2. Add the red wine and let half of it evaporate.
3. At this point, add the tomato paste, the pureed tomatoes, four glasses of beef broth, the bay leaves, and a pinch of salt and pepper.
3. After mixing everything, let it simmer for at least 3 hours without a lid. Halfway through cooking, add the rest of the broth.

For Béchamel:
1. Cook the butter in a saucepan until it melts.
2. Add the flour and mix to form a paste. Let it cook for about 1 minute.
3. Slowly add half of the milk, stirring constantly. When it becomes thick, add the rest of the milk, Parmesan, nutmeg and a pinch of salt and pepper.
4. Continue stirring the sauce until it thickens enough. Remove from heat and set aside.

For Lasagne:
1. Preheat the oven to 350° F | 180°C | Fan 160°C.
2. To begin, pour a small amount of ragù into the bottom of the pan. Subsequently, cover the ragù with an even layer of lasagna sheets, trying to adapt them to the pan.
3. Add a few tablespoons of meat sauce again to cover the pasta and then two spoons of bechamel.
4. Repeat the same procedure a little while ago, in the following order: pasta (lasagne), ragù and béchamel (white sauce), until you run out of everything.
5. Finally, cover the last layer of the lasagne with the cut mozzarella and bake for 45 minutes (or until golden brown).
6. Enjoy!

NUTRITION:

calories: 389 | fat: 14g | protein: 13g | carbs: 65g | fiber: 8g | sodium: 100mg

1015. Guacamole

Prep time: 65 minutes | Cook time: 15 minutes | Serves: 6

INGREDIENTS:

- 3 sweet yellow peppers
- 1 1/2 sweet red pepper
- 1 1/2 green pepper
- 30 broken in half pretzel sticks
- 1 1/2 cup. guacamole
- 24 oz. of the crescent dough sheet
- 6 oz. softened cream cheese
- 2 1/4 tsp. taco seasoning
- Chopped. Cilantro

DIRECTIONS:

1. Preheat oven to 375° F | 190°C | Fan 170°C
2. Unroll the dough tube into an oiled baking sheet and press into a rectangle.
3. Use a fork to prick the potatoes before sprinkling with 3/4 teaspoon taco spice, continue with this step for the rest of the dough and spices.
4. Bake in the oven for 10-12 minutes once golden brown, cool completely on wire racks.
5. Cut across each of the four strips into an 8x4-inch rectangle, then cutting each strip into 5 triangles for the trees.
6. Now insert a pretzel piece into the base of each triangle for trunks, in a medium-size bowl mix cream cheese and guacamole, beat until smooth, spread over trees.
7. Peppers should be halved and seeded. Using a 3/4-inch star-shaped cookie cutter, cut 40 stars from the peppers.
8. Make tree decorations, dice, and julienne the peppers that are left while adding some cilantro.
9. Refrigerate until ready to serve.

NUTRITION:

calories: 244 | fat: 14g | protein: 8g | carbs: 23g | fiber: 12g | sodium: 100mg

1016. Easy Cucumber Sandwiches

Prep time: 25 minutes | Cook time: 0 minutes | Serves: 6

INGREDIENTS:

- Slivered red pearl onions
- 3 tbsp. mayonnaise
- 3 tsp. Italian salad dressing
- 45 slices of pumpernickel bread
- 12 oz. of softened cream cheese
- 90 thin cucumber slices
- Dill springs

DIRECTIONS:

1. Inside a medium bowl mix cream cheese, mayonnaise with the dressing, and set aside for 30 minutes.
2. Spread the cream cheese mixture onto two bread slices.
3. Top with two cucumber slices, dill and red onion slivers if desired.
4. Refrigerate until ready to serve.

NUTRITION:

calories: 287 | fat: 9g | protein: 9g | carbs: 15g | fiber: 3g | sodium: 100mg

1017. Artichoke Caprese Platter

Prep time: 20 minutes | Cook time: 0 minutes | Serves: 6

INGREDIENTS:

- 3 tbsp. red wine vinegar
- 3 tbsp. olive oil
- Coarsely ground pepper
- 3 cups. basil leaves
- 22 1/2 oz. of marinated artichokes
- 1 1/2 lb. mozzarella cheese, diced
- 9 plum tomatoes, diced

DIRECTIONS:

1. Drain the artichokes and put aside 1/2 cup. of the marinade
2. In a small bowl whisk vinegar, oil, and reserved marinade.
3. Arrange the artichokes, tomatoes, mozzarella cheese, and basil on a large serving plate.
4. Drizzle vinaigrette on top and season with coarsely ground pepper if preferred and serve.

NUTRITION:

calories: 2180 | fat: 4g | protein: 1g | carbs: 6g | fiber: 4g | sodium: 100mg

1018. Skewers

Prep time: 25 minutes | Cook time: 0 minutes | Serves:

INGREDIENTS:

48 grape tomatoes
24 pimiento-stuffed Queen olives
24 thin slices of 1/2 lb. hard salami
16 oz. mozzarella cheese
Italian vinaigrette

DIRECTIONS:

1. Thread tomatoes, mozzarella, salami slices, and olives onto wooden skewers.
2. Refrigerate until ready to serve. If preferred before serving, sprinkle the skewers with vinaigrette.

NUTRITION:

calories: 240 | fat: 6g | protein: 4g | carbs: 7g | fiber: 1g | sodium: 100mg

1019. Italian Farfalle

Prep time: 15 minutes | Cook time: 30 minutes | Serves: 6

INGREDIENTS:

3 cloves of garlic, minced
1 1/2 cup. chopped tomato
3/4 cup. pine nuts
18 oz. farfalle pasta
1 1/2 lb. crumbles of chorizo sausage
3/4 cup. Parmesan cheese, shredded
3/4 cup. red wine vinegar
3/4 cup. olive oil
3/4 cup. basil leaves

DIRECTIONS:

1. Boil pasta in salted water until well-done.
2. While the pasta is cooking brown the chorizo over medium heat. Proceed to add the nuts making sure not to let them burn. Remove the pan from the heat and add garlic.
3. Remove the pasta from the pot, toss the pasta, chorizo mixture, basil, cheese, and tomatoes together in a large bowl.
4. Finally, combine the olive oil and vinegar ready to be poured over the pasta, and toss and serve.

NUTRITION:

calories: 365 | fat: 11g | protein: 10g | carbs: 60g | fiber: 4g | sodium: 100mg

1020. Feta Cheese Spread

Prep time: 20 minutes | Cook time: 0 minutes | Serves: 4

INGREDIENTS:

1/4 cup. red bell pepper, minced
1/4 cup. green pepper, minced
2/3 dozen Greek olives, minced
1/3 lb. feta cheese
1/3 cup. softened butter
1/3 cup. onion, minced
1/4 cup. of toasted pine nuts
2/3 tsp. dill, diced

DIRECTIONS:

1. In a food processor finely blend the cheese and butter until frothy and creamy.
2. Place in a mixing bowl before stirring in the olives, onions, peppers, and dill.
3. Proceed to fill mold with 2 cups of the mixture then to refrigerate until solid.
4. When solid remove from the mold and top with pine nuts before serving with crackers or a baguette as preferred.

NUTRITION:

calories: 136 | fat: 8g | protein: 10g | carbs: 5g | fiber: 4g | sodium: 100mg

1021. Butter Cookies

Prep time: 40 minutes | Cook time: 12 minutes | Serves: 4

INGREDIENTS:

2/3 egg yolk
2/3 tsp. vanilla extract
2/3 lb. salt-free melted butter
4 cups. plain flour
1/3 tsp. baking powder
2 1/3 cups. confectioners' sugar

DIRECTIONS:

1. Preheat oven to 400°F | 200°C | Fan 180°C
2. In a large bowl mix butter and confectioners' sugar until smooth. Then whisk in egg yolk and the vanilla extract.
3. In another bowl, mix flour and the baking powder. Slowly mix with prepared butter mixture until fully combined.
4. Then proceed to heap tbsp. of dough within crescents.
5. Place the crescents 1-inch apart into baking trays for 8-12 minutes.
6. Remove from oven, then sprinkle sugar as required.

NUTRITION:

calories: 213 | fat: 4g | protein: 17g | carbs: 8g | fiber: 4g | sodium: 100mg

1022. Couscous Salad

Prep time: 20 minutes | Cook time: 10 minutes | Serves: 6

INGREDIENTS:

2 2/3 cups. whole-grain couscous
21 3/4 oz. canned chicken broth
6 green onions, diced
9 3/4 oz. ripe olives, diced
1 1/2 cup. parsley, minced
1 1/2 cucumber, sliced
3 cups. of grape tomatoes
3/4 cup. feta cheese, crumbled
3/4 cup. extra virgin olive oil
3/4 tsp. salt
1 1/2 tsp. adobo seasoning
2 1/4 tsp. grated lemon zest
3/4 cup. lime juice

DIRECTIONS:

1. In a large-size saucepan bring the broth to a boil then toss in the couscous. Remove and place aside to allow the broth to soak in.
2. Take a bowl and place cucumber with tomatoes, parsley, olives, and green onions then gently whisk in the dressing with feta cheese.
3. Combine and serve.

NUTRITION:

calories: 155 | fat: 8g | protein: 17g | carbs: 11g | fiber: 4g | sodium: 100mg

1023. Rice Bowls

Prep time: 20 minutes | Cook time: 10 minutes | Serves: 6

INGREDIENTS:

1 1/8 cup. of cherry tomatoes
3/4 cup. Greek olives, sliced
3/4 cup. feta cheese, crumbled
12 3/4 oz. brown rice medley
3/4 cup. Greek vinaigrette
3/4 avocado, sliced
Parsley, chopped

DIRECTIONS:

1. Mix rice with 2 tsp. vinaigrette inside a microwave-proof bowl.
2. Cook for 2-3 minutes (covered) until fully cooked.
3. Place into two bowls.
4. Finally, garnish with avocado, tomatoes, cheese, olives and the remaining dressing, with chopped parsley.

NUTRITION:

calories: 263 | fat: 12g | protein: 7g | carbs: 11g | fiber: 9g | sodium: 100mg

1024. Tomato Bites

Prep time: 25 minutes | Cook time: 20 minutes | Serves: 6

INGREDIENTS:

2 1/4 cups. feta cheese crumbled
3/4 cup. ripe olives, pitted and coarsely chopped
9 plum tomatoes, thinly sliced
26 1/4 oz. thawed, frozen puff pastry
2 1/4 cups. grated Gouda cheese
Basil, chopped
Oregano, chopped

DIRECTIONS:

1. Preheat oven to 325°F. | 170°C | Fan 150°C
2. With the puff pastry, make a cutting for each sheet into 16 squares, place in parchment-lined baking sheets.
3. Sprinkle over Gouda cheese, topped with tomatoes, olives followed by feta cheese
4. Bake it for 18-20 minutes or until golden brown then sprinkle with herbs.

NUTRITION:

calories: 246 | fat: 1g | protein: 9g | carbs: 10g | fiber: 6g | sodium: 100mg

1025. Chicken and Olives

Prep time: 20 minutes | Cook time: 20 minutes | Serves: 6

INGREDIENTS:

1 1/2 tbsp. olive oil
3/4 tsp. salt and 1/2 tsp. pepper
1 1/2 tbsp. drained capers
6 chicken thighs
3/4 cup. pimiento-filled olives
3/4 cup. chicken broth
1 1/2 tsp. rosemary, dried and crushed

DIRECTIONS:

1. Season chicken with dried rosemary, salt, and ground pepper.
2. In a large size pan on medium heat, drizzle oil and brown the chicken on each side.

3. Toss in olives, chicken broth, and capers.
4. On low heat cook, covered for 2-4 minutes.
5. Remove and serve.

NUTRITION:

calories: 224 | fat: 10g | protein: 3g | carbs: 5g | fiber: 1g | sodium: 100mg

1026. Roasted Potatoes and Feta Cheese

Prep time: 20 minutes | Cook time: 45 minutes | Serves: 4

INGREDIENTS:

2 tbsp. lemon juice
1/2 cup. water
2 lb. Yukon Gold potatoes
1/2 cup. feta cheese, crumbled
2 2/3 garlic cloves, minced
1/3 cup. olive oil
2/3 tsp. salt
1/3 tsp. pepper
1 1/3 tsp. dried oregano
DIRECTIONS:

1. Preheat oven to 450°F.| 230°C | Fan 210°C
2. All items must be whisked together leaving salt and pepper.
3. Using a shallow size grill skillet, evenly place the potatoes.
4. Pour the water mixture in and roast for 35-40 minutes, or until potatoes are golden brown.
5. Grate some cheese on top and serve.

NUTRITION:

calories: 121 | fat: 4g | protein: 4g | carbs: 1g | fiber: 1g | sodium: 100mg

1027. Easy Turkey Panini

Prep time: 15 minutes | Cook time: 20 minutes | Serves: 6

INGREDIENTS:

11 1/4 oz. artichokes, diced
3 plum tomatoes, sliced
1 lb. deli turkey, sliced
6 oz. feta cheese, crumbled
36 oz. spaghetti sauce
Ciabatta rolls
DIRECTIONS:
1. Spread 2 tbsp. marinara sauce on each ciabatta roll.

2. Garnish with ½ cheese, artichokes, sliced tomato, sliced deli turkey.
3. Cook for 3-5 minutes Panini machine until cheese is melted.
4. In a medium-size microwave-proof dish, put in leftover marinara sauce and cook on high.
5. Serve alongside with sandwiches.

NUTRITION:

calories: 300 | fat: 9g | protein: 6g | carbs: 22g | fiber: 4g | sodium: 100mg

1028. Aioli

Prep time: 15 minutes | Cook time: 15 minutes | Serves: 6

INGREDIENTS:

8 1/4 oz. mayonnaise
1 1/2 tsp. Dijon mustard
1 1/2 garlic clove, crushed

3 tbsp. lemon juice
A pinch of saffron

DIRECTIONS:

1. In a small bowl combine the garlic, lime juice, and a sprinkle of salt.
2. Inside another bowl, combine a pinch of saffron and 1 tablespoon of boiled water, then put aside for 5 minutes.
3. Toss the saffron with mayo and Dijon mustard.
4. Sieve the mixture over lime juice and discard garlic bits.
5. Combine and serve.

NUTRITION:

calories: 221 | fat: 4g | protein: 4g | carbs: 1g | fiber: 1g | sodium: 100mg

1029. Pany Tomato

Prep time: 15 minutes | Cook time: 0 minutes | Serves: 6

INGREDIENTS:

6 slices of sourdough bread
Olive oil

3 ripe tomatoes, halved
1 1/2 garlic clove, halved

DIRECTIONS:

1. Toast each side of the bread and brush with garlic clove, then tomatoes.
2. Sprinkle with oil and season with salt.
3. Serve up.

NUTRITION:

calories: 124 | fat: 4g | protein: 3g | carbs: 3g | fiber: 2g | sodium: 100mg

1030. Chorizo Sauce and Cod with Tomato

Prep time: 20 minutes | Cook time: 30 minutes | Serves: 6

INGREDIENTS:

Green beans
1 1/2 garlic clove, sliced
3 cod fillets
6 chorizo sausages, minced

21 oz. tomatoes, chopped
Olive oil
A pinch of dried chili flakes

DIRECTIONS:

1. In a saucepan, warm 1 tbsp. oil and add garlic and chorizo for few minutes. Then add chili with tomatoes and boil for 9-10 min.
2. Meanwhile, brush the fish with some oil, season with salt and pepper and proceed to grill or steam till cooked through, approximately 4-6 minutes.
3. Now combine and serve.

NUTRITION:

calories: 270 | fat: 10g | protein: 1g | carbs: 12g | fiber: 3g | sodium: 100mg

1031. Prawn Paella

Prep time: 20 minutes | Cook time: 30 minutes | Serves: 6

INGREDIENTS:

1 1/2 onion, minced
1 1/2 red pepper, diced
1 1/2 garlic clove, minced
600 ml. chicken stock
8 1/4 oz. cooked prawns
8 1/4 oz. paella rice

5 1/4 oz. frozen peas
Olive oil
A pinch of saffron
A pinch of smoked paprika
Bunch of chopped parsley
Lemon wedges

DIRECTIONS:

1. Inside a skillet add 1 tbsp. oil, fry the onion and sliced pepper, then the garlic, until soft.
2. Whisk in rice with saffron then paprika and combine well.
3. Now add stock and boil for 14-15 min.
4. Include prawns with peas within the last 4 minutes.
5. Serve with diced parsley and lemon. Enjoy!

NUTRITION:

calories: 284 | fat: 9g | protein: 12g | carbs: 40g | fiber: 3g | sodium: 564mg

1032. Arroz con Leche

Prep time: 10 minutes | Cook time: 35 minutes | Serves: 6

INGREDIENTS:

Sugar to taste
A pinch of salt
1 1/2 cinnamon stick
1 1/2 cup. rice

6 3/4 cups. milk
3 lemon slices
1 1/2 tsp. ground cinnamon

DIRECTIONS:

1. Wash the rice with cold water then place in a pot, fill with water just enough to cover rice. Place it over moderate flame.
2. Add lime rind with a cinnamon stick. (Make sure to keep stirring till all the water has been absorbed).
3. Pour in ½ cup. of milk while stirring until it is completely absorbed. Keep adding milk until it reaches the litre mark.
4. When it's done, remove from heat.
5. Season with a touch of salt and a dash of cinnamon. Adding sugar as desired.
6. To finish, sprinkle a little more cinnamon over the top!

NUTRITION:

calories: 272 | fat: 8g | protein: 5g | carbs: 38g | fiber: 3g | sodium: 564mg

1033. Cucumber Salad

Prep time: 15 minutes | Cook time: 0 minutes | Serves: 6

INGREDIENTS:

5 1/4 oz. green bell pepper
5 1/4 oz. red onion
3/4 cup. of red wine vinegar
15 3/4 oz. Lebanese cucumbers
5 1/4 oz. Anthotyro cheese

1 1/2 lb. truss tomatoes
5 1/4 oz. barley rusks
1/2 cup. olive oil
Salt and pepper
1 1/2 tsp. dry oregano

DIRECTIONS:

1. Wash all veggies and discard the cores, tops and bottoms.
2. Thinly slice tomatoes cucumbers, green peppers and the onion.
3. Inside a large size mixing bowl, combine all the ingredients.
4. Sprinkle the shredded cheese on top of veggies and tear the barley rusks into medium chunks.
5. Sprinkle with salt, add oil, red wine vinegar, dried oregano and toss.

6. Taste and adjust spices as needed.
7. Toss everything together in a salad dish and serve.

NUTRITION:

calories: 278 | fat: 22g | protein: 8g | carbs: 12g | fiber: 4g | sodium: 572mg

1034. Chocolate Cake

Prep time: 20 minutes | Cook time: 35 minutes | Serves: 6

INGREDIENTS:

8 1/4 oz. grated coconut
15 ml. black coffee
12 oz. caster sugar
10 1/2 oz. dark chocolate
13 1/2 oz. salt-free butter
9 small eggs
5 1/4 oz. breadcrumbs

DIRECTIONS:

1. Preheat oven at 375°F | 190°C | Fan 170°C
2. In a mixing bowl whip, the butter and sugar until light and fluffy.
3. Include yolks one by one.
4. Now melt the chocolate, combining it with the coffee.
5. Whip the egg whites until they are stiff.
6. Toss the melted chocolate, coconut and fine breadcrumbs in the butter/sugar mixture.
7. Now fold the beaten eggs into the mixture, put over an oiled tray.
8. Cook for 25-30 min until done, then serve.

NUTRITION:

calories: 320 | fat: 15g | protein: 6g | carbs: 34g | fiber: 7g | sodium: 572mg

1035. Grated Carrot with Orange Salad

Prep time: 15 minutes | Cook time: 10 minutes | Serves: 6

INGREDIENTS:

8 1/4 tbsp. thyme honey
3 tbsp. of pine nuts
1 1/2 tbsp. of ground almonds
1 1/2 lb. carrots, grated
3 peeled oranges
3 tbsp. of orange juice
1 1/2 tbsp. of orange flower water
4 1/2 tbsp. lemon juice
1 1/2 tbsp. of olive oil
3/4 tsp. salt
Mint leaves

DIRECTIONS:

1. In a serving dish, combine honey, floral water, lemon and orange juice.
2. Also place almonds, salt, carrots and oranges, then toss well.
3. Using a skillet fry the pine nuts within oil until golden, then add to the salad.
4. Mix the salad (sprinkle with mint if wanted) and serve.

NUTRITION:

calories: 192 | fat: 5g | protein: 4g | carbs: 9g | fiber: 3g | sodium: 572mg

1036. Oatmeal Cookies

Prep time: 15 minutes | Cook time: 20 minutes | Serves: 6

INGREDIENTS:

2 1/4 tsp. baking soda
3 large eggs
1 1/2 tbsp. molasses
3 tsp. vanilla extract
3 cups. instant-cooking oats
2 1/4 cups. softened butter
2 1/4 cups. chocolate chips
3 cups. plain flour
2 1/4 cups. brown sugar
1 1/2 cup. sugar
3/4 cup. pecans, diced
1 1/2 cup. raisins
3/4 tsp. salt
1 1/2 tsp. ground cinnamon

DIRECTIONS:

1. Preheat oven at 350°F | 180°C | Fan 160°C
2. Combine butter and sugars together inside a large size bowl and mix until creamy.
3. Inside another bowl, stir eggs, molasses and the vanilla extract.
4. Now in a medium bowl put the flour, oats, baking soda, ground cinnamon, and then salt, combine well.
5. Finally, pour into the sugar mixture.
6. Include pecans with chocolate chips and mix thoroughly.
7. Spoon the mixture over an oiled baking tray, 2 inches apart.
8. Now bake for 8-10 minutes.
9. Allow cooling for 3 minutes within the tray, then move to wire racks.

NUTRITION:

calories: 287 | fat: 14g | protein: 6g | carbs: 41g | fiber: 2g | sodium: 572mg

1037. Holiday Cappuccino

Prep time: 15 minutes | Cook time: 10 minutes | Serves: 6

INGREDIENTS:

6 tsp. instant hot chocolate mix
1 1/2 fluid oz. vanilla extract
18 fluid oz. hot brewed espresso
18 fluid oz. half-and-half
6 tsps. whipped cream
1 1/2 tsp. chocolate shavings
3 fluid oz. brandy
3 fluid oz. amaretto liqueur
6 tsp. white sugar

DIRECTIONS:

1. In a medium-size saucepan over the medium-low heat whisk together some hot espresso and half-and-half followed by brandy and amaretto.
2. Add vanilla extract along with hot chocolate mix and add sugar.
3. Now cook till the sugar is completely dissolved.
4. Lastly, divide the mixture into four mugs, top with whipped cream or some chocolate shavings.

NUTRITION:

calories: 162 | fat: 8g | protein: 8g | carbs: 4g | fiber: 4g | sodium: 572mg

1038. Greek Pizza

Prep time: 20 minutes | Cook time: 25 minutes | Serves: 4

INGREDIENTS:

1 1/3 pizza crusts
2/3 tbsp. extra virgin olive oil
2/3 tsp. Italian seasoning
2/3 tbsp. sugar
4 oz. can of tomato paste
3 2/3 cups. red wine
2/3 tsp. salt
1 cup. spinach leaves
3 2/3 oz. chopped black olives
1/3 red onions, finely diced
2/3 lb. mozzarella cheese, grated
3 2/3 oz. feta cheese, crumbled
1/3 red bell pepper, finely diced
Black pepper

DIRECTIONS:

1. Preheat oven to 400°F | 200°C | Fan 180°C
2. Place the pizza dough over two oiled pizza pans.
3. Mix all the sauce items until smooth and distribute between crusts.
4. Garnish pizzas with 1/2 mozzarella cheese, then other items, to your liking.
5. Bake for 20-minutes until the cheese becomes browned bubbly. Serve right away.

NUTRITION:

calories: 362 | fat: 12g | protein: 11g | carbs: 55g | fiber: 8g | sodium: 572mg

1039. Pizza with Feta Cheese

Prep time: 15 minutes | Cook time: 25 minutes | Serves: 6

INGREDIENTS:

3 tbsp. green onions, diced (if liked)
4 1/2 diced red peppers, roasted
3 cups. feta cheese, crumbled
2 1/4 lb. pizza dough
1/2 cup. pizza sauce
1/2 cup. Kalamata olives
1/4 tsp. pepper
1/3 tsp. paprika
A dash of cayenne pepper
2 1/4 cups. chickpeas, minced

DIRECTIONS:

1. Preheat oven to 450°F | 230°C | Fan 210°C
2. In a medium bowl, mix olive oil and spices. Then add the chickpeas, whisk to coat and place aside.
3. Dress the cornmeal over a baking tray. Slice dough into two pieces. Shape a circle from both pieces and distribute pizza sauce, then spread it evenly over the tops, except 1 inch across the sides.
4. Garnish every pizza with half of the spiced chickpeas, red peppers and olives
5. Then bake the pizzas until just golden from the sides about 10-15 minutes then add feta cheese and bake again until cheese melts.
6. Remove pizza from the oven, allow cool and garnish with diced green onions (if liked).

NUTRITION:

calories: 355 | fat: 11g | protein: 10g | carbs: 51g | fiber: 8g | sodium: 572mg

1040. Veggie Pizza Squares

Prep time: 15 minutes | Cook time: 20 minutes | Serves: 6

INGREDIENTS:

1/2 cup. sour cream
3 cups. chopped mixed veggies
1 1/2 can of crescent rolls
9 oz. feta cheese, crumbled
9 oz. cream cheese

3 tsp. of lemon juice
2 1/4 tsp. garlic powder
1 1/2 tsp. dry dill

DIRECTIONS:
1. Within an oiled skillet place crescent rolls equally (cook as per box instructions) allow cooling completely.
2. Inside a small bowl mix cream cheese, sour cream, lemon juice, dill, and garlic powder then whisk until smooth.
3. Distribute the prepared mixture on crusts and garnish with chopped veggies, then feta cheese.
4. Slice and serve right away.

NUTRITION:
calories: 377 | fat: 15g | protein: 14g | carbs: 45g | fiber: 8g | sodium: 572mg

1041. Gluten-Free Keto Pizza
Prep time: 20 minutes | Cook time: 50 minutes | Serves: 4

INGREDIENTS:

1/3 cup. Parmesan cheese, grated
3 cups. cauliflower rice
1/3 cup. mozzarella cheese, shredded
2/3 egg, beaten
1/3 cup. mushrooms, finely sliced
2/3 bunch of baby spinach
1/8 cup. diced black olives

1/3 cup. mozzarella cheese, shredded
1 1/3 ripe tomatoes, finely sliced
1/3 yellow onion, finely sliced
1 1/3 garlic cloves, diced
1 2/3 tbsp. olive oil
2/3 tsp. rosemary

DIRECTIONS:
1. Preheat oven to 400°F | 200°C | Fan 180°C
2. Cover a large skillet with parchment paper
3. Now steam cauliflower rice just until soft, about 8-10 minutes and remove extra liquid.
4. In a medium-size bowl, stir together rice and the cheese with the egg.
5. Pour the mixture into the skillet, then gently press downwards, leaving the sides slightly thicker.
6. Then place inside the oven for 20-25minutes and prepare the topping while you wait.
7. Inside a medium bowl, mix topping items, leaving out the mozzarella. Then distribute the topping on pizza crust and garnish with mozzarella cheese.
8. Serve and enjoy!

NUTRITION:
calories: 370 | fat: 12g | protein: 14g | carbs: 49g | fiber: 8g | sodium: 572mg

1042. Porcini, Sausage, and Black Truffle Pizza
Prep time: 20 minutes | Cook time: 35 minutes | Serves: 4

INGREDIENTS:

1 cup. black celery pesto
2 2/3 tbsp. truffle oil
2 2/3 balls of pizza dough
1 2/3 tbsp. olive oil
2 2/3 tbsp. truffle paste

2 2/3 cups. porcini mushrooms, diced
4 cups. mozzarella cheese, shredded
2/3 cup. pecorino cheese, shredded
2 2/3 sausages

DIRECTIONS:
1. Preheat oven to 450°F | 230°C | Fan 210°C
2. In a medium-size skillet, warm 2 tbsp. of oil and sauté mushrooms until softened and lightly browned; remove the mushrooms and place aside.
3. Place the sausage meat in the frying skillet and sauté until lightly browned. Then remove meat from skillet.
4. Flatten all dough balls within a 12 1/2-inch flatbread with your fingers and put it over a cornmeal-dusted tray.
5. Put a 1/3 of the mozzarella over the flatbread and garnish with 1/3 of the mushrooms and the sausages.
6. Now spoon a little bit of pesto equally over the top; season with 1/3 of the pecorino.
7. Bake for 15-20 minutes or just until bubbly and browned.
8. Whisk the truffle oil and truffle paste together, then dribble some of it around the pizza before serving.

NUTRITION:
calories: 342 | fat: 10g | protein: 12g | carbs: 51g | fiber: 8g | sodium: 572mg

1043. Pizza Bianca
Prep time: 20 minutes | Cook time: 20 minutes | Serves: 4

INGREDIENTS:

4 cups. of arugula
2 2/3 balls of pizza dough
2 2/3 ripe tomatoes, finely sliced

10 2/3 thin pieces of prosciutto
Olive oil, as needed
Spiced olive oil

DIRECTIONS:
1. Preheat oven to 450°F | 230°C | Fan 210°C
2. Flatten dough balls within a 12 1/2-inch flatbread with your fingers.
3. Put each flatbread over a baking tray covered with cornmeal, then rub with olive oil over each one.
4. Bake the dough for 15-20 minutes until browned, then garnish with tomatoes, followed by arugula and prosciutto.
5. Dribble every pizza with olive oil, then serve.

NUTRITION:
calories: 342 | fat: 9g | protein: 12g | carbs: 49g | fiber: 12g | sodium: 572mg

1044. Whole Wheat Pizza
Prep time: 20 minutes | Cook time: 15 minutes | Serves: 6

INGREDIENTS:

3 tbsp. diced Kalamata olives
1 1/2 whole-grain pizza crust
2 1/4 cups. crumbled feta cheese
2 1/4 cups. artichoke hearts, separated

and drained
3 tbsp. diced pepperoncini, drained
6 oz. jar of basil pesto

DIRECTIONS:
1. Preheat oven to 450°F | 230°C | Fan 210°C
2. Sprinkle flour onto a board and place pizza crust, then spread with pesto.
3. Garnish with artichoke heart pieces, olives, pepperoncini slices and feta cheese.
4. Cook inside the oven until the crust becomes crispy and also the cheese melts, about 8-10 minutes.
5. Serve!

NUTRITION:
calories: 312 | fat: 15g | protein: 12g | carbs: 61g | fiber: 14g | sodium: 572mg

1045. Spinach, Chicken and Cherry Tomato Flatbread
Prep time: 20 minutes | Cook time: 25 minutes | Serves: 4

INGREDIENTS:

1 lb. pizza dough
5 1/3 oz. mozzarella, sliced into pieces
2-cups. fried spinach
Baked chicken breast, sliced within 1-inch dice

2/3 pint of cherry tomatoes, cut in half
2 2/3 oz. sliced taleggio cheese
Olive oil, as needed
Red pepper flakes
Sea salt

DIRECTIONS:
1. Preheat oven to 450°F | 230°C | Fan 210°C
2. Line 2 baking trays with parchment paper.
3. Now divide pizza dough into two equal balls, roll each ball within 14 x 7 inches oval, place in trays.
4. Finely rub the edges of each flatbread with oil and garnish with cheese.
5. Garnish with the spinach, chicken and tomatoes evenly among every flatbread; sprinkle with red pepper strips and sea salt (as desired).
6. Bake flatbreads for 15-20 minutes, until bubbly also browned.
7. Allow cooling for 6-minutes.
8. Serve and enjoy!

NUTRITION:
calories: 322 | fat: 16g | protein: 17g | carbs: 51g | fiber: 5g | sodium: 572mg

1046. Mini Pizzas
Prep time: 20 minutes | Cook time: 25 minutes | Serves: 6

INGREDIENTS:

2 1/4 cups. of tomato sauce
3/4 recipe of potato focaccia dough
2 1/4 cups. mozzarella cheese, shredded

1/3 cup. extra virgin olive oil
9 basil leaves

DIRECTIONS:
1. Preheat oven to 400°F | 200°C | Fan 180°C
2. Dust two baking trays with cornmeal.
3. Then with a medium-size round cup., cut the dough into individual pieces.
4. Now place them into the trays.
5. Rub oil over the edges of the pizza dough, followed by some tomato sauce.
6. Cut the basil and garnish the pizzas, then finally the mozzarella.
7. Bake the pizzas 10-15 minutes until golden also bubbly.

NUTRITION:

calories: 351 | fat: 11g | protein: 8g | carbs: 48g | fiber: 8g | sodium: 572mg

1047. Flavorful Panzerotti
Prep time: 120 minutes | Cook time: 15 minutes | Serves: 6

INGREDIENTS:

1/3 tsp. dried oregano	2/3 tbsp. olive oil
Basic pizza dough	Salt and pepper
6 2/3 oz. mozzarella cheese, sliced	Canola oil
9 1/3 oz. diced tomatoes	Salt and pepper
1 1/3 garlic cloves, chopped	1 1/3 tbsp. basil, thinly chopped

DIRECTIONS:
1. Preheat oven to 375°F | 190°C | Fan 170°C
2. Grab a small saucepan and warm the oil, fry the garlic just until aromatic.
3. Include the tomatoes, dry oregano, Kosher salt, and black pepper, then cook for 10-15minutes.
4. Now divide the dough into ten pieces and form into balls.
5. Flatten dough balls within a 4 1/2-inch round shape.
6. Scoop the prepared tomato mixture over each dough ball, seasoning with basil, Kosher salt, and black pepper, then coat with 1 1/2 tbsp. mozzarella.
7. Finely moisten the sides with water and pinch to seal.
8. Place skillet in the oven to warm oil, then sauté in batches until golden browned.
9. Serve warm.

NUTRITION:

calories: 220 | fat: 10g | protein: 8g | carbs: 49g | fiber: 7g | sodium: 572mg

1048. Calzone Spinach and Ricotta Cheese
Prep time: 20 minutes | Cook time: 30 minutes | Serves: 4

INGREDIENTS:

1/3 cup. mozzarella cheese, shredded	1/4 cup. crispy pancetta, chopped
1 cup. Parmesan cheese, grated	A pinch of red pepper flakes
3 1/3 oz. diced spinach	2/3 organic egg
1 cup. ricotta cheese	Salt and pepper
1 1/3 balls of pizza dough	

DIRECTIONS:
1. Preheat oven to 450°F | 230°C | Fan 210°C
2. Dust a baking tray with cornmeal.
3. Flatten dough balls within the 8.5-inch round shape.
4. Grab a bowl, whisk together spinach, ricotta, mozzarella, parmesan, kosher salt, black pepper, and red pepper flakes.
5. Add 1/2 of the prepared filling over one-half of every flatbread. Keeping the borders clean.
6. Roll the other half with moist hands, then pinch to seal.
7. Put every calzone into prepared baking trays.
8. Break the egg within a bowl, include 1 1/2 tbsp. of water and beat using a fork until blended. Rub the egg on every calzone, season with Parmesan cheese.
9. Bake for 20-25 minutes or just until bubbly and golden brown.
10. Serve and enjoy.

NUTRITION:

calories: 370 | fat: 12g | protein: 14g | carbs: 52g | fiber: 8g | sodium: 572mg

1049. Pizza Marinara with Arugula
Prep time: 20 minutes | Cook time: 20 minutes | Serves: 6

INGREDIENTS:

3 3/4 cups. tomato sauce	3 balls of pizza dough
3 garlic cloves, thinly chopped	2 1/4 cups. shaved Parmesan cheese
6 3/4 cups. arugula	6 tbsp. olive oil

DIRECTIONS:
1. Preheat oven to 450°F | 230°C | Fan 210°C
2. Finely flour a surface, flatten the dough balls within a 13-inch round shape.
3. Put in a baking tray finely dusted with cornmeal.
4. Distribute 1 cup. of tomato sauce evenly over the top, keeping a 1-inch border clean.
5. Now divide 1/2 minced garlic over the top and dribble with oil.
6. Bake for 10-15 minutes, or until puffy and browned.
7. Garnish with arugula and Parmesan, then serve.

NUTRITION:

calories: 377 | fat: 11g | protein: 9g | carbs: 47g | fiber: 8g | sodium: 572mg

1050. Pizzette
Prep time: 20 minutes | Cook time: 20 minutes | Serves: 6

INGREDIENTS:

1 1/8 cup. walnuts, diced	3 ripe pears
1/2 cup. artisan honey	2 1/4 lb. pizza dough
4 1/2 cups. young pecorino, grated	1/2 cup. olive oil
2 1/4 cups. aged pecorino, shaved	

DIRECTIONS:
1. Preheat oven to 450°F | 230°C | Fan 210°C
2. Divide the dough in half and then form into 1/4-inch thickness with a rolling pin.
3. With a 3 1/2-inch circular cutter, slice out round shapes; place aside for 10 minutes.
4. Finely slice the pears. With moist fingers, stretch the dough within a 4 1/2-inch circle and put it into a baking tray.
5. Rub the edges of the pizza crust with oil, then garnish with cheese and 2 pear pieces per pizzette, including aged pecorino shavings.
6. Sprinkle with diced walnuts; dribble with some honey.
7. Bake for 10-15 minutes or until bubbly and golden brown.

NUTRITION:

calories: 355 | fat: 11g | protein: 8g | carbs: 51g | fiber: 8g | sodium: 572mg

1051. Pizza with Cherry Tomatoes
Prep time: 20 minutes | Cook time: 20 minutes | Serves: 6

INGREDIENTS:

5 1/4 oz. goat cheese	diced
1 1/2 garlic clove, chopped	3 tbsp. basil pesto
2 1/4 cups. cherry tomatoes, halved	3 tbsp. olive oil
1 1/2 ball of pizza dough	Salt and pepper
2 1/4 cups. mozzarella cheese, finely	1/3 cup. diced basil

DIRECTIONS:
1. Preheat oven to 450°F | 230°C | Fan 210°C
2. In a mixing bowl whisk together the tomatoes, garlic, olive oil, kosher salt, and pepper, along with diced basil then place aside.
3. Using moist hands, spread the dough within a 13-inch round shape and put into a tray dusted with cornmeal.
4. Stir together the oil and pesto, then rub it over the pizza, and keep a 1 1/2 -inch border clean.
5. Top with mozzarella, then tomatoes and garnish with crumbled goat cheese.
6. Bake for 12-15 minutes or until the crust becomes lightly browned; the cheese is bubbly.

NUTRITION:

calories: 388 | fat: 11g | protein: 10g | carbs: 47g | fiber: 8g | sodium: 572mg

1052. Pizza Quattro Formaggi
Prep time: 20 minutes | Cook time: 20 minutes | Serves: 6

INGREDIENTS:

6 3/4 oz. white cheese	9 oz. mozzarella, shredded
6 tbsp. Parmesan cheese, grated	5 1/4 oz. gorgonzola cheese crumbles
3 balls of pizza dough	9 oz. spicy pepperoni

DIRECTIONS:
1. Preheat oven to 450°F | 230°C | Fan 210°C

2. Put a pizza stone inside the oven for 10-15 minutes.
3. Form the dough within a 13-inch round shape, then put it over a tray dusted with cornmeal.
4. Season 1/2 of the cheese on the pizza, followed by pepperoni.
5. Transfer the prepared pizza over the pizza stone, then bake for 8-10-minutes or until also browned bubbly.
6. Remove and serve

NUTRITION:

calories: 455 | fat: 22g | protein: 20g | carbs: 45g | fiber: 9g | sodium: 572mg

1053. Pizza Venture

Prep time: 20 minutes | Cook time: 25 minutes | Serves: 4

INGREDIENTS:

4 zucchinis, diced and grilled
9 oz. fried baby-Bella mushrooms
3 cups. fried spinach
4 tbsp. capers
4 balls of pizza dough
4 cups. mozzarella cheese, diced
2 eggplants, diced and grilled
5 cups. tomato sauce
6 roasted sweet peppers, sliced into strips
8 tbsp. diced pitted black olives

DIRECTIONS:

1. Preheat oven to 450°F | 230°C | Fan 210°C
2. Put a pizza stone inside the oven for 10 minutes.
3. Form the dough within a 13-inch round shape, then put it over a tray finely dusted with cornmeal.
4. Over all the pizza doughs, distribute 1 1/2 cups. of tomato sauce, organize the veggies evenly on the sauce.
5. Season the edges with 1/2 of the capers, olives, and mozzarella cheese.
6. Bake for 10-minutes, or just until pizza crust is lightly browned also cheese melts.
7. Slice into wedges, then serve hot.

NUTRITION:

calories: 381 | fat: 13g | protein: 11g | carbs: 52g | fiber: 7g | sodium: 572mg

1054. Escarole Pizza

Prep time: 15 minutes | Cook time: 35 minutes | Serves: 6

INGREDIENTS:

3 cups. mozzarella cheese, grated
1 1/2 garlic clove, chopped
7 1/2 escarole leaves, soak-drain
1 1/2 prepared pizza crust
2 1/4 cups. pizza sauce
1 1/2 tbsp. olive oil
Salt and pepper

DIRECTIONS:

1. Preheat oven to 350°F | 180°C | Fan 160°C.
2. Finely rub the crust with oil and distribute pizza sauce, then season with garlic.
3. Remove stiff stems of escarole; place leaves on pizza, then garnish with mozzarella.
4. Bake for 25-30 minutes, or just until the cheese melts.
5. Serve right away.

NUTRITION:

calories: 289 | fat: 15g | protein: 13g | carbs: 51g | fiber: 5g | sodium: 572mg

1055. Pesto Pizza

Prep time: 20 minutes | Cook time: 15 minutes | Serves: 4

INGREDIENTS:

2 tbsps. Parmesan cheese, grated
1/3 cup. prosciutto
1/3 cup. pesto
6 2/3 oz. container of refrigerated pizza crust
4 oz. marinated mozzarella cheese, diced
1/8 cup. parsley, chopped
2 tbsp. basil, chopped

DIRECTIONS:

1. Preheat oven to 400°F | 200°C | Fan 180°C
2. Roll out the dough according to box instructions.
3. Distribute the pesto equally over the dough.
4. Place mozzarella pieces onto the pesto and dress with prosciutto, season with parsley, diced basil, and Parmesan.
5. Bake for 10 minutes until the pizza crust also becomes browned bubbly.

NUTRITION:

calories: 377 | fat: 11g | protein: 12g | carbs: 50g | fiber: 8g | sodium: 572mg

1056. Tuna Pizza

Prep time: 15 minutes | Cook time: 25 minutes | Serves: 4

INGREDIENTS:

1 cup. mozzarella cheese, grated
1/3 cup. red onion, minced
3 1/3 oz. can of tuna drained well and flaked
9 1/3 oz. package of prebaked pizza crust
5 1/3 oz. package of cream cheese softened
Smashed red pepper flakes

DIRECTIONS:

1. Preheat oven to 400°F | 200°C | Fan 180°C
2. Distribute the cream cheese equally over the dough.
3. Garnish with tuna, onions, mozzarella and red pepper flakes.
4. Bake for 15-20 minutes until the pizza crust also becomes browned bubbly.

NUTRITION:

calories: 314 | fat: 12g | protein: 17g | carbs: 47g | fiber: 8g | sodium: 572mg

1057. Zucchinis Pizza

Prep time: 15 minutes | Cook time: 20 minutes | Serves: 4

INGREDIENTS:

2 1/4 cups. tomato sauce
1/4 tsp. red pepper flakes
1 1/2 zucchini, diced within 1/3-inch pieces
1 1/2 cup. grated Mexican 4-cheese blend
1/3 cup. pecorino cheese, shredded
2 1/4 cups. olive oil
1/4 tsp. garlic salt
1/4 tsp. onion salt

DIRECTIONS:

1. In a large pan on medium heat warm olive oil then add zucchini pieces in the hot oil.
2. Season the pieces with red pepper, garlic salt and then onion salt.
3. Sauté until tender, around 3-5-minutes on each side.
4. Garnish each piece with cheese, then a spoonful of sauce; fry until cheese starts to melt, again around 3-5-minutes.
5. Garnish with cheese again, fry until cheese melts.
6. Then serve.

NUTRITION:

calories: 344 | fat: 13g | protein: 13g | carbs: 58g | fiber: 8g | sodium: 572mg

1058. Spaghetti Pizza

Prep time: 55 minutes | Cook time: 30 minutes | Serves: 4

INGREDIENTS:

1/3 cup. Parmesan cheese, grated
2/3 cup. milk
2/3 lb. vermicelli pasta
2 1/3 cups. spaghetti sauce
6 oz. package of diced pepperoni sausage
1 1/3 cups. mozzarella cheese, grated
1 1/3 eggs, beaten
2/3 tbsp. garlic salt
Black pepper
2/3 tbsp. dried parsley

DIRECTIONS:

1. Preheat oven to 400°F | 200°C | Fan 180°C
2. In a large size casserole dish start boiling salted water.
3. Gently break the vermicelli pasta around two 1/2-inch thin pieces, then boil for 8-10 minutes and drain well.
4. After draining place pasta inside a 9x13-inch baking tray finely oiled with vegetable spray.
5. In a medium bowl combine milk, eggs, garlic salt, parsley, black pepper and 1 1/2 cups. of mozzarella.
6. Add the pasta to the bowl, then season with Parmesan.
7. Bake for 15-minutes.
8. Then lower heat to 350°F | 180°C | Fan 160°C.
9. Add spaghetti sauce to the pasta and garnish with pepperoni, then remaining mozzarella. Now cook until cheese melts.
10. Serve and enjoy!

NUTRITION:

calories: 389 | fat: 12g | protein: 14g | carbs: 65g | fiber: 8g | sodium: 572mg

1059. Sunrise Pizza

Prep time: 20 minutes | Cook time: 20 minutes | Serves: 4

INGREDIENTS:

- 1 cup. ricotta cheese
- 1 cup. red onion, diced
- 1 cup. tomato, diced
- 1 cup. red bell pepper, diced
- 8 2/3 inches instant-made pizza crust
- 3 2/3 oz. pork sausage, crumbled
- 3 2/3 oz. mozzarella cheese, grated
- 1 cup. green bell pepper, diced
- 4 eggs, finely beaten

DIRECTIONS:

1. Preheat oven to 375° F | 190°C | Fan 170°C
2. Place sausage inside a large size deep pan.
3. In a pan cook the sausage until finely browned, remove fat on the surface, if any, then add eggs.
4. Now cook eggs with sausage together just until the eggs are cooked through.
5. Put the crust into a baking tray.
6. Sprinkle ricotta cheese over the crust, making sure the border is clean.
7. Spread the prepared egg/sausage mixture on the ricotta cheese and garnish with onion, tomato, red pepper, green pepper and mozzarella.
8. Bake for 10-15 minutes just until bubbly and golden brown.

NUTRITION:

calories: 301 | fat: 13g | protein: 15g | carbs: 52g | fiber: 5g | sodium: 572mg

1060. Mozzarella Cornbread Pizza

Prep time: 30 minutes | Cook time: 25 minutes | Serves: 4

INGREDIENTS:

- 1/3 tsp. pepper
- 2/3 tsp. salt
- 2 cups. grated part-skim mozzarella cheese
- 1/2 cup. sweet red or green pepper, diced
- 1 2/3 oz. can, sliced ripe olives
- 2 2/3 green onions, diced
- 1 1/3 packages of 8 1/2 oz. each cornbread
- 2 cups. grated zucchinis
- 2 lightly beaten large eggs
- 9 1/3 oz. jar pizza sauce
- 1/4 cup. fresh basil, coarsely diced
- 2/3 tsp. diced fresh oregano or 1 tsp. dried oregano

DIRECTIONS:

1. Preheat oven to 450°F | 230°C | Fan 210°C
2. Meanwhile, take a colander over a basin by placing the zucchinis and stir with ¾ teaspoon of salt the letting it cool for around 15 minutes.
3. Place the zucchinis into a large mixing bowl after pressing, blotting dry with paper towels, and stir in the cornbread mixes, eggs, pepper, and remaining salt until well combined.
4. In a greased baking sheet, spread evenly and bake for 8-10 minutes until lightly browned.
5. Now lower temperature to 350°F | 180°C | Fan 160°C and spread the pizza sauce on top of the crust and garnish with the red pepper, olives, and green onions.
6. And serve!

NUTRITION:

calories: 321 | fat: 17g | protein: 18g | carbs: 59g | fiber: 8g | sodium: 572mg

1061. Coca Pizza

Prep time: 75 minutes | Cook time: 30 minutes | Serves: 4

INGREDIENTS:

- 1/4 tsp. salt
- Onion
- Yellow bell pepper
- Tomato
- 1 cup. whole-grain flour
- 1/3 tsp. instant yeast
- Water
- 2/3 tsp. olive oil
- Salt and pepper

DIRECTIONS:

1. Preheat oven to 275°F | 135°C | Fan 115°C
2. Take a small mixing dish, add flour, salt, and yeast, now mix them well while adding enough water for producing a soft dough.
3. Proceed to knead it gently for 5-10 minutes or until the dough is elastic; put it aside in to a bowl so the volume to double.
4. Meanwhile slice the onions, peppers, and tomatoes.
5. Place the dough into the baking dish and shape it into a rectangle. At this stage, you can add the sliced onions peppers and tomatoes over the top.
6. Finally, add salt and pepper on top.
7. Bake for 20 to 25 minutes or until golden brown. Slice, serve, and enjoy.

NUTRITION:

calories: 379 | fat: 11g | protein: 12g | carbs: 51g | fiber: 8g | sodium: 572mg

1062. Pesto Pizza

Prep time: 15 minutes | Cook time: 9 minutes | Serves: 6

INGREDIENTS:

- Kalamata olives, pitted
- 3 6-inch Greek pita flatbreads
- 3 tsp. prepared pesto
- 3/4 cup. feta cheese
- 3 small tomatoes, diced

DIRECTIONS:

1. Preheat oven to 350°F | 180°C | Fan 160°C.
2. Top each pita with pesto, feta cheese, tomatoes, and Kalamata olives.
3. Place all the pittas into a baking tray.
4. Finally, bake for 6 to 8 minutes until the cheese has been fully melted.

NUTRITION:

calories: 362 | fat: 12g | protein: 11g | carbs: 55g | fiber: 8g | sodium: 572mg

1063. Tomato Pizza

Prep time: 20 minutes | Cook time: 20 minutes | Serves: 6

INGREDIENTS:

- 22 1/2 oz. canned artichoke hearts
- 1 1/8 cup. sun-dried tomatoes
- 3/4 cup. pitted and halved Kalamata olives
- 3/4 cup. cherry tomatoes, halved
- 1 1/2 12-inch pizza dough
- 2 1/4 cups. mozzarella, grated
- 1 1/8 cup. red onion, sliced
- 6 tsp. olive oil
- 3/4 tsp. salt
- 1/3 tsp. black pepper
- 3/4 tsp. dried basil
- 3/4 cup. fresh parsley, diced
- 1 1/2 tsp. thyme

DIRECTIONS:

1. Preheat oven to 375° F | 190°C | Fan 170°C
2. Place the pizza stone in the oven for around 10 minutes.
3. Now neatly roll out the pizza dough to 12 inches on a baking sheet or a pizza peel.
4. Brush the dough with extra virgin olive oil and nicely season with salt, thyme, a pinch of black pepper, and the dried basil.
5. Now garnish with artichoke hearts, sun-dried tomatoes, olives, red onion, and mozzarella.
6. Place the pizza on a pizza stone and bake for 15 to 18 minutes, until the cheese is melted and bubbling.
7. Garnish with diced parsley and fresh tomatoes before serving right away.

NUTRITION:

calories: 366 | fat: 10g | protein: 10g | carbs: 54g | fiber: 8g | sodium: 572mg

1064. Pizza Bites

Prep time: 20 minutes | Cook time: 20 minutes | Serves: 6

INGREDIENTS:

- 3/4 cup. sundried tomatoes packed in olive oil
- 3/4 cup. Kalamata olives, pitted and diced
- 1/ cup. golden raisins
- 3 packets of sausage patties
- 3/4 cup. feta cheese, crumbled
- 12 oz. mozzarella cheese
- 3/4 cup. pine nuts
- 3/4 cup. basil, diced

DIRECTIONS:

1. Preheat oven to 375° F | 190°C | Fan 170°C
2. Place the sausages on a cookie sheet.
3. Proceed to make 12 pieces of mozzarella and place one on top of each sausage patty.
4. Inside a medium-sized mixing bowl toss together the sundried tomatoes and Kalamata olives followed by golden raisins and pine nuts as well as basil and feta cheese.
5. Place a spoonful of the mixture on top of each sausage patty then bakes for 15 minutes.
6. Finally garnish it with diced basil and serve.

NUTRITION:

calories: 377 | fat: 9g | protein: 11g | carbs: 60g | fiber: 8g | sodium: 572mg

1065. Chicken Pizza

Prep time: 25 minutes | Cook time: 20 minutes | Serves: 6

INGREDIENTS:

1 1/2 small tomato, diced
1 1/2 red pepper, diced
3/4 cup. balsamic vinaigrette dressing
3/4 cup. red onions, thinly sliced
4 1/2 cups. torn mixed salad greens
1 1/2 instant-bake whole-grain 12-inch pizza crust
3 3/4 cups. grated cooked chicken
2 1/4 cups. mozzarella cheese, grated
4 1/2 cloves of garlic, diced

DIRECTIONS:

1. Preheat oven to 450°F | 230°C | Fan 210°C
2. Grab medium-size skillet and heat it with 3 tsp. of dressing on medium heat.
3. Start by adding peppers and garlic, then allowing to cook covered on low heat for 10 min. Until peppers are tender.
4. In the meantime, garnish with chicken, onions, tomatoes followed by mozzarella toppings onto the pizza crust.
5. Bake for 12 min until the mozzarella is melted.
6. Finally, toss the salad greens with the remaining dressing over the pizza.
7. Serve immediately.

NUTRITION:

calories: 388 | fat: 16g | protein: 19g | carbs: 55g | fiber: 8g | sodium: 572mg

1066. Pizza Moons

Prep time: 20 minutes | Cook time: 20 minutes | Serves: 6

INGREDIENTS:

6 cups. mozzarella cheese, grated
24 slices pepperoni
3 oz. package refrigerated crescent rolls
3/4 cup. Parmesan cheese

DIRECTIONS:

1. Preheat oven to 375° F | 190°C | Fan 170°C
2. Place crescents on a flat surface and unroll them.
3. Now sprinkle grated cheese and pepperoni slices over each piece of dough before rolling into a crescent shape adding additional cheese on top.
4. Place on a baking sheet, assemble pizza moons.
5. Bake for 12 to 15 minutes until golden brown, remove from the oven and sprinkling of Parmesan cheese.
6. Serve!

NUTRITION:

calories: 387 | fat: 14g | protein: 12g | carbs: 54g | fiber: 5g | sodium: 572mg

1067. Lumberjack Pizza

Prep time: 25 minutes | Cook time: 15 minutes | Serves: 6

INGREDIENTS:

3 garlic cloves, diced
7 1/2 tsp. olive oil
3/4 tsp. fennel seed
12-inch pizza crust
9 trimmed and thinly sliced Brussels sprouts
15 oz. mozzarella cheese, grated
13 1/2 slices pancetta

DIRECTIONS:

1. Preheat oven to 450°F | 230°C | Fan 210°C
2. Take a skillet over medium heat with 1 tablespoon olive oil, place in the pancetta, cook for around 3-5 minutes until the fat has been released.
3. After place pancetta on a dish lined with paper towels.
4. In the same skillet, pour the remaining 5 tablespoons of olive oil and sauté garlic until fragrant, around 20 seconds.
5. Now add Brussels sprouts to the garlic and simmer, stirring regularly, cook for 6-12 minutes until they begin to brown.
6. At this point, place the sprouts and garlic in a mixing bowl topped with crumbled cold pancetta, mozzarella cheese and fennel seed, now toss.
7. Place the pizza crust on a baking pan topped with the Brussels sprouts mixture and bake for 10 minutes until the cheese is melted.
8. Now slice, serve and enjoy.

NUTRITION:

calories: 375 | fat: 11g | protein: 11g | carbs: 55g | fiber: 8g | sodium: 572mg

16-Week Flexible Meal Plan

I bet you have been looking for a meal plan that is easy to follow and, above all, is effective for a long time. Well, today, I will introduce you to a new type of meal plan that is effective and flexible. It will make you forget you are on a diet.

In this 16-week meal plan, I have introduced all the most important principles of the Mediterranean diet with many different recipes and new dishes every day to make weight loss effective and realistic even for busy people.

The calories have been limited to about 1300kcal per day. This is because, as I have already explained to you, there must be a calorific deficit important enough to begin to see tangible results and have a healthy and fast weight loss. With this calorific deficit, you should be losing around two pounds per week. In case you feel too hungry, I have included adjustments to increase calories to 1500, 1800, and 2000kcal. I will also explain a less fast but equally effective method to lose weight without being too hungry. However, I recommend that you discuss this with your doctor before following any diet plan. This is because each person can have different health conditions. Therefore, it would be better to consult a specialist before starting.

It is important to make some clarifications before starting to follow this food plan:

1) You must drink at least two liters of water every day. Our body often confuses the sense of thirst with that of hunger. Consequently, water helps create more volume in our stomach, so that we feel the stimulus of hunger less. It is important to drink with meals, but it is even more important between meals.
2) Vegetables can be eaten in unlimited quantities. This is because they are rich in fiber and highly hydrated. Therefore, they will help you feel less hungry.
3) Consume a maximum of five teaspoons (25ml) of olive oil to flavor your meals.
4) Don't fill your house with foods that could tempt you.
5) Indulge yourself when you can, by going to the movies, shopping, or even indulging in a small portion of dessert every now and then.
6) Move as much as possible, take the stairs, and walk a lot throughout the day. Stay active!

Flexible Meal Plan Tips and Tricks

It is possible to change the meals with those of another day, to your liking. The recipes I have selected can easily be replaced by another, as long as they are part of the same category. For example, I can change a dish that I don't like with another that I like, even if I have already eaten it during the week.

It is advisable to drink a lot during meals for the reasons I explained previously.

The recipe must be respected. If the recipe calls for a quantity of ingredients for six people, you can also cook for your family or save the meal for the next day. It is absolutely not a problem to eat the same meal for several days.

Even if not specified in the recipes, it is preferable to use whole grain products due to their high fiber content.

Finally, have fun cooking and turning your life upside down forever!

1 WEEK

Day 1:
BREAKFAST: Pancakes with Berry Sauce - pag 33
LUNCH: Spanish Chicken and Rice - pag 149
SNACK: 1 Apple
DINNER: Fish Fillet on Lemons - pag 37
TOT CALORIES: 1367

Day 2:
BREAKFAST: Greek Yogurt with Nuts - pag 26
LUNCH: Shrimp Lemon and Basil Pasta - pag 146
SNACK: 1 Banana
DINNER: Spinach Salad - pag 164
TOT CALORIES: 1333

Day 3:
BREAKFAST: Pistachio Smoothie - pag 23
LUNCH: Mushroom Parmesan Risotto - pag 138
SNACK: 1 Orange
DINNER: Lemon Rosemary Branzino - pag 39
TOT CALORIES: 1391

Day 4:
BREAKFAST: Bulgur Bowls with Fruits - pag 25
LUNCH: Simple Pesto Pasta - pag 153
SNACK: 1 Apple
DINNER: Detox Salad - pag 165
TOT CALORIES: 1324

Day 5:
BREAKFAST: Vanilla Raspberry Oats - pag 25
LUNCH: Fusilli with Chickpea Sauce - pag 147
SNACK: 1 cup. Fruit Salad
DINNER: Fish and Tomato Sauce - pag 40
TOT CALORIES: 1343

Day 6:
BREAKFAST: Mini Frittatas - pag 25
LUNCH: Lasagna Rolls - pag 140
SNACK: 1 cup. Blueberries
DINNER: Tomato Hummus Soup - pag 159
TOT CALORIES: 1302

Day 7:
BREAKFAST: Sweet Potato Toast - pag 25
LUNCH: Free
SNACK: 2 Kiwi
DINNER: Lemon Rainbow Trout - pag 49
TOT CALORIES: 1335

2 WEEK

Day 1:
BREAKFAST: Veggie Sandwiches - pag 29
LUNCH: Mushroom Parmesan Risotto - pag 138
SNACK: 1 Orange
DINNER: Pasta Bean Soup - pag 160
TOT CALORIES: 1312

Day 2:
BREAKFAST: Avocado Toast with Poached Eggs - pag 29
LUNCH: Simple Pesto Pasta - pag 153
SNACK: 1 Apple
DINNER: Olive Tuna - pag 42
TOT CALORIES: 1402

Day 3:
BREAKFAST: Scrambled Eggs with Feta and Olives - pag 30
LUNCH: Couscous Confetti Salad - pag 138
SNACK: 1 cup. Fruit Salad
DINNER: Bulgur Salad - pag 143
TOT CALORIES: 1294

Day 4:
BREAKFAST: Vegetables and Goat Cheese Frittata - pag 30
LUNCH: Pearl Barley Risotto with Parmesan Cheese - pag 139
SNACK: 2 Kiwi
DINNER: Tilapia Fillet with Avocado - pag 43
TOT CALORIES: 1360

Day 5:
BREAKFAST: Orange French Toast - pag 31
LUNCH: Spanish Chicken and Rice - pag 149
SNACK: 1 Orange
DINNER: Sweet Potato Salad - pag 163
TOT CALORIES: 1306

Day 6:
BREAKFAST: Avocado with Eggs Toast - pag 31
LUNCH: Farro Risotto with Fresh Sage - pag 139
SNACK: 1 cup. Blueberries
DINNER: Chickpea Salad - pag 163
TOT CALORIES: 1289

Day 7:
BREAKFAST: Marinara Poached Eggs - pag 32
LUNCH: Free
SNACK: 1 Apple
DINNER: Sicilian Tuna - pag 142
TOT CALORIES: 1433

3 WEEK	4 WEEK
### Day 1: BREAKFAST: Spicy Almond and Pistachio Smoothie - pag 33 LUNCH: Red Wine Risotto - pag 145 SNACK: 1 Apple DINNER: Cod Fillet with Swiss Chard - pag 45 TOT CALORIES: 1404	### Day 1: BREAKFAST: Avocado Smoothie - pag 35 LUNCH: Mushroom Bolognese - pag 147 SNACK: 1 Apple DINNER: Tuna Salad - pag 158 TOT CALORIES: 1380
### Day 2: BREAKFAST: Salad Sandwich with Tuna and Avocado- pag 33 LUNCH: Linguine with Tomato Sauce - pag 145 SNACK: 1 Orange DINNER: Greek Vegetable Salad - pag 158 TOT CALORIES: 1276	### Day 2: BREAKFAST: Orange French Toast - pag 31 LUNCH: Farro Risotto with Fresh Sage - pag 139 SNACK: 1 cup. Fruit Salad DINNER: Cod Fillet with Swiss Chard - pag 45 TOT CALORIES: 1354
### Day 3: BREAKFAST: Pistachio Smoothie - pag 23 LUNCH: Pasta with Fresh Tomato - pag 144 SNACK: 2 Kiwi DINNER: Fish Sticks - pag 44 TOT CALORIES: 1343	### Day 3: BREAKFAST: Salad Sandwich with Tuna and Avocado - pag 33 LUNCH: Simple Pesto Pasta - pag 153 SNACK:1 Apple DINNER: Israeli Salad - pag 156 TOT CALORIES: 1363
### Day 4: BREAKFAST: Bulgur Bowls with Fruits - pag 25 LUNCH: Turkey and Quinoa - pag 148 SNACK: 1 cup. Fruit Salad DINNER: Pistachio-Parmesan Kale and Arugula Salad - pag 158 TOT CALORIES: 1361	### Day 4: BREAKFAST: Scrambled Eggs with Feta and Olives- pag 30 LUNCH: Whole-Wheat Fusilli with Chickpea Sauce - pag 152 SNACK: 1 Orange DINNER: Smoked Salmon and Watercress Salad - pag 48 TOT CALORIES: 1299
### Day 5: BREAKFAST: Apple-Tahini Toast - pag 34 LUNCH: Spanish Chicken and Rice- pag 149 SNACK: 1 Banana DINNER: Shrimp and Beans Salad - pag 47 TOT CALORIES: 1332	### Day 5: BREAKFAST: Apple-Tahini Toast - pag 34 LUNCH: Triple-Green Pasta with Parmesan - 152 SNACK: 2 Kiwi DINNER: Avocado and Hearts of Palm Salad - pag 157 TOT CALORIES: 1342
### Day 6: BREAKFAST: Pumpkin Muffins - 3 muffins- pag 34 LUNCH: Tortellini Salad - pag 149 SNACK: 1 cup. Blueberries DINNER: Greek Vegetable Salad - pag 158 TOT CALORIES: 1365	### Day 6: BREAKFAST: Mini Frittatas - pag 25 LUNCH: Lasagna Rolls - pag 147 SNACK: 1 Banana DINNER: Creamy Curry Salmon - pag 48 TOT CALORIES: 1331
### Day 7: BREAKFAST: Banana Corn Fritters - pag 28 LUNCH: Free SNACK:1 Apple DINNER: Pasta Bean Soup - pag 160 TOT CALORIES: 1301	### Day 7: BREAKFAST: Sweet Potato Toast - pag 25 LUNCH: Free SNACK: 1 cup. Blueberries DINNER: Grilled Salmon Summer Salad - pag 161 TOT CALORIES: 1322

5 WEEK	6 WEEK
### Day 1:	### Day 1:
BREAKFAST: Avocado Smoothie - pag 35 LUNCH: Lasagna Rolls - pag 147 SNACK: 1 Apple DINNER: Mahi Mahi and Pomegranate Sauce - pag 48 TOT CALORIES: 1344	BREAKFAST: Avocado Smoothie - pag 35 LUNCH: Fried Rice - pag 148 SNACK: 2 Kiwi DINNER: Fig, Prosciutto and Arugula Salad - pag 159 TOT CALORIES: 1377
### Day 2:	### Day 2:
BREAKFAST: Orange French Toast - pag 31 LUNCH: Spanish Chicken and Rice - pag 149 SNACK: 1 cup. Fruit Salad DINNER: Zesty Spanish Potato Salad - pag 159 TOT CALORIES: 1327	BREAKFAST: Orange French Toast - pag 31 LUNCH: Israeli Couscous with Asparagus - pag 152 SNACK: 1 Orange DINNER: Lemon Rainbow Trout - pag 49 TOT CALORIES: 1297
### Day 3:	### Day 3:
BREAKFAST: Salad Sandwich with Tuna and Avocado - pag 33 LUNCH: Simple Pesto Pasta - pag 153 SNACK: 2 Kiwi DINNER: Salmon and Mango Mix - pag 48/49 TOT CALORIES: 1361	BREAKFAST: Salad Sandwich with Tuna and Avocado - pag 33 LUNCH: Pasta with Fresh Tomato - pag 144 SNACK: 1 Banana DINNER: Citrus Fennel and Pecan Salad - pag 158 TOT CALORIES: 1401
### Day 4:	### Day 4:
BREAKFAST: Scrambled Eggs with Feta and Olives - pag 30 LUNCH: Israeli Couscous with Asparagus - pag 152 SNACK: 1 Banana DINNER: Shrimp and Beans Salad - pag 47 TOT CALORIES: 1367	BREAKFAST: Scrambled Eggs with Feta and Olives - pag 30 LUNCH: Simple Pesto Pasta - pag 153 SNACK: 1 Apple DINNER: Calamari and Dill Sauce - pag 50 TOT CALORIES: 1358
### Day 5:	### Day 5:
BREAKFAST: Apple-Tahini Toast - pag 34 LUNCH: Mediterranean Lentils and Brown Rice - pag 151 SNACK: 1 Orange DINNER: Trout and Tzatziki Sauce - pag 49 TOT CALORIES: 1369	BREAKFAST: Apple-Tahini Toast - pag 34 LUNCH: Pesto Pasta and Shrimps - pag 143 SNACK: 1 cup. Fruit Salad DINNER: Italian-Style Baked Beans - pag 135 TOT CALORIES: 1321
### Day 6:	### Day 6:
BREAKFAST: Mini Frittatas - pag 25 LUNCH: Mushroom Barley Pilaf - pag 138 SNACK: 1 cup. Blueberries DINNER: Greek Vegetable Salad - pag 158 TOT CALORIES: 1345	BREAKFAST: Mini Frittatas - pag 25 LUNCH: Lasagna Rolls - pag 147 SNACK: 1 Apple DINNER: Salmon and Green Beans - pag 50 TOT CALORIES: 1366
### Day 7:	### Day 7:
BREAKFAST: Sweet Potato Toast - pag 25 LUNCH: Free SNACK: 1 Apple DINNER: Cilantro pork and Olives - pag 102 TOT CALORIES: 1381	BREAKFAST: Sweet Potato Toast - pag 25 LUNCH: Free SNACK: 1 cup. Blueberries DINNER: Greek Lemon Chicken Kebabs - pag 60/61 TOT CALORIES: 1390

7 WEEK	8 WEEK
### Day 1:	### Day 1:
BREAKFAST: Spicy Almond and Pistachio Smoothie - pag 33 LUNCH: Spaghetti with Pine Nuts and Cheese - pag 142 SNACK: 2 kiwi DINNER: Scallions and Salmon Tartar - pag 50 TOT CALORIES: 1280	BREAKFAST: Spicy Almond and Pistachio Smoothie - pag 33 LUNCH: Herb Polenta - pag 144 SNACK: 1 apple DINNER: French Green Lentils with Chard - pag 135 TOT CALORIES: 1323
### Day 2:	### Day 2:
BREAKFAST: Salad Sandwich with Tuna and Avocado - pag 33 LUNCH: Simple Pesto Pasta - pag 153 SNACK: 1 Banana DINNER: Zucchini Soup - pag 170 TOT CALORIES: 1400	BREAKFAST: Salad Sandwich with Tuna and Avocado - pag 33 LUNCH: Herb Rice - pag 143 SNACK: 1 cup. Fruit Salad DINNER: Salmon, Calamari and Mango Mix - pag 52 TOT CALORIES: 1395
### Day 3:	### Day 3:
BREAKFAST: Pistachio Smoothie - pag 23 LUNCH: Triple-Green Pasta with Parmesan - 152 SNACK: 1 Apple DINNER: Cayenne Cod and Tomatoes - pag 51 TOT CALORIES: 1365	BREAKFAST: Pistachio Smoothie - pag 23 LUNCH: Risotto with Parmesan Cheese - pag 142 SNACK: 1 Orange DINNER: Herb Lentil-Rice Balls - pag 134 TOT CALORIES: 1420
### Day 4:	### Day 4:
BREAKFAST: Bulgur Bowls with Fruits - pag 25 LUNCH: Garlic Shrimp Fettuccine - pag 153 SNACK: 1 Orange DINNER: French Onion Soup - pag 172 TOT CALORIES: 1343	BREAKFAST: Bulgur Bowls with Fruits - pag 25 LUNCH: Shrimp Fettuccine - pag 142 SNACK: 2 kiwi DINNER: Octopus and Radish Salad - pag 52 TOT CALORIES: 1388
### Day 5:	### Day 5:
BREAKFAST: Apple-Tahini Toast - pag 34 LUNCH: Asparagus and Grape Tomato Pasta - pag 154 SNACK: 1 Cup Bluebarries DINNER: Shrimp and Calamari Mix - pag 51 TOT CALORIES: 1387	BREAKFAST: Apple-Tahini Toast - pag 34 LUNCH: Couscous Confetti Salad - pag 138 SNACK: 1 Banana DINNER: Oregano Lentil and Carrot Patties - pag 135 TOT CALORIES: 1337
### Day 6:	### Day 6:
BREAKFAST: Pumpkin Muffins - pag 34 LUNCH: Spanish Chicken and Rice - pag 149 SNACK: 1 cup. Fruit Salad DINNER: Greek Vegetable Salad - pag 158 TOT CALORIES: 1312	BREAKFAST: Pumpkin Muffins - pag 34 LUNCH: Mushroom Parmesan Risotto - pag 138 SNACK: 1 Cup Bluebarries DINNER: Minty Sardines Salad - pag 51 TOT CALORIES: 1365
### Day 7:	### Day 7:
BREAKFAST: Banana Corn Fritters - pag 28 LUNCH: Free SNACK: 1 Apple DINNER: White Cannellini Bean Stew - pag 136 TOT CALORIES: 1369	BREAKFAST: Banana Corn Fritters - pag 28 LUNCH: Free SNACK: 1 Apple DINNER: Cilantro pork and Olives - pag 102 TOT CALORIES: 1333

9 WEEK	10 WEEK
### Day 1: BREAKFAST: Spicy Almond and Pistachio Smoothie - pag 33 LUNCH: Fried Rice - pag 148 SNACK: 1 Apple DINNER: Orange Roasted Salmon - pag 53 TOT CALORIES: 1367	### Day 1: BREAKFAST: Spicy Almond and Pistachio Smoothie- pag 33 LUNCH: Moroccan-Style Brown Rice and Chickpea - pag 151 SNACK: 1 Apple DINNER: Greek Lemon Chicken Kebabs - pag 60/61 TOT CALORIES: 1377
### Day 2: BREAKFAST: Salad Sandwich with Tuna and Avocado- pag 33 LUNCH: Lentils and Brown Rice - pag 150 SNACK: 1 Orange DINNER: Octopus and Radish Salad - pag 52 TOT CALORIES: 1322	### Day 2: BREAKFAST: Salad Sandwich with Tuna and Avocado - pag 33 LUNCH: Mushroom Parmesan Risotto - pag 138 SNACK: 1 Banana DINNER: Olive Oil-Poached Tuna - pag 54 TOT CALORIES: 1392
### Day 3: BREAKFAST: Pistachio Smoothie - pag 23 LUNCH: Mushroom Parmesan Risotto - pag 138 SNACK: 2 kiwi DINNER: Cilantro Lemon Shrimp - pag 54 TOT CALORIES: 1343	### Day 3: BREAKFAST: Pistachio Smoothie - pag 23 LUNCH: Wild Mushroom Farro - pag 150 SNACK: 2 Kiwi DINNER: Citrus Fennel and Pecan Salad - pag 158 TOT CALORIES: 1332
### Day 4: BREAKFAST: Bulgur Bowls with Fruits - pag 25 LUNCH: Lasagna Rolls - pag 147 SNACK: 1 Banana DINNER: Italian-Style Baked Beans - pag 135 TOT CALORIES: 1346	### Day 4: BREAKFAST: Bulgur Bowls with Fruits - pag 25 LUNCH: Whole-Wheat Fusilli with Chickpea Sauce - pag 152 SNACK: 1 cup. Fruit Salad DINNER: Shrimp Pesto Rice Bowls - pag 46 TOT CALORIES: 1366
### Day 5: BREAKFAST: Apple-Tahini Toast - pag 34 LUNCH: Turkey and Quinoa - pag 148 SNACK: 1 cup. Fruit Salad DINNER: Salmon with Tomatoes and Olives - pag 54 TOT CALORIES: 1352	### Day 5: BREAKFAST: Apple-Tahini Toast - pag 34 LUNCH: Spanish Chicken and Rice - pag 149 SNACK: 1 cup Bluebarries DINNER: Kale Salad with Anchovy Dressing - pag 158 TOT CALORIES: 1369
### Day 6: BREAKFAST: Pumpkin Muffins - pag 34 LUNCH: Shrimp Fettuccine - pag 142 SNACK: 1 Cup Bluebarries DINNER: Minty Sardines Salad - pag 51 TOT CALORIES: 1321	### Day 6: BREAKFAST: Pumpkin Muffins - pag 34 LUNCH: Tortellini Salad - pag 149 SNACK: 1 Orange DINNER: Grilled Lemon Shrimp - pag 53 TOT CALORIES: 1289
### Day 7: BREAKFAST: Banana Corn Fritters - pag 28 LUNCH: Free SNACK: 1 Apple DINNER: Tabouli Salad - pag 157 TOT CALORIES: 1303	### Day 7: BREAKFAST: Banana Corn Fritters - pag 28 LUNCH: Free SNACK: 1 Apple DINNER: Fig, Prosciutto and Arugula Salad - pag 159 TOT CALORIES: 1345

11 WEEK

Day 1:
BREAKFAST: Spicy Almond and Pistachio Smoothie - pag 33
LUNCH: Wild Mushroom Farro - pag 150
SNACK: 1 Banana
DINNER: Pollock and Vegetable Pita - pag 55
TOT CALORIES: 1398

Day 2:
BREAKFAST: Salad Sandwich with Tuna and Avocado - pag 33
LUNCH: Spaghetti with Pine Nuts and Cheese - pag 142
SNACK: 1 orange
DINNER: Pastina Chicken Soup - pag 161
TOT CALORIES: 1303

Day 3:
BREAKFAST: Pistachio Smoothie - pag 23
LUNCH: Asparagus and Grape Tomato Pasta - pag 154
SNACK: 2 Kiwi
DINNER: Honey-Garlic Glazed Salmon - pag 57
TOT CALORIES: 1362

Day 4:
BREAKFAST: Bulgur Bowls with Fruits - pag 25
LUNCH: Garlic Shrimp Fettuccine - pag 153
SNACK: 1 Apple
DINNER: Zesty Spanish Potato Salad - pag 159
TOT CALORIES: 1363

Day 5:
BREAKFAST: Apple-Tahini Toast - pag 34
LUNCH: Simple Pesto Pasta - pag 153
SNACK: 1 cup. Fruit Salad
DINNER: Easy Tuna Steaks - pag 43
TOT CALORIES: 1378

Day 6:
BREAKFAST: Pumpkin Muffins - pag 34
LUNCH: Triple-Green Pasta with Parmesan - 152
SNACK: 1 cup Blueberries
DINNER: Parmesan Chicken and Cream - pag 76
TOT CALORIES: 1321

Day 7:
BREAKFAST: Banana Corn Fritters - pag 28
LUNCH: Free
SNACK: 1 Apple
DINNER: Beef and Potatoes with Tahini Sauce - pag 88
TOT CALORIES: 1332

12 WEEK

Day 1:
BREAKFAST: Spicy Almond and Pistachio Smoothie - pag 33
LUNCH: Squash and Eggplant Casserole - pag 147
SNACK: 2 kiwi
DINNER: Lentil Stuffed Tomatoes - pag 134
TOT CALORIES: 1365

Day 2:
BREAKFAST: Salad Sandwich with Tuna and Avocado - pag 33
LUNCH: Spanish Rice - pag 148
SNACK: 1 Banana
DINNER: Pressure-Cooked Mussels - pag 57
TOT CALORIES: 1312

Day 3:
BREAKFAST: Pistachio Smoothie - pag 23
LUNCH: Fried Rice - pag 148
SNACK: 1 Apple
DINNER: Mashed Beans with Cumin - pag 136
TOT CALORIES: 1377

Day 4:
BREAKFAST: Bulgur Bowls with Fruits - pag 25
LUNCH: Spanish Chicken and Rice - pag 149
SNACK: 1 Orange
DINNER: Octopus and Radish Salad - pag 52
TOT CALORIES: 1334

Day 5:
BREAKFAST: Apple-Tahini Toast - pag 34
LUNCH: Brown Rice Bowls with Roasted Vegetables - pag 150
SNACK: 1 cup Blueberries
DINNER: Pesto Chicken Mix - pag 63
TOT CALORIES: 1369

Day 6:
BREAKFAST: Pumpkin Muffins - pag 34
LUNCH: Israeli Couscous with Asparagus - pag 152
SNACK: 1 cup. Fruit Salad
DINNER: Oregano Shrimp Puttanesca - pag 45
TOT CALORIES: 1311

Day 7:
BREAKFAST: Banana Corn Fritters - pag 28
LUNCH: Free
SNACK: 1 Apple
DINNER: White Cannellini Bean Stew - pag 136
TOT CALORIES: 1367

13 WEEK

Day 1:
BREAKFAST: Spicy Almond and Pistachio Smoothie - pag 33
LUNCH: Linguine with Tomato Sauce - pag 145
SNACK: 1 Banana
DINNER: Salmon with Broccoli Rabe and Cannellini Beans - pag 57
TOT CALORIES: 1315

Day 2:
BREAKFAST: Salad Sandwich with Tuna and Avocado- pag 33
LUNCH: Shrimp Paella Made with Quinoa - pag 144
SNACK: 1 Apple
DINNER: Minty Sardines Salad - pag 51
TOT CALORIES: 1322

Day 3:
BREAKFAST: Pistachio Smoothie- pag 23
LUNCH: Israeli Couscous with Asparagus - pag 152
SNACK: 1 cup. Fruit Salad
DINNER: White Cannellini Bean Stew - pag 136
TOT CALORIES: 1412

Day 4:
BREAKFAST: Bulgur Bowls with Fruits - pag 25
LUNCH: Farro Risotto with Fresh Sage - pag 139
SNACK: 1 cup Bluebarries
DINNER: French Onion Soup - pag 172
TOT CALORIES: 1302

Day 5:
BREAKFAST: Apple-Tahini Toast - pag 34
LUNCH: Lasagna Rolls - pag 147
SNACK: 1 Orange
DINNER: Balsamic Shrimp on Tomato and Olive - pag 58
TOT CALORIES: 1349

Day 6:
BREAKFAST: Pumpkin Muffins - pag 34
LUNCH: Tortellini Salad - pag 149
SNACK: 2 kiwi
DINNER: Pesto Chicken Mix - pag 63
TOT CALORIES: 1351

Day 7:
BREAKFAST: Banana Corn Fritters - pag 28
LUNCH: Free
SNACK: 1 Apple
DINNER: Parmesan Chicken and Cream - pag 76
TOT CALORIES: 1323

14 WEEK

Day 1:
BREAKFAST: Spicy Almond and Pistachio Smoothie - pag 33
LUNCH: Red Wine Risotto - pag 145
SNACK: 1 Apple
DINNER: Zesty Spanish Potato Salad - pag 159
TOT CALORIES: 1299

Day 2:
BREAKFAST: Salad Sandwich with Tuna and Avocado - pag 33
LUNCH: Pasta with Fresh Tomato - pag 144
SNACK: 1 cup. Fruit Salad
DINNER: Shrimp, Mushrooms, Basil Cheese Pasta - pag 56
TOT CALORIES: 1287

Day 3:
BREAKFAST: Pistachio Smoothie - pag 23
LUNCH: Shrimp Fettuccine - pag 142
SNACK: 1 Banana
DINNER: Fig, Prosciutto and Arugula Salad - pag 159
TOT CALORIES: 1333

Day 4:
BREAKFAST: Bulgur Bowls with Fruits - pag 25
LUNCH: Creamy Parmesan Garlic Polenta - pag 138
SNACK: 1 Apple
DINNER: Dill and Garlic Stuffed Red Snapper - pag 45
TOT CALORIES: 1348

Day 5:
BREAKFAST: Apple-Tahini Toast - pag 34
LUNCH: Mushroom Parmesan Risotto - pag 138
SNACK: 1 cups Bluebarries
DINNER: Greek Vegetable Salad - pag 158
TOT CALORIES: 1365

Day 6:
BREAKFAST: Pumpkin Muffins - pag 34
LUNCH: Couscous Confetti Salad - pag 138
SNACK: 2 kiwi
DINNER: Pollock and Vegetable Pitas - pag 55
TOT CALORIES: 1363

Day 7:
BREAKFAST: Banana Corn Fritters - pag 28
LUNCH: Free
SNACK: 1 Orange
DINNER: Pesto Chicken Mix - pag 63
TOT CALORIES: 1388

15 WEEK	16 WEEK
### Day 1:	### Day 1:

Day 1 (Week 15):
BREAKFAST: Spicy Almond and Pistachio Smoothie - pag 33
LUNCH: Couscous with Asparagus - pag 140/141
SNACK: 1 Apple
DINNER: Pollock and Vegetable Pita - pag 55
TOT CALORIES: 1244

Day 2:
BREAKFAST: Salad Sandwich with Tuna and Avocado - pag 33
LUNCH: Asparagus & Grape Tomato Pasta - pag 154
SNACK: 1 Banana
DINNER: French Green Lentils with Chard - pag 135
TOT CALORIES: 1412

Day 3:
BREAKFAST: Pistachio Smoothie - pag 23
LUNCH: Greek Rice - pag 143
SNACK: 2 Kiwi
DINNER: Honey-Garlic Glazed Salmon - pag 57
TOT CALORIES: 1342

Day 4:
BREAKFAST: Bulgur Bowls with Fruits - pag 25
LUNCH: Wild Mushroom Farrotto with Parmesan - pag 139
SNACK: 1 cups Bluebarries
DINNER: Garbanzo and Fava Bean Ful - pag 134
TOT CALORIES: 1377

Day 5:
BREAKFAST: Apple-Tahini Toast - pag 34
LUNCH: Pasta with Parmesan - pag 141
SNACK: 1 Orange
DINNER: Easy Tuna Steaks - pag 43
TOT CALORIES: 1367

Day 6:
BREAKFAST: Pumpkin Muffins (3 muffins) - pag 34
LUNCH: Fusilli with Chickpea Sauce - pag 140
SNACK: 1 cup. Fruit Salad
DINNER: Zesty Spanish Potato Salad - pag 159
TOT CALORIES: 1354

Day 7:
BREAKFAST: Banana Corn Fritters - pag 28
LUNCH: Free
SNACK: 1 Apple
DINNER: Chicken Kebabs - pag 74/75
TOT CALORIES: 1398

---

16 WEEK

Day 1:
BREAKFAST: Spicy Almond and Pistachio Smoothie - pag 33
LUNCH: Pearl Barley Risotto with Parmesan Cheese - pag 139
SNACK: 2 Kiwi
DINNER: Italian-Style Baked Beans - pag 135
TOT CALORIES: 1399

Day 2:
BREAKFAST: Salad Sandwich with Tuna and Avocado - pag 33
LUNCH: Prosciutto with Beans - pag 140
SNACK: 1 cups Bluebarries
DINNER: Pressure-Cooked Mussels - pag 57
TOT CALORIES: 1375

Day 3:
BREAKFAST: Pistachio Smoothie - pag 23
LUNCH: Bow Ties with Zucchini - pag 139/140
SNACK: 1 cup. Fruit Salad
DINNER: Mashed Beans with Cumin - pag 136
TOT CALORIES: 1323

Day 4:
BREAKFAST: Bulgur Bowls with Fruits - pag 25
LUNCH: Quinoa - pag 140
SNACK: 2 Kiwi
DINNER: Octopus and Radish Salad - pag 52
TOT CALORIES: 1302

Day 5:
BREAKFAST: Apple-Tahini Toast - pag 34
LUNCH: Easy Pasta with Pesto - pag 141
SNACK: 1 Banana
DINNER: Greek Vegetable Salad - pag 158
TOT CALORIES: 1313

Day 6:
BREAKFAST: Pumpkin Muffins (3 muffins) - pag 34
LUNCH: Chicken Rice - pag 68
SNACK: 1 Orange
DINNER: Oregano Shrimp Puttanesca - pag 45
TOT CALORIES: 1375

Day 7:
BREAKFAST: Banana Corn Fritters - pag 28
LUNCH: Free
SNACK: 1 Apple
DINNER: Chicken with Mushrooms - pag 67
TOT CALORIES: 1369

Calorie Supplementation

Below you'll find a list of all the foods that can be integrated to reach 1500kcal, 1800kcal, or 2000kcal.

1500kcal (choose only one of this snacks): 2 tsp of dried fruit or 1 energy bar (80/100kcal, you can choose the one you like more) or one Greek yogurt with 1 tsp of honey.

1800kcal (choose only one of this snacks): 1/2 slice of wholemeal bread with 2 tsp of ricotta and 1 tsp of honey or 1 energy bar with 15g of protein (can choose the one you like more) or 1 fruit yogurt.

2000kcal (choose only one of this snacks): 1 slice of wholemeal bread with 3 tsp of ricotta and 2 tsp of honey or 1 energy bar of 30g of protein or 1 Greek yogurt with 2 tsp of cereals and 1 tsp of honey.

The Pyramid Method

If you think that the meal plan (around 1300 kcal) I have created for you sounds too drastic or stressful, don't worry: here's the solution! As you may have seen, the 16-week meal plan is about 4 main 1300 kcal meals per day.

Well, today I'm going to teach you another method to start your weight loss process in a less drastic and fun way. The pyramid scheme is about gradually reducing the calories we consume over the weeks.

Of course, this process is slower than the previous one, but it turns out to be more sustainable and easier to follow.
Well, let's get started. The first thing we need to do is to divide the meal plan into four phases, focusing specifically on the first weeks.

During the first week we will be through a phase that involves a "normocaloric approach": basically, we're going to "shock" our body to start getting used to the diet.
At this stage it will be sufficient to integrate one of the snacks I have created for you in our food plan to reach 2000kcal.

During the second phase (Week 2) we're going through a gradual reduction in calories, passing from 2000 to 1800kcal.

Obviously, during this second phase, you will have to integrate one of the snacks I have selected in the 1800kcal section.

In the third phase we will move on to snacks in the 1500 kcal section.

In the fourth stage, we will take away the fifth meal (the snack) and move on to our original meal plan.

Thanks to this process, our body will be able to better adapt to change, you will not be overly hungry and you're not going to feel weak.

You will start this process with more serenity and motivation!

Cooking Measurement Chart

Weight

Imperial	Metric
1/2 oz	15 g
1 oz	29 g
2 oz	57 g
3 oz	85 g
4 oz	113 g
5 oz	141 g
6 oz	170 g
8 oz	227 g
10 oz	283 g
12 oz	340 g
13 oz	369 g
14 oz	397 g
15 oz	425 g
1 lb	453 g

Measurement

Cup	Onces	Milliliters	Tablespoons
8 cup	64 oz	1895 ml	128
6 cup	48 oz	1420 ml	96
5 cup	40 oz	1180 ml	80
4 cup	32 oz	960 ml	64
2 cup	16 oz	480 ml	32
1 cup	8 oz	240 ml	16
3/4 cup	6 oz	177 ml	12
2/3 cup	5 oz	158 ml	11
1/2 cup	4 oz	118 ml	8
3/8 cup	3 oz	90 ml	6
1/3 cup	2.5 oz	79 ml	5.5
1/4 cup	2 oz	59 ml	4
1/8 cup	1 oz	30 ml	3
1/16 cup	1/2 oz	15 ml	1

Temperature

Farenheit	Celsius
100 °F	37 °C
150 °F	65 °C
200 °F	93 °C
250 °F	121 °C
300 °F	150 °C
325 °F	160 °C
350 °F	180 °C
375 °F	190 °C
400 °F	200 °C
425 °F	220 °C
450 °F	230 °C
500 °F	260 °C
525 °F	274 °C
550 °F	288 °C

Conclusion

Thanks for making it to the end of the book.
I hope you enjoyed it.

As you have seen, the Mediterranean diet is about having a healthy lifestyle, not being too restrictive with calories. The main goal you need to have is stop worrying about trying to be thin or losing weight in the shortest period of time, but to have a healthy lifestyle that you are satisfied with.

Having the body you want is a consequence of healthy habits and nothing else!
It's about being active every day and not overeating.
I can't stress enough the concept of avoiding processed foods, instead preferring to use fresh foods.
You can eat all the delicious dishes of the Mediterranean diet and now you no more excuses to improve your lifestyle for the better.

Here are some tips for maintaining this diet all the time:
- Balance the calories in your diet to find the right balance
- Eat at least 4-5 meals a day
- Don't skip meals
- Maintain a healthy consistency in meals
- Give your body time to adapt to new foods and ingredients
- Make the change realistic and achievable
- Eliminate processed and refined foods from your diet
- Don't be afraid to eat a variety of foods
- Do not deprive yourself of pleasures (they help a lot psychologically)
- Keep a food diary
- Don't be too hard on yourself
- Take a walk after meals (at least 30 minutes)
- Be positive. Cook and enjoy. You are not obliged to follow what I have written here.

Thanks to this diet you will notice your body start changing in a few weeks.
It will improve metabolism and digestion within days.

You will also find out an increase in your sense of satiety, your energy and improve your mood. These are among the most significant benefits anyone who tries this diet has if followed correctly.

Thank you again for reading my book and I hope it will help you change your life and that of your loved ones in a very positive way.

To your health and happiness!